THE ASHGATE RESEARCH COMPANION TO MODERN WARFARE

ASHGATE
RESEARCH
COMPANION

The *Ashgate Research Companions* are designed to offer scholars and graduate students a comprehensive and authoritative state-of-the-art review of current research in a particular area. The companion's editors bring together a team of respected and experienced experts to write chapters on the key issues in their speciality, providing a comprehensive reference to the field.

Other Research Companions available in Politics and International Relations:

The Ashgate Research Companion to US Foreign Policy
Edited by Robert J. Pauly, Jr.
ISBN 978-0-7546-4862-8

The Ashgate Research Companion to Political Leadership
Edited by Joseph Masciulli, Mikhail A. Molchanov and W. Andy Knight
ISBN 978-0-7546-7182-4

The Ashgate Research Companion to Ethics and International Relations
Edited by Patrick Hayden
ISBN 978-0-7546-7101-5

The Ashgate Research Companion to Federalism
Edited by Ann Ward and Lee Ward
ISBN 978-0-7546-7131-2

The Ashgate Research Companion to the Politics of Democratization in Europe
Concepts and Histories
Edited by Kari Palonen, Tuija Pulkkinen and José María Rosales
ISBN 978-0-7546-7250-0

The Ashgate Research Companion to Modern Warfare

Edited by

GEORGE KASSIMERIS AND JOHN BUCKLEY

University of Wolverhampton, UK

ASHGATE

Published by
Ashgate Publishing Limited
Wey Court East
Union Road
Farnham
Surrey GU9 7PT
England

Ashgate Publishing Company
Suite 420
101 Cherry Street
Burlington,
VT 05401-4405
USA

www.ashgate.com

British Library Cataloguing in Publication Data
The Ashgate research companion to modern warfare.
  1. Military art and science--History--20th century.
  2. Military art and science--History--21st century.
  3. War--Moral and ethic aspects. 4. War and society.
  I. Research companion to modern warfare II. Kassimeris,
  George. III. Buckley, John.
  355'.02-dc22

Library of Congress Cataloging-in-Publication Data
The Ashgate research companion to modern warfare / [compiled] by George Kassimeris and John Buckley.
     p. cm.
  Includes bibliographical references and index.
  ISBN 978-0-7546-7410-8 (hardback) -- ISBN 978-0-7546-9177-8 (ebook) 1. Military art and science--History--20th century. 2. Military art and science--History--21st century. 3. Military history, Modern--20th century. 4. Military history, Modern--21st century. I. Kassimeris, George. II. Buckley, John (John D)
  U42.A84 2010
  355.02--dc22
                                                                        2009033062

ISBN 9780754674108 (hbk)
ISBN 9780754691778 (ebk)

Mixed Sources
Product group from well-managed forests and other controlled sources
www.fsc.org Cert no. SA-COC-1565
© 1996 Forest Stewardship Council

Printed and bound in Great Britain by
MPG Books Group, UK

Contents

List of Figures

List of Tables

Notes on Contributors

Stephen Badsey, MA(Cantab) FRHistS, is Reader in Conflict Studies at the University of Wolverhampton, UK. Educated at Cambridge University, he has held research positions for the Imperial War Museum, the BBC, the Royal Military Academy Sandhurst and for several British and overseas universities. An internationally recognised specialist on the history of military–media relations, his books include *The Gulf War Assessed* (with John Pimlott); *Modern Military Operations and the Media*; *Doctrine and Reform in the British Cavalry 1880–1918* and *The British Army and Its Image 1914–18*. Further details may be found on his website, <www.stephenbadsey.com>.

Jeremy Black is a professor of history at the University of Exeter, UK. He is a senior fellow at the Center for the Study of America and the West at the Foreign Policy Research Institute. He graduated from Queens' College, Cambridge, did postgraduate work at St John's and Merton at Oxford, and then taught at Durham from 1980 as a lecturer, then professor before moving to Exeter in 1996. He was awarded an MBE for services to stamp design. Black is also an advisory fellow of the Barsanti Military History Center at the University of North Texas. He has lectured extensively in Australasia, Canada, Denmark, France, Germany, Italy and the US. Professor Black is the author of over 90 books, especially on eighteenth-century British politics and international relations, including the most recent: *Crisis of Empire: Britain and America in the Eighteenth Century* (2008); *War: A Short History* (2009); *The War of 1812: A Napoleonic Perspective* (2009); *War in the Nineteenth Century 1800–1914* (2009); and *Naval Power* (2009).

Brett Bowden is an associate professor of politics and international studies. He holds appointments at the University of Western Sydney, the Australian National University and the University of New South Wales at the Australian Defence Force Academy. He is the author of *The Empire of Civilization: The Evolution of an Imperial Idea* (University of Chicago Press, 2009); and editor of the four volume major work *Civilization: Critical Concepts in Political Science* (Routledge, 2009).

John Buckley is Professor of Military History at the University of Wolverhampton, UK. He has written widely on many aspects of air power and on the British Army in the Second World War. His next book will be *Monty's Men: The British Army and the Liberation of Northwest Europe 1944–45*.

Helena Carreiras is an assistant professor of sociology at ISCTE-Lisbon University Institute, where she has taught since 1989, mainly in the fields of epistemology and methodology of the social sciences and research methods and techniques on all study levels, and is also a senior researcher at the Centre for Research and Studies in Sociology (CIES-ISCTE-IUL). She obtained a PhD from the European University Institute in Florence in 2004. Her research interests are in gender politics, defence and armed forces. She has been a visiting scholar at the University of California, a guest lecturer in Spain and Brazil, and a vice-president of the Portuguese Sociological Association.

James S. Corum (MLitt Oxford, PhD Queen's University, Canada) is Dean of the Baltic Defence College, located in Tartu, Estonia. He is a military historian and author of seven books and more than 50 major journal articles and book chapters. He has written extensively on counterinsurgency. His latest book on the subject is *Bad Strategies: How Great Powers Fail in Counterinsurgency* (Zenith Press, 2008). Dr Corum is a retired lieutenant colonel in the US Army Reserve and is one of the primary authors of the US Army and Marine Corps Counterinsurgency Doctrine (FM 3-24 Counterinsurgency).

Myriam Dunn Cavelty is Head of the New Risk Research Unit at the Center for Security Studies, ETH Zurich, and a lecturer in the Department of Social Sciences and Humanities at ETH Zurich, Switzerland. Her recent publications include *Cyber-Security and Threat Politics: US Efforts to Secure the Information Age*; *Securing the Homeland: Critical Infrastructure, Risk, and (In)Security* (co-edited with Kristian Søby Kristensen); and *Handbook of Security Studies* (co-edited with Victor Mauer).

Antulio J. Echevarria II is Director of Research at the US Army War College. He holds a PhD in history from Princeton University and is a graduate of the US Army War College. He has written extensively on military history and military theory. His most recent book is *Clausewitz and Contemporary War* (Oxford University Press, 2007).

Jari Eloranta is an associate professor of comparative economic and business history at Appalachian State University in North Carolina. He received his PhD from the European University Institute in Florence, Italy in 2002. He has published widely on the topic of military spending, armaments production, and the arms trade from the late nineteenth century to the Second World War.

John Ferris is Professor of History at the University of Calgary, Honourary Professor in the Department of International Politics at the University of Wales, Aberystwyth, UK and Adjunct Professor at the Department of War Studies of the Royal Military College of Canada. He was Cryptologic Scholar in Residence at the National Security Agency in 2008–09. He writes widely in strategic and intelligence history, and strategic studies.

Patrick Finney teaches in the Department of International Politics, Aberystwyth University, UK. His publications include *Remembering the Road to World War Two: International History, Collective Memory, National Identity* (London: Routledge, 2010). He is currently writing a book for Oxford University Press on the global collective memory of the Second World War.

James A. Green has been a lecturer at the University of Reading, School of Law since 2006. He is the author of *The International Court of Justice and Self-Defence in International Law* (Hart Publishing, 2009) and has additionally published various articles on international law in journals in both Europe and North America. In 2005, he was a visiting research scholar at the University of Michigan, USA.

Steven Haines is Head of the Security and Rule of Law programme at the Geneva Centre for Security Policy and formerly Professor of Strategy and the Law of Military Operations within the University of London. From 1971 to 2003 he was an officer in the Royal Navy, his most recent operational deployments being to Kosovo and Sierra Leone in 2001. His research spans the twin fields of international relations and international law in general, and strategic studies and the law of military operations in particular. While a staff officer in the Ministry of Defence he wrote the UK's strategic doctrine (British Defence Doctrine, 2001) and chaired the editorial board of the official *Manual of the Law of Armed Conflict*, published in 2004. While a visiting fellow at St Antony's College, Oxford, he was invited to participate in the work of the International Commission on Intervention and State Sovereignty and was a named contributor to its report (*Responsibility to Protect*) presented to UN Secretary General Kofi Annan in December 2001.

Joel Hayward is Dean of the Royal Air Force College. He is also Head of Air Power Studies at King's College London and a director of the Royal Air Force Centre for Air Power Studies. He is the author or editor of six books as well as many book chapters and journal articles, some of which have appeared in German, Russian, Portuguese, Spanish and Serbian translations. He lectures widely throughout Europe and beyond.

Thomas M. Kane lectures on international politics and security issues at the University of Hull, UK. He further explores ethical issues in twenty-first-century international relations in his recent work *Emerging Conflicts of Principle: International Relations and the Clash between Cosmopolitanism and Republicanism* (Aldershot: Ashgate, 2008). Dr Kane expands his work applying Machiavelli's thought to issues in American foreign policy in *Theoretical Roots of US Foreign Policy* (London: Routledge, 2006).

George Kassimeris, a Senior Research Fellow in Conflict and Terrorism at the University of Wolverhampton, is the author/editor of five books, including *Europe's Last Red Terrorists*; *Playing Politics with Terrorism*; *The Barbarisation of Warfare*; and *Warrior's Dishonour: Barbarity, Morality and Torture in Modern Warfare*.

Chris Kinsey is a lecturer in international security with King's College London, Defence Studies Department at the Joint Services Command and Staff College, where he teaches military officers from around the world. His research examines the role of contractors in war. He has published widely on the subject in leading academic journals. His present work examines the impact on the military of outsourcing logistical support to front-line operations, cultural links between private security companies and the military, and how military values can influence the behaviour of armed contractors. He is author of *Corporate Soldiers and International Security* (London: Routledge, 2006); *Private Contractors and the Reconstruction of Iraq: Transforming Military Logistics* (London: Routledge, 2009); and is editing a forthcoming book with Dr Malcolm Patterson titled *Contractors and War* that will be published by Stanford University Press.

Andrew Lambert is Laughton Professor of Naval History in the Department of War Studies at King's College, London. His books include: *The Crimean War: British Grand Strategy against Russia 1853–1856* (Manchester, 1990); *'The Foundations of Naval History': Sir John Laughton, the Royal Navy and the Historical Profession* (London, 1997); *Nelson: Britannia's God of War* (London, 2004); and *Franklin: Tragic Hero of Polar Navigation* (London, 2009).

George R. Lucas is Professor of Philosophy at the US Naval Academy (Annapolis, MD) and Director of Navy and National Programs in the Vice Admiral James B. Stockdale Center for Ethics and Leadership. He is also Visiting Professor of Ethics at the Naval Postgraduate School (Monterey, CA) and Research Associate in the Center for Ethics at the French Military Academy (Saint-Cyr). His most recent book is *Anthropologists in Arms: The Ethics of Military Anthropology* (AltaMira Press, 2009).

Lucy Noakes is a historian at the University of Brighton, UK. Her research focuses on war, memory, gender and nationhood in twentieth-century Britain; and publications include *War and the British: Gender and National Identity 1939–1991* (1998); and *Women in the British Army: War and the Gentle Sex 1907–1948* (2006).

Mark Phythian is Professor of Politics in the Department of Politics and International Relations at the University of Leicester, UK. His research interests are in the area of intelligence and security. He is the author or editor/co-editor of nine books on intelligence and security topics, as well as numerous journal articles and book chapters.

Jonathan Pieslak is an associate professor at the City College of New York and the Graduate Center, CUNY. Jonathan has published among the top music journals in the field on topics including critical theory, popular and metal music, and music and war. He is the author of the first interview-based book to explore the relationship between American soldiers in Iraq and music, *Sound Targets: American Soldiers and*

Music in the Iraq War (Bloomington and Indianapolis: Indiana University Press, 2009), <www.soundtargets.com>.

Thomas Rid is a visiting scholar at Hebrew University, Jerusalem. Previously he was a fellow at John Hopkins University/SAIS, the RAND Corporation in Washington, DC, the Institut français des relations internationales in Paris, and the Stiftung Wissenschaft und Politik in Berlin. Among his books are *War 2.0* (Praeger, 2009); and *War and Media Operations: The U.S. Military and the Press from Vietnam to Iraq* (Routledge, 2007). He published several articles on nineteenth-century colonial campaigns.

Tony Shaw is Professor of Contemporary History at the University of Hertfordshire, UK. He is an international historian who specialises in the fields of political propaganda and public diplomacy. He is the author of *Eden, Suez and the Mass Media: Propaganda and Persuasion during the Suez Crisis* (I.B. Tauris, 1996); *British Cinema and the Cold War: The State, Propaganda and Consensus* (I.B. Tauris, 2000); and *Hollywood's Cold War* (University of Massachusetts Press, 2007).

Philip M. Taylor is Professor of International Communications in the Institute of Communications Studies at the University of Leeds, UK. His many publications include *War and the Media: Propaganda and Persuasion in the Gulf War* (2nd edn, 1997); *Munitions of the Mind: A History of Propaganda from the Ancient World to the Present Day* (3rd edn, 2003); *Global Communications, International Affairs and the Media Since 1945* (1997); and *British Propaganda in the 20th Century: Selling Democracy* (1999). His latest books are *Shooting the Messenger: The Political Impact of War Reporting* (co-authored with Paul Moorcraft, Potomac, 2008) and the *Routledge Handbook of Public Diplomacy* (co-edited with Nancy Snow, 2008).

Christopher P.M. Waters is Associate Dean of the Faculty of Law, University of Windsor, Canada. Prior to that, he was a senior lecturer at the University of Reading, and a visiting research fellow at Oxford's Changing Character of War programme. He frequently addresses military audiences on the use of force in international law and has extensive field experience with intergovernmental and non-governmental organisations.

David Whetham joined the Defence Studies Department of King's College London in 2003. Based at the UK Joint Services Command and Staff College, David primarily concentrates on the ethical, legal and moral dimensions of war while retaining a keen interest in medieval warfare. As well as academia, David has worked for BBC History and with the OSCE in Kosovo, contributing to the 2001 and 2002 elections. His book *Just Wars and Moral Victories: Surprise, Deception and the Normative Framework of European War in the Later Middle Ages* was published by Brill in 2009.

Introduction

George Kassimeris and John Buckley

When the Cold War between West and East drew to a close in the early 1990s many believed, or perhaps hoped, that, in the new global order, conflict and violent confrontation between modern nations might be a thing of the past. There was even an expectation of a peace dividend which would result in those states damaged by the pressures and stresses of confronting the forces of communism, recovering, rebuilding and reinvesting resources to make good the price of victory, whilst the nations of the former Eastern bloc looked forward to a world in which they could determine their futures without the burden of heavy military expenditure and the spectre of war. For a time these highly optimistic views and hopes swept world opinion along, famously fuelled by Francis Fukuyama's infamous thesis about the conclusion of the Cold War and the end of history.[1] To those caught up in conflicts across the globe in the early 1990s such hollow triumphalism resonated with irony; indeed, in the midst of the celebrations, in Europe itself, a ghastly and brutal series of wars driven by nationalist politics, religion and race erupted in the Balkans which poisoned Europe's recovery for many years. On a wider scale, to those embroiled in long-running and bitter wars across the globe, the end of the confrontation between East and West impacted upon them little, in the short term at least.

Indeed, as we have journeyed into the twenty-first century human civilisation seems no closer to solving the problem of war and conflict. New threats to security have emerged, new enemies to confront, and warfare, in its many forms and guises, remains a part of the lives of the majority of the world's populations. Moreover, to some, the nature of warfare has degenerated and its ferocity intensified in modern times, ironically a direct consequence of the growth of capitalism and competition. Eric Hobsbawm pointed to an ongoing process of barbarisation of warfare since the nineteenth century fuelled by imperialism and the rise of the West, and thus, far from witnessing the end of history, we have merely seen change and not for the better: the world wars were followed by the Cold War, and then the 'war on terror'.[2] Arms trading with questionable states, the use of torture for intelligence gathering, and the rise of unrelenting extremism are viewed as manifestations of

---

1   Francis Fukuyama, 'The End of History?' *The National Interest* (Summer, 1989); *The End of History and the Last Man* (London: Free Press, 1992).
2   Eric Hobsbawm, 'Barbarism: A User's Guide', *New Left Review*, 206 (July–August 1994).

this downward spiral, exacerbated by the emergence of a multi-polar world and a plethora of new threats since the collapse of the Cold War.

This vision of an increasingly dissonant and insecure world is perhaps overly pessimistic when one considers the reality of the devastation and loss of life as a result of warfare in the twentieth century. Moreover, the view that warfare has degenerated is also open to question: that it has changed is not, as demonstrated by this volume. Atrocity and violence has been conditioned across history by capacity and need, and states, nations and groups have employed whatever measures necessary to achieve political objectives, even when driven by factors many would today regard as abhorrent or extreme. What perhaps remains a greater paradox is the divergence in the West between rhetoric and practice in attitudes to and the conduct of war; where one might have expected a rejection of certain forms of violence as modern states and societies have matured, we have in reality seen little change in the degree of conflict, even if its nature has modified.

In essence this volume aims to provide an opportunity for understanding and interpreting the many facets and manifestations of modern warfare, and how they have changed since the emergence of the industrial age. The manner in which land, sea and air forces have been deployed to fight conventional wars, and on occasion unconventional ones, remains the most obvious example of how warfare has been and will be fought, but the underpinning strategies behind these methods have been shaped by new approaches and interpretations in the modern era. Few Western perspectives on war are deemed legitimate without recourse to Clausewitz and many modern armed forces employ his writing to a greater or lesser extent in defining themselves, though the degree to which he is actually understood is questionable. Indeed, the ambiguities in interpreting Clausewitz are perhaps the very reasons his writing endures. Moreover, our understanding of warfare is reflected through the prism of Western attitudes and thought, which shape our understanding and interpretation of conflict. To some, John Keegan most famously, Clausewitzian philosophy cannot be disentangled from its Western roots and this, fused with the West's overtly technocentric, individualistic, libertarian and fiercely competitive nature, has shaped our attitudes to interpreting and understanding war in all its guises. Clearly, such views contrast sharply with those that argue for the universality of Clausewitz's philosophies.[3]

The conduct of war on land, sea and in the air, are pivotal aspects of how war has been fought and remain our most enduring manifestations of war. All three areas demonstrate how interstate warfare has changed radically and how all three areas need to be understood and integrated successfully into any strategy for the prosecution of a modern war. Sea and land warfare have become industrialised and, in parallel, increasingly shaped by technology, whilst air power has been largely defined by technological change and developments since its inception. Such reliance on production, machinery and technology has caused many changes

---

3   John Keegan, *A History of Warfare* (London: Hutchinson, 1993); and Christopher Bassford, 'John Keegan and the Grand Tradition of Trashing Clausewitz: A Polemic', *War in History*, no. 4 (1994).

to the nature of warfare. Some have indeed argued that we have encountered a revolution in military affairs (RMA) in which the conduct of war has been driven increasingly by technological change, particularly in the field of intelligence and information. Command, control and communications have increasingly been determined by intelligence gathering and interpretation as the twentieth century has progressed; those who adopted modern approaches to the vital nature of intelligence tended to fair better. Indeed, states and armed forces, of all types and hue, have become so dependent on the movement and control of information that this itself has become a weakness to be targeted. The ultimate manifestation of this, though as yet unrealised, is the concept of cyberwar, an attack on a state's ability to interact with the world on virtual or electronic terms. It remains to be seen if this apocalyptic vision of conflict will emerge to the degree some have stated, or whether, as with many other revolutionary forms of warfare, the impact is lessened by countermeasures and other developments.

On land the conduct of war has become increasingly a product of management and organisation rather than simple tactical flair, though it took some time for this crucial factor to be fully appreciated in many armies. Well into the mid-twentieth century many armies considered warfare as being defined by combat in isolation from the politico-strategic environment. The transition away from semi-independent armies functioning largely in isolation from their governments and societies was driven by growing reliance on the home front to maintain the increasingly voracious appetite of armies for resources, and the development of communications networks, which allowed stakeholders such as governments and peoples to gain direct access to information.

This change also affected naval forces as centralised control became possible through radio, and the need for the latest cutting-edge warships made navies increasingly dependent on the support of state and society to fund such developments. The situation was exacerbated by the enhanced vulnerability of iron warships to modern gunfire, mines and torpedoes; in contrast it had always been harder to sink a wooden sailing ship with cannon. The relevance of naval strength was also threatened by the supposed decline in value of maritime power, driven by the growth in continental industry and transport networks in the late nineteenth and early twentieth centuries. Moreover, the emergence of air power provided a real threat to the viability of warships from the moment of the Mitchell trials in 1921 to the crushing blows delivered at Taranto and Pearl Harbor in 1940 and 1941 respectively. Yet sea power proved adaptable and flexible, and was fundamental to success in both world wars and crucial in the Cold War. In the contemporary world, in the likely absence of nuclear threats, naval forces provide obvious political and diplomatic statements of intent, alongside effective conventional power projection.

Air power has provided the most radical change to the dynamics of the conduct of war in the modern age. Air forces have seriously altered the battlefield by adding a third dimension, both on land and at sea, and by World War II aircraft could seriously compromise an enemy lacking the means to resist in the skies over the battlefield. By the 1990s technological development even seemed to have produced the ability for a state to win a war without recourse to ground forces, though this remains contested. Air power has also extended the reach of warfare in a direct physical sense by bringing civilians into the sphere of combat and has greatly expanded the capacity of major industrial and technological powers, most obviously the USA, to impose their will by distant means. What took weeks in the nineteenth century through the use of naval forces now takes hours, or even minutes, with the application of air power and the power relationship between modern states wielding air forces and those resisting them has changed as a result, fuelling moves towards the adoption of guerrilla and insurgency strategies.

The greatest challenge confronting all armed forces, but perhaps land forces most pertinently, has been insurgencies and people's war. Armies have long been structured and conditioned to winning conventional interstate wars, yet in the post-Cold War world much military action has been in the field of counterinsurgency warfare, peacekeeping and peace implementation, and the ongoing adaptation has proved painful and difficult. Nevertheless, armed forces have still struggled with this change and force structures still largely reflect the historical baggage carried by the services.

Terrorism, insurgency warfare and air attack have all brought the civilian directly into the realm of physical combat to a degree hitherto unknown, simultaneous with the growing requirement for modern war to be supported and facilitated by the societies from which armed forces are drawn. Indeed reliance on populations, economies, scientists and states has become essential, increasingly so in the age of total war (c. 1916–1945) and since. Harnessing a nation's resources, managing them effectively and productively, and shaping the will of a nation through control of how warfare is understood, have become vital to modern interstate wars; those states which managed this process more successfully tended to win, whilst those which did not, often failed. Harnessing or deploying all of a nation's resources and the incorporation of all parts of society into warfare has precipitated a shift in the gender balance of war. Prior to the twentieth century women were allowed in generally patriarchal Western societies only peripheral roles in warfare, but with the expansion of the electoral franchise, heightened popular nationalism and the increasing need for labour in war industries, women were drawn much further into the sphere of war. By World War II the experience and place of women in war had changed dramatically through mobilisation and identification with war aims, and in the latter half of the twentieth-century women were integrating in greater numbers into professional armed forces, though not without much anguished debate; traditional armed forces have rarely been noted for their progressive thinking on social issues. To the consternation of many in male-oriented services, females now play an increasingly important role in warfare, even to the extent of front-line combat.

In part this has been driven by the increasing costs of training and maintaining military personnel derived from societies reluctant to surrender themselves to the excesses of war; in this situation women provide a further pool for recruitment. In addition, pressures on personnel resources and costs have been eased by the growth of private security firms, which can provide, in theory, a reasonable level of moderate-to-low security at lower cost than deploying highly trained military personnel. There are, of course, considerable questions to be asked of such organisations and the concept sits uncomfortably with human rights groups and monitors, but it can be seen to be a consequence of the high levels of training and increasingly high-cost technology employed in armed forces impacting upon numbers.

The increasing reliance on technology and industry to provide the needs of resource hungry armed forces has fuelled the development of arms industries across the globe, but particularly in the US, UK, France, Russia and China, and these in turn have sought markets for weapons and arms technologies beyond their own national borders. This trade began to flourish during the Cold War as the superpowers endeavoured to increase pressure on each other through client states, which in turn required weapons bought from their backers, be they East or West. Since the collapse of the USSR the trade has not diminished and in response to burgeoning threats from terrorist groups, insurgents and instability, weapons manufacturers have continued to win high-cost export contracts, and provide income and employment in their home states. Despite reservations about the politics and morals of the end-users of some of these arms deals, few in Western regimes have challenged or actively sought to curtail the industry.

The first time the phrase 'media war' was heard was during the First Gulf War in the weeks after the US and its allies initiated Operation Desert Storm back in 1991. It was, as Stephen Badsey writes in this volume, coined to reflect a new adversarial relationship between the media and the Western armed forces. Fighting a 'media war' is not, of course, about the armed forces waging a war against the national or international media establishments but about the systematic attempts by the military to influence, dictate and ultimately exploit the news media agenda in order to achieve military victory on the battlefield and away from it in the context of public diplomacy and public opinion. The key questions here are: Where are the lines drawn? When does it become propaganda rather than news? In the case of the First Gulf War, after the war was over 17 of the major US news organisations, including the Associated Press, *The New York Times*, *The Washington Post* and others protested to the then Secretary of Defense, Dick Cheney against the 'real censorship' during the war which confirmed 'the worst fears of reporters in a democracy'.[4]

The arrival of new technologies and changes in telecommunication have made journalism more intrusive, faster and to a certain degree independent from military logistics. It has also led to new methods, purposes and technologies of warfare. In an information age that has now become global, digital and instantaneous, fighting also takes place with email, blogs, instant-messaging digital cameras, and the Internet; non-state actors somewhat inevitably have also adapted and are able to use media and communications as their own 'battle space'. The attacks on New York and Washington in 9/11 illustrated the significance of this new global information battle space. For the jihadists, having understood only too well the utility of twenty-first-century media and communications in their campaign, they

---

4   See *The New York Times* (3 July 1991).

were waging not only asymmetric strikes against the US but also a sophisticated information assault. 'More than half of this battle', Osama bin Laden's chief lieutenant, Ayman al-Zawahiri declared soon after the attack, 'is taking place on the battlefield of the media ...'.

One of Osama bin Laden's intentions back in 2001 surely must have been to portray the West as emotionally vulnerable, over-reactive, decadent and hypocritical about liberal values. The West has done a very good job in the years following 9/11 of proving him right. The invasion of Iraq, the images of torture and the widely documented abuse of prisoners at Guantanamo and other US facilities left the US reviled not only in the Arab world but throughout the West, undercutting the moral authority which is vital for any democracy in dealing effectively with persistent national security threats.

Excesses in wars have always been commonplace; armies, both invading and occupying, have always behaved badly. The Belgians in Congo, the French in Algeria, the Germans, Russians and Japanese during the Second World War, the British in Kenya; even the Dutch during the colonial wars committed atrocities and practised torture and sexual humiliation on despised, recalcitrant natives. But most did it before the age of the digital pocket camera. Images like the photograph of naked Iraqi prisoners cowering in front of barking dogs in Abu Ghraib have forced us to come face-to-face with warfare's undiminished brutality and indiscriminate excess. Be that as it may, at the start of the twenty-first century, we should not be debating the use of torture. Questions such as whether torture works and whether the Geneva conventions still hold should not have become central moral issues of our age. It falls outside the parameters of this introduction to provide an analysis of whether of not the occupation of Iraq turned out – to use the words of the liberal American magazine *The Nation* – to be a morally corrosive imperial adventure but it needs to be said that the sight of Americans torturing Iraqis in the same prison that Saddam Hussein used to torture Iraqis destroyed the credibility of the assumption that American and British troops would help to build a stable, representative democracy that respected human rights and the rule of law. Now that the truth about the hidden prisons and the beatings and the torture chambers has come out, we can no longer identify so easily the moral differences between Saddam's regime and the rule of the American and British militaries which followed.

As Coffer Black, the one-time director of the CIA's counter-terrorist unit, put it in testimony to Congress in early 2002, there was 'a before 9/11 and an after 9/11'. The problem stems in part from a moral equivalent that emerged after the events of 9/11 when America found itself under attack by a brutal, amorphous enemy which would go to extraordinary lengths and use whatever means it could to destroy the West. Former president George Bush would repeatedly declare that we were 'in a different kind of war'. Yet, however 'different' that war was going to be, universal (and American) values required that civilised standards be maintained. A country as powerful as the United States had many choices, even when struck by a blow as heavy as that of 9/11. Playing fast and loose with international law and the norms of civilised behaviour as the Bush administration chose to do after 9/11 was always going to be a self-defeating strategy. In its casual disregard for international public opinion and cavalier approach to human rights, the United States damaged not only the nation's moral standing but, more crucially, undermined the very values that the war against both 'terror' and al-Qaeda was supposed to encourage. Francis Fukuyama may have exaggerated in the past with his 'end of history' assertions but he hardly did when he wrote that the world's perception of [George Bush's] America's image was no longer the Statue of Liberty but the hooded prisoner and Abu Ghraib.

When morality vanishes from the battlefield, a war can never be won. It does not really matter a great deal whether you choose to call this kind of treatment abuse or some other euphemism, the fact remains that torture, like any other atrocity, lives on in the minds of the tortured. And, as any abused prisoner at Abu Ghraib, Guantanamo or Bagram will tell you, every time a person is reduced to a howling beast by deliberately inflicted pain, our civilisation crumbles a little more, until in the end there will only be barbarism. Because the maltreatment of detainees and 'terrorists' dehumanises not just those who man the cages and take the callous photos, but also the societies in whose name the cages and gaols were built. The Abu Ghraib snapshots and the hundreds of prisoners held beyond the rule of law in Guantanamo, Bagram and Diego Garcia tell us that despite the profound and largely positive sociocultural changes that have taken place in Western society since 1914, barbarity, atrocity and torture still loom large. What links twentieth-century warfare with the current history of conflict in the 'war against terror' is the notion that warfare is a state of being, not a state of conflict. People do have a choice, even if they have opted to march into battle. In the same way there are just wars and unjust wars, forms of killing that are necessary and forms that shame us all, there are human and inhuman warriors.

Reflecting on Raymond Aron's insight that what matters most in a modern war is the way it is fought, 'the battle in and for itself', the principal aim of the essays which follow in this collection is to take a fresh look at key issues in modern warfare, not only in terms of the conduct of war and the wider complexities and ramifications of modern conflict but also of concepts of war, the crucial shifts in the structure of warfare and the utility, morality and legality of the use of force in a post-9/11 age. Ultimately, it is intended that the chapters will provide provocative, enlightening and thought-provoking studies and introductions to the key issues, concepts, strategies and dilemmas that have confronted and continue to confront those engaged in the conduct and process of war in the modern world.

PART I
STRATEGY AND
CONDUCT OF WAR

The Western Way of War

Jeremy Black[1]

The conceptualisation of war and of military history is a sparse field. This might appear a surprising remark given the number of words deployed about Clausewitz, Jomini, Sun Tzu, Mahan, Corbett and others, but is in fact the case. Firstly in comparative terms, the writing on the theory of social, gender or cultural history, for example, is far more extensive. Secondly, although particular writers, themes and episodes in military affairs and history have attracted conceptual literature, many have not. Moreover, the conceptualisation has frequently been fairly simple. Whiggish notions of improvement in terms of a clear teleology are rampant, not least with regards to weapons technology. War and Society approaches have also attracted teleological treatment, not least with the idea of improved social mobilisation in modern industrial warfare. Alongside teleology came determinism, notably with the assumption that superior resources explained results. Thus, determinism has become bound up with the material-culture approach to war.

A contrary approach, albeit one related in its simplicity, was the notion of national or cultural ways of war. This was an approach that drew on a number of roots, but particularly on the organic ideas of identity that became more prominent in the nineteenth century, which was very much an age influenced by biological approaches and Darwinian ideas of competition. These organic ideas of a distinctive response to environmental circumstances creating a synergetical basis for identity proved particularly interesting for those concerned with international competition. They led, moreover, to vitalist notions in which 'environment' was linked to 'will'. The concept of a national will proved especially conducive to commentators considering the nature of capability in an age of mass-conscript armies. The idea of superior national will seemed to offer a method for ensuring success, not least through better morale.

A separate strand contributing to the same end emerged from the idea of cultural competition. The concept of distinctive cultures appeared to match that of different national identities. Each drew on a notion of essentialism, which can be seen as indicative of the strength of neo-Platonic ideas. Cultural essentialism was potent

---

1   I am most grateful to John France, Stephen Morillo and Rich Schneid for their comments on an earlier draft.

in the nineteenth century as a description of both present and past. It appeared to provide an explanation for Western expansion and also to link it with past conflicts that could be seen in cultural terms. The key rivalry was between civilisation and barbarism and, to that, all else could be subordinated. This idea drew on the attractive notion that the then modern West was the embodiment of the Classical world. This linkage between Classical Greece and Rome and modern Europe and the USA seemed obvious to commentators reading the Classics in their original languages and seeing their legislators emerge from neo-Classical buildings. If the neo-Gothic Palace of Westminster did not appear to match this, prime ministers such as Derby and Gladstone not only read the Classics in the original Greek and Latin, but also wrote knowledgeably about them.

The idea of a linkage was scarcely new at this juncture. While important during the Middle Ages, the idea had received a powerful boost from the Classical revival that had been so significant during the Renaissance. This had a direct military manifestation with interest in writers, such as Machiavelli, who employed Classical ideas and models. The practice was taken forward by the Princes of Orange during what was later seen as the Military Revolution of 1560–1660, and again by Maurice of Saxe and French commentators in the early eighteenth century. The sense of parallelism emerged through varied manifestations over the following century, ranging from the response to Edward Gibbon's *Decline and Fall of the Roman Empire* (1776–88), indicating that Britain in the age of the American Revolution was moving in the same direction, to the conscious use of Classical echoes by the French Revolutionaries and Napoleon. Indeed, the latter was a modern Caesar, with his coup, his legions and his imperial aspirations.

Western imperialism during the post-Napoleonic century took this cultural approach to new heights. It drew on a revived Romanitas, with modern Western Proconsular generals and governors seeing themselves as successors of the Romans. Napier's *'Peccavi'* ['I have sinned'] in response to his conquest of Sind in 1843 was commentary as much as joke: *Punch* portrayed him sending this telegram; he never did it. Here was another view of the modern Caesar, not a Napoleon making war on fellow Europeans, but a warrior bringing barbarians to heel. This idea also drew on a strong notion of religious superiority and, in particular, on an activist pulse that was also seen in large-scale missionary activity.

The amalgam of these ideas was important because war was waged outside Europe, not only with those who could be presented as barbarians (not least by the application of a stadial [stages] theory of development), but also because there was conflict with states that were seen as products of decayed civilisations. It was thus that China and Persia, Burma and Egypt, Turkey and Ethiopia were presented. Only Japan escaped this conceptual trap, and then because it Westernised so rapidly. Thus, the modern Europeans were akin to the Classical Greeks resisting Persia under Xerxes and Darius, while their generals were latter-day Alexanders the Great. The notion of Western warfare therefore drew on strong cultural impulses and these gave it an identity that helped explain and justify success. Christian providentialisation and cultural superiority were also present in the explanation of technological progress, which, in turn, was held to demonstrate them. Different commentators presented this account with contrasting emphases, but it was, nevertheless, a key element in the positioning and explanation of warfare.

The Western interpretation of warfare in terms of Christian providentialism and cultural superiority became far less prominent in the twentieth century, although again for varied reasons that were of different importance for particular commentators. First, the emphasis from 1914 to 1989 on struggle or confrontation within the developed world – Sarajevo to the fall of the Berlin Wall – did not encourage such a clear-cut and consistent cultural and moral approach. Looked at differently, such approaches were deployed during both the two world wars and the Cold War, but they were short-term and particularly associated with one or other side. Thus, German assumptions of a right to rule and of cultural superiority were discredited, as were Communist counterparts. These changes underlined the extent to which there is also a philosophical and conceptual problem with defining 'Western'. Indeed, what counts as Western is always a particular political construction, and depends on the writer and the context. Thus, Western is not a natural category, a point that needs emphasis over against essentialist (and nationalist and racist) claims.

Secondly, the failure of the West in sustaining imperial rule or even post-imperial power across the Third World was a prominent feature of the period 1919 to 1975 and, more particularly, 1945 to 1975. Ideologies of cultural superiority did not provide victory for the French in Indo-China and could not sustain the Portuguese in their resistance to insurgencies in their African colonies. Lastly, the warfare of the age of total war appeared so different to what had come before that historicist accounts of conflict seemed redundant.

The Western way of war was thus not to the fore in the late twentieth century. Indeed, one of the key concepts of the 1990s, the revolution in military affairs (RMA) was particularly unreceptive to such a designation, because its technological impetus and definition were presented as possibly for diffusion across cultural boundaries.

The 2000s witnessed a rediscovery of the concept, most prominently with the writings of the American historian Victor Davis Hanson, although not only with him. This rediscovery was very presentist in character, resting as it did on the concatenation of expeditionary warfare and the 'war on terror' with the need to provide a new doctrine and exegesis to replace, or at least supplement, the RMA. Hanson, an expert on warfare in Classical Greece, sought to provide reassurance and certainty, arguing that cultural factors brought strength and success and that, once this was understood, it should encourage a firmness of purpose. He also proposed a clear lineage, linking the ancient world to modern conflict. To Hanson, two elements of Greek warfare were central to Western warfare: first, the civic militarism of warfare conducted by a population of citizen soldiers whose participation in war reflects democratic political engagement; and second, a tradition of the search for decisive battle and an accompanying practice of warfare. To Hanson, these two elements combined to produce an unmatched effectiveness.

The details of Hanson's approach have been much criticised and its lacunae and flaws are clearly highlighted. Thus, there was not the continuity that Hanson asserts:

civic militarism was absent for much of the period 0–1790 AD; Western forces were frequently unsuccessful; some Western militaries favoured the avoidance of battle; and Hanson's combination was more truly demonstrated by Eurasian nomads such as the Mongols of the thirteenth century. Less attention has been devoted to a more central flaw, that of essentialism or a central identity. In short, whatever the questionable nature of the belief in a Western way of war having certain characteristics, there is the issue of whether there is something that can be defined as a Western way of war. The questioning of the latter can come from a number of directions. It can be argued that the key element is national military culture and that there was/is such a powerful variety among the latter that the idea of an aggregate Western way of war falls to the side. It can also be suggested that the national dimension has been overplayed, not in order to privilege a Western way of war but, instead, because most military development is task-driven, and changes in the context that condition and affect tasks are crucial. For example, talk of a way of war means little for militaries and societies that have to adapt to the changes entailed by switching into and out of the practice and consequences of conscription. Variety occurs across space as well as time. A Western way of war in 1650 would have to encompass the 'regular' forces of Western Europe, the greater role for cavalry in Eastern Europe, colonial forces, most obviously in Latin America, and those thrown forward by civil wars. Moreover, it would be necessary to show that these were recognisably different in type to the forces seen elsewhere in Eurasia. Once external contrasts are taken out of consideration, were the force structures and doctrines sufficiently contrasting to think in terms of distinctive European patterns, whether or not they were to be aggregated in terms of a Western way of war? The answer is probably not. In particular, there was considerable overlap between methods of war-making and fighting in Eastern Europe across the Christian-Moslem divide and comparisons with the Ottoman Empire (Turkey) can then be extrapolated by asking about the extent of contrast between, say, the armies of Tsar Alexis of Russia and John Sobieski of Poland and those of the Kangzi Emperor in China or Aurangzeb, his Mughal counterpart in India. If contrasts emerge more clearly by 1750 and, even more, by 1850, it can be asked whether this was due to essential differences or to stages in a developmental process, the latter a thesis advanced by those interested in Westernisation and diffusion, and, notably, in some of the writing on Indian military history, or to contingency. Moreover, contrasts between West and non-West have to be set alongside a reality of variety in both West and non-West, with these variations also involving overlap with the other category. This has remained the case throughout the nineteenth and twentieth centuries and into the present age.

Parallels are also instructive. The ability of governments, not limited to Western, to impose their will on the state or nation in order ultimately to achieve their objectives, and the extent to which they are willing to expend resources, including population, to achieve that end, are crucial. If this war-making is defined as a 'Western' characteristic, then it has to be noted that war among states beyond the West, such as Ottomans and Persians, or the modern Iran–Iraq and India–Pakistan wars, are conducted in an analogous fashion. Indeed, the ability and willingness of these governments to sustain heavy casualties to achieve their objectives suggests that the notion of a Western way of war should be questioned or perhaps simply stated as the way governments wage war, irrespective of geographic region.

If the idea of a distinctive Western way of war is therefore suspect from a number of different directions, this does not mean that a Western-dominated mindset has not conditioned much of our understanding of warfare, with war understood as a largely Western vision. A similar point can be made elsewhere. The Chinese understanding of war in the nineteenth century was even more flawed because the relevant range of experience was more limited (no recent trans-oceanic or naval warfare), and the same point can be made about other states and 'cultures', whatever the latter are to be understood as meaning.

Whether a Western-dominated mindset can be successfully detached from belief in a Western way of war is unclear, but the freedom of expression in the West and the breadth of scholarly discussion (within the academy but also outside it) offer some encouragement on this head. The extent of sophisticated debate within the American military and related military academies and think tanks is particularly impressive. In large part, there has been a strong critique not only of the RMA but also of any notion of technological determinism. There has also been much call for a need for task-based warfare rather than the capability-centred emphasis on output. An interest in outcome entails an attempt to place warfare more centrally in its political context. All this can be seen as conforming to or clashing with the/a Western way of war, which simply highlights the questionable nature of the latter concept if it is to be employed as a coherent analytical tool and building block.

Yet, approached differently, it is precisely because the idea of a Western way of war is so loose, that it has proved so valuable, not least to broad-brush writers such as Hanson. Indeed, it is the very looseness of concepts that makes them useful. It can be argued that this is particularly the case with military history, not least because many of the writers are popular historians or military figures who are not adept at, or interested in, sophisticated (or any) conceptual discussions. The latter point suggests that the Western way of war still has considerable mileage. Like many ideas it fills a gap. As such, it offers a parallel to such concepts as the early-modern European military revolution. The extension of the idea of military revolution indicates the value attached to any concept that is available. This, again, is a reflection of the degree to which the field lacks intellectual sophistication, although, looked at differently, the treatment of military developments by specialists in more conceptual fields, such as sociology and politics, is scarcely encouraging. Moreover, it would be inaccurate to suggest that military affairs lack a changing vocabulary. The large-scale diffusion from the 1980s of the concept of the operational dimension of conflict is particularly instructive, as is a more general engagement with doctrine. Furthermore, in the 2000s, the range of discussion of COIN (counterinsurgency) doctrine and methods repays attention as evidence of a capacity for a considered response to circumstances and experience.

Whether other societies have different response methods and models is unclear, for one of the problems that is worth considering is the extent to which there is a lack of published critical discussion of the situation by many other societies. Indeed,

15

however much Western-centric perspectives are to be criticised, they are less flawed than what appears to be on offer elsewhere. For example, it is unclear how much the insurgents in Iraq or the Taliban have a sense of the wider parameters of military change. Looked at differently, they locate their own activities in an experience that provides not only motivation but also an ability to respond to challenges. This was seen in Afghanistan with the response, firstly, to the Red Army in the 1980s and, secondly, to Western military power in the 2000s.

Yet, considered in another light, the Iraqi insurgents, like the Taliban, found that their ideas and practices brought less success than they had anticipated, contributing to a major general failure of war-making in 2001–08 to achieve desired results. The extent to which this failure reflected widespread conceptual limitations, both in the West and in the non-West (in so far as they can be aggregated and distinguished) repays attention. The more general failure of war-making also suggests that criticism of simple practices of Western-centred analysis should be set in a wider context of failure. This suggestion underlines the need for comparative assessment when judging capability. That is not simply the case for historians but also for those considering war today as well as its likely future development.

References

Black, Jeremy, *Why Wars Happen* (London: Reaktion, 1998)
———, *War: Past, Present and Future* (London: Sutton, 2000)
———, 'Western Warfare, 1792–1918', *New Perspective on Modern History*, vol. 8, pt 2 (2002)
———, *Rethinking Military History* (London: Routledge, 2004)
Hughes, Matthew and William Philpott, eds, *Palgrave Advances in Modern Military History* (London: Palgrave, 2006)
Keegan, John, *A History of Warfare* (London: Hutchinson, 1993)
Kennedy, Paul, *The Rise and Fall of the Great Powers* (London: Unwin, 1988)
Wawro, Geoffrey, *Warfare and Society in Europe 1792–1914* (London: Routledge, 1999)

Strategic Thought:
The Relevance of Clausewitz

Antulio J. Echevarria II

Prussian military thinker Carl von Clausewitz (1780–1831) developed his theories some 200 years ago, after witnessing first-hand the effectiveness of Napoleon's way of waging war. Nonetheless, they have proven remarkably resilient. One reason for this durability is undoubtedly, as historian Hew Strachan suggests, that the ideas expressed in Clausewitz's masterwork, *On War* (*Vom Kriege*), are ambiguous enough to lend themselves to reinterpretation when new circumstances emerge.[1] Yet, there is another, equally valid reason. As the late American strategic theorist Bernard Brodie once argued, the analyses underpinning the Prussian's ideas penetrate to the very fundamentals of war.[2] It is the desire to understand those fundamentals that draws serious readers to *On War*, whether or not what they ultimately see is largely a reflection of the assumptions and concerns of their times. Brodie went on to say that *On War* was the only military text to have plumbed war's depths so thoroughly. That is still true today, and it makes the earnest study of *On War* all the more rewarding.

Brodie's views have, however, come under fire, particularly of late. Numerous critics contend that the nature of war is fundamentally different from what it was in the industrial age, and thus Clausewitz's theories are no longer relevant.[3] Of

---

1   Hew Strachan, *Clausewitz's On War: A Biography* (New York: Atlantic Monthly Press, 2007). The edition of *On War* used throughout this essay is Carl von Clausewitz, *Vom Kriege. Hinterlassenes Werk des Generals Carl von Clausewitz*, 19th edn, ed. by Werner Hahlweg (Bonn: Dümmlers, 1991); hereafter, *Vom Kriege*. Due to its popularity, references will also be made to Carl von Clausewitz, *On War*, ed. and trans. by Michael Howard and Peter Paret (Princeton: Princeton University, 1976); hereafter, *On War*.

2   Bernard Brodie, 'The Continuing Relevance of *On War*,' in *On War*, pp. 45–50.

3   For the con side, see: Herfried Münkler, *The New Wars* (Malden: Polity, 2005); Mary Kaldor, *New and Old Wars: Organized Violence in a Global Era* (Stanford: Stanford University, 1999); Kalev J. Holsti, *War, the State, and the State of War* (Cambridge: Cambridge University, 1996); John Keegan, *A History of Warfare* (New York: Alfred Knopf, 1994); Martin van Creveld, *The Transformation of War* (New York: Free Press, 1991). For the pro side, see: Jan Angstrom and Isabelle Duyvesteyn, eds, *Rethinking the*

course, to make that argument successfully, one must first show that the nature of war has, in fact, changed fundamentally and, second, that Clausewitz's ideas no longer apply. In truth, Clausewitz's critics have not yet done either convincingly. Newer, more destructive weapons are obviously available now, and a global, real-time media brings immediate attention to even the smallest acts of violence. However, the basic components of war's nature, as Clausewitz described them, have hardly become obsolete. It is also worth pointing out that the argument over whether Clausewitz's theories are relevant is somewhat misleading. Relevance comes and goes with the passage of time: what is relevant today may not be so tomorrow. Resilience, on the other hand, implies that a particular idea has some durability due to its fundamental soundness; it could thus claim a certain validity in any age. Examining the resilience or durability of a theory is thus more beneficial than debating its relevance.

Clausewitz's *On War* is by no means the sum of his thinking. Nonetheless, it is where any serious study of his theories must begin, and so it is the focus of this essay. Clausewitz's chief ambition was to develop a scientific theory of war, an organized body of universally valid observations some of which might qualify as principles. This is essentially what *On War* is, or was intended to be. It remains incomplete in form, though—as the author indicated—the basic ideas are there. He clearly felt that arranging his observations in a coherent system was just as important as their content: proper arrangement distinguished a unified body of knowledge, a theory, from a mere collection of impressions.[4] *On War* is not unlike Copernicus's attempt to order the planets according to their orbital patterns; in fact, the text itself has been referred to as Copernican in nature.[5] Whereas Copernicus's heliocentric system was based on observations of planetary orbits, Clausewitz's theory of war is based on observations of the central importance of combat or fighting, which weaves "its way through the whole fabric of military activity and holds it together."[6] In short, *On War* is where we find Clausewitz's definition of war, his ideas concerning the nature of war and the relationship between war and politics, his definition of strategy, and several of his strategic principles. These are his most durable theories.

Nature of War (London: Frank Cass, 2005); and *The Nature of Modern War: Clausewitz and His Critics Revisited* (Stockholm: Swedish National Defense College, 2003); David J. Lonsdale, *The Nature of War in the Information Age: Clausewitzian Future* (London: Frank Cass, 2004); Gert de Nooy, ed., *The Clausewitzian Dictum and the Future of Western Military Strategy* (The Hague: Kluwer, 1997).

4   'Ueber den Zustand der Theorie der Kriegskunst,' in *Carl von Clausewitz: Schriften—Aufsätze—Studien—Briefe*, 2 vols, ed. by Werner Hahlweg (Göttingen: Vandenhoeck, 1990), vol. 2, part 1, pp. 28–9.

5   Hans Rothfels, 'Clausewitz,' in *Makers of Modern Strategy: Military Thought from Machiavelli to Hitler*, ed. by Earle Meade (Princeton: Princeton University, 1943), p. 101.

6   *Vom Kriege*, I/2, p. 225; *On War*, p. 97.

A Word on Method

On War is, as its critics claim, notoriously difficult to understand. Many would-be readers fail to advance beyond the book's first chapter. Part of the difficulty can be reduced by understanding Clausewitz's purpose in writing *On War*, and the form he attempted to use in presenting his ideas.

It is generally accepted that Clausewitz used military history as a sort of crucible to examine potential principles and concepts.[7] However, until recently his system for validating and presenting those concepts has received little attention. Clausewitz evidently borrowed his system from the German philosopher Immanuel Kant or, more precisely, from the lectures and textbooks of Johann Kiesewetter, a German professor of mathematics and logic.[8] The method required that Clausewitz conduct parallel lines of inquiry, one logical and one material, which were more comparative than dialectical in nature; as a third step, it also required that any valid concept be located within the established hierarchy of other known concepts.[9] Clausewitz's celebrated statement that "war is the continuation of political activity by other means" essentially satisfies that requirement: it situates war firmly and precisely within the field of politics (*Politik*) or what today might be called international relations. Much of the philosophical terminology Clausewitz used in *On War* is defined in Kiesewetter's textbooks. Those definitions help to shed light on Clausewitz's methodology and enable us to resolve the time-honored complaint that *On War* is too theoretical or too wrapped in philosophical jargon to be deciphered by the general reader.

---

7   Beatrice Heuser, *Reading Clausewitz* (London: Pimlico, 2002); Hugh Smith, *On Clausewitz: A Study of Political and Military Ideas* (New York: Palgrave, 2005); and Raymond Aron, *Penser la Guerre, Clausewitz*, 2 vols (Paris: Gallimard, 1976). The English translation of Aron, *Clausewitz: Philosopher of War*, trans. by C. Booker and N. Stone (Englewood Cliffs: Prentice-Hall, 1985), is considered inadequate. See also *A Short Guide to Clausewitz's On War*, ed. with an introduction by Roger Ashley Leonard (New York: Putnam, 1967). For examples see: Clausewitz, 'Strategic Critique of the Campaign of 1814 in France' (c. early 1820s), in *Historical and Political Writings*, 205–19.

8   Johann G.K. Kiesewetter (1766–1819): his principal text was *Grundriss einer Allgemeinen Logik nach Kantischen Grundsätzen zum Gebrauch für Vorlesungen*, 2 vols, 3rd and 4th edns (Leipzig: H.A. Kochly, 1824–25): vol. I deals with pure logic (or reason), while vol. II pertains to applied logic. For discussion of Kiesewetter's value to Clausewitz see: Peter Paret, *Clausewitz and the State: The Man, His Theories, and His Times* (Princeton: Princeton University, 1985), p. 69; Hans Rothfels, *Carl von Clausewitz: Politik und Krieg* (Berlin: Dümmler, 1920), pp. 23–4; and Werner Hahlweg, 'Philosophie und Theorie bei Clausewitz,' in U. De Maizière, ed., *Freiheit ohne Krieg? Beiträge zur Strategie-Diskussion der Gegenwart im Spiegel der Theorien von Carl von Clausewitz* (Bonn: Dümmler, 1980), pp. 325–32. See also Roger Parkinson, *Clausewitz: A Biography* (New York: Stein and Day, 1971), p. 35.

9   Kiesewetter, *Grundriss*, vol. I, pp. 46–7, 109–11; Michael Handel, *Masters of War: Classical Strategic Thought*, 3rd edn (London: Frank Cass, 2001), Appendix C, pp. 327–44; and Aron, *Philosopher of War*, esp. pp. 89–175 overemphasize the use of the dialectical method in Clausewitz's approach.

Defining War

We find Clausewitz's definition of war stated boldly in the opening paragraphs of *On War*: "war is an act of violence to force an opponent to fulfill our will." While war's purposes might vary, violence, or the threat of violence, is war's only proper means. It is, Clausewitz insisted, violence or the potential for producing it that distinguishes war from other human endeavors.

By advancing a theory of war in which violence or combat is the fundamental cause-and-effect relationship, Clausewitz offered an alternative to several of the theories offered by his contemporaries, such as Henry Lloyd, Heinrich von Bülow and Antoine-Henri Jomini.[10] These theories either did not establish the centrality of violence or did not address the role of combat directly. Whereas Copernicus's revolution shifted astronomy away from a geocentric view of the universe, Clausewitz's revolution attempted to move military theory away from artificial geometric or geographic devices toward combat.

War's Nature

If violence is the heart of armed conflict, it might seem that the best approach to waging war would be to maximize the use of violence, in the style of Napoleon. Indeed, this appears to have been the direction of Clausewitz's thinking, particularly after the Prussian army's resounding defeat at Jena in 1806. However, his experiences in the campaigns of 1812 through 1815, combined with his broader historical studies, caused him to revise his thinking.[11] The Russians were able to defeat Napoleon by denying him an opportunity to win a decisive battle, except at Borodino; there, Napoleon, who had always been willing to take risks, held back his reserves and the opportunity—if there had truly been one—was lost.

Moreover, many wars, as Clausewitz had to admit, did not escalate at all, but settled more or less into a state of hostile observation. If war were a simple matter of applying more violence than one's opponent, waging it would be fairly straightforward and its outcomes would be essentially predictable. War's nature, too, would be simple: every war would tend to escalate toward violent extremes, stopping only when physical limits were reached. However, as his historical studies revealed, wars often had periods of little or no violence and generally unfolded according to the political conventions of the day. This was the case, for instance, for the bulk of the wars of the feudal period and of the eighteenth century.

---

10   *Vom Kriege*, II/2, pp. 281–4; *On War*, pp. 134–6. See Martin van Creveld, *The Art of War: War and Military Thought* (London: Cassell, 2005); and Azar Gat, *The Origins of Military Thought from the Enlightenment to Clausewitz* (Oxford: Clarendon, 1989).

11   Andreas Herberg-Rothe, *Das Rätsel Clausewitz: Politische Theorie des Krieges im Widerstreit* (Munich: W. Fink, 2001).

A theory of war's nature would thus have to account for such polar opposites—that is, armed conflicts with little violence and those with a much higher level—otherwise it would fail to represent reality. While history shows that wars can assume any number of forms, Clausewitz identified three elemental forces—hostility, chance and purpose—which he found to be common in all wars. The first, hostility, can take two forms: hostile feelings and hostile intentions. Hostile feelings need not exist for war to occur; however, hostile intentions—one party advancing its interests at the expense of another—are present in every war. Chance, which can be expressed as a function of probability, not only affects the conduct of war at the highest levels, distinguishing it from war on paper, but also influences the activities of units and individual soldiers. It is the exploration of chance and related intangibles, such as friction, that make Clausewitz's theory much more realistic than those of his contemporaries. Although other works of military theory in Clausewitz's day, such as *Reflections on the Art of War* by the Prussian officer and diplomat Georg Heinrich von Berenhorst (1733–1814), also stressed the importance of psychological factors and chance, Clausewitz was evidently the first to dissect friction.[12] He saw friction and psychological factors as the principal influences separating practice from theory, and he believed that correct knowledge could help commanders to improve their judgment and, in effect, close that gap. Purpose is probably the decisive factor in shaping war's nature because it defines (or should define) the military goal. War's purpose can vary in kind from total conquest to negotiated settlement. Thus, it was developed after taking a broad, historical view of wars.

The dynamic nature of these forces and their sometimes antagonistic interactions meant that war's nature, too, had to be dynamic and changeable. Clausewitz captured these forces in a single, enduring conception which he referred to as a wondrous trinity (*wunderliche Dreifaltigkeit*). To be sure, arguing that war's nature is diverse and changeable comes close to saying that war has no nature of its own. Clausewitz realized this, claiming that war is like a true chameleon which can change not only its external features, but its internal ones as well, being shaped through and through by circumstances. Such a broad definition and conception leaves little room for those who argue that Clausewitz's theory of the nature of war is too narrow or is rooted in a Napoleonic paradigm.

Interestingly, Clausewitz went on to argue that the laws of logical necessity do not apply to real war; they are reserved for the fiction that is war in the abstract. Real war, true to its variable and complex nature, is governed by the laws of probability, in so far as such laws actually govern at all. This conclusion carries some weighty implications for both the theorist and the practitioner. It means, above all, that war's ability to achieve the purposes of policy begins as a 50–50 proposition: war is a risky business, regardless of the stakes. One can, of course, take actions which

---

12   Georg Heinrich von Berenhorst, *Betrachtungen über die Kriegskunst*, 3 vols (Osnabrück: Biblio Verlag, 1796–99); see Wilhelm Rüstow, *Feldherrnkunst des Neunzehnten Jahrhundert: Zum Selbststudium und für den Unterricht an höheren Militärschulen*, 2nd edn (Leipzig: F. Schultheiss, 1867), pp. 181–7.

will increase one's odds of success, but so can one's foe. The complexities of the larger political situation are generally such that rarely, if ever, can we expect the chances of success to be 100 percent.

Moreover, since war does not obey the laws of logical necessity, arguments advocating a particular course of action based on military (or political) necessity are assailable. Such arguments depend upon a logical imperative which cannot exist in reality. In other words, what we tend to think of as military (or political) necessity is often merely a matter of subjective judgment on the part of a commander or policymaker. That judgment may, in fact, be correct; but it cannot be considered an absolute certainty.

Rather than reducing war's probabilities to a series of algorithms, as in game or decision theory, Clausewitz maintained that courage and self-assurance, qualities of genius which Enlightenment theorists tended to marginalize, are indispensable. They balance the inhibiting influence of uncertainty. Clausewitz was actually the first military theorist to attempt a scientific dissection of military genius. He believed genius to be a balance of intellectual and emotional traits, so that each aids rather than impairs judgment. However, he also saw it as an innate talent which establishes the rules, methods and models for art, whether music, painting, sculpture or military art. Genius, for Clausewitz, was more than the proverbial soldier marching to a different beat. The rules which genius established had to prove effective on a consistent basis, which would in turn lead others to emulate them. Otherwise, as Clausewitz acknowledged, we might mistake a lucky fool for a genius.

War and Politics

Even in his early writings, Clausewitz revealed his belief that all wars are driven by political purposes.[13] However, this belief was essentially common knowledge at the time and certainly not unique to Clausewitz. Where he went farther than his contemporaries, however, was in his use of policy's potential power to reconcile war's various and conflicting forms and represent them as part of a coherent, yet dynamic nature. Here the influence of the German philosopher G.F.W. Hegel might indeed be evident, as politics becomes the means of reconciling two seemingly contradictory ideas, namely, wars of conquest versus wars of observation. Clausewitz's statement that "war is a continuation of political activity by other means thus does more than reiterate common knowledge"; it actually situates armed conflict within a larger, and ultimately proper, context. War is not to be considered a separate activity with its own laws, but an integral part of political activity, which is itself essentially continuous and capable of assuming multiple forms. Moreover, war is at once

---

13   Clausewitz, 'Observations on the Wars of the Austrian Succession' (c. early 1820s), 'Notes on History and Politics' (c. 1803–7), and 'Letter to Fichte' (1809), in *Historical and Political Writings*, 22, 245, 279–84 respectively.

existential (for the soldier and citizen) and instrumental (for the head of state), an activity as well as a process. Clausewitz defines political activity (or politics) as the interaction of governments and peoples—what today might be referred to as international and domestic relations. War—it is important to note—does not interrupt this interaction, but continues it, albeit through violent means. Finally, the formulation makes an important statement as to war's place in any aspiring theory or body of knowledge. Importantly, it makes the theory complete (even if the text is still unfinished), taking his revolutionary emphasis on the role of violence full circle.

However, Clausewitz's formulation has caused considerable confusion because some of his critics have taken policy and politics, both expressed in German as *Politik*, to be essentially interchangeable. While war will sometimes get away from its original policy aims, either escalating or de-escalating contrary to the wishes of its political masters, it does so only because a greater political dynamic is at work. It is not possible to separate war from its political context, Clausewitz maintained, without making the concept itself nonsensical. It simply cannot occur. Political activities, which Clausewitz appears to have conceived very broadly, are what, in all cases, give rise to armed strife. Even in situations where military aims might appear to drive events, they function more as symptoms than as causes. Military aims are shaped by political activities and can only supersede political objectives to the extent that political conditions allow. In this sense, political conditions are what enable military classes to cultivate certain values, create particular means and, in effect, develop specific styles of warfare. Militaristic societies are but particular expressions of political conditions; conversely, the same is true for societies in which militaries exercise less influence.

To be sure, there is a certain amount of political determinism—circular reasoning based on politics as first cause—evident in Clausewitz's thinking, particularly in several of the chapters of Book VIII of *On War*, where he is wrestling with the relationship between war and politics and attempting to reconcile what appear to be the two conflicting natures of war.[14] Nonetheless, this political determinism does not diminish the validity of his observation that war's proper milieu is that of political activity and that, indeed, war is political maneuvering with the addition of violent means. Cultures, ideologies, and economic and social systems can all be said to be products of, or integral components of, political activity. Clausewitz was no political scientist and his understanding of political processes was far from sophisticated; yet he indeed appears to have arrived at one of war's very fundamentals, as Brodie believed.

---

14   Antulio J. Echevarria II, "On the Clausewitz of the Cold War: Reconsidering the Primacy of Policy in *On War*," *Armed Forces & Society* (2007).

Strategy and its Principles

Clausewitz defined strategy as the use of engagements for the purpose of war. This definition is admittedly limited in several critical respects, but it is one that many contemporary strategic theorists and practitioners still regard as valid. It does not address how economic power might be used in war, for instance, or how economic and military power might be integrated. However, it does establish the premise of aligning the military aim (*Ziel*) with the war's overall purpose (*Zweck*) and thus offers a rare example of one of Clausewitz's subjective or normative departures from his endeavor to build objective knowledge. Once the military aim is in line with the political purpose, strategists and war planners can, presumably, simply focus on the former.[15]

However, Clausewitz also insisted that strategy performed another critical function, namely, that of setting the conditions for battle—"when, where, and with what forces, the fighting will occur"—so as to maximize the probability of victory.[16] Strategy was to provide every possible advantage to the military commander, whose task, in turn, was to win the battle. Such advantages included, but were not limited to: having the greatest possible numerical superiority over one's opponent, making the best use of the geographic circumstances of the theater of war, and implementing measures to protect one's lines of communication and supply.

Clausewitz actually identified five elements of strategy which, in his view, affect the outcome of engagements: (1) intellectual and psychological factors, such as the genius of the commander and the experience and spirit of the military force; (2) physical elements, including the size, composition and nature of its arms of the military force; (3) mathematical or geometrical factors, such as lines of operation and converging attacks; (4) geographical elements, such as the influence of rivers, mountains and other types of terrain; and (5) statistical factors, such as logistical support and maintenance.[17] Clausewitz warned that while these elements are easy to comprehend, they are not necessarily easy to apply: "Everything in war is very simple, but the simplest thing is difficult."[18] That intangible quality, judgment, becomes once again the key.

When referring to achieving tactical victory or winning a battle, Clausewitz means destroying the adversary's physical and psychological forces, and occupying the battlefield.[19] Specifically, victory occurs when an opponent (1) suffers a greater loss of physical forces; (2) suffers a greater loss of psychological forces (morale);

---

15   *Vom Kriege*, III/1, p. 345; II/1, p. 277; *On War*, pp. 176–7.
16   *Vom Kriege*, III/8, p. 373; *On War*, pp. 194.
17   *Vom Kriege*, III/2, p. 354; *On War*, p. 183. He discussed psychological elements further in Book III, Chapters 3–7, 10; physical elements in Book III, Chapters 8, 9, 11–14; geometric elements in Book III, Chapter 15 and Book VI, Chapters 4, 14, 24; statistical elements in Book III, Chapters 16, 18, and in Book V, Chapters 14–16; and geographic elements are discussed in several chapters in Books V, VI, and VII.
18   *Vom Kriege*, I/7, p. 261; *On War*, p. 119.
19   *Vom Kriege*, I/2, pp. 214–15; *On War*, p. 90.

or (3) visibly abandons his intentions.[20] This last condition provides the only real proof of victory, in Clausewitz's view.

It is clear from the above that Clausewitz's definition of strategy, like his concept of war in general, holds destruction or the threat of destruction at its center. At first glance, it might seem to exclude those forms of war, such as insurgency or guerrilla warfare, in which fighting is not considered to be the central element. T.E. Lawrence, who guided and advised Arab tribes in partisan activities against the Turks in the First World War, once described guerrilla wars as only one-third military and two-thirds political.[21] Yet, Clausewitz was no stranger to insurgencies, guerrilla wars and partisan activities either. He referred to such conflicts collectively as an "observable fact (*Erscheinung*) of the nineteenth century," and provided some valuable insights into their nature.[22] In 1810–1, he delivered a series of lectures at the War College, on the subject of small wars (*Kleinkrieg*), which were based on his analyses of French operations in the Vendee and the Spanish insurrection against Napoleon.[23] The lectures were aimed, for the most part, at instructing junior officers in tactics and techniques appropriate for countering guerrillas and partisans.[24] He did, however, strongly urge the Prussian monarchy to pursue a strategy of insurrection against Napoleon after the defeat at Jena-Auerstadt; he was, thus, clearly aware of the advantages of that form of war. Clausewitz, like Jomini, also acknowledged that such small wars were an effective means of resisting an invading force by disrupting its lines of communication, harassing and attacking its small detachments, and destroying its supply depots.[25]

Hence, as Clausewitz added: "Every strategic act eventually comes back to the idea of an engagement, because strategy is the use of military forces, and the idea of the engagement lies at the root of that use."[26] Therefore, whether fighting actually occurred or its outcomes were merely imagined, the cause-and-effect relationship, the law, of combat remained in his eyes universally valid.

---

20 *Vom Kriege*, IV/4, p. 433; *On War*, pp. 233–4. He also defined victory as: (1) the complete or partial destruction of the enemy's armed forces; (2) the occupation of his country; and (3) breaking his will to fight. However, these applied only to war in its pure *concept*, and not to actual war. *Vom Kriege*, I/2, pp. 214–15; *On War*, p. 90.

21 T.E. (Thomas Edward) Lawrence, *Seven Pillars of Wisdom: A Triumph* (London: M. Pike, 1926).

22 *Vom Kriege*, VI/26, p. 799; *On War*, p. 479.

23 For the lectures see "Meine Vorlesungen über den kleinem Krieg, gehalten auf der Kriegs-Schule 1810 und 1811," in *Schriften — Aufsätze — Studien — Briefe*, vol. I: 208–599.

24 Werner Hahlweg, "Clausewitz and Guerrilla Warfare," in *Clausewitz and Modern Strategy*, 127–33, which is an English translation of "Clausewitz und der Guerilla-Krieg," in *Freiheit ohne Krieg*, 349–58.

25 Robert B. Asprey, *War in the Shadows: The Guerrilla in History* (London: Macdonald, 1975), p. 164.

26 *Vom Kriege*, IV/3, p. 423; *On War*, p. 227.

Defense and Attack

Clausewitz maintained throughout *On War* that defense is the stronger form of war.[27] This argument, he realized, contradicted the rather fiercely held assumption — which many still consider valid today — that attack is stronger than defense. If attack were truly stronger, he asked, would not both parties opt for the offensive directly at the outset of a conflict? Why would either party opt to defend rather than attack? If defense did not offer intrinsic advantages, which at least partially offset a deficiency in military strength, it would be a pointless undertaking.

Superiority of Numbers

Clausewitz wrote that bringing the greatest possible number of troops into action at the decisive point was the "first principle of strategy."[28] Strategy, he explained, determines the place, the time and the forces with which the battle is to be fought; strategy's role, therefore, is to calculate space and time so as to have a preponderance of force at the decisive point. His historical observations, which ranged from ancient times to his own day, reveal that numerical superiority is the "most common" element in tactical and strategic victory, though it is never the only factor. Others include the purpose of the engagement, the means used, circumstances of terrain and weather, the skill of the commander and the fighting value of the troops.

Concentration of Forces in Space and Time

In Clausewitz's view, military commanders should divide their forces only on rare occasions.[29] He railed against the customary practice of dividing and sub-dividing one's forces in the field and sending them off to perform ancillary tasks. Instead, the purpose of the campaign and the nature of the means to be used should dictate the extent to which one's forces might be divided. Moreover, he urged that, since the best strategy was always to be strong at the decisive point, commanders should commit their forces simultaneously rather than sequentially.

Economy of Force

Clausewitz used the phrase "economy of force" literally — meaning to get the most out of one's forces. "We must always keep in mind," he warned, "that no part of

---

27   The defense receives special attention in *Vom Kriege*, Book VI, "Defense," Chapters 1–5; see also Book I, Chapter 1; Book VII, "Attack," Chapters 1–2; and Book VIII, "The Plan of War," Chapter 8.
28   *Vom Kriege*, III/8, p. 374; *On War*, p. 195.
29   *Vom Kriege*, III/11, p. 388; *On War*, p. 204.

one's forces should be idle." "We should not waste forces by sending them on trivial missions and we should have as many forces engaging our opponent as possible. Nor should we allow the enemy to tie down a large number of our forces with a minimum number of his own."[30] In other words, Clausewitz's principle is the converse of its modern counterpart.

Surprise

Clausewitz maintained that the principle of surprise underpins all military activity, for, without it, one could not achieve superiority at the decisive point.[31] He saw surprise as one of the means by which superiority is attained and, because of the psychological effect it creates, tending to compound material superiority, ranked surprise as a principle in its own right. In his view, surprise is best achieved through secrecy and speed of execution; indeed, in his chapter on "Cunning" (*Der List*), he suggested that all surprise owes itself to at least some degree of deception or use of a ruse.[32] He also stressed that only large-scale surprises bring about major results, but cautioned that basic friction makes it difficult to achieve large-scale surprise consistently. The greater the intended surprise, the more difficult it is to accomplish. Overall, he appeared to feel that cunning is less important to a commander than genuine understanding and penetrating insight.

Perseverance

For Clausewitz, "perseverance" signified a commander's ability to remain psychologically steadfast in battle, even when inundated by a multitude of negative impressions.[33] High "courage and stability of character," the principal components of perseverance, were considered essential qualities for any commander. Clausewitz's principle of perseverance thus concerned only the mind of the commander.

The Culminating Point of Victory

Clausewitz determined that the moral and physical superiority gained through a victory generally augments the strength of the victor, adding to his superiority, but only to a point, and this he called "the culminating point of victory."[34] This, he pointed out, is particularly evident in wars in which it is not possible for the victor to defeat his opponent completely.

---

30   *Vom Kriege*, III/14, p. 401; *On War*, p. 213.
31   *Vom Kriege*, III/ 9, p. 379; *On War*, p. 198.
32   *Vom Kriege*, III/10, p. 386; *On War*, p. 202.
33   *Vom Kriege*, III/7, "Beharrlichkeit," p. 371; *On War*, p. 193.
34   *Vom Kriege*, VII/(22), p. 935; *On War*, p. 566.

Center of Gravity

Clausewitz also developed the concept of the center of gravity as a tool for military planning. He defined it as the focal point of force and movement, upon which the larger whole depends. It is the thing that, if struck, would lead to the total collapse of the foe. The concept was evidently inspired by the center of gravity as it is represented in elementary physics. Accordingly, it is best thought of as a focal point, rather than as a source of strength or a specific strength or weakness. Similarly, centers of gravity exist only where separate parts are connected enough to form a single entity. Moreover, centers of gravity tend to come into play—and are only truly evident—in wars in which a decisive victory is sought, because such conflicts unleash powerful forces, which in turn require focus and direction. In wars where such a victory is not sought, collapsing an opponent's entire system might not serve one's political purposes and might even run counter to them; hence, striking a center of gravity might not be desirable.

Clearly, *On War*'s strategic principles are closer to today's notion of operational art than to strategy. Yet, contemporary military doctrine still considers the bulk of these principles to be valid, despite the fact that some clearly pertain to linear rather than nonlinear combat environments. Furthermore, as Clausewitz admitted, he was less than satisfied with having been unable to discern principles for wars fought for negotiated settlements. In such wars, centers of gravity, as one example, may be present, but the physical and psychological forces of the belligerent parties are unlikely to be strong enough to cause such focal points to emerge. When wars tend toward nonviolent observation, so Clausewitz reasoned, principles and concepts become less useful. In a sense, this logic is valid, for, when such operations occur today, rules of engagement tend to take the place of doctrinal principles. Nonetheless, it seems that Clausewitz was less than satisfied with having found no universal principles for such wars. Contemporary efforts to develop principles for so-called "operations other than war" have not fared much better.

In addition, today—unlike in Clausewitz's day—military strategy also covers the use of military forces in peacetime. In the absence of war, military forces do not stand idle but routinely accomplish important tasks, such as training with allies and coalition partners, which advance national interests and further the ends of strategy without using battles or campaigns to do so. Whereas peace may be the ultimate object of war, as Clausewitz also believed, peacetime activities are clearly not the subject of *On War*. His masterwork is, in any case, more about war than strategy.

Conclusion

Certainly, not all of Clausewitz's ideas contribute to our knowledge of war or can be said to offer something of enduring value. Nor did Clausewitz address every aspect of war. Careful readers will discover important gaps and inconsistencies in *On War*.

He did not write about naval warfare, for instance; nor did he address the roles that economic power, diplomacy and information play in war. Such shortcomings are only partially remedied by studying his many other works. However, as we have seen, Clausewitz did establish a number of what one might call first, or fundamental, principles, just as Brodie claimed. Many of the principles introduced here can be found in the doctrines of modern militaries, though perhaps modified.

As we have said, Clausewitz's overall concern was to replace the artificial systems of his day with one that was grounded in the reality of war, that is, fighting or combat, including the threat of combat. Unfortunately, he never finished the manuscript to his satisfaction, despite more than a decade of effort. He began composing the work sometime after 1815, but died of cholera, in 1831, before bringing the product of his long labor to final form. Most scholars agree that the unfinished state of *On War* does not diminish its overall value; nonetheless, a finished manuscript would have precluded a great many debates. The ambiguity of *On War* may well have contributed to its appeal over time; but that is not its strongest attribute.

Ironically, just as Clausewitz predicted, his revolution has been largely misunderstood, not only in his own era, but for the better part of two centuries. His nineteenth-century heirs, for instance, inspired more by Napoleon's battlefield victories than by the ideas in *On War*, tended to tie theory, which rested on the centrality of combat, directly to the pursuit of decisive victory on the battlefield.[35] Perhaps no less surprisingly, scholars from the early twentieth century to the present, all too aware of war's growing apocalyptic potential, have seen in Clausewitz's discussion of the relationship between war and policy the complete antithesis of the nineteenth-century view. Each group also misread his observations concerning absolute war. The former saw it as a description of war's true nature, which strategies and war plans may not violate. The latter have perceived it as a threat to the rational control of war by policy, and hence have argued that strategies should be designed in ways that restrict war's nature. Neither group so far, however, has put much effort into evaluating Clausewitz's revolution nor has taken seriously his attendant search for the best form for presenting his ideas. Both, in short, have succumbed to the temptation of finishing an unfinished symphony. The problem with doing that is that the final product never quite satisfies anyone.

---

35 Martin Kitchen, "The Political History of Clausewitz," *Journal of Strategic Studies*, vol. 11, no. 1 (March 1988): 27–50.

Development of Modern Counterinsurgency Theory and Doctrine

James S. Corum

Insurgency, the effort to overthrow the government of a state carried out by internal groups using violence, has been with us since organized states have been in existence. Although insurgency has been one of the most common forms of conflict, no theories of counterinsurgency appeared until the end of the nineteenth century. To well into the twentieth century insurgency was commonly seen as a military problem which simply required the government to send troops to defeat the insurgents. However, as states, societies, and economies grew in complexity and organization, so did insurgencies.

Historically, most insurgencies have failed due to the military and political weakness of the insurgents when facing substantially larger military forces and economic resources of the ruling state. However, some insurgencies have been spectacularly successful and enough have succeeded so that it remains a reasonable option for a group wishing to overthrow a government. Yet, although insurgency has remained one of the most common forms of conflict, the literature on the subject is surprisingly thin—especially when one compares it to the vast literature on conventional war. Still, enough theoretical work has published to provide a foundation for analyzing this highly complex form of conflict. This essay will focus on the development of counterinsurgency theory and doctrine among the Western powers from the late nineteenth century to the present.

The Beginnings of Counterinsurgency Theory

Sometimes insurgents have adopted the organization, strategies and tactics of conventional states and armies and fought in a highly conventional manner—the American War of Independence is a good example of this. However, in most cases, insurgents have been forced by necessity to fight the war of the weak and eschew conventional tactics and organization, and employ irregular or guerrilla warfare against the government. But insurgents can still win by employing a better strategy than the defending government. One effective strategy is to engage in a prolonged war in which the insurgent succeeds simply by wearing down the government's will to the point where a political settlement is possible. Insurgents have often employed guerrilla tactics to wear down government forces and force the government to spend far more in money and resources than it can reasonably afford.

General Carl von Clausewitz briefly addressed the subject of "people's war" with the example of Spain before him. In 1808 Napoleon overthrew the Spanish kingdom and replaced it with a puppet regime headed by his brother. This inspired a spontaneous revolt of thousands of Spaniards who organized irregular forces to fight a guerrilla war [from the Spanish, meaning "little war"] of ambush and harassment against the French forces. While the Spanish guerrillas were too weak to fight major battles, they nevertheless inflicted a large number of casualties by their constant raids against rear garrisons and supply lines. Eventually, the French were defeated by the British and Allied armies on the battlefield, but not before being greatly weakened by guerrilla war. For Clausewitz this irregular form of warfare could, under the right circumstances and given strong popular support, be highly dangerous for the forces of a conventional power.

Although Clausewitz addressed the subject only briefly, he recognized that a conflict fought by non-state forces against conventional armies constituted a different type of war than one fought between conventional states and armies.[1] The great theorist of war understood that war between state and non-state forces required its own theory, but never followed this line of thought further. Despite numerous military operations in their colonial empires throughout the nineteenth century, there was no theory of insurgency and counterinsurgency until the end of the century. The first author to seriously address the issue of conflict with non-state enemies was British Major General C.E. Callwell in the book *Small Wars: Their Principles and Practice*, published in 1896. Callwell's book went through several editions and was popular reading in the British Empire, where the military and political leaders had to deal with numerous rebellions in the colonies.

Callwell defined small wars as "campaigns undertaken to suppress rebellions and guerrilla warfare in all parts of the world where organized armies are struggling against opponents who will not meet them in the open field."[2] The forms of conflict that Callwell described would be classified today as insurgencies. In Callwell's study the enemy consisted mainly of "irregular forces," which included everything from semi-organized armies to tribal levies and bandits. Callwell's method was

---

1   Clausewitz's main discussion of guerrilla war is found in Book 6, Chapter 26 of *On War*. He touches on aspects of insurgency in Book 3, Chapter 5; Book 5, Chapter 17; and Book 8, Chapter 3. For the best edition of Clausewitz in English see Carl von Clausewitz, *On War*, ed. and trans. by Michael Howard and Peter Paret (Princeton, NJ: Princeton University Press, 1976).

2   Major C.E. Callwell, *Small Wars: Their Principles and Practice* (London: Harrison and Sons, 1899; reprinted 1903), p. 1.

highly historical and he cited many colonial military operations conducted by the major powers to illustrate his points. Callwell emphasized that the nature of the enemy and the politics that drove the conflict made a "small war" a fundamentally different kind of conflict. He began his study by describing the many different forms that irregular warfare could take.[3] "But the conditions of small wars are so diversified, the enemy's mode of fighting is often so peculiar, the theatres of operations present such singular features, that irregular warfare must generally be carried out on a methods totally different from the stereotyped system [meaning state on state warfare]."[4]

One of the most important differences between Callwell's small war and conventional warfare was the greater role of intelligence in fighting irregular forces. Not only did the counterinsurgent power have to find the military forces of the rebels, but it also had to understand the whole of the society that it was dealing with—from the economy to the tribal organization. The counterinsurgent power had to thoroughly understand the groups and factions of a region in order to win their open support, or at least their neutrality, in an irregular conflict. Callwell's description of the difficulties of intelligence collection and analysis still rings true in today's conflicts.[5] Callwell's book was a useful first step towards helping Western powers to understand counterinsurgency. It is foremost a practical book and was highly influential in its day. Leaving the strategy to the politicians, he concentrated on the operational and tactical side of counterinsurgency campaigns.

When American troops occupied the Philippines after the 1898 war with Spain they became embroiled in a campaign to suppress Philippine nationalists and had to quickly develop a counterinsurgency doctrine. Although the Philippine Insurrection (1899–1908) was America's first major colonial war, the US Army was not completely devoid of useful experience to serve as a guide. American commanders drew upon their experience of fighting the Indians as well as the British experience of colonial warfare as recounted by Callwell. The US military leaders adapted quickly and developed a sophisticated strategy to defeat the Filipinos. While waging an aggressive military and police campaign to defeat rebel forces in the field, US military commanders also stressed the non-military aspects of the campaign. American regional commanders established local self-government, and began civic action programs such as schools and medical care that visibly improved the lives of the people. An important part of the American strategy was a policy to co-opt rebel leaders by granting amnesty to those willing to lay down their arms and recognize American sovereignty. Former guerrillas were readily accepted into the ranks of the local and regional governments once they had proven their loyalty. Although not formally codified in regulations, the US

---

3   Ibid., pp. 21–42.
4   Ibid., p. 3.
5   Ibid., pp. 43–56.

strategy included a "hearts and minds" campaign that addressed the causes of discontent among the population.[6]

Transition from Rebellion to People's War

The first insurgency that can properly be described as a "people's war" in the modern sense was the rebellion of the Irish nationalists against British rule from 1916 to 1922, during which the Irish waged a guerrilla war of small raids and skirmishes across Ireland. Small groups of rebels assassinated British officers and agents, raided police stations and ambushed army patrols. Clumsy sweep operations by conventional forces failed to clear areas of rebels, as the IRA columns evaded the British conventional forces and chose battle only on their terms. Though the Irish inflicted little damage to the British military, they created enough casualties to cause dissatisfaction in Britain over the cost of holding Ireland in the Empire.

In the Irish nationalist strategy the establishment of an underground government — complete with finances, law courts, and an underground press — was just as important as their military operations. Rebel violence forced the British governmental authorities to retreat into protected enclaves so that the day-to-day managing of the country, especially in the rural areas, was taken over by the well-organized, nationalist civil authorities. Eventually the Irish nationalists were accepted by the majority of the Irish as the legitimate government, while the British were seen as foreigners lacking true legitimacy. Although the Irish nationalists never won any major military victories, they won the war by simply staying in the field.

While the British failed in Ireland, they also fought a series of successful counterinsurgency campaigns in the colonies, the largest of these being the suppression of a major revolt in Iraq in 1920. For Britain and the European powers the insurgent threat in the colonies consisted mostly of poorly organized nationalist factions that attempted to fight a conventional war against their foreign occupiers. The European powers, equipped with the latest technology and able to deploy well-trained and well- supplied forces, had an insurmountable advantage against rebels when it came to fighting in Syria, Morocco, the Sudan and elsewhere. Because the European forces possessed such huge military advantages over irregular forces, little effort was made by European armed forces to develop a more sophisticated counterinsurgency doctrine. The counterinsurgency thinking that did occur was almost all in the military and tactical realm.

In contrast, the American military developed a relatively sophisticated doctrine for counterinsurgency in this era. The US government carried out numerous military interventions in the Caribbean and Central American region between 1914 and 1934, with the intent of creating stability and propping up pro-American

---

6   For the best historical account of the US counterinsurgency campaign in the Philippines, see Brian Linn, *The Philippine War 1899–1902* (Lawrence, KS: University Press of Kansas, 2000).

regimes rather than imposing direct colonial rule. The US Marine Corps, which served as the primary American intervention force in the Caribbean and Central America, developed new doctrines that brought the counterinsurgency and military occupation missions to the level of high art. For one thing, the American thinking focused on a more comprehensive approach to counter irregular enemies. In the administration of Haiti (1914–1934), during the interventions in Nicaragua from 1925 to 1933, and in other interventions, the Marine Corps gained considerable experience in conducting a variety of missions against irregular enemies. Marine Corps operations included fighting insurgents, supporting pro-American indigenous governments, training local constabularies, building local infrastructures, and even administering small countries. This experience was collected and edited by a group of Marine officers and published in 1940 as the *USMC Small Wars Manual*.

The *Small Wars Manual* has long been considered one of the classics of counterinsurgency literature. While some sections dealing with the specific tactics of infantry operations are dated, most of the *Small Wars Manual* deals with fundamental issues of military operations and strategy that have remained largely unchanged. Sections of the doctrine deal with coordinating the civilian and military arms of the US government, the requirement for US political leaders to set clear political objectives, and linking military operations to the political objections. The *Small Wars Manual* discusses the conduct of intelligence operations in counterinsurgency, the training of local forces, and even organizing the military occupation of a country. Throughout the Marine doctrine there is an emphasis on conducting operations within the framework of international, American, and local law. Developing and maintaining good relations with the local population is held to be an essential part of successful operations. The *Small Wars Manual* reminds the reader of the importance of establishing the political legitimacy of US-supported local government and institutions. The *Small Wars Manual* also rules out a heavy-handed approach toward counterinsurgency.[7] The minimum practical amount of force is recommended, with the understanding that maintaining good long-term political relations with the local inhabitants is always the paramount goal.

Mao's Model of Revolutionary War

Mao Tse Tung, the leader of the Chinese Communist Party, developed a comprehensive theory of insurgency as he fought the Nationalist government of Chiang Kai-Shek during the 1930s and 1940s. It was a quantum leap forward in establishing a practical theory for an insurgent. In a series of essays written over a decade, Mao developed a "people's war" strategy to enable the militarily weaker insurgents to defeat superior government forces. Mao's model was drawn from

---

7   For a good overview of the USMC policies in Nicaragua, see Wray Johnson, "Airpower and Restraint in Small Wars: Marine Corps Aviation in the Second Nicaraguan Campaign, 1927–1933," *Aerospace Power Journal* (Fall, 2001).

classical military and Marxist theory, military history, and an analysis of China's conditions. Mao's theory of people's war has influenced, and continues to influence, insurgent groups throughout the world.[8]

Mao's theory assumes that revolutionary wars are likely to be protracted wars. Even where there is widespread dissatisfaction with the government, revolutionaries are rarely strong enough in terms of the military forces or economic resources needed to mount an effective military campaign early in the insurgency. Mao believed that the revolutionaries' best hope was to develop a superior political organization, to win the mass of people to their side, to build up "liberated areas" as bases for continued operations, to continually attrite and weaken government forces by guerrilla war and, finally, to defeat the government by force once the measures of relative strength favored the insurgents.

Mao put his priority not on building military forces, but in first building a strong revolutionary organization. With a strong central organization the insurgent could gain control of the populace, no matter how strong the government was in terms of military power. For Mao, military power was an outgrowth of a strong civil organization and in revolutionary warfare it was the population, not the armed forces, which provided the centre of gravity. For Mao, the revolutionary organization had to be continuously expanded and nurtured by propaganda and education. Well-organized insurgents could absorb military setbacks and still prevail in the long run as long as the organization was preserved. Mao's victory in the Chinese civil war was largely due to his brilliance in building a powerful organization.

Many post-World War II insurgencies followed a variation of Mao's "people's war" model and the Maoist model was found to be a highly effective means for conducting insurgency in countries whose populations consisted mostly of peasants. The Vietnamese insurgency against French rule (1946–1954) provides a good example of adapting the Maoist model to local conditions. Truong Chinh, a Vietnamese communist theoretician, understood the necessity for a protracted war to defeat the French, but disagreed with Mao's concept of guerrilla forces. Truong Chinh developed a particularly Vietnamese strategy of a "war of interlocking," in which both guerrilla and regular insurgent forces would conduct simultaneous operations against the French government forces.[9]

---

8   The most useful overview of Mao's works on revolutionary warfare theory in English is found in the *Selected Military Writings of Mao Tse-Tung* (Peking, 1963).

9   James Corum and Wray Johnson, *Airpower and Small Wars* (Lawrence, KS: University Press of Kansas, 2003), pp. 230–233. For a thorough study of the Vietnamese approach to revolutionary war doctrine, see Wray Johnson, *Vietnam and the American Doctrine for Small Wars* (Bangkok: White Lotus Press, 2001).

New Models of Counterinsurgency

After World War II France, Britain and other European powers faced a variety of insurgent challenges by nationalists eager to overthrow colonial rule. In other cases weak, pro-Western governments such as those in Greece and the Philippines were threatened by communist revolutionary insurgents with support from the Soviet Union. The post-war wave of insurgencies was a greater threat than anything the Western powers had faced within their empires. The successes of Mao's revolutionary insurgency theory and its variants compelled the non-communist powers to find an effective counterinsurgency doctrine. With the start of the Cold War, defeating local insurgent movements took on an international significance.

Among the first challenges to be faced by Britain and the United States was the communist insurgency in Greece between 1944 and 1949. Greece had been devastated and impoverished by the world war and had a large and dissatisfied rural population with legitimate grievances. Such a population provided many willing recruits to the Greek Communist Party, which had used the wartime occupation to organize and arm itself. By the end of the war the Greek Communist Party possessed a large military force and controlled much of Greece. To help the newly established pro-Western Greek government, Britain and the United States provided considerable military and economic support. Britain and the United States sent military advisors, trainers and equipment to help the Greek government build an effective army. President Truman understood that it was essential for the Greek government to address the economic privation of the Greek populace, so along with military support the Americans provided hundreds of millions of dollars of financial aid to help the Greek economy. In Greece the British and American strategy proved successful. British and American military equipment and training gave the Greek armed forces the necessary superiority to defeat the communist forces in the field and US economic aid helped the Greek government meet the basic needs of the populace.

In the Philippines a communist rebellion challenged the newly independent Philippine government from 1946 to 1954. As in Greece, the insurgency had its roots in long-standing social problems, notably in the high level of poverty among the peasant laborers. The Philippine Communist Party and its military arm, called the Huks, developed from wartime resistance movements and were well-equipped and prepared to launch an insurgency at the end of the world war. The initial reaction of the Philippine government was a heavy handed military campaign against the rebels, which only served to further alienate the rural peasants and win more recruits for the insurgents. By 1949 the insurgency was growing rapidly.

As in Greece, the United States provided military advisors, trainers and equipment to improve and enlarge the Philippine military. The American military advisor to the Philippine defence ministry, Lieutenant Colonel Edward Lansdale, USAF, worked closely with the highly capable Defence Minister Ramon Magsasysay to craft a comprehensive counterinsurgency strategy. Realizing that the key to success lay in winning over the rural peasantry, the US financed development programs in the countryside where the insurgency had its roots. The Philippine

Army combined military operations with civic action activities that visibly improved the lives of the Filipino peasants. Magsasysay demonstrated inspired leadership as he worked tirelessly to visit the rural people and address their most pressing issues. Land reform ensured that many formerly landless peasants were granted title to plots of public land. An amnesty program not only encouraged the guerrillas to surrender, but also provided them with financial help to get started as independent farmers.[10] As the government addressed many of the concerns of the rural populace, the insurgency receded.

In the British colony of Malaya, post-war disorder and the rise of the Malayan Communist Party during the world war set the stage for a major insurgency that broke out in 1948. At first, the British dealt with the insurgency by military action. Forty thousand army troops were committed to Malaya, the 10,000-man police force was increased to 40,000, and tens of thousands of Malayan home guards were recruited to guard the mines and rubber plantations that produced Malaya's wealth. Yet, even with the massive application of military power, the insurgent army continued to grow and had reached more than 10,000 fighters, backed up by many thousands of active sympathizers, by 1951.

A new cadre of military and civilian leaders sent out in 1952 quickly turned a bad situation around. The new governor general and military commander, General Gerald Templer, made political and economic reform the key elements of the British strategy. Another key element of the British strategy was to Malayanize the conflict by training an effective Malayan army and reforming the police.[11] Large unit sweep operations that had little effect against the insurgents were replaced with a military plan centred on small unit offensive operations and a major effort to provide basic security for the population. The British defused the nationalist issue by promising independence to the Malayans and systematically preparing the Malayans to take responsibility for their own security. More than anything else, the British effort was based on a program of building sound Malayan institutions. The British strategy quickly turned the situation to the advantage of the government and by 1955 the insurgency was fading quickly and was virtually gone when Malaya became independent in 1959. Although Britain lost a colony much earlier than expected, the newly independent Malaya had a pro-Western and anti-communist government. Strategically, it was a good outcome for Britain.

In the aftermath of insurgencies in Greece, Malaya, and the Philippines, a major conflict was heating up in Vietnam that featured both an internal insurgency and an outside conventional attack by North Vietnam. Largely to meet the challenge of insurgency in Vietnam, several of the most successful British and American practitioners of counterinsurgency wrote books that discussed the

---

10 For an overview of the successful counterinsurgency strategies of the Huk campaign see Douglas Blaufarb, *The Counterinsurgency Era: U.S. Doctrine and Performance* (New York: The Free Press, 1977), pp. 24–40.

11 On the program to Malayanize the war and build effective Malayan security forces, see James Corum, *Training Indigenous Forces in Counterinsurgency: A Tale of Two Insurgencies* (Carlisle, PA: US Army War College Strategic Studies Institute, 2006).

strategic, operational, and tactical lessons learned in recent campaigns. Sir Robert Thompson, who had served as a senior civilian in Malaya, wrote several important books dealing with the basic principles of counterinsurgency operations. Colonel Lansdale, who had served in the Philippines, wrote his memoirs of the campaign and described the development of a successful strategy.[12] Taken together, the works of these British and American practitioners amount to a comprehensive theory and doctrine model for counterinsurgency operations against insurgents employing variations of Mao's revolutionary warfare strategy. Some of the basic principles outlined by the American and British authors were:

> *1. The civilian population is the centre of gravity in an insurgency. One cannot defeat insurgents without winning the support of the population. Counterinsurgency strategy should be geared to driving a wedge between the population and the rebels. 2. Successful counterinsurgency requires a comprehensive strategy that combines military and police operations with social, political and economic action. Since insurgencies grow out of large-scale dissatisfaction with the government, the social, political and economic problems that provide the fuel for insurgency need to be addressed. 3. There needs to be a unity of effort by the government forces, that is, close coordination between the military and civilian agencies at every level. 4. Effectively fighting the insurgents, who usually live among and draw support from the civilian population, requires good intelligence. Military and police action without good intelligence is largely a wasted effort. 5. Military and civic action campaigns need to proceed simultaneously, and be coordinated with each other. 6. The government needs to wage an effective media campaign to reassure the population and undermine support for the insurgents. 7. Military and police power needs to be applied carefully and with discrimination. A "heavy-handed" approach is wasteful and can cause discontent among the populace.*

As the British and Americans carried out their post-war counterinsurgency campaigns the French fought two major campaigns in Indochina (1946–1954) and Algeria (1954–1962). To address the conditions posed by these conflicts several French officers developed their own line of counterinsurgency theory. One of the most important French works on the subject was written by French Army

---

12   Some of the best works on counterinsurgency operations include Sir Robert Thompson, *Defeating Communist Insurgency* (London: Chatto & Windus, 1966); also important is Thompson's *No Exit From Vietnam* (London: Chatto & Windus, 1969). An outline of basic counterinsurgency theory and practice is Frank Kitson, *Low Intensity Operations* (London: Faber and Faber, 1971). An important American work is John J. McCuen, *The Art of Counter-Revolutionary War* (London: Faber and Faber, 1966). See also the memoir of one of America's leading counterinsurgency practitioners, Edward Lansdale, *In the Midst of Wars: An American's Mission to Southeast Asia* (1972; repr. New York: Fordham University Press, 1991).

Colonel Roger Trinquier and published as *Modern Warfare* in 1961. Trinquier, who had served in several counterinsurgency campaigns, outlined some useful tactics for dealing with urban rebellion, including a discussion of how to seal off a city district, collect comprehensive data on the population, and register the population as a means to limit the ability of insurgents to move within the country. Trinquier's doctrine differed from the British/American model on several points. First of all, Trinquier viewed counterinsurgency primarily in military terms. Establishing a military presence and crushing the insurgents by force was his first priority. In contrast to the British and American view that military action should be carried out simultaneously with civic action programs, Trinquier argued first for military action to crush the insurgents. Only then would the government carry out its civic action programs. Whereas British and American theorists of the 1950s and 1960s believed that building up a legitimate civilian government and supporting indigenous institutions were key elements of counterinsurgency strategy, there is little of this in Trinquier's work. Essentially, Trinquier believed in strong-arming the population into compliance with French rule.[13]

A French counterinsurgency specialist with an approach closer to the British/American views was Lieutenant Colonel David Galula, who published several important works on counterinsurgency in the early 1960s.[14] Galula had extensive service in Algeria and described the French army tactics that had been generally successful in winning control of most of the Algerian countryside from the FLN rebels. For Galula, presence was essential and the French civic action teams of the SAS provided an effective model of bringing a positive government presence to rural Algeria. For Galula, the essential thing for the soldier was to work closely with the population. As the campaign in Algeria progressed, local home guard groups proved highly effective in defending the villages from FLN influence.

Although Galula's theory of placing the priority of effort in winning over and protecting the population proved to be a sound approach to counterinsurgency, the French campaigns in Indochina and Algeria ultimately failed because the French strategy of trying to maintain a colonial empire in the post-World War II world was simply impossible. Excellent operational techniques and tactics could not substitute for a national strategy that never had a chance for success. Britain in Malaya followed a more realistic strategy of allowing independence, but ensuring that the independent Malaya would be stable and pro-British.

---

13   Roger Trinquier, *Modern Warfare: A French View of Counterinsurgency* (London: Pall Mall Press, 1964). The French version was published as *La Guerre Moderne* (Paris: Editions de la Table Ronde, 1961). An important work outlining the French approach to counterinsurgency in Algeria is General Paul Aussaresses, *Services Speciaux: Algerie, 1955–1957* (Paris: Perrin, 2001); English translation: *The Battle of the Casbah: Terrorism and Counter-Terrorism in Algeria 1955–1957* (London: Enigma Books, 2003).

14   See David Galula, *Counterinsurgency Warfare: Theory and Practice* (London: Praeger, 1964); and David Galula, *Pacification in Algeria 1956–1958* (Rand Study, 1963).

America's Failure in Vietnam

In Vietnam from 1961 to 1973 the US government and military signally failed to apply lessons from recent successful counterinsurgency campaigns. While there were many unique aspects to Vietnam many were also remarkably similar to the conditions in the Philippines and Malaya. In all these cases the counterinsurgent was working with similar rural societies and the rebel forces had a similar ideology, organization and tactics. In the early 1960s Edward Lansdale, now an Air Force general, and Sir Robert Thompson, appointed as chief of the British advisory mission to Vietnam from 1961 to 1965, urged the US military to undertake a concerted counterinsurgency campaign in that country. They argued for a comprehensive civil/military strategy based on the model of the campaigns in Malaya and the Philippines and a strategy that would enable the South Vietnamese to defend themselves rather than rely on US military forces.[15] Unfortunately, US military leaders at the time could only think in terms of large-scale conventional war. Starting with the introduction of American combat divisions to Vietnam in 1965, the counterinsurgency side of the conflict was largely ignored by the American military as it concentrated on the big battles against the North Vietnamese Army. While the US was usually successful in the battlefield, such success failed to support the legitimacy of the South Vietnamese state or provide security to the peasant villagers of South Vietnam.[16]

In 1969 Thompson told the US military commanders that their conventional war strategy was "a failure" and argued that the US should have concentrated on building up the South Vietnamese Army from the start.[17] Thompson, along with several American experts, pointed to the US Marine Corps program of training local defense forces in the northern sector of the country. The USMC policy of putting small detachments to live among the Vietnamese villagers and to train local home guard forces had made the rural areas of the north secure from Vietcong activity. Although such a program would have increased the security for the rural population in the south, the conventionally-minded General Westmoreland

---

15   On the US experience in Vietnam and the failure to employ a coherent counter-insurgency campaign, see W. Scott Thompson and Donaldson D. Frizzell, eds, *The Lessons of Vietnam* (New York: Russak and Co., 1977). In it are articles by Maj. Gen Edward Lansdale on counterinsurgency and an article on the small but successful US program to train local self-defense forces by Col. Robert Rheault, "The Special Forces and the CIDG Program," pp. 246–55. See also Thomas Thayer, "Territorial Forces," pp. 256–62.

16   A good overview of the US counterinsurgency doctrine in the Vietnam era is Andrew Birtle, *U.S. Army Counterinsurgency and Contingency Operations Doctrine 1942–1976* (Washington, DC: US Army Center for Military History, 2006).

17   Thompson's sharp critique of American strategy in Vietnam is found in *No Exit from Vietnam*, pp. 122–144. However, Thompson also pointed out that some potentially effective counterinsurgency programs were weak because the effort was too thin and spread out and that programs to build the economic and social infrastructure lacked coherence. See pp. 152–55.

would hear none of it.[18] Westmoreland, the US military commander in Vietnam from 1965 to 1969, had no interest in operations that did not rack up impressive body counts and refused to deploy army forces for activities such as securing the rural population. When Thompson argued that the Malaya strategy of clearing and pacifying one district at a time was also appropriate for South Vietnam he was again ignored.[19]

In 1969 General Creighton Abrams replaced General Westmoreland as American commander in Vietnam and dramatically changed the American strategy. Where Westmoreland had focused on fighting a conventional war against the North Vietnamese units, Abrams made securing the South Vietnamese rural population the primary American mission. Under Abrams rural economic development under the CORDS program became a top priority. The new strategy, aimed at undermining the Vietcong insurgency, soon showed dramatic results. Vietcong insurgent presence in the countryside diminished as the rural areas became more secure and more prosperous. By 1972 the Vietcong insurgency in the countryside was essentially defeated. But the Abrams strategy came too late to change the course of the war. American public opinion had turned against the Vietnam War by the summer of 1968 and the American public was insisting on reducing the US forces in Vietnam. In taking over direction of the war effort in 1965, the Americans had ignored the vital mission of helping the South Vietnamese build sound institutions. When the Americans pulled out of Vietnam in 1973 the South Vietnamese government and military were not strong enough to resist the North Vietnamese. In April 1975 South Vietnam fell, not to the Vietcong insurgents, but to a conventional armoured *Blitzkrieg* carried out by North Vietnamese conventional forces.[20]

After the Vietnam War most of the American military leaders—the same leaders that refused to employ a counterinsurgency strategy in Vietnam—took away the false lesson that counterinsurgency strategies did not work. The prevailing attitude in the US military and government was "no more counterinsurgency wars."[21] The many positive lessons of Vietnam, such as the effectiveness of the rural pacification policy from 1969 to 1972, were forgotten in the mainstream military as it focused its attention on developing conventional war doctrine to oppose the Warsaw Pact. Counterinsurgency courses were cut out of the curricula of the American military staff colleges, and the study of the subject was relegated to the Special Forces and a few military academics.[22] The key parts of the military essential

---

18   Thompson, *No Exit From Vietnam*, pp. 122–39.

19   Ibid., pp. 197–8.

20   Possibly the best critique of the US Army's failure in Vietnam is Andrew Krepinevich, *The Army and Vietnam* (Baltimore: Johns Hopkins Press, 1986).

21   See Richard Locke-Pullan, "'An Inward-Looking Time': The United States Army, 1973–1976," *Journal of Military History* (April 2003), vol. 67, no. 2: 483–512. On the thinking on counterinsurgency in the post-Vietnam US Air Force, see Dennis Drew, "U.S. Airpower Theory and the Insurgent Challenge: A Short Journey to Confusion," *Journal of Military History* (October 1998), vol. 62, no. 4: 809–32.

22   US Army Lieutenant Colonel John Nagl argues that the US Army in Vietnam was not an effective learning institution. See John Nagl, *Learning to Eat Soup With a Knife:*

for counterinsurgency operations were gutted. Special operations forces were greatly reduced and the human intelligence expertise, the most important form of intelligence for counterinsurgency, was drastically cut as money and personnel were transferred to high-tech intelligence systems best suited for conventional war.

A Counterinsurgency Success

In the aftermath of Vietnam, a remarkable counterinsurgency success in El Salvador went almost unnoticed in the US military establishment. From 1981 to 1992 the US provided military advisors and trainers to El Salvador, as well as several billion dollars in military and economic assistance, and helped that country defeat a strong Marxist insurgency. The small group of American military and State Department personnel who served in El Salvador developed a strategy that generally followed the classic British/American doctrines of counterinsurgency—all of which were validated by the outcome of the war.

At the start of their involvement the American advisors determined that the Salvadorans had to initiate broad reforms in the military and civilian spheres; that the economic problems of the nation had to be addressed; that Salvadoran security forces had to be retrained and reformed; and that an emphasis had to be placed upon civic action and human rights throughout all levels of government—something alien to the tradition of military dictatorship that had long prevailed in El Salvador. After Vietnam the US Congress would not allow the US military to commit large conventional forces to the conflict, so the US support to El Salvador was restricted to advisors, trainers, equipment and supplies. The military advisors and State Department officials on the ground used American aid as a lever to push the Salvadoran government to accept the changes that were needed to defeat the insurgents.[23]

The El Salvador experience added to the corpus of Western counterinsurgency theory.[24] Max Manwaring, who served for several years in El Salvador helping to craft a comprehensive strategy for the Salvadorans and Americans, argued for a "new people-oriented model. Every policy, program, and action—military, political, economic, opinion making—must contribute directly to the maintenance or enhancement of political legitimacy. As much must be focused on pre-conflict and

---

Counterinsurgency Lessons from Malaya and Vietnam (Chicago: University of Chicago Press, 2005).

23 For the background of the war and the US policies in El Salvador, see James Corum, "The Air War in El Salvador," Airpower Journal (Summer, 1998).

24 For a good overview of the lessons from El Salvador, see Edwin Corr and Courtney Prisk, "El Salvador: Transforming Society to Win the Peace," in Edwin Corr and Stephen Sloan, eds, Low Intensity Conflict (Boulder, CO: Westview, 1992), pp. 223–54.

post-conflict periods as on the conflict itself."[25] Manwaring was mainly restating essential principles of counterinsurgency that had been forgotten after Vietnam. Manwaring argued that the war in El Salvador was not just about military action but equally about social, political and economic reform: "The ultimate outcome of any effort to deal with a given conflict is not primarily determined by the skilful manipulation of violence in one of the many military/police battles that might take place."[26] El Salvador was compared with other insurgencies and a useful matrix was drawn up outlining the many tasks that a nation needed to address in order to successfully defeat the insurgents.[27] While the success in El Salvador led to a renewed interest in counterinsurgency among a small group of American military officers, the mainstream US military leaders still expressed little interest in such conflicts.

It should be noted that at the same time that some Americans were learning lessons in El Salvador, the British military was gaining broad experience in counterinsurgency in Northern Ireland. Tactically and operationally it was a very different kind of war from the campaigns recently fought by British troops in Aden and Oman. In Northern Ireland the British forces had to operate in an urban environment and develop a sophisticated human intelligence system capable of tracking down the small IRA terrorist cells.[28]

Insurgency Evolves

While the Maoist model of insurgency still remains common—witness the ongoing Marxist insurgency in Colombia—groups in the Middle East developed a new insurgent strategy and organization to carry on the fight against Israel during the 1980s and 1990s. In 1987 Palestinians in the territories occupied by Israel rose up in a rebellion called the *Intifada*, which has been conducted at varying levels of intensity ever since. In contrast to the highly centralized leadership of the Palestinian Liberation Organization (PLO), some of the Palestinians developed a new and very loose form of organization. The *Intifada* became a popular rebellion organized through a network of small local groups. The local committees and the leaders of the United National Command of the *Intifada* followed a different path than the guerrilla leaders in the past who emphasized personal charisma and leadership. Handbills produced by the local committees were simply signed "UNC" (United

---

25 Max Manwaring, "The Threat of the Contemporary Peace Environment: The Challenge to Change Perspective," in *Low Intensity Conflict*, pp. 46–59. See also pp. 52–3.

26 Ibid., p. 54.

27 See Max Manwaring and John Fishel, "Insurgency and Counter-Insurgency: Toward a New Analytical Approach," *Small Wars and Insurgencies* (Winter, 1992), 272–305. The authors provide a matrix of requirements needed to oppose insurgency successfully.

28 On the British counterinsurgency experiences of this period, see Ian Beckett, *Modern Insurgencies and Counter-insurgencies* (London: Routledge, 2001), pp. 217–31.

National Command) and *Intifada* leaders chose to remain anonymous. With an insurgent leadership that was difficult to identify, the usual Israeli tactic of arresting the local and national PLO leaders failed to cripple the organization. The new form of guerrilla organization proved highly resilient against all the Israeli efforts to suppress it.[29] The Palestinian rebels also showed a new sophistication in their ability to work through various media to publicize the Palestinian cause to the world and to place Israel under intense international pressure.[30] With only a few regular fighters and little chance of striking any serious military blows against Israel, the Palestinian insurgents have had considerable success in winning legitimacy in the eyes of the world.

After the Israeli invasion of Lebanon to defeat the PLO in 1982, the Israelis faced a new style of insurgent group in the form of Hezbullah, the organization of the Lebanese Shiites that led the resistance to Israel in the occupied zone of southern Lebanon. Hezbullah was originally organized around Shiite clerics, and based its popularity on being a combination of an ethnic and a religious organization. As with the Palestinian *Intifada*, Hezbullah is loosely organized into many semi-independent cells under a large central council. Military activity is kept on a small scale, with most military raids against the Israelis carried out by no more than a squad. Beginning in the early 1980s, Hezbullah pioneered the use of suicide bombers as a standard tactic against the Israeli forces. The decentralized nature of the Hezbullah organization also made it difficult for the Israelis to strike any decisive blows against the leaders or military forces. After 18 years of desultory warfare in southern Lebanon, the Israeli public was frustrated with the ongoing conflict and in 2000 Israel simply pulled its forces out of Lebanon. Hezbullah was left in effective control of the southern third of the country. The conflicts in the Middle East inspired a small group of thinkers within the US military to analyze the new tactics and strategies developed by Hezbullah and the Palestinians. One of the leading thinkers looking at the changes in insurgency conflict was Colonel T.X. Hammes, USMC, who described the new, loosely-organized forms of insurgency as "fourth generation warfare" in a series of articles in the *Marine Corps Gazette*. In 2004 Hammes refined his analysis in *The Sling and the Stone*, which laid out the challenge of modern insurgency as that the US and Western powers are facing today in Iraq and Afghanistan.

Counterinsurgency Lessons from Iraq and Afghanistan

After taking down the Taliban regime in Afghanistan in 2001 and Saddam Hussein's army in Iraq in 2003 the United States armed forces found themselves singularly

---

29   Col. Thomas X. Hammes, USMC, *The Sling and the Stone: On War in the 21st Century* (St Paul: Zenith Press, 2004), pp. 100–101.

30   See Lt. Col. T. X. Hammes, USMC, "The Evolution of War: A Fourth Generation," Thesis of the National Defence College, Kingston, Ontario (June 1994), 25–7.

unprepared to fight insurgents or irregular enemies, or to carry out any operation other than a high-tech conventional war. From 2001 to 2006 the US military leadership was generally slow to respond and adapt to the challenge of fighting insurgents.

After the remarkable victory over Iraq during the Gulf War of 1991 there appeared a kind of euphoria among many of the top US military leaders. The rapid and decisive victory over Saddam Hussein's large army was won through the application of superior technology and at a price of less than 200 fatalities on the American side. Decades of training and preparing for the high-tech conventional war had paid off handsomely. For most of the US military, and most of the American public, the Gulf War seemed to prove that American technology presented such an overwhelming advantage that the US could apply the same formula to defeat almost any potential enemy quickly, efficiently, and decisively — and at minimal cost.[31] Richard Cheney, secretary of defense during the First Gulf War, was highly impressed with this vision of warfare and commented shortly after the Gulf War: "This war demonstrated dramatically the new possibilities of what has been called the 'military technological revolution in warfare'."[32] Through the 1990s the limited conflicts in Bosnia in 1995 and Kosovo in 1999 seemed to confirm that technology was the primary factor in warfare. Claims were made by the top officers in the US military that high technology had fundamentally changed warfare; that modern technology had overcome the fog and friction of the battlefield that Clausewitz described as the normal condition of war.

Largely because such fallacious thinking was so prevalent in the US military in the 1990s there was little planning for the occupation of Iraq. After the US and coalition forces won the conventional victory against Saddam Hussein's forces in 2003 Iraq quickly descended into chaos and civil war. For a long time after the start of the insurgency, the US military and civilian leadership failed to understand the conditions in Iraq.[33] Despite the recent experience of the interventions in Bosnia and Kosovo in the 1990s, when large forces on the ground had been necessary to stabilize the situation, US Secretary of Defense Donald Rumsfeld and the Chairman of the Joint Chiefs General Myers insisted upon occupying Iraq with a force far too small to establish order.[34] The view of many in the American military

---

31 On the US military's lessons from Gulf War One and the belief that the conflict represented a fundamental change in the nature of war, see James S. Corum, *Fighting the War on Terror* (St Paul: Zenith Press, 2007), pp. 51–82.

32 Cited in Thomas Keaney and Eliot Cohen, *Revolution in Warfare?* (Annapolis, MD: Naval Institute Press, 1995), p. 188.

33 There are many recent accounts of the failure of US strategy and leadership in Iraq. For one of the best accounts see Thomas Ricks, *Fiasco: The American Military Adventure in Iraq* (London: Penguin, 2006).

34 On the historical troop requirements needed for interventions and stability operations, see James T. Quinlivan, "Force Requirements in Stability Operations," *Parameters* (Winter, 1995), 59–69. Quinlivan points out that Northern Ireland, Malaya, Bosnia, and a host of other stability operations required as many as 20 soldiers per 1,000 civilians to effectively control the population. The US force ratio in Iraq from 2003 to 2005 was less than five soldiers to every 1,000 of the population.

leadership was that America's high-tech advantage made numbers on the ground unnecessary. What they forgot was that successful counterinsurgency requires constant human interaction, and that requires troops on the ground rather than sophisticated space surveillance or airplanes at 30,000 feet.

Failing to stabilize the situation, various factions in Iraq had the freedom to organize and initiate violence against each other and the coalition forces. With no plan or strategy the US and coalition forces failed to build effective Iraqi institutions and security forces. A few intermediate commanders showed some talent for counterinsurgency, the most notable being General David Petreaus, commander of the 101st Airborne Division in Iraq in 2003 to 2005. Promoted to lieutenant general in 2005 he took over the US Army Combined Arms Command and organized a specially selected group of Army and Marine Corps officers and civilian experts to develop a new, comprehensive counterinsurgency doctrine to respond to the challenges facing the US military in Iraq and Afghanistan. In late 2006 the Army and Marine Corps published their first comprehensive counterinsurgency doctrine since the Vietnam War, Field Manual FM 3-24: Counterinsurgency.

FM 3-24 was published as capstone army doctrine, that is, one of the six primary manuals upon which all army doctrine is based. Over 220 pages long, the manual is essentially a book-length treatise on the theory and practice of counterinsurgency. It begins with a chapter on the principles of counterinsurgency, which are essentially the same as the principles established in British and American doctrine in the 1960s. The techniques of intelligence are discussed in detail and extensive advice is provided on the techniques of building host nation institutions and security forces. Most of the work follows the well-known and highly effective counterinsurgency techniques of the past and all the points are illustrated by brief historical vignettes. What is new about the doctrine in FM 3-24 is its emphasis on understanding the new, networked type of insurgent organization. The doctrine contains an extensive annex written by a sociologist to provide the counterinsurgency planner with a basic social network analysis model. Most importantly, the doctrine stresses the importance of a comprehensive strategy for counterinsurgency in which the military is only one of the elements—and perhaps not the most important one. Basically, the doctrine more than adequately fulfills its purpose of providing practical guidance for the commander and staff planner.

While FM 3-24 is a big step forward for the American military, one still wonders if the US and its allies will continue to develop their understanding of what is likely to be a prevalent form of warfare in the twenty-first century, or whether the institutional preference of the civilian and military leadership for the high-tech conventional war approach will derail the progress made in counterinsurgency theory and doctrine. Even at the time of this writing (2008) there is considerable resistance within the US military leadership, notably in the US Air Force, to abandoning the high-tech/minimal manpower strategy that failed to live up to its promise in both Afghanistan and Iraq.[35]

---

35   An example of a critique on the US Army's classical approach to counterinsurgency doctrine and the advocacy of the high-tech/low manpower strategy comes from a general on the US Air Force Staff. See Major General Charles Dunlap, "Air-Minded Considerations for Joint Counterinsurgency Doctrine," *Air and Space Power Journal* (Winter, 2007).

Air Power: The Quest to Remove Battle from War

Joel Hayward[1]

Warfare is among humans' oldest collective activities. Etched in clay or carved in stone within our earliest writings, depictions and descriptions of war reveal armed competitions between communities which seem, in their nature although not in their technology, little different to many of today's wars. Records of conflicts occurring in all of the last 50 centuries teach us that by far the most common forms of warfare, and most of history's decisive battles, have involved small or large armies inflicting lethal violence upon each other and, sometimes, disregarding ideals, upon civilian communities. Battles and wars have occurred at sea far less frequently. Navies have more often served as trade protectors and as transporters of soldiers to more distant regions where, once ashore, the soldiers fought on battlefields. Indeed, throughout the last 50 centuries armies have dominated warfare. Ideas on how to raise, train, sustain, deploy and command armies have dominated military thinking. It is unsurprising, then, that the word 'strategy' comes from the Greek words for 'army leadership'.

By the time the Wright Brothers pioneered powered flight in the decade before the guns of August roared in 1914 the centrality of the battlefield in war and the key functions of army components – including infantry, cavalry and artillery – had become deeply ingrained in what we might call the Western way of war. Periods of significant technological and organisational development had added such influential things as horses, gunpowder, mass-mobilisation and the industrial production of ordnance, yet the concepts, strategies and practices of soldiers throughout the ages retained a remarkable degree of similarity. A leading Crusader was as likely to recognise and draw ideas and inspiration from strategies and tactics within Caesar's *Gallic Wars* as was a general of the French Revolution or the Boer War. In short, 50 centuries of evolutionary trial and error had given army leaders a fairly consistent set of ideas on how best to compete against opposing forces.

---

1   Dr Joel Hayward is the Dean of the Royal Air Force College. He is a director of the Royal Air Force Centre for Air Power Studies. He also heads King's College London's Air Power Studies Division.

The advent of powered flight gave some non-military authors, pundits and futurists dramatic new and frightening ideas about the vulnerability of urban populations to assault from airships and aircraft which would operate away from, and independently of, battlefields. H.G. Wells, aware of the horrors inflicted unusually on cities by artillery during the American Civil War and the Franco-Prussian War, is perhaps the best-known of those who wrote that the British Isles were no longer safe behind their moat and that all great cities would soon face peril.

On the other hand, the consensus among military practitioners, thinkers and commentators in the decade before the Great War seems to be that these new machines, if they were to have any significant military role (and of that there was no consensus), would operate within the very same strategic and ethical framework of war that had developed throughout 5,000 years. Naval thinkers saw them as potentially better eyes for seeing afar than anything that existed aboard ships. Army officers, depending on their corps backgrounds and inclinations, saw them potentially as scouts, alongside the cavalry, for observation and reconnaissance, and perhaps (as technology developed) as a means of applying fires à la artillery.

Very few professional military men argued that airships or aircraft could or should conduct decisive campaigns against civilian populations and none argued for the creation of separate air organisations for that purpose. However novel and fantastic flying seemed in those early days, one single decade of flying could scarcely affect 500 decades of strategic and ethical thinking. In the last years of peace before 1914 it was clear to most military professionals that the flying machines would mainly serve in armies on and around battlefields in customary roles assigned to them by army leaders whose concepts, strategies and tactics would look much like those seen in previous generations.

Many army officers were nonetheless excited at the prospect of enhanced capabilities in these crucial functions. Training and actual missions revealed that aircraft could locate and observe enemies and make sense of their dispositions and likely intentions faster than conventional cavalry patrols. The largest European armies purchased aircraft primarily with these roles in mind. By war's outbreak close to 1,000 aircraft were imbedded within the various opposing armies (and, in some cases, within the navies). They constituted function-oriented corps like the other army corps: of infantry, cavalry and artillery. With only slight variations in name (Royal Flying Corps, *Corpo Aeronautico Militare*, *Luftstreitkraefte*, *Aviation Militaire*, United States Army Air Service, and so forth) they were army air corps, intended to contribute to the armies' combined-arms battle.

The first significant contributions aircraft made on both sides reinforced early army notions that aircraft were best suited to reconnaissance as flying cavalry patrols. In the great manoeuvrist Battle of Tannenberg, in August 1914, the Germans responded to intelligence gained from aircraft as well as from radio interception and moved artfully and very successfully against attacking Russian armies. Weeks later, in the West, French and British commanders were shocked to learn from French aviators that the German First Army had unexpectedly turned to the southeast, away from Paris. This left an exposed and porous flank and a relatively weak front for the French and British to attack if they risked all and wasted no time. They took the risk and moved quickly. It worked. In grim battle they stopped German advances and, after a series of attempts at flanking manoeuvres by both sides, the front began to solidify, finally settling into so-called 'trench stalemate' by Christmas 1914.

Army reliance on aerial reconnaissance remained high throughout the war, but when combat fluidity gave way in late 1914 to static warfare the dispositions and movements of enemy armies ceased to be the primary things that army commanders wanted aviators to observe.[2] The increasingly pressing need for accuracy prompted artillerists to seek from aviators photographs for map-making as well as targeting and range-finding information and feedback. They gained the latter mainly from spotters in tethered balloons but also from spotters in aircraft. Whereas semaphore and similar flag systems had allowed artillery spotters standing on hills in previous generations to see and sometimes influence the effectiveness of artillery, during the Great War no one found an easy means of creating two-way, or even one-way, communication between ground troops and observers in aircraft. Experiments with radio telegraphy eventually led to a rudimentary system. Yet by far the most common and workable arrangement involved ground troops laying out coloured panels in certain patterns, or using flares and smoke pots, to send messages to aviators whose options for sending back spontaneous useful instructions or targeting advice remained poor.

Armies on both sides quickly realised the importance of preventing the enemy from gaining and exploiting information provided by aviators and of ensuring that the enemy could not impede their own intelligence gathering and dissemination. Armed by late 1915 with weapons that fired forward through the propellers, machine-gun-equipped 'fighters' soon patrolled the skies above battlefields. Army commanders initially distributed fighters among reconnaissance units so that they could protectively escort them on photo-reconnaissance or artillery-spotting sorties. Within a year they were assembling large formations of fighters and sending them, not on escort missions but, by themselves, to target observation balloons and comb the skies for enemies to attack, on what we would today call campaigns for control of the air or 'air superiority'.

Many scholars argue that the key contribution made throughout the Great War by these large formations – most famous of them being Manfred 'Red Baron' von Richthofen's Flying Circus – was their interference with reconnaissance. One can argue with equal confidence that the other profoundly important contribution was psychological. They provided national morale-boosting heroes in a war unusually characterised by waves of nameless young soldiers, dying en masse, whose individual courage and fighting skills seemingly made no real impact. Armies provided few national heroes and, aside from leading generals, only a small number of soldiers became household names. Despite the bestowal of innumerable

---

2   See Lee Kennett, *The First Air War, 1914–1918* (New York: Free Press, 1991); and John H. Morrow Jr, *The Great War in the Air: Military Aviation from 1909 to 1921* (Washington: Smithsonian Institution Press, 1993).

well-earned medals, many commentators complained that chivalrous combat – the competition of single champions whose courage and skill made them distinct – had largely disappeared.

Like jousting knights, airmen reportedly often broke off collective action to duel at close range against their foes in single combat that seemed to be, but was not especially, framed by chivalrous codes of honour. Dubbed 'aces' by the French and then their allies, and *Überkanone* ['top guns'] by the Germans, these airmen became national heroes, and idols in some cases, to patriotic populations struggling to form positive empathetic bonds with the millions of men dying along lines stretching from the Channel to Switzerland. Thanks to adulatory newspapers and smart military publicists, the lives, exploits and habits of dozens of highly-decorated heroes became well-known to civilians throughout their own and even their enemies' states. At least some war, it seemed, was still heroic.

Airmen on both sides also sought to contribute more conventionally to the land battle not only through targeting railheads and march-routes, but also through bombing and strafing enemy troops on the battlefield. Distinguishing between friends and foes was not routinely difficult. The linear and commonly static nature of battle kept opponents separate except during particular assaults. Yet levels of fratricide remained troublesome. Accurately firing guns and dropping bombs on troops and defences was very difficult. The first crude aiming devices did not help much. Moreover, an increasing amount of small-arms fire, including newly designed anti-aircraft guns placed protectively around balloons and key strong points, combined with enemy aircraft to make the skies above battlefields highly dangerous for the flying artillery.

General Hugh Trenchard, Officer Commanding the Royal Flying Corps in the Field (a long-serving army officer, like most early air leaders), conceptualised warfare in traditional soldiering terms. Defeating the enemy's forces in decisive battle, he believed, provided strategic victory that ordinarily led to the imposition of conclusive political conditions. The best use of his increasing number of aircraft, he therefore argued, was first to have them attempt to clear the skies of enemies and then to throw them into combined-arms battle with as much coordination and cooperation with the army's other corps as possible. This view was pleasing to his boss, Field Marshal Douglas Haig, in charge of the entire BEF (British Expeditionary Force), who appreciated air power's ability to perform some army roles much faster or more thoroughly than regular infantry, cavalry or artillery could (at least alone). Unfortunately, circumstances were not always conducive to relentless offensive action, particularly when defending enemy air units were ready and more numerous. Frightful attrition in the air corresponded proportionately with that on the ground. RFC losses at Arras were so high that April 1917 became known as 'bloody April'.

Bombing soldiers, positions and equipment on the battlefield was very difficult and dangerous. Increased inter-service coordination brought greater effectiveness to both sides' efforts by war's end. Yet neither side proved masterful at what later became known as close air support. Impermanence of presence, lack of lethality, high fratricide and excessive casualty rates characterised attempts at army support and ground attack. Yet bombing military things closely behind or leading to the battlefield proved less difficult and dangerous and altogether more effective. This established an air–land integration focus (and operational ratio) that favoured interdiction over close air support. This logical favouritism – airmen preferring to avoid close joint battle and strike instead at people and things away from battlefields – has never significantly changed and has always confused and disappointed soldiers who have expected friendly aircraft continuously overhead or on call.

Bombing things far further from the battlefield, indeed entirely unconnected to the battlefield, proved even less troublesome. Bombing cities that were not fortresses or populations that were not garrisons was morally unusual, resembling only aberrant excesses in occasional previous wars. Yet national frustrations and enmities and tit-for-tat cycles of actions and reactions caused on both sides a degree of moral apathy and a barely perceived steady weakening of stances.

These independent (of the battlefield) missions actually started very early in the war. Attacks on German airships and their hangars to prevent their use for army and navy reconnaissance, and perhaps reciprocally to repay Germans for a Zeppelin raid on the strongly-garrisoned fortress-city of Liège (then being bombarded by the German Army's largest artillery pieces) in the war's earliest days, led to tit-for-tat attacks by German airships against English and French urban targets. Exaggerated claims within German leadership that British morale was plummeting, as opposed to the actuality of resistance and hostility rising, led Germany to design 'heavy' Gotha bomber aircraft and deploy them, from May 1917, against English cities.

These Zeppelin and then Gotha raids against British towns and cities never did much damage or killed many people, and never constituted more than one per cent of all German air sorties during the war, but they led to the creation of a partially successful British air-defence system that eventually included observers, fighters, balloons and anti-aircraft guns. More importantly, the villainy of the civilian deaths in the German raids did not cause British political and public demands for superior moral behaviour, but caused widespread British demands for retribution in kind. The creation of the Royal Air Force in April 1918, the first anywhere to break free of army and navy, flowed directly from the perceived need for protection and a desire for retribution. The RAF almost immediately gained an 'Independent Force' of bombers – appropriately named, given that it would operate independently of war's traditional home, the battlefield – with which to make German civilians pay for their aviators' wicked attacks on innocent British people. Initially under Trenchard's command, the Independent Force struck cities including Frankfurt, Mannheim and Cologne for the war's remaining months. Ostensibly to destroy factories and logistical infrastructure, but in reality to convey vengeance, these raids were no more discriminate or accurate than the German attacks and similarly killed civilians and created bitterness.

It is ironic that, although they were soldiers or former soldiers, some prominent airmen during the first years after the Great War overlooked the significant integrated contribution made by aircraft to joint battle (at sea and on land), ignored the fantastic potential in this area, and focused their attention on the 'independent' missions which had been morally and strategically unusual and relatively unimportant militarily. The Great War had not demonstrated that, contrary to 5,000 years of thinking, strategic decision would occur away from battlefields and battles. Nothing had shown that, even in this age of industrialisation, whole national populations were so culpable of criminality that they should be subject to collective responsibility and targeted and punished as 'the enemy'. There was very little evidence that aircraft could (and no new moral reasoning that they should) severely damage either industrial production or the national will to resist. Yet, primarily because of an understandable revulsion of trench warfare's unparalleled slaughter, these ideas, and especially those about production and national will, seemed strangely compelling to some thinkers.

Nowadays, scholars and practitioners looking at this period tend to focus their attention on three air power advocates and call them things like 'the classical theorists' or even 'prophets'.[3] These three were Giulio Douhet, an Italian, Hugh Trenchard, a Briton, and William Mitchell, an American. They also ascribe to them influential 'theories', which implies that the airmen articulated logical and self-consistent models of action based on empirical observation; certainly something stronger than speculation or conjecture. On closer examination, this was not entirely the case.

With his 1921 book in Italian, *The Command of the Air*, Douhet came closest of the three to expressing a comprehensive framework for understanding and optimally applying air power during warfare. Douhet felt shocked by what he considered as the horrendously attritional nature of land warfare, seeing the Great War not as aberrational but as typically modern. With industrial states now and henceforth mobilising their entire populations in war efforts, Douhet claimed, those populations were collectively responsible for the continuance of resistance. Their vulnerability to air attack logically made them far easier and, in his view, more directly strategic, targets than soldiers in defensive positions. Aircraft should strike civilian populations away from war's customary habitat, the battlefield, and destroy them and their civil organisation, key transport infrastructure and production means so that survivors as well as observers in other centres will, in fear and anger, create ungovernable civil circumstances or even pressure governments to surrender. Ignoring the traditional concept of innocence that had generally protected civilians, Douhet expressed an unusual logic for a warrior: winning wars quickly by killing or terrorising concentrations of civilians, who were anyway collectively culpable of state resistance, was more humane than allowing armies to slaughter each other in protracted industrialised competitions.

Douhet's views were not easily accessible or widely known, let alone generally palatable, to most of his contemporaries in other army air corps and emerging air forces. In Britain, Hugh Trenchard adopted similar ideas, albeit for his own reasons and with a different rationale. He increasingly argued in speeches, memoranda and reports the need for air forces (his own anyway) to remain independent. By this he meant free of the armies and navies to which military aircraft had earlier

---

3   David R. Mets, *The Air Campaign: John Warden and the Classical Airpower Theorists* (Air University, AL: Air University Press, 1999).

belonged, and free of their land and sea battles to which he had earlier insisted they were ideally suited to contributing.

Trenchard passionately advocated various novel roles independent of battles primarily because he could not contemplate the loss of the RAF's independence. He despaired at the rapid shrinking of squadron numbers and felt he needed to counter some mooted high-level suggestions to save money and reduce duplication by reabsorbing air assets into armies and navies. Not all the independent roles he identified and championed were conceptually consistent, proven during war or morally conventional. Among his unorthodox recommendations were the punishment of misbehaving indigenous communities in some parts of the Empire (even with poison gas if they remained recalcitrant) and the suppression of workers during industrial disturbances in Britain. His belief that air units could patrol and police some parts of the Empire more easily and cheaply than army units – an idea that again placed aircraft into conventional army roles, this time by what he called 'substitution' – actually worked rather well on some occasions and did save money and effort. Yet this type of operation, and Trenchard's increasingly vocal argument that the RAF might one day have to wage war against France or any other peer-competitor, and fight them by striking main cities, also shows that Trenchard no longer believed that civilians were innocents and therefore exempt from direct violence.[4]

His views were consistent in many ways with Douhet's and those of William 'Billy' Mitchell, who had commanded American air combat units during the Great War and became a public advocate of air power's efficacy in the first years of peace. Like Trenchard (with whom he had regular contact), Mitchell had earlier believed that aircraft should be used to best effect on an integrated battlefield but later, as Trenchard did, he revised his position to argue that aircraft could and should perform independent roles that would by themselves prove strategically decisive. Mitchell claimed that aircraft could protect American coasts from enemy warships at a fraction of the cost of maintaining huge and dreadfully expensive fleets, and that air attacks could break enemy morale by destroying infrastructural, industrial and even agricultural targets. Mitchell was less keen to see civilians targeted directly than Douhet and Trenchard (who was himself not quite as emphatic about this as the Italian), but he agreed with the others that, in any future wars of total state mobilisation, civilians were subject to collective responsibility and could save themselves from harm only by refusing to uphold the state and its war effort.

During the interwar years these views tended to dominate thinking on air power, even though aviators in many small and large wars (none of these wars being 'total') continued to provide close air support and interdiction on and around traditional battlefields. Even airmen in the United States, which intervened in several Central and South American conflicts and used air power most often

---

4   An excellent starting point, despite some internal conceptual inconsistencies, is Tami Davis Biddle, *Rhetoric and Reality in Air Warfare: The Evolution of British and American Ideas about Strategic Bombing, 1914–1945* (Princeton, NJ: Princeton University Press, 2002).

during them for reconnaissance and as flying artillery, favoured the theoretical but unproven potential of independent missions against purportedly strategic objects over these sorts of activities. Wanting separation from the Army, the US Army Air Corps sought separate roles and articulated a belief that its increasingly fine bombers, with impressive speed, range, survivability and load-carrying capability, should be used against enemy nodes far away from, and ideally *instead* of, battle.

When Adolf Hitler won power in 1933 he began freeing Germany of the crippling economic burden of the Treaty of Versailles and of its severe military constraints. With German air power assets and structures outlawed since 1919, and with no cadre of German air force officers learning and pushing ideas of independent decisive contributions, the dictator and Germany's senior military planners had relatively few and only weak experiential, conceptual and organisational reasons to think that air power had been, or would be, best used independently of traditional battlefields. When Hitler's military leaders created a new air force in 1935, named the Luftwaffe, they gave it a focus on decisive battle that largely represented the traditional strategic thinking of most German military men. Hitler, a soldier by both experience and inclination, and new air commander-in-chief Hermann Göring, a former above-the-trenches fighter ace, likewise saw air attack on and around the customary battlefield as heroic, essential and potentially strategic.

Göring and senior commanders immediately commenced developing the Luftwaffe into a physically resilient force with men and machines capable of enduring long periods of high stress in a variety of environments. Rather than creating separate, essentially mono-functional commands as the Royal Air Force did in 1936 (with the Bomber Command being primarily for deterrence by threatening attacks on the enemy's 'heartland' and with Fighter Command for home defence against the enemy bombers that would 'always get through'), the Luftwaffe formed huge, self-contained and far more flexible *multi*-functional operational commands called Luftflotten (Air Fleets).[5]

Each Luftflotte comprised all types of air combat units (reconnaissance, transport, fighter, ground-attack, dive-bomber, and bomber) as well as ground-based signals and flak units. The transfer of the latter from the Army to the Luftwaffe, in order to protect forward airfields and to aid in the air superiority contest that the Luftwaffe saw as a prerequisite to all air and land operations, greatly strengthened the physical toughness of each Luftflotte. This mutually supporting integration of aircraft and anti-aircraft artillery was years ahead of its time. A Luftflotte was immense, growing throughout World War II to become the air equivalent of an entire German Army group. It was nonetheless capable of being deployed in full to any European and Mediterranean theatre of operations, where it would partner an army group. Or it could be deployed in subordinate, army-sized commands called Fliegerkorps (Air Corps). Each Fliegerkorps was itself a smaller version of its parent; self-contained and fully multi-functional, capable of undertaking

---

5   Joel Hayward, 'The Luftwaffe's Agility: An Assessment of Relevant Concepts and Practices', in N. Parton, ed., *Air Power: The Agile Air Force* (Royal Air Force, 2007), pp. 40–49.

– either sequentially or simultaneously, cooperatively or independently – virtually the entire range of air missions from air superiority to reconnaissance, close air support, interdiction and even some 'indirect' bombing. Fliegerkorps were, in that sense, not entirely dissimilar to the Expeditionary Air Wings that several air forces, including the RAF, are currently creating.

During the first aggressive German campaigns of World War II the Luftwaffe sought and gained at least local air superiority and then synchronised its operations with those of the Army to a degree never before seen in war. Its reconnaissance aircraft (of which it had proportionately far more than any other air force) provided the Army with invaluable battlefield awareness and its bombers and dive-bombers interdicted the battlefield and applied firepower – commonly as flying artillery – unusually close to forward friendly troops. At tactical and operational levels Luftwaffe and Army commanders routinely met and coordinated their forces' efforts in time and space, creating joint focal points.

If winning wars is strategic and if, as the Nazis leaders believed, their joint campaigns of 1939 and 1940 were each intended as 'complete' wars in their own right, the Luftwaffe's contribution to battle was strategically successful (as was the Army's). Conversely, when it proved difficult to contain war within a traditional battlefield on which a decisive victory could be gained – as it did during the Battle of the Atlantic and then the assault on the Soviet Union – industrial insufficiency meant that comparative numerical inferiority rendered this formula inadequate. The result was seemingly endless attrition without decision.

After proving comparatively poor in joint contexts in France in 1940 and in the Balkans and North Africa in 1941, British and Empire armies and air forces emulated their enemy's war-fighting style, worked far harder at combining and coordinating their intellectual and physical efforts, and duly experienced more success. Enhanced integration at the tactical level eventually included the development of rudimentary but highly useful two-way (both land-to-air and air-to-land) radio communication systems as well as the embedding of small and specialist air liaison teams within army units – in essence a copy of the German 'Flivo' system – which were able to assist army leaders with close air support decision-making.

In those theatres that offered the possibility of contained and decisive battle – in North Africa in 1942 and 1943, then in Sicily and Italy in 1943 and 1944, and finally in North-West Europe during the global conflict's final year – British and then American 'tactical' air operational art came to resemble the Luftwaffe's earlier modus operandi and, indeed, to prove similarly strategic. By comparison with the inability of mono-functional RAF commands to work together effectively in France in 1940, the Desert Air Force and later 'tactical' air forces in Europe were multi-functional and thus far more flexible, versatile and lethal. In Europe, for example, after gaining local and eventually general air superiority, Allied air forces' reconnaissance, battlefield interdiction and flying artillery created intolerable difficulties for the German armed forces. Their campaign to drive the Luftwaffe from the French skies had a fabulous side effect (to which modern 'manoeuvrist' armed forces should perhaps pay close attention). It not only provided Allied soldiers with a reasonably benign air environment but, by destroying most German tactical reconnaissance aircraft that ever risked flying low and slow, it also left both the Luftwaffe and the German Army operationally and tactically blind.[6]

As in the Great War, and for the same reasons, aviators preferred interdiction missions over direct battlefield attack. This again led to accusations by some soldiers, including famously on one occasion in 1943 by Major General George Patton, that armies received inadequate support from air forces. Eighteen months later he found himself paired with an air commander who more successfully demonstrated that the absence of aircraft directly overhead most of the time was probably the result of the aircraft working elsewhere on interdiction missions that, by interrupting resupply and reinforcement, actually made the job of his soldiers far easier and safer. This need for mutual understanding of each service's limitations, capabilities and priorities still lies at the heart of effective air–land integration.

The Soviets, who understood war in fairly traditional terms as pursuit of the destruction of the enemy's forces in decisive battle, undoubtedly gained highly positive results by using ground-attack aircraft and light and medium bombers in ever closer integration with the Red Army.[7] Massive industrial output of aircraft focused on *battle*-winning types allowed the Red Air Force to contribute mightily to *war*-winning combined-arms fighting. Willing to take significant losses, and accepting higher fratricide rates than Western counterparts, they flew as many close support missions as interdiction missions. They saw these missions as interdependent and complementary. By sealing the battlefield with close interdiction missions they prevented German concentrations from dispersing when attacked. The impact of this integrated use of air power, mistakenly dismissed as 'tactical' by some pundits, should not be underrated. The Soviets killed almost seven-eighths of all German troops who died in battle during the Second World War, and their hard-won victories in battle were directly strategic. Their use of air power, which directly caused around one-quarter of all German soldiers' deaths and facilitated yet more, was thus also highly strategic in effect.

Beginning in a 1940 milieu of fear, frustration and asserted retribution, Great Britain and later the United States attempted to break the will to persist of the German people (and, in the US case, of the Japanese people) through increasingly massive air attacks directly upon them, and to significantly damage their physical means to persist through air attacks on industry and infrastructure. Germany conducted raids on garrisons and fortress-cities like Warsaw and Rotterdam, but also, in similar fashion to Anglo-American forces but on a lower scale (owing to lack of resources, not lack of desire), the Luftwaffe also deliberately targeted civilians who did not constitute garrisons or inhabit fortresses. With retributive temper and various other angers among national leaders prompting both departures from military doctrine and unusual decisions, the Luftwaffe attacked civilians in English cities, and also, less notoriously, occasionally in the Balkans and in the East. The Luftwaffe's Blitzes on Belgrade and Moscow were as heavy as upon London and Coventry. All were

---

6   Donald Caldwell and Richard Muller, *The Luftwaffe over Germany: Defence of the Reich* (London: Greenhill, 2007).

7   James Sterrett, *Soviet Air Force Theory, 1918–1945* (Oxford: Routledge, 2009).

dwarfed by Luftwaffe attacks on Kharkov, Sevastopol, Stalingrad and many other cities being besieged by the German Army. The German justification for these terrible raids is that civilians were joining soldiers in resistance, thus forfeiting their position as innocents.

Both sides' explanations for shifting an enormous weight of military effort away from its customary home, the battlefield, and for their moral strides away from respecting the sanctity of civilian life, focused on assertions that they were now reluctantly embroiled in unwanted 'total war' (explained ambiguously as contests of both industrialisation and irreconcilable ideologies). According to their logic, war could no longer be contained within battle.

One can of course ask whether 'total war' was, conceptually, a justification of the bombing of civilians, the industrial intensification necessary to facilitate this, the notion of collective responsibility, and various other unusual factors. Conversely, one can ask whether the independent bombing was a response to, and symptom of, the extraordinary societal mobilisation supposedly inherent in 'total war'. In other words, did various extremes of strategy and action create total war, or did total war create various extremes of strategy and action?[8]

In any event, Allied policy-makers at the time devoted considerable effort to assuring the public that factories, not families, were the primary targets. Distressed in the war's first years by setbacks and defeats, and understanding that their enemies had started these sorts of brutal attacks anyway, the public generally accepted this and seldom expressed concern about any weakening of moral stances. Of course, in those days before real-time television coverage by an unrestricted media beamed horrific images into living-rooms, the public received highly sanitised news and, while in some cases people experienced some of war's violence themselves (during the Blitz, for example), almost everyone lacked the information necessary to make reasonably informed judgements.

Practitioners and commentators claimed at the time and in the first decades afterwards that the so-called Allied 'strategic' air campaigns, so named because of their independence of battles and battlefields, justified their title. Yet increasing numbers of scholars of those highly destructive campaigns nowadays argue that their strategic contribution was far less significant than originally claimed. Germany did have to divert resources away from other crucial areas in order to counter the bombing offensives, but Britain and the United States had to divert as many resources of their own away from joint battle in order to prosecute the offensives. Germany's production of armaments and related war-stuffs did suffer interruptions and overall decreases in *potential* output quantities. Yet the effect never proved as crucial as the loss of key joint battles and, in actuality, production levels increased steadily throughout the war until the last final months. By that stage a series of catastrophic battlefield losses had already sealed the Reich's fate.

There is less merit than resilience in the claim that battle-obsessed German leaders stymied the creation of a heavy bombing force possessing long-range

---

8   A fabulous starting point, even if the author does not share all his views, is John Buckley, *Air Power in the Age of Total War* (London: University College London Press, 1999).

aircraft and that the absence of this force severely limited Germany's military prospects. Germany had relatively little steel, chromium, rubber and oil. Even if, hypothetically, it did create a good heavy bomber, for instance, it could never have produced them in anywhere near sufficient numbers to cripple its enemies' industries or broken their will to resist (if such a thing was ever possible short of genocide-scale attacks). The Allies *did* have a staggering quantity, but never achieved those results. Moreover, even if the Germans had magically designed and produced aircraft comparable to the greatest bombers of the era they could not have flown far enough to reach the key industrial areas of the Soviet Union or, even more impossibly, of the United States.

War did not occur only on, or above, land. The war at sea involved the commitment of prodigious capital and industrial effort by all the main belligerents, who, with one or two exceptional occasions in the Pacific and Mediterranean theatres, avoided Nelsonian decisive battle between fleets or flotillas. More predictably, and purportedly necessarily, they concentrated on thwarting their enemies' efforts to impose coercive economic blockades that could potentially starve their peoples or deny them war-making materials. In all maritime theatres aircraft became indispensable, although, largely because of priorities based on conceptual traditions, they were rarely the primary achiever of strategic or operational accomplishment.

In the uncontainable and attritional Battle of the Atlantic the Luftwaffe used shore-based aircraft around coastlines offensively to strike at Allied convoys, defensively to protect its own convoys from air and naval and coastal gunfire attacks, and, during both types of operations, as a provider of vital reconnaissance information to the German Navy. Yet, because Germany believed that its joint campaigns on land would ultimately provide all war-winning decisions (which at least partly explains why it had never commissioned aircraft carriers), it prioritised its air effort greatly in favour of those land-based joint campaigns and allocated far fewer aircraft and less aviation fuel to the war at sea. British priorities were equally unbalanced, although in different ways. The Royal Navy had a credible air component and the Royal Air Force had its own zealous and punchy Coastal Command, of which the Admiralty effectively exercised operational command after 1941. However, even during the Battle of the Atlantic's worst months, when German submarines caused genuine fear, frustration and economic pain, the independent bombing of German cities remained Britain's air power priority. Overall, the most significant contribution made by both sides' maritime air power – even more important than its eventually effective attack capabilities – was probably information-gathering. Aerial reconnaissance permanently transformed the character of sea power by finally giving fleets reasonable chances of locating elusive enemy ships (and of course submarines) in the oceans' expanses.[9]

Particularly in the vast Pacific theatre, where neither side had sufficient forward air bases on land within useful distances of the many major joint battlefields, or of enemy infrastructural or civilian targets (until quite late in the war), aircraft carriers

---

9   Geoffrey Till, 'Maritime Airpower in the Interwar Period: The Information Dimension', *Journal of Strategic Studies*, vol. 27, no. 2 (2004): 298–323.

became the most important warships. Without their aircraft all other vessels in fleets, flotillas and convoys were vulnerable to attack by the aircraft of their rivals. Great control-of-the-air battles occurred as fleets approached each other. Decisions in these battles and in the air attacks that they denied or facilitated significantly extended the fighting distances between fleets from around 15 miles to 150 miles or more. Sometimes – for example, in the Battles of the Coral Sea and Midway – these actions meant that surface vessels did not directly engage at all. Likewise, without similar air superiority battles and the flying artillery provided by carrier-borne aircraft, which pummelled and pinned down dug-in enemy troops in conjunction with naval gunfire, it would have been highly perilous for either side's amphibious assault forces to attempt landings on defended islands.

The Second World War reveals that, in theatres with decisive battles, air power's contribution, like those of other services and branches, can rightly be called strategic. Yet in theatres that were uncontainable and had no decisive battles, it would be exaggerating to consider any tactical outputs, not just air power's, to be strategic, except perhaps in an indirect and cumulative sense. Moreover, in multi-theatre warfare (and the Germans sometimes had to fight in and coordinate as many as five interdependent theatres at once), it is hard to see any battles as war-winning except for the final one. Yet this observation does not weaken a growing recognition by air power scholars that the type of integrated air power we customarily describe as 'tactical' profoundly contributed to the joint battles that, more than other factors including the independent coercive or attritional campaigns which we traditionally label as 'strategic', provided the Allies with complete victory.

One cannot deny that, as emotions calm and factual knowledge grows with each passing decade, public opinion on those so-called 'strategic' air attacks has become more negative. A large percentage of Britons, for example, feel pleased that the Allies defeated unquestionably wicked regimes but they worry that some of their methods, whilst undeniably requiring courage and sacrifice, were morally questionable and distasteful. The Combined Bomber Offensive and USAF raids on Japanese cities have certainly not fared as well in the public's mind as those air campaigns that seemed more closely both to match their national warrior codes – like the famous 'few' of the Battle of Britain, hailed as duelling knights in similar fashion to the Great War dogfighters – and to adhere to long-held ethical standards of proportionality and discrimination.[10]

It is interesting that the ideas underpinning the air missions that now seem most disproportionate and indiscriminate – the independent wrecking of German and Japanese cities and the atomic bombing of Hiroshima and Nagasaki – dominated post-war air power thinking for at least several decades, whereas the invaluable and often decisive contribution of so-called 'tactical' air power to battle received less intellectual interest, economic resourcing and technical developmental effort. This can be explained. First, it became psychologically important to justify (meaning the attempt to make just) the worst of attacks that air forces had undertaken, especially

---

10   See Anthony C. Grayling, *Among the Dead Cities: The History and Moral Legacy of the WWII Bombing of Civilians in Germany and Japan* (New York: Walker, 2006).

as they did not seem to fit the established criteria for justice during war. Their effect, as opposed to their ethics, was thus heavily stressed and possibly unintentionally exaggerated in some memoirs and official after-action surveys and analyses. Second, the aircraft-carried atomic bomb seemed finally to offer air power the means to coerce enemies strategically – with the likely foe being the fearfully strong Soviet Union (which, ironically, built an impressive nuclear deterrent capability but still favoured battle-centric air power) – without the need for massive casualty-heavy joint battles which the Soviets believed formed the heart of war.

Just as it did after the Great War, a natural revulsion for the human cost of battle created ideas about air power that once again threatened to place the burden of punishment, paradoxically, on the civilians who had once been considered innocent by professional warriors.

War started in Korea in 1950, three years after the birth of an independent, army-free United States Air Force that had configured its forces into huge mono-functional commands (à la RAF in 1936) and proclaimed that it no longer needed to concern itself greatly with supposedly anachronistic 'tactical' battle. Like its British counterpart, the USAF developed stronger-than-ever technical and doctrinal emphases on 'strategic' missions that would be waged away from, and more importantly *instead of*, conventional battle. Yet the political context of the Korean War, with its grave risk of regional or even global escalation, created a need for the belligerents to contain the conflict within the Korean peninsula. Despite the urgings of some military leaders within both the USAF and the US Army (one of them sacked for appearing insubordinate and supportive of nuclear intervention), they also desperately wanted to keep it non-nuclear. Consequently, despite the excellence and significance of their 'tactical' operational art in North-West Europe back in 1944 and 1945, American and British Commonwealth air forces under the United Nations banner struggled in the first year of the Korean War to make a positive contribution within the war's very traditional but no longer anticipated type of force-on-force battle.

Their main developmental and doctrinal focus was on nuclear bombers and high-performance and high-altitude jet fighters (intended for both the inevitable air superiority contest and bomber escorting, but unsuited to attacking or defending anything on the ground). The UN air forces initially had to make do with new but not very useful aircraft types and ordnance, and – pulling them out of the military equivalent of mothballs – with old and no longer suitable or competitive aircraft. World War II-era bombers waged both coercive and national interdiction campaigns but found the enemy's relatively undeveloped economy and logistics systems, which were based less on mechanisation and more on manpower, virtually impossible to break and keep broken. And almost all ground-attack aircraft brought back into service were equally old and flown by pilots with far less experience than they would have had only five or six years earlier. North Korean jet fighters, most of Soviet design and many flown by Chinese pilots, outperformed these types before competitive UN jets appeared in greater numbers and began duelling credibly for air superiority. Perhaps because it was inherently joint and had steadfastly refused to consider removing its aircraft from sectors in which its land and maritime troops would be fighting, only the US Marine Corps retained its World War II level of competence in close air support and did not need to re-learn the lessons that had been so quickly forgotten by others in only five years. For the others, including the USAF's tactical airmen, the re-education process was slow and awkward. By war's end in 1953 things were undoubtedly better. Reorientation on traditional battle involved, again, specialised aircraft and ordnance, joint planning and the employment of liaison officers and forward air controllers.

The only truly meaningful air campaigns in Korea had been both sides' air superiority efforts and the UN's eventually adequate air–land integration. The might of so-called strategic air power, much of it nuclear, could not contribute to this historically typical war that had immediately made total war seem more aberrational. Yet, in terms of air power concepts it was as if the Korean War had never occurred. Explaining it as merely an anomaly, or arguing that it had not been fought the way it should have been, Western air forces continued to argue that they possessed the strategy and means, both nuclear and conventional, to deter wars or to win them without having to undertake the battles that had determined their outcomes for 5,000 years. More so in the West than in the Soviet Union and wider Eastern sphere, the emphasis of most influential air force thinkers on 'strategic' air power once again left the minority 'tactical' commands and elements without adequate specialised aircraft and ordnance and with fewer opportunities and less funding for research, training, experimentation and doctrinal development.

Yet air power during the next major war – the Vietnam War – did not involve the world's two superpowers undertaking what they had ceaselessly prepared and rehearsed since the 1940s: conducting nuclear attacks on each other in a great intercontinental holocaust. Indeed, mutual nuclear deterrence had apparently limited the likelihood of such an unlimited conflagration but increased that of traditional limited wars. None occurred directly between the superpowers, but several arose between or within smaller troubled states, the Vietnam War being perhaps the largest and (certainly for the purposes of this essay) most influential. Like in the Korean War, it involved the attempt of a Western industrial superpower (this time without the legitimacy of a UN banner) to defeat a relatively undeveloped Asian nation that had commenced a national reunification struggle that the interloper misunderstood and found unacceptable.

In 1965, following and alongside its huge ground troop build-up in South Vietnam, the United States commenced its gloriously titled Operation Rolling Thunder, a staggeringly heavy but graduated air campaign against North Vietnam aimed at signalling American resolve, imposing a paralysing strain and boosting morale in South Vietnam.[11] Despite its larger weight of bombs dropped than its World War II predecessors, in one regard Rolling Thunder represented a more sophisticated air campaign. Although incorporating elements of the concept of collective responsibility and a casual attitude towards incidental civilian deaths,

---

11   Mark Clodfelter, *The Limits of Air Power: The American Bombing of North Vietnam* (New York: Free Press, 1989); Ronald Bruce Frankum, *Like Rolling Thunder: The Air War in Vietnam, 1964–1975* (Lanham: Rowman & Littlefield, 2005).

Rolling Thunder did not make the enemy's civilian population and its morale a key (or publicly articulated) target. More artfully, but equally experimentally, Rolling Thunder comprised a series of carefully nuanced pauses and escalations designed to convince the enemy leaders that, should they not abandon their armed struggle for unification, much worse would befall their nation.

Yet the strategy contained a weakness. Even if heavily industrial states were as critically vulnerable to attacks designed to destroy their means of production and distribution as the strategic air power advocates insisted – and World War II had only partially supported their thesis – North Vietnam was a very different type of nation to urbanised, industrialised and centralised Germany and Japan. This target nation's subsistence economy rested mainly on peasant agriculture, not primary industries, and its people's and army's limited reliance on roads, rails, petroleum and electricity meant that the degradation of those systems from the air did not prove catastrophic. The four-year campaign failed to coerce the North Vietnamese but, with grim television reports beamed into homes every evening, did help to turn many American people off the war. Retributively bombing the infrastructure, industry and people of cruelly expansionist Germany and Japan during a 'total war' had been one thing; bombing a peasant people back to the Stone Age was quite another.

After failing to coerce the leadership politically, or defeat the North Vietnamese and Vietcong forces militarily, the war-weary Americans conducted two heavy 'Linebacker' bombing campaigns in 1972. The first was a sustained interdiction campaign waged mainly by fighter-bombers trying to blunt powerful North Vietnamese military offensives and to prevent supplies and weapons from flowing into theatre. The second, after subsequent peace talks collapsed, was a shorter coercive one waged mainly by heavy bombers. Particularly during the second the targets included things and places that had previously been too politically awkward to target, such as the oil, road and rail infrastructures in the north of the country, the key port-city and even the capital city. This distressed many Americans, whose media exposure to the effects of bombing was vastly greater than, say, those of the World War II generation who had known almost nothing about the effects of their air campaigns. Certainly during 1972 their public protests increased after newspaper and television reports showed (albeit often inaccurately) that aiming imprecision was causing many civilian deaths and much suffering.

As with Rolling Thunder, the air planners did not deliberately try to kill civilians. (Notions that civilian morale was fragile and should be broken by targeting the people themselves had quietly disappeared from Western non-nuclear strategic thinking.) Yet the campaign planners clearly still believed that the best use of air power was against things that kept states functional. Despite the widespread suffering that the destruction of those things caused, there was no moral dilemma, they argued, because the population's consent and labour upheld the state. Especially during the second campaign the American air forces struck fast and furiously, trying not to drag out a domestically unpopular campaign and needing a quick result. They got one. The North Vietnamese returned to negotiations and promptly signed an agreement that ended the war.

Many airmen since then have thus proclaimed that the air campaign 'worked' in the way that previous generations had always anticipated one could. If a similar campaign had occurred in 1965, they argue, instead of the failure of Rolling Thunder, the war may have ended in that same year. Yet their claims hold less water than they think. Back in 1965 the war was an unconventional insurgency that relied to a large degree on decentralised support, minimal logistics and widespread but low-level human labour. Even if air power had broken and stopped the repair of virtually every oil tank, electricity station, factory, railway marshalling yard and highway it would not have adequately coerced the government or ended the insurgency. By 1972 the emboldened North Vietnam was fighting a different war; far more symmetrical, with forces needing conventional long and thorough logistics tails. Despite remarkable and deadly innovations in ground-based air defence (including improved detection and warning systems and radar-guided surface to air missiles, or SAMs), North Vietnam's new and more conventional production and logistics chains proved highly vulnerable to powerful air interdiction. Their wreckage seemed swiftly strategic, especially following the 'tactical' destruction by air of tanks, trucks, guns and troops during Linebacker I. Yet by 1972 the political context of, and reasons for, the American air campaigns were markedly different to those of 1965. Because of a political thawing the US no longer anxiously predicted that China and the Soviet Union would intervene if it used massive force. The US was also no longer trying to defeat the enemy to 'win' the war, let alone on its one-sided terms. By 1972 it had already withdrawn most of its ground troops and was more realistically trying to find a way of withdrawing completely with the semblance of honour from a seriously unpopular war through getting the North Vietnamese to accept a compromise settlement. The North Vietnamese acceded. They were in genuine pain from American air power, which had delivered a double-whammy. First, attacks on national infrastructure, coupled with a naval blockade and the mining of their key port, did hurt. Second, even if they could survive those wounds, air attacks on their army and its supply chain had significantly reduced their military options. When they had attempted to augment guerrilla war with conventional decisive battle – a premature and unwise political decision – air power had proven truly punishing in the interdiction and close air support roles. Even so, one should not see American reduced strategic ambitions and increased military violence as the only cause of the North Vietnamese leaders' compromise decision. They were well aware of how close they were, if they acted shrewdly, to attaining their goal of reunification but this needed the Americans entirely out of the picture. By agreeing to terms that involved them giving away almost nothing, they quickly moved into a position of unopposed strength.

The controversies and media coverage of the Rolling Thunder and especially the Linebacker campaigns commonly disguise something that most participating soldiers had known for years: battlefield air power, more and more of it in US Army ownership, had vastly improved the way they performed their customary functions. Informed by forward air controllers and liaison teams, rugged ground-attack aircraft and fighter-bombers added unusually accurate fires to joint battle. This often involved contributing to small-scale firefights or to preparatory barrages (as flying artillery) before ground assaults, routinely with adequate coordination with ground troops. Helicopters, including some with fantastic heavy-lift capabilities, vastly improved the mobility of troops, being able to insert, support, supply and evacuate them in regions far from runways and often in enemy-held areas. Their growing use in battlefield medical evacuations significantly improved the life expectancy of the wounded. Their increasing employment in search and destroy missions, which had historically been a key function of horse cavalry, earned them the evocative title, 'air cavalry'. Their vulnerability to ground fire prompted the development of specialised armoured helicopters designed around vicious guns as well as fixed-wing equivalents – both called gunships – which boasted such things as infrared night-vision sensors, advanced computer-targeting capabilities and astonishingly accurate and fast guns.

By the mid-1970s most of the influential World War II bomber generals had left service and a new breed, proportionately more of them with fighter backgrounds and 'tactical' combat experience, began to appear within and then to dominate upper command echelons. New concepts began to emerge alongside the prevailing nuclear theories (which 'strategic' air thinkers still considered valid in some contexts, perhaps not for denial or coercion but certainly for deterrence). Aware that their predecessors' ideas had not all proven especially useful, and that air power would certainly contribute as mightily to conventional limited war at the tactical and operational levels as it might conceivably at the strategic level, many of these airmen began to reassess the relationship between battle and war. Despite earlier excitable beliefs, air power had not allowed war to exist, let alone reach resolution, away from its usual habitat, the battlefield, and attempts to remove it had not worked wonderfully and had proved domestically disconcerting to various degrees. As well as looking to Vietnam for lessons, Western airmen prodigiously studied the ferocious Arab-Israeli Wars of 1969 and 1973 (more accessible to Western observers than, say, the Indian-Pakistan Wars) as they sought to change the configuration of air forces and the utility of air power.

Acutely aware that it lacked any viable strategic depth, and without the luxury of time to devote to any potentially drawn-out campaigns against the enemy's governance, morale and production, Israel wisely constructed all its strategic ideas around the conventional battlefield and on the time-proven concept of decisive battle. Acting on thorough intelligence and pre-empting enemies about to do harm, in 1967 the Israelis undertook a remarkable Blitzkrieg-like campaign on several fronts and beat their foes with stunning tactics and operational art.[12] Air power, used first to win air superiority (masterfully through the annihilation of the enemy air force, mostly on the ground) and then to interdict the battlefield and strike enemy troops and vehicles directly, allowed the partnering army to sweep its enemies away. In 1973 its attempt to replicate this success started with disastrous results. Soviet-supplied SAMs inflicted high losses and denied the Israeli Air Force the entire airspace above and immediately in front of the Egyptian Army. Only by

---

12   Eliezer Cohen, *Israel's Best Defense: The First Full Story of the Israeli Air Force* (New York: Orion, 1993).

drawing that army out from beneath its SAM protection, and employing hastily supplied electronic countermeasures, could the Israelis contribute air power to the battle with any influence.

That widely-observed lesson – that ground-based systems contributed to the air superiority contest as significantly as air-to-air combat – reinforced painful lessons learned by the Americans when they had began to strike in and around Hanoi and Haiphong in 1972. Losses to strong and lethal SAM defences prompted the rapid development of radar detection, suppression and destruction aircraft and ordnance. Now, after both Vietnam and the Yom Kippur War of 1973, the suppression of enemy air defences became integral to all air campaigning. Israel got it right in the Bekaa Valley in 1982, when its air force destroyed Syrian SAM-based air defences in a successful air-to-ground and air-to-air campaign[13]. Likewise, the US-led coalition managed quickly in 1991 to incapacitate and render irrelevant Iraq's supposedly impregnable integrated air-defence system through a powerful and artful air campaign.

The recognition of battle-centric airmen that nuclear deterrence had not eradicated major conventional conflicts, and that one could still occur in Europe between NATO and the Soviet Union, encouraged them to think of new ways of winning decisive battle. They were not alone in wrestling with these issues. Bothered by its mixed successes in Vietnam, the US Army also searched its soul. The Army's Training and Doctrine Command (TRADOC) and the USAF's Tactical Air Command (TAC) unusually combined their conceptual efforts for several years to form in 1982 a new army doctrine called the AirLand Battle. Aimed at blunting any major westward thrust by Warsaw Pact forces, it placed air and land forces into an interdependent high-tempo, offensive-oriented partnership. As well as providing the lion's share of operational reconnaissance and surveillance information, air power would wage an air superiority contest aimed at both providing the US Army with an acceptably benign airspace and freeing that airspace for its own various uses. Air power (Army aviation and Air Force) would then assist the Army to fix the enemy ground forces in place while interdicting all second-echelon ('follow-up') forces to prevent them from reinforcing the front as well as to create 'time windows' for rapid offensive actions. All this required effective joint planning and training, integrated control, careful coordination and willing cooperation, none of it possible without a spirit of harmony and trust.

Many independence-oriented airmen found these ideas unpalatable and suspected their tactical brethren of becoming the Army's battle-obsessed handmaidens. One such American airman, John Warden, designed a system of air attack based on his argument that a nation-state is like an organism.[14] According to Warden, a state has interdependent life systems, including its digestion (its reliance on petroleum, electricity and other essential energy sources), nervous

---

13   Matthew M. Hurley, 'The Bekaa Valley Air Battle June 1982: Lessons Mislearned?' *Airpower Journal*, vol. 3, no. 4 (Winter, 1989): 60–70.

14   John A. Warden III, *The Air Campaign: Planning for Combat*, rev. edn (San Jose, CA: toExcel, 2000).

system (critical national infrastructure), body (society) and limbs (the armed forces). All could be hurt independently, but, for maximum effect, should be struck simultaneously. Most importantly, the nation-state also has a brain (its leadership), which should be the primary target. An artful and hard headshot could alone paralyse or kill the organism. Warden never advocated targeting civilians directly but still included an emphasis on weakening civilian morale (or 'will'). He also eschewed traditional battle, considering its effects to be indirect at best. He believed, like many independent bomber advocates in every previous generation but now with different targets in mind, that, if used directly against the systems that made the enemy state functional, air power could be decisive by itself.

His ideas on independent air power, like those of both predecessors and successors, include few well-developed and consistent ethical considerations; not even an attempt to explain the grave implications of 'paralysing' a nation (even temporarily until its capitulation or acceptable compromise). National decapitation or paralysis inevitably plunges civil society into chaos and possibly ruin, particularly if the things that underpin ordinary life are broken or severely disrupted. This can only be tolerable to the attackers (and their own populations) if they accept the notion of collective responsibility – that is, that the people of the state with whom they disagree are themselves partly or wholly responsible for the grievance, even if only by lack of resistance to their own leaders – or if they genuinely judge that, as well as there being no other viable and timely options than the use of military force, the good created by their actions will outweigh their evil and that the harm done to civilians is strenuously minimised.

Many pundits and even some scholars attribute the American-led coalition air force's startling success in the Gulf War of 1991 to the application of Warden's theory. This is certainly an overstatement. The huge phased air campaign masterfully degraded the Iraqi integrated air-defence system, gained control of the air and created a surprisingly benign air environment for coalition forces. In combination with cruise missiles, its attacks on leadership targets and associated communication systems noticeably reduced Iraqi command and control capabilities (but did not paralyse them). Its degradation of critical energy sources temporarily crippled the state. Yet the coalition theatre commander's requirement of the destruction of a large percentage of enemy fielded forces – which he conceived as a key enabler of successful decisive battle – gave the overall air campaign a character and emphasis quite unlike that recommended by Warden. And when land and air forces finally struck, after almost 40 days of relentless preparation by air power, enemy resistance in the joint battle-space was weak, easy to manoeuvre against and quick to defeat. Decisive battle worked. The champions of AirLand Battle doctrine must have felt satisfied that air power's role in the final joint war-fighting phase was very effective. Interdiction sealed the battlefield and, with nothing much moving forward into it and, no less importantly, with no means of withdrawing or fleeing safely without attracting devastating air strikes, Iraqi forces found themselves trapped, pinned down and hammered by close air support provided by army and air force aviators as well as, of course, by powerful infantry, artillery and armour.

Far from demonstrating that air power could achieve strategic decision away from the battlefield the Gulf War showed that it worked wonderfully when utilised in partnership with ground forces in decisive battle. Yet the independent air power advocates focused mainly on the impressively quick, heavy, dramatic and accurate devastation of Iraqi infrastructure, seeing it as more significant. One commentator famously noted that politicians, the media and the public also seemed so unusually impressed by those aspects of the air campaign (and especially by air power's ability to devastate something with unprecedented speed and its apparently 'surgical precision') that air power had regained a 'mystique' almost like it had in its infancy.[15] Certainly through the 1990s the United States favoured air power as its main instrument of coercion. Its sophisticated technology lent itself, more than land warfare or sea power, to America's self-perception as the world's most advanced nation. Phenomenal information-gathering, electronic warfare, stand-off range, futuristic stealth aircraft, advanced satellite-guided cruise missiles and precision-guided munitions created an expectation of total accuracy and effectiveness, safety for pilots and crews, and made it the most politically attractive instrument of coercion and denial.

To a far greater degree than land warfare or sea power, air power seems to neutralise the Western intolerance for 'friendly' casualties, growing concern about enemy civilian suffering, and fear of domestic dissatisfaction caused by reports of either. Sensitivity to casualties was manifest on many occasions in the decades after the Vietnam War, with the clearest case being the dramatic drop in public support following the October 1993 deaths of 18 American soldiers in Mogadishu, Somalia. Likewise, grave public concern for the plight of civilians, both friends' and enemies', revealed that, with the collective memory of 'total war' receding, stronger ethical concerns were attaching themselves to military activity. Even 'accidents' now caused problems. For example, when an Allied air raid on a command and control bunker in Baghdad in 1991 killed several hundred civilians using it as a shelter, the fear of a public backlash in America was so strong that air commanders had to suspend the strategic air campaign against Baghdad for 10 days.

The Gulf War of 1991 and Operation Deliberate Force in 1995 (NATO's punitive air attacks on Serb positions in Bosnia) seemed to 'prove' that, in the age of cruise missiles, stealth technology and precision-guided munitions, air power could indeed achieve strategic results for few casualties and little 'collateral damage'. Further evidence of a mounting belief in the supposedly ideal nature of air power as an instrument of coercion came during 1998. In August, the United States launched strong air assaults against Osama bin Laden's suspected terrorist bases in Afghanistan and an alleged chemical weapons plant in Sudan. Four months later, American and British air power assets undertook Operation Desert Fox, a four-night torrent of cruise missiles and 'smart bombs' poured upon ever-troublesome Iraq. Despite their dubious legality and purpose, those punitive missions again seemed to provide high returns for low costs (at least in terms of casualties). A more

---

15   Eliot A. Cohen, 'The Mystique of U.S. Air Power', *Foreign Affairs*, vol. 73, no. 1 (January–February 1994): 109–24.

reasonable assessment is that, while the strikes may have demonstrated leadership resolve for domestic consumption, they had very little real coercive or preventative effect on the enemies.

The United States and Britain obviously wanted to repeat their formula in the case of Yugoslavia, whose clumsily excessive counterinsurgency campaign in Kosovo caused accusations of ethnic cleansing. In 1999 their air forces and others within NATO commenced what they intended as a quick coercive campaign which would force Serbia to adopt a more humane and reasonable course of action. Largely because of NATO's misjudgement of the Serbian leadership's resolve, the attempt at quick coercion failed, forcing a tough choice upon NATO: give up or escalate. Unable to concede defeat, NATO escalated, massively. The struggling air campaign steadily gained far more air assets, less constrained rules of engagement, and a far wider spread of targets. This package ushered in a 'new' offensive; a parallel operation à la Warden's theory. Especially throughout the final five or six weeks, NATO aircraft systematically targeted Serbia's interdependent life systems (and also destroyed many objects of national prestige that had no military, economic or governmental functions), effectively paralysing the nation and causing medium-term economic and long-term ecological wreckage. Unable to tolerate further destruction, and suddenly aware of their total political isolation, Serbian leaders threw in the towel and accepted what they considered to be a compromise and what NATO called a capitulation. The operation that had started as an attempt at quick coercion and transformed into a war of denial and punishment ended after 78 days.

It would be ungenerous to say that air power did not eventually achieve coercive results in concert with various political pressures. Yet it was far from a model campaign. NATO acted with questionable legitimacy and with apparent haste. After trying and failing initially to coerce using proportionate force, it eventually resorted to very *dis*proportionate force (inflicting more violence and creating more harm than the foe in the original grievance). It caused economic and environmental damage to non-involved neighbouring states, and it created significant international disagreement.[16]

Some of the controversy grew directly from increasing Western ethical considerations about what happens during wars, especially wars of choice. Even though NATO's air campaign was the most precise application of air power in history, the use of depleted uranium ammunition and cluster bombs proved controversial, as did the ecologically harmful wreckage of oil refineries and chemical plants. With environmentalism at the forefront of political activism in almost all Western states, the days of air forces bombing oil infrastructure without severe protests were over.

---

16   Joel Hayward, 'NATO's War in the Balkans: A Preliminary Analysis', *New Zealand Army Journal*, no. 21 (July 1999): 1–17; Joel Hayward, 'Air Power and the Environment: The Ecological Implications of Modern Air Warfare', *Air Power Review* (forthcoming, Winter 2009).

Moreover, the campaign also involved a relatively small number of dreadful accidents that earlier in the century would barely have raised an eyebrow during air campaigns. Yet they now proved almost war-ending for NATO. These included wiping out a civilian refugee convoy, scattering cluster bombs in a busy marketplace, wrecking a full passenger train, and bombing the Chinese embassy. At times, these unfortunate, widely broadcast events threatened not only to undermine the much-proclaimed morality underpinning NATO's intervention in Kosovo, but also to escalate the conflict. This reveals the inherent problem with 'smart' weapon technology. It raises public expectation that air attacks will cause no civilian casualties. In fact, as weapons becoming increasingly precise, public disgust at any accidents becomes correspondingly stronger.

The terrorist attacks in the United States on 11 September 2001 composed a significant grievance for the United Sates and its friends to address. The attacks' ingenuity, audacity, indiscrimination, scale and symbolic power meant that retribution would be quick and severe. It was. Later in 2001 American-led coalition forces overthrew Taliban leadership in Afghanistan and, despite a dubious linking rationale, deposed Saddam Hussein in Iraq in 2003. Air power played significant roles in both wars and has continued to do so in the counterinsurgency conflicts that grew from both. The 'shock and awe' attacks at the start of Iraq's invasion were powerful, precise and impressive. They positively influenced the joint battle that gave the coalition its initial victory. Yet, after war in Iraq changed from conventional combat to the type of awkward counterinsurgency that was already plaguing the coalition in Afghanistan, coalition air forces found themselves without any high-technology and target-rich enemies to fight. Instead, they found themselves fighting amorphous, stateless networks of guerrilla fighters, who lacked both the centralised leadership (the brain in Warden-esque terminology) and the infrastructural, economical and governmental structures (the 'central nervous system') that 'strategic' air power had targeted for at least six decades.

Air power has nonetheless made a significant contribution to the counterinsurgency conflicts. Airborne reconnaissance, surveillance, intelligence-gathering and battle management capabilities have proven critical.[17] From large and sophisticated Airborne Warning and Control System (AWACS) aircraft and Joint Surveillance and Target Attack Radar System (JSTARS) aircraft to the apparent abundance of various electronic 'pods' and sensors on strike and other aircraft, the ability of air assets to collect and synthesise data and to find and target insurgent groups rapidly and from long distances has greatly aided the coalition joint forces. Equally importantly, greater tactical integration between ground forces, army attack helicopters and fixed-wing aircraft and those of air forces has made the counterinsurgency battle – which the media routinely depicts as a 'soldier's battle' – as a truly joint battle. Interdiction and close air support are no longer on a grand scale, covering vast battlefields, or even routinely on the size contributed to

---

17 Christopher Bolkcom and Kenneth Katzman, *Military Aviation: Issues and Options for Combating Terrorism and Counterinsurgency* (Congressional Research Service Report for Congress, 2005).

most Vietnam battles. In Iraq and especially in Afghanistan the scale of air strike missions in partnership with ground troops is generally low (on-contact firefights, not planned battles) but their number and simultaneity are very high. Some comparisons with Vietnam would not be frivolous; in both Iraq and Afghanistan army and air force aviation assets provide crucial logistical, heavy-lift, mobility and medical support.

Looking beyond the current operations, practitioners and theorists of air power – whether they identify with the 'independent' camp or with the 'integrated' camp – will doubtless continue to disagree about the relative importance in past and future wars of their own contributions. The author of this essay finds the evidence most compelling in support of the argument that air power works best (meaning that it makes its greatest contribution to the defeat of foes) when integrated in partnership with ground forces in the very type of decisive battle that some pundits once claimed (inaccurately as it happens) would no longer be typical in war. Independent of battle, the value of air power's contributions has varied markedly throughout the experimental campaigns of the twentieth century. Yet, even in its most effective moments, independent air power has never entirely (or even nearly) lived up to the prophecies of its first major advocates. It has proven no more 'strategic' than the so-called 'tactical' air campaigns that have occurred alongside them. Indeed, the latter has more often provided stronger direct war-winning effects. Independent air power's use as a coercive tool, especially outside of a recognised state of war, has also not yet produced the desired results, at least without the coercion involving vastly disproportionate force, heavy damage and tumultuous controversy, as in the case of NATO in 1999 and Israel against Hezbollah in Lebanon in 2006.

Regardless of whether integrated or independent air power will prove most influential in the future, all air power thinkers will doubtless continue to wrestle with the issue of air superiority, which is the only type of independent air campaign, in this author's assessment, that has ever proven essential and directly decisive. The struggle to gain at least local air superiority used to be a staple requirement; a prerequisite for and facilitator of all surface and other air operations. Since the end of the Cold War, however, Western air forces have faced no robust or sustained contest for control of the air. From the Gulf War of 1991 and the 12 years of no-fly-zone policing through to the Balkans Wars and the high-end and counterinsurgency campaigns against Iraq and Afghanistan, ground-based air defences and enemy fighter forces have had minimal or no effect on the progress of operations. The Taliban's air assets were woefully non-competitive. During the 2003 invasion of Iraq, the Iraqi Air Force did not undertake a single sortie. Air power thinkers will need to reflect deeply on the likelihood that this pattern will continue and, if it does, whether Western air forces will still need to retain large and expensive forces of fighters in case of scenarios involving any peer-competitors who might seek to own the airspace or deny its use to others.

Sea Power

Andrew Lambert[1]

Definitions

Although it has ancient origins and is widely talked about, the concept of sea power lacks a universally accepted definition. This matters because it is studied for two quite distinct reasons: firstly, as part of the development of military education and political understanding; and, secondly and far more recently, in terms of the disinterested study of history, the attempt to comprehend what happened in the past on its own terms. Modern 'sea power' was developed by naval educators to describe strategic choice, making sea power relative, a military/strategic tool within the grasp of many states. While this usage dominates contemporary usage it should not obscure the original historical definition. Historians remain uncertain about the meaning of 'sea power' which they should adopt, notably when examining states in which the sea was the dominant fact of life. Such concepts have little utility for modern strategists.

Despite being deeply rooted in history, writing on sea power is invariably present-minded and agenda-led, characteristics that have seen it develop along very different lines to the older historical concept. Most authors avoid definition, or assume a broad, flexible approach. Consequently the term is frequently used loosely. The *OED* offers:

1. 'A nation or state having international power or influence on sea'.
2. 'The strength and efficiency of a nation (or of nations generally) for maritime warfare'.[2]

These are vague and signally fail to explore the dichotomy that lies at the heart of the subject. They do not address a core concern of historians: why some states become sea powers and how this affects economic and political development. An

---

1   I would like to thank my colleagues Dr Alan James and Professor Theo Farrell for their valuable input.
2   *Oxford English Dictionary*, online edition.

examination of historical and political science literature will indicate the nature of the problem and suggest some solutions.

Mahan: Strategic Thought

Although strategists often assume that 'sea power' was invented by Captain Alfred Thayer Mahan USN (1840–1914) nothing could be further from the truth. He was not the first to employ the concept in the nineteenth century, though he was the first to use the two-word form as a title designed for maximum impact. That said, his 1890 work, *The Influence of Sea Power upon History, 1600–1783*, remains the founding text.[3] Mahan argued that sea power, the key to world power, could be acquired by countries following his strategic programme of battle-fleet based sea control. While history provided examples, his argument was essentially based on a political science approach. Sea power depended on assets. Without coasts and harbours, seamen and ships, and the sustained support of the state it was no more than an interesting idea. Mahan set out six constituent elements of sea power: geographical position, physical conformation, extent of territory, number of population, character of the people, and character of the government. He held up Britain as the example, hardly surprising at a time when Britain, the only world power, used the Royal Navy to connect and control a unique global empire of trade. Less favoured nations, those with exposed land frontiers, poor harbours and few sailors were not 'natural' sea powers.

In the second of his three-book series, Mahan examined the wars of the French Revolution and Empire, 1792–1812, the last 'Great' War. The first volume focused on the struggle for sea power, and the second on the use of sea power, largely through economic blockade, to defeat Napoleon's Continental System.[4] Mahan described sea power as: 'wonderful and mysterious … a complex organism … Not quite defying investigation …, but rendering it exceedingly laborious'.[5] He did not undertake those labours. Mahan's third sea power study, his most 'historical' work, used the War of 1812 to argue the case for a powerful American fleet, but appeared a decade after that need had been addressed. Consequently it had little impact.[6] After 1890 Mahan developed and broadened the sea power argument, without adding theoretical insight. At the same time he produced a stream of articles arguing for the contemporary case for American sea power.[7] It is important to stress that Mahan was also a pioneering writer on naval strategy, the use of naval

---

3   Alfred T. Mahan, *The Influence of Sea Power upon History, 1600–1783* (Boston, MA: Little, Brown, 1890).

4   Mahan, *The Influence of Sea Power upon the French Revolution and Empire, 1793–1812*, 2 vols (Boston, MA: Little, Brown, 1892).

5   Ibid., vol. II, p. 372.

6   Mahan, *The Influence of Sea Power upon the War of 1812*, 2 vols (Boston, MA: Little, Brown, 1905).

7   Mahan, *The Interest of America in Sea Power: Present and Future* (Boston, MA: Little, Brown, 1897). For a full list of Mahan's essays see Hattendorf's bibliography.

forces to contest 'Command of the Sea'.[8] The two subjects should not be conflated. Sea power defines a strategic or cultural approach at the grand strategic level; naval strategy concerns the struggle to control the sea, or to deny its use to others, within the wider context.

Influences

Mahan popularised sea power and linked naval strategy with the far larger body of writing on military strategy. His intellectual debt to the Swiss strategist Antoine Henri Jomini and mid-nineteenth century French writers on naval power and national strategy was considerable. Mahan modified Xavier Raymond's proto 'strategic culture' argument into a more proscriptive model, replacing his response to strategic reality with an element of choice.[9] Mahan had originally conceived the 1890 text as a historical narrative to support the teaching of naval strategy and command at the new United States Naval War College. At a late stage, the passage of the British Naval Defence Act of 1889 and public controversy about the Navy in the United States prompted the hurried addition of the distinctive Raymond influenced opening section about sea power to the book. The link with current events was obvious: Mahan argued that naval power was a key element in national strength, and addressed his remarks to an American audience. This additional material caught the attention of a global audience. Recognising that after 1865 the United States had ceased to be a sea power, in either sense of the term, Mahan called for the recovery of strategic sea power. His message was entirely divorced from the national cultural construction of sea power employed by contemporary historians, who saw sea power as an organic outgrowth of national interest in and dependence upon the sea. Mahan knew such definitions excluded the continental United States, which may explain his reluctance to advance a conclusive definition of sea power.[10]

Studies

Mahan has attracted a considerable body of scholarly literature, much of it generated by the United States Navy, especially at the institution where he taught,

---

8   Mahan, *Naval Strategy: Compared and Contrasted with the Principles and Practice of Military Operations on Land* (Boston, MA: Little, Brown, 1911). This book contains Mahan's original 1880s War College lectures, essentially unmodified.

9   Antione H. Jomini *The Art of War* (1862), trans. by G.H. Mendell and W.P. Craighill (Phildelphia: J.B. Lippincott) – it remains the standard English edition and is frequently reprinted. Xavier Raymond, *Les Marines de la France et de l'Angleterre, 1815–1863* (Paris, 1863) – Raymond argues that France is not a maritime state like Britain. Richild Grivel, *De la Guerre maritime avant et depuis les novellas inventions. Attaque et défense des côtes et des ports. Guerre du large. Etude Historique et stratégique* (Paris, 1869) – Grivel advocates an anti-sea power strategy for France.

10   See fn 5 and 6.

the Naval War College, Newport, Rhode Island.[11] Leading Mahan scholar Professor John Hattendorf has generated a complete bibliography of the entire, varied output of Mahan as educator, strategist and political commentator, including variant editions and reprints down to 1986.[12] Robert Seager, Mahan's biographer, produced an edition of Mahan's correspondence, but restricted himself to Mahan's letters, ignoring those of his correspondents.[13] His correspondence with Professor Sir John Laughton, the British naval historian, published in 2003, emphasises the point that he did not see himself as a historian, defining his work in terms closely approximating to political science.[14]

Professor Jon Sumida's *Inventing Grand Strategy and Teaching Command* of 1997, the most important book about Mahan for two generations, places his writing in a more sophisticated context. Sumida includes an excellent guide to Mahan's use of concepts and themes.[15] Azar Gat's study of nineteenth-century military thinking provides an excellent guide to the international context for the early sea power theorists, placing Mahan and Corbett in the context of the much larger military strategic literature.[16] Another critical context has been provided by Roland, Bolster and Keyssar's American maritime history *The Way of the Ship*, which demonstrates that America had ceased to be a classic historical sea power long before Mahan began work.[17]

Geopolitics

Concepts like sea power reflect the age in which they were developed. Mahan's sea power studies emphasised the global power potential and superior economics of sea transport over land transport as key advantages for expanding empires. The British relied on a combination of naval and commercial strength to generate sea power; either alone was insufficient. Such analysis makes him the father of modern geopolitics. The 1900 collection *The Problem of Asia* assembled half a dozen essays linking imperial activity in China, Persia and Africa with global strategy and the

11 J.B. Hattendorf, ed., *The Influence of History on Mahan* (Newport, RI: Naval War College Press, 1991). This is taken from a 1990 Naval War College conference.

12 J.B. Hattendorf and L.C. Hattendorf, *A Bibliography of the Works of Alfred Thayer Mahan* (Newport, RI: Naval War College Press, 1986).

13 R. Seager and D. Macguire, *The Letters and Papers of Alfred Thayer Mahan*, 3 vols (Annapolis, MD: Naval Institute Press, 1977).

14 A.D. Lambert, *Letters and Papers of Professor Sir John Knox Laughton, 1840–1915* (Aldershot: Navy Records Society, 2003).

15 J.T. Sumida, *Inventing Grand Strategy and Teaching Command: The Classic Works of Alfred Thayer Mahan Reconsidered* (Washington: Woodrow Wilson Centre Press, 1997).

16 Azar Gat, *The Development of Military Thought: The Nineteenth Century* (Oxford: Clarendon Press, 1992).

17 Alex Roland, Jeffrey Bolster and Alexander Keyssar, *The Way of the Ship: America's Maritime History Re-envisioned, 1600–2000* (Hoboken, NJ: John Wiley, 2008).

superior utility of sea power as a power-political instrument.[18] If Mahan was the apostle of sea power, of an oceanic/colonial world-view he did not have the field to himself for long. In 1904, English geographer Halford Mackinder argued that Mahan's 'Columbian epoch' dominated by sea communications was about to end. Consequently the hitherto untapped resources of the Eurasian land mass, located far from the sea and invulnerable to sea power would be mobilised by railways. Mackinder delivered his polemic, 'The Geographical Pivot of History', to the Royal Geographical Society in London as part of a political campaign to change the economic policy of the British Empire.[19]

In the third quarter of the twentieth century, historians trying to explain the collapse of the British power cited Mackinder's paper and argued that sea power had been a waning asset. Paul Kennedy's *The Rise and Fall of British Naval Mastery* (1976) provided the most powerful exposition of this approach, combining Mackinder with the work of military historians Sir Michael Howard and Correlli Barnett.[20] Kennedy argued that Mackinder had anticipated the development of global strategy. Sea power was in decline, land power in the ascendant, and the future belonged to the Soviet Union. In fact, Mackinder's hasty political alarmism had been generated for very different reasons. Furthermore, when read in detail, Mackinder did not claim that sea power was waning; he set up a potential future threat in order to persuade his country to change fundamental economic policies from free trade to industrial protection. He used the vague menace of a Eurasian land power, invulnerable to sea power, to alarm his listeners; the reality was, as he knew, very different. He did not say that sea power was waning; he wanted to rebuild British sea power on an imperial basis. Despite the pessimistic tone he did not differ fundamentally from Mahan: both advocated a peripheral maritime strategy to contain a resurgent Russia. By 1905 Russia had been humiliated by Japanese sea power, and Britain had rejected Mackinder's policy recommendations. Since the end of the Cold War the utility of sea power has been acknowledged and geopolitics, after decades out of fashion, is currently in vogue.[21]

Mahan's contribution to modern strategic thought was immense. He outlined the concept of sea power, although he did not define it, and deployed it to explain past and present, with an eye to the future and America's place in that future. However, he was writing on the cusp of massive changes in the nature of history in the Anglophone world. By the time he died, in 1914, English and American history had assumed modern academic form, leaving such polemical, present-minded writing to other disciplines. Sea power and naval history were dropped from the mainstream historical discourse, their use restricted to naval education. Only in

---

18   Mahan, *The Problem of Asia* (Boston, MA: Little, Brown, 1900).
19   Halford Mackinder, 'The Geographical Pivot of History', *Geographical Journal XXIII* (1904).
20   Paul M. Kennedy, *The Rise and Fall of British Naval Mastery* (London: Allen Lane, 1976).
21   Colin Gray and Geoffrey Sloan, eds, *Geopolitics: Geography and Strategy* (London: Frank Cass, 1999).

recent years have historiographical trends and the development of multidisciplinary approaches to the study of war reconnected the original elements of this debate.

The British Response

Although Mahan's was the first book to be catalogued by the British Library with the title 'Sea Power', he inspired others. Among the more significant British 'sea power' authors of the Edwardian era were sea-minded soldier Colonel George Clarke, who took Mahan's ideas into the heart of British policy. By contrast, *Fighting Ships* founder Fred Jane launched a counter-attack and Thomas Gibson Bowles focused on the threat posed to the exercise of sea power by international law. This present-minded literature subordinated the past to the present.[22]

This trend was reversed by Sir Julian Corbett (1854–1922), a legally educated historian, who deployed modern strategic theory and sophisticated historical case studies to develop the first fully formulated British strategy. He did so between 1902 and 1914, while teaching the Royal Navy war course, supporting war planning and contributing to the public debate on national policy.[23] Corbett created both a historical template to inform thinking about future wars and a persuasive analysis of the maritime nature of British strategy, notably in a case study of the conduct of global war for his naval students.[24] Like Mahan, the key to his work lay in a close and sustained connection with the educational needs of mid-career and senior naval officers, a task that played a central role in the development of sea power studies.[25]

Anxious to avoid the opaque terminology deployed by his contemporaries, Corbett did not use 'sea power', preferring 'command of the sea' – 'nothing but the control of maritime communications, whether for commercial or military purposes' to describe the strategic dimension of sea power.[26] He emphasised that this was not a universal panacea: 'we are inclined to forget how impotent it is of itself to decide a war against great continental states'.[27]

---

22   George S. Clarke and James T. Thursfield, *The Navy and the Nation, or Naval Warfare and Imperial Defence* (London: John Murray, 1897); George S. Clarke, *Russia's Sea Power: Past and Present* (London: John Murray, 1898); George S. Clarke, *Studies of an Imperialist* (London, 1928); Fred T. Jane, *Heresies of Sea Power* (London: Longman, 1906); Thomas Gibson Bowles, *Sea Law and Sea Power as they would be Affected by Recent Proposals; with Reasons against those Proposals* (London: Longman, 1910); British Library electronic catalogue: title words 'sea power' period 1890–1914.

23   Donald S. Schurman, *Julian S. Corbett: 1854–1922* (London: Royal Historical Society, 1981). This is the only full-length study of this critical thinker.

24   J.S. Corbett, *England in the Seven Year's War* (London: Longmans, 1907).

25   D. Schurman, *The Education of a Navy: The Development of British Naval Strategic Thought 1867–1914* (London: Cassell, 1965). Mahan and Corbett are prominent.

26   J.S. Corbett, *Some Principles of Maritime Strategy* (London: Longman, 1911). See also the edition edited by E. Grove (Annapolis, MD, 1988).

27   Corbett (1907), vol. 1, p. 5.

This critical disclaimer from the foremost strategic analyst of sea power requires further elaboration. Corbett was addressing a specific audience, at a specific time. Furthermore, his object was not the development of timeless principles, but the foundation of a coherent and soundly-based national, strategic concept, which would be understood and applied by British statesmen and armed forces. His 1911 text, *Some Principles of Maritime Strategy*, was a carefully crafted argument for a limited war strategy based on, but not exclusively composed of, sea power. It was put forward as both an alternative to the narrowly naval strategies and the continental vision of the army.

After Corbett's death his friend, Admiral Sir Herbert Richmond, continued his work and provided a classic definition: 'Sea Power enables its possessor to send his troops and trade across those spaces of water which lie between nations and the objectives of their desires and to prevent his opponents from doing so.'[28] It should be stressed that Richmond understood the difference between Mahanian or 'strategic' sea power and broadly based 'historical/cultural' sea power.[29]

During the Cold War Corbett's ideas were at a discount in Britain. In *The Continental Commitment: The Dilemma of British Defence Policy in the Era of Two World Wars* (1972), Professor Howard provided a historical explanation of Britain's current strategic posture, dominated by a British army on the Rhine and an air force in West Germany. He dismissed Corbett and sea power as both irrelevant to modern conditions and historically unimportant. Paul Kennedy went further, arguing that both Britain and the Royal Navy had been consigned to history, an assumption overtaken by the transformation of Britain under Prime Minster Margaret Thatcher (1979–1990).[30] Such arguments were rendered obsolete by the end of the Cold War and the collapse of the Soviet threat. It was highly significant that the United States Navy re-examined these two British thinkers as part of the intellectual response to the end of the Cold War.[31] Professor Baugh provided a persuasive counter to the Howard/Kennedy argument.[32]

Corbett's concept continues to inform British strategy in the twenty-first century because it was soundly based and reflected a clear grasp of long-term continuities. It

---

28 Admiral Sir Herbert W. Richmond, 'The Objects and Elements of Sea Power in History', *Naval Review* (1943), p. 8; and *Statesmen and Sea Power* (Oxford: Oxford University Press, 1946).

29 Admiral Sir Herbert W. Richmond, *Sea Power in the Modern World* (London: George Bell, 1934). At this time Richmond was the Vere-Harmsworth Professor of Naval History at Cambridge. *Statesmen and Sea Power* remains his best-known work.

30 M. Howard, 'The Continental Commitment: The Dilemma of British Defence Policy in the Era of Two World Wars' (London, 1972; taken from the 1971 Ford Lectures at Oxford); Kennedy, *The Rise and Fall of the British Naval Mastery*.

31 John B. Hattendorf and James Goldrick, eds, *Mahan is not Enough: The Proceedings of a Conference on the Works of Sir Julian Corbett and Admiral Sir Herbert Richmond* (Naval War College Press, 1993); taken from Naval War College Conference of 1992, it provides useful essays and important bibliographies of both Corbett and Richmond.

32 D. Baugh, 'British Strategy during the First World War in the Context of Four Centuries: Blue-Water versus Continental Commitment' in D.M. Masterson, ed., *Naval History* (Annapolis, MD: Naval Institute Press, 1986).

is Howard's continental argument that has been shown to be a short-term aberration by the *Strategic Defence Review*.[33] Since 1989 Britain has engaged in a number of expeditionary operations, ranging from high-end warfare to disaster relief in the Gulf Wars, and longer-term Gulf region deployments, former Yugoslavia, Belize, East Timor, Sierra Leone and Afghanistan. Since the sixteenth century England, and later Britain, has been a maritime state, dominated by commercial interest, resource dependency and the singular geostrategic fact that it is an island. It was at once a cultural/historical and a strategic sea power, possibly the last such state.

In reality historical/cultural sea power is not a question of strategic choice: it is largely a factor of those characteristics that Mahan outlined. Corbett recognised that Britain could not avoid being a sea power. Depending on the sea for her very survival Britain was desperately vulnerable to sea power and would be forced to surrender if she lost control of the ocean routes. A thorough blockade would signal her defeat. While the ideas are Corbett's they were best summed up by his friend, Admiral Lord Fisher: 'It's not *invasion* we have to fear if our navy is beaten, it's *starvation!*'[34]

Political Science

Strategists of Sea Power

Texts in the political science, strategy/naval education fields are, as a rule, more concerned with clarity and exposition; they are anxious to teach and happy to simplify. They are often dominated by numerous small case studies – which are intended to prove something. Of course, such bleeding morsels prove nothing, beyond the intent of the author/s, and the singular fact that the less we know the easier it is to understand. Such texts frequently use 'Sea Power' as a title, distil discussions of strategic thought over time, without providing anything as banal as context, and direct the audience towards the future. While this literature is large, the underlying themes were established a century ago; subsequent elaboration has done little more than update the examples and introduce ever more tedious terminology. Most of what passes for sea power studies is didactic writing on maritime strategy, tracing 'sea power' across long periods, picking out the obvious highlights, creating a history lesson. Such works fit neatly into a line of argument that stretches back to Mahan, in English, and somewhat further in French. Headline contributors include

---

33   *The Strategic Defence Review*, 2 vols (London: HMSO, 1998); *The Strategic Defence Review: How strategic? How much of a review?* (London: Brassey's, 1998). These texts establish the underlying Corbettian nature of contemporary British strategy. See also *The Fundamentals of British Maritime Doctrine*, 2nd edn (London: HMSO, 1998).

34   Fisher (1904); Arthur J. Marder, *The Anatomy of British Sea Power: A History of British Naval Policy in the pre-Dreadnought Era, 1880–1905* (New York: Alfred Knopf, 1940), p. 65.

Gorshkov, Gray and Till.[35] These titles, aimed at naval officers and analysts, employ borrowed historical examples to demonstrate principles and practices – they do not derive them from history. This Mahanian sea power remains slightly diffuse, relative and inclusive. States that rely on the sea are classified as maritime powers. When historians use sea power as a title they assume a Mahanian definition.[36]

History and Sea Power

Mahan understood the relationship between history and sea power, and recognised that the development of his naval educational product depended on an accurate understanding of the past. He observed:

> [H]istory gives you the whole. ... But you approach history with powers developed to appreciate what it gives, if you have beforehand the light which is given by principles, clearly enunciated. You come to it provided with standards ...

> My own lectures form a desirable preparation for works such as those of Corbett. Corbett himself has the advantage, as a military – or naval – historian, of approaching his subject provided with clearly formulated principles, drawn, as he continually allows to transpire, from standard military writers.[37]

This was something of a confessional. Where Corbett used theory to interpret and analyse his evidence, a critical phase in the evolution of higher understanding, Mahan used it to inform the construction of a teaching text.

Historians have been using the concept of sea power for 2,500 years. The ancient Athenians understood the concept, while one of the first things Mahan discovered after adumbrating his concept was that sixteenth-century Englishman Francis Bacon, taking his cue form Thucydides, had deployed a sea power concept: 'he that commands the sea is at great liberty, and may take as much and as little of the war as he will; whereas those that be strongest by land are many times nevertheless in great straits' and managed to convey his meaning in a few deft phrases, as opposed to Mahan's bulky book.[38] The ancient Greeks were probably

---

35   Stephen W. Roskill, *The Strategy of Sea Power: Its Development and Application* (London: Collins, 1962); the Lees-Knowles Lectures; the official historian of the British naval war 1939–1945 updated Mahan, Corbett and Richmond for the Cold War. See also Sergie Gorshkov, *The Seapower of the State* (London: Pergamon Press, 1979) for the thoughts of the man who created the Soviet fleet.

36   Marder; Christopher Bartlett, *Great Britain and Sea Power 1815–1853* (Oxford: Oxford University Press, 1963).

37   Mahan, *Naval Strategy*, pp. 16–17.

38   Francis Bacon, 'Of the true Greatness of Kingdoms and Estates' (1597), in P. Mattheson and E. Mattheson, eds, *Francis Bacon* (Oxford: Oxford University Press, 1929), pp. 85–6 – based on Pericles' Funeral Oration.

the first to speak of sea power and, even if they were not, their words inspired modern usage.[39] Herodotus, Thucydides and others had formulated the concept to explain the fundamental differences between Athens and Sparta, land versus sea, democracy against autocracy, progress and stasis. Plato equated the sea with moral and political corruption.[40] Professor Momigliano linked the emergence of a 'searching analysis' of the nature of sea power to post-Peloponnesian War attempts to comprehend the disaster that had befallen the Athenian state, a debate revived at intervals as the city slowly slid into obscurity. Ancient sea power had a political and cultural significance that has frequently been revived across the ages to invest the concept with meanings far broader than those encompassed by strategists.

Greek sea power was revived by Victorian historians George Grote (1894–1871) and John Robert Seeley (1832–1895) who connected ancient Athens, Venice and modern Britain.[41] Seeley contrasted British sea power with the two great land powers, Russia and America: 'Between them, equally vast, but not as continuous, with the ocean flowing through it in every direction, lies, like a world-Venice, with the sea for streets, Greater Britain.'[42] Many who adopted Mahan's analysis had been predisposed to sea power by Seeley and Grote, Thucydides and Herodotus. It is highly probable that he had read their works.

While historians from Herodotus to the modern age have used sea power to describe a cultural reality the meaning is constantly reshaped to address new ages and new concerns. By contrast, strategists and political scientists treat sea power as a policy choice, a strategy aimed at securing control of the sea, or the product of that policy. They are concerned with the utility of sea power rather than its meaning. While this construction is frequently borrowed by historians, it needs to be distinguished from the historical/cultural definition that historians continue to use, notably when deployed as an alternative to land power, a fundamental question of national interests and culture. This historical sea power is a question of the totality of a nation's response to the ocean; it is only employed to describe states in which the sea occupies a dominant position in all aspects of national life, from commerce and strategy to art and language. This dependence is reflected across cultural life broadly defined, sea powers have maritime heroes, maritime ceremonies, use maritime words in common speech and see the sea in every aspect of national life. For them strategic sea power is not a choice, it is a necessity: they simply cannot exist without the sea.

To describe states that dominate the sea the Greeks coined the term *thalassocracy* [sea empire]. Once again the *Oxford English Dictionary* definition 'mastery of the sea; the sovereignty of the sea' does not do justice to the original concept. The

---

39   Arnaldo Momigliano, 'Sea Power in Greek Thought', *The Classical Review*, (May 1944), vol. 58, no. 1: 1–7.

40   P. Horden and N. Purcell, *The Corrupting Sea: A Study of Mediterranean History* (Oxford: Basil Blackwell, 2000).

41   G. Grote, *A History of Greece: Volume V* (London: John Murray, 1849); J.R. Seeley, *The Expansion of England* (London, 1883). The latter is the best-selling imperialist tract.

42   Seeley, pp. 291–2.

Greeks stressed that *thalassocracies* were vulnerable to the sea. They did not occupy extensive hinterlands or acquire, with the odd exception, extensive land empires, and would be exposed to disaster if they lost command of the sea. Athens, Carthage, Venice and Britain are classic examples. In the 1970s Reynolds, working across the scholarly boundaries between history and defence education, revived the term as an analytical classification to help distinguish sea powers from land powers. His argument was weakened by the decision to include late twentieth-century America in his list of *thalassocracies*: modern America is a classic continental empire, not a maritime state. Significantly, the American economy is less globalised than the average of world nations.[43] This is why the United States Navy focuses on strategic issues and does not examine the totality of Mahanian sea power.

Writing on sea power reflects the methodological and conceptual division between history and political science/strategy. The former can be characterised as the systematic analysis of evidence from some defined period or region, in which sea power is used as an analytical tool in developing some contingent conclusions about the subject under review, conclusions which are not intended to have any current value. Larger, more profound conclusions tend to be based on substantial focused research. While historians like Braudel and Lane have profound things to say about sea power, embedded in works of monumental scholarship, they do not offer 'lessons'. Braudel's detailed study of an age and a region dominated by sea power – from the French *Annales* school – stresses the importance of *la longue durée* above specific events. Lane, a historian with experience of modern sea power, was never afraid to make analogies. Current practitioners of this approach Horden and Purcell are similarly reflective, qualifying definitions and emphasising the specific and the contingent.[44] Such work provides a useful counter to the history gobbets served up in most strategic writing on sea power.

Modern Developments

Strategic Culture

Understanding sea power requires the key texts to be re-read in ways that their authors did not intend. A literature devised for naval education and doctrine development can only be assessed in context. These texts are cultural artefacts, each unique, contingent and specific. Even so, there remains a real need for a broad

43   K.R. Ross, 'The Fragility of Thalassocracy: Pericles to Heinlein' [online] <http://www. friesian.com/thalasso.htm>; C.G. Reynolds, *History and the Sea: Essays on Maritime Strategies* (Columbia, SC: University of South Carolina Press, 1989), pp. 20–65.
44   Fernand Braudel, *The Mediterranean and the Mediterranean World in the Age of Philip II*, 2 vols (London: Collins, 1975); Frederick Lane, *Venice: A Maritime Republic* (Baltimore: Johns Hopkins, 1973).

definition of sea power. Historians have provided a useful concept to encapsulate this approach, 'culture'. Within the broad definition of culture it is possible to identify 'strategic culture', but here again political science has reinvented an old historical concept in a form that hampers interdisciplinary discussion.[45]

Strategic culture, coined by Jack Snyder four decades ago to explain Soviet thinking on nuclear weapons, has been debated and perpetuated in a thoroughly postmodern sense.[46] The argument is that each state has a unique strategic culture, reflecting location, politics, economics, geography, population, history and other variables – intimately connected to national culture, reflecting the same concerns, values and ambitions in a more specific form. It is, according to Colin Gray, 'modes of thought and action with respect to force'.[47] When Alistair Iain Johnston attempted to add a new layer of elaboration, separating beliefs from behaviour in order to establish the causal impact of culture, as distinct from other variables, Gray dismissed such distinctions as nonsense.[48]

Historians would not find the idea of viewing strategic choice through the lens of national culture unusual. The Greeks located sea power in a cultural context, highlighting the distinction between authoritarian, militaristic Sparta, and dynamic, seafaring, democratic Athens. Their words inspired countless historians and political theorists, from Francis Bacon to the pioneer military historian Hans Delbrück. For Delbrück war was an integral part of cultural history:

> For the art of war is an art like painting, architecture, or pedagogy, and the entire cultural existence of peoples is determined to a high degree by the military organisations, which in turn are closely related to the technique of warfare, tactics, and strategy. All these things have mutual influence on one another.[49]

Lawrence Sondhaus's analysis of strategic culture literature linked it with the concept of national 'ways of war' developed from Basil Liddell Hart's 'British Way in Warfare' of the early 1930s, a significant reiteration of the fundamentally maritime nature of British strategy. Historians remain divided on the utility of 'strategic culture' and 'ways of war'. Jeremy Black argues that they are too simplistic and rational to deal with the complex and contingent nature of the past.[50] Although strategic culture has been developed by political scientists trying to understand current behaviour and provides some predictive capability, it can also be a 'useful

---

45 H. Delbrück, *The History of the Art of War: Volume IV – The Modern Era* (Berlin, 1919), trans. by W. Renfroe (Lincoln, NB, 1985), p. x; L. Sondhaus, *Strategic Culture and Ways of War* (Abingdon: Routledge, 2006). This is a bold attempt to harmonise history and political science by a noted naval historian.

46 Sondhaus, pp. 1–6.

47 Quoted in T. Farrell, 'Strategic Culture and American Empire', *SAIS Review* (Summer/Fall, 2005), no. 2: 3.

48 Farrell, p. 10.

49 Delbrück, p. x.

50 Sondhaus, pp. 11–12.

framework for understanding the recent as well as the more distant past'.[51] One of the core problems, as Colin Gray observed, is that the people who use these concepts operate within the military and political community: they are 'particularly encultured people and organisations'. Cultural assumptions pervade every level of analysis, and those of political scientists are probably not the best basis for analysing history or strategy. Treating history as a source of 'proof' or example, and unwilling to engage with complex, contingent pasts, they are, to quote Paul Schroeder, 'indifferent to context and deeper meaning, concerned only with taking what can be immediately used'.[52] Little wonder that there are problems defining sea power.

Navies and State-Building

Historians have taken a different perspective to Mahan, arguing that sea powers tend to be democratic and commercial. In Athens, Venice, Holland and Britain the political and economic development of the state was driven by the resource demands of naval power. Brewer and Glete argue that Holland and Britain, the first northern European states to develop modern tax-raising, bureaucratic government systems, used central banks, national debts and representative institutions to harness national wealth to fund naval power. Rival powers denied the commercial classes a significant role in government; their sea power did not prosper.[53]

Sea Power in the Post-Cold War World

Despite occasional challenges by Germany, Japan and the Soviet Union, sea power has been held by Britain, the United States and the Western world since 1890. Since 1989 the ocean has been a Western dominated space and sea power has never been more ubiquitous. A series of conflicts in the Balkans, the Middle East and Afghanistan have been dominated by power projection from the sea. With safe sea communications the West has been able to impose economic sanctions, carry troops and logistic back-up, and deploy sea based forces with impunity against non-naval adversaries.

The result has been a steady shift in naval analysis of sea power, moving from contests for command of the sea to power projection. This has the benefit of ensuring

---

51   Sondhaus, pp. 12–13.
52   Sondhaus, pp. 129–30.
53   J. Brewer, *The Sinews of Power: War, Money and the English State, 1688–1783* (London: Unwin Hyman, 1989); Jan Glete, *Navies and Nations: Warships, Navies and State Building in Europe and America, 1500–1860*, 2 vols (Stockholm: Almquist & Wiksell, 1993); Jan Glete, *War and the State in Early Modern Europe: Spain, the Dutch Republic and Sweden as Fiscal-Military States* (London: Routledge, 2002); Alan James, *Navy and Government in Early Modern France, 1572–1661* (Woodbridge: Royal Historical Society, 2004).

that the role of the sea in warfare be seen in a wider context, avoiding the danger of a narrow focus on purely naval events at the expense of their true significance. Most of these texts are more concerned with naval strategy than with sea power.[54]

Conclusion

Sea power is a useful concept (not a theory or a model) that can be deployed to organise and qualify evidence and ideas, but only if we accept agreed meanings that work for history, strategy and political science. It should never be used as a term without clarification. Current academic trends suggest that any individual discipline-based construction would sever the intellectual connection between historians and political scientists, to the considerable detriment of both communities. It is essential that the interface between political science and history respects the intellectual development of both. Harding provides an explicit analysis of the link between historical writing and sea power theory.[55] The latest historical thinking emphasises the contingent: it is defiantly anti-theoretical and widens the divergence between history and theory-based disciplines such as political science. However, most historians have abandoned grand designs in favour of the unique and focus on the role of human agency 'because we have developed an increased sensitivity to the complexities that differentiate one society or one subculture from another'.[56]

At the most basic level it is essential to distinguish between historical and strategic sea power. In attempting to reconcile these variant forms it is essential to recall that, although sea power began life in texts we now treat as history, these texts were originally conceived as political science and strategy. The inability of individual disciplines to produce an agreed definition for such a key concept suggests that the multidisciplinary approach of 'war studies' may be the natural home of sea power. The latest analysis of British history certainly implied as much.[57] Only

---

54   Eric Grove, *The Future of Seapower* (London: Routledge, 1990). This is a timely text for the end of the Cold War. See also Colin Gray, *The Leverage of Sea Power: The Strategic Advantage of Navies in War* (New York: Free Press, 1992), a classic text by a fine strategist, who normally pushes the case for air power; G. Till, *Seapower: A Guide for the Twenty-First Century* (London: Frank Cass, 2004), a recognised educational text across the Anglophone world, intended to officers undergoing mid to senior level education.

55   Richard Harding, *Seapower and Naval Warfare 1650–1850* (London: University College Press, 1999).

56   R. Darnton, 'History Lessons', *Perspectives* (September 1999); ,<http://.www.historians. org/perspectives/issues/1999/9909/9909pre.cfm>[viewed 10 March 2008]. An impressive, short think-piece by the then president of the American Historical Association, which sums up the core of what makes history different and valuable. It has the unusual quality of having been written quickly, in response to current events that were leading some in public life to look for the 'lessons of history'.

57   Bentley (2005), p. 85.

within such a multidisciplinary context can sea power retain the utility that Mahan intended, speaking to a broad audience that includes naval officers, statesmen and historians.

Land Warfare:
Attrition and Manoeuvre

John Buckley

On 30 July 1864 Union troops of the Army of the Potomac launched a daring attack on the Confederate lines defending Petersburg in an effort to break the growing deadlock. Employing a mine packed with some 8,000lb of powder the plan was intended to break the siege and eliminate the need for a further attritional struggle in an increasingly casualty-intensive campaign, which was draining both Union and Confederate armies. The plan was, however, an ad hoc effort, an attempt to alter the shape that the US Civil War had become in the summer of 1864, a drawn out and bitter struggle founded upon the mobilisation of industry, personnel and national resources. Ulysses Grant may have grasped the nature of the war in 1864 better than his contemporaries and the advantages conferred by the North's greater wealth in population and output, but it was not a development that sat easily with the approach of military practitioners and the historic flow of strategy and doctrine. The plan to break the siege failed due to poor prosecution, caused some 5,000 casualties, and contributed to the growing stalemate around Petersburg which lasted into 1865.

For many historians the US Civil War remains the point at which the conduct of war began its inexorable descent into attrition. In the age of mass production, industry and popular mobilisation, wars between the world's great powers increasingly became battles of resources such that, by the First World War, wealth and lives were consumed at an appalling rate and in a profligate manner. For the commanders of great armies trained to deliver decisive battlefield victories in the style of Napoleon, these developments were unwelcome and threatened to undermine the role and status of armed forces. Indeed, the impact of industrialisation and new technology from the 1860s onwards has been viewed as the principal factor in determining the failure of the armies in the US to deliver rapid success. For some, this signalled the emergence of industrial war, later referred to as total war, in which whole societies, economies and national resources had to be mobilised to achieve victory, and in which resources and technology overwhelmed military doctrine and strategic thought.[1] Historians have pointed to the inability of military commanders to adapt the prosecution of campaigns to the new environment, which consequently was a major contributory factor to the dramatically increased casualties inherent in modern wars. Others have argued that armies did adapt, albeit slowly at times, but that the impact of industrialisation and new technology often ran ahead of the capacity of commanders to cope with it.[2]

What is apparent over the period of the mid-nineteenth century through to the present is that armies and military theorists have wrestled with the problem of attrition and have endeavoured to energise warfare by injecting pace and decisiveness through manoeuvre. The problems apparently thrown up by the emergence of new weaponry and mass mobilisation on the battlefields of the US in the 1860s led some to believe that the age of Napoleonic style thinking and warfare was at an end and that wars would naturally become attritional. Practitioners, however, tried to meet this challenge in the early twentieth century and as new communications technology began to emerge, coupled with air power and increasingly efficient combustion engines, the problem of how to achieve sufficient manoeuvre to bring about decisive action began to appear solvable. This process has determined much of the development of land warfare in the twentieth century and has markedly shaped modern approaches to warfare. A now dominant theory in this field is the concept of the revolution in military affairs (RMA), which emerged in the closing years of the twentieth century as a means of conceptualising rapid developments in military capability and technology, particularly in the aftermath of the First Gulf War in 1991.[3] Retrospectively, it was noted by analysts that there had been a series of RMAs dating back many centuries, sometimes referred to in historical writing as military revolutions, the most famous being that of the mid-seventeenth century.[4] However, the concept of the RMA was narrower than that of the military revolution as discussed by Roberts in the 1950s and was predominantly focused on military doctrine and technology. The RMA concept is essentially concerned with the advantage gained by one side over another, usually through the implementation of new technology and the opponents' efforts to close the gap; where and when a state gains advantage by

---

1   See Arthur Marwick, *The Deluge: British Society and the First World War*, 2nd edn (London: Palgrave, 2006); Arthur Marwick, ed., *Total War and Social Change* (London: Palgrave, 1988); Stig Forster and Jorg Nadler, *On the Road to Total War: The American Civil War and the Wars of German Unification* (Cambridge: Cambridge University Press, 1997); and Forster and Nadler, *Great War, Total War: Combat and Mobilization on the Western Front, 1914–1918* (Cambridge: Cambridge University Press, 2000).

2   Brent Nosworthy, *The Bloody Crucible of Courage: Fighting Methods and Combat Experience of the Civil War* (London: Basic, 2003) is a good example of these issues.

3   Cf. Steven Metz and James Kievit, *Strategy and the Revolution in Military Affairs: From Theory to Policy* (US Army War College, Strategic Studies Institute, 1995); Donald Kagan and Frederick W. Kagan, *While America Sleeps: Self-Delusion, Military Weakness and the Threat to Peace Today* (New York: St Martin's Press, 2000).

4   Michael Roberts, *The Military Revolution, 1560–1660*, An inaugural lecture delivered before the Queen's University of Belfast (Belfast: Boyd, 1956).

the harnessing of innovation, an RMA can be said to have taken place. Historical examples often cited are the gunpowder revolutions of the early-modern era, Western naval developments of the ocean-going and exploration era, and the mass mobilisation of the Napoleonic period.[5] However, it should not be accepted as established historical understanding that there has ever been anything that conforms neatly to the notion of the RMA: all the cited examples are contentious and many historians have argued that there are so many other factors than technology and doctrine in play, and that periods either side of the supposed RMA are equally important, that the RMA concept is of limited use.[6]

Nevertheless, where imbalance has occurred it is true that new technology and thinking has often played a crucial role. More specifically, in the early twentieth century, the debate has centred on the technological imbalance between command, control and communications, alongside combat capability on the battlefield: it has been contended that in the period of the First World War such an imbalance occurred, with command structures and methods unable to control mass armies and new technology, thus resulting in the attritional carnage of the Western front.[7] An RMA may well have been the reaction to this in the interwar era leading to the apparent dynamism of the Second World War, often rather fallaciously described as the German 'concept' of *Blitzkrieg* [lightning war]. More recently, there is some validity in the view that technology and smart weaponry played a crucial role in the 'AirLand Battle' and 'network- centric warfare' concepts and their consequent impact on the conduct of air-ground operations in the closing decade of the twentieth century and the opening decade of the twenty-first. Arguably, this has now caused a major redefinition in the interrelationship between the use of force and political expediency. Indeed, the ease with which American-led coalitions can now overcome many conventional global opponents has clearly emphasised and underpinned the worldwide order and limited available options, if indeed there are any, open to potential opponents of the US.

The Road to Stalemate 1865–1916

Although it can now be seen that there was much to be learned from the US Civil War, it appeared to many European analysts that the amateurism of the American armies and the indecision of the war between 1861 and 1865 demonstrated little of

---

5   Clifford Rogers, ed., *The Military Revolution Debate: Readings on the Military Transformation of Early Modern Europe* (London: HarperCollins, 1995); and Geoffrey Roberts, *The Military Revolution: Military Innovation and the Rise of the West, 1500–1800*, 2nd edn (Cambridge: Cambridge University Press, 1996).

6   Jeremy Black, *A Military Revolution? Military Change and European Society, 1551–1800* (London: Palgrave, 1990), pp. 1–34.

7   Richard Bryson, 'The Once and Future Army', in Brian Bond et al., eds, *Look to Your Front: Studies in the First World War* (Staplehurst: Spellmount, 1999).

worth. Although a debate continues to the present day over how modern the US Civil War actually was, and whether it was truly the first 'total war', there were certainly indications of what a future industrial war might become, especially if it lingered longer than a few months. Even if one can accept that there was a degree of inefficiency in the conduct of battles and campaigns in the 1861–63 period there was clear evidence of the kind of problems that might be encountered by other nations' armies during the campaigns of 1864. A technocentric argument for the stalemate is based on the increased ranges and capabilities of rifled small arms, which prevented the decisive employment of artillery and greatly impeded rapid and potentially crushing pursuits in the wake of battle. However, it is by no means certain as to the importance of new combat technologies in the difficulties in attaining decisive victories in the civil war. Paddy Griffith has contentiously argued that truly professional armies of the period would not have found battlefield victory so elusive, irrespective of new technology which he regards as of less importance.[8]

The period after 1865 also demonstrates that, despite the first indications of emerging battlefield problems that would ultimately lead to stalemate, decision in war was not unattainable. Germany fought successful wars against Denmark (1864), Austria (1866) and France (1870–71) incorporating new practices and technology, but all driven by the notion of the *Vernichtungsschlact* [battle of annihilation] in which, in the Clausewitzian tradition, greatest force would be brought against the enemy's main force and in the *Kesselschlacht* [in essence, the double envelopment of the enemy]. Such concepts informed German operational planning and campaign strategies well into the Second World War. Throughout the mid-to-late nineteenth century other nations, Britain and France in particular, were concerned with maritime and imperial military affairs, and it was only in the closing years of the century that the unstable international situation prompted the Great Powers to focus attention on a possible confrontation in Europe. However, the ability of major industrial powers to produce vast numbers of soldiers resulted in the major European land armies each being able to muster in excess of three million soldiers and in Russia's case, around six million. New technology had also been introduced with long-range, rapid firing artillery, such as the French 75mm and German 150 mm guns, machine guns, and magazine-fed rifles. All such developments threatened to change the nature and scale of the battlefield, and conflicts such as the Boer War (1899–1902) and the Russo-Japanese War (1904–05) gave indications of future potential tactical difficulties.[9]

However, as war loomed large in the pre-1914 era, few believed that a future war could be anything other than short, and indeed some, such as Ivan Bloch, argued that a modern war was simply untenable due to the likely tactical stalemate

---

8   Paddy Griffith, *Battle Tactics of the American Civil War*, 2nd edn (London: Crowood, 1996). See introduction in particular.

9   Thomas Pakenham, *The Boer War* (London: Weidenfeld & Nicolson, 1979); and Richard Connaughton, *The War of the Rising and the Tumbling Bear* (London: Routledge, 1988).

caused by rapid rifle fire.[10] Armies still worked to plans and assumptions based on offensive action. France's Plan XVII called for mass assaults shot in by artillery, heavily reliant on morale or élan as a driving force. German planning was partly centred upon the famous Schlieffen Plan, a meticulous and carefully considered stratagem intended to deliver a quick knockout blow to France before Russia could intervene seriously on the Eastern front; in this way Germany would avoid a two-front war. Tactics in all armies had developed in the decade prior to 1914 but remained essentially linear, with limited immediate or organic fire support. Artillery was only just beginning to come to terms with indirect firing and no one was at all sure how logistical support could be maintained for armies in the medium to long term. Mobility was another key issue, particularly in the East where road networks were poor and railways limited in scope. However, as noted previously, command and control was a limiting factor in large armies, fighting over great distances and across 'empty' battlefields where the enemy often remained largely out of sight and in cover. With only a limited grip on these many factors, with a hazy idea of how command could be wielded in such circumstances, and with conscript troops of limited capability, generals were forced to prepare for the war they imagined they would get, which ultimately proved not to be the one that was eventually thrust upon them in the summer of 1914.[11]

The first few weeks of the Great War proved to be a chastening experience and, soon, many tactical problems began to confound commanders and soldiers alike. The emphasis on the offensive was rapidly exposed as being so costly as to be almost untenable. France's summer offensives (Plan XVII) resulted in severe casualties, numbered at some 160,000 and achieved little, whilst further to the north German troops enjoyed greater, if also costly, success. German strategy supposedly conformed to the Schlieffen Plan, though the degree to which this informed operations is now contested, but the rate and scale of the German advance caused considerable panic in Allied quarters. However, although Paris was temporarily threatened, German forces had overextended themselves and were forced to retreat to safer defensive positions. By the end of the year it was clear that neither side had been able to solve the difficulties in successfully prosecuting offensives with tolerable casualties.[12]

The basic tactical conundrum that confounded armies in the Great War, effectively until 1918, though there is evidence of progress in 1917, was that considerable tactical advantages were conferred on defenders, replacements of troops and equipment were sufficient to support large-scale and widespread operations, and commanders were forced to cope with a variety of complex tactical and operational issues that emerged at the same time that they were dealing with intense political pressures. It was little wonder that in the midst of absorbing the

---

10   Ivan S. Bloch, *Is War Now Impossible? Being an Abridgement of the War of the Future in Its Technical, Economic and Political Relations* (London: Gregg, 1992, repr.).

11   John Gooch, *Armies in Europe* (London: Routledge, 1980), Chapters 5 and 6.

12   Hew Strachan, *The First World War: Volume One: To Arms* (Oxford: Oxford University Press, 2001).

impact of recent technological innovations alongside the demand for immediate success, commanders made errors, though perhaps criticism is more justified in the willingness to continue with operations when casualties were great and success unlikely.[13]

In essence, the tactical environment greatly diminished the successful offensive use of infantry on the battlefield, as soldiers were hopelessly vulnerable to rapid firing artillery and machine guns. Relative safety was only achievable by 'digging-in', ultimately in complex trench systems, which resulted in predominantly static warfare. The only way to get forward was to suppress opposing artillery and eliminate the threat of entrenched enemy troops to such an extent that an attack across the ground between enemy lines – soon titled 'no-man's-land' – could be conducted with a reasonable chance of success and limited losses. Firepower was the key to this and in 1914–1918 artillery the only means of delivering it: unfortunately, a series of tactical issues had to be solved first in order for artillery to become effective enough. Only then could armies begin to cope with the wider operational issues of getting their own armies moving forward in a co-ordinated and integrated fashion. Artillery in the first years of the Great War was only just beginning to come to terms with the concept of 'indirect fire' and crews had yet to master environmental issues, the effects of wear and tear on accuracy, problems of mobility, and balancing ranging fire against surrendering surprise. In addition, armies had to learn how to manage large-scale battles in which command and control issues were vitally important and, until the closing stages of the war, there were no immediate answers. By 1918 armies had developed integrated operational plans in which supporting arms such as artillery, infantry, air power and tanks co-operated closely on the battlefield, all co-ordinated by more sophisticated command structures and communications developments, such as radio, and supported by greatly enhanced intelligence gathering. Offensives could now yield reasonable rewards, though dramatic advances had to be reined in to prevent troops advancing beyond the cover of their own artillery and within range of supply lines.[14]

The effectiveness of these new techniques can be ascertained by comparing battles of 1916 – the Somme and Verdun – with the methods employed in 1918, particularly by the British and notably in the Hundred Days' Campaign. In 1916 the failings of firepower and command resulted in heavy casualties on all sides with little apparent indication of progress. The most famous example remains the

---

13   Gary Sheffield and Dan Todman, eds, *Command and Control on the Western Front: The British Army's Experience 1914–1918* (Staplehurst: Spellmount, 2004) is a good example of the issues.

14   Shelford Bidwell and Dominick Graham, *Firepower: The British Army: Weapons and Theories of War 1904–45* (London: HarperCollins, 1982); Tim Travers, *The Killing Ground: The British Army, The Western Front and the Emergence of Modern Warfare 1900–1918* (London: HarperCollins, 1987); and Martin Samuels, *Command or Control? Command, Training and Tactics in the British and German Armies, 1888–1918* (London: Routledge, 1996) provide a selection of interpretations.

first day of the Somme battle (1 July 1916) in which some 57,000 British soldiers became casualties, with around 19,000 dead, but the battles around Verdun between French and German forces were also clear indications of the huge losses incurred in prosecuting offensives in the prevailing tactical and operational environment. Confronted by such heavy casualties, commanders and general staffs fell back on measuring success in terms of attrition. By 1918 the new approaches and techniques had produced much better results. The Battle of Amiens (August 1918) is perhaps the starting point for the emergence of more mobile warfare in which all arms co-ordination was the key. In many ways the summer of 1918 saw the beginnings of mechanised warfare.[15]

The historiographical debate surrounding military effectiveness in the Great War has been fierce indeed, certainly since the 1960s. The prevailing and orthodox interpretation has maintained that generalship was poor in the Great War and that commanders were too willing to commit armies to battle knowing casualties would be severe with little realistic chance of success other than inflicting attrition. This, perhaps, is best captured in the much quoted expression 'lions led by donkeys'.[16] However, since the 1980s there has been a growing revisionist body of historians who have developed the notion of the 'learning curve': that though mistakes were made they were explainable by the prevailing circumstances; that generals were not congenitally stupid; and that armies developed and learned how to deal with the rapid changes to modern warfare. Casualties were huge but this was in large part due to the scale of industrial warfare. It is interesting to note that many modern studies of military operations in the Great War have focused on the supposed effectiveness of the German Army, perhaps a retrospective reflection of the German Army's performance in World War II; yet, many historians now contend that it was the British Army that made the most progress in the 1916–1918 era and it was here that the roots of modern warfare were to be found. It should also be noted that the Hundred Days' Campaign was not a *Blitzkrieg*: Allied methods relied heavily on firepower and careful planning, and more accurately presaged Allied methods employed in the 1942–45 era, not the risky and aggressive manoeuvring of the Germans in 1939–42.[17]

---

15   Paddy Griffith, ed., *Battle Tactics of the Western Front: The British Army's Art of Attack* (New Haven, CT: Yale University Press, 1996); Tim Travers, *How the War Was Won: Command and Technology in the British Army on the Western Front 1917–1918* (London: Routledge, 1992).

16   Alan Clark, *The Donkeys* (London: Morrow, 1962); and John Laffin, *British Butchers and Bunglers of World War One* (Stroud: Alan Sutton, 1988).

17   Paul Harris, *Amiens to the Armistice: The BEF in the Hundred Days' Campaign* (London: Brassey's, 1999).

The Search for Manoeuvre 1918–1939

Although the Great War had ended with Allied armies making considerable advances, it was also true that the defending German forces had been exhausted by conducting a two-front war until 1917, then faced with a huge influx of American troops into Europe in 1918, and were concerned about collapsing support for the war at home. Consequently, the Allied armies may have demonstrated the future of land warfare in 1918, but it was unclear as to how important these techniques had actually been in winning the war. Moreover, in the wake of the horrendous losses and the calamitous aftermath of the war there was little political stomach for serious widespread contemplation about the future of war. Nevertheless, for military theorists and practitioners there was considerable interest in exploring ways in which the attritional battles of the Great War could be avoided. Despite the popular sentiment of 'never again' it was clear that future wars were still possible and that a repeat of the Great War was highly undesirable.

One of the lessons drawn from the First World War, and in particular 1918, was the importance of mobility through mechanisation as a means of breaking deadlock. This was a partial view, as it was all arms co-ordination after a period of attrition that had resulted in the advances of 1918, but, nevertheless, analysts such as Colonel J.F.C. Fuller of the British Army saw mass mechanisation of armies as the next logical step in warfare. This concept had formed a major part in Fuller's famous 'Plan 19', a vision of the 1919 campaign if the First World War had continued based on rapid advances by mobile troops bypassing enemy centres of strength. It was a rather utopian vision but, nonetheless, has since been considered prescient by later writers.[18] Another Briton, Captain Basil Liddell Hart also wrote widely on the future of warfare and cultivated an image of being the pioneer of mobile, mechanised warfare, though it is clear that Liddell Hart was by no means as important as he later claimed. In the aftermath of the Second World War he attempted to use the testimony of German generals to bolster his importance as a military pioneer, but there is little evidence that his writing directly shaped or influenced German military developments in the interwar years. The British Army itself lost its lead in mechanised warfare developments when cost-cutting hit hard in the 1930s and disagreements over how armoured forces should be constituted resulted in tank-heavy formations emerging in the years leading up to World War II. The Second World War demonstrated clearly that armour had to be part of a balanced force of mechanised infantry, mobile artillery and air support to be effective.

It was in other European nations, such as Germany and the Soviet Union, that theories of land warfare really developed in the 1930s, leaving Britain behind. In the Soviet Union theories of modern or mobile warfare based on mechanisation emerged when industry began to produce enough equipment to make it viable.

---

18   Brian Holden Reid, *JFC Fuller: Military Thinker* (London: Palgrave, 1987); and Azar Gat, *Fascist and Liberal Visions of War: Fuller, Liddell Hart, Douhet and other Modernists* (Oxford: Oxford University Press, 1998).

Dramatic increases in amounts of equipment such as artillery, tanks and aircraft radically altered the nature of the Soviet Army, and this mixed with emerging theories of how best to employ it. The most famous term employed in discussions of Soviet doctrine in this period was 'deep battle'. This vision of war focused on the operational level linked to strategic objectives and described the battlefield more holistically than German notions, which focused too closely on tactical issues. In the Soviet concept the whole enemy army needed to be tackled rather than just the front line: restricting the enemy's ability to respond to offensives was a crucial and important lesson from the Great War. This could be achieved by targeting the enemy's command and control structure with air power and fast moving units which would induce 'operational shock'. Once the enemy was so paralysed resistance would falter and thus a greater level of victory could be attained. Notably, Soviet thinking foresaw that a series of linked operational successes would be required to win a campaign; there was no vision of a knockout blow. In addition, great importance was placed on logistical support, planning and intelligence.[19]

Much of this thinking emerged from the work of Mikhail Tukhachevski, K.B. Kalinovsky and Vladimir Triandafillov and in the late 1920s and early 1930s official doctrine began to be based on the principles of 'deep battle'. By the middle of the 1930s Soviet doctrine was advanced and modern, while the army was well supplied with *materiel* [equipment]. However, Stalin's paranoia over a possible Red Army coup intervened in 1936 and, over the next two years, some 35,000 Soviet officers were executed in a mass purge. The leading exponents of modern military doctrine, including Tukhachevski, were liquidated in a move that, in effect, destroyed the Soviet Army's ability to wage modern warfare. Ill-prepared junior officers were over-promoted and ill-informed political interference grew. When war came in 1941 the Red Army was hopelessly ill-equipped, both structurally and conceptually, for the nature of the conflict that was thrust upon the Soviet state.

The most famous exponents of modern mechanised warfare in the 1930s and the Second World War, however, were the Germans, and the speed with which Hitler's forces overwhelmed large parts of Europe in the 1939–42 period led many post-Second World War analysts to seek out the roots of this success, widely referred to in the Anglophone world as *Blitzkrieg*. They particularly examined the developments in doctrinal thinking in the German Army in the aftermath of defeat in the Great War, particularly under the tutelage of Hans von Seeckt. Despite being denuded of modern equipment and restricted to some 100,000 troops, the German Army and its core staff carefully evaluated the lessons of the 1914–18 war in whole series of studies in the 1920s and 1930s. What emerged from this work was an emphasis on combined arms, devolved battlefield command, mobility and the avoidance of static warfare. These key factors underpinned existing German military philosophy in still aiming to fight decisive battles of annihilation (*Vernichtungsschlachten*), and there remained the devotion to *Kesselschlachten* – battles of encirclement. There was also an underlying desire to avoid the attritional battles and campaigns of the

---

19   Richard Simpkin and John Erickson, *Deep Battle* (London: Brassey's, 1987); and David M. Glantz, *Soviet Military Operational Art: In Pursuit of Deep Battle* (London: Cass, 1991).

Great War, in part in the pursuit of delivering efficient military victories but also because Germany's parlous economic and geostrategic position rendered victory in a refight of the Great War highly unlikely.[20]

After Hitler's ascent to power new, more aggressive, technically-minded commanders began to come to the fore in the German Army, men such as Heinz Guderian, who placed greater emphasis on armoured formations as a means of driving the initial phase of the battles of encirclement. Such formations, the Panzer divisions, still conformed, however, to the concept of all arms co-ordination and, in this way, they differed from the British and French. It should be noted, however, that the doctrinal debate was not done and dusted in 1939, nor was there ever a single *Blitzkrieg* doctrine. Indeed, the term was not used in the German Army and the nearest military expression to it would be *Bewegungskrieg* [manoeuvre warfare]. Moreover, despite the popular view that the German Air Force, the Luftwaffe, was an army support arm, it was a multi-purpose service with only some 10 per cent given over to direct ground support.[21] The Luftwaffe would, however, contribute significantly to the early successes of World War II by providing operational and campaign level support, and in particular in contributing to the imposition of strategic paralysis on an enemy by attacking lines of communication and control networks. In this way the enemy would be unable to react quickly enough to German offensives and would thus bring about more rapid victory.

In essence, when war came in 1939 the German Army was by no means the finished article. It had a better grasp of many tactical issues and some, though by no means the majority, in the army had seized upon possible options for delivering quick operational level success should it become a necessity. In 1939, forced into a war on two fronts when heavily outnumbered and outmatched in resources, that is precisely what Germany fell back on. However, early successes merely concealed the severe deficiencies and weaknesses in the German Army's approach to war, rather than battle.

The Second World War 1939–1945

In terms of military theory and doctrine, the Second World War will forever be associated with *Blitzkrieg*, even though many historians have now rightly rejected the notion that there was a tactical or operational approach with that name. In many popular works, however, the term and concept is casually employed to

---

20 James S. Corum, *The Roots of* Blitzkrieg: *Hans von Seeckt and German Military Reform* (Lawrence, KA: Kansas University Press, 1992).

21 James S. Corum, *Creating the Operational Air War 1918–1940* (Lawrence, KA: Kansas University Press, 1997); and Williamson Murray, *Strategy for Defeat: The Luftwaffe 1933–45* (London: Brassey's, 1996).

explain the rapid success the German Army achieved up to late 1942.[22] During this time German forces overran Poland, Norway, Denmark, The Netherlands, Belgium, Luxembourg, France, Yugoslavia, Greece, much of the Soviet Union west of the Urals, and advanced to within 60 miles of Cairo. Most spectacularly, France fell after a campaign of less than two months, in sharp contrast to the four years of attritional stalemate in the Great War. For many at the time and since, these victories demonstrated that the German Army had devised a new approach to war, based on new tactics, backed with liberal use of armour and close air support. Even if the Germans themselves did not use the term *Blitzkrieg* (it was introduced into the lexicon of war by *Time* magazine), it nevertheless captured the essence of something new which had resulted in the end of attrition and the triumph of manoeuvre.

German operations in this period were undoubtedly prosecuted at such a high tempo that enemies were quickly overwhelmed, or at least were for as long as the limited German resources available could support such high-speed operations. It should be noted, however, that some German campaigns did not rely on armour, that air support was general pitched at the campaign-operational level rather than tactical, and that the great majority of the German Army remained non-mechanised throughout the war. Moreover, German doctrine was initially far from tied to concepts of dynamic, thrusting, armoured warfare, and deployments and plans for the invasion of Poland show that German operational thinking was far from certain; even the early plans for the campaign in the West demonstrated little adherence to popular visions of *Blitzkrieg*. In reality, German methods drew more from the past than might be imagined; considerable attention was still given to the battle of encirclement concept, much as had long been employed historically by German armies. However, by the 1930s through the application of limited mechanisation supported by air power, tactical flexibility and battlefield opportunism, the German Army was able to achieve its short-term objectives at a faster rate than hitherto. By the time of the campaign against France and the Low Countries in May 1940, a central aim was to break through enemy lines in a few key locations, and to drive hard in to the enemy's rearzone in order to sow chaos. Retaining the initiative and imposing a high tempo on operations to prevent the enemy from recovering was crucial. If German forces could deliver enough such operational victories before resources began to dwindle and front-line troops began to tire, an enemy would not be afforded enough time to recover and collapse might follow. Until the invasion of the Soviet Union in 1941 these methods were enough to score quick victories over lesser powers. The result of German actions appeared new because of the speed of the successes, but operational methods continued to develop and change in the 1939–42 period and at no time would troops or commanders have been aware of the introduction of a new doctrine; merely the more effective prosecution of previous notions at high speed, often referred to as *Bewegungskrieg* [manoeuvre warfare].

---

22   J.P. Harris, 'Debate – The Myth of *Blitzkrieg*', *War in History*, vol. 2, no. 3 (1995); Charles Messenger, *The Art of* Blitzkrieg (London: Ian Allan, 1976).

Nevertheless, although there was no new formal doctrine, the *Blitzkrieg* era appeared to have ushered in a new era in land warfare, one in which manoeuvre appeared to have returned to triumph over attrition. Indeed, if the German state had halted prior to June 1941, prepared fully for a longer campaign in the East against the USSR and maximised the resources then available, this estimation may have appeared accurate. However, the very nature of Hitler's regime and his commanders prevented this and when launched at the Soviet Union in 1941 the weaknesses in Germany's approach to the conduct of war were ruthlessly exposed. German methods relied heavily on delivering victory through a series of operational successes rather than the prosecution of a campaign composed of actions intended to deliver an identified strategic goal, underpinned by good intelligence, long-term planning and logistical support. The victories scored certainly depleted the Red Army considerably, but proved insufficient to knock out the Soviet state, partly because there was no clear strategy of how this was to be achieved within the time frame rendered feasible and sustainable by the available resources. When the initial rush of spectacular but disconnected victories failed to topple Stalin, Germany became locked into a long war in which firepower and attrition proved to be the decisive factors once again, a war for which the Third Reich was woefully underprepared and structurally deficient.[23]

In many ways, Germany's conduct of the war and its army's approach to operations was, in fact, remarkably backward-looking rather than modern: the victors of World War II were those armies that husbanded resources, linked operations into a grand design, and planned the war from top to bottom and front to rear, rather than relying on close combat tactics and abilities, and operational mobility. It was the Allies that fought a more modern war and viewed the battlefield not just as a front line but as a total theatre, in which the long term predominated over short-term opportunism. As the war turned against Germany in 1942 it was the application of firepower – most obviously land-based artillery and air forces – that formed the cornerstone of victory and against which the Germans had no answer.[24] Yet the cost was still high. Even though the Western Allies attempted to limit friendly casualties through the liberal if costly application of machinery and resources, the battlefield of 1944–45 was still very dangerous for the rifleman at the sharp end of war, more so than the killing fields of the Great War. Additionally, Allied front-line troops had to develop their own battlefield craft to a sufficient level to work alongside their supporting firepower assets in order to defeat their battle-hardened and grimly determined German opponents.

By the end of hostilities in 1945, the war, which had accounted for millions of civilian lives on a scale never before seen, had also cost the lives of millions of

---

23   Evan Mawdsley, *Thunder in the East: The Nazi-Soviet Struggle 1941–45* (London: Hodder Arnold, 2005).

24   David French, *Raising Churchill's Army: The British Army and the War Against Germany 1919–1945* (Oxford: Oxford University Press, 2000); Williamson Murray and Allan R. Millett, *A War to be Won: Fighting the Second World War* (Cambridge, MA: Harvard University Press, 2000).

soldiers and had, in many ways, appeared to have become a refight of the Great War with the application of firepower and the imposition of attrition winning out against operational mobility.

The Cold War 1945–1991

In the aftermath of the Second World War it was in Central Europe that the most likely collision of land forces seemed likely, if the Cold War between the West and East ever erupted into open, high-intensity conflict. Such a war would directly involve the armed forces of NATO (North Atlantic Treaty Organisation) led by the USA, and the Warsaw Pact led by the Soviet Union, and both sides planned and prepared for a showdown along the Iron Curtain in Europe, the border between East and West. The principal battleground however, was expected to be Germany, then divided between the western Federal Republic and the eastern German Democratic Republic. Prevailing military theories about how best to conduct such a campaign, should it ever come to it, contrasted between NATO and the Warsaw Pact, and were shaped and defined by the ebb and flow of the Cold War, prevailing attitudes to the emergence of nuclear weapons, financial constraints, and the need to prosecute a variety of more limited operations around the globe.

Soviet approaches to the conduct of major land operations built on their experiences of the Second World War and were firmly based on the successful methods that had crushed the German Army in 1943–45. Following on from the ideas of interwar deep battle theory, which then crystallised in the Second World War, Soviet plans for fighting NATO were based on superiority in numbers, the application of firepower, attacking enemy positions in depth and the employment of fast-moving forces to plunge far into the enemy's rearzones to facilitate collapse. However, operations would be seen as building blocks with the expectation that a series of such battle would be needed to bring about victory. The Soviets imagined being able to overwhelm NATO's conventional forces through the application of force and tempo and, in particular, the knockout blows delivered by the following second echelon forces designed to exploit breakthroughs (later referred to as 'operational manoeuvre groups' (OMGs)).[25]

Western military thinking was in many ways defined by the experience of fighting the Germans in World War II as well as the prospect of fighting the Soviets, and in applying the lessons of one to the plans for combating the other. The US Army in particular had been greatly impressed by the operational methods employed by the German Army in World War II, initially in the *Blitzkrieg* era and then in fending off much larger armies backed by greater resources in the last two

---

25   David M. Glantz, *Soviet Military Operational Art: In Pursuit of Deep Battle* (London: Cass, 1991); and Richard E. Simkin, *Race to the Swift: Thoughts on Twenty-First Century Warfare* (London: Brassey's, 2000).

years of the war. It appeared that this was the closest approximation to the situation in which NATO found itself in the Cold War: facing a larger enemy force reliant on firepower and conforming to a firm plan. Western armies, already interested in adopting methods other than firepower and attrition, examined how the often numerically inferior Germans had employed tactical flexibility, devolved command structures and high-tempo operations to outmanoeuvre opponents, seized fleeting opportunities on the battlefield, and prevailed against superior numbers. Indeed, for many Allied commanders, impressed by German determination and tactics in the Second World War, there was much to learn from their defeated enemies which could be applied to battling the Warsaw Pact, especially if married to more modern and sophisticated approaches to intelligence, logistics and strategic planning, areas in which the Allies had proved superior. In many ways, however, this was a very partial reading of the German Army's methods and 'successes', and many of their attributes simply did not transfer easily to NATO; the obduracy of the German soldier owed much to desperation, desensitisation to combat, and ideological fervour, resulting in atrocity and excess, aspects of military affairs unwelcome in liberal democratic states.

NATO methods were therefore to rely on superiority in command and control structures, leadership and initiative, and the application of mobile firepower. The most significant weaknesses were in resources and numbers; conventional armies properly equipped were hugely expensive and, in the aftermath of World War II, few in Europe were able or willing to afford large armies. The experience of the Korean War (1950–53) emphasised how costly conventional forces could be, and a balance had to be struck between military security and economic rebuilding. Consequently, it was estimated that NATO forces would be unlikely to deliver a spectacular victory in Europe but that they could blunt any Soviet attack in order to buy time for Western mobilisation, politics and diplomacy to achieve a solution.[26]

US policy in the 1950s recognised, however, that any successful defence of Central Europe was unlikely until such time that NATO's conventional forces could offer a realistic chance of success against an invasion, and this was considered unlikely for some time to come. In the interim a nuclear-reliant defence was implemented, referred to as the 'trip wire' policy, in which conventional weakness would be met by a large-scale nuclear response. This was later expanded and offered some flexibility by the intention of using tactical nuclear weapons to bolster NATO's conventional forces in Europe. Nuclear weapons were considerably cheaper and European powers, in particular, were keen to incorporate them into defence planning. However, the great weakness of tactical nuclear weapons was that any first use would probably produce a similar response from the Soviets and could cause still further escalation, leading to an exchange of strategic nuclear weapons. This greatly undermined credibility: did the Soviets really believe that the US would risk nuclear holocaust to defend

---

26   Robert R. Bowie and Richard H. Immerman, *Waging Peace: How Eisenhower Shaped an Enduring Cold War Strategy* (Oxford: Oxford University Press, 1997).

Europe? Consequently, tactical nuclear weapons held a limited deterrent value as the Soviets were sceptical that they would ever be used against their conventional forces, especially as West Germany was also openly hostile to the use of tactical nuclear weapons on its territory.

The only realistic route open to NATO was to develop sufficiently powerful conventional forces to render the use of nuclear defence unnecessary. Without a hugely expensive and politically damaging expansion of conventional forces there appeared to be no solution, but in the 1970s a new concept began to emerge, named AirLand Battle, in which new technologies might be developed and harnessed to balance out the disparity in numbers between NATO and Warsaw Pact forces.[27] Initial development centred on the use of new anti-tank guided missiles, which considerably increased the effectiveness of smaller formations against armour heavy forces, but it was General Don Starry who pushed the idea of an integrated battlefield zone in which air and land forces would work together closely, aided by sophisticated communications systems to co-ordinate offensive actions against Soviet forces, and in particular against the second echelon and follow-up units the Red Army intended to exploit situations on the battlefield. Attacks on these forces using increasingly sophisticated smart weapons would cripple the Warsaw Pact's ability to drive offensives home whilst, simultaneously, making the job of front-line or first echelon formations that much more difficult. Moreover, by enhancing mobility, manoeuvre, targeting and firepower, NATO forces would be able to dictate and impose the pivotal moments in an operation and ensure success. In essence, the harnessing of new emerging technology was to be the determining factor in eliminating the Warsaw Pact's superiority in numbers.

As a concept 'AirLand Battle', which became increasingly dominant in NATO thinking in the early 1980s, caused major problems for the Soviet armed forces. Without a dramatic increase in investment or acquisition of new technology the balance of conventional power seemed to be about to switch from East to West and there was little that could be done. By the mid-1980s the USSR was beginning to implode anyway, but AirLand Battle remained the cornerstone of NATO warfighting doctrine well into the 1990s and the results, though far from definitive. were seen in the First Gulf War in 1991.

Contemporary Military Doctrine

Since the end of the Cold War technology has developed apace and the results have been adopted by an enthusiastic military, most obviously in the USA. With huge sums

---

27   Robert A. Doughty, *The Evolution of US Army Tactical Doctrine, 1946–76* (Ft Leavenworth: US Army Command and General Staff College, 1979); John L. Romjue, 'The Evolution of the AirLand Battle Concept', *Air University Review* (May–June 1984); and Robert Leonhard, *The Art of Maneuver: Manuever-Warfare Theory and AirLand Battle* (New York: Presidio, 1991).

of money to invest the US military have furthered the impact of communications technology in warfare and the successor to AirLand Battle has become network-centric warfare or operations. This is an attempt to link all aspects of conflict into a networked system that manages and filters information and intelligence to enhance dramatically the effectiveness of operations and actions. By having a much greater ability to know what to attack and with what force, fused with an ability to hit a target ever more accurately, military action can be better controlled and focused and becomes less personnel and equipment-intensive. Between the Gulf Wars (1991 and 2003) smaller US forces are now capable of delivering much more in the way of effective targeted action intended to deliver political results.[28]

However, according to some critics, a fundamental problem with high-intensity concepts of war such as current network-based operations is that they are doctrines for wars that are no longer likely. Of much greater significance are and will be methods and doctrines to combat insurgencies, terrorism, or asymmetric conflicts, known as 'fourth generation warfare', and, however sophisticated and all-encompassing network-centric doctrines may be, they are rendered increasingly redundant by the global strategic environment. In part, this notion supports the growth of interest in effects-based operations, an approach to war which attempts to incorporate all methods of achieving political objectives in conflicts alongside direct military force. Where force is to be used it should be directly proportional to the likely effects of the destruction and should not ideally be counterproductive. The application of overwhelming military force might solve an immediate problem but could create greater military, political or social problems later in a campaign and should thus be very carefully evaluated.[29]

Conclusion

The battle between attrition and manoeuvre, however simplistic this notion is, appears by the early twenty-first century to be over. Owing to the emergence of highly sophisticated technology, which facilitates very rapid intelligence gathering and evaluation, and which is capable of targeting enemy forces and assets with great precision, the need for heavy and relentless firepower as a means of inflicting attrition is diminishing. The employment of sufficient, yet decisive, amounts of

---

28   David S. Alberts, John J. Garstka and Frederick P. Stein, *Network Centric Warfare: The Face of Battle in the 21st Century* (National Defense University Press, 2001); James R. Baker, *Transforming Military Force: The Legacy of Arthur Cebrowski and Network Centric Warfare* (New York: Praeger, 2007).

29   Paul K. Davis, *Effects Based Operations: A Grand Challenge for the Analytical Community* (Santa Monica: RAND, 2001); E. Mann, G. Endersby and Thomas Searle, *Thinking Effects: Effects-Based Methodology for Joint Operations* (Alabama: Air University Press, 2002); and Edward R. Smith, *Effects Based Operations: Applying Network Centric Warfare in Peace, Crisis and War* (CCRP Information Age Transformation Series, 2002).

force and firepower at critical moments and locations, guided and monitored by information gathering and dissemination systems, is now attainable; ground forces in modern armies are capable of a great deal more with a good deal less. This is in clear and marked contrast to the previous wars of attrition when, despite the fallacious claims of many writers, there were no realistic answers to the problem of prosecuting large-scale industrial warfare. However, despite the increased capabilities of modern armies, their targets have largely changed and, when confronted with insurgents and acts of terrorism, even the most sophisticated of forces struggles to utilise all its assets with sufficient force to manage these new threats easily.

PART II
ASPECTS OF MODERN WAR

After the RMA: Contemporary Intelligence, Power and War

John Ferris

Intelligence is not just espionage. It is the collection, collation and analysis of information so to help one use resources well in competitions with rivals. Intelligence is not a form of power, but a guide to its use. Intelligence is not collected for its own sake, but to support action. It does not win wars, but it can help generals to do so, by serving as a force multiplier, or by letting one know one's options and choose a good one. It has offered advantages to States for millennia, though not consistently—here essential to events, there irrelevant. Most States have received some intelligence sometimes, but not always from permanent and specialized agencies, and they have not always assessed it through bureaucracies. Until 1860, staffs were a secretariat, while commanders handled even minor functions of command. They organized the collection of their own intelligence, working through ad hoc means and a few aides; so did prime ministers and kings. This approach had advantages. Decision-makers could direct their intelligence and receive exactly the information they wanted; despite their lack of technological resources, the best personalized systems matched any bureaucratized ones of the twentieth century. Most pre-modern systems, however, were worse than mediocre modern ones, because intelligence was not thoroughly collected and assessed. By 1914, bureaucracy and technology enabled a revolution in intelligence, which rose sharply in significance and, along with other factors, transformed the nature of power and the working of war. Some see another such revolution in military intelligence occurring today.

Intelligence is collected through open sources and secret ones, including agents, signals intelligence and imagery. Before 1914, secret sources were of most use in peace, while open ones were central during war. Superiority in light cavalry produced mastery in tactical intelligence, as the side with better skirmishers monitored and blinded its foe. Since 1914, the power of secret sources (especially those with a technological base) has risen in peace and war. Each source has power and limits. Open sources, including one's own troops in war, offer the most information on the widest range of topics, but are stymied by security—their limits define the need for secret intelligence. Agents produce vast amounts of unreliable intelligence, as well as the rarest gems—documents from key decision-makers and inside commentary on their meaning. Imagery provides accurate material in such quantities that a mass of trivialities may mask the significant point. Signals intelligence yields the greatest stream of valuable and reliable data, but, often, it is hard to acquire, or else produces first-rate material on second-rate issues. Sources are valuable not because of secrecy or technical complexity, but because they provide accurate, relevant and timely information for action. A primitive source may equal a sophisticated one in value, an open source a secret one. Their value also varies with the competition and the competitors. Two first-rate intelligence services may neutralize each other, while, when fighting an incompetent adversary, a mediocre espionage agency may give its master a remarkable edge. Even the best sources rarely tell the whole truth and nothing else. More often, they offer masses of material, of uncertain accuracy or marginal relevance, fragmentary and hard to use, illustrating issues such as the quartermaster's accounts or the views of second-rate figures, which can illuminate their master's voice.[1]

The best intelligence is useless without an efficient link between the organs which collect, evaluate and act upon it. Flaws are possible anywhere along the chain. When one link breaks, so will the whole. Accurate intelligence may not be collected or assessed properly. It may not reach a commander in time; they may be unable to use knowledge or mishandle the attempt. A good army with bad information may beat a bad army with good intelligence. At Jutland and Midway, signals intelligence let two navies ambush an ambusher, but only one of them won its battle. Fluke so affected both battles that they could have gone either way, yet still Jutland aided the loser more than it did the victor. Knowledge has different effects when mobile forces operate over large spaces, rather than in long and slow campaigns of attrition. Where force to space ratios are low, flanks open, breakthrough easy and maneuver possible, espionage can contribute to epic victories—letting an attacker concentrate its strength against an enemy's weakness, or a defender place its reserves precisely where the foe plans to attack. In circumstances marked by high force to space ratios, equilibrium and attrition, intelligence provides only a series of small advantages. A mediocre intelligence service may affect a war of maneuver more than a good service does a struggle of attrition. Intelligence rarely shapes the formulation of policy but often guides its execution. Intelligence affects operations and bargaining more than strategy, and war differently than it does the inchoate spheres of politics and diplomacy, where it guides influence, by showing whom to manipulate and how, rather than power.[2]

---

1   Michael Herman, *Intelligence Power in War and Peace* (Cambridge: Cambridge University Press, 1996) and Michael Handel, *War, Strategy and Intelligence* (London: Frank Cass, 1989) are excellent introductions to intelligence.

2   For operational intelligence, cf. Michael Handel, *Intelligence and Military Operations* (London: Frank Cass, 1989); John Ferris and Michael Handel, "Clausewitz, Intelligence, Uncertainty and the Art of Command in Modern War," *Intelligence and National Security (INS)* (January 1995), 10/1: 1–58; and the special issue of *INS* (2007), 22/5, ed. by Huw Davies.

The modern age of intelligence began in 1914, as a function of developments in sources, organization and communication. Imagery and signals intelligence, joined to the general staff system, telegraph and radio, produced more powerful means of collecting, assessing and using intelligence. Operational intelligence and signals intelligence emerged suddenly, for the first time and the same reason. The rise of radio enabled operational control but raised new problems for security. Control was possible only by giving the enemy intelligence; many organizations, like the *Kriegsmarine*, would have been better served by not using radio at all. During August to October 1914, simply through exploitation of radio messages sent in plain language by the attacker, signals intelligence shaped the defensive victories which set the pattern in East and West, leading to the destruction of a Russian Army in East Prussia and the German failures between the "miracle of the Marne," and the "race to the sea." Thereafter intelligence, much of it produced at the leading edge of technology, became central to the working of military machines. States, however, proved unable even to approach the maximum use of the material available to them. Even so, by 1918, intelligence used virtually every technique deployed between 1939 and 1945 and, in two areas, affected events as much as it ever has done. The military surprise of the war—Germany's ability to smash a numerically far larger Russian enemy—stemmed from superiority in command, operational art and signals intelligence, which constantly, and in a one-sided way, uncovered Russian defensive weaknesses and offensive intentions. The dominant German commander on the front, Max von Hoffman, later claimed: "We were always warned by the wireless messages of the Russian staff of the positions where troops were being concentrated for any new undertaking"; only once "were we taken by surprise."[3] Meanwhile, American entry into the war was triggered by British intelligence, especially its solution of the "Zimmerman telegram" (by which Germany offered Mexico an offensive alliance against the United States).

This war rested on a long struggle between great armies. Intelligence affected it everywhere, varying with operational circumstances. In Russia, Palestine and Iraq, intelligence shaped victories on an epic scale. There, force to space ratios were low, breakthrough and exploitation possible, and the weight of intelligence lay heavily with one side, Austria and Germany on the Eastern front and Britain in the Middle East. The Western front between 1915 and 1917, conversely, was characterized by dense force to space ratios, elaborate defensive systems and firepower which could kill but not move. Breakthrough was extremely difficult to achieve; exploitation impossible. Both sides also possessed intelligence services of high skill. Each penetrated the other's intentions and capabilities, making surprise rare. Hence, intelligence canceled much of its own effect: but not all. It affected thousands of small actions and dozens of great ones, increasing one's chances for final victory, and reducing its price. Signals intelligence traced enemy deployments and movements, aircraft monitored enemy forces and photographed its defences, other sources produced much tactical information, while armies learned to deceive

---

3   Max von Hoffman, *The War of Lost Opportunities* (London, 1924), p. 132; David Kahn, *The Codebreakers: The Story of Secret Writing* (New York: Macmillan, 1967), pp. 622–34.

the enemy. Intelligence gave defenders advance warning of the British attack at the Somme in 1916 and the German one at the second Battle of the Marne in 1918; deception covered the surprise assaults of German forces during March to May 1918 and Commonwealth armies a few months later.[4]

At sea, British intelligence acquired an edge its master could not easily apply. The Admiralty tried to use signals intelligence hundreds of times, exactly as between 1940 and 1945, almost always without success; most spectacularly at Jutland, most routinely against U-boats. Aircraft were too slow and their ordnance too primitive to deliver the killing blows guided by signals intelligence until 1943. If one gauged effect through operations alone, Room 40 would be a failure—more British than German warships sank in the battles it brought about; but Britain had battleships to burn and its reward was above the battle. At the strategic level, intelligence, security and deception were fundamental to the war at sea for both sides, their fleets hours from Armageddon. Simple procedures of security could achieve surprise for a fleet operation, 24 hours warning could eliminate that edge—and Britain easily won the war of knowledge. For most days of the war, it knew what the main elements of the German Navy were doing and whether or not it was planning to leave harbour. This situation, combined with each side's fear that it might lose a main fleet action, the German reluctance to fight except on their own best terms and the substantial British advantage in warships, were fundamental to the war at sea—to stalemate in operations and Teutonic defeat in strategy. Room 40 denied Germany the advantage of intelligence or surprise and wrecked its only (however faint) chance to win the naval war, the "whittling" strategy it defined in autumn 1914, aiming to provoke warships into ambushes by submarines or larger but hidden forces. Intelligence strengthened the stronger navy, by removing the faint chance that German strategy could upset its weakness in seapower; less by multiplying force than by preventing its multiplication.[5]

Thus, control of the seas bolstered the bigger side, letting the allied powers wield the world's resources as a weapon in Europe, and damage the enemy's economy. The maritime blockade of the Central Powers rested on Anglo-French seapower, and control over transatlantic cables. The combination of signals intelligence at home and human sources abroad was central to this power and its execution, providing

---

4   J.R. Ferris, ed., *The British Army and Signals Intelligence During the First World War* (Army Records Society, 1992); pp. 14; Michael Occleshaw, *Armour Against Fate: British Military Intelligence in the First World War* (London: Columbus, 1989); John Schindler, "Steamrollered in Galicia: The Austro-Hungarian Army and the Brusilov Offensive, 1916," *War in History* (2003), 10/1: 27–59; and "A Hopeless Struggle: Austro-Hungarian Cryptology during World War I," *Cryptologia* (2000), 24/4: 339–50; Yigal Sheffy, *British Military Intelligence in the Palestine Campaign, 1914–1918* (London: Frank Cass, 1998).

5   Heinrich Walle, "Die Anwendung der Funktelegraphie bein Ensatz deutscher U-boote im Ersten Weltkrieg," *Revue Internationale d'Histoire Militaire* (1985), no. 62: 111–39; Korvettenkapitan Kleikamp, *Der Einfluss der Funkaufklarung auf die Seekriegsfuhrung in de Nordsee 1914–1918* (Kiel, 1934); Patrick Beesley, *Room 40, British Naval Intelligence, 1914–1918* (London: Harcourt, 1984).

knowledge, evidence and means for leverage.[6] The interception of letters, and telegraph or wireless messages let Britain know when firms were trying to break the blockade, often triggering the use of detectives or consuls in neutral countries to gather further information, which could be given to foreign authorities to justify actions against their own. Thus, blockade struck as many enemies as possible and as few innocents. Blockade was a battleaxe rather than a scalpel; it could wreck relations with firms and states. Intelligence helped Britain to wield it with accuracy. The blockade harmed the enemy significantly, more than it did the allies; neither outcome might have happened without the edge of intelligence.

In a war where power was measured by the ability to produce hundreds of thousands of soldiers and millions of tons of steel, intelligence mattered, far more than in any previous conflict, as much as in any later one. Yet its limits were equally notable. Intelligence proved hard to use everywhere. The army best served by signals intelligence, that of Austria-Hungary, was mediocre in quality—it was smashed by the Brusilov offensive even though its code-breakers warned of the onslaught. For signals intelligence in particular, this was a war of lost opportunities. Again, the Entente surpassed the Central Powers in intelligence, but not by much. By making blockade work without alienating Washington, and by influencing American elite and public opinion through censorship, propaganda and the Zimmerman telegram, intelligence eased, and may have been essential, to allied victory. Yet these allied triumphs were balanced by Austrian and German operational and subversive successes against Russia. Even more, these victories occurred at the same times, each countering the other before it led anywhere: in 1914, Tannenburg matched the Marne, in 1917 the Zimmerman telegram countered the Russian collapse. The greatest successes of intelligence in the First World War exceed those of the Second and, in the aggregate, their quality was equal. But intelligence affected the Great War less because, at the strategic level, each side's successes cancelled each other out, while it was harder to use for dramatic results in operations.

In the Second World War, the effect of intelligence was more one-sided. Axis intelligence ranged from incompetent to good, mostly mediocre. Allied services were mediocre to great, mostly good. In 1939 to 1941, however, their forces were operationally too poor to use that material, and their governments made disastrous failures of assessment—the Soviets failed to anticipate the German attack of June 1941, the British and American to understand that Japan was likely to start the Pacific War. Before 1942, intelligence did little to prevent Axis successes; instead, it worked marginally in their favour. Axis intelligence scored several successes, while the Allies did less well than often is supposed. This story is distorted because it usually is told from the perspective of Allied sword against Axis shield at Ultra's

---

6   Archibald C. Bell, *A History of the Blockade of Germany and of the Countries Associated with Her in the Great War, Austria, Bulgaria and Turkey, 1914–1918* (London: HMSO, 1937); Jonathan Clay Rendel, *Information for Economic Warfare: British Intelligence and the Blockade, 1914–1918* (PhD diss., University of North Carolina at Chapel Hill, 1993); Greg Kennedy, "Intelligence and the Blockade, 1914–1917: A Study in Friction, Administration and Command," *INS* (2007), 22/5: 699–721.

peak. Intelligence served Japan better in the run-up to the Pacific War than it did Britain or the United States, though still the biggest intelligence failure of 7/8 December 1941 occurred in Tokyo, not in Washington or London. German armies gained from low-level signals intelligence and imagery, but not much, given their other advantages, merely speeding maneuver. The Axis won the intelligence war in the Mediterranean, the North Sea and the Atlantic for much of 1940–42; and used their victories well. Intelligence backed an aggressive German naval campaign, and sustained an Italian strategy of fleet in being, combined with attack by submarines, mines and the Luftwaffe. Signals intelligence shaped the destruction of more large British than Axis warships, and multiplied the power of U-boats against commerce. Yet, at a strategic level, these successes were minor—specialists have downgraded the effect even of the U-boat campaign.[7] Their pursuit, in an equal exchange with Britain, broke the German Navy and smothered the Italian one, which still had battleships to burn, if fewer than in 1914. Ultimately, Britain won that war at sea because its seapower was greater; Ultra merely matched its competition. That was all it had to do.

From 1942, however, successes in intelligence multiplied the power of the stronger side and eased allied victory. Following a British lead, the Western allies organized their intelligence to unprecedented effect, through centralized assessment and the rapid and secure delivery of material to commanders. They applied more brains and resources to intelligence than did the Axis because they had more of them, and regarded the matter as fundamental. This edge was honed by cooperative competition in the pursuit of common tasks. British services worked better with American ones than German agencies did with each other.[8] The payoff was most particular in signals intelligence. Ultra, material derived from the solution of high-grade Axis cryptographic systems, was the most important and sophisticated source of intelligence during this war. It was never perfect, however, nor always the best source. Imagery, other forms of signals intelligence, prisoners, spies and captured documents remained valuable. Ultra took words straight from the enemy's mouth; but those words were not always straightforward, and its value differed with time and theatre. Ultra became more successful and useful as years went by, although its history was replete generally with sudden successes, defeats, and reversals of fortune. The allies never read every important enemy message, or

---

7   Marc Milner, "The Battle of the Atlantic," in John Gooch, ed., *Decisive Campaigns of the Second World War* (London: Frank Cass, 1990), pp. 45–64; David Syrett, *The Defeat of the German U-Boats, The Battle of the Atlantic*, (Columbia, SC: University of South Carolina Press, 1994); W.J.R. Gardner, *Decoding History: The Battle of the Atlantic and Ultra* (Annapolis, MD: Naval Institute Press, 2002).

8   Bradley Smith, *The Ultra-Magic Deals and the Most Secret Special Relationship, 1940–1946*, (Novato, CA: Presidio, 1993); Alan Bath, *Tracking the Axis Adversary, The Triumph of Anglo-American Naval Intelligence* (Lawrence, KS: University Press of Kansas, 1998).

indeed most of them.[9] Even in 1944, Ultra often failed: before Overlord, it could not even define the number of German tanks in France.[10]

Nor were technical achievements in cryptanalysis and battlefield success linked in a simple way. In the African campaign Ultra would have been most useful when it was technically most primitive rather than most mature, because of operational conditions. When it was most primitive, force to space ratios were low, as were both sides' strengths; hence, victories with decisive consequences were possible. Once Ultra became mature, large and good armies were locked in prolonged and high-intensity struggles of attrition on narrow fronts—like the Great War, though more fluid. Even so, intelligence budged the balance of attrition toward the allies. The war was won by the big battalions, guided by intelligence. In Europe, intelligence provided an excellent grasp of German capabilities, perceptions and intentions, letting Western commanders use their resources efficiently. Between 1942 and 1944, Allied amphibious operations against North Africa, Sicily, and Normandy, hit the enemy at weak points, and by surprise, transforming the front, because German intelligence was incompetent and its command manipulated by British deception. On the Eastern front during 1941–42, extraordinary success in imagery and signals intelligence initially gave Germany as great an edge as Ultra ever provided. Given its other advantages, however, and constant errors in the assessment of Soviet strength and intentions, intelligence was tertiary in German success. From late 1942, that edge vanished. Germany, increasingly, fell victim to Soviet intelligence and deception, which found Nazi weaknesses and hid key redeployments from rear to front, which enabled smashing and cost-effective attacks.[11] On the Eastern front, intelligence aided the stronger side, especially the Soviets during 1943–45, and perhaps helped to destroy more German forces than in Western Europe, although, relative to other factors, it mattered less.

In the Pacific, Ultra—of lesser quality than in Europe—enabled greater operational triumph because conditions on the battlefield gave intelligence a more dramatic effect. Intelligence affected this war more than any other in history. Radio dominated communications for small forces scattered over millions of square miles. Prisoners and agents were less useful sources than usual; signals intelligence, radar and imagery more so. In these disciplines, the Japanese were poor and their enemies good. Force to space ratios were low, most elements of either side rarely

---

9 F.H. Hinsley, with E.E. Thomas, C.F.G. Ransom and R.C. Knight, *British Intelligence in the Second World War: Its Influence on Strategy and Operation*, Volumes I—III (London: HMSO, 1979–81); and Ralph Bennett, *Ultra in the West* (London: Hutchinson, 1979) and *Ultra and Mediterranean Strategy* (New York: William Morrow, 1989).

10 John Ferris, "Intelligence and Overlord: A Snapshot from 6 June, 1944," in John Buckley, ed., *The Normandy Campaign 1944: Sixty Years On* (London: Routledge, 2006).

11 David Kahn, *Hitler's Spies and German Military Intelligence, 1939–45* (Bethesda, MD: University Publications of America,1984); for the Soviets, cf. David Glantz, *Soviet Military Deception in the Second World War* (London: Frank Cass, 1989) and *Soviet Military Intelligence in War* (Novato, CA: Presidio, 1990) and Robert Stephan, *Stalin's Secret War, Soviet Counter Intelligence Against the Nazis, 1941—1945* (Lawrence, KS: University Press of Kansas, 2004).

were in contact with the other, and their dispositions were masked. Rarely has the initiative had such power. Unexpected blows were hard to handle—weeks might be required to redeploy naval or air forces from one base to another, months to build the infrastructure to maintain large forces in a new area or to move soldiers by sea or by land. To destroy 20,000 men or 200 airplanes, capture one base or outmaneuver two divisions, often transformed operations in New Guinea, a theatre the size of the Mediterranean. The ability to concentrate against the enemy's weakness, to catch it by surprise, and to profit from knowledge of its intentions, were unusually large, especially for that most complex of operations, amphibious assaults. Failures in these areas were unusually expensive. Ultra gave American power a razor edge, by showing how to execute lines of strategy, where to begin major operations, how to force the enemy into disadvantageous battle, and how to prevent it from returning the favor.[12] Poor signals security and intelligence left the Japanese vulnerable to surprise, defeat in detail, and loss of the initiative.

During 1942 the United States Navy (USN) in the Pacific was outnumbered by a good enemy, but excellent intelligence and command twice let it concentrate its strength against fractions of Japan's navy. This produced the Battles of the Coral Sea, an American tactical defeat and strategic victory, and of Midway, and the exchange of four Japanese for one American carrier, after which the USN was no longer outnumbered. Intelligence enabled the great American victories of attrition between August 1942 and February 1944, starting with the seizure of Guadalcanal and the 18-month-long Solomon Islands campaign, and culminating in a terrible campaign of maritime interdiction, where it guided small forces of aircraft and submarines precisely on to Japanese vessels over a large area. In 1944, the "island- hopping" strategy, which broke Japanese defences on the cheap, was possible only because intelligence showed how to strike where the enemy was weakest. The United States won the Pacific war because of the quality of its forces and commanders and the scale of its resources, but intelligence let it win far more speedily and cheaply than otherwise could have happened.

Underlying these developments was another one between weapons, intelligence and communications. Between 1914 and 1918, C3I (command, control, communications, and intelligence) was well-suited to support operations, better than forces were to fight them. Problems of signals declined faster than did those of action. Still, systems of C3I and ISR (intelligence, surveillance, and reconnaissance) filled the tactical needs of strike warfare, via distant or predictive gunfire. At sea, telephone links between commanders, gun turrets, range finders, spotters, plotters, and fire control officers, controlled fire on individual ships. On land, fire plans

---

12   John Prados, *Combined Fleet Decoded: The Secret History of American Intelligence and the Japanese Navy in World War Two* (Annapolis, MD: Naval Institute Press, 1995); Gordon Prange, *Miracle at Midway* (New York: McGraw-Hill, 1982); Ronald Spector, ed. *Listening to the Enemy: Key Documents on the Role of Communications Intelligence in the War with Japan* (Wilmington, DE: Scholarly Resources, 1988); and Edward J. Drea, *MacArthur's ULTRA: Codebreaking and the War against Japan, 1942–1945* (Lawrence, KS: University Press of Kansas, 1992).

defined the actions of thousands of guns over 10-day periods, while deep, thick and simultaneous connections joined batteries, and their intelligence services, like sound rangers, signals intelligence, imagery, spotting aircraft, and commanders. In its most flexible and powerful form, as practiced by the Canadian Corps in 1918, intelligence and firepower were fused at all levels. Direction of fire was centralized during breakthrough, unleashed to subordinates in open phases, and recovered when counter-attack loomed. However labour intensive and convoluted, C3I and ISR combined the leading edges of technique and technology as well as ever has been done.[13] Yet these C3I systems were stronger than the weapons they supported. Whether on land or at sea, they made artillery as effective as it could be; but that just strengthened a weapon with limited range, accuracy and destructive capacity, attacking the most hardened targets in the world, in a large number of exchanges against an enemy of equal capabilities. This outcome simply sharpened the process of attrition by both sides at once, changing the margins rather than the nature of operations. Twenty years later, revolutions occurred in operations and strike warfare, as commanders and forces, especially aircraft, caught up with the opportunities enabled by C3I. In some cases, like strategic air defence or carrier aviation, intelligence was turned into target acquisition and operations into strike warfare. Strike ceased to be a chisel of war and became a sledgehammer. Signals intelligence, radio, aircraft and aircraft carriers created a new form of maritime war centred on strike against soft targets, thin hulls or decks rather than armoured turrets. Strike by aircraft and guns (more powerful because of enhanced organization) was central to land warfare, through close support against soldiers and interdiction against soft and distant targets central to enemy power, like units on the move, logistics, communications and transport. Aircraft delivered heavy and one-sided blows, reshaping operations and the power of one army (or navy) against another.[14]

The intelligence services of the Cold War were the largest and most sophisticated ever seen. In 1780, Austria's code-breaking bureau had 20 employees; during 1980, 100,000 worked in American signals intelligence. Intelligence alliances of unprecedented sophistication linked both coalitions, locked in a continuous struggle which shaped the Cold War. They focused on supporting millions of soldiers in a worldwide competition of power politics against a peer, with the trump suit being the collection of data on strategic issues through highly technical means.[15] Signals intelligence and imagery minimized ignorance, uncertainty and

---

13   Dan Jenkins, "The Other Side of the Hill: Combat Intelligence in the Canadian Corps, 1914–1918," *Canadian Military History* (Spring 2001), 10/2; Albert Palazzo, "The British Army's Counter-Battery Staff Office and Control of the Enemy in World War 1," *The Journal of Military History*, 63/1 (1999), pp. 55–74.

14   Brad Gladman, *Intelligence and Anglo-American Air Support in World War II* (London: Palgrave Macmillan, 2009).

15   James Bamford, *The Puzzle Palace, A Report on America's Most Secret Agency* (Boston, MA: Suffolk University, 1982) and *Body of Secrets, Anatomy of the Ultra-Secret National Security Agency* (New York: Anchor, 2001); John R. Schindler, *A Dangerous Business: The U.S. Navy and National Reconnaissance During the Cold War* (CCH, 2004); Jeffery Richelson

alarm about nuclear forces and stabilized the balance of terror—here, intelligence affected strike warfare more than at any other time, though fortunately not in practice. Intelligence shaped conventional conflict as it did in both world wars, but was less useful against guerrillas. These strengths came at a cost. More is not always better. Intelligence and strategic bureaucracies could not handle the host of material they received—photographic analysts were routinely six to 18 months behind in their examination of imagery. Intelligence services faced a new problem, which continued after the Cold War ended. Once most pieces of intelligence were false; now, they were true, but trivial in quality and overwhelming in quantity, producing bewilderment and information overload.

Intelligence might affect power and war in the twenty-first century differently than it did in the twentieth. The pace of technology may cripple old sources of intelligence as much as it helps new ones. Some argue that developments in public key cryptography may wreck communications intelligence; others that we confront a revolution in military intelligence. Since 1989, American military policy has been driven by efforts to ride a revolution in military affairs (RMA). Through a marriage between precision weapons and information technology, it advocates forces of unprecedented precision, speed, lethality and comparative advantage: "frictional imbalance" or "decision superiority."[16] Its advocates assume that this marriage will transform the knowledge available to armed forces, their nature and that of war. Intelligence and communication, not command and discipline, will be the heart of armed forces. Intelligence will be an engine fit for a finely tuned, high performance machine—reliable, understood, useful, usable, on-call. One can learn exactly what one wants to know when one needs to do so, and verify its accuracy with certainty and speed. The truth and only the truth can be known. It will show what should be done and what will happen if one does it. Action taken on knowledge will have the effect one intends, nothing more or less. Armed forces will act without friction on near-perfect knowledge, through the fusion of command, control, communications, intelligence, surveillance and reconnaissance (C4ISR). They will jettison traditional hierarchies, adopt interconnected and flat structures based on the Internet, and conduct net-centric warfare (NCW). All forces and intelligence will be linked to each other through a thick web of communications, which automatically will send the right information straight from sensor to shooter; through S2S, all command and intelligence will become target acquisition and all forms of operations, strike warfare. If these advocates of an RMA are right, conventional force has more power

and Desmond Ball, *The Ties That Bind: Intelligence Cooperation between the UKUSA Countries-the United Kingdom, the United States of America, Canada, Australia and New Zealand*, 2nd edn (Boston: Allen & Unwin, 1990); Matthew M. Aid and Cees Wiebe, eds, "Secrets of Signals Intelligence during the Cold War and Beyond," *INS* (Spring, 2001), 16/1; Michael Herman, J. Kenneth McDonald and Vojtech Mastny, "Did Intelligence Matter in the Cold War?" *Institute for forsvarsstudier* [Norwegian Institute for Defence Studies], (Oslo, 2006).

16   Joint Vision 2010 and Joint Vision 2020, Joint Chiefs of Staff, July 1996 and May 2000, <www.dtic.mil/doctrine>.

and the leading powers greater superiority in it, than ever since the heyday of European imperialism.[17]

These ideas were tested in three recent conflicts. They failed in Kosovo during 1999, a limited war where forces suffering from political interference, over-centralization and confusion between levels of command, engaged an enemy with good strategy, camouflage and air defence: strike did little damage, nor did the allies achieve clear victory. In Afghanistan and Iraq during 2001 and 2003, limited wars for the attacker but total ones for the defenders, Western forces found it hard to convert military to political success. Still, larger forces, better used, unleashed against worse conventional foes, coordinated command and intelligence with unprecedented skill. This multiplied the strength of all forms of centralized firepower and rapid, precise and long-distance weapons. These leaps in the quality and sheer quantity of aircraft and precision-guided munitions (PGMs) let strike forces matter far more than ever before. Strike turned from hammer to rapier. Aircraft equalled the power of armour or infantry in land warfare. Iraqi command was easily shattered, and its forces in open country broken. Yet classic problems of information overload, friction between headquarters, and inexperienced personnel swamped coalition commands. For all the talk of NCW and C4ISR, command and intelligence were no better than in 1944, although the enemy was worse.[18]

The main, if paradoxical, lesson to be taken from these campaigns is that Western powers cannot easily defeat any enemy even with a competent leadership and army, and fair public consent. Nor are Americans the only people who can learn lessons and improve their performance. It is convenient when an enemy chooses to be foolish and weak, but that is its choice, not yours. A smart but weak foe may refuse any game where you can apply your strengths, and make you play another one. A tough and able foe might turn the characteristics of your game into a strength of its own by attacking any precondition for your machine to work and imposing its rules on you. By doing what suits them, they change their strengths and weaknesses—and yours. Precisely that has happened in Iraq and Afghanistan since 2004, where NCW has failed while Western intelligence has had a mixed performance, often worse than its enemies.

In order to understand the contemporary value of intelligence, one must turn from slogans to basics. Power and war have social roots, many forms, and a competitive nature—your system against the enemy's in specific circumstances. The edge of the razor is comparative advantage, your strengths, and your ability to force them on the enemy. Numbers and technology matter, but not enough to win every time. Able armies with no material edge can whip larger enemies. A belligerent able to take heavy losses can beat one with high technology and low

---

17 For differing views, cf. William Lahneman, "Is a Revolution in Military Affairs Occurring?" *International Journal of Intelligence and Counter Intelligence*, (March 2007), 20/1: 1–17; John Ferris, "NCW, C4ISR, IO and RMA: Toward a Revolution in Military Intelligence?" in John Ferris, *Intelligence and Strategy, Selected Essays* (London: Frank Cass, 2005), pp. 288–325.

18 Ferris, *Intelligence and Strategy*.

willpower. Politics and willpower can defeat firepower and technology, or vice versa. Small elite forces can crush large half-trained ones, or not. It varies with the circumstances. So, too, the value of intelligence varies in every form of war and power politics—deterrence, compulsion, diplomacy and crisis; high-intensity operations; the formulation of strategy; strike; limited wars; counterinsurgents against guerrillas. The historical record illuminates these issues, but not in a simple way. Overgeneralization from any form to another is dangerously easy. RMA enthusiasts assume that lessons drawn from strikes, characterized by a steady rise in power driven by technology, or from the direct effect of information on conventional operations, define the role of intelligence in all competitions. War is not so simple, nor intelligence, nor C4ISR.

Since 1990, intelligence failures (and successes) at the strategic-diplomatic levels of war, or peace, have followed old patterns. Neither the problems nor the solutions have changed. Nothing suggests that NCW and C4ISR will transform those levels. They will not improve the influence of intelligence on the formulation of policy. They may well, however, distort command and the use of intelligence in diplomatic crises and limited wars, reinforcing attempts by figures at home to control tactical details abroad, increasing micromanagement, friction and information overload.

In operations, NCW, intelligence and C4ISR may make every cog of the machine work well at the same time, reducing friction so far as possible. They will not surpass the best past performances, but might make these more common. Strike warfare, however, has been transformed, and with it some forms of conventional power, more because of changes in weapons than systems. In 1917, Allied intelligence constantly located U-boats, prompting immediate air or surface strikes, which failed because units were slow and their ordnance weak. By 1943, intelligence on U-boats was little better but Allied forces far more able to kill. In 1944, Allied air forces could reportedly strike any target immediately, but not accurately. In 2003, aircraft launched instant, precise and devastating strikes, at fleeting chances which once would have been lost, based on information acquired 10 minutes earlier by headquarters 10,000 miles away. Strike weapons let conventional forces hit harder, further and more accurately than ever before. They reshape power at sea and in the air. They enable a new version of gunboat diplomacy, by letting one destroy select targets from a distance, so to make a political point, exercise coercive diplomacy or sustain deterrence. These gains are real, but restricted. They increase the strength of any superior force over an inferior one in conventional war or hard politics. Little will change where equals engage, because each would attack the other's ability to fight at this level. Even weak foes can attack their enemies' C4ISR, or boost their own camouflage or air defence. If NCW fails in any instance in which it is relied upon, disaster will be redoubled; and fail NCW ultimately must. It will force your adversaries to find solutions by evading your strength or making you play to your weaknesses.

Such weaknesses are particular in counterinsurgency, where many types and levels of war and intelligence overlap: guerrillas, conventional and strike forces, and politics in villages and capitals. Intelligence is even more important to counterinsurgency than it is to conventional war, but it works as much through politics as through operations (which is also true of limited war). Counterinsurgents can have good intelligence; yet most guerrillas lose their wars. Able guerrillas, however, are hard to beat, partly because intelligence tends to work in their favor. During the Vietnam War, American human and signals intelligence was good, but was outmatched by the enemy. In Algeria, France began with poor intelligence, which became better, partly through the routine use of torture, with political consequences. In Malaya, British intelligence matched its foe early on and then surged ahead, but it was hard to use.[19] Britain escaped that dilemma in Northern Ireland only because its population and government were willing to tolerate a dirty campaign of murder against murderers (and innocents). Unfortunately, when Western forces engage guerrillas, it will be from necessity, and thus only in the hardest cases, when foes are powerful and friends weak. The enemy will start stronger at intelligence. Western forces will not even know their vulnerabilities, or understand local languages, culture or society. They must graduate kindergarten, and develop basic social and cultural understanding against an enemy with a PhD. In guerrilla war, human intelligence is unusually valuable. There, the enemy will have a head start. Western forces cannot routinely use another source, with proven power in counterinsurgency. Contrary to cant, torture is an effective source of intelligence, though like any of them it has limits. To abandon torture is not to jettison a bad source, but to reject a strong one. Jettison it we must, although the enemy will not.

Nor will integrating strike into counterinsurgency be easy. This was first done during 1920, by Britain in Somaliland, but the combination of intelligence and strike offers new problems and power. It enables long hits at enemy forces and leaders, making assassination a form of war as well as politics. Yet anything short of perfect target acquisition may make strikes tragic and counterproductive, while the power of the combination will lead to its overuse. Its record is mixed in Afghanistan, Iraq, Pakistan, Somalia, Sudan and Yemen, with effective strikes balanced by bad attacks and missed opportunities. The record has been better in Gaza, an optimum case for the attacker, because the territory is small, penetrated by several sources and close to weapons. S2S links join Israeli intelligence, which locates and identifies targets, often teams readying to fire missiles, to pre-assigned PGMs ready to strike, enabling instant attacks without need for authorization from above. Such strikes generally hit good targets, even if they miss tactically, or kill 'unfortunates' yards away. The Gaza standard, the best practicable in counterinsurgency, will not easily be achieved in larger territories, for that reason. Tension will exist between the most transformed type of military power, strike, and its role in counterinsurgency. While intelligence may become target acquisition, politics cannot become just strike.

---

19   Robert J. Hanyok, *Spartans in Darkness: American SIGINT and the Indochina War, 1945–1975* (Ft George Meade, MD: National Security Agency, Center for Cryptologic History, 2002); Martin Alexander and John Kieger, *France and the Algerian War, 1954–1962: Strategy, Operations and Diplomacy* (London: Frank Cass, 2002); John Coates, *Suppressing Insurgency: An Analysis of the Malayan Emergency, 1948–1954* (Boulder, CO: Westview, 1992).

Intelligence changed less between 1989 and 2008 than it did during 1914 and 1918, or between 1850 and 1870, with the combination of telegraph and general staff. Most matters have not changed at all, but some have done so dramatically. Intelligence must be ready to aid play in several different games, which will be harder for some sources and States than others. Imagery has a universal ability to monitor certain kinds of capabilities; but signals intelligence, though powerful in all these games (even guerrillas rely on cell phones) requires the maintenance of appropriate linguistic capacity, and so, too, human intelligence. In order to meet these needs, one must be able in general, and prepared in particulars, but even just to gauge your quality or readiness will be hard. Intelligence is a competitive process, involving many players, boards and games. Comparative quality is easiest to judge for operational intelligence in conventional war, where sources and forces must take specific forms, especially for a country with narrow concerns and just a few enemies. It is harder with limited war and guerrilla war, where politics intervene dramatically and frequently, or in cases when one organization must prepare for many foes and locales. Even great powers can play well on just a few boards at once. Most States can do so only on their home board. Failure to prepare your intelligence for the right locale and foe will be costly, doubly so if you get your war wrong too, as the United States did in Iraq, since 2003. The rule for intelligence is, know your enemy and your war. It also helps to know yourself.

Cyberwar

Myriam Dunn Cavelty

Introduction

Since RAND researchers John Arquilla and David Ronfeldt suggested that 'Cyberwar is coming!' in 1993,[1] the *jinni* has been out of the bottle: Cyberwar has become the most prominent buzzword in the debate surrounding computers, national security and cyberspace. Indeed, if there is any major hacker intrusion nowadays, it is certain to be labelled as an instance of cyberwar by the media and government officials alike. Such usage is far removed from the one intended by Arquilla and Ronfeldt, but such mislabelling is not uncommon; the term 'cyberwar' shares this fate with all the other expressions from the information age arsenal, all of which have been created by simply placing prefixes such as 'cyber-', 'information', 'e-', or 'digital' before another word.[2] Under-defined and under-contextualized, these terms have acquired so many meanings and nuances over the years that they have become confusing or have even lost their meaning altogether.[3]

Whether we regard the terminological quandary as a sign of immaturity of the field or just as part of a normal process of continuous semantic reflection, evolution, and revision that accompanies every new phenomenon, the first problem with any discussion about cyberwar is definitional. The major focus of this contribution will thus be on the different meanings of 'cyberwar' and the different contexts in which these meanings have arisen. To understand meanings and contexts will also help the researcher to grasp causes and implications of cyberwar-related issues. This chapter is based on the premise that the importance and emergence of the concept of cyberwar can only be understood in the larger context of the information revolution, which has shaped – and is still shaping – perceptions of opportunities and dangers

---

1   John Arquilla and David F. Ronfeldt, 'Cyberwar is Coming!' *Comparative Strategy*, 12/2 (1993): 141–65.

2   Uri Fisher, 'Information Age State Security: New Threats to Old Boundaries', *Journal for Homeland Security* (November 2001).

3   Geoffrey S. French, 'Shunning the Frumious Bandersnatch, Current Literature on Information Warfare and Deterrence', TRC Analysis (The Terrorism Research Center, 2000).

and has made developments possible.[4] In particular, the information revolution and related organizational innovations seemed to alter the nature of conflict and the kinds of military structures, doctrines and strategies needed. Thus, it seemed to imply the rise of a 'new' kind of warfare in which the factor of information was to grow more and more important. This development was facilitated (if not driven) by the end of the Cold War and the ensuing reorientation in terms of enemies, strategic thought and defence spending.

This chapter starts off with a short overview of the relevant literature available to any scholar delving into the issue of cyberwar. This issue warrants special attention in the context of this research compendium because there are some difficulties involved: the specialist literature is mostly policy-oriented, and only very rarely informed by theory, whether from the international relations (IR) discipline or any other field. The second section looks at definitional issues in more depth and will trace how the meaning of 'cyberwar' evolved from the narrow conception referring exclusively to military interaction to its broad meaning, which has become detached from 'war' and encompasses almost every activity linked to the aggressive use of computers. The third section investigates four cases between 1999 and 2007 that have been labelled 'cyberwar' by a variety of actors. In the fourth section, a reality check based on these cases is performed. We see that while cyber-vandalism is an everyday reality, cyberwar is not. After speculating on possible restraints for the use of cyberwar tools in the future, the chapter concludes with thoughts on the danger inherent in cyberwar ideas due to the realities of a globalized, interdependent and networked world.

The Cyberwar Literature

There are some difficulties in studying cyberwar from an academic perspective, mainly because the books and articles on cyberwar and related topics published over the last 10 to 15 years tend to be highly specific and policy-oriented, and do not communicate with more general international relations theory and research.[5] The US is the main and often exclusive arena and target of this literature, even though some American strategists have focused on China and Russia (but only in

---

4   Cf. David S. Alberts and Daniel S. Papp, eds, *The Information Age: An Anthology of Its Impacts and Consequences* (Washington, DC, 1997).

5   Prominent examples include: Alan D. Campen, *The First Information Warfare* (Fairfax, 1992); Alan D. Campen, Douglas Dearth and Thomas Goodden, eds, *Cyberwar: Security, Strategy and Conflict in the Information Age* (Fairfax, 1996); Alan D. Campen and Douglas H. Dearth, eds, *Cyberwar 2.0: Myths, Mysteries and Reality* (Fairfax, 1998); John Arquilla and David F. Ronfeldt, eds, *In Athena's Camp: Preparing for Conflict in the Information Age* (Santa Monica, 1997); Ryan Henry and Edward Peartree, eds, *Information Revolution and International Security* (Washington, DC, 1998).

order to reflect on US strategy in this domain).[6] Furthermore, cyberwar has lost some prominence after 11 September 2001, after which various aspects of terrorism became the main focal point in the strategic literature, with the result that the majority of cyberwar studies date from the late 1990s and the early 2000s.

Literature that could be considered more academic, and is produced outside of specific US military journals and think tanks, is fragmented and rather disorganized. The topic is situated at the crossroads of various issues, including computer studies, information technology, and the information revolution in general, but also strategic studies, threat construction, and policy design, to name just a few. While disciplines such as media, communication, or cultural studies have long discovered the information age as a topic, the discipline of international relations (IR), one of the more obvious candidates for explaining aspects of cyberwar has been very slow to come to grips with the challenge of the information revolution. One of the most dynamic sub-fields of IR, security studies, is also surprisingly silent on questions concerning the information revolution, despite the breakthrough that broadened perspectives of security had in the last decade. The policy-oriented literature described above is only implicitly influenced by the realist thought paradigm when it looks at whether the information revolution has the ability to change capabilities, resources and therefore power relationships between states. The book *Bombs and Bandwidth: The Emerging Relationship between IT and Security* contains several articles bearing directly on the topic of security in the information age, but there is only modest effort to link findings to the major IR theories.[7] The same is true for other volumes such as *Power and Security in the Information Age: Investigating the Role of the State in Cyberspace.*[8]

Apart from books like International Relations and Security in the Digital Age,[9] which are deliberately broad but contain some chapters of interest for scholars of cyberwar, there is some research focusing on the construction of information-age security threats by using frameworks informed by constructivism, especially securitization

---

6   See for example: Timothy L. Thomas, *Dragon Bytes: Chinese Information-War Theory and Practice* (Ft Leavenworth, 2004); Timothy L. Thomas, *Like Adding Wings to the Tiger: Chinese Information War Theory and Practice* (Ft Leavenworth, 2000); James C. Mulvenon and Richard H. Yang, eds, *The People's Liberation Army in the Information Age* (Santa Monica, 1998); Mary C. FitzGerald, 'Russian Views on Electronic Signals and Information Warfare', *American Intelligence Journal,* 15 (1994): 81–7; Timothy L. Thomas, 'Russian Views on Information-based Warfare', *Airpower Journal,* Special Edition (1996): 26–35.

7   Robert Latham, ed., *Bombs and Bandwidth: The Emerging Relationship between IT and Security* (New York, 2003).

8   Myriam Dunn Cavelty, Sai-Felicia Krishna-Hensel and Victor Mauer, eds, *Power and Security in the Information Age: Investigating the Role of the State in Cyberspace* (Aldershot, 2008).

9   Johan Eriksson and Giampiero Giacomello, eds, *International Relations and Security in the Digital Age* (London, 2007); see also Johan Eriksson and Giampiero Giacomello, 'The Information Revolution, Security, and International Relations: (IR)Relevant Theory?' *International Political Science Review,* 27/3 (2006): 221–44.

theory.[10] From this, valuable insights can be gained with regard to threat perceptions and policy reactions; in particular, various meanings of cyberwar and changes in its implementation can be explained. More research is warranted, however, particularly comparative studies of threat constructions in countries other than the US. Post-structuralism (borrowing from French philosophers such as Foucault and Virilio) has influenced another body of literature, which focuses on so-called 'postmodern war'.[11] It is seen as a discourse on technical-military interaction that focuses on the centrality of information. Information becomes the 'new metaphysics of power',[12] with various implications of such a conceptualization for the military itself and society as a whole.

In conclusion, even though the state of the art of this field makes it difficult explicitly to contribute to an identifiable scholarly body of literature, there also is a great chance for scholars to make unique contributions: first, there are a lot of unquestioned assumptions in both expert and official writings about the topic, which can be illuminated and evaluated; second, although the topic is of such urgency to security policy, it has received little scholarly attention outside of specialized journals and think tanks so far; and third, the issue presents an opportunity to apply theories designed for a specific purpose in one body of literature to solve an existing problem of a different kind. As this chapter mainly focuses on definitional and conceptual issues of cyberwar, it draws predominantly on the policy-oriented literature, which also deals most closely with cyberwar. The researcher is also greatly dependent on media coverage for cases, as there is little scholarly literature containing case studies.

Contexts and Meanings of Cyberwar

It was the Second Persian Gulf War of 1991 that created a watershed in US military thinking about cyberwar. That conflict was seen by military strategists as the first of a new generation of conflicts where victory is no longer ensured only by physical force, but also by the ability to win the information war and to secure 'information dominance'. As a result of the conflict, American military thinkers began to publish scores of books on the topic and stressed the importance of developing a concept

---

10   Ralf Bendrath, 'The American Cyber-Angst and the Real World – Any Link?' in Robert Latham, ed., *Bombs and Bandwidth: The Emerging Relationship between IT and Security* (New York, 2003), pp. 49–73; Johan Eriksson, 'Cyberplagues, IT, and Security: Threat Politics in the Information Age', *Journal of Contingencies and Crisis Management*, 9/4 (2001): 211–22; Myriam Dunn Cavelty, *Cyber-Security and Threat Politics: US Efforts to Secure the Information Age* (London, 2008).

11   Chris Hables Gray, *Postmodern War – The New Politics of Conflict* (London, 1997); James Der Derian, *Virtuous War: Mapping the Military-Industrial-Media-Entertainment Complex* (Boulder, CO, 2001); Chris Hables Gray, *Peace, War, and Computers* (London, 2005).

12   Michael Dillon and Julian Reid, 'Global Liberal Governance: Biopolitics, Security and War', *Millennium Journal of International Studies*, 30/1 (2001): 59.

that, until then, had only been loosely articulated, in which the ability to degrade or even paralyze an opponent's communications systems was emphasized.[13] Among these thinkers were Arquilla and Ronfeldt; their seminal text on cyberwar was the focus of the first sub-chapter. The reaction to the technological developments after the Gulf War also manifested itself in the publication of new doctrinal papers that included an information component – the information warfare and information operations doctrine, which was the focus of the second sub-chapter. But cyberwar also leads a life outside of military confinements and has been studied by scholars trying to differentiate between different kinds of online activity, which will be the focus of the third sub-chapter.

Cyberwar: The First Coinage

Like other strategists, Ronfeldt and Arquilla attributed the success of the US and its international allies in the Gulf War to the preservation of their own networks coupled with the disruption of the enemy's. Subsequently, Arquilla and Ronfeldt developed the concepts of 'cyberwar' and 'netwar', which in the words of the authors were 'comprehensive approaches to conflict based on the centrality of information [combining] organizational, doctrinal, strategic, tactical and technological innovations for both offense and defense'.[14] The two concepts revolve around information and communications matters, are instances of war about knowledge, and are mainly network-based. Neither of these modes necessarily depends on information and communication technology (ICT), nor do they occur only in cyberspace or the infosphere, but they are facilitated by these aspects. Both cyberwar and netwar are important in the context of this chapter, because the two concepts have greatly influenced the way in which the military and the larger national security apparatus have come to understand conflict in the information age.

Cyberwar is described as a set of new operational techniques and a new mode of warfare. It is used in conflicts at an intense level of escalation to target opponents' military and control. It is thus a new form of 'command and control warfare' (C2W), depending less on geographic terrain than on the nature of the electronic cyberspace.[15] It refers to conducting and preparing military operations according to information-related principles. It features formal military forces pitted against each other, and aims at disrupting or destroying the (military) information

---

13   Greg Rattray, *Strategic Warfare in Cyberspace* (Cambridge, 2001), pp. 314–15; Michael O'Hanlon, *Technological Change and the Future of Warfare* (Washington, DC, 1999).

14   John Arquilla and David F. Ronfeldt, 'A New Epoch – and Spectrum – of Conflict', in John Arquilla and David F. Ronfeldt, eds, *In Athena's Camp: Preparing for Conflict in the Information Age* (Santa Monica, 1997), p. 6.

15   John Arquilla and David F. Ronfeldt, 'Cyberwar is Coming!' in John Arquilla and David F. Ronfeldt, eds, *In Athena's Camp: Preparing for Conflict in the Information Age* (Santa Monica, 1997), pp. 30–31.

and communications systems on which the adversaries rely in order to 'know' themselves. In the first instance, the concept of cyberwar was thus very clearly associated with the military, the state and war.

Netwar, on the other hand, has been used to describe the emergence of diffuse, often transnational, distributed forms of warfare, in which the players are largely hidden among the general population to avoid conventional attack.[16] This concept includes low-intensity conflict, operations other than war, and other non-military modes of conflict and crime. Clearly, it also involves non-state actors, including paramilitary and irregular forces. It aims at disrupting, damaging or modifying what the target population knows or thinks, with a focus on public or elite opinion, or both. It may involve public diplomacy, propaganda, psychological campaigns, political/cultural subversion, interference with local media, or infiltration of computer systems.

The concepts of cyberwar and netwar as developed by Arquilla and Ronfeldt have become part of the official military information operations doctrine in modified form. As will be shown below, while the notion of cyberwar played an important role in the beginning, doctrinal concepts were gradually expanded more towards the idea of netwar, with a greater appreciation of a globalized information environment.

Development of the Information Warfare Doctrine

'Information warfare' (IW) as a concept was formally launched in December 1992 with the dissemination of DoD Directive 3600.1, classified Top Secret. As is apparent from allusions to it,[17] and as was later revealed by an unclassified version,[18] the document depicted information warfare as being almost synonymous with the 'C4I for the warrior' vision released by the Joint Chiefs of Staff in 1992.[19] This also closely resembles Arquilla and Ronfeldt's concept of cyberwar. In the following years, a variety of formal and informal doctrine documents about conflict based on the centrality of information were published.[20] For a while, information warfare remained essentially

---

16   Ibid., 28–30; John Arquilla and David F. Ronfeldt, *The Advent of Netwar* (Santa Monica, 1996); John Arquilla and David F. Ronfeldt, eds, *Networks and Netwars: The Future of Terror, Crime, and Militancy* (Santa Monica, 2001).

17   Defense Science Board, *Report of the Defense Science Board Summer Study Task Force on Information Architecture for the Battlefield* (Washington, DC, 1994).

18   Department of Defense, *Directive Number 3600.1, Information Operations*, Revision One (October 2001).

19   C4I stands for Command, Control, Communications, Computer, and Intelligence. Joint Staff, C4 Architecture & Integration Division, *C4I for the Warrior* (Washington, DC, 12 June 1992).

20   United States Air Force, *Cornerstones of Information Warfare* (Washington, DC, 1995); Department of the Army, *Information Operations, Field Manual No. 100-6* (Washington, DC, 27 August 1996); Chairman of the Joint Chiefs of Staff, *US Armed Forces, Joint Vision 2010* (Washington, DC, 1996).

limited to military measures in times of crisis or war. This began to change around the mid-1990s, when the activities began to be understood as actions targeting the entire information infrastructure of an adversary – political, economic and military – throughout the continuum of operations from peace to war.

Acknowledging this, the DoD and Joint Chiefs of Staff moved to adopt the term 'information operations' (Info Ops) instead of information warfare in 1997.[21] Individual building blocks and ideas were assembled into a coherent strategy in 1998, when the US Joint Chiefs of Staff released Joint Publication JP 3-13, 'Joint Doctrine for Information Operations'. Since then, the category of information operations is defined as 'the integrated employment of electronic warfare (EW), computer network operations (CNO), psychological operations (PSYOP), military deception (MILDEC), and operations security (OPSEC), in concert with specified supporting and related capabilities, to influence, disrupt, corrupt, or usurp adversarial human and automated decision making while protecting our own'.[22] Cyberwar as such is not part of this doctrine.

The Cyber-Threat Escalation Ladder

As previously mentioned, the term 'cyberwar' also exists outside the military discourse. The popular usage of the word has come to refer to basically any phenomenon involving a deliberate disruptive or destructive use of computers by anyone. The following definition might serve as a representative example: 'Cyberwar is information warfare waged over the Internet. It involves disseminating information via websites or email in order to raise awareness, mobilise support and create global networks of supporters. Beyond this propaganda aspect, cyberwar can also involve infiltrating and disrupting an enemy's computer networks and databases.'[23]

In general, the media loves the idea of 'cyber-doom' and repeatedly features sensationalist headlines about it. This has resulted in a widespread tendency to 'hype' the issue with rhetorical dramatization and alarmist warnings even in official circles. More cautious voices usually belong to technically-educated political advisors and journalists, who try to be deliberately more specific in their estimates of the threat to national security. While some question the underlying assumption of vulnerability,[24] others have introduced differentiations between online activities

---

21 Myriam Dunn, *Information Age Conflicts: A Study on the Information Revolution and a Changing Operating Environment*, Zürcher Beiträge zur Sicherheitspolitik und Konfliktforschung, no. 64 (Zurich, 2002), pp. 118–19.

22 Joint Chiefs of Staff, *JP 3–13, Joint Doctrine for Information Operations* (Washington, DC, 2006), p. ix. In fact, the official DoD Dictionary of Military and Associated Terms does not even provide a definition of cyberwar.

23 Giles Trendle, 'Cyberwars: The Coming Arab E-Jihad', *The Middle East* (1 April 2002).

24 James A. Lewis, *Assessing the Risks of Cyber-terrorism, Cyber War and Other Cyber Threats* (Washington, DC, 2002).

by focusing on the effects of the cyber-activity, the actors behind it, and/or the objectives of an attack. For example, Dorothy Denning, a US information security researcher, introduces a useful distinction between three classes of politically motivated activity involving the Internet – activism, hacktivism, and cyber-terrorism:[25]

- (Cyber-)activism: Is the normal, non-disruptive use of the Internet in support of a (political) agenda or cause. Examples are: browsing the Web for information, posting materials online, using the Internet to discuss issues, form coalitions, and plan and coordinate activities.
- Hacktivism: Is the marriage of hacking and activism, including operations that use hacking techniques against a target's Internet site with the intention of disrupting normal operations, but not causing serious damage. Examples are: web 'sit-ins' and virtual blockades, automated email bombs, web hacks, computer break-ins, and computer viruses and worms.
- Cyber-terrorism: Consists of unlawful attacks against computers, networks, and the information stored therein, to intimidate or coerce a government or its people in furtherance of political or social objectives. Such an attack should result in violence against persons or property, or at least cause enough harm to generate the requisite fear level to be considered 'cyber-terrorism'.[26]

In a similar vein, Bruce Schneier, an internationally renowned security technologist and author, differentiates between cyber-vandalism, which includes the defacing of websites; cybercrime, which includes theft of intellectual property, extortion based on the threat of 'distributed denial of service' attacks (DDoS) attacks, fraud based on identity theft, and so on; cyber-terrorism, for example, hacking into a computer system to cause a nuclear power plant to melt down, a dam to open, or two airplanes to collide; and cyberwar.[27] Schneider uses 'cyberwar' to refer to the use of computers to disrupt the activities of an enemy country, especially carrying out deliberate attacks on communication systems. This understanding closely resembles the concept of 'computer network attacks' (CNA), which is part of the official information operations doctrine and connotes 'actions taken through the use of computer networks to disrupt, deny, degrade, or destroy information

---

25   Dorothy Denning, 'Activism, Hacktivism, and Cyberterrorism: The Internet as a Tool for Influencing Foreign Policy', in John Arquilla and David F. Ronfeldt, eds, *Networks and Netwars: The Future of Terror, Crime, and Militancy* (Santa Monica, 2001), pp. 239–88.

26   Ibid.; Myriam Dunn Cavelty, 'Cyber-Terror – Looming Threat or Phantom Menace? The Framing of the US Cyber-Threat Debate', *Journal of Information Technology and Politics*, 4/1 (2007): 19–36.

27   Bruce Schneier, 'Schneier on Security: A Blog Covering Security and Security Technology', <http://www.schneier.com/blog/archives/2007/06/cyberwar.html> [accessed 2 June 2008].

resident in computers and computer networks, or the computers and networks themselves'.[28]

Both Denning's and Schneier's classifications construct a cyber-threat escalation ladder – from rung to rung the potential effects get worse. The advantage of such a 'severity of effects' view is that it helps policy-makers to prioritize. Only computer attacks whose effects are sufficiently destructive or disruptive should be regarded as a national security issue.[29] Attacks that disrupt nonessential services, or that are mainly a costly nuisance, are not.[30] Nonetheless, it must be noted that the lines of demarcation between the different activities are greatly blurred. First of all, when a particular detrimental event occurs, it is often difficult to determine whether it is the result of a malicious attack, a failure of a component, or an accident.[31] Secondly, although their goals are different, the tools and tactics used by armies, terrorists, and criminals in cyberspace are the same.

What, then, is cyberwar? Bruce Schneier captures the crux of the matter when he writes:

> … [J]ust as every shooting is not necessarily an act of war, every successful Internet attack, no matter how deadly, is not necessarily an act of cyberwar. A cyberattack that shuts down the power grid might be part of a cyberwar campaign, but it also might be an act of cyberterrorism, cybercrime, or even – if it's done by some fourteen-year-old who doesn't really understand what he's doing – cybervandalism. Which it is will depend on the motivations of the attacker and the circumstances surrounding the attack … just as in the real world.[32]

Thus, an attack on computer systems should only be called cyberwar if it is carried out by a state actor with warlike intentions. The more narrowly we define and use the term, the better the phenomenon can be grasped. A narrow and precise definition also helps to circumvent other dangers inherent in calling something 'war', like exculpating the victims of an attack from their own responsibility for the consequences of their negligence in terms of computer security, or creating pressure to retaliate against 'hackers', real or imagined.[33]

---

28   DOD Dictionary of Military and Associated Terms, <http://www.js.mil/doctrine/jel/doddict/data/c/01183.html> [accessed 2 June 2008].
29   Clay Wilson, *Computer Attack and Cyber-terrorism: Vulnerabilities and Policy Issues for Congress*, Congressional Research Report for Congress, RL32114, 17 October 2003 (Washington, DC, 2003).
30   Denning, 'Activism, Hacktivism, and Cyberterrorism: The Internet as a Tool for Influencing Foreign Policy'.
31   R.J. Ellison, D.A. Fisher, R.C. Linger, H.F. Lipson, T. Longstaff and N.R. Mead, 'Survivable Network Systems: An Emerging Discipline', Technical Report, CMU/SEI-97-TR-013. ESC-TR-97-013 (November 1997), p. 3.
32   Schneier, 'Schneier on Security: A Blog Covering Security and Security Technology'.
33   Martin Libicki, *Defending Cyberspace* (Washington, DC, 1997), p. 38.

Reality Check – Is Cyberwar Here or Still Coming?

In this chapter, the various aspects of cyberwar as introduced above are subjected to a reality check by looking at the following cases: 1) NATO's intervention against Yugoslavia, code-named Operation Allied Force, which marked the first sustained use of the full spectrum of information operations components in combat; 2) cyber-confrontations between Chinese and US hackers in 2001, which were labelled the first Cyber World War by some observers; 3) expectations for the use of cyberwar tools in the Iraq War; and 4) the three-week wave of cyber-attacks on Estonia, which were attributed to Russia by some.[34]

Operation Allied Force

During Operation Allied Force, both sides used information warfare aspects to harm the enemy. Much of this involved the use of propaganda and disinformation via the media, but there were also extensive efforts to intercept the other side's communications, to jam or deceive sensors, and to conduct other forms of electronic warfare.[35] However, the most important component of NATO's Info Ops in this conflict was the rather traditional bombing of Serbia's command-and-control infrastructure. Apart from bombings, the conflict also saw the widespread use of PSYOPS.

The increasing use of the Internet during the conflict also gave it the distinction of being the 'first war fought in cyberspace' or the 'first war on the Internet'.[36] It was the first armed conflict in which all sides, including a variety of actors who were not directly involved, had an active presence on the Internet, and the first conflict where the Internet was used extensively for the exchange and publication of conflict-relevant information. There also were numerous incidents of hacktivism. The question remains whether any of these attacks were state-sponsored and therefore fall under the definition of strategic information warfare, with most sources maintaining that it is rather doubtful whether the Yugoslav government orchestrated any of the attacks.[37]

---

34   Computer intrusions (which are sometimes subsumed under the heading of computer network exploitations) are excluded. Even though they were instrumental in shaping the threat perception that the US was asymmetrically vulnerable (due to the high dependence of the entire society on vulnerable civilian infrastructures), they are not considered to be part of cyberwar. Examples are the 'Rome Lab incident' in 1994 or 'Solar Sunrise and Moonlight Maze' in 1998. Just as significant were exercises such as 'The Day After' in 1996, or 'Eligible Receiver' in 1997.

35   A.H. Cordesman, *Defending America. Redefining the Conceptual Borders of Homeland Defense. Critical Infrastructure Protection and Information Warfare* (Washington, DC, 2000).

36   Denning, 'Activism, Hacktivism, and Cyberterrorism: The Internet as a Tool for Influencing Foreign Policy'.

37   F. Wolfe, 'Pentagon Analyzing Serb Attacks on DoD Web Sites', www.infowar.com (22 June 1999).

There is also rather substantive evidence against the rumours that during Operation Allied Force, the US launched the first offensive 'cyberwar' in history. The numerous publications and press releases on this topic, as well as military rhetoric before and even during the conflict, raised expectations that this new warfare tool would be employed. The rumours reached their first apex at the end of May 1999, when a *Newsweek* article reported that the US had launched computer attacks on Yugoslav systems.[38] Later in the year, *The Washington Times* took the story up and wrote that while details still remained classified, top US military officials had confirmed that the US had launched a computer attack on Yugoslav systems during NATO's bombing campaign, in the first such broad use of offensive cyberwarfare during a conflict, and had thus 'triggered a superweapon that catapulted the country into a military era that could forever alter the ways of war and the march of history'.[39]

There are at least two strong points contradicting most of these claims: first, cyberwarfare against a relatively low-tech enemy cannot be expected to be overly effective;[40] and second, according to a number of reports, the US found that there was neither a clear basis in law for carrying out computer attacks, nor was there any legislation that would allow retaliation against possible Serbian attacks. The uncertainty surrounding international law, especially because of the continuing unpredictability of the effects of information attacks, evoked fears that their use might make US military commanders liable to prosecution on war crimes charges.[41] Other reports state that while the US Air Force had planned such cyber-attacks in depth, their execution was blocked by some exponents of the US intelligence community, who felt that such measures would do more to corrupt the quality of intelligence collection than to damage Serbian operations.[42]

'Cyber World War I'

The year 2001 witnessed the first Cyber World War, if we can believe some experts and government officials. The cause was a US reconnaissance and surveillance plane that was forced to land on Chinese territory after a mid-air collision with a Chinese jet fighter. Initially, the online controversy over the diplomatic handling of the incident was limited to chat rooms in China and the US. Soon after, however, large-scale defacement of Chinese and US websites and waves of denial-of-service attacks began. Individuals from many nations joined in, with Saudi Arabia, Pakistan, India, Brazil, Argentina, and Malaysia on the US side and Korean, Indonesian, and

---

38   G.L. Vistica, 'Cyberwar and Sabotage', *Newsweek* (31 May 1999), p. 22.
39   Lisa Hoffmann, 'U.S. Opened Cyber-War During Kosovo Fight', *Washington Times* (24 October 1999), p. C1; Robert Burns, 'Computer Warfare Used in Yugoslavia', *Associated Press* (7 October 1999).
40   Maria Seminerio, 'Infowar Part of NATO Arsenal?' *ZDNet* (25 March 1999).
41   Steven Metz, 'The Next Twist of the RMA', *Parameters*, 30/3 (2000): 40–53.
42   Cordesman, pp. v and 47.

Japanese hackers supporting China. In some countries, such as Brazil, supporters of both sides were found.[43]

Some of the government officials seemed to take the hacktivism activities very seriously. The US government and military stated that they had sharply stepped up network security in response to an FBI-led National Infrastructure Protection Center warning. Other sources reported that the Navy was at INFOCONALPHA, a cyber version of real-world military Defense Readiness Level (DEFCON).[44] That US officials reacted particularly strongly to this case of hacktivism is less surprising if we take into account that China is considered America's prime nemesis in the field of information operations.[45] The DoD repeatedly points to the intense fascination China seems to have with information warfare. Experts state that 'Chinese military journals are replete with articles that either directly or indirectly address the subject.'[46] Only recently, the US has claimed that China is developing offensive weapons for cyberwar and a first-strike capability. Beijing has often criticized such reports as an attempt to exaggerate its military modernization and demonize China.[47]

Iraq War 2003–

Despite claims to the contrary,[48] the Iraq campaign saw little activity in the cyberwar domain,[49] apart from large-scale attempts at perception management or PSYOP, the primary goal of which was to turn the Iraqi army and population against the regime of Saddam Hussein. This aspect of Info Ops is not the focus of this chapter, but it is important to note that PSYOP or perception management has gained more influence since the events of 11 September 2001,[50] while the prominence of cyberwar

---

43   Michelle Delio, 'Is this World Cyber War I?' *Wired* (1 May 2001); Michelle Delio, 'It's (Cyber) War: China vs. U.S.' (30 April 2001).

44   Timothy L. Thomas, 'The Internet in China: Civilian and Military Uses', *Information & Security: An International Journal*, 7 (2001): 159–73.

45   Ehsan Ahrari, 'U.S. Military Strategic Perspectives on the PRC: New Frontiers of Information-Based War', *Asian Survey*, 37/12 (1997): 1,163–80; Toshi Yoshihara, *Chinese Information Warfare: A Phantom Menace Or Emerging Threat?* (Carlisle, 2001).

46   James C. Mulvenon, 'The PLA and Information Warfare', in James C. Mulvenon and Richard H. Yang, eds, *The People's Liberation Army in the Information Age* (Santa Monica, 1998), p. 175.

47   Office of the Secretary of Defense, *Military Power of the People's Republic of China 2006*, A Report to Congress (Washington, DC, 2006); Josh Rogin, 'DOD: China Fielding Cyberattack Units', *Federal Computer Week* (25 May 2006).

48   Associated Press, 'Fierce Cyber War Predicted: Strides in Technology Magnify Info War Potential', *CNN.com* (3 March 2003).

49   Brian McWilliams, 'Iraq's Crash Course in Cyberwar', *Wired* (22 May 2003); Matthew French, 'Bandwidth in Iraq a Subject of Debate', *Federal Computer Week* (20 October 2003).

50   Cf. Donald H. Rumsfeld, *Information Operations Roadmap* (30 October 2003).

is decreasing. This is due to the fact that after 11 September 2001, the focus shifted towards terrorist organizations and their supposedly skilful use of ICT and new media. At the same time, in the broader context of the so-called 'war on terrorism', it seemed more and more important to exert a positive influence on public opinion in the Muslim world, while simultaneously convincing a global audience that this 'war' is justified.

While there were the usual hacktivism activities, there has been no reported deployment of viruses, government-trained hackers, or special electromagnetic pulse bombs to knock out Iraq's computers and other sensitive electronic equipment. In truth, Iraq does not have much of an information infrastructure to attack. This backwardness is a direct result of trade sanctions, which make it difficult to obtain current versions of software or up-to-date training.[51] Deploying cyberwar tools against countries with such degraded information infrastructures and such low dependence on it seems, to put it bluntly, pointless.

Estonia

When the Estonian authorities began removing a Second World War memorial – a bronze statue of a Soviet soldier – from a park at the end of April 2007, a three-week cyber-battle ensued in which a wave of DDoS swamped various websites – among them the websites of the Estonian parliament, banks, ministries, newspapers and broadcasters – disabling the sites by exceeding the bandwidths for the servers running the sites.

The Estonian-Russian online squabble made headlines,[52] and various officials pounced on the cyberwar theme. It was claimed both implicitly and explicitly that the Russian Federation was behind the attack and that this was the first known case of one state targeting another using cyberwarfare.[53] One NATO official reportedly said: 'I won't point fingers. But these were not things done by a few individuals. This clearly bore the hallmarks of something concerted. The Estonians are not alone with this problem. It really is a serious issue for the alliance as a whole.'[54]

A sober look at the plain facts after the uproar reveals the usual pattern of such incidents: it seems unlikely that the 'attacks' were initiated by the Russian government or its security service. Fake Internet protocol (IP) addresses – in this case, a Russian government computer was supposed to have been involved in the

---

51   Brian McWilliams, 'Unleashing the Dogs of Cyber-War on Iraq!' *Salon.com* (6 March 2003).

52   See, for example, Steven Lee Myers, 'Cyberattack on Estonia Stirs Fear of "Virtual War"', *International Herald Tribune* (18 May 2007); BBC News, 'The Cyber Raiders Hitting Estonia' (17 May 2007); Agence France-Presse/Sydney Morning Herald, 'Estonia Urges Firm EU, NATO Response to New Form of Warfare: Cyber-attacks' (16 May 2007).

53   Ian Traynor, 'Russia Accused of Unleashing Cyberwar to Disable Estonia', *The Guardian* (17 May 2007).

54   Ibid.

DDoS attack – are a routine part of any 'hacktivist' attack. Furthermore, the attacks were so low-tech and old-school that they were almost certainly carried out by people with relatively little real computer expertise, who use readily available techniques and programs to search for and exploit weaknesses in other computers on the Internet. And finally, despite the uproar, the attacks had a relatively negligible effect (a usual feature of DDoS attacks). The most important outcome of these incidents may have been their effect on a broader public and its perception of the issue.

The (Present and Future) Reality of Cyberwar

That every political tension or conflict is accompanied by heightened activity in cyberspace (in the form of hacktivism) is the norm today, and more of the same should be expected. In addition to the examples given above, many other cases confirm this pattern: the number of pro-Pakistan defacements of Indian websites has risen markedly in recent years; in the Middle East, hacktivism onslaughts broke out in October 2000 shortly after the second *Intifada* erupted on the ground.[55]

But despite the high attention devoted to denial-of-service and defacement attacks, they are only directed against the public face of selected organizations and are relatively harmless, even though they are considered to be an inconvenience as well as an embarrassment. By defacing an opponent's web page and replacing it with propaganda, pictures and slogans, attackers seek to produce a sense of lack of control on behalf of network operators. The main effect is humiliation. Apart from an economic impact that is very hard to measure, hacktivism attacks have a highly questionable political impact. It is therefore not justified to regard hacktivism as a national security threat – at the most, such attacks are a case for law enforcement, but only in exceptional cases.

While such break-ins, including computer network exploitations, are real, they are far from constituting an 'Electronic Pearl Harbor'.[56] So far, cyber-attacks resulting in deaths and injuries remain the stuff of Hollywood movies or conspiracy theory. But what about the future? In the estimate of one expert, 'there should be no doubt that the smarter and better-funded militaries of the world are planning for cyberwar, both attack and defense'.[57] There are various indications that this is indeed the case. The US, for example, is reportedly developing national-level

---

55 Michael A. Vatis, *Cyber Attacks during the War on Terrorism: A Predictive Analysis* (Hanover, 2001).

56 Winn Schwartau was the first to use this term in 1991 in a Congress hearing, as he states in Winn Schwartau, *Information Warfare. Chaos on the Electronic Superhighway* (New York, 1994), p. 43; an interesting article on the hype surrounding the issue: David Isenberg, 'An Electronic Pearl Harbor? Not Likely', in T.E. Copeland, ed., *The Information Revolution and National Security* (Carlisle Barracks, 2000), pp. 92–102.

57 Schneier, 'Schneier on Security: A Blog Covering Security and Security Technology'.

guidance for determining when and how to launch cyber-attacks against enemy computer networks.[58] More recent reports tell of the founding of the US Air Force Cyber Command, tasked with both offensive and defensive cyber-activities.[59] On the other hand, US military strategy experts assert that strategic rivals such as China and Russia have offensive information warfare programs.

It seems logical that, until cyberwar is proven to be ineffective, states and non-state actors who have the ability to develop such 'weapons' will most likely try to do so, because they appear to be cost-effective and less risky than other forms of armed conflict. However, the mere existence of these capabilities does not necessarily mean that they will be used. Even if the technology existed and could really be targeted specifically at enemy infrastructures, its use raises a mass of legal, ethical, but also strategic issues.

Legal Restraints?

Even though information operations have gained a great deal of importance in recent years, the concept as such remains controversial. As far as democratic states with rule of law are concerned, this is true in particular for the offensive aspects of such operations, of which computer network attacks are part. The problem is that the spectrum of intentions of Info Ops is total, since they are aimed at the entirety of the global public. In addition, information in this context refers simply to the entire communication infrastructure of an opponent, including military *and* civilian data networks, telecommunications installations, and the mass media. As a result, it is no longer possible to draw a clear distinction between combatants and non-combatants, and the boundaries between war and peace become largely blurred. The consequence of this is that the majority of countries attribute greater importance to defensive measures than to possible offensive operations, including cyberwar.

Some countries obviously have the political determination or capabilities to apply the entire range of instruments – within certain limits, however. As mentioned, during the Kosovo conflict, some US officials were reportedly worried about the legal implications of launching the world's first 'cyberwar', for which they found no clear basis in law.[60] A 50-page booklet with guidelines for waging cyberwar issued in May 1999 mainly warns commanders to be cautious of targeting institutions that are essentially civilian.[61] There are also many more ambiguous

---

58 Graham Bradley, 'Bush Orders Guidelines for Cyber-Warfare: Rules for Attacking Enemy Computers Prepared as U.S. Weighs Iraq Options', *Washington Post* (7 February 2003), p. A01.

59 Henry S. Kenyon, 'Cyberspace Command Logs In', *Signal online* (August 2007).

60 Reuters, 'U.S. Military Grapples With Cyber Warfare Rules' (8 November 1999).

61 Department of Defense, Office of General Counsel, *An Assessment of International Legal Issues in Information Operations* (Washington, DC, 1999).

legal parameters involved, such as the unclear role of third nations or 'neutrals' in preventing the use of their cyber-facilities and information systems.

In truth, however, the rules of international law and the law of war are likely to provide only insufficient guarantees for the non-utilization of 'cyber-weapons' in the future. Most technical possibilities are not adequately regulated by existing agreements, since many aspects do not fall under the traditional understanding of violence.[62] In addition, the Iraq campaign has shown that existing legal constraints can be a very weak inhibitor. The option of pre-emption as detailed in the US National Security Strategy of 2002 (and 2006) could also, theoretically, be expanded to cyberspace. The possibility of use of force by the US in response to potential cyber-attacks is conceivable, though unlikely.[63]

International law is, at best, a voluntary guideline for the selection of offensive, defensive, or retaliatory action in information battles, but never an obstacle for political resolution or military willingness to engage in 'cyberwar' activities.[64] The more likely constraint for the use of 'cyber-weapons' might be the fear of giving away a strategic advantage.

Strategic Restraints?

Cyberwar experts Arquilla and Libicki believe that the Pentagon actually did hack into Serbian computers to spy during the Kosovo conflict, but refrained from causing chaos principally for strategic reasons. Widespread use of these new weapons and tools would probably have accelerated and focused foreign military research on them and threaten to deprive the US of its information warfare edge in a field where foes could catch up quickly and cheaply.[65]

In addition, nobody can be truly interested in allowing the unfettered proliferation and use of cyberwar tools, not even (or maybe least of all) the country with the offensive lead in this domain. Quite to the contrary, very strong arguments can be made for the overall strategic interest of the world's big powers in developing and accepting internationally agreed norms on the use and non-use use of cyberwar, that is, computer network attacks, and in creating agreements that might pertain to the development, distribution, and deployment of cyber-weapons or to their use.[66] The most obvious reason is that the countries that are currently

---

62 Andrew Rathmell, 'Controlling Computer Network Operations', *Information & Security: An International Journal*, 7 (2001): 121–44.

63 Dawn M. Gibson, *A Virtual Pandora's Box: Anticipatory Self-Defense In Cyberspace*, online paper.

64 Rathmell, 'Controlling Computer Network Operations'; William J. Bayles, 'The Ethics of Computer Network Attack', *Parameters*, 31/1 (2001): 44–58.

65 Julian Borger, 'Pentagon Kept the Lid on Cyberwar in Kosovo', *The Guardian* (9 November 1999).

66 Dorothy Denning, 'Obstacles and Options for Cyber Arms Controls', paper presented at Arms Control in Cyberspace Conference, Heinrich Böll Foundation 9Berlin, Germany, 29–30 June 2001).

openly discussing the use of cyberwar tools are precisely the ones that are the most vulnerable to cyberwarfare attacks due to their high dependency on information infrastructure.

Conclusion

This chapter has attempted to provide a balanced picture of the phenomenon of cyberwar. It looked at the change in the conception of the phenomenon, which was first understood as C2I (or C4I) warfare and which today more closely refers to computer network attacks by state actors, that is, military actors. The above cases point to the reality of cyber-vandalism, cyber-activism, and hacktivism, but they show that computer network attacks, also known as 'cyberwar', remain science fiction for the time being. This could be due to technical issues: even though it is often claimed that hacker tools are simple to use, inexpensive, and widely available on computer bulletin boards and various websites, sophisticated cyber-weapons would need to be a lot more powerful than that to be effective and to deliver 'effect' to a particular geographic conflict zone or enemy. We would need to see a qualitative leap in the ability to penetrate and manipulate ICT, but also to directly control aspects of the information infrastructure. Furthermore, dependence on ICT would still have to substantially increase.[67]

But even if technical impediments can be overcome, cyberwar is not a dream come true for a technologically advanced nation. Apart from legal and strategic restraints that will certainly be factored into any consideration of whether to use these tools or not, the biggest impediment should be fears of uncontrollable blowback.[68] Clearly, there is a disjunction between the technological and market realities of a globalized, interdependent and networked world, and the idea of using cyberwar tools. Cyberwar is not about a game of seeking strategic advantage from a new technology. There are a number of ways in which computer network attacks could – and most likely would! – 'blow back' on Western societies. First of all, repercussions could emerge directly through the interdependencies between various critical assets that characterize the environment. Second, blowback may be felt through the more intangible effect of undermined trust in cyberspace, with damaging repercussions for the global economy. In this sense, let us hope that cyberwar remains science fiction for a while longer.

---

67   Cf. Johan Eriksson and Giampiero Giacomello, 'Conclusion: Digital-Age Security in Theory and Practice', in Johan Eriksson and Giampiero Giacomello, eds, *International Relations and Security in the Digital Age* (London, 2007), pp. 173–84.

68   Rathmell, 'Controlling Computer Network Operations'.

References

Agence France-Presse/Sydney Morning Herald, 'Estonia Urges Firm EU, NATO Response to New Form of Warfare: Cyber-attacks' (16 May 2007), <www.smh.com.au/news/Technology/Estonia-urges-firm-EU-NATO-response-to-new-form-of-warfarecyberattacks/2007/05/16/1178995207414.html> [accessed 2 June 2008]

Ahrari, Ehsan, 'U.S. Military Strategic Perspectives on the PRC: New Frontiers of Information-Based War', *Asian Survey*, 37/12 (1997): 1,163–80

Alberts, David S. and Daniel S. Papp, eds, *The Information Age: An Anthology of Its Impacts and Consequences* (Washington, DC: National Defense University, 1997)

Arquilla, John and David F. Ronfeldt, 'Cyberwar is Coming!' *Comparative Strategy*, 12/2 (1993): 141–65

— — —, *The Advent of Netwar* (Santa Monica: RAND, 1996)

— — —, eds, *In Athena's Camp: Preparing for Conflict in the Information Age* (Santa Monica: RAND, 1997)

— — —, eds, *Networks and Netwars: The Future of Terror, Crime, and Militancy* (Santa Monica: RAND, 2001)

Arquilla, John, David F. Ronfeldt and Michele Zanini, *Networks, Netwar and the Information Age* (Santa Monica: RAND, 1996)

Associated Press, 'Fierce Cyber War Predicted: Strides in Technology Magnify Info War Potential', *CNN.com* (3 March 2003), <http://www.cnn.com/2003/TECH/ptech/03/03/sprj.irq.info.war.ap/index.html> [accessed 2 June 2008]

Bayles, William J., 'The Ethics of Computer Network Attack', *Parameters*, 31/1 (2001): 44–58

BBC News, 'The Cyber Raiders Hitting Estonia' (17 May 2007), <news.bbc.co.uk/1/hi/world/europe/6665195.stm> [accessed 2 June 2008]

Borger, Julian, 'Pentagon Kept the Lid on Cyberwar in Kosovo', *The Guardian* (9 November 1999), <http://www.infowar-monitor.net/modules.php?op=modload&name=News&file=article&sid=15> [accessed 2 June 2008]

Burns, Robert, 'Computer Warfare Used in Yugoslavia', *Associated Press* (7 October 1999), <http://transnational.org/SAJT/features/computerwarfare.html> [accessed 2 June 2008]

Campen, Alan D., *The First Information Warfare* (Fairfax: AFCEA International Press, 1992)

Campen, Alan D., Douglas H. Dearth and Thomas Goodden, eds, *Cyberwar: Security, Strategy and Conflict in the Information Age* (Fairfax: AFCEA International Press, 1996)

Campen, Alan D. and Douglas H. Dearth, eds, *Cyberwar 2.0: Myths, Mysteries and Reality* (Fairfax: AFCEA International Press, 1998)

Chairman of the Joint Chiefs of Staff, *US Armed Forces, Joint Vision 2010* (Washington, DC: US Department of Defense, 1996)

Copeland, T.E., ed., *The Information Revolution and National Security* (Carlisle Barracks: Strategic Studies Institute, 2000)

Cordesman, A.H., *Defending America. Redefining the Conceptual Borders of Homeland Defense. Critical Infrastructure Protection and Information Warfare* (Washington, DC: Center for Strategic and International Studies, 2000)

Defense Science Board, *Report of the Defense Science Board Summer Study Task Force on Information Architecture for the Battlefield* (Washington, DC: Department of Defense, 1994)

Delio, Michelle 'It's (Cyber) War: China vs. U.S.', *Wired* (30 April 2001), <http://www.wired.com/politics/law/news/2001/04/43437> [accessed 2 June 2008]

———, 'Is this World Cyber War I?' *Wired* (1 May 2001), <http://www.wired.com/politics/law/news/2001/05/43443> [accessed 2 June 2008]

Denning, Dorothy, 'Obstacles and Options for Cyber Arms Controls', paper presented at Arms Control in Cyberspace Conference, Heinrich Böll Foundation (Berlin, Germany, 29–30 June 2001), <http://www.cs.georgetown.edu/~denning/infosec/berlin.doc> [accessed 2 June 2008]

Department of Defense, *Directive Number 3600.1, Information Operations*, Revision One (October 2001), <http://www.iwar.org.uk/iwar/resources/doctrine/DOD36001.pdf > [accessed 2 June 2008]

Department of Defense, Office of General Counsel, *An Assessment of International Legal Issues in Information Operations* (Washington, DC: Department of Defense, May 1999)

Department of the Army, *Information Operations, Field Manual No. 100-6* (Washington, DC: Department of the Army, 27 August 1996)

Der Derian, James, *Virtuous War: Mapping the Military-Industrial-Media-Entertainment Complex* (Boulder, CO: Westview, 2001)

Dillon, Michael and Julian Reid, 'Global Liberal Governance: Biopolitics, Security and War', *Millennium Journal of International Studies*, 30/1 (2001): 41–66

Dunn Cavelty, Myriam, *Information Age Conflicts: A Study on the Information Revolution and a Changing Operating Environment*, Zürcher Beiträge zur Sicherheitspolitik und Konfliktforschung, no. 64 (Zurich: Center for Security Studies, 2002)

———, 'Cyber-Terror – Looming Threat or Phantom Menace? The Framing of the US Cyber-Threat Debate', *Journal of Information Technology and Politics*, 4/1 (2007): 19–36

———, Cyber-Security and Threat Politics: US Efforts to Secure the Information Age (London: Routledge, 2008)

Dunn Cavelty, Myriam, Sai-Felicia Krishna-Hensel and Victor Mauer, eds, *Power and Security in the Information Age: Investigating the Role of the State in Cyberspace* (Aldershot: Ashgate 2008)

Ellison, R.J., D.A. Fisher, R.C. Linger, H.F. Lipson, T. Longstaff and N.R. Mead, 'Survivable Network Systems: An Emerging Discipline', Technical Report, CMU/SEI-97-TR-013. ESC-TR-97-013 (November 1997), <http://www.cert.org/research/97tr013.pdf> [accessed 2 June 2008]

Eriksson, Johan and Giampiero Giacomello, 'The Information Revolution, Security, and International Relations: (IR)Relevant Theory?' *International Political Science Review*, 27/3 (2006): 221–44

— — —, eds, *International Relations and Security in the Digital Age* (London: Routledge, 2007)

Eriksson, Johan, 'Cyberplagues, IT, and Security: Threat Politics in the Information Age', *Journal of Contingencies and Crisis Management*, 9/4 (2001): 211–22

Fisher, Uri, 'Information Age State Security: New Threats to Old Boundaries', *Journal for Homeland Security* (November 2001), <http://www.homelandsecurity. org/journal/articles/fisher.htm> [accessed 2 June 2008]

FitzGerald, Mary C., 'Russian Views on Electronic Signals and Information Warfare', *American Intelligence Journal*, 15/1 (1994): 81–7

French, Geoffrey S., 'Shunning the Frumious Bandersnatch, Current Literature on Information Warfare and Deterrence', *TRC Analysis* (The Terrorism Research Center, 2000), <http://www.terrorism.com/modules.php?op=modload&name =News&file=article&sid=5648&mode=thread&order=0&thold=0> [accessed 2 June 2008]

French, Matthew, 'Bandwidth in Iraq a Subject of Debate', *Federal Computer Week* (20 October 2003), <http://www.fcw.com/print/9_39/news/81220-1.html> [accessed 2 June 2008]

Gibson, Dawn M., *A Virtual Pandora's Box: Anticipatory Self-Defense In Cyberspace*, online paper, <http://www.uiowa.edu/~cyberlaw/csl03/dgcsl03.html> [accessed 2 June 2008]

Graham, Bradley, 'Bush Orders Guidelines for Cyber-Warfare: Rules for Attacking Enemy Computers Prepared as U.S. Weighs Iraq Options', *Washington Post* (7 February 2003), p. A01

Hables Gray, Chris, Postmodern War – The New Politics of Conflict (London: Routledge, 1997)

— — —, *Peace, War, and Computers* (London: Routledge, 2005)

Henry, Ryan and Edward Peartree, eds, *Information Revolution and International Security* (Washington, DC: Center for Strategic and International Studies, 1998)

Hoffmann, Lisa, 'U.S. Opened Cyber-War During Kosovo Fight', *Washington Times* (24 October 1999), p. C1

Joint Chiefs of Staff, *JP 3–13, Joint Doctrine for Information Operations* (Washington, DC: Department of Defense, 2006)

Joint Staff, C4 Architecture & Integration Division, *C4I for the Warrior* (Washington, DC: Joint Staff, 12 June 1992)

Kenyon, Henry S. 'Cyberspace Command Logs In', *Signal online* (August 2007), <http://findarticles.com/p/articles/mi_qa5438/is_200708/ai_n21293976> [accessed 2 June 2008]

Latham, Robert, ed., *Bombs and Bandwidth: The Emerging Relationship between IT and Security* (New York: The New Press, 2003)

Lewis, James A., *Assessing the Risks of Cyber-terrorism, Cyber War and Other Cyber Threats* (Washington, DC: Center for Strategic and International Studies, 2002)

Libicki, Martin, *Defending Cyberspace* (Washington, DC: National Defense University, 1997)

McWilliams, Brian, 'Unleashing The Dogs of Cyber-War on Iraq!' *Salon.com* (6 March 2003), <http://dir.salon.com/story/tech/feature/2003/03/06/iraq_geeks/> [accessed 2 June 2008]

———, 'Iraq's Crash Course in Cyberwar', *Wired* (22 May 2003), <http://www.wired.com/politics/law/news/2003/05/58901?currentPage=2> [accessed 2 June 2008]

Metz, Steven, 'The Next Twist of the RMA', *Parameters*, 30/3 (2000): 40–53

Mulvenon, James C. and Richard H. Yang, eds, *The People's Liberation Army in the Information Age* (Santa Monica: RAND, 1998)

Myers, Steven Lee, 'Cyberattack on Estonia Stirs Fear of "Virtual War"', *International Herald Tribune* (18 May 2007), <www.iht.com/articles/2007/05/18/news/estonia.php> [accessed 2 June 2008]

O'Hanlon, Michael, *Technological Change and the Future of Warfare* (Washington, DC: Brooking Institute, 1999)

Office of the Secretary of Defense, *Military Power of the People's Republic of China 2006: A Report to Congress* (Washington, DC: Office of the Secretary of Defense, 2006)

Rathmell, Andrew, 'Controlling Computer Network Operations', *Information & Security: An International Journal*, 7 (2001): 121–44

Rattray, Greg, *Strategic Warfare in Cyberspace* (Cambridge, MA: MIT Press, 2001)

Reuters, 'U.S. Military Grapples With Cyber Warfare Rules' (8 November 1999), <http://www.hartford-hwp.com/archives/27a/021.html> [accessed 2 June 2008]

Rogin, Josh, 'DOD: China Fielding Cyberattack Units', *Federal Computer Week* (25 May 2006), <http://www.fcw.com/online/news/94650-1.html> [accessed 2 June 2008]

Rumsfeld, Donald H., *Information Operations Roadmap* (30 October 2003), <http://www.gwu.edu/~nsarchiv/NSAEBB/NSAEBB177/info_ops_roadmap.pdf> [accessed 2 June 2008]

Schneier, Bruce, 'Schneier on Security: A Blog Covering Security and Security Technology', <http://www.schneier.com/blog/archives/2007/06/cyberwar.html> [accessed 2 June 2008]

Schwartau, Winn, *Information Warfare: Chaos on the Electronic Superhighway* (New York: Thunder's Mouth Press, 1994)

Seminerio, Maria, 'Infowar Part of NATO arsenal?' *ZDNet* (25 March 1999), <http://www.infosecnews.org/hypermail/9903/1564.html> [accessed 2 June 2008]

Thomas, Timothy L., 'Russian Views on Information-based Warfare', *Airpower Journal*, Special Edition (1996): 26–35

———, Like Adding Wings to the Tiger: Chinese Information War Theory and Practice (Ft Leavenworth: Foreign Military Studies Office, 2000)

———, 'The Internet in China: Civilian and Military Uses', *Information & Seucrity: An International Journal*, 7 (2001): 159–73

———, *Dragon Bytes: Chinese Information-War Theory and Practice* (Ft Leavenworth: Foreign Military Studies Office, 2004)

Traynor, Ian, 'Russia Accused of Unleashing Cyberwar to Disable Estonia', *The Guardian* (17 May 2007), <www.guardian.co.uk/frontpage/story/0,2081512,00.html> [accessed 2 June 2008]

Trendle, Giles, 'Cyberwars: The Coming Arab E-Jihad', *The Middle East* (1 April 2002), <http://findarticles.com/p/articles/mi_m2742/is_2002_April/ai_n25045470> [accessed 2 June 2008]

United States Air Force, *Cornerstones of Information Warfare* (Washington, DC: Department of the United States Air Force, 1995)

Vatis, Michael A., *Cyber Attacks during the War on Terrorism: A Predictive Analysis* (Hanover: Institute for Security Technology Studies, 22 September 2001)

Vistica, G.L., 'Cyberwar and Sabotage', *Newsweek* (31 May 1999), p. 22

Wilson, Clay, *Computer Attack and Cyber-terrorism: Vulnerabilities and Policy Issues for Congress*, Congressional Research Report for Congress, RL32114, 17 October 2003 (Washington, DC: Congressional Research Service, 2003)

Wolfe, F., 'Pentagon Analyzing Serb Attacks on DoD Web Sites', *www.infowar.com* (22 June 1999), <http://www.tla.ch/TLA/NEWS/1999sec/19990622serb.htm> [accessed 2 June 2008]

Yoshihara, Toshi, *Chinese Information Warfare: A Phantom Menace Or Emerging Threat?* (Carlisle: Strategic Studies Institute, November 2001)

Twentieth Century Military Spending Patterns

Jari Eloranta

Introduction

The causes, impacts, and scope of twentieth-century military spending and conflicts have been debated widely among scholars.[1] One can distinguish a pessimistic tradition as well as a more optimistic interpretation of the conflicts and legacies pertaining to this century. Scholars like Eric Hobsbawm would view the extreme political and military outcomes of the period of world wars as indicative of the decadence and economic failures of the twentieth century. For Hobsbawm, mankind's descent into anarchy and degradation began in Sarajevo in 1914 and culminated in the Balkan madness of the 1990s. His twentieth century was an era of total warfare in its perverse perfection, with state-sanctioned genocides, ethnic cleansing, and totalitarianism; a world brought to the brink of extinction during the Cold War arms race.[2] Is this an accurate and/or fair depiction of the twentieth century? And what are the implications of these factors for twentieth-century military spending?

According to the prominent historical sociologist Charles Tilly, the twentieth century was the most bellicose in human history, featuring hundreds of bloody conflicts and over a hundred million battle deaths. He argued that the reasons included the rapid development of more deadly weapons, along with more centralized and powerful nation states.[3] Niall Ferguson has agreed with Tilly, saying that the hundred years after 1900 "were without question the bloodiest century

---

1   Some of the ideas and data analyzed here have already been touched on in Jari Eloranta, *Military Spending Patterns in History* (EH.Net, 2006). This article, however, is a more specific analysis of the twentieth-century military spending patterns instead of a broad overview of long-run changes.

2   E.J. Hobsbawm, *The Age of Extremes: A History of the World, 1914–1991* (New York: Vintage, 1996).

3   Charles Tilly, *Coercion, Capital, and European States, AD 990–1990* (Cambridge, MA: Basil Blackwell, 1990), pp. 67, 74.

in modern history, far more violent in relative as well as absolute terms than any previous era."[4] He has pointed out that the average yearly amount of (Great Power) war was highest in the sixteenth and lowest in the nineteenth century. During the nineteenth and twentieth centuries, the industrialized nation states found new ways to mobilize their manpower and resources for warfare, and the technological advances of the age, in particular railroads, often served both the civilian as well as military production and planning.[5]

As argued by Charles Tilly, the number of Great Power wars has declined over centuries—wars have become shorter and fewer—yet the deadliness of these conflicts has increased. Ferguson has attempted to explain the twentieth-century violence in terms of economic volatility, disintegrating empires, and ethnic conflicts. Moreover, the twentieth-century mayhem featured two of the deadliest conflicts in human history. The world wars were unparalleled in their severity and concentration, and pioneered the widespread use of genocides, or democides, in this century.[6] The First World War (1914–1918) thrust more than 30 countries into conflict with each other and led to 20 million premature deaths, only to be dwarfed by the Second World War (1939–1945), in which more than 60 countries waged war and prematurely ended the lives of more than 55 million people.[7] The European region, as well as many other battlefields around the globe, was decimated by these conflicts, a situation that did not improve until after the Second World War.

However, the pessimistic perspectives on the twentieth century do not tell the whole story. Bradford DeLong and Alex Field have stressed the underlying continuities of technological change through the first half of the century that eventually made possible the massive increases in living standards in the second half.[8] Europe was certainly not an exception in this regard. Despite macroeconomic shocks, technological development continued at a fast pace and exceeded the nineteenth-century European experiences. Ferguson has also mentioned this paradox of massive conflicts alongside tremendous economic progress, which

---

4   Niall Ferguson, *The War of the World: Twentieth-Century Conflict and the Descent of the West* (New York: Penguin, 2006), p. xxxiv.

5   Niall Ferguson, *The Cash Nexus: Money and Power in the Modern World, 1700–2000* (New York: Basic, 2001).

6   Ferguson, *The War of the World: Twentieth-Century Conflict and the Descent of the West*; R.J. Rummel, *Power Kills: Democracy as a Method of Nonviolence* (New Brunswick, NJ: Transaction, 1997).

7   Stephen Broadberry and Mark Harrison, "The Economics of World War I: An Overview," in *The Economics of World War I*, ed. by Stephen Broadberry and Mark Harrison (Cambridge: Cambridge University Press, 2005), pp. 3–40.

8   J. Bradford DeLong, *Cornucopia: The Pace of Economic Growth in the Twentieth Century* (National Bureau of Economic Research, 2000), <http://papers.nber.org/papers/W7602. pdf>; Alexander J. Field, "The Most Technologically Progressive Decade of the Century," *American Economic Review*, 93 (September 2003); Alexander J. Field, "Technical Change and U.S. Economic Growth: The Interwar Period and the 1990s," in *The Global Economy in the 1990s: A Long Run Perspective*, ed. by Paul Rhode and Gianni Toniolo (Cambridge: Cambridge University Press, 2006).

manifested itself especially in terms of incomes, improved nutrition, life expectancy, and political voice.[9] This economic expansion was linked to the technological advances of the period, some of which were spurred on by the conflicts.

In fact, Niall Ferguson has argued provocatively that military expenditures have been the principal cause of fiscal innovation for most of history, leading to the adoption of four key institutions from the eighteenth century onwards: tax bureaucracy, parliament, system of national debt, and central bank.[10] Respectively, even though there does not seem to be a linear or exponential growth trend in military spending in history over the long run, the "bang for the buck," that is, the destructive effectiveness of military spending, has increased over time, particularly in the twentieth century. At the same time, the more cohesive and ambitious nation states of the post-Napoleonic era have been able to achieve high absolute military spending while keeping the relative economic burden of this spending fairly low. The industrial revolutions of the nineteenth century have made this possible. On the other hand, the warfare states of the early twentieth century have been severely challenged in the late twentieth century by the rise of the welfare states. Even though linear substitutions of one type of spending for another are relatively rare, the budgetary challenges posed by such spending choices, as well as the criticism of Keynesian policies and greater economic role of the state in the 1980s and 1990s, have forced the warfare state into a limited retreat in the post-Cold War climate.

These influences can be seen in the twentieth-century military spending patterns. The age of total war in the nineteenth and twentieth centuries finally pushed the dominant nation states, mostly in Europe, to adopt more and more efficient fiscal systems and enabled some of them to dedicate more than half of their GDP (gross domestic product) to the war effort during the world wars. Comparatively, even though military spending was regularly the biggest item in the budget for most states in the beginning of the twentieth century, it still represented only a modest amount of their GDP. The Cold War period again saw high relative spending levels, due to the enduring rivalry between the West and the Communist bloc. Finally, the collapse of the Soviet Union alleviated some of these tensions and lowered the aggregate military spending in the world. Newer security challenges such as terrorism and various interstate rivalries have again pushed the world towards growing overall military spending.

Here, I will first elaborate on some of the research trends in studying military spending and the multitude of theories attempting to explain the importance of warfare and military finance in recent history. This will be followed by a more or less chronological survey, starting with the military spending leading to the world wars and ending up with discussion of the current behavior of states in the post-Cold War international system. By necessity, this chronological review

---

9   Ferguson, *The War of the World: Twentieth-Century Conflict and the Descent of the West*, pp. xxxv–xxxvi. See also Peter H. Lindert, *Voice and Growth: Was Churchill Right?* (Cambridge, MA: National Bureau of Economic Research, 2003).

10   See Ferguson, *The Cash Nexus: Money and Power in the Modern World, 1700–2000* for further discussion.

will be selective at best, given the enormity of the time period in question and the complexity of the topic at hand. In general, I will attempt to put the military spending patterns in the twentieth century in the context of the preceding debate over the nature of the twentieth century. In particular, did military spending, in the form of arms races, contribute to the severity of the conflicts in this period? Moreover, did military expenditures have an impact on the economic performance of the period?

Theoretical Approaches

Military spending is a crucial component in order to understand various aspects of economic and political history: the cost, funding, and burden of conflicts; the creation of nation states; and, in general, the increased role of the state. Nonetheless, certain characteristics can be distinguished from the efforts to study twentieth-century conflicts and spending patterns among different fields of science; mainly in history, economics, and political sciences. Historians, especially diplomatic and military historians, have preferred to study the origins of the two world wars and perhaps certain other massive conflicts. Equally, many of the historical studies on war and societies have analyzed developments at a remote macro-level, often without a great deal of elaboration on the "lesser" conflicts and the quantitative evidence pertaining to military spending. For example, Paul Kennedy argued, in his famous *The Rise and Fall of the Great Powers: Economic Change and Military Conflict from 1500 to 2000*, that military spending by hegemonic states eventually becomes excessive and a burden on its economy, finally leading to economic ruin. But Kennedy has been criticized by many economists and historians, since he seems to lack the proper quantitative evidence to support his notion of interaction between military spending and economic growth.[11] Economic historians, respectively, have not been particularly interested in the long-term economic impacts of military spending. Usually, economic historians have focused on the economics of global conflicts—of which a good example of recent work combining the theoretical aspects of economics with historical case studies is *The Economics of World War II*, a

---

11   See Paul Kennedy, *The Rise and Fall of the Great Powers. Economic Change and Military Conflict from 1500 to 2000* (London: Fontana, 1989). On criticism of Kennedy's "theory," see especially Todd Sandler and Keith Hartley, *The Economics of Defense*, ed. by Mark Perlman, *Cambridge Surveys of Economic Literature* (Cambridge: Cambridge University Press, 1995) and the studies listed in it. Other examples of long-run explanations can be found in, for example, Maurice Pearton, *The Knowledgeable State: Diplomacy, War, and Technology since 1830* (London: Burnett, 1982) and William H. McNeill, *The Pursuit of Power: Technology, Armed Force, and Society since A.D. 1000* (Chicago: University of Chicago Press, 1982). A recent global study of similar scope is Jeremy Black, *European Warfare in a Global Context, 1660–1815* (London: Routledge, 2007).

volume edited by Mark Harrison—as well as the immediate short-term economic impacts of wartime mobilization.[12]

Defense economics, in turn, has been imprinted by the immense expansion of military budgets and military establishments in the Cold War era. At least three aspects in defense economics set it apart from other fields of economics: 1) the actors (both private and public spheres of influence, for example in contracting); 2) theoretical challenges introduced by the interaction of different institutional and organizational arrangements, both in the budgeting and the allocation procedures; and 3) the nature of military spending as a tool for destruction as well as providing security.[13] Defense economists have been, at least so far, fairly complacent about studying periods other than the age since the Second World War.[14]

Among peace and conflict sciences, a broader yet overlapping field comparable to defense economics, the focus in research has been to find the causal factors behind the most destructive conflicts. A typical feature in most studies of this type is that they are focused on finding those sets of variables that might predict major wars and other conflicts, in a way similar to the historians' origins of wars approach, whereas studies investigating the military spending behavior of various kinds of states in particular are quite rare. Moreover, even though some cycle theorists and conflict scientists have been interested in the formation of modern nation states and the respective system of states since 1648, they have not expressed any real interest in long-run analysis of the causes of warfare.[15]

How can theories of state behavior at the system level be linked to the analysis of military spending? According to George Modelski and William R. Thompson,

---

12 See Mark Harrison, ed., *The Economics of World War II: Six Great Powers in International Comparisons* (Cambridge: Cambridge University Press, 1998). See also Stephen Broadberry and Mark Harrison, eds, *The Economics of World War I* (Cambridge: Cambridge University Press, 2005). Classic studies of this type are Alan Milward's works on the European war economies; see, for example, Alan S. Milward, *The German Economy at War* (London: Athlon, 1965) and Alan S. Milward, *War, Economy and Society 1939–1945* (London: Allen Lane, 1977).

13 Sandler and Hartley, *The Economics of Defense*, p. xi; Jari Eloranta, *Different Needs, Different Solutions. The Importance of Economic Development and Domestic Power Structures in Explaining Military Spending in Eight Western Democracies During the Interwar Period* (Licentiate Thesis, University of Jyväskylä, 1998).

14 See Jari Eloranta, *External Security by Domestic Choices: Military Spending as an Impure Public Good among Eleven European States, 1920–1938* (Dissertation, European University Institute, 2002) for details.

15 See, for example, Jack S. Levy, "Theories of General War," *World Politics*, vol. 37, no. 3 (1985). For an overview, see especially Daniel S. Geller and J. David Singer, *Nations at War. A Scientific Study of International Conflict*, vol. 58, *Cambridge Studies in International Relations* (Cambridge: Cambridge University Press, 1998). A classic study of war from the holistic perspective is Quincy Wright, *A Study of War* (Chicago, IL: University of Chicago Press, 1942). See also Geoffrey Blainey, *The Causes of War* (New York: Free Press, 1973). On rational explanations of conflicts, see James D. Fearon, "Rationalist Explanations for War," *International Organization*, vol. 49, no. 3 (1995).

proponents of Kondratieff waves and long cycles as explanatory forces in the development of world leadership and conflict patterns, the key aspect in a state's ascendancy to prominence via such cycles in such models is naval power, that is, a state's ability to vie for world political leadership, colonization, and domination in trade.[16] One of the less explored aspects in most studies of hegemonic patterns is the military expenditure component in the competition between the states for military and economic leadership in the system. It is often argued, for example, that uneven economic growth levels cause nations to compete for economic and military prowess. The leader nation(s) thus has to dedicate increasing resources to armaments in order to maintain its position, while the other states, the so-called "followers," can benefit from greater investments in other areas of economic activity. Therefore, the follower states act as free-riders in the international system stabilized by the hegemon. A built-in assumption in this hypothesized development pattern is that military spending eventually becomes harmful for economic development, a notion that has often been challenged in empirical studies.[17]

Overall, the assertion arising from such a framework is that economic development and military spending are closely interdependent, with military spending being the driving force behind economic cycles. Moreover, based on this development pattern, it has been suggested that a country's poor economic performance is linked to the "wasted" economic resources represented by military expenditures. However, as recent studies have shown, economic development is often more significant in explaining military spending rather than vice versa. The development of the US economy since the Second World War certainly does not connote the type of hegemonic decline predicted by Kennedy.[18] As some of the hegemonic theorists reviewed above suggest, economic prosperity might be a necessary prerequisite for war and expansion. Thus, as Brian M. Pollins and Randall L. Schweller have indicated, economic growth would induce rising government expenditures, which, in turn, would enable higher military spending—therefore, military expenditures would be "caused" by economic growth at a certain time lag.[19] In order for military spending to hinder economic performance, it would have to surpass all other areas of an economy, such as is often the case during wartime. In peacetime, this is unlikely to happen.

---

16   George Modelski and William R. Thompson, *Leading Sectors and World Powers: The Coevolution of Global Politics and Economics, Studies in International Relations* (Columbia, SC: University of South Carolina Press, 1996), pp. 14–40.

17   George Modelski and William R. Thompson, *Seapower in Global Politics, 1494–1993* (Basingstoke: Macmillan, 1988).

18   Eloranta, *External Security by Domestic Choices: Military Spending as an Impure Public Good among Eleven European States, 1920–1938*; Sandler and Hartley, *The Economics of Defense*.

19   Brian M. Pollins and Randall L. Schweller, "Linking the Levels: The Long Wave and Shifts in U.S. Foreign Policy, 1790–1993," *American Journal of Political Science*, vol. 43, no. 2 (1999): 445–6. Moreover, Alex Mintz and Chi Huang, "Guns Versus Butter: The Indirect Link," *American Journal of Political Science*, vol. 35, no. 1 (1991) suggest an indirect (negative) growth effect via investment at a lag of at least five years.

The Age of World Wars

A new kind of mobilization, which became a more or less permanent state of affairs in the nineteenth century—associated with industrialized, more centralized governments as well as large, conscripted armies—required new ways of financing. The fiscal reforms included centralized public administration; reliance on specific, balanced budgets; innovations in public banking and public debt management; and reliance on direct taxation of income for revenue. These activities were also supported by the spread of industrialization and rising productivity. The nineteenth century was also the century of the industrialization of war, starting in the mid-century and quickly gathering breakneck speed. By the 1880s, military engineering began to forge ahead even of civil engineering. More and more international armaments firms were established: first to serve the domestic markets, and then to enter into the growing international markets for arms. Furthermore, a revolution in transportation with steamships and railroads made massive, long-distance mobilizations possible, as seen in the Prussian victory over the French in 1870–71.[20]

The demands posed by these changes on the state finances and economies differed. In the French case, the defense share mean (= *military spending, percent of central/federal government expenditures*) stayed roughly the same throughout the nineteenth and early twentieth centuries, at little over 30 percent, whereas its military burden (= *military spending, percent of GDP*) increased circa one percent to 4.2 percent. The British defense share mean declined circa two percent to 36.7 percent in 1870–1913 compared to the early nineteenth century. However, the strength of the British economy made it possible that the military burden actually declined a little to 2.6 percent, which is similar to what Germany was spending in the same period (1870–1913). For most countries, the period leading to the First World War meant higher military burdens than that, such as Japan's 6.1 percent. The United States, the new global economic leader by the closing decades of the century, however, spent a meager on 0.7 percent of its GDP, on average, for military purposes, a trend that continued throughout the interwar period as well, resulting in a military burden of 1.2 percent. Furthermore, the aggregate, systemic (based on a 16-country total), real military spending in this period increased consistently. The impact of the Russo-Japanese war (1904–05) was immense for the Great Powers' military spending behavior: the unexpected defeat of the Russians, along with the arrival of dreadnoughts, launched an intensive arms race.[21]

---

20 See especially McNeill, *The Pursuit of Power. Technology, Armed Force, and Society since A.D. 1000*.

21 Eloranta, *External Security by Domestic Choices: Military Spending as an Impure Public Good among Eleven European States, 1920–1938*; Jari Eloranta, "National Defense," in *The Oxford Encyclopedia of Economic History*, ed. by Joel Mokyr (Oxford: Oxford University Press, 2003). Military spending patterns preceding the First World War are discussed in Jari Eloranta, "From the Great Illusion to the Great War: Military Spending Behaviour of the Great Powers, 1870–1913," *European Review of Economic History*, vol. 11, no. 2 (2007). See also Ferguson, *The Cash Nexus: Money and Power in the Modern World, 1700–2000*.

This military potential was unleashed in Europe with horrible consequences in 1914 in a war that many of the participants expected to win quickly; yet they ended up fighting a war of attrition in the trenches, at least in the Western front. The age of total war, which was probably already initiated during the Napoleonic conflicts, became a reality.[22] It has been estimated that circa nine million combatants and 12 million civilians died during the so-called "Great War," with property damage especially in France, Belgium, and Poland. According to Rondo Cameron and Larry Neal, the direct financial losses arising from the Great War were circa 180–230 billion 1914 US dollars, whereas the indirect losses of property and capital rose to over 150 billion dollars.[23] According to the most recent estimates, the economic losses arising from the war could be as high as 692 billion 1938 US dollars.[24] But how much of their resources did they have to mobilize and what were the human costs of the war?

As Table 9.1 displays, for example, the French military burden was fairly high, in addition to the size of its military forces and the number of battle deaths. France mobilized the most resources in the war and, subsequently, suffered the greatest losses. The mobilization by Germany was also quite efficient, because almost the entire state budget was used to support the war effort. On the other hand, for example, the United States barely participated in the war, and its personnel losses in the conflict were relatively small, as was its economic burden. In comparison, for example, the massive population of Russia enabled fairly high personnel losses, in a way quite similar to the Soviet experience in the Second World War.

In the interwar period, especially in the 1920s, public spending was very static. New strains on spending were, however, imposed by the pension and healthcare concerns arising from the war, as well as reconstruction expenses. This meant that, although in many countries except the authoritarian regimes, defense shares dropped noticeably, their respective military burdens stayed either at similar levels or even increased—for example, the French military burden rose to a mean level of 7.2 percent in this period. In Great Britain, also, the defense share mean dropped to 18 percent, although the military burden mean actually increased compared to the pre-war period, despite the military expenditure cuts and the "Ten-Year Rule" in the 1920s. The mid-1930s marked the beginning of intense rearmament for the reluctant democracies, whereas many of the authoritarian regimes had begun earlier in the decade. Germany under Hitler increased its military burden from 1.6 percent in 1933 to 18.9 percent in 1938, a rearmament program combining creative financing and promising both guns and butter for the Germans. Mussolini was not quite

---

22 The practice of total war, of course, is as old as civilizations themselves, ranging from the Punic Wars to the more modern conflicts. Here the term total war refers to the twentieth-century evolution of warfare, embodying the use of all economic, political, and military might of a nation to destroy another in industrialized conflict.

23 Rondo Cameron and Larry Neal, *A Concise Economic History of the World From Paleolithic Times to the Present*, 4th edn (Oxford: Oxford University Press, 2003), p. 339. Thus, the estimate in, for example, Eloranta, "National Defense" is the minimum estimate expressed in Gerard J. de Groot, *The First World War* (New York: Palgrave, 2001).

24 See Table 13 in Broadberry and Harrison, "The Economics of World War I: An Overview." The figures are, as the authors point out, only tentative.

as successful in his efforts to recreate the Roman Empire, with a military burden fluctuating between four and five percent in the 1930s. The Japanese rearmament drive, driven by a militaristic elite, was perhaps the most impressive, with a military burden as high as 22.7 percent and a defense share of over 50 percent in 1938. For many countries, such as France and Russia, the rapid pace of technological change in the 1930s unfortunately rendered many of the earlier armaments obsolete only two or three years later.[25]

Table 9.1 Resource mobilization by the great powers in the First and Second World War

Country and years in the war	Average military burden	Average defense share	Military personnel as a percentage of population	Battle deaths as a percentage of population
France:				
1914–1918	43	77	11	3.5
1939–1945	–	–	4.2	0.5
Germany:				
1914–1918	–	91	7.3	2.7
1939–1945	50	–	6.4	4.4
Russia/ Soviet Union:				
1914–1917	–	–	4.3	1.4
1939–1945	44	48	3.3	4.4
UK:				
1914–1918	22	49	7.3	2.0
1939–1945	45	69	6.2	0.9
USA:				
1917–1918	7.0	47	1.7	0.1
1941–1945	32	71	5.5	0.3

Source: For the First World War: Historical Statistics (*Historical Statistics of the United States, Colonial Times to 1970*, 1975), Fontvieille (1976), Mitchell (1998), Morgan (1952), Singer and Small (1993), Correlates of War Inter-State War Data, 1816-1997. Version 3.0. Available from: http://www.umich.edu/~cowproj/dataset.html#IntraStateWar, 2003. For the Second World War: In addition to the sources listed in the Appendix, Broadberry and Howlett (1998), Harrison (1998, 2000). The Soviet defense share only applies to years 1940–1945, whereas the military burden to 1940–1944. These two measures are not directly comparable, since the former is measured in current prices and the latter in constant prices. Note: Military burden: Military spending, per cent of GDP. Defense share: Military spending, per cent of central or federal government spending.

---

25 Eloranta, *External Security by Domestic Choices: Military Spending as an Impure Public Good among Eleven European States, 1920–1938*; Eloranta, "National Defense"; Carolyn Webber and Aaron Wildavsky, *A History of Taxation and Expenditure in the Western World* (New York: Simon and Schuster, 1986).

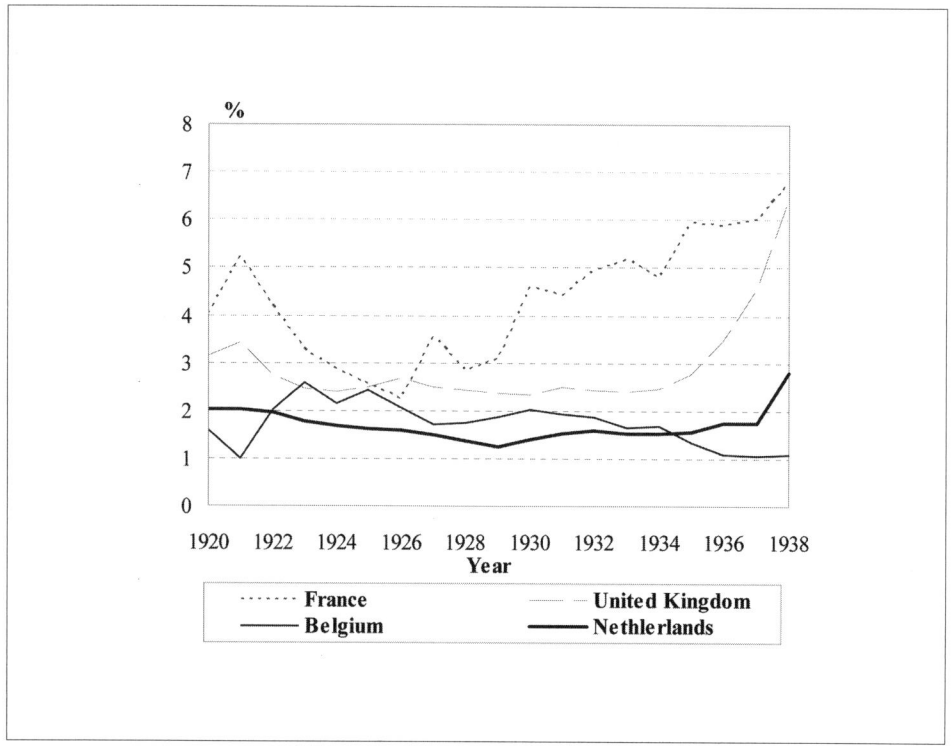

Figure 9.1 Military burdens of Belgium, France, the Netherlands, and the UK, 1920–1938

Source: Eloranta (2002).

There were differences between democracies as well, as seen in Figure 9.1. Some smaller countries behaved similarly to the UK and France, which belonged to a higher spending group among European democracies. This was also akin to the actions of most East European states. Belgium and the Netherlands were among the low-spending group, perhaps owing to the futility of trying to defend their borders amidst probable conflicts involving their giant neighbors, France and Germany. Overall, the democracies maintained fairly steady military burdens throughout the period. Their rearmament was, however, much slower than the effort amassed by most autocracies. This is also amply displayed in Figure 9.2.

In the ensuing conflict, the Second World War, the initial phase, from 1939 to early 1942, favored the Axis as far as strategic and economic resources and performance were concerned. After that, the war of attrition, with the United States and the USSR joining the Allies, turned the tide in favor of the Allies. For example, in 1943 the Allied total GDP was 2,223 billion international dollars (in 1990 prices), whereas the Axis accounted for only 895 billion. It seems plausible that the "rich" countries, which often were democracies, ultimately won this conflict owing to their superior resources and ability to mobilize even further than their more agricultural and authoritarian enemies. Also, the impact of the Second World War was much more profound for the participants' economies. For example, Great Britain at the height of the First World War incurred a military burden of circa 27 percent, whereas the military burden level consistently held throughout the Second World War was over 50 percent.[26]

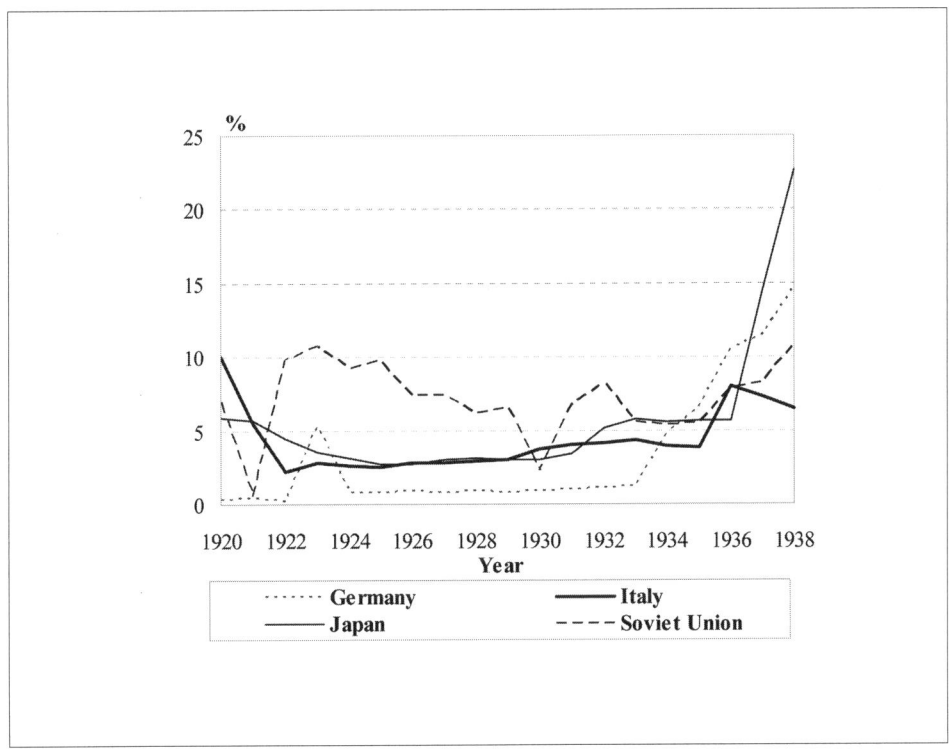

Figure 9.2 Military burdens of Germany, Italy, Japan, and Russia/USSR, 1920–1938

Source: Eloranta (2002), see especially Appendices for data sources. There are severe limitations and debates related to for example the German (see e.g. Abelshauser, 2000) and the Soviet data (see especially Davies, 1993, and Davies and Harrison 1997).

As Figure 9.2 shows, the greatest military burden was most likely incurred by Germany, even though the other Great Powers experienced similar levels. Only the massive economic resources of the United States made possible its lower military burden. Also the UK and the United States mobilized their central/federal

26   Eloranta, "National Defense."

government expenditures efficiently for the military effort. In a way, the Soviet Union fared the worst and, additionally, the share of military personnel out of the population was relatively small compared to the other Great Powers. On the other hand, the economic and demographic resources that the Soviet Union possessed ultimately ensured its survival during the German onslaught. On the aggregate, the largest personnel losses were incurred by Germany and the Soviet Union, in fact many times those of the other Great Powers.[27] In comparison with the First World War, the Second was even more destructive and lethal, and the aggregate economic losses exceeded even 4,000 billion 1938 US dollars. After the war, the European industrial and agricultural production amounted to only half of the 1938 total.[28]

The Cold War and Beyond

The end of the Second World War also brought with it a new role for the United States in world politics, a military-political leadership role warranted by its dominant economic status, established over 50 years earlier. With the establishment of NATO in 1949, a formidable defense alliance was formed by the major capitalist countries. The USSR, rising to new prominence owing to the war, established the Warsaw Pact in 1955 to counter these efforts. The war also meant a change in the public spending and taxation levels of most Western nations. The introduction of welfare states brought the OECD (Organization for Economic Co-operation and Development) government expenditure average from just below 30 percent of the GDP in the 1950s to over 40 percent in the 1970s. Military spending levels followed suit and peaked during the early Cold War. The American military burden climbed over 10 percent in 1952–54, and the United States retained a high mean value for the post-war period of 6.7 percent. Great Britain and France followed the American example after the Korean War.[29]

The Cold War embodied a relentless armaments race, with nuclear weapons now the main investment item, between the two superpowers (see Figure 3), with the USSR, according to some figures, spending circa 60 to 70 percent of the American level in the 1950s, and actually spending more than the United States in the 1970s. Nonetheless, the United States maintained a massive advantage over the Soviets

---

27   Mark Harrison, "The Economics of World War II: An Overview," in *The Economics of World War II: Six Great Powers in International Comparisons*, ed. by Mark Harrison (Cambridge: Cambridge University Press, 1998); Eloranta, "National Defense."

28   Cameron and Neal, *A Concise Economic History*; Mark Harrison, "The Economics of World War II: An Overview," in *The Economics of World War II: Six Great Powers in International Comparisons*, ed. by Mark Harrison (Cambridge: Cambridge University Press, 1998); Broadberry and Harrison, "The Economics of World War I: An Overview." Again, the same caveats apply to the Harrison-Broadberry figures as disclaimed earlier.

29   Eloranta, "National Defense."

in terms of nuclear warheads. Figures collected by SIPRI (Stockholm International Peace Research Institute) suggest an enduring, though dwindling, lead for the USA even in the 1970s. On the other hand, the same figures point to a 2-to-1 lead in favor of NATO countries over Warsaw Pact members in the 1970s and early 1980s. Part of this armaments race was due to technological advances that led to increases in the cost per soldier—it has been estimated that technological increases produced a mean annual increase in real costs of circa 5.5 percent in the post-war period. Nonetheless, spending on personnel and their maintenance remained the biggest spending item for most countries.

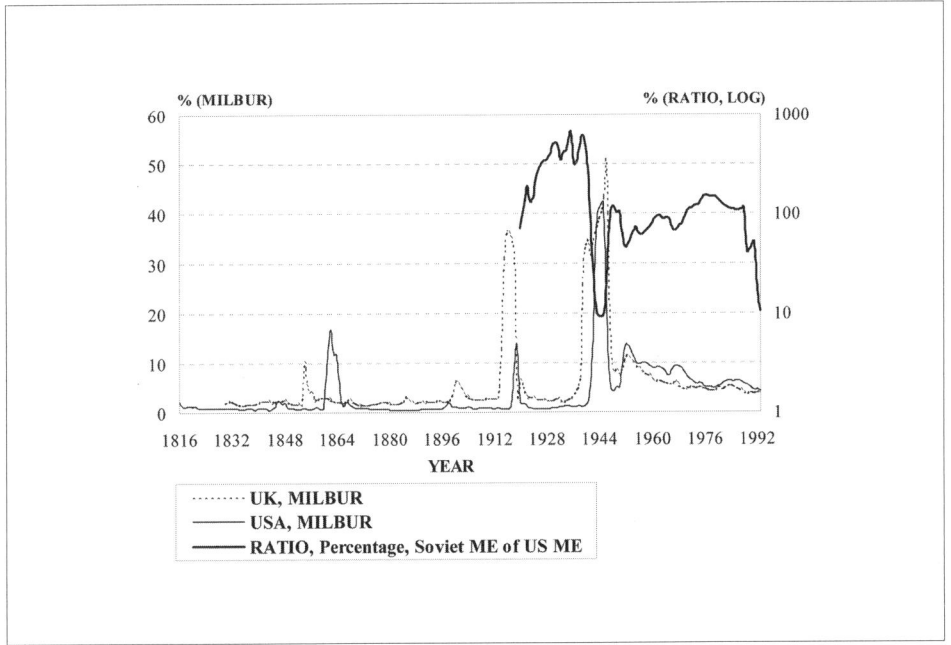

Figure 9.3 Military burdens (MILBUR) of the United States and the United Kingdom, and the Soviet Military spending as a percentage of the US military spending (ME), 1816–1993

Source: References to economic data can be found in Eloranta (2003). ME (Military Expenditure) data from Singer and Small (1993), supplemented with the SIPRI data for 1985-1993. Details available from the author by request. Exchange rates from Global Financial Data (Global Financial Data 2003). The usual caveats apply to using currency conversion instead of PPPs.

One outcome of this Cold War arms race that is often cited is the so-called "military industrial complex" (MIC), made famous by President Eisenhower in his farewell speech in 1961. This term usually refers to the influence that the military and industry have on each other's policies. The more nefarious connotation refers to the unduly large influence that military producers might develop over tax revenue and foreign policy, in particular, in such a collusive relationship. In fact, the origins of this type of interaction can be found further back in history, as far back as the late nineteenth century. As Paul Koistinen has emphasized, the First World War was a watershed in business–government relationships, since businessmen were often brought into government, to make supply decisions during such a massive conflict. Most governments, as a matter of fact, needed the expertise of the core business elites during the world wars. In the United States, some form of an MIC came into existence before 1940. Similar developments can be seen in other countries before the Second World War, for example in the Soviet Union. The Cold War simply reinforced these tendencies.[30] Findings by, for example, Robert Higgs indicate that the financial performance of the leading defense contracting companies was, on average, much better than that of comparable large corporations during the period 1948–1989. Nonetheless, his findings do not support the normative conclusion that the profits of defense contractors were "too high," arising from the possible emergence of MIC.[31]

The world military spending levels began a slow decline from the 1970s onwards, with the Reagan years being an exception for the USA. In 1986, the US military burden was 6.5 percent, whereas in 1999 it was down to three percent. During the period 1977–1999, the French military burden declined from the post-war peak levels in the 1950s to a mean level of 3.6 percent at the turn of the millennium. This was mostly the outcome of the reduction in tensions in the post-Cold War climate, as well as the downfall of the USSR and the communist regimes in Eastern Europe. The USSR was spending almost as much on its armed forces as the United States up until the mid-1980s, and the Soviet military burden was still 12.3 percent in 1990. Under the Russian Federation, with a declining GDP, this level dropped rapidly to 3.2 percent in 1998. Similarly, other nations downscaled their military spending in the late 1980s and the 1990s. For example, German military spending in constant USD was over 52 billion in 1991, whereas in 1999 it had declined to less than 40 billion. In the French case, the decline was from little over 52 billion in 1991 to below 47 billion USD in 1999, with its military burden decreasing from 3.6 percent to 2.8 percent.[32]

Overall, according to SIPRI figures, there was a reduction of circa one-third in real terms in world military spending in 1989–96. In the global scheme, world military expenditure was still highly concentrated in the hands of a few countries at the end of the twentieth century, with the 15 major spenders accounting for 80 percent of the world total in 1999. The newest military spending estimates, as seen

---

30 Mark Harrison, "Soviet Industry and the Red Army under Stalin: A Military-Industrial Complex?" *Les Cahiers du Monde russe*, 44, no. 2–3 (2003); Paul A.C. Koistinen, *The Military-Industrial Complex: A Historical Perspective, with a Foreword by Congressman Les Aspin* (New York: Praeger, 1980).

31 Robert Higgs, "The Cold War Economy: Opportunity Costs, Ideology, and the Politics of Crisis," *Explorations in Economic History*, vol. 31, no. 3 (1994).

32 Eloranta, "National Defense."

in Table 9.2, display a growth trend in the world military expenditures, once again owing to new threats such as international terrorism and interstate rivalries in the twenty-first century. In terms of absolute figures, the United States still dominates the world of military spending with a 47 percent share of the world total in 2003, although the US spending total becomes slightly less impressive when purchasing power parities (PPPs) are utilized. Nonetheless, the United States has entered the third millennium as the world's only real superpower—a role that it embraces sometimes awkwardly. Whereas the United States was an absent hegemony in the late nineteenth and first half of the twentieth centuries, it now has to maintain its presence in many parts of the world, sometimes despite objections from the other players in the international system.

Table 9.2 World military spending trends, 1988–2005

Region	1988	1992	1996	2000	2005
Africa	12.1	10.7	10.0	13.0	15.3
Americas	525	457	374	381	549
Asia and Oceania	102	118	128	139	176
Europe	513	326	279	287	309
Middle East	40.2	49.0	40.7	55.8	70.5
World	1193	960	831	876	1119

Source: Information from the Stockholm International Peace Research Institute (SIPRI) <http://www.sipri.org/contents/milap/milex/mex_wnr_table.html>. Figures are in constant 2005 US dollars, in billions.

Conclusions

The basic goals of this article were not only to review the military spending patterns in the twentieth century in light of the conflicting scholarly views on the period, but also to explore whether military spending contributed to the conflicts and economic performance of this era. It seems clear that the age of total war and industrial revolutions in the nineteenth and twentieth centuries finally pushed the most prominent nation states to adopt more efficient fiscal systems and enabled some of them to dedicate more than half of their GDP to the war effort during the world wars. Although military spending was regularly the biggest item in the budget for most states in the beginning of the twentieth century, it still represented only a modest amount of their respective GDPs. The Cold War period again saw high relative spending levels, owing to the enduring rivalry between the West and the Communist bloc. Finally, the collapse of the Soviet Union alleviated some of these tensions and lowered the aggregate military spending in the world, if only temporarily. Newer security challenges such as terrorism and various interstate rivalries have again pushed the world towards a growth path in terms of overall military spending.

The cost of warfare has increased in the last centuries. The adoption of new technologies and massive standing armies has kept military expenditures in a central role for modern fiscal regimes. Although the growth of welfare states in the twentieth century has forced some trade-offs between "guns and butter," usually the spending choices have not been mutually exclusive. Thus, the size and spending of governments have increased. Even though the growth in welfare spending has abated somewhat since the 1980s, according to Peter Lindert they will most likely still experience at least modest expansion in the future. Nor is it likely that military spending will be displaced as a major spending item in national budgets. Various international threats and the lack of international cooperation will ensure that military spending will remain the main contender to social expenditures.[33] As the recent Iraq war and several articles on the costs of the war and deficit spending prove, this debate over "guns versus butter" is alive and well.[34]

Military spending (or any kind of government spending) is often argued to crowd out investment, although the evidence on the economic impacts of military spending is conflicting. The analysis of the conversion of military resources into civilian use, in order to achieve the so-called "peace dividend," implying a positive economic growth effect from the said conversion, seems to yield contradictory results as to whether this has any significant economic consequences.[35] Moreover, advocates of hegemonic perspective, for example Paul Kennedy, have argued that uneven economic growth "inevitably" causes the world's leading states to embark on increasing, costly military spending, opening opportunities for challengers. The results of empirical research on hegemonic cycles are, however, still quite mixed. Research on the economic growth impact of military spending, mostly performed with post-Second World War data, has discovered, based on the argument that military spending crowds out investment, a negative demand-side growth impact.

---

33 For more, see especially Ferguson, *The Cash Nexus: Money and Power in the Modern World, 1700–2000*; Peter H. Lindert, *Growing Public: Social Spending and Economic Growth since the Eighteenth Century*, 2 vols (Cambridge: Cambridge University Press, 2004), vol. 1. On tradeoffs, see, for example, David R. Davis and Steve Chan, "The Security-Welfare Relationship: Longitudinal Evidence from Taiwan," *Journal of Peace Research*, vol. 27, no. 1 (1990); Herschel I. Grossman and Juan Mendoza, "Butter *and* Guns: Complementarity between Economic and Military Competition," *Economics of Governance*, no. 2 (2001), Alex Mintz, "Guns Versus Butter: A Disaggregated Analysis," *The American Political Science Review*, vol. 83, no. 4 (1989); Mintz and Huang, "Guns Versus Butter: The Indirect Link;" Kevin Narizny, "Both Guns and Butter, or Neither: Class Interests in the Political Economy of Rearmament," *American Political Science Review*, vol. 97, no. 2 (2003).

34 See, for example, Holman W. Jenkins Jr, "An Oldie but Goodie: Guns Plus Butter," *The Wall Street Journal* (November 26, 2003); Christopher DeMuth, "Guns, Butter and the War on Terror," *The Wall Street Journal* (April 29, 2004).

35 See, for example, Steve Chan, "Grasping the Peace Dividend: Some Propositions on the Conversion of Swords into Plowshares," *Mershon International Studies Review*, vol. 39, no. 1 (1995).

Nonetheless, in contrast, most supply-side models have pointed toward a small positive growth impact or none at all.

Certainly, research on the twentieth-century military spending trends has contributed, at best, conflicting results. One cannot deny that arms races have contributed greatly to the severity and scope of the conflicts in this period, but it seems probable that investments in military technology have had positive economic outcomes as well. Unfortunately, the rapid technological development has also increased the "bang for the buck," that is, the destructive efficiency of military spending, leading to larger and more destructive conflicts.

References

Black, Jeremy, *European Warfare in a Global Context, 1660–1815* (London: Routledge, 2007)

Blainey, Geoffrey, *The Causes of War* (New York: Free Press, 1973)

Broadberry, Stephen and Mark Harrison, eds, *The Economics of World War I* (Cambridge: Cambridge University Press, 2005)

Cameron, Rondo and Larry Neal, *A Concise Economic History of the World From Paleolithic Times to the Present*, 4th edn (Oxford: Oxford University Press, 2003)

Chan, Steve, "Grasping the Peace Dividend: Some Propositions on the Conversion of Swords into Plowshares," *Mershon International Studies Review*, vol. 39, no. 1 (1995): 53–95

Davies, R.W., "Soviet Military Expenditure and the Armaments Industry, 1929–33: A Reconsideration," *Europe-Asia Studies*, vol. 45, no. 4 (1993): 577–608

Davies, R.W. and M. Harrison, "The Soviet Military-Economic Effort under the Second Five-Year Plan 1933–1937," *Europe-Asia Studies*, vol. 49, no. 3 (1997): 369–406

Davis, David R. and Steve Chan, "The Security-Welfare Relationship: Longitudinal Evidence from Taiwan," *Journal of Peace Research*, vol. 27, no. 1 (1990): 87–100

De Groot, Gerald J., *The First World War* (New York: Palgrave, 2001)

DeLong, J. Bradford, *Cornucopia: The Pace of Economic Growth in the Twentieth Century* (National Bureau of Economic Research, 2000), <http://papers.nber.org/papers/W7602.pdf>

DeMuth, Christopher, "Guns, Butter and the War on Terror," *The Wall Street Journal* (New York, Eastern edn, April 29, 2004), p. A16

Eloranta, J., *Different Needs, Different Solutions: The Importance of Economic Development and Domestic Power Structures in Explaining Military Spending in Eight Western Democracies During the Interwar Period* (Licentiate Thesis, University of Jyväskylä, 1998)

———, *External Security by Domestic Choices: Military Spending as an Impure Public Good among Eleven European States, 1920–1938* (Dissertation, European University Institute, 2002)

–––, "National Defense," in J. Mokyr, ed., *The Oxford Encyclopedia of Economic History* (Oxford: Oxford University Press, 2003), pp. 30–33

–––, (2006) "Military Spending Patterns in History," in *EH.Net Encyclopedia*, ed. by R. Whaples, <http://eh.net/encyclopedia/article/eloranta.military> [accessed March 16, 2008]

–––, "From the Great Illusion to the Great War: Military Spending Behaviour of the Great Powers, 1870–1913," *European Review of Economic History*, vol. 11, no. 2 (2007): 255–83

Fearon, James D., "Rationalist Explanations for War," *International Organization*, vol. 49, no. 3 (1995): 379–414

Ferguson, N., *The Cash Nexus: Money and Power in the Modern World, 1700–2000* (New York: Basic, 2001)

–––, *The War of the World: Twentieth-Century Conflict and the Descent of the West* (New York: Penguin, 2006)

Field, Alexander J., "The Most Technologically Progressive Decade of the Century," *American Economic Review*, 93 (September 2003): 1,399–1,414

–––, "Technical Change and U.S. Economic Growth: The Interwar Period and the 1990s," in Paul Rhode and Gianni Toniolo, eds, *The Global Economy in the 1990s: A Long Run Perspective* (Cambridge: Cambridge University Press, 2006), pp. 89–117

Fontvieille, L., *Evolution Et Croissance De L'etat Français: 1815–1969, Economies Et Sociétés* (Paris, 1976)

Geller, Daniel S. and J. David Singer, *Nations at War: A Scientific Study of International Conflict*, vol. 58, *Cambridge Studies in International Relations* (Cambridge: Cambridge University Press, 1998)

Global Financial Data (2003), <http://www.globalfindata.com> [accessed January 3, 2003]

Grossman, Herschel I. and Juan Mendoza, "Butter *and* Guns: Complementarity between Economic and Military Competition," *Economics of Governance*, no. 2 (2001): 25–33

Harrison, M., ed., *The Economics of World War II: Six Great Powers in International Comparisons* (Cambridge: Cambridge University Press, 1998)

–––, "Soviet Industry and the Red Army under Stalin: A Military-Industrial Complex?" *Les Cahiers du Monde russe*, 44, no. 2–3 (2003): 323–42

Higgs, Robert, "The Cold War Economy. Opportunity Costs, Ideology, and the Politics of Crisis," *Explorations in Economic History*, vol. 31, no. 3 (1994): 283–312

Historical Statistics of the United States, Colonial Times to 1970 (Washington, DC, 1975)

Hobsbawm, E.J., *The Age of Extremes: A History of the World, 1914–1991* (New York: Vintage, 1996)

Jenkins Jr, Holman W., "An Oldie but Goodie: Guns Plus Butter," *The Wall Street Journal* (New York, Eastern edn, November 26, 2003), p. A17

Kennedy, P., *The Rise and Fall of the Great Powers. Economic Change and Military Conflict from 1500 to 2000* (London: Fontana, 1989)

Koistinen, Paul A.C., *The Military-Industrial Complex: A Historical Perspective, with a Foreword by Congressman Les Aspin* (New York: Praeger, 1980)

Levy, Jack S., "Theories of General War," *World Politics*, vol. 37, no. 3 (1985): 344–74

Lindert, Peter H., *Voice and Growth: Was Churchill Right?* (Cambridge, MA: National Bureau of Economic Research, 2003)

———, *Growing Public: Social Spending and Economic Growth since the Eighteenth Century*, 2 vols (Cambridge, 2004), vol. 1

McNeill, William H., *The Pursuit of Power: Technology, Armed Force, and Society since A.D. 1000* (Chicago: University of Chicago Press, 1982)

Milward, Alan S., *The German Economy at War* (London: Athlon, 1965)

———, *War, Economy and Society 1939–1945* (London: Allen Lane, 1977)

Mintz, Alex, "Guns Versus Butter: A Disaggregated Analysis," *The American Political Science Review*, vol. 83, no. 4 (1989): 1,285–93

Mintz, Alex and Chi Huang, "Guns Versus Butter: The Indirect Link," *American Journal of Political Science*, vol. 35, no. 1 (1991): 738–57

Mitchell, B.R., *International Historical Statistics: Europe 1750–1993*, 4th edn (Basingstoke: Macmillan, 1998)

Modelski, George and William R. Thompson, *Seapower in Global Politics, 1494–1993* (Basingstoke: Macmillan, 1988)

———, *Leading Sectors and World Powers: The Coevolution of Global Politics and Economics, Studies in International Relations* (Columbia, SC: University of South Carolina Press, 1996)

Morgan, E.V., *Studies in British Financial Policy, 1914–1925* (London: Macmillan, 1952)

Narizny, Kevin, "Both Guns and Butter, or Neither: Class Interests in the Political Economy of Rearmament," *American Political Science Review*, vol. 97, no. 2 (2003): 203–20

Pearton, Maurice, *The Knowledgeable State: Diplomacy, War, and Technology since 1830* (London: Burnett, 1982)

Pollins, Brian M. and Randall L. Schweller, "Linking the Levels: The Long Wave and Shifts in U.S. Foreign Policy, 1790–1993," *American Journal of Political Science*, vol. 43, no. 2 (1999): 445–6

Rummel, R.J., *Power Kills: Democracy as a Method of Nonviolence* (New Brunswick, NJ: Transaction, 1997)

Sandler, Todd and Keith Hartley, *The Economics of Defense*, ed. by Mark Perlman, *Cambridge Surveys of Economic Literature* (Cambridge: Cambridge University Press, 1995)

Singer, J.D. and M. Small, *National Material Capabilities Data, 1816–1985* (Ann Arbor, MI: J. David Singer, University of Michigan; Detroit, MI: Melvin Small, Wayne State University [producers], 1993) [accessed January 5, 2003]

Tilly, Charles, *Coercion, Capital, and European States, AD 990–1990* (Cambridge, MA: Basil Blackwell, 1990)

Webber, Carolyn and Aaron Wildavsky, *A History of Taxation and Expenditure in the Western World* (New York: Simon and Schuster, 1986)

Wright, Quincy, *A Study of War* (Chicago, IL: University of Chicago Press, 1942)

The Politics of the Contemporary Trade in Major Conventional Weapons

Mark Phythian

Introduction

Andrew J. Pierre memorably termed arms sales 'foreign policy writ large'.[1] This characterisation reflected the fact that, during the era of the Cold War and decolonisation, for a number of suppliers, but especially the two superpowers, the transfer of arms was a highly political act. At the same time, recipients viewed certain types of weapon – particularly jet fighter aircraft – as symbols of statehood. Arms transfers conferred a mark of legitimacy on the recipient and served as a signal of superpower support. Even amongst second-tier suppliers, such as the UK and France, political factors were far from absent from calculations concerning the transfer of arms, even though economic imperatives were more pressing here than at the superpower level. Although economic justifications came to assume a greater importance in the less ideological post-Cold War era, a time during which the arms market increasingly came to be a buyers' market, as this chapter indicates the arms trade remains highly politicised. In making this point, the chapter offers a guide to key issues in the study of the contemporary arms trade. It discusses arms trade statistics, analyses the nature of the contemporary market, including the impact of the post-9/11 'war on terror', as well as human rights and ethical issues. Finally, it discusses the progress that has been made in introducing a degree of transparency to the trade in major conventional weapons over the last decade.

---

1   Andrew J. Pierre, *The Global Politics of Arms Sales* (Princeton, NJ: Princeton University Press, 1982), p. 3.

Arms Trade Statistics

For those looking to gain an understanding of the scale and nature of the international arms trade, various sets of statistics exist to aid the endeavour, although all have their limitations. While some figures are based on the value of orders, the most reliable are those based on actual weapons deliveries, as not all orders translate into sales for a range of economic and political reasons. A general trend towards greater transparency on the part of exporters, particularly those who are members of (or seek membership of) the European Union (EU) (discussed below) has meant that arms trade statistics are becoming more authoritative. The most detailed breakdown is to be found in the figures published by some national governments, although the thoroughness of these and regularity with which they are published are variable.

While these provide important sources of information at a national level, for comparative purposes, in order to understand the relative significance of exports and imports two further sets of statistics are important. The US Congressional Research Service's annual survey of *Conventional Arms Transfers to the Developing World*, produced by Richard Grimmett,[2] gives a US dollar value for both arms agreements and arms transfers to the developing world. Although, as the publication's title indicates, it excludes transfers to developed countries, Grimmett's reports are authoritative statements on the contemporary arms market. The second set is that provided by the Stockholm International Peace Research Institute (SIPRI). These figures are based on deliveries and are expressed in what SIPRI calls 'trend indicator values' (TIV). These aim to give a reliable picture of trends in the international arms trade but are not simply based on the actual financial value of arms deliveries. Although SIPRI has recently begun to offer broad financial values for the annual trade,[3] which do not reveal any significant changes to its existing, TIV-based, top rankings of arms exporters or importers, arriving at financial values is complicated by the absence of a common definition of 'arms' or 'weapons' amongst the states that compile and publish the data from which an overall estimate can be attempted.[4]

---

2   These are available via the Federation of American Scientists' Arms Sales Monitoring Project: <http://www.fas.org/programs/ssp/asmp/index.html>. Grimmett's report on the period 2000–2007 is available at <http://www.fas.org/sgp/crs/weapons/RL34723.pdf>.

3   As SIPRI explains: 'TIVs do not represent the financial value of goods transferred. Instead, TIVs are an indication of the volume of arms transferred. Hence, TIVs can be used to measure trends in international arms transfers, such as changes in the total flow of weapons and the geographic pattern of arms exports or imports. The data can also be used to measure a particular country's share of the overall import or export market or the rate of increase or decline in its imports or exports. However, since TIVs do not represent the financial value of the goods transferred, they are not comparable to official economic data such as gross domestic product or export/import figures.' <http://www.sipri.org/contents/armstrad/output_types_TIV.html>.

4   See Paul Holtom, Mark Bromley and Pieter D. Wezeman, 'International Arms Transfers', in *SIPRI Yearbook 2008: Armaments, Disarmament and International Security* (Oxford: Oxford University Press, 2008), p. 296.

Hence, there is considerable merit to SIPRI's TIV approach, especially in terms of its reliability as trend analysis.

The major limitation with regard to SIPRI's figures is that they are of deliveries of *major* conventional weapons and do not include, for example, small arms and light weapons, ammunition, or the supply of spare parts and training.[5] By definition, however, these would have little impact on the statistics that SIPRI produces. SIPRI's data is both authoritative and openly accessible via the SIPRI website.[6] However, the best way to develop a thorough understanding of the nature and scale of the international arms trade is to view all of these sets of data in conjunction with each other, rather than to simply rely on any one set.[7]

Market Issues

The international arms market has been through several phases in the years since 1945, with an overall trend of a shift from a suppliers' market to a buyers' market.[8] This shift has become more pronounced since the end of the Cold War, reflecting the collapse of the Cold War barriers to trading across the old power blocs as well as continued growth in the number of suppliers. In part, this has been a consequence of the number of post-Soviet republics seeking to sell arms, of which Ukraine, Belarus and Uzbekistan have become leading exporters (see Table 10.1). All of this means that the contemporary trade in major arms is highly competitive. However, within this, suppliers can specialise in either types of equipment (for example, aircraft, naval vessels, armoured vehicles, and so on) or at different levels of technological sophistication, allowing for the development (or, at least, pursuit) of market niches.

After years of constant decline, the international market in major conventional weapons is, according to SIPRI data, once again on the rise. As Table 10.1 indicates, the actual value of the trade in major conventional weapons declined in 2007 from 2006, but the general post-2002 upward trend in the market looks set to continue. SIPRI estimates that the financial value of the trade in 2006 was US$45.6 billion, a mere 0.4 per cent of total world trade.[9] The top five leading suppliers of major conventional weapons during 2006 included four of the five permanent members of the UN Security Council – the US, Russia, France and the UK. Along with Germany, these states have consistently comprised the leading suppliers, as measured by

---

5   For an explanation of what the figures do and do not cover, see <http://www.sipri.org/contents/armstrad/coverage.html>.

6   <www.sipri.org/>.

7   Having said that, given the overview nature of this chapter and the inevitable limitations of space, the data and analysis here will be based solely on SIPRI TIVs.

8   For a detailed overview, see Mark Phythian, *The Politics of British Arms Sales Since 1964* (Manchester: Manchester University Press, 2000), Ch. 1.

9   Holtom et al., 'International Arms Transfers', in *SIPRI Yearbook 2008*, p. 295.

SIPRI, since 1993, collectively accounting for approximately 80 per cent of the trade. Although Russian weapons exports were at roughly the same level as those of the US in the years 2001–04 (and exceeded the value of those from the US in 2002), trend analysis highlights the dominance of the US, whose weapons exports for the period 1997–2007 were greater than those of the next three lead exporters (Russia, France and Germany) combined.

In short, the post-Cold War years have seen the US entrench its position as the world's leading supplier of choice of military hardware, as measured in both the range of states to which it supplied weapons (it supplied major weapons to 95 states in the 1997–2007 period, with France and Germany both supplying 68 and Russia 63), as well as the volume of deliveries. The post-9/11 'war on terror' has helped cement this position by loosening restrictions on the export of US weapons or leading to the lifting of embargoes in order for states to be able to assume their share of 'war on terror' partnership.[10] Nowhere has this impact been clearer than in relation to the US arms export relationship with Pakistan, which has seen a return to the kind of relationship that pertained under the rule of General Zia where, for geopolitical reasons relating to prioritising the arming of the mujahidin opposing the Soviet occupation of neighbouring Afghanistan, the US sought to ignore Pakistan's contravention of nuclear non-proliferation norms in favour of short-term strategic calculations.[11] In return for its role in the 'war on terror' Pakistan has been rewarded via the lifting of the embargo imposed on it and India following their 1998 tit-for-tat nuclear tests. Moreover, in June 2004 Pakistan was designated a major non-NATO ally, freeing it up to receive second-hand US weapons. In 2006, the Bush administration succumbed to an increasingly technologically advanced Pakistani weapons wishlist and agreed to supply it with 26 second-hand F-16 combat aircraft (capable of delivering Pakistani nuclear weapons), despite congressional unease at the prospect. The first of these were delivered in mid-2007.[12]

The official rationale for the sale of F-16 combat aircraft to Pakistan was their usefulness in counter-terrorist operations, even though they are hardly the archetypal counter-terrorist weapon. As Donald Camp, the Principal Deputy Assistant Secretary for South and Central Asian Affairs, told the House of Representatives in July 2008: 'The new and enhanced F-16s will provide Pakistan the ability to attack fleeing targets with precision during all weather conditions.'[13] The 'war on terror', and in particular the argument that regional allies need to be

---

10 For an early analysis, see Human Rights Watch, 'Dangerous Dealings: Changes to US Military Assistance After September 11' (February 2002), <http://www.hrw.org/reports/2002/usmil/>.

11 For an analysis, see Adrian Levy and Catherine Scott-Clark, *Deception: Pakistan, the United States and the Global Nuclear Weapons Conspiracy* (London: Atlantic Books, 2007).

12 See Richard F. Grimmett, *US Arms Sales to Pakistan* (CRS Report for Congress, 8 November 2007), <http://www.fas.org/asmp/resources/110th/CRS22757.pdf>.

13 Donald Camp, Principal Deputy Assistant Secretary for South and Central Asian Affairs, 'Defeating al-Qaeda's Air Force: Pakistan's F-16 Program in the Fight against Terrorism', Statement Before the US House of Representatives Foreign Affairs Subcommittee on South Asia (16 September 2008), <http://www.state.gov/p/sca/ci/af/2008/109757.htm>.

armed to face a resurgent and threatening Iran, has also been used to justify a new round of US weapons sales to the Gulf region. It has also been employed to counter concern expressed in some quarters of Congress that sales of weapons to Saudi Arabia, such as the Joint Direct Attack Munition (JDAM) guided bomb, widely used by US forces in the conflicts in Iraq and Afghanistan, might endanger Israel or even the US.[14]

Table 10.2 illustrates the way in which Asia has supplanted the Middle East as the primary market for major conventional weapons over the last decade, with Asian states accounting for four of the top five importers and all of the top three. In the period 1997–2007, the world's leading importer of major weapons by some margin was China. Ninety-two per cent of these came from Russia (France, Ukraine, the UK, Israel and Germany accounting for most of the remaining eight per cent), and accounted for 42 per cent of all Russian exports of major conventional arms in the same period.[15] China has little option but to source its arms from Russia given the continued existence of EU and US 'embargoes' on the sale of weapons to China, imposed in the wake of the Chinese state response to protests in Tiananmen Square in 1989, although it is making progress in further developing its own domestic weapons industry. While the EU embargo has restricted China's access to military technology and products, it is hardly watertight and has allowed EU states such as France, the UK, and Germany to export a range of military equipment, with France and UK emerging as the second and fourth most valuable exporters of major weapons to China in the 1997–2007 period after Russia and separated only by the Ukraine. This reflects the fact that there is no common EU definition of what constitutes 'weapons, and equipment which could be used for internal repression' – the wording of the June 1989 EU embargo – in relation to China. Hence, each EU member has interpreted this in its own way, creating export space. It also reflects the fact that, with 27 member states who must all agree before an EU embargo can be imposed or lifted, the enlarged EU is one in which consensus on embargoes is more and more difficult to obtain, meaning that it will be more difficult to implement them in the future and perhaps even more so to lift them.

With regard to China, a division has emerged within the EU between those states which believe that the embargo should be maintained, and those states such as France and Germany (that is, the more significant arms exporters), which argue that it should be lifted. In January 2004, French President Jacques Chirac went so far as to talk of the embargo as being something that 'no longer corresponds with the political reality of the contemporary world'.[16] The position of the UK is complicated by the fact that it is both a major exporter and, at the same time, somewhat constrained in

---

14   William Matthews, 'Lawmakers Caution White House on Proposed JDAM Sale to Saudi Arabia', *Defense News* (19 November 2007); Tony Cappacio, 'Lawmakers Question Sale of Boeing's Smart-Bomb Kit to Saudis', *Bloomberg News* (19 November 2007).

15   Information from the SIPRI Arms Transfer Database, <http://armstrade.sipri.org/>.

16   Cited in Siemon T. Wezeman and Mark Bromley, 'International Arms Transfers', in *SIPRI Yearbook 2005: Armaments, Disarmament and Security* (Oxford: Oxford Universiy Press, 2005), p. 439.

calling, along with Germany and France, for a lifting of the embargo by its alliance with the US (as well as by a domestic human rights lobby).

The US has been insistent that the embargo remain, and the pressure it has been able to bring to bear on some newer EU members is one factor in the absence of an EU consensus on lifting the embargo.[17] This US insistence has several sources, but is particularly felt on the conservative right, perhaps less because of the legacy of Tiananmen Square and more because lifting it would help to accelerate China's military modernisation, thus hastening the arrival of the global challenge to the US that many conservatives anticipate and also heightening Taiwanese insecurity.[18] Hence, the embargo is formally retained and while at one level it prevents the export of major offensive weapons systems, at another it is becoming something of a polite fiction, as well as a clear source of transatlantic dispute.

The second largest market for major conventional weapons between 1997 and 2007 was India, also Russia's largest market. India accounted for 22 per cent of Russia's exports during this period, while Russia supplied 71 per cent of India's imports. Other significant Indian suppliers have included Israel, France and the UK. US efforts to penetrate the market have been hampered by both the US arms export relationship with Pakistan and the premium that India attaches to the need for unbroken supply in times of tension or conflict. In this respect, the history of US sanctions applied to India to indicate displeasure at its behaviour – for example, over its 1998 nuclear tests – has had a negative impact on its arms sales prospects, with India preferring Russian arms, despite periodic frustrations over delivery times and technical problems, to US arms which carry with them the risk of interrupted supply.

Post-9/11 US weapons exports to Pakistan have certainly done nothing to improve the US's prospects of penetrating the Indian market, thereby lessening Russian influence. The status of the US-Pakistan arms sales relationship is monitored closely in India, as is Pakistani use of US weapons. As US-Pakistani tensions grew over the covert use of US forces and weapons in and over Pakistani territory in 2008, the Indian media was able to report on the possibility that US forces might well be attacked with the very combat aircraft they had just delivered to Pakistan, after the Pakistan Air Force reportedly deployed its F-16s to challenge US drones operating in its airspace as well as an unsanctioned airborne mission that landed US Navy Seals inside Pakistan.[19]

---

17   For a US perspective, see Kristin Archick, Richard F. Grimmett and Shirley Kan, *European Union's Arms Embargo on China: Implications and Options for US Policy* (CRS, April 2005), <http://fpc.state.gov/documents/organization/45458.pdf>.

18   For a US conservative perspective, see, for example, Peter Brookes, 'The Lifting of the EU Arms Embargo on China: A US Perspective' (March 2005), on the Heritage Foundation website, at <http://www.heritage.org/research/europe/hl866.cfm>.

19   'US Faces the F-16s It Supplied Pakistan', *The Times of India* (14 September 2008), <http://timesofindia.indiatimes.com/File_US_faces_the_F-16s_it_supplied_Pakistan/articleshow/3482718.cms>.

Table 10.1 Leading exporters of major conventional weapons, 1997–2007*

		1997	1998	1999	2000	2001	2002	2003	2004	2005	2006	2007	1997–2007
1.	USA	14280	15376	11476	7505	5801	4984	5581	6616	7026	7821	7454	93921
2.	Russia	2958	2046	3924	4190	5631	5458	5355	6400	5576	6463	4588	52590
3.	France	3085	3340	1788	1033	1235	1342	1313	2267	1688	1586	2690	21367
4.	Germany	872	1754	1719	1622	825	910	1707	1017	1879	2891	3395	18591
5.	UK	2393	1211	1129	1356	1116	772	624	1143	871	978	1151	12743
6.	Netherlands	606	584	318	259	192	243	342	218	611	1575	1355	6302
7.	Ukraine	566	655	760	280	661	244	397	354	308	563	109	4898
8.	Italy	440	420	512	192	224	408	311	210	818	694	562	4793
9.	China	458	401	299	228	507	561	580	288	271	562	355	4512
10.	Sweden	84	319	372	308	850	125	468	287	536	437	413	4199
11.	Israel	229	191	124	316	298	365	309	561	280	246	238	3157
12.	Spain	638	164	30	46	7	120	158	56	133	825	529	2705
13.	Canada	89	34	75	109	129	182	276	302	206	210	343	1955
14.	Belarus	416	58	476	293	299	56	80	50	24	35		1788
15.	Switzerland	66	43	82	104	102	102	120	217	196	208	211	1451
16.	Poland	20	1	67	43	70	43	72	43	17	255	135	766
17.	South Korea	60	72		8	165		104	20	32	80	214	755
18.	Uzbekistan						73	340	170	4			587
19.	Belgium	90	39	39	22	36	34	15	47	171	58	10	561
20.	Slovakia	54	10	151	92	73	44		79		7		510
	Others	699	309	655	271	457	692	599	743	609	728	456	6218
	Total	28105	27026	23997	18278	18677	16759	18750	21089	21256	26223	24210	244369

Note: Values are SIPRI trend indicator values expressed in US$m at constant (1990) prices. * Information from the SIPRI Arms Transfer Database <http://armstrade.sipri.org/>. The absence of a figure indicates that the value of deliveries is less than US$0.5m.

Table 10.2 Leading importers of major conventional weapons, 1997–2007*

		1997	1998	1999	2000	2001	2002	2003	2004	2005	2006	2007	1997–2007
1.	China	741	292	1684	1874	3234	2636	2068	2906	3346	3719	1424	23923
2.	India	1659	749	1056	826	924	1613	2870	2331	1182	1404	1318	15933
3.	Taiwan	4936	4066	1725	598	416	299	101	341	794	608	3	13887
4.	Greece	804	1681	863	651	700	480	2226	1498	540	817	2089	12348
5.	South Korea	1048	1404	1548	1266	583	336	575	967	661	1527	1807	11721
6.	Turkey	1485	2464	1593	1042	430	887	433	174	984	317	944	10755
7.	UAE	686	754	414	309	182	208	700	1436	2224	2067	1040	10020
8.	Saudi Arabia	2805	2518	1226	81	59	550	159	952	148	185	72	8755
9.	Egypt	1060	523	509	826	804	827	816	752	736	1020	418	8291
10.	Israel	68	1370	1217	364	147	325	292	845	1108	1102	891	7730
11.	Japan	880	1511	1276	431	499	426	465	412	299	477	519	7195
12.	Australia	27	523	634	366	1237	711	864	558	560	765	685	6930
13.	UK	675	897	57	808	1227	713	787	135	16	332	698	6346
14.	Pakistan	705	703	859	160	397	528	592	385	333	321	715	5699
15.	USA	575	258	206	268	391	430	501	523	476	514	587	4728
16.	Singapore	576	740	241	612	210	235	70	384	543	47	707	4365
17.	Canada	311	107	199	560	522	389	127	317	110	120	623	3384
18.	Iran	192	385	325	413	496	320	198	136	86	450	297	3299
19.	Italy	544	45	20	241	262	168	516	434	136	702	176	3246
20.	Algeria	35	103	411	428	554	233	197	272	152	125	700	3209
	Others	8295	5932	7933	6154	5403	4443	4191	5331	6824	9602	8495	72604
	Total	28105	27026	23997	18278	18677	16759	18750	21089	21256	26223	24210	244369

Note: Values are SIPRI trend indicator values expressed in US$m at constant (1990) prices. * Information from the SIPRI Arms Transfer Database <http://armstrade.sipri.org/>.

Table 10.3 Leading markets of leading suppliers, 1997–2007

	USA	Russia	France	Germany	UK
1.	Taiwan: 9895	China: 22074	UAE: 5203	Turkey: 2744	S. Arabia: 1803
2.	S. Korea: 8619	India: 11379	Taiwan: 3939	Greece: 2282	USA: 1675
3.	Japan: 6795	Iran: 2076	Greece: 1399	Australia: 1653	Canada: 1266
4.	Israel: 6600	Algeria: 2009	S. Arabia: 1313	S. Africa: 1298	Malaysia: 854
5.	Egypt: 6275	Venezuela: 1334	S. Korea: 1059	Israel: 1088	India: 600
6.	Turkey: 5849	Greece: 1278	Pakistan: 1041	S. Korea: 993	Jordan: 516
7.	Greece: 5353	Vietnam: 1271	Turkey: 913	Spain: 963	Italy: 509
8.	S. Arabia: 5289	Yemen: 1119	Brazil: 743	Sweden: 755	Australia: 506
9.	UK: 4753	Egypt: 1082	Singapore: 717	UK: 671	Chile: 472
10.	UAE: 3351	Eritrea: 779	Qatar: 659	Italy: 642	Romania: 422

Note: Values are SIPRI trend indicator values expressed in US$m at constant (1990) prices.

Emblematic of India's problems with Russia as its principal weapons supplier is the saga of the *Admiral Gorshkov*, a Kiev class aircraft carrier sold to India in 2004, to be delivered by 2008. This was originally sold at a price of US$1.5 billion, which the Russians subsequently raised by some US$1.2 billion while at the same time putting the delivery date back to 2011 or 2012, placing considerable strain on the arms sales relationship.[20] Still, Russia remains the preferred supplier of combat aircraft to India, and in late 2007 the two countries signed an agreement to jointly develop a fifth generation multi-role jet fighter.[21] India is not the only recipient to voice dissatisfaction with Russian arms. Aside from this saga, dissatisfaction with Russian arms has been most evident with regard to Algeria which, in 2008, took the drastic step of returning 15 MiG-29s bought under reasonably favourable terms and delivered during 2006–07, and refusing to accept delivery of a scheduled further 15 owing to the low-quality parts used in the aircraft.[22]

Elsewhere, Russia has sought to lessen its export dependence on China and India by developing its arms export ties with Iran, Malaysia, and Venezuela,[23] where the oil-rich government of Hugo Chavez hinted that it might turn to Russian MiG-29 combat aircraft after the US refused to allow Israel to upgrade Venezuela's ageing fleet of US F-16 aircraft. Given the frosty relationship the Chavez government has with the US, on present trends Venezuela is likely to see its arms relationship with Russia develop to the point where it exceeds those with Algeria and Iran in value. It is the South American state's only realistic source of major combat weapons apart from China, and as such accounted for 76 per cent of Venezuela's arms imports in the 1997–2007 period. Already, the entente between Chavez and the Russians has led to the purchase of a range of military helicopters, 24 Su-30MK combat aircraft and 100,000 AK-103 rifles (to facilitate large-scale resistance to the anticipated US invasion, according to the official rationale), and has led to agreement being reached on the sale of at least five Project 636 diesel submarines. Whilst irritating for the US, this hardly poses a threat to the US nuclear submarine fleet. As one analyst put it: 'In the submarine world, it's the equivalent of a Lada. It's non-nuclear, runs on diesel-electric, and has a snorkel. Russia simply doesn't have the technology to produce modern torpedoes.'[24] Nevertheless, it may well auger an era of heightened Russian-Venezuelan military co-operation that could be even more of an irritant to the US. Chavez supported the August 2008 Russian incursion into Georgia and

---

20   See, for example, 'India Owns Admiral Gorshkov: Navy Chief', *The Times of India* (3 December 2007), <http://timesofindia.indiatimes.com/India_owns_Admiral_Gorshkov_Navy_chief/articleshow/2592064.cms>; 'India, Russia: A No-Win Resolution on the Gorshkov', *Stratfor* (20 February 2008).

21   Vladimir Radyuhin, 'India, Russia Sign Pact to Build Combat Aircraft', *The Hindu* (19 October 2007).

22   'Algeria Lays Down Russian Arms', *Kommersant* (18 February 2008), <http://www.kommersant.com/p854040/r_1/military_hardware_foreign_relations/>.

23   See, for example, Tony Halpin and Alexi Mostrous, 'Russia Ratchets up US Tensions with Arms Sales to Iran and Venezuela', *The Times* (19 September 2008).

24   Luke Harding, 'Venezuela Strikes £500m Deal to Buy Russian Submarines', *The Guardian* (15 June 2007).

shortly afterwards announced that one of Russia's most prestigious warships, the 28,000 ton nuclear-powered *Peter the Great* (formerly the *Yuri Andropov*), would head a visit by Russian ships to Venezuela and conduct joint exercises. 'Go ahead and squeal, Yankees', was Chavez's message to the US.[25]

The third-largest importer during the 1997–2007 period was Taiwan, which depends overwhelmingly on US weapons systems, with the US supplying some 71 per cent of Taiwan's imports of major conventional weapons and France most of the remainder. The continuation of the US military relationship with Taiwan is of fundamental importance to the garrisoned island democracy as it acts as a clear signal to China of the US commitment to Taiwan's continued independence. As such, in the 1997–2007 period, the US has sold Taiwan a bevy of advanced weaponry that can be regarded as defensive, including thousands of anti-tank, surface to air and air-launched missiles, hundreds of tanks, combat helicopters and, between 1997 and 1999, 150 F-16C fighter aircraft (although some remained based in the US for training Taiwanese pilots). At the same time, the US is engaged in a delicate balancing act with China over Taiwan, as evidenced by the private assurances given to Chinese leaders by US officials since the time of Richard Nixon that they would oppose Taiwanese independence or admission to the United Nations and continue to follow the 'one China' policy essential to a constructive relationship with China.[26] As such, the US has always presented its sales to Taiwan as being a response to Chinese acquisitions, has carefully calibrated all arms offers, and in some cases has continued to hold the weapons it has sold to Taiwan, even though this approach has done little to lessen Chinese displeasure at such sales. To give a flavour of this: in October 2008 the US finally approved the export of almost US$6.5 billion worth of arms to Taiwan, including Apache attack helicopters and Patriot land-to-air missiles.[27] These had been offered by the Bush administration back in 2001 when the President committed himself to doing 'whatever it takes' to defend Taiwan.[28] Yet, after a lengthy delay, this represented fewer Patriot missile batteries and missiles than Taiwan had wanted, while the US continued to stall on a request for Black Hawk helicopters, ignore a separate request for F-16 fighter aircraft and do nothing about a vague 2001 commitment to facilitate Taiwanese acquisition of submarines.[29]

---

25 BBC News, 'Russian Navy to Visit Venezuela' (8 September 2008), <http://news.bbc.co.uk/2/hi/americas/7602530.stm>.

26 On this, see James Mann, *About Face: A History of America's Curious Relationship with China, From Nixon to Clinton* (New York: Knopf, 1999).

27 Jonathan Adams, 'Taiwan Arms Deal Sours US-China Relations', *Christian Science Monitor* (6 October 2008), <http://www.csmonitor.com/2008/1006/p99s01-duts.html>.

28 Jonathan Adams, 'Delay in US Arms Sale to Taiwan Stirs Concerns', *Christian Science Monitor* (24 July 2008), <http://www.csmonitor.com/2008/0724/p99s01-duts.html/>.

29 On the submarine question see, for example, Joseph Fitchett, 'US Offer of Submarines is Seen as "Snub": Europeans Reject Role in Taiwan Arms Deal', *International Herald Tribune* (27 April 2001), <http://www.iht.com/articles/2001/04/27/uboat_ed3__0.php>; Kirsten McNeil, 'Long-Delayed Arms Sales to Taiwan Announced', *Arms Control Today* (November 2008), <http://armscontrol.org/act/2008_11/Taiwan>.

Nevertheless, in response, China cancelled a number of military and diplomatic contacts with the US, including a scheduled visit by a senior Chinese general and port calls by naval vessels, and indefinitely postponed a series of meetings to discuss stopping the spread of weapons of mass destruction. A Defense Department spokesman professed surprise at this reaction, warning that: 'China's continued politicization of our military relationship results in missed opportunities.'[30]

While Israel and Egypt remain key markets most of their purchases from the US are provided via US military aid. Moreover, the US is by far the biggest supplier to these two states, supplying some 85 per cent of Israel's major conventional weapons imports and some 75 per cent of Egypt's in the 1997–2007 period.[31] Elsewhere in the Middle East, the UAE and Saudi Arabia remain major markets, the former dominated by France during this period, although there has been a resurgence in US deliveries in the last few years, which has seen the US become the largest supplier to the UAE over the 2005–07 period. While the Saudi market has been dominated by the US over the last few years, this situation looks set to change with the Saudi decision to go ahead with Project Salam by ordering 72 Eurofighter Typhoon aircraft from the UK (that is, assembled in the UK from the sections built by companies from the Eurofighter consortium countries – the UK, Germany, Italy and Spain), to be delivered from 2011. This represents a follow-up to the 1985 Al Yamamah deal with the UK – the largest in British arms export history prior to the Typhoon deal. Project Salam could be worth as much as £20 billion over the life of the contract,[32] although the Saudi desire to assemble the aircraft in-country may affect the profitability of the deal.

However, while this deal has been vital to the continued corporate health of BAE Systems, the company created by the 1999 merger of British Aerospace and Marconi Electronic Systems, the history of the UK's arms sales relationship with Saudi Arabia has come to be regarded as emblematic of the ethical problems that have come to be associated with the weapons trade (see Timeline, below). These, in turn, form an important plank of opposition to the weapons trade by non-governmental organisations such as Campaign Against Arms Trade, Oxfam, Amnesty International and Human Rights Watch,[33] which is also grounded in concerns over human rights and the unavoidable fact that the purpose of the commodities in question revolves around the capability to kill and/or repress, and that the best markets for weapons do not always have the best records in these areas. Given this, exporters can find themselves trapped in a cycle of targeting for

---

30   'China Rebuffs United States Over Taiwan Arms Deal', *International Herald Tribune* (7 October 2008), <http://www.iht.com/articles/2008/10/07/asia/military.php>.

31   Information from the SIPRI Arms Transfer Database, <http://armstrade.sipri.org/>.

32   David Robertson, 'Eurofighters Head Towards Saudi Arabia as BAE Completes £4.4bn Order', *The Times* (18 September 2007).

33   See, for example, the CAAT website, at <http://www.caat.org.uk/>.

sales countries with poor human rights records and downplaying the significance of ethical or human rights concerns relating to key markets in international fora.[34]

The Typhoon deal with Saudi Arabia was particularly controversial as it was only confirmed in the wake of the December 2006 decision to abandon a Serious Fraud Office (SFO) investigation into allegations that BAE Systems operated a 'slush fund'. This was abandoned on the grounds that Saudi Arabia would withhold 'war on terror' intelligence co-operation if the investigation proceeded, and as such there was a 'national interest' in its termination. However, it was widely believed that termination of the investigation was primarily a response to Saudi Arabia's threat to abandon the proposed purchase of Typhoon fighter aircraft in favour of a French alternative unless the investigation was dropped, and the 'war on terror' dimension merely provided the most convenient cloak. However, in announcing the decision at 5.21 p.m. on a day that had already seen Tony Blair became the first serving prime minister to be interviewed as part of a criminal investigation as part of the 'cash for peerages' inquiry, the government announce the closure of 2,500 post offices, and Lord Stevens publish his report into the death of Diana, the late Princess of Wales, the Attorney General, Lord Goldsmith, denied that 'commercial interests or the national economic interest' had been factors in the decision.[35] Such a rationale offered the government its best feasible line of defence when it came to explain to its international partners why it appeared to be compromising its anti-bribery commitments under the OECD Convention on Combating Bribery of Foreign Public Officials in International Business Transactions.[36]

Timeline: BAe/BAE Systems–Saudi Arabia Arms Controversy[37]

1985/86: Conservative Secretary of State for Defence Michael Heseltine agrees and then signs the first phase of the Al-Yamamah arms deal with the Saudi government. The contract covers the supply of Tornado and Hawk jets and an airbase construction programme.

1988: The UK and Saudi Arabia agree a further understanding over the Al-Yamamah deal.

1989: The National Audit Office launches a probe into the contract amid bribery allegations. The report is never published.

---

34   See, for example, Antony Barnett, 'MoD Targets Libya and Iraq as "Priority" Arms Sales Targets', *The Observer* (24 September 2006).
35   Hansard (14 December 2006), cols 1,711–12.
36   See <http://www.oecd.org/document/21/0,3343,en_2649_34859_2017813_1_1_1_1,00.html>.
37   Based on <http://www.telegraph.co.uk/news/worldnews/middleeast/saudiarabia/2473238/ BAEs-arms-deals-with-Saudi-Arabia-Timeline.html>. For more detail on the period from 1965–97, see Phythian, *The Politics of British Arms Sales Since 1964*, pp. 198–226.

May 2004: Allegations of a secret BAE 'slush fund' used as part of the Saudi deal are printed by *The Guardian* newspaper.

November 2004: BAE Systems reveals that it is the subject of a Serious Fraud Office (SFO) investigation.

December 2006: Attorney General Lord Goldsmith announces that the SFO is discontinuing its probe.

June 2007: BAE Systems announces that it is under investigation by the US Department of Justice over its arms deal payments with Saudi Arabia.

November 2007: Campaign groups Corner House Research and the Campaign Against Arms Trade win permission for a judicial review into the SFO's decision to drop the case.

April 10, 2008: The High Court rules that the UK government and SFO acted unlawfully in dropping the case. Senior judges condemn the UK government's 'abject surrender' to the 'blatant threats' that Saudi co-operation in the fight against terror would end unless the probe into corruption was halted.

April 13, 2008: Lord Goldsmith, the UK government's chief legal advisor at the time of the decision in 2005, attacks the ruling. He accuses the judges of failing to live in the real world and undermining a key legal principle.

April 22, 2008: The SFO says it will appeal against the ruling.

April 24, 2008: The High Court gives the SFO permission to appeal to the House of Lords.

July 30, 2008: The House of Lords, the highest court in the land, rules that the decision taken by the director of the SFO was lawful.

France also maintains a close interest in the Saudi Arabian market, and in 2008 secured contracts to sell military helicopters and fast-patrol boats. Following the October 2004 lifting of the EU arms ban on Libya,[38] France, alongside the UK, was prominent in trying to generate weapons business with the Gadafy regime, with

---

38   An additional UN embargo was applied in 1992 in relation to the 1988 bombing of Pan Am Flight 103 over Lockerbie, over which Libya came to be identified as the chief suspect and refused to co-operate with the investigation. It was lifted after Libya finally agreed to hand over two suspects for trial. The EU embargo had been a response to earlier Libyan support for international terrorism, and so remained in force beyond 1999. See the text of the 1986 decisions underpinning the EU arms embargo at <http://www.sipri.org/contents/expcon/eu_libya8601.html> and <http://www.sipri.org/contents/expcon/eu_libya86.html>.

both the British prime minister and the French president travelling to Tripoli to meet Colonel Gadafy. In the case of Nicolas Sarkozy this fuelled speculation that the sale of Milan anti-tank missiles had been linked to the negotiations through which the French successfully secured the release from a Libyan prison of five Bulgarian nurses and a Palestinian doctor convicted of knowingly infecting Libyan children with HIV.[39] In both cases, Libya's willingness to enter into arms agreements with the UK and France – under the embargo it relied on the Ukraine to supply its major conventional arms – helped to lubricate its re-entry into what President George H.W. Bush once termed the 'family of nations' after years of isolation. Given Libya's oil wealth, it has the capacity to become a major importer of weapons systems in the coming years now that the embargo has been lifted, a fact not lost on either the US or Russia, both of which are seeking to develop strategic links with Libya as a prelude to becoming key armourers.[40]

In addition to these markets, France has also been a major supplier to Turkey, which has been involved in a form of arms-racing with Greece, and which has looked to focus its purchases less on the US and more on European suppliers, arguably in order to improve its chances of acceptance into the EU. However, French arms sales to Turkey have lagged behind those of Germany. German exports to Turkey in the 2005–07 period accounted for over half the total value of German exports of major weapons systems across the entire 1997–2007 period. Moreover, showing what Andrew Undershaft in George Bernard Shaw's *Major Barbara* called 'the true faith of the armourer' ('To give arms to all men who offer an honest price for them, without respect of persons or principles'),[41] Germany has also been a prominent supplier to Greece – indeed, the two countries account for 27 per cent of Germany's exports of major conventional weapons in the 1997–2007 period.

Transparency

A further research area involves the development, future direction, potential and limitations of arms transparency initiatives at the international, regional and national levels. At the international level, a general sense of Western responsibility for the 1980s arming of Iraq which helped facilitate the August 1990 invasion of Kuwait and required a war to reverse it, led to calls for greater transparency regarding the hitherto secretive world of arms exporting once that war was over. Indeed, a number of national political figures claimed authorship of the concept of the transparency mechanism that emerged in 1991–92 as the UN Register of Conventional Arms. The UN Register was conceived as a means by which the

---

39   Kim Willsher, 'France denies Libyan Arms Trade-Off', *The Guardian* (4 August 2007).
40   See, for example, Julian Borger, 'Gadafy Gets His Reward as Rice Visits Libya', *The Guardian* (6 September 2008); Tom Parfitt, 'Gadafy Offers Russia a Naval Base in Libya', *The Guardian* (1 November 2008).
41   George Bernard Shaw, *Major Barbara* (London: Penguin, 1988 ed., originally 1905), p. 138.

UN could exercise its determination to 'prevent the excessive and destabilizing accumulation of arms, including conventional arms, in order to promote stability and strengthen regional or international peace and security, taking into account the legitimate security needs of States and the principle of undiminished security at the lowest possible level of armaments'.[42]

While there is no doubt that the UN Register succeeded in casting light on arms exports and imports it has, to date, been only a qualified success. Reporting is via seven broadly-defined weapons categories (battle tanks, armoured combat vehicles, large calibre artillery systems, combat aircraft, attack helicopters, warships, and missiles or missile systems), reflecting the initial need to proceed on the basis of broad consensus and accept something approaching a lowest common denominator starting position. There have been regular revisions to the substance of the UN Register since its inception, with regular meetings of groups of governmental experts to discuss how the Register might be expanded so as to provide still greater transparency.

However, as memories of the Iraq example have receded, so too has international commitment to the Register concept, something which was never universal to begin with. It has been undermined by inconsistencies in national reporting, even amongst its most committed supporters. From the outset, the 18 states of the Arab League, plus Palestine, announced their support for the concept, but announced that they would not participate because the Register did not require states to make a return on nuclear weapons holdings – an objection clearly aimed at Israel. There have been variations in Arab state participation in the years since, but overall this participation has been low, while the question of the inclusion of nuclear weapons has served to block developments in other areas of the Register. Participation by African states has also been disappointing – highly significant in terms of the number of conflicts and potential for instability that exists on the continent. The consistency of Chinese reporting has also been affected by its decision not to report for a time in response to the US inclusion of its exports to Taiwan in its return (given that it is not a member of the UN, Taiwan is not covered by the Register). As a consequence, it might be suggested that the UN Register has achieved all that it can, and even that the high watermark of the Register's potential has now passed.[43] However, the UN Register is still capable of consolidation and further development. It has developed in important ways since 1992, to the extent that it

---

42　United Nations General Assembly, 65th Plenary Meeting (6 December 1991), <http://disarmament.un.org/cab/ares4636l.html>.

43　The annual SIPRI Yearbook can be counted on for a gloomy assessment of the Register's prospects. See, for example, Bjorn Hagelin, Mark Bromley and Siemon T. Wezeman, 'International Arms Transfers', in *SIPRI Yearbook 2006: Armaments, Disarmament and International Security* (Oxford: Oxford University Press, 2006), p. 471; and Siemon T. Wezeman et al., 'International Arms Transfers', in *SIPRI Yearbook 2007: Armaments, Disarmament and International Security* (Oxford: Oxford University Press, 2007), pp. 413–14.

now offers the potential for states to provide a broad range of information going well beyond the original and narrower remit.

At a regional level, there have been examples of significant developments over the last decade, in particular with regard to the 1998 EU Code of Conduct for Arms Exports, which laid down eight criteria by which member states should assess export licences for military equipment, and required the sharing of information in cases where a member declined to issue an export licence, and for any member issuing such a licence after a refusal by another member or members to explain to those members why the licence had been granted. Hence, the EU Code combined transparency with a clear set of criteria for what constituted 'responsible' export policy – the former reinforcing adherence to the latter. The process results in what is now a detailed annual report,[44] has set a standard that other states have committed to, and has allowed the EU to act as a powerful advocate of the Arms Trade Treaty initiative being pursued through the UN in the face of US opposition.[45]

While the type and extent of information contained in them varies considerably, an increasing number of states now also produce their own national reports on arms imports and exports, albeit not always on an annual basis – the ideal which would allow for fullest scrutiny and transparency and hence go furthest in building confidence and lessening tension. As noted earlier, EU states and those seeking accession to the EU, have been at the forefront of this process. As of 2007, approximately 30 states have produced reports with varying degrees of regularity. Nevertheless, this represents a firm basis for future developments and a transformation in the situation that existed in the mid-1990s when such reporting was exceptional.[46] Nevertheless, its development requires careful monitoring and analysis to encourage continued development at this level.

Conclusion

As the foregoing indicates, the study of the trade in major conventional arms is dominated by issues of market analysis, human rights, ethics, and transparency and arms control. Notwithstanding the possibility of the odd future year in which Russian weapons exports might slightly outstrip those of the US because of significant business with China, there seems little prospect of the US being displaced from its position as the world's leading supplier of weapons. At the same time, while predictions of Russia's demise as a leading arms exporter have been a feature of post-Cold War commentary, they have been confounded by the resilience of the Russian export sector. While this has been based on a high level

---

44   The annual reports have been published since 1999, and are available via <http://www. sipri.org/contents/armstrad/atlinks_gov.html>.

45   See <http://www.armstradetreaty.com/att/aboutatt.php>.

46   For a list of reporting countries and to access their reports, see <http://www.sipri.org/ contents/armstrad/atlinks_gov.html>.

of dependence on the Chinese and Indian markets, there is evidence that Russia has enjoyed some success in developing additional markets and so will be able to lessen this dependence and maintain its overall position as the world's second-largest exporter. Despite concerns about the performance and reliability of some of its weapons systems, Russia will continue to benefit from the business of those states for whom dealing with the US is either undesirable or infeasible, and so need to identify a reliable (in this context, non-NATO) alternative.[47] As with so much else in world politics, a key variable is the future role of China. While it declined as a weapons exporter during the 1990s and has, of necessity, focused on the sale of less technologically advanced weapons systems, one would expect this position to begin to change as the twenty-first century wears on. It may reasonably be expected that China will come to assume a more prominent position as an exporter, expanding beyond its current key markets in Pakistan, Iran and Burma. The rise of collaborative production within the EU and the existence of the EU Code of Conduct have meant that European exporters act in unison more often than in the past, but analyses that emphasise European co-operation can underestimate the degree to which intra-European competition remains a feature of the market.

The arms trade remains a highly controversial one. Where this controversy was originally rooted in human rights considerations, today these are joined by concerns about the ethical implications of involvement in the trade and the impact of support for the trade on governments' national policies and ethical standing in the international community. Certainly, all those states involved in the trade in major conventional weapons adopt something of a schizophrenic approach to the arms issue: on the one hand, generally supporting calls for restraint and the emergence of legally-binding frameworks designed to limit the trade; on the other, seeking to maximise the economic and diplomatic advantages they can derive from it. This paradox is partly a consequence of the different constituencies (both internal and external) that governments must attempt to satisfy simultaneously, with the resulting need at times to pursue contradictory objectives. This paradox and the fact that the trade in major conventional weapons arises from the nature of the international system, guarantee that there will be a need for thoughtful analysis of the trade for some time to come.

---

47   In 2008 the US operated 26 arms embargoes, of which just 11 were UN-mandated.

Turning War into Business: Private Security Companies and Commercial Opportunism

Chris Kinsey

Introduction

There is nothing new about the role of contractors in warfare. In the case of England, for example, the English Ordnance Department is older than the Army of which it became part in the late nineteenth century. The post of Master of Ordnance (later known as Master General) dates back to the fifteenth century, the first officially recorded holder of the appointment being Nicholas Merbury in the year 1414.[1] Napoleon was also forced to rely on contractors for his supplies, though he detested them for profiting from war, referring to them as 'rogues … [who] roll in … insolent luxury, while my soldiers have neither bread nor shoes'.[2] Contractors also played a part in the American Civil War. Indeed, America has a history of turning to the market for military support services. For instance, KBR (formerly Kellogg Brown & Root) continue to supply logistical support for the US and UK militaries on overseas operations.[3] In this respect, little has changed over the centuries, with contractors still playing an important, if somewhat controversial, role in warfare. As Herbst has written, 'the private provision of violence was a routine aspect of international relations before the twentieth century'.[4]

---

1   Brigadier A.H. Fernyhough CBE MC (Retd), *A Short History of the RAOC* (Great Britain: Europrint, 1980), p. 7.

2   Edgar Sanderson, ed., *Bourrienne's Memoirs of Napoleon Bonaparte*, Hutchinson's Library of Standard Lives, pp. 302–3.

3   For a detailed discussion of contractors on deployed military operations see Matthew Uttley, *Contractors on Deployed Military Operations: United Kingdom Policy and Doctrine* (US: US Army War College, 2005).

4   Jeffery Herbst, 'The Regulation of Private Security Forces', in Greg Mills and John Stremlau, eds, *The Privatisation of Security in Africa* (Pretoria: South African Institute of International Affairs, 1997), p. 117.

The presence of armed contractors in places such as Iraq and Afghanistan is, however, novel in that it stands in stark contrast to their absence from the battlefield during the Cold War. Mercenaries, as some scholars prefer to call them, are as old as war itself,[5] but today's private security companies (PSCs)[6] are different. While the mercenaries of the 1960s and 1970s involved themselves in political intrigue, especially in Africa, PSCs are now seen as a tool of government and international organisations. This is in contrast to mercenaries who operate in an ad hoc fashion, coming together to satisfy a single contract, as was the case with Simon Mann who, along with South African mercenaries attempted to overthrow the government of Equatorial Guinea.[7] PSCs are permanent corporate structures, or as permanent as any corporate structure can be. They are, according to Spicer,[8] the official military transformed into the private sector in a business guise.[9] Furthermore, according to the industry itself, they have a practical and potentially beneficial role to play in helping to resolve what Kaldor calls 'new' wars.[10] The following chapter examines the nature of that role.

In its narrowest sense, PSCs represent nothing more than the commoditisation of security in conflict zones, thus separating them from the much larger, commercial security companies that operate globally and prefer to provide security for shopping malls, banks and corporate offices. That said, both are no more than economic actors, driven by profit. The concern of this chapter is the former group of private actors, those PSCs that operate in conflict zones.

The first part of the chapter examines the early years of the industry, focusing on Watchguard International, the company credited with being the first modern

---

5   For example see Abdel Fatau Musah and J 'Kayode Fayemi, 'Africa in Search of Security: Mercenaries and Conflicts – an Overview', in Abdel Fatau Musah and J 'Kayode Fayemi, eds, *Mercenaries: An African Security Dilemma* (London: Pluto, 2000).

6   The term 'private security companies' is used throughout the chapter, while the term 'private military companies' is used only to describe companies which offer combat/ military support operations of the type undertaken by Executive Outcomes.

7   In early 2004 the South African business partner of President Obiang's brother and Security Chief, Armengol Ondo Nguema, was arrested and sentenced without trial on charges of plotting a coup, along with 14 others. At the same time Simon Mann, a retired British Army officer who had served in the Special Air Service, and former members of the South African security forces, some of whom were EO veterans, were arrested when their plane landed in Harare to collect weapons that were supposed to have been purchased from the government-run Zimbabwean Defence Industries. The men always denied that they were on their way to Equatorial Guinea to participate in the coup, claiming that they were actually going to work as security officers in the Congo. For an account of the Equatorial Guinea plot see Angela McIntyre and Taya Weiss, 'Weak governments in search of strength: African experience of mercenaries and private military companies', in Simon Chesterman and Chia Lehnardt, eds, *From Mercenaries to Market: The Rise and Regulation of Private Military Companies* (Oxford: Oxford University Press, 2007), p. 77. Also see Adam Roberts, *The Wonga Coup* (London: Profile Books, 2006).

8   Tim Spicer was Sandline International's first chief executive officer and a retired Lt Colonel from the Scots Guards.

9   Tim Spicer, *An Unorthodox Soldier* (London: Mainstream Publishing, 1999), p. 165.

10 Mary Kaldor, *New & Old Wars* (Cambridge: Polity Press, 2002).

PSC by those who now work in the industry, and going on to discuss how, during the 1970s and 1980s, globalisation and international terrorism created the very opportunities necessary for the fledgling industry to expand while distancing itself from the mercenary activities that were still going on in places such as Africa. The second part of the chapter is concerned with the role of PSCs in the post-Cold War era. The industry has experienced its most rapid growth during this period, with most of that growth coming immediately after the invasion of Iraq by coalition forces in 2003. Part two first examines the impact of Executive Outcomes (EO) in Angola's civil war in the early 1990s, before touching on the roles of Military Professional Resources Incorporated (MPRI) and DynCorp for the US government. It then briefly discusses Sandline International's involvement in Papua New Guinea and the 'arms to Africa' affair,[11] before finally looking at the impact of PSCs on Kaldor's new wars, while paying particular attention to Afghanistan and Iraq.

Establishing a PSC Industry: The Early Years

The idea of setting up a PSC came to David Stirling, the founder of the Special Air Service (SAS), after he helped to recruit British and French mercenaries to fight in the Yemen civil war in the early 1960s.[12] This is not the place for a detailed discussion of the war other than to observe that the operation gave Stirling a very good understanding of what could be accomplished with a small group of retired Special Forces personnel, with their superior training in the use of weapons, communication and medical skills.

> *Stirling knew roughly the cost of using a mercenary force and he felt there was scope for setting up a private force, whose main function would be to have a controllable political effect, but which must produce an operating profit: politics was the driving force but it had to be financially viable. ... Stirling conceived the idea of forming a commercial company to operate in areas of paramount interest to the highest national figures – the heads of state.*[13]

---

11 The 'arms to Africa' affair was a sequence of events in 1997 that saw the exiled President Tejan Kabbah of Sierra Leone turn to Sandline International for help in returning him to power. The affair concerned the importation of weapons and ammunition into Sierra Leone by Sandline in contravention of Security Council Resolution 1132 and whether the British government was aware of the weapons assignment as well as giving it official approval. For a detailed discussion of the affair see Christopher Kinsey, *Corporate Soldiers and International Security: The Rise of Private Military Companies* (London: Routledge, 2006), pp. 72–93.

12 For an account of the role of British and French mercenaries in the civil war in Yemen see Clive Jones, *Britian and the Yemen Civil War, 1962–1965* (Brighton: Sussex Academic Press, 2004).

13 Alan Hoe, *David Stirling: The Authorised Biography of the Creator of the SAS* (London: Warner Books, 1994), p. 369.

Thus by the late 1960s everything was in place for him to establish Watchguard International, the first modern PSC.

The aim of the company was to protect British interests in those areas around the world where the British government felt it was undesirable to have a presence, for whatever reason, and therefore would not be able to act if there was a threat to its interests. Importantly, there may be the need for the government to deny having any involvement in the company's operation to protect its reputation. Hoe points out that 'the company would provide a service aimed at preventing the violent overthrow of a government, but that it would not thereafter seek to exert political influence'.[14] Stirling registered the company in the Channel Islands in 1967. Watchguard's area of operation was initially the Middle East, later extending into Africa. At the time, the African continent was going through the process of decolonisation; and therefore a potential market for the company emerged, as leaders sought to protect themselves from political rivals and their own militaries. As with PSCs today, the company initially provided three types of services: military surveys and advice; close protection for heads of state friendly to the British government; and training of special forces.

The company, however, would only take on an operation with the consent of the British government. Stirling knew that selling military advice could not run counter to UK national interests. Consequently, it would always be necessary to gain the consent of the government before taking on an operation. In a private interview given in 1979, he confirmed that the government had approved of Watchguard: 'The British government wanted a reliable organisation without any direct identification. They wanted bodyguards trained for rulers they wanted to see survive.'[15] Furthermore, the statement bears out the fact that whichever party was in government during this period would be ready to use private actors to expand the range of covert operations beyond government agencies to support foreign policy objectives.[16]

The start of the 1970s saw a different set of social conditions start to emerge, which were directly linked to changes in the international environment. The result of these changes was to see the legitimate growth in the sale of private military/security services offered by PSCs. As Westbury explains, 'globalisation and international terrorism created opportunities for companies to engage in private military security as legitimate security companies'.[17] The oil and extraction industries, in particular, were now operating in areas of the world where the risk of attack on their staff and assets was much higher than in the places where they normally operated. They therefore needed the type of protection that only former Special Forces personnel were trained to provide; in this case, close protection involving the use of firearms. Also, by the late 1960s international terrorism was

---

14   Ibid., pp. 371–2.
15   J. Bloch and P. Fitzgerald, *British Intelligence and Covert Action* (London: Junction Books, 1983), p. 48.
16   Ibid., p. 48.
17   Interview with Lord Richard Westbury, Chief Executive, Hart GMSSCO Cyprus Ltd (1 April 2004).

on the increase as the number of terrorist acts mounted. According to US State Department records for 1970, there were over 3,000 terrorist acts worldwide, while the number of acts continued to grow through the 1970s.[18] Even though Watchguard had identified commercial opportunities for military style security for international clients, it was left to a new breed of security company to exploit this burgeoning market. Control Risks Group,[19] Kroll and, later, Defence Systems Ltd[20] and Saladin all benefited from the commercial opportunities that the need for private military security now offered.[21] According to Lord Westbury, Control Risks provided political risk analysis and hostage negotiation experts for international corporations, while Kroll supplied investigation services for the same customers; Saladin concentrated on close protection for corporate executives and other political elites, and Defence Systems Ltd focused on providing security services to supranational agencies and multinational corporations.[22] Thus by the 1980s these four companies were transforming the industry as they started to distance themselves from the clandestine operations that were the hallmark of British mercenaries during the 1960s and 1970s.

During the Cold War, the role of PSCs was very much restricted to those functions mentioned above. While state militaries relied on commercial companies to supply logistical support services during this period, PSCs were rarely to be seen. They certainly did not undertake the types of role that they are now being asked to take on in Iraq by the US government, notably convoy protection, perimeter protection and close protection of government officials. The industry was also centred in London and dominated by UK companies, while their relations with the government were informal. The reason that London was chosen as the focal point had to do with the country's history, the SAS and the fact that London was also one of the financial centres of the world. As with any government in the Cold War, the UK needed to protect the country's national interests, of which access to oil and minerals was one. Moreover, many of the countries where oil and minerals were to be found were former colonies of Britain. Thus, it is not hard to understand why the British government sought to protect the new heads of state of these new countries in order to ensure access for British multinational corporations to their oil and mineral deposits. At the same time, security for the multinationals was guaranteed by PSCs whose members properly had intimate knowledge of the countries where the multinationals were operating because of their time in the SAS. This arrangement worked very well during the Cold War, but particularly for PSCs

---

18   Ken Connor, *Ghost Force: The Secret History of the SAS* (London: Orion, 1999), p. 306.

19   The company is now called Control Risks. Interestingly, Lieutenant Colonel Jim Johnson, a retired Special Forces officer, was responsible for organising and administering the Yemen operation and later set up Control Risks with David Walker and Arish Turle. See Kevin O'Brien, 'Private Military Companies and African Security 1990–1998', in Abdel Fatau Musah and J 'Kayode Fayemi, op. cit., p. 47.

20   Defence Systems Ltd is now ArmorGroup International.

21   Christopher Kinsey, 'Problematising the Role of Private Security Companies in Small Wars', *Small Wars and Insurgencies* (2007), vol. 18, no. 4: 590.

22   Westbury interview (see n. 17).

able to exploit the political/social instability found in these countries for economic reward.[23] The end of the Cold War saw a new set of challenges for PSCs as the international environment changed.

Making Business Out of War: The Start of the Post-Cold War Era

The post-Cold War period has seen PSCs expanding into controversial areas of the market from which the industry had stayed away during the Cold War. During this period, however, the number of PSCs has grown considerably, particularly in the US.

Singer points to a number of reasons for demand for military/security services having soared since the end of the Cold War. He first points to the massive increase in the global leaves of conflict. Of particular concern is the huge increase in the number of civil wars now being fought, especially in Africa. Second, he argues that the rise in non-state violence such as international terrorism has also led to an increase in demand for private military/security services. The third reason relates to the downsizing of state militaries in the West and the end of the apartheid regime in South Africa. In all cases, the result has been the flooding of the market for international security with former soldiers and military equipment, which has led to increasing competition which invariably forced down prices to a level that private actors could also afford. Fourth, there was reluctance on the part of the West to intervene in the civil wars that were now being fought, unless their national interests were at stake.[24] Finally, in the case of the US government, using PSCs carries far less political risk in circumstances where there is a high risk of something going wrong than their own military assets. Furthermore, the US military in Iraq made it clear from the start that it now only does war fighting, leaving other US agencies and contractors to purchase their own security.

Most academics, when examining the immediate post-Cold War period, focus on the role of EO (Executive Outcomes)[25] in Angola in the early 1990s. At the same time, nothing has been said about the role of private contractors who were employed to clear the landmines from Kuwait's oil and gas fields in the aftermath of the First Gulf War in 1991. However, there has been very little research into that operation and nothing of substance has been written about it. What we do know is that, instead of employing coalition soldiers to clear the landmines laid by the Iraqi troops and the cluster bombs dropped by the coalition air forces, the government

---

23   For an interesting discussion on how London and Washington have been able to control Nigeria's oil over the years and the part played by private security see Andy Rowell et al., *The Next Gulf: London, Washington and Oil Conflict in Nigeria* (London: Constable & Robinson, 2005).

24   Peter Singer, *Corporate Warriors: The Rise of the Privatized Military Industry* (London: Cornell University Press, 2003), pp. 49–70.

25   The company finally closed its door to business 1 January 1999.

of Kuwait turned to private contractors. The British company Royal Ordnance was one of the companies to be awarded a $90 million contract to clear landmines in the country. They accomplished the task using 200 former British soldiers, many of whom had served in the Royal Engineers and former Ghurkhas. Numerous PSCs now working in mine clearance are doing so as a consequence of contractors who gained their experience working in Kuwait after the Gulf War.

While Royal Ordnance was arguably one of the first companies to exploit the commercial opportunities on offer following a major conflict immediately after the end of the Cold War, it was EO's operation in Angola that drew the attention of the international community. Eben Barlow, a former officer in 32 Reconnaissance Battalion before joining the South African Civil Cooperation Bureau (CCB), founded the company in 1989 after leaving the military. Barlow's aim in establishing the company was to build Africa's biggest military advisory company in order to work all over the world, training armies and getting involved in conflict resolution, but related more to the battlefield instead of the political scene.[26] The company also provided combat support for its clients, a key factor in its success.

According to Barlow, in 1993 the company was approached, through a friend, by an international oil company that needed help in Soyo, in north-west Angola, to recover equipment that had been lost, or laid waste, but which the oil company wanted recovered because of its value. Barlow agreed to help the oil company, although at the time he did not know that Soyo was in the hands of *Uniao Nacional para a Independencia Total do Angola* (UNITA).[27] The operation took two months, turning into a serious battle between UNITA and EO. As Barlow explains, 'for the first five days … all our guys did at Soyo was defend, until through probably very disciplined fire control they had worn UNITA down'.[28] UNITA finally withdrew, leaving EO temporarily in control of the area. However, UNITA recaptured Soyo when EO pulled out leaving a battalion from the Angolan army in charge. According to Shearer, though, 'the operation was nevertheless significant in that it was the first real demonstration of EO's combat capabilities'.[29]

As a consequence of its success, no doubt, the company was again approached later the same year. General Faceira, a senior officer in the *Forças Armadas Angolanos* (FAA), wanted to know if EO was interested in a one-year contract to train soldiers from the FAA's 16th Regiment and pilots, but also to give combat support to operations against UNITA. The contract, worth US$40m, was later renewed for a further year in September 1994 and then again for three months in 1995.[30] By

---

26   Christopher Kinsey,' Private Security Companies: Agents of Democracy or Simply Mercenaries', in Thomas Jäger and Gerhard Kümmel, eds, *Private Military and Security Companies: Chances, Problems, Pitfalls and Prospects* (Germany: VS Verlag Für Sozialwissenschaften, 2007), p. 97.

27   Transcript of interview between Eben Barlow and Jim Hooper (26 January 1996).

28   Ibid.

29   David Shearer, 'Private Armies and Military Intervention', *Adelphi Paper 316* (Oxford: Oxford University Press, 1998), p. 46.

30   Ibid., p. 46

supplementing local forces with veterans of South Africa's Special Forces from the apartheid era, the Angolan government drew on tactical advice based on a solid understanding of UNITA's weakness. After all, many of EO's men had intimate knowledge of UNITA, having spent years working alongside them during Angola's civil war. The company also had the advantage of intelligence on UNITA's activities leaked via South African sources.[31]

EO's reputation as an organisation able to achieve military success soon spread throughout the African continent and led to it receiving a contract from the Sierra Leone government in May 1995 to help it defeat the Revolutionary United Front (RUF). This time the company signed three contracts that covered a period of 21 months and were worth US$35m.[32] With the RUF only 20 miles from Freetown when EO arrived it certainly had its work cut out, stopping the RUF from overrunning the capital. However, after eight months of fighting, the company was able to force the RUF to the negotiating table for the first time in five years.

Other companies also sought to profit from international instability during the early 1990s. MPRI, for example, has become a proxy military/security training company for the US government. The company was established in 1987 by a group of former senior US military officers who realised the business opportunities available to them in utilising the experiences of retired military personnel to support US foreign and military policy. The company is directly involved in training foreign militaries on behalf of the US government. It also organises security sector reform (SSR)[33] programmes and law enforcement services that focus on stabilisation and reconstruction efforts.[34] However, the company is best known for the contract it signed with the Croatian government in 1994 to help transform the country's military from a Warsaw Pact-style force to a NATO-style force. MPRI was responsible for designing the Long-Range Management Programme for the Croatian Ministry of Defence, establishing a strategic long-term capability to improve its chances of becoming a NATO member.[35] DynCorp, on the other hand, has supplied personnel for the International Police Task Force in Bosnia and Haiti. In the former case, the responsibility of the force was to monitor, advise and train law enforcement officers in the country. However, while turning to the market may provide government with flexibility along with a surge capacity, to mention only two advantages, the market also holds problems for governments that rely on it. As Avant notes, 'the private option … is harder to control and frequently more costly than its public alternative and reduces incentives to reorganise the force'.[36] Moreover, regarding the

---

31   Ibid., p. 48.
32   Alex Vines, 'Mercenaries, Human Rights and Legality', in Abdel Fatau Musah and J'Kayode Fayemi, op. cit., p. 175.
33   For a detailed discussion of the problems associated with outsourcing SSR programmes to the market see Elke Krahmann, 'Transitional States in Search of Support', in Simon Chesterman and Chia Lehnardt, eds, op. cit., pp. 94–112.
34   See MPRI website <www.mpri.com/index.html> [accessed 4 July 2007].
35   David Shearer, op. cit., p. 58.
36   Deborah Avant, *The Market for Force: The Consequence of Privatizing Security* (Cambridge: Cambridge University Press, 2005), p. 127.

reorganisation of the force, using the market to field an international civilian police force for Haiti, which the US government was unable to field itself, has allowed them to avoid creating an international civilian police capacity. Furthermore, much of the evidence suggests that using contractors has resulted in poor training, little strategic vision and, ultimately, less effective policy.[37]

The company, properly, most associated with economic opportunism and war is Sandline International.[38] In January 1997 the prime minister of Papua New Guinea, Sir Julius Chan, signed a contract with Sandline in the hope that the company would be able to help the military defeat the Bougainville Revolutionary Army (BRA). The BRA had been fighting since 1989 to take control of Bougainville and its lucrative copper mine. The contract, worth US$36m, would see Sandline provide direct combat support and procurement assistance to help end the rebellion. As soon as the contract became know to the public it drew international outrage, while the Australian government, a major provider of aid to the country, called the use of mercenaries 'totally unacceptable'.[39] In the end, the prime minister was forced to resign, while those working for Sandline were deported from the country, with the exception of Spicer, who was arrested and charged with illegally possessing a pistol and ammunition. The charge was eventually dropped and Spicer was released when Judge Andrew and the Commission decided they no longer needed him.[40] A judicial inquiry later revealed that the contract issued to Sandline was legal; the company was eventually paid in full even though it had not actually done any of the work the contract required. What the incident highlights are the lengths those in power will go to in order to resolve internal turmoil when international support is not forthcoming. It is also a classic case of an attempt to maintain power backfiring, and prejudicing internal and external respect for the government, according to Mandel.[41]

No sooner was the Papua New Guinea incident resolved than Sandline was again embroiled in controversy, but this time it was over the company's involvement in the civil war in Sierra Leone. In December 1997 Spicer met with exiled president Ahmad Tejan Kabbah to discuss how the company might help Kabbah regain power in the country. Kabbah was not only aware of the constraints placed on the Economic Community of West African States Monitoring Group (ECOMOG) but was also concerned with the lack of an explicit UN mandate and a crucial lack of logistics and armaments.[42] The latter was obviously necessary for him to regain power. At the meeting Spicer proposed a military plan that would restore civilian rule to the country, a plan which, as noted above, became known as the 'arms to

37   Ibid., p. 127.
38   The company closed down its operations 16 April 2004.
39   Robert Mandel, *Armies without States: the Privatization of Security* (London: Lynne Rienner, 2002), p. 111.
40   Tim Spicer, *An Unorthodox Soldier: Peace and War and the Sandline Affair* (London: Mainstream, 1999), p. 186.
41   Ibid., p. 112.
42   John Hirsch, *Sierra Leone: Diamonds and the Struggle for Democracy* (London: Lynne Rienner, 2001), p. 66.

Africa' affair. Spicer considered Sandline well-placed to supply the type of military support that Kabbah's government needed to eject the junta from power. After all, the company was close to EO and had been successful once before against the Revolutionary United Front (RUF). In the event, the company broke a UN arms embargo when it imported 35 tons of ammunition and weapons into the country, embarrassing the new Labour government in the UK. The following inquiry by Sir Thomas and Sir Robin Ibbs found that the Foreign and Commonwealth Office (FCO) had been informed, while Sandline argued that some officials had given it their approval, a claim dismissed by the FCO but accepted by the Legg inquiry. The inquiry noted that elements in the FCO might have unintentionally given the impression that the operation had government support, when in fact it did not.[43]

These were not the only PSC operations during the early to mid-1990s. However, they were probably the most reported in the media, normally by human rights organisations. Throughout this period Control Risks, Kroll, ArmorGroup International and Saladin continued to focus on security-related activities for commercial organisations, while staying away from the type of military/security services offered by EO, MPRI and Sandline. Indeed, in the case of the UK, this approach typified the security industry. Occasionally a company might take on a training contract with the knowledge of the government, as ArmorGroup did in Mozambique when they trained a tea plantation security force from 1986 to 1992,[44] but usually they concentrated their efforts on providing security for the commercial market. What is more, the focus on the provision of security and not military activity is typical of the British companies and has its roots in the industry's commercial activities during the 1970s and 1980s. As Donald explains: 'British PSCs will not in the short to medium term undertake combat tasks because it would wreck their business. The sector has spent too long separating itself from the combat end of the private security spectrum to jeopardise it all with dogs of war headlines.'[45]

This view is different to that held by some US PSCs. Cofer Black, the vice chairman of Blackwater, has even gone as far as to suggest using private contractors to help stop the fighting in Darfur. He proposed sending a brigade-sized private force to the region as part of the UN peacekeeping effort. According to Donald, the company may have quietly dropped the idea because of a lack of support from the US government.[46] That said, the African Union force commander for Darfur,

---

43 For an account of the affair see Foreign Office Committee, Second Report, *Sierra Leone* (London: The Stationery Office, 1999). Also see Sir Thomas Legg KCB QC and Sir Robin Ibbs KCB, *Report of the Sierra Leone Arms Investigation* (London: The Stationery Office, 1998); and Kinsey (2006), op. cit., Chapter 4.

44 The project came to an end when EMOCHA (the Mozambique tea company) was unable to continue funding the project. Email communication with Patrick Toyne Sewell, Communications Director, ArmorGroup International (4 January 2008).

45 Dominick Donald, 'After the Bubble: British Private Security Companies after Iraq', (RUSI, Whitehall Paper Series 66, 2006), p. 36.

46 Interview with Dominick Donald, Aegis, London (17 July 2007).

General Martin Agwai, has a number of advisors, staff officers and 'military' observers from DynCorp, paid for by the US State Department.[47]

While the industry did not go through any rapid growth during the 1990s, business was slowly increasing with more companies being set up to take advantage of the growing political instability in places such as Africa. With every new intra-state war, by the mid-1990s the numbers were growing, offering new business opportunities for the industry, from supporting weak or failing governments, as in the case of EO, to protecting corporate assets and rebuilding State militaries. Some companies were also developing new markets for themselves. Prior to 1990 the only private organisations to undertake mine clearance in worn-torn countries were charities, the Mines Advisory Group (MAG) being one of the first, if not the first, to develop this specialist area of humanitarianism. As mentioned above, the humanitarian mine clearance operation in Kuwait changed all that. Thus, by the mid-1990s PSCs were starting to become heavily involved with mine clearance to such an extent that today the UN frequently utilises its expertise for some of its own mine clearance operations.[48] At the same time, the industry's customer base was also expanding as more international organisations turned to the market for the type of security solutions only PSCs could offer. The 1990s marked a period of growth for the industry as companies sought new markets and customers. Even so, industry participation in areas such as peace support operations (PSO) at the time was still ad hoc with little or no attempt to integrate PSCs into the operational side of UN missions. Also, the focus was on logistical support and not on the provision of physical security which companies are now taking on in Afghanistan and Iraq. Finally, the tragic events of 9 November 2001 not only changed the international security environment, they changed the role of private security forever.

The Business of Terror:
The Market for Private Security Just Got Bigger

As with terrorism in Western Europe in the 1970s and 1980s, the 9/11 attacks on the Twin Towers in New York and the Pentagon were the beginning of an economic bonanza for the private security market. Whereas the international economy faced an economic slowdown, the share prices of leading security companies saw a 50 per cent increase in their value and some security companies actually saw their shares double in price.[49] As one journalist mentioned at the time, the rise in share prices levied the equivalent of a 'security tax' on the global economy.[50] The 9/11 attacks

---

47   Confidential source.
48   See <www.armorgroup.com/services/servicesmineaction/> [accessed 4 January 2008].
49   E. Scharder, 'US Companies Hired to Train Foreign Armies', *Los Angeles Times* (14 April 2002).
50   S. Lunday, 'Firms Joing Security Drive', *Charlotte Observer* (13 February 2002).

made security a priority for every business leader who placed it at the top of his or her agenda and effectively fuelled demand for protection that PSCs could only benefit from. Ensuring staff and assets were properly protected was now a priority for businesses, as they began to reassess the risks associated with operating in an international marketplace that was vulnerable to attacks.

The response from international corporations, international organisations and governments to 9/11, and the constant threat of terrorist attacks, led to a sudden increase in business for PSCs, while at the same time helping to consolidate the industry. As a spokesman for the Pentagon's Defense Security Cooperation Agency noted at the time, 'the war on terror is the full employment act for these guys. A lot of people have said, "ding ding ding, gravy train"'.[51]

Iraq: The Icing on the Cake for PSCs

While 9/11 may have been responsible for the boom in business for PSCs, Iraq put 'the icing on the cake' for the industry. This should not surprise us when we look at the roles the industry has been asked to perform for the UK, US and Iraqi governments as well as international organisations and transnational corporations. The decision of the US government to use PSCs to protect US government officials and reconstruction projects was not thought of before the war but afterwards, when it was realised that victory on the battlefield was simply a prelude to a post-war insurgency operation. As Bensahel noted, 'expecting US forces to be greeted as liberators instead of occupiers is much more than just a semantic issue; it contains an implicit assumption about the nature of the post-war environment'.[52] By conceptualising their forces as liberators, US officials marginalised or even ignored potential security problems and popular resistance in the post-war period, while the situation was ruthlessly exploited by PSCs looking for opportunities to make money.[53]

US military planners failed to realise, argues Bensahel, 'that the ultimate political objectives of the operation – establishing a peaceful and democratic Iraq – would either succeed or fail depending on how events unfolded after the military objectives had been achieved'.[54] Troop estimates, for example, were based on combat requirements instead of the need to maintain order in the country after the invasion. With too few troops on the ground to counter popular resistance, a security void soon occurred that PSCs were more than happy to fill, in doing so lending

---

51   E. Scharder, op. cit.
52   N. Bensahel, 'Mission Not Accomplished: What Went Wrong With Iraqi Reconstruction', *The Journal of Strategic Studies*, vol. 29, no. 3 (2006): 457.
53   Christopher Kinsey, 'Problematising the Role of Private Security Companies in Small Wars', *Small Wars and Insurgencies*, vol. 18, no. 4 (2007): 599.
54   N. Bensahel, op. cit., p. 467.

additional support to troops on the ground.[55] Importantly, through concentrating on war fighting and not the general provision of security, the US government had little option but to turn to PSCs to provide the security for government agencies, including their own, and multinational corporations involved in rebuilding the country's infrastructure. The employment of approximately 25,000 security contractors is no small number, but was necessary if the reconstruction was to go ahead.[56] Moreover, the PSCs allowed the US military to concentrate their efforts on fighting the insurgency instead of protecting personnel responsible for rebuilding the country's shattered infrastructure. The PSCs they believe they have demonstrated in Iraq that they can play a role in supporting nation-building in the mist of a civil war.

What Commercial Opportunities Next?
The Role of PSCs in Supporting Nation-Building

It is generally agreed among those who study the industry that it has a future, and that that future lies in four distinct areas: intelligence provision and analysis for governments and commercial organisations; support to stabilisation and post-conflict reconstruction operations; security sector reform programmes; and humanitarian and development assistance. While both the commercial sector and government agencies are concerned with the first two areas, the last two are the responsibility of governments and non-governmental organisations (NGOs). In the UK, PSCs will likely start to push for more UK government contracts, if they are not already doing so, particularly given the fact that some already do a lot of work for the US government.[57] Furthermore, if the British government wants to achieve its foreign and security policy goals in places such as Iraq and Afghanistan then it

---

55 Global Security was one of the first PSCs to take over from US troops guarding US military establishments, releasing much-needed troops to fight the insurgency. Interview with Bob Cole, Minimal Risks Consultancy Limited, Joint Services Command and Staff College (6 February 2008).

56 United States Government Accounting Office, 'Rebuilding Iraq: Actions Needed to Improve Use of Private Security Providers', Government Report: GAO-05-737 (July 2005), p. 8.

57 Aegis Specialist Risk Management won the renewal of the US Department of Defense's (DoD) contract to provide reconstruction security support services in Iraq. This two-year contract, the largest single security contract awarded by DoD, is anticipated to be valued up to $475 million. Since 2004, Aegis provided a command, control, communication, intelligence and security framework to Gulf Regional Division (GRD) – enabling the reconstruction effort to take place in as secure an environment as possible. See <www.aegisworld.com/> [accessed 25 February 2008]. ArmorGroup International, on the other hand, has contracts to protect US embassies around the world. See <www.armorgroup.com/mediacentre/newsarchive/> [accessed 25 February 2008].

may have no option but to let the MOD employ PSCs to take on security tasks that an overstretched army can no longer carry out.[58]

There are certainly advantages to using PSCs, though they have to be carefully weighed against the problems associated with employing them. For example, PSCs give governments greater policy flexibility, because they are not bound by the same set of responsibilities that apply to troops. Their use is supposed to free the government of the political cost of employing troops. PSCs can also tap into the resources of former military/government personnel to which governments may no longer have access.[59] They are able to give governments a surge capacity that can alleviate pressure on troops, freeing them up to concentrate on core tasks. In this respect they are able to offer governments a quick, flexible answer to the types of problem which materialise suddenly and which government sectors may struggle to respond to because of insufficient troop levels, or because drawing troops from elsewhere might compromise another operation in a different theatre.[60] Critics of the industry, though, point to the fact that governments may be going too far with unreflective outsourcing to private security, and that it could have a serious impact on the combat effectiveness of soldiers as a consequence of handing over responsibility for armed services to private contractors. Worse still would be a contractor underperforming on a mission-critical task, placing not only the lives of troops in jeopardy but also the operation. Finally, since PSCs are not bound by military law, they can leave their jobs at any moment, further risking mission effectiveness.

Even though these and other problems remain, governments are already turning to PSCs for services that in the past would have been provided by the military. The question, therefore, is not whether we should be using them, but what roles governments should allocate them when operating in the battle-space.[61]

In the case of intelligence, the area most likely to be exploited by PSCs is the provision of analysis to support a government's own analytical capacity. PSCs will be used to provide additional analytical insight into established or emerging threats, especially threats associated with regions engulfed in civil wars such as West Africa. Another area they may choose to take advantage of is supplying local information collected from their areas of operation. In Iraq, for example, all the companies have their own network of local individuals who keep them informed about what is happening on the ground and about intended attacks against them. Such tactical information is a force multiplier and is frequently used by personal security details (PSDs) to prepare them properly for threats, while allowing managers to allocate resources more efficiently. Such information, because it is coming from individuals living in the local community who hear and see things that foreign intelligence officials may not know about, can help develop a wider and more detailed picture

---

58   Michael Evans, 'Half Trained Troops to Fight the Taleban', *The Times* (31 January 2008).

59   Kinsey, op. cit., p. 603.

60   Donald, op. cit., pp. 45–6.

61   Ibid.

of an insurgency, which, in turn, can lead to a more effective response from force commanders on the ground. This, however, will need greater cooperation between government intelligence agencies and PSCs than is currently the case.

At present, PSCs are heavily involved in post-conflict reconstruction and stabilisation operations as is evident in Iraq and Afghanistan. This is also an area suitable for future expansion. PSCs feel comfortable in this area of the market for two reasons: first, they can offer some of the functions that are necessary for the successful transition of a country plagued by war to peace; and second, many of their staff will already be familiar with this area, having served in the military and been involved in many peacekeeping/peace enforcement operations. They will have first-hand experience of the types of problem that government agencies, international organisations, corporations and NGOs will face trying to work in a post-conflict environment that can be potentially hostile.

Neither are PSCs new to this market. US PSCs, in particular, have been involved in post-conflict reconstruction through the US State Department for over a decade. For example, the Department, through DynCorp, provided a force of international civilian police in Haiti that otherwise would not have been fielded.[62] The same company also provides police trainers to train the Afghanistan national police forces.[63] According to Avant, over the long term, outsourcing to DynCorp has meant that the US government has been able to avoid the creation of an international civilian police capacity, while evidence suggests that relying on contractors has resulted in poor training, little strategic vision and ultimately, less effective policy.[64]

The British government has been slower to engage with PSCs in this area of the market, preferring to keep its distance instead. Needless to say, it may have little option other than to change its position, given the manpower shortage it faces.[65] Whether it chooses to outsource to the same extent as the US government is questionable, but it is considering possibilities, while decisions are likely to be made on a case-by-case basis. Operationally-based activities that may be considered for outsourcing could include specialist advisors in infrastructures and how to rebuild them, de-mining, munitions disposal, command and coordination of PSCs operating in conflict zones (akin to Aegis's matrix contract in Iraq)[66] and armed protection of MOD civil servants. Finally, as Donald point out, UK and US PSCs already have their eyes on peacekeeping and enforcement support roles such as offering rotary and fixed-wing air lift capacity, and signalling/engineering capabilities, which could enhance UN and African Union operations.[67]

Security sector reform (SSR) is the third area where PSC involvement is likely to increase. To be fair, US companies are already involved in this area of the market.

---

62   Deborah Avant, *The Market for Force: The Consequence of Privatising Security* (Cambridge: Cambridge University Press, 2005), p. 127.

63   See DynCorp <www.dyn-intl.com/pm_home.html> [accessed 26 February 2008].

64   Deborah Avant, op. cit., p. 127.

65   See n. 58.

66   See n. 57.

67   Donald, op. cit., pp. 56–7.

As mentioned earlier, MPRI has been involved with training foreign militaries for more than a decade, while recently running SSR programmes in Afghanistan and Iraq.[68] This is not the case, however, in the UK, where foreign military training is still the responsibility of the British Army, though for how long this will remain so in light of troop shortages is unclear. The last area where more PSC participation may occur is humanitarian and development assistance. It is also the most contentious of the four areas examined, with numerous NGOs unhappy with the idea of sharing their space with what some see as nothing more than corporate mercenaries.[69] Indeed, it is an area where the UK government, in particular, has become reliant on NGOs and international organisations, funnelling funding through such organisations as Oxfam, Save the Children UK and numerous UN agencies. Using these organisations does, though, allow services to reach the most needed, since it is at this level that NGOs and UN agencies usually operate.

Working so close to those that are in most need of help also means that they know what is required and how to make it work. Importantly, funnelling funds through them normally has an immediate impact at the grass-roots level. Even so, there are also disadvantages, including the risk of becoming too reliant on them. This can create problems for government departments if the NGO community, for example, chooses not to support a particular operation or actually withdraws support after an operation is underway. This was the case in Iraq when NGOs refused to support the operation or receive funding from any of the coalition partners because they believed that the operation was illegal and therefore that working in Iraq for the coalition would compromise their integrity. Using PSCs can also create the wrong type of perception among the victims of humanitarian disasters, that is, that the safety of their staff is more important than the safety and well-being of the victims, thus notably distancing the two groups concerning the principles behind humanitarianism.

Conclusion

Since the end of the Cold War, PSCs have become significant actors in international security. They are likely to remain so for the foreseeable future, though their guise may change. It has been the US government which has taken the PSC concept the furthest and substituted regular soldiers with private contractors in training roles and numerous security functions; what some critics see as outsourcing military responsibility to the market. The main reasons for this have to do with political expediency and overstretch. In the first instance, fewer people care about dead contractors as opposed to seeing their soldiers coming home in body bags. Second, both the US and UK militaries are struggling to retain soldiers while their commitments continue to increase, creating overstretch. Private contractors have

---

68   See MPRI <www.mpri.com/main/securitysectorreform.html> [accessed 26 February 2008].
69   See War on Want <www.waronwant.org/> [accessed 26 February 2008].

been able to reduce overstretch by taking on some responsibilities that would otherwise fall to the military.

The 9/11 attacks not only changed the face of the industry forever, though in many respects change was already on its way, they also ensured the future of the industry in the medium term. PSCs have become a tool in the war against terror as governments, international organisations and business corporations place security at the top of their agendas. It was their role in the Second Gulf War that really demonstrated to governments their utility, as well as the problems associated with using them. In Iraq, they have complemented the US military, engaging in close protection for government officials, convoy protection, static guarding and military/police training. Without them the military would have had to perform these tasks themselves and would probably have required an additional army division. At the same time, their presence offers extra capacity for governments, while the challenge will be deciding what services they should undertake.

Women in the Armed Forces of Western Democracies

Helena Carreiras

Introduction

The situation of women in the armed forces of Western democracies has been changing during the past four decades. By the beginning of the twenty-first century, all NATO countries had admitted and increased the number of women in their armed forces; many restrictions had been lifted; women had been progressively allowed to enter military academies and given access to a wider variety of positions and functions; gender awareness had grown within most military structures; and integration policies had been designed and implemented.

In the year 2008 more than 300,000 women served in NATO forces.[1] While the majority were[2] employed in support functions, many had already been accepted in operational or close-to-combat areas. In countries such as Norway, women had served aboard submarines and a woman had already occupied the position of submarine commandant. Some others, namely Canada, Germany or the UK had experienced rather strong external pressures to achieve gender equality in the armed forces. In spite of a rather late start, Southern European nations such as Portugal or Spain had also made significant progress in the integration of women in their militaries.

The factors that induced these convergence effects (or at least fostered synchronization of policies) derive from macro-sociological trends – from a rather strong pressure to achieve gender equality in most of the Western world, to changes

---

1   Information retrieved from country national reports and other documents at <http://www.nato.int/issues/women_nato> [accessed 22 September 2008].

2   Christopher Dandeker and Mady W. Segal, 'Gender Integration in Armed Forces: Recent Policy Developments in the United Kingdom', *Armed Forces and Society*, 23/1 (1996): 30–47; Donna Winslow and Jason Dunn, 'Women in the Canadian Forces: Between Legal and Social Integration', *Current Sociology*, 50/5 (2002): 641–67; Gwyn Harries-Jenkins, 'Women in Extended Roles in the Military: Legal Issues', *Current Sociology*, 50/5 (2002): 745–69.

in the military towards force reduction and professionalization – which affected all these countries, even if with diverse rhythms and degrees. The growing number and the diversification of women's military roles is both a symptom and one of the most visible consequences of change in the armed forces during the late modern and postmodern periods.[3]

There is, however, the reverse side of the coin. Despite the tendency to eliminate discrimination and equalize status between service members, occupational restrictions still exist and women are mostly excluded from combat-related areas and functions; they are clearly under-represented in international peacekeeping operations; they have limited representation in higher hierarchical posts and power positions within the military system; and last but not least, they are not always accepted and often have to face hostile reactions. Empirical data show that even when formal/legal integration has been accomplished, real social integration does not necessarily follow.[4] In addition, progress made in the past has not always shown a linear pattern. Women's military participation has been subject to cycles of expansion and contraction, and tendencies to reinstate exclusionary policies have been observed.[5]

Diversity between countries is also clear: while some have integrated women, granting them real (and not only formal) access to a wide range of positions and occupations, others keep women in little more than symbolic positions. As has already been noted in the past,[6] there is still great variation regarding the extent to which different countries have promoted the integration of women. Such variation ranges from a very limited numerical presence, rank limitations, segregated training and severe functional restrictions, to relatively open career patterns, fully integrated training and access to combat roles.

In any case, from the moment women started joining the military with full military status, a historical pattern of exclusion and invisibility has been dramatically challenged. This process was depicted as a revolution,[7] a threat to the military,[8] and even as a deeper transformation than the introduction of nuclear weapons.[9] Independently of how extensive we consider the impact of this new

---

3   Charles Moskos, Jay Williams and David R. Segal, eds, *The Postmodern Military* (New York, 2000).

4   Winslow and Dunn, 'Women in the Canadian Forces'.

5   Mady Segal, 'Gender and the Military', in Janet S. Chafetz, ed., *Handbook of the Sociology of Gender* (New York, 1999), pp. 563–81; Helena Carreiras and Gerhard Kummel, eds, *Women in the Military and in Armed Conflict* (Wiesbaden, 2008).

6   Sandra Stanley and Mady W. Segal, 'Military Women in NATO: An Update', *Armed Forces and Society*, 14/4 (1988): 559–85.

7   Jeanne Holm, *Women in the Military: An Unfinished Revolution* (Novato, CA, 1993).

8   Brian Mitchell, *Women in the Military, Flirting With Disaster* (Washington, 1998); Martin Van Creveld, *Men, Women and War: Do Women Belong in the Front Line?* (London, 2001).

9   The challenge this meant to the military establishment is well illustrated by a famous statement of a former US Joint Chiefs of Staff Chairman, who said: 'the influx of women has brought greater change to the US military than the introduction of nuclear weapons', quoted in Berenice Carroll and Barbara W. Hall, 'Feminist Perspectives on

pattern of women's military participation to be – and there are reasons to suppose that the descriptions above overstate the real effects of gender integration – one thing seems clear: this is no longer a change only for the duration of conflicts, as previously happened. However unequal their status, however occupationally segregated and culturally discriminated against, women are no longer peripheral to the armed forces. And, to some extent, the amplification of women's military roles has meant a challenge to the common view of the armed forces as a male domain and the male–warrior paradigm.[10]

This chapter starts by reviewing the debate over women in the military, underlying its intensity, pervasiveness and confrontational character. The relevance of this debate resides less in its contents than on the impact it has had on policy decisions, from recruitment and selection standards, to women's functions and assignments, as well as on the overall sociopolitical construction of the issue of women soldiers. The chapter proceeds with an analysis of current patterns of gender integration in the armed forces of NATO countries, reviewing the factors which account for the variety of policies, practices and results they have achieved. The final section of the chapter looks at the participation of military women in peacekeeping missions, highlighting both the significance of these new contexts for the exercise of military professionalism and the way in which, following the debates around UN Resolution 1325, a new 'naturalistic' discourse but also new opportunities, have emerged regarding the role of women in conflict situations. The chapter ends with some conclusive remarks about the paradoxical nature of discourses and practices with regard to women in the military.

Women in the Armed Forces: The State of the Debate

The issue of women in the military has always been one of the most controversial in the study of military institutions. It has been a focus of political conflict whenever questions such as citizenship rights, conscription, or wartime mobilization have been discussed; it is also an extremely sensitive topic in debates of cultural conceptions of gender or women's social status. Positions range from those who vehemently oppose the presence of women in the armed forces, to those who accept women's presence in some areas, to those who welcome full integration. Within the multiplicity of perspectives, some 'strange quasi coalitions' have been identified.[11] This is the

---

Women and the Use of Force', in Ruth H. Howes and Michael R. Stevenson, eds, *Women and the Use of Military Force* (Boulder, CO, 1993), p. 19.

10   Dunivin, Karen O., 'Military Culture: Change and Continuity', *Armed Forces and Society*, 20/4 (1994): 531–47.

11   Gerhard Kummel, 'When Boy Meets Girl: The "Feminization" of the Military. An Introduction Also to be Read as a Postscript', *Current Sociology*, 50/5 (2002): 617; Fabrizio Battistelli, 'Presentazione', in Fabrizio Battistelli, ed., *Donne e Forze Armate* (Roma, 1997), p. 31.

case of the apparently surprising convergence between military conservatism and pacifist feminism, both opposing the military participation of women. Behind these extreme standpoints there is usually an essentialist perspective on gender which equates men with power, aggression, physical strength and domination, and women with powerlessness, peacefulness, weakness and submission.[12] In this respect, as noted by Elshtain, stereotypes of men as 'just warriors' and women as 'beautiful souls' have frequently been used to secure women's status as non-combatants and men's identity as warriors.[13]

Most confrontations regarding the military participation of women, or the roles and functions they should perform, operationalized this controversy by opposing citizenship concerns to military efficiency. Democratic values concerning civil rights and citizenship are set in opposition to military readiness and efficiency, as if endorsing one set of values would involve denying the competing claims of the other. A civil society equal rights discourse is set in opposition to a discourse of military readiness and national security.

The 'effectiveness' argument's extreme position assumes that the military are different from the rest of society: their mission, to provide security, is singular and takes precedence over all others; therefore the role of the military is not to grant equal rights to all individuals and the institution should not be transformed into a 'laboratory for social experimentation'. The 'civil rights argument', on the contrary, underlines the way in which the military in a democratic polity is (or should be) a reflection of the society it is supposed to protect, including the defence of its core values such as citizenship and equality.

Even if positions have varied significantly between these two ideal types, the intensity, pervasiveness and confrontational character of the 'rights versus readiness' debate are striking. It is remarkable and simultaneously puzzling to note that the arguments do not seem to have changed significantly since the 1970s. Segal already pointed to this at the beginning of the 1980s and at the start of the twenty-first century, a revision of current debates leads to the same conclusion.[14]

On one side of the divide there are those who believe that women represent a danger to military readiness. Because the presence of women is seen as jeopardizing the effectiveness of the forces, their access to combat functions is considered a risk for the security of the nation. Tuten has put it bluntly:

---

12 Sharon Macdonald, Pat Holden and Shirley Ardener, eds, *Images of Women in Peace and War* (London, 1987).

13 Jean B. Elshtain, *Women and War* (Chicago, 1995).

14 Mady W. Segal, 'The Argument for Female Combatants', in Nancy L. Goldman, ed., *Female Soldiers: Combatants or Non-Combatants? Historical and Contemporary Perspectives* (Westport, CT, 1982), pp. 267–90; Mady W. Segal, 'Women's Roles in the US Armed Forces: An Evaluation of Evidence and Arguments for Policy Decisions', in Robert K. Fullinwider, ed., *Conscripts and Volunteers: Military Requirements, Social Justice and the All-Volunteer Force* (New Jersey, 1983), pp. 200–13; Carreiras and Kummel, *Women in the Military and in Armed Conflict*.

> [T]he primary function of the US armed services is to provide for common
> defense – not to redress perceived social and sexual inequalities in our society
> … The primary function of the military services is to defend the American
> society, not to change it. To the extent that we use the military as a testbed for
> social experimentation we risk the security of the nation.[15]

In a similar vein, Marlowe sustained that 'if we are serious about the missions
that are mandated for the combat arms, we cannot afford to make them a locus of
social experimentation'.[16] This position is usually accompanied by controversial
statements such as that there are no fundamental discontinuities between modern
war and modes of successful warfare in the past, or that the influx of women into
military services was not the product of military need but the result of external
political pressure.[17]

Resistances have been expressed from the very start of female recruitment in
the 1970s and seem to be gaining new impetus at present. Carreiras and Kummel
noted that in recent years and, more specifically, in the wake of the terrorist suicide
attacks of 9/11, together with a renaissance of the cult of direct ground combat in
military operational thinking, 'the issue of integrating females into the military
and granting them access even to combat occupations and specialties has been
[re]moving up on the agenda and reinvigorating a debate that has actually never
faded away'.[18]

Critics often focus explicitly and exclusively on the combat-related functions,
with opponents of female involvement in combat showing nevertheless some
tolerance for the assignment of women to support and combat support roles.[19] Other
times the mere presence of women, independently of the function they perform, is
seen as a fundamental threat to the functionality, if not survival, of the military
organization.[20] Some have even argued that the influx of women into the militaries
of advanced countries does not represent a gain for women but it represents in fact
part-symptom/part-cause of the decline of the advanced military. Israeli military
historian Martin van Creveld, who maintains that the feminization of the military
is equivalent to its weakening and decline, stated that 'if only because research
shows that going into combat is the last thing most military women want, the more
of them there are around the less capable those military are of acting as effective

---

15   Jeff M. Tuten, 'The Argument against Female Combatants', in Goldman, *Female Soldiers*,
      p. 261.
16   David H. Marlowe, 'The Manning of the Force and the Structure of Battle. Part 2: Men
      and Women', in Fullinwider, *Conscripts and Volunteers*, p. 195.
17   Marlowe, 'The Manning of the Force and the Structure of Battle', p. 198; Tuten, 'The
      Argument against Female Combatants', p. 260.
18   Carreiras and Kummel, *Women in the Military and in Armed Conflict*, p. 30.
19   Marlowe, 'The Manning of the Force and the Structure of Battle'.
20   Mitchell, *Women in the Military, Flirting With Disaster*; Tuten, 'The Argument against
      Female Combatants'.

combat units'.[21] Others, like Stephanie Gutmann (2000), Brian Mitchell (1998) or Stephan Maninger (2008) basically sustain these ideas.

At the other end of the ideological spectrum are those who believe that citizenship rights and responsibilities are paramount and should have priority in the whole discussion. Liberal feminists have been among those who more strongly emphasized the need to bring 'citizenship' concerns into the debate on women soldiers' roles. Feld has argued that 'the case for accepting women for combat assignments cannot be argued on a pragmatic basis; nor at least on strictly military terms'.[22]

Likewise, Lorry Fenner claimed that the focus of discussions should not be the particular conditions of service and the inclusion of specific groups, but the fundamental issues of citizenship and the role of the military in a democratic society. She argued that the debate has excessively focused around the question of military effectiveness, and that:

> we resist discussing the disjuncture between our cultural ideology and democratic political philosophy; or how discrimination and inconsistent and contradictory restrictions hurt efficiency; or how constantly changing, non-reality-based standards militate against cohesiveness and damage the credibility of policy-makers; or how failure to live up to our rhetoric affects morale and integrity.[23]

Defenders of this position usually underline the fact that arguments to exclude women from the military or limit their roles and functions are reminiscent of those used in the past to exclude other categories, or of those used to justify excluding women from other occupations.[24] They also point to the connections between concepts of citizenship and military participation, stressing the way in which excluded groups have achieved more equal citizenship rights through military service.[25]

Four main sets of arguments have been exposed and confronted on each side of the 'rights versus readiness' divide. First, there are concerns about women's individual characteristics, their bodies and psychological characteristics that supposedly make them less effective combatants (physical strength, menstruation, pregnancy, emotionality and ability to perform under stress). Second, there are

---

21   Van Creveld, Men, Women and War, p. 442.

22   M.D. Feld, 'Arms and the Women: Some General Considerations', Armed Forces and Society, 4/4 (1978): 559.

23   Lorry Fenner, 'Either You Need These Women or You Need Not: Informing the Debate on Military Service and Citizenship', in Rita J. Simon, ed., Women in the Military (New Brunswick, 2000), p. 19.

24   Segal, 'The Argument for Female Combatants'; Segal, 'Women's Roles in the US Armed Forces'.

25   Emmanuel Reynaud, Les Femmes, La Violence et L'Armée (Paris, 1988); Sheila Tobias, 'Shifting Heroisms: The Uses of Military Service in Politics', in Jean B. Elshtain and Sheila Tobias, eds, Women, Militarism and War (Savage, MD, 1990), pp. 163–85.

questions related to the effects of women's presence on cohesion and morale of military units (interpersonal processes bearing on performance, impact on 'male-bonding'); third, arguments regarding cost-effectiveness (attrition, job migration, lost duty time, personnel selection costs); finally, there are the consequences of women's participation in the military in terms of social and cultural values (preservation of gender ideals, public opinion, perception of the military by allies and potential adversaries). Recent evaluations of this debate have confirmed the continued centrality of the two first sets of arguments. Focusing on the positions assumed by military traditionalists, Carreiras and Kummel examined in detail what they referred to as 'discursive weapons' targeting gender integration in the military: the cult of the body and the cult of social homogeneity.[26]

As far as the cult of the body is concerned, the military traditionalists primarily stress women's psychological characteristics such as lack of physical (upper body) strength, menstruation and pregnancy as limiting women's capabilities to perform military tasks, especially those related to combat. The issue has raised and continues to raise deeply emotional reactions, partially because of the perceived injustice of gender-norming the physical fitness and training standards. Referring to men's average higher levels of physical strength, resistance and speed, Tuten noted that 'few would deny that these physical attributes are essential to the soldier or marine in ground combat. Therefore ... the exclusion of women from front-line ground combat is mandated by their lesser physical capabilities'.[27]

Opponents of this view emphasize the need to develop job-related physical tests:

> [I]f a certain level of physical strength is required for a particular job, then this would serve as one of the selection criteria for the job. Rather than assuming that all women are incapable of performance by virtue of the average women's lack of capacity, specific requirements should serve as the selection criteria, not gender.[28]

But it has also been pointed out that different physical standards and tests may have problematic consequences. On the one hand, when gender-specific physical tests are implemented, change associated with gender integration may be interpreted as a lowering of standards. On the other hand, physical performance becomes one important source of perception of inequity and inequality. Referring to the physical fitness test soldiers have to go through for admission and training, Segal noted that, 'since a women can pass the test with a performance for which a man would fail, many male soldiers believe that women are given unfair advantage'.[29]

Change in standards is itself a difficult issue; usually pre-existing standards are reified as if they are something outside anyone's agency or ability to challenge.

26   Carreiras and Kummel, Women in the Military and in Armed Conflict.
27   Tuten, 'The Argument against Female Combatants', p. 248.
28   Segal, 'Women's Roles in the US Armed Forces', p. 206.
29   Segal, 'Gender and the Military', p. 576.

Since physical tests were initially conceived to measure men's physical fitness with limited equipment, this reinforces perceptions of inequality. Not only are women being evaluated by traits on which average men score higher than average women, but those physical traits in which women would outperform men (such as measures of flexibility) are not routinely included. In the same vein, Vogel believes that, so far, there is only:

> an insufficient basis to recommend common service-wide fitness test standards since acceptable objective criteria are lacking. The future development of appropriate criteria upon which to base general physical fitness standards, along with proper considerations of training potential, should lead to more objective and supportable standards. These standards would be based on justified requirements rather than subjective levels that are empirically derived.[30]

Nevertheless, the fact remains that perceptions of women's physical inferiority by both men and women, military and civilians, lay at the basis of much of the opposition to women in various military functions especially those related to ground combat.

As far as the cult of social homogeneity is concerned, the debate is no less sharp. Behind the argument that the presence of women affects male bonding and thus performance is the belief that effective or successful performance is the result of cohesion, and this, in turn, is a result of social homogeneity. By interfering in the unit cohesion of male-bonded groups women would thus represent a threat to effectiveness, especially in combat situations. Gabriel has clearly expressed this point of view:

> [T]he fact is that combat effectiveness is only partially, and probably only a small part, the result of well-applied technical skills.... [M]ilitary unit effectiveness and cohesion are far more the result of socio-psychological bonding – anthropologically, male bonding – among soldiers in combat groups. Without this crucial bonding units disintegrate under stress no matter how technically proficient or well-equipped they are.[31]

Strong arguments have been put forward against these assumptions. One of them regards the evidence of women's prominent role in terrorist and guerrilla groups, in which strong patterns of male bonding would be expected to exist.[32] Others derive from the results of various empirical studies. Two important

---

30   James A. Vogel, *Summary Report Research Workshop on Physical Fitness Standards and Measurements within the Military Services, 31 August – 2 September 1999* (Herndon, VA; Fort Detrick, MD: US Military Operational Medicine Research Program, 1999), p. 11.

31   Richard Gabriel, 'Women in Combat? Two Views', *Army Magazine*, 44/2 (1980): 54–60; quoted in Tuten, 'The Argument against Female Combatants', p. 251.

32   Martin Binkin and Shirley Bach, *Women and the Military* (Washington, 1977), p. 91.

programmes conducted by the US Army Research Institute for Behavioral and Social Sciences in the mid 1970s examined the performance of women both in non-combatant units during training programs (MAXWAC) and while away from home installations during extended field exercises (REFWAC). In both cases results showed no significant relationship between the proportion of women and the readiness and operational capability of the units. Similar findings can be retrieved with regard to the Gulf War in the early 1990s where the role of servicewomen within the American troops was substantial. The US General Accounting Office summarized that:

> [O]verall, the unit commanders and focus group participants gave primarily positive assessments of women's performance in the Persian Gulf War.... [W]omen and men endured similar harsh encampment facilities and conditions. Health and hygiene problems during the deployment were considered inconsequential for both men and women. Cohesion in mixed gender units was generally considered to be effective during deployment; ... and gender homogeneity was not reported by focus group participants as a requirement for effective unit cohesion during the deployment.[33]

More recently, the participation of women in peacekeeping missions has also been a source of information regarding the performance of mixed groups in field situations. Research results have shown that men and women seem to work better together under the difficult and stressful field conditions than often in the barracks environment. The fact that they are sharing tasks and goals presumably makes integration easier and increases the possibility that people are seen as individuals more than members of a group or sexual category.[34]

But even if we admit that the presence of women or other minority categories may have disruptive effects in the cohesiveness of all-male groups, and that this is an important issue to be addressed by policy-makers, the question remains to assess the relationship between cohesion and performance. Contradicting intuitive ideas, research results in this field seem to be extremely elusive and inconclusive. Kier has underlined the fact that cohesion is only one of multiple factors that may affect group performance and that its contribution may be considerably both less significant and more complex than often assumed. For instance, there is little evidence of a causal relationship between cohesion and performance. Only a modest

---

33   General Accounting Office (GAO), National Security and International Affairs Division, *Women in the Military: Deployment in the Persian Gulf War: Report to the Secretary of Defense (GAO/NSIAD-93-93)* (Washington, DC: GAO, 1993), p. 3.

34   M.C. Devilbiss, 'Gender Integration and Unit Deployment: A Study of GI Joe', *Armed Forces and Society*, 11/4 (1985): 523–52; Charles Moskos and Frank Wood, eds, *The Military, More Than Just a Job?* (Washington, 1998); Laura Miller and Charles Moskos, 'Humanitarians or Warriors? Race, Gender and Combat Status in Operation Restore Hope', *Armed Forces and Society*, 4 (1995): 615–37; M.L. Maniscaldo, 'Operazione Diverse Della Guerra: Il Ruolo Delle Donne', in Battistelli, *Donne e Forze Armate*.

positive correlation has been identified and, even in this case, analysts seem to be more confident that successful performance leads to cohesion than the contrary. Additionally, cohesion can be beneficial or damaging to a group's performance. Group cohesion can be dysfunctional to organizational performance whenever the group goals are contrary to those of the organization, or when the group develops a subculture that makes acts of resistance feasible. This was observed during the Vietnam War, where certain groups developed a powerful ideology of their own that was more likely to reinforce dissent from, than commitment to, the service's larger goals and normative claims.[35]

Moreover, some changes seem to be taking place regarding the nature of the debate itself. In certain policy-making contexts the emphasis put on military effectiveness is fading as a rationale for preventing women's access to certain positions within the military structure. Results of a study conducted by Dandeker and Segal (1996) in the UK indicated that military effectiveness could decline as a basis for excluding women from certain positions and functions, to be replaced by arguments concerning rights of privacy and decency: 'The main reason for such a change is the vagueness of arguments based on operational effectiveness, especially those concerning the supposed effects of male bonding.'[36]

Facing a growing tendency on the part of service members to use law courts to pursue their grievances, military policy-makers would thus tend to use rights to privacy, which are easier to justify in court.

Patterns of Gender Integration in the Armed Forces of Western Democracies

Notwithstanding the difficulties of gender integration in the military – of which old and current debates are just one visible expression – this is an area in which, in recent decades, notable developments have occurred.[37] In 2008 more than 300,000 women served as volunteer soldiers in NATO countries. With some

---

35 John Helmer, *Bringing the War Home: The American Soldier in Vietnam and After* (New York, 1974); Stephen D. Westbrook, 'The Potential for Military Disintegration', in Sam C. Sarkesian, ed., *Combat Effectiveness: Cohesion, Stress and the Volunteer Military* (Beverly Hills, CA,1980), pp. 244–78; quoted in Elizabeth Kier, 'Discrimination and Military Cohesion: An Organizational Perspective', in Mary F. Katzenstein and Judith Reppy, eds, *Beyond Zero Tolerance: Discrimination in Military Culture* (Lanham, 1999), p. 42.

36 Dandeker and Segal, 'Gender Integration in Armed Forces', p. 33.

37 Stanley and Segal, 'Military Women in NATO'; Marina Nuciari, 'Women Soldiers in a Transcultural Perspective', in Giuseppe Caforio, ed., *Social Sciences and the Military: An Interdisciplinary Overview* (London and New York, 2007); Kummel, 'When Boy Meets Girl'; Helen Carreiras, *Gender and the Military: Women in the Armed Forces of Western Democracies* (London and New York, 2006); Carreiras and Kummel, *Women in the Military and in Armed Conflict*.

minor exceptions, percentages of women have been increasing steadily and some countries reached the first decade of the twenty-first century with an overall female military representation of around 20 per cent. Others, however, still had relatively low levels of women in their armed forces (Table 12.1).

Table 12.1 Percentage of Female Soldiers in the Armed Forces of NATO countries 1986–2008

	1986	2000	2004	2008
Belgium	3.9	7.6	8.3	
Bulgaria			4.2	10.3
Canada	9.2	11.4	12.3	11.0
Czech Republic*	2.7	3.3	12.3	12.4
Denmark	3.0	4.2	5.0	5.8
France	3.7	8.5	12.8	14.2
Germany	0.0	1.4	5.2	7.6
Greece	1.0	3.8	4.2	11.7
Hungary*	5.7	6.8	10.0	20.0
Italy			0.5	3.3
Latvia			13.5	16.5
Lithuania			6.0	12.2
Luxembourg	0.0	4.2		
Netherlands	1.5	8.0	8.6	9.0
Norway	1.4	3.2	6.3	7.5
Poland*	0.0	0.1	0.5	1.2
Portugal	0.0	6.6	8.4	14
Romania			3.9	4.0
Slovakia			6.1	
Slovenia			19.2	15.8
Spain	0.0	5.8	10.5	12.3
Turkey	0.0	0.1	3.9	
United Kingdom	5.1	8.1	8.8	10.2
United States	10.2	14.0	15.0	15.5

Note: * Data for the first period refers to years 1990/2.
Source: Stanley and Segal (1988: 563); CWINF Annual Reports of the Committee of Women in the NATO Force <http://www.nato.int/issues/women_nato/index.html>.

211

A comparative study conducted in 2000 revealed a diversity of gender integration patterns and proposed an analytical framework to explain differences and similarities between countries.[38] The study highlighted the following aspects:

- From the point of view of service distribution, female representation was higher in the most specialized services: Navy and Air Force. At that moment women made up for 6.3 per cent of Army personnel, 10.2 per cent of the Navy and 12.2 per cent of the Air Force.
- Although in some cases, the possibility of women's conscript recruitment was foreseen in case of general mobilization or war, all countries had decided to incorporate women on a strictly volunteer basis.
- From the point of view of global representation, two different patterns were identified. On the one hand, in a larger group of countries, formal mechanisms such as rank restrictions and the establishment of maximum ceilings or regulatory quotas had contributed to limit or condition the overall representation of women. Even if, in 2000, the overwhelming majority of countries did not have formal quantitative limitations, 'informal' ceilings existed in many cases when assignments were considered. The gap between formal policies and actual practices was thus notorious, leading to the conclusion that 'the absence of *formal* restrictions was most probably related to existing anti-discriminatory laws, in the light of which such explicit limitation policies are (or have become) unsustainable'. On the other hand, there were cases where recruitment difficulties had forced the military to define recruitment 'goals' in terms of female representation.
- The occupational distribution of military women revealed a strong cross-national segregation pattern: more than two thirds (70.4 per cent) of military women were concentrated in support (personnel/administration/logistics) and medical functions; 17.5 per cent in technical areas (engineering, communications); and only 7 per cent occupied positions in the more operational areas in combat arms (artillery, infantry, cavalry). According to the author, reasons for disparities between men and women were to be found in both the characteristics of women's choices and in the conservative occupational assignment policies that had been followed by a majority of countries.
- Despite the absence of legal limitations to hierarchical progression, female representation in the various ranks and promotion conditions were still limited in formal and informal ways. First, in some countries women had not served long enough to attain higher ranks; second, some countries did not recruit women for specific categories; and third, in other instances, combat exclusion and occupational segregation prevented women from acquiring the experience and fulfilling the functions that would serve as the basis for promotion.

---

38 Carreiras, *Gender and the Military.*

- Finally, there was also great variation between countries in terms of social policies aiming at eliminating discrimination and promoting gender integration. Those countries that had made more progress in terms of representation and occupational and hierarchical desegregation were also those where specific policies concerning the conciliation of work and family, equity monitoring and sexual harassment had been implemented. In other countries these policies were totally absent.

Using multiple indicators concerning policies and practices for each of the countries in the sample, the author went on to build an index of gender inclusiveness from which those different patterns clearly emerge.[39]

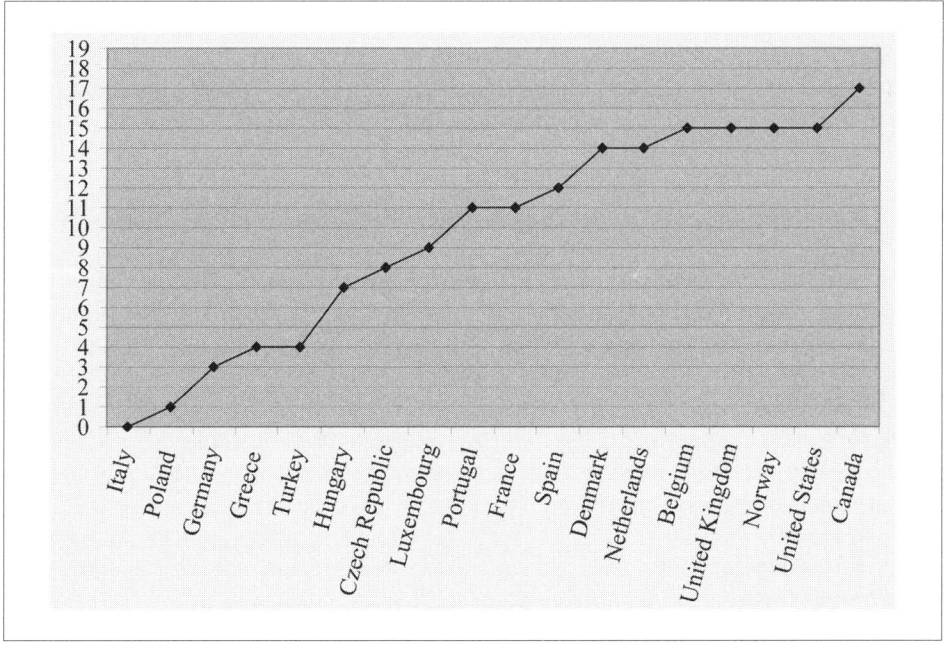

Figure 12.1 Index of gender inclusiveness in the armed forces
Source: Carreiras (2006).

---

39 The index includes structural variables relative to the overall representation of women in active duty forces, occupational sex segregation and rank distribution, but also variables aimed at capturing the impact of policies: existence of segregation practices, presence or absence of formal limitations in occupational and hierarchical terms, programs for conciliation between family and a military occupation and sexual harassment and gender equity monitoring.

An analysis of the factors that might help explain such diversity highlighted three main conclusions. The first conclusion regards the effects of time on inclusiveness. Results revealed that, against existing expectations, a longer presence of women in the ranks did not imply a consistent increase in their relative numbers. Although time was positively correlated to the overall degree of gender inclusiveness, this was only true for the group of countries that scored higher in inclusiveness. This meant that time seemed to be positively related to the integration process only when other conditions were met: 'Data support the idea that time, by and in itself, does not automatically foster gender integration or contribute to eliminate existing discriminations in terms of occupational or hierarchical segregation.'[40]

The second conclusion regards the relation between the organizational format of the armed forces and the level of inclusiveness. As expected, evidence showed that the organizational format affected representation: the more a force relied on volunteer personnel, the higher was the percentage of women. Inversely, the closer a military was to the mass-army format, the lower the female representation.

The third conclusion refers to the impact of some external variables related to the socio-economic and political structures and revealed one of the most striking results of the study: while this type of variable had a negligible influence over numerical representation of women in the military, it had a very significant impact on their global integration. Against expectations, indicators of women's 'simple' presence in the system, such as women's labour force participation, did not relate either to women's representation or to gender inclusiveness, whereas indicators of women's 'qualified' presence such as UNDP's Gender Empowerment Measure revealed a much stronger relationship.[41]

In sum, the author concluded that gender integration:

> clearly reached higher levels in countries more exposed to the democratization
> of gender relations in society at large and to external political pressures to
> achieve gender equality in the military. Likewise, gender inclusiveness is higher
> where the military has opened up to society due to organizational shifts towards
> professionalization and where gender equality policies have been implemented
> in the armed forces. Contrarily, and regardless of the moment when women
> joined the military, in countries where those external influences have not
> been felt with the same intensity, where the military remains closer to a mass-

---

40   Carreiras, *Gender and the Military*, p. 200.

41   GEM is a combined index measuring gender inequality in three basic dimensions of empowerment – economic participation and decision-making, political participation and decision-making, and power over economic resources. It includes the following indicators: 'seats in parliament held by women', 'female legislators, senior officials and managers', 'female professional and technical workers' and 'ratio of estimated female to male earned income' (cf. UNDP, Human Development Report 2001 (New York: UNDP, 2001), pp. 244–5).

army format, were women have not reached a 'qualified' position in the social structure, there are lower levels of gender inclusiveness in the military.[42]

Recognizing that these results point to potential spill-over effects from society into the military organization, it was then hypothesized that change towards greater gender equality in the armed forces would not occur automatically as a consequence of time or the increase in relative numbers. On the contrary, it would probably depend more on the extent to which women's 'controlling' presence in society at large might influence policy orientations and decision-making processes within the armed forces.[43]

This conclusion was also supported by an analysis of the difficulties and hardships that military women had to face when seeking integration in the military. Drawing on studies that stress the persistence of integration problems – ranging from performance pressures and blocked mobility to social isolation or sexual harassment – Carreiras concluded that 'empirical results do not allow for optimism.... [T]here is evidence that women are still *tokens* in the military and are likely to remain so in the near future. Besides minority status, gender "inappropriateness" in a profession that is normatively defined as masculine still accounts for women's lack of organizational power and influence.'[44] This sociological pessimism is anchored on the idea that many tensions of gender integration in the military are not revocable by decree and result from two main factors which exist also beyond the military context. The first one is the persistence of a shared cognitive model that supports gender asymmetries and is reproduced in military culture. As Katzenstein and Reppy have argued: 'Persistent gender discrimination suggests that there are aspects of military culture that actively promote intolerance. Military culture is at odds with official policy on gender integration because masculinity has traditionally been central to military identity and culture.'[45]

The second factor regards the difficult conciliation between family and the military profession, both seen as 'greedy' institutions.[46] Even if this affects men and women alike, the disproportionate share of work and family responsibilities between men and women still accounts for the fact that women are more affected than men by such 'greediness' (Gerson, 1985; Shields, 1988; Reynaud, 1988; Moskos and Wood, 1988). This is why it has been sustained (Carreiras, 2006) that overcoming integration problems will not depend strictly on the existence of formal regulations and policies. Greater inclusiveness might instead result from the combined effect of

---

42 Carreiras, *Gender and the Military*, p. 200.

43 Anna G. Jonasdottir, 'On the Concept of Interest: Women's Interests and the Limitations of Interest Theory', in Kathleen B. Jones and Anna G. Jonasdottir, eds, *The Political Interests of Gender* (London, 1990), pp. 33–65.

44 Carreiras, Gender and the Military, p. 206.

45 Katzenstein and Reppy, Beyond Zero Tolerance, p. 2.

46 Lewis Coser, Greedy Institutions: Patterns of Undivided Commitment (New York, 1974); Mady W. Segal, 'The Military and the Family as Greedy Institutions', Armed Forces and Society, 13/1 (1988): 9–38.

women's qualified presence in the social and political realms, its impact on cultural conceptions of gender relations and on a more balanced distribution of domestic and paid work between the sexes. A similar view is shared by Williams (2000). While recognizing that those states that have made more formal commitments are more likely to carry out integration, the author also notes that '*de jure* policies do not automatically translate into de facto opportunities, and domestic interest groups know they must use both legal and political instruments to ensure that they do'.[47]

Women in Peacekeeping

The changing role of the military in complex multifunctional, multinational and multicultural peacekeeping operations has been identified as providing new opportunities for women in the military. Indeed, women's participation in international operations has been intensifying since the early 1990s, after the start of the conflicts in the Balkans. In the context of peacekeeping expansion into areas of humanitarian relief, refugee return, de-mining, civilian policing, demobilization, human rights monitoring, elections and nation-building, women have been ascribed an ever-growing range of tasks.[48]

As far as the military domain is concerned, in the year 2000 all NATO countries had already deployed women in UN and NATO international and peacekeeping missions. However, levels of participation have varied significantly among member nations: data from 2006 show that while in some cases it is almost symbolic, in other cases women's presence in peacekeeping operations has reached very impressive levels.[49] In general, though, the proportion of women soldiers in the military component of peacekeeping missions is still much lower than their representation in the respective national armed forces. Data from the United Nations Department of Peacekeeping Operations (DPKO) show that female presence ranges from a mere one to three per cent of the military personnel in these missions.

This situation has been widely acknowledged in the frame of the debates on the implementation of UN Security Council Resolution 1325, which recognized the urgent need to mainstream gender perspectives into peacekeeping operations.[50] Fox argued that 'the relatively recent concept and practice of peacekeeping have

---

47 Jay Allen Williams, 'The Postmodern Military Reconsidered', in Moskos, Williams and Segal, The Postmodern Military, p. 270.

48 Judith Hicks Stihem, 'Women, Peacekeeping and Peacemaking: Gender Balance and Mainstreaming', in Louise Olsson and Torunn L. Tryggestad, eds., *Women and International Peacekeeping* (London, 2001) pp. 39–48.

49 <http://www.nato.int/issues/women_nato/personnel_comparison_in_deployments_2006.pdf> [accessed 27 October 2008].

50 Olsson and Tryggestad, *Women and International Peacekeeping*, pp. 39–48; Dyan Mazurana, Angela Raven-Robert and Jane Parpart, eds, *Gender, Conflict and Peacekeeping* (Lanham, 2005).

been a predominantly male concern, in the same way as war and military matters in general. Efforts to introduce gender mainstreaming into peacekeeping missions is notable, yet they are long overdue, since they are hardly a new idea'.[51]

Table 12.2 Women in the Military Component of UN Peacekeeping Operations

Mission	Male	Female	Total	Percentage Female
MONUC	17,109	229	17,338	1.3
UNMIL	11,380	262	11,642	2.2
UNIFIL	11,743	552	12,295	4.5
UNMIS	9,210	125	9,335	1.3
UNOCI	7,920	102	8,022	1.3

Source: UNDPKO, Gender Statistics <http://www.un.org/Depts/dpko/dpko/contributors/gender/2008 gender/aug08.pdf>, accessed on 12 October 2008.

In fact, empirical studies conducted mainly during the 1990s had already highlighted the importance of a gender perspective to this type of mission, stressing the way in which the gender-integrated nature of military units deployed to conflict areas accounted significantly for the success of the operations.[52]

More recently, a common concern to a variety of studies and analysis which have aimed at evaluating the impact of Resolution 1325 has been the need to stress the distinct advantages of women's involvement in this type of operations.[53] Hendricks and Hutton synthesized the reasons why female peacekeepers can contribute to the effectiveness of the missions. Their description is worth a full quote:

> [L]ocal men and women tend to see female peacekeepers as more approachable and less threatening than male peacekeepers; female military personnel are needed at roadblocks, airports, etc. ... to perform body searches on women; the ability to work with local women's organizations and to gather information from local women enables the data for decision-making to be more detailed and accurate and therefore more useful; female peacekeepers may, when off duty,

51   Mary-Jane Fox, 'The Idea of Women in Peacekeeping: Lysistrata and Antigone', in Olsson and Tryggestad, *Women and International Peacekeeping*, p. 4.

52   Miller and Moskos, 'Humanitarians or Warriors?'; Maniscaldo, 'Operazione Diverse Della Guerra'; Helena Carreiras, 'A Participação Militar Feminina em Operações de Peacekeeping: Nota de Reflexão Com Ilustração Empírica', *Revista de Psicologia Militar*, 11 (1999): 107–13; Olsson and Tryggestad, *Women and International Peacekeeping*.

53   Gerard J. DeGroot, 'A Few Good Women: Gender Stereotypes, the Military and Peacekeeping', in Olsson and Tryggestad, *Women and International Peacekeeping*, pp. 23–38; Kari H. Karamé, 'Military Women in Peace Operations: Experiences of the Norwegian Battalion in UNIFIL 1978–98', in Olsson and Tryggestad, *Women and International Peacekeeping*, pp. 85–96.

> socialize with local women and talk with them about 'life behind the scenes'.
> This is another way for the mission to get valuable information about what is
> going on in the host country; female military personnel serve as monitors of
> excessive behaviour among male soldiers; female peacekeepers provide positive
> role models for local women to join armed and security forces; both men and
> women who have been victims of sexual abuse are more likely to disclose this
> to female peacekeepers.[54]

Analysing the UN mission to South Africa in the frame of a comparative study of peacekeeping missions, Anu Pillay also states that during the mission there were no incidents of abuse of local women or undisciplined behaviour, which have frequently been reported in peacekeeping operations. She cites women members who noted that 'the mission drew strength from what they termed *feminine traits*, including concern for the wider needs of community, shedding symbols of status and power; networking; sharing information; making intuitive decisions; and using a hands-on approach'.[55] Likewise, in a case study of the Nordic Battalion (NORBAT) experience in Lebanon (UNIFIL), Karamé concluded that female staff contributed to a good mission environment as well as an increased access to local information.[56] In the same vein, Al-Hussein argued that 'the presence of more women in a mission especially at senior levels will help to promote an environment that discourages sexual exploitation and abuse, particularly of the local population'.[57]

All of these analyses point towards the idea that women's presence in peacekeeping actually makes a difference. What is interesting about this discourse is that the supposed peacefulness of women, or at least the social perception of female stereotypical characteristics, is now being used to legitimate the inclusion of women, while in other instances it has been, and continues to be, used to sustain the opposite claim.[58] Dittmer and Apelt note this paradox when they contend that these arguments, 'which were used previously to exclude women from military service, are now being used to force their inclusion'.[59] The authors further note that we seem to witness an inversion of the traditional associations of 'women as nature' and 'men as culture', since the inclusion of women is now seen as a requirement to help control men's supposedly more aggressive behaviour and uncontrolled biological needs. In the face of what appears to be a re-naturalization of the debate about women in the military, De Groot has clearly summed up the

---

54   Cheryl Hendricks and Lauren Hutton, 'Defence Reform and Gender', in Megan Bastick and Kristin Valasek, eds, *Gender and Security Sector Reform Toolkit* (Geneva, 2008), p. 4.

55   Quoted in Hendricks and Hutton, 'Defence Reform and Gender', p. 4.

56   Karamé, 'Military Women in Peace Operations'.

57   Prinz Zeid Ra'ad Zeid Al-Hussein, 'A Comprehensive Strategy to Eliminate Future Sexual Exploitation and Abuse in United Nations Peacekeeping Operations', A/59/710 (New York: United Nations General Assembly, 2005), p. 19.

58   DeGroot, 'A Few Good Women'; Cordula Dittmer and Maja Apelt, 'About Intervening in Vulnerable Societies: Gender in Military Peacekeeping of the Bundeswehr', in Carreiras and Kummel, *Women in the Military and in Armed Conflict*.

59   Dittmer and Apelt, 'About Intervening in Vulnerable Societies', p. 71.

paradox: '[M]ilitaries of the future might want women for the very same reasons they have rejected them in that past.'[60]

Conclusion

Women's military activities have changed during the past decades, as they have been formally integrated into military structures in unprecedented ways. Despite heterogeneity in integration patterns and the existence of cycles of expansion and contraction in women's military roles, their presence in the armed forces has meant a significant challenge to the ethos and identity of the military organization. However, throughout this process contradictory dynamics were set in motion, both in the material and symbolic dimensions.

The debate over women in combat roles illustrates this well. It shows that cultural conceptions of gender and war still account for many of the difficulties surrounding gender integration and that, in many instances, representations of maleness and femaleness remain relatively untouched by objective changes in men's and women's activities. The participation of women (including women soldiers) in peacekeeping missions and the discourses on the advantages of female presence in this type of operation are probably the best example of the contradictions and paradoxes the topic raises. Parallel to a widespread request to increase women's participation in peacekeeping – both in the field and in the decision-making processes – there is a discourse that justifies such a claim on the basis of women's stereotypical natural or social characteristics. As noted above, women's supposedly (and perceived) gentle nature, peacefulness, ability to control aggression and conciliatory attitude are exactly the same characteristics that have been used to sustain women's exclusion in the past. In the face of this paradox, the question might be raised as to whether the association of women and peace will, as some authors believe, lend support to an idealized masculinity that implies constructing women as passive victims in need of protection and help to sustain traditionalist claims concerning separate spheres,[61] or whether, on the contrary, the 'gender stereotypes which previously acted as a barrier for female participation in war might actually enhance the potential for women in the military today'.[62]

The problem still remains for research to investigate the extent to which an increasing representation of women, their access to a wider variety of military functions and their participation in major deployments will contribute to alter perceptions of women's roles in the military, the acceptance of women, the

---

60   DeGroot, 'A Few Good Women', p. 133.
61   J.A. Tickner, *Gender in International Relations* (New York, 1992); Richards, Radcliffe, 'Why the Pursuit of Peace Is Not Part of Feminism', in Elshtain and Tobias, *Women, Militarism and War*, pp. 211–25.
62   DeGroot, 'A Few Good Women', p. 24.

effectiveness of gender-integrated units and, last but not least, the share of power women will have in decision-making about the vital issues of collective defence.

References

Al-Hussein, Prinz Zeid Ra'ad Zeid, 'A Comprehensive Strategy to Eliminate Future Sexual Exploitation and Abuse in United Nations Peacekeeping Operations', A/59/710 (New York: United Nations General Assembly, 2005)

Bastick, Megan and Kristin Valasek, eds, *Gender and Security Sector Reform Toolkit* (Geneva: DCAF, OSCE/ODIHR, UN-INSTRAW, 2008)

Battistelli, Fabrizio, ed., *Donne e Forze Armate* (Roma: Franco Angeli, 1997)

Binkin, Martin and Shirley Bach, *Women and the Military* (Washington: The Brookings Institution, 1977)

Caforio, Giuseppe, ed., *Social Sciences and the Military: An Interdisciplinary Overview* (London and New York: Routledge, 2007)

Carreiras, Helena, 'A Participação Militar Feminina em Operações de Peacekeeping: Nota de Reflexão Com Ilustração Empírica', *Revista de Psicologia Militar*, 11 (1999): 107–13

———, Gender and the Military: Women in the Armed Forces of Western Democracies (London and New York: Routledge, 2006)

Carreiras, Helena and Gerhard Kummel, eds, *Women in the Military and in Armed Conflict* (Wiesbaden: Vs Verlag, 2008)

Chafetz, Janet S., ed., *Handbook of the Sociology of Gender* (New York: Kluwer Academic/Plenum, 1999)

Coser, Lewis, *Greedy Institutions: Patterns of Undivided Commitment* (New York: Free Press, 1974)

Dandeker, Christopher and Mady W. Segal, 'Gender Integration in Armed Forces: Recent Policy Developments in the United Kingdom', *Armed Forces and Society*, 23/1 (1996): 30–47

Devilbiss, M.C., 'Gender Integration and Unit Deployment: A Study of GI Joe', *Armed Forces & Society*, 11/4 (1985): 523–52

Dunivin, Karen O., 'Military Culture: Change and Continuity', *Armed Forces and Society*, 20/4 (1994): 531–47

Elshtain, Jean B., *Women and War*, 2nd edn (Chicago: University of Chicago Press, 1995)

Elshtain, Jean B. and Sheila Tobias, eds, *Women, Militarism and War* (Savage, MD: Rowan and Littlefield, 1990)

Feld, M. D., 'Arms and the Women: Some General Considerations', *Armed Forces and Society*, 4/4 (1978): 557–68

Fullinwider, Robert K., ed., *Conscripts and Volunteers: Military Requirements, Social Justice and the All-Volunteer Force* (New Jersey: Rowan & Allanheld, 1983)

Gabriel, Richard, 'Women in Combat? Two Views', *Army Magazine*, 44/2 (1980): 54–60

General Accounting Office (GAO), National Security and International Affairs Division, *Women in the Military: Deployment in the Persian Gulf War: Report to the Secretary of Defense (GAO/NSIAD-93-93)* (Washington, DC: GAO, 1993)

Gerson, K., *Hard Choices: How Women Decide About Work, Career and Motherhood* (Berkeley: University of California Press, 1985)

Goldman, Nancy L., ed., *Female Soldiers: Combatants or Non-Combatants? Historical and Contemporary Perspectives* (Westport, CT: Greenwood Press, 1982)

Goldstein, Joshua S., *War and Gender: How Gender Shapes the War System and Vice Versa* (Cambridge: Cambridge University Press, 2001)

Gutmann, Stephanie, *The Kinder, Gentler Military: Can America's Gender-Neutral Fighting Force Still Win Wars?* (New York: Scribner's, 2001)

Harries-Jenkins, Gwyn, 'Women in Extended Roles in the Military: Legal Issues', *Current Sociology*, 50/5 (2002): 745–69

Helmer, John, *Bringing the War Home: The American Soldier in Vietnam and After* (New York: The Free Press, 1974)

Holm, Jeanne, *Women in the Military: An Unfinished Revolution* (Novato, CA: Presidio, 1993)

Howes, Ruth H. and Michael R. Stevenson, eds, *Women and the Use of Military Force* (Boulder, CO: Lynne Rienner, 1993)

Isaksson, Eva, ed., *Women and the Military System* (New York: St Martin's Press, 1988)

Jones, Kathleen B., and Anna G. Jonasdottir, eds, *The Political Interests of Gender* (London: Sage, 1990)

Katzenstein, Mary F. and Judith Reppy, eds, *Beyond Zero Tolerance: Discrimination in Military Culture* (Lanham: Rowan and Littlefield, 1999)

Kummel, Gerhard, 'When Boy Meets Girl: The "Feminization" of the Military: An Introduction Also to be Read as a Postscript', *Current Sociology*, 50/5 (2002): 615–39

Macdonald, Sharon, Pat Holden and Shirley Ardener, eds, *Images of Women in Peace and War* (London: Macmillan, 1987)

Mazurana, Dyan, Angela Raven-Robert and Jane Parpart, eds, *Gender, Conflict and Peacekeeping* (Lanham: Rowan and Littlefield, 2005)

Miller, Laura and Charles Moskos, 'Humanitarians or Warriors? Race, Gender and Combat Status in Operation Restore Hope', *Armed Forces and Society*, 4 (1995): 615–37

Mitchell, Brian, *Women in the Military, Flirting With Disaster* (Washington: Regnery, 1998)

Moskos, Charles, 'Battleground of Confusion', *Guardian Weekly* (18 January 1998)

Moskos, Charles and Frank Wood, eds, *The Military, More Than Just a Job?* (Washington: Pergamon-Brassey's, 1998)

Moskos, Charles, Jay Williams and David R. Segal, eds, *The Postmodern Military* (New York: Oxford University Press, 2000)

Olsson, Louise and Torunn L. Tryggestad, eds, *Women and International Peacekeeping* (London: Frank Cass, 1996)

Reynaud, Emmanuel, *Les Femmes, La Violence et L'Armée* (Paris: Fondation pour les Etudes de Defense Nationale, 1988)

Sarkesian, Sam C., ed., *Combat Effectiveness: Cohesion, Stress and the Volunteer Military* (Beverly Hills, CA: Sage,1980)

Segal, Mady W., 'The Military and the Family as Greedy Institutions', *Armed Forces and Society*, 13/1 (1988): 9–38

Simon, Rita J., ed., *Women in the Military* (New Brunswick: Transaction, 2001)

Stanley, Sandra and Mady W. Segal, 'Military Women in NATO: An Update', *Armed Forces and Society*, 14/4 (1988): 559–85

Tickner, J.A., *Gender in International Relations* (New York: Columbia University Press, 1992)

UNDP, Human Development Report 2001 (New York: UNDP, 2001)

Valenius, Johanna, 'Gender Mainstreaming in ESPD Missions', Chaillot Paper, no. 101 (Paris: Institute for Security Studies, 2007)

Van Creveld, Martin, *Men, Women and War: Do Women Belong in the Front Line?* (London: Cassell, 2001)

Vogel, James A., *Summary Report Research Workshop on Physical Fitness Standards and Measurements within the Military Services, 31 August–2 September 1999* (Herndon, VA; Fort Detrick, MD: US Military Operational Medicine Research Program, 1999)

Winslow, Donna and Jason Dunn, 'Women in the Canadian Forces: Between Legal and Social Integration', *Current Sociology*, 50/5 (2002): 641–67

Women and World War II

Lucy Noakes

Introduction

In July 2005, as one of many acts marking the 60th anniversary of the end of World War II, a new memorial was unveiled in Whitehall, London, the traditional civic and national site for official acts of war commemoration. As a result of a long-standing campaign by female veterans and their representatives, the Queen unveiled a statue to commemorate the work of British women in World War II. Unlike many of the other statues and memorials in Whitehall, this was not a figurative sculpture. Instead, the 22-feet-high bronze sculpture takes the form of a cenotaph, around which hang, as if on pegs, 17 different uniforms representing the variety of war work undertaken by women in World War II. Alongside uniforms from the various women's services are canteen overalls, a nurse's cape and a welder's helmet.

The memorial, designed by the artist John Mills, was, as Betty Boothroyd MP pointed out at the opening ceremony, not intended to commemorate the work of just one woman or one group of women. Instead, Boothroyd said, 'it is not by its nature purely a military memorial. It depicts the uniforms of women in the forces alongside the working clothes of those who worked in the factories, the hospitals, the emergency services and the farms'.[1] The decision to create a memorial which commemorated the work of civilians in World War II alongside the military, and to place it close to Lutyens' Cenotaph, the key site for acts of war remembrance in Britain, is perhaps a reflection of the wider understanding and representation of World War II in British culture as the 'people's war', a war that drew on the labour of much of the population, and in which the contribution of the factory worker or ARP warden ranked alongside that of the soldier. However, there is also another, gendered reading of this memorial. The uniforms and other wartime accoutrements which are represented there are empty; there are no women's bodies filling them. These empty uniforms suggest wartime occupations and identities which were temporary, which could be literally 'put on' for the duration of the war and then 'taken off' at the war's end, when the women who had been wearing them resumed their peacetime identities. The aim of this chapter then is twofold: firstly, it is to

---

1   <http://news.bbc.co.uk/1/hi/england/london/4667705.stm> [accessed 27 May 2008].

examine what these wartime roles were, and the extent to which they were shaped by considerations of gender; and, secondly, it is to revisit the debates around the impact of the war on women and on notions of gender, and to consider the extent to which women's wartime roles in Britain can be understood as temporary, as just being 'for the duration'.

In Britain, pre-war planning by the State reflected and was shaped by an assumption that men would fight, and women would care for the home. However, this simplistic gender binary was complicated by two important factors. Firstly, it had become clear during the 1930s that the front line in any coming war would run through towns and cities as aerial bombardment became a widely expected aspect of modern warfare. Being in the home, or on the home front, was no guarantee of safety. Secondly, drawing on the lessons of World War I, the three military services and other government departments all recognised to a greater or a lesser degree that they were going to need to draw on women's organised labour in order to support the work of the combatant man and to replace his labour in the civil sphere. Thus, official State policy towards women's labour was driven by two contradictory forces: there was a perceived need to maintain women's link with the home and with traditional conceptions of femininity and a woman's role; whilst, at the same time, women's labour had to be utilised by the State wherever and whenever it was needed for the successful prosecution of the war effort. Women's movement into wartime work, and their eventual conscription in Britain, was shaped by attempts to balance and reconcile these two needs.

Women's Wartime Work

Women's paid work in wartime was shaped by two contradictory forces: the material need for women's labour to be fully mobilised to meet the demands of the wartime economy; and the ideological need for women's wartime role to disturb the gendered equilibrium as little as possible. As Antonia Lant has argued, the conflict between these two opposing demands can be seen especially clearly in the figure of the 'mobile woman', the (usually) young, single woman, living away from the home and occupied in war work.[2] Women were addressed as active, mobile citizens, able to travel to where they were needed for the war effort through posters, women's magazines, film and government policy. Posters were produced which encouraged women to 'Come into the Factories' to undertake industrial work, to 'Free a man for the Front' in the Army, and to 'Serve with the men who fly' in the Air Force. Women's magazines encouraged women to move into new areas of work and to place the collective needs of the nation above their own, individual needs. Films such as *Millions Like Us* and *The Gentle Sex* acted as effective recruiting

---

2   A. Lant, 'Prologue: Mobile Femininity', in C. Gledhill and G. Swanson, eds, *Nationalising Femininity: Culture, Sexuality and British Cinema in the Second World War* (Manchester: Manchester University Press, 1996), pp. 13–34.

tools for the relatively unpopular occupations of factory work and the Auxiliary Territorial Service (ATS), the women's auxiliary branch of the Army. In all of these sites, a tension can be observed between the material need for women's labour and the ideological need to maintain existing gender relations, a difficult balancing act when women were moving in their tens of thousands into civilian and military occupations which had previously been understood as the preserve of men. In part, the endeavour to preserve gender relations can be discerned in the exhortations to women to maintain their feminine appearance, even when occupied in distinctly 'masculine' work. For example, the magazine *Woman's Own* advised recruits to the ATS on ways to 'keep smart in hair, nails and complexion', while an advert for P & B Knitting Wools reminded its audience: 'They look to you ladies! They expect you to stay lovely and feminine, shining like a good deed in a naughty world.'[3] Other attempts to encourage women to enter paid work in areas such as industry, however, chastised women for 'taking their household duties over-seriously' or spending their time 'gently ambling around the shops' instead of dedicating themselves to the war effort.[4] The attempt to preserve the existing relationship between masculinity and femininity, however, can be discerned most clearly through an examination of the construction of the policy of female conscription, introduced in 1941, and in the work allocated to women when they were in wartime employment.

Although the British State had recognised the need for women's wartime labour before the war, discussions about female mobilisation in the War Office and in other government departments had been based around the voluntary principle; unlike men, women would not be subject to conscription and direction, but instead the State would rely upon their patriotism and sense of duty as a means of ensuring that they volunteered their labour. Despite warnings from women's auxiliary military organisations that 'it would be impossible to create an organisation on recognised lines of official procedure on a large scale entirely by voluntary peacetime effort', women were not to be directed into military, agricultural or industrial work in the early years of the war.[5] However, by 1941, a reluctance amongst women to move into industrial work or to join the ATS, both of which were predominantly staffed by working class women and which, in the case of the ATS, had an unwarranted reputation for promiscuity, led the government to begin to register women for war work, introducing a registration for employment order (REO) so that they could be directed into areas of employment where there was a labour shortage. The debate was ongoing, in 1941, about women's wartime role. Under the auspices of the REO the Ministry of Labour could direct women aged between 18 and 24, who were unemployed or working in occupations designated non-essential, into industry but not into the women's auxiliary forces. These new powers were perceived by some as an attack on fundamental social values; the intrusion into the private life of family and home by an autocratic state. In an argument that singularly failed

---

3   *Woman's Own* (4 May 1940); *Picture Post* (13 April 1940).
4   *Picture Post* (1 February 1941).
5   The National Archive (TNA), London War Office (WO), WO32/10652, *Women's Reserve 1937–1938*.

to recognise the realities of modern warfare, Agnes Hardie MP contended in the House of Commons that 'it has been a tradition for generations that war is a man's job and women have the bearing and raising of children and should be exempt from war'.[6] The Woman-Power Debate that took place in the House of Commons in March 1941 contrasted a discourse of female war work, which positioned it as both heroic and as liberating, with concerns that increasing State management of women's lives threatened to undermine both family life and femininity itself. Whilst two Conservative MPs, Thelma Cazalet and Irene Ward, argued that 'women will not be found wanting' and that 'this debate creates another milestone in British parliamentary history', Hardie emphasised the importance of women's maternal role over and above their role as wartime workers, arguing that mothers were 'doing a far more important job for the future generations ... than filling shells with which to kill some other mother's son'.[7] Debates around the formalisation of women's war work thus illustrate the tension between the demands of patriarchy and the demands of production identified by Penny Summerfield.[8]

By the end of 1941 it had become clear that the REO alone was not sufficient to provide the numbers of women needed for wartime work, especially in the less popular occupations of industry and the ATS. In August 1941, for example, only 6,647 women volunteered for service with the ATS, whilst 15,827 applied to join the far smaller Women's Auxiliary Air Force (WAAF).[9] Conscription was extended to women by the National Service (No. 2) Act, passed in December 1941. The Act initially enabled the government to call up all unmarried women aged between 20 and 30, beginning with women born in 1920 and 1921. However, unlike conscription for men, introduced on the outbreak of war in 1939, women's national service was hedged about with a variety of clauses that were designed to enable the co-existence of a mobilised, and often militarised, femininity alongside a conception of a woman's wartime role which continued to emphasise the importance of home and family. Whilst the exemption of women with childcare responsibilities for children under 14 from conscription was a recognition of the need for some stability to be maintained in the family home, where the father was often absent on military service, the regulations that surrounded the employment of married women without childcare responsibilities are less easy to explain in practical terms. Married women without young children and with husbands absent on war work or military service could be conscripted, but only into part-time, local work. The maintenance of the domestic home thus superseded the needs of production, demonstrating the importance attributed to retaining links

---

6   Hansard, House of Commons, 5th series, vol. 376 (1941–1942), Parliamentary Debates November 12–December 19, 1941, Debate on Maximum National Effort 2/12 (1941), col. 1,079.

7   Hansard, vol. 370 (March–April 1941), Woman-Power Debate, cols 351–3.

8   Penny Summerfield, *Women Workers in the Second World War: Production and Patriarchy in Conflict* (London: Croom Helm, 1984).

9   TNA, Department of Labour and National Service (LAB), LAB 76/3, J.L. Brooke-Wavell, *Women's Auxiliary Services* (1956), p. 26.

between femininity and domesticity in wartime, even when this link threatened the efficiency of the war effort.

When women were conscripted and directed into war work, the types of work, and the rates of pay accorded to them, were again shaped by gender. Women working in industry were subject to the process known as dilution, by which the employment of skilled and semi-skilled men was replaced by the employment of larger numbers of less skilled and unskilled female employees. A task formerly completed by one or two skilled male workers was typically broken down into its constituent parts, with a less skilled worker employed to do one or two of these parts, rather than being trained (and paid) to complete the entire process. In part, dilution was a pragmatic means of managing the need for large numbers of replacement workers to be trained quickly, in order to keep the factories producing when the male workers were conscripted into the forces. However, dilution was also the result of agreements between employers and trades unions, looking to protect the wages of male workers from being undercut by female employees paid at a lower rate. Predicated on the idea of 'men's work' and 'women's work', dilution demonstrated both the naturalised idea of gender and of types of occupation suitable to men and to women, and the belief that women's war work was temporary, imagined as being 'just for the duration'.

Women who joined the auxiliary services were similarly subject to dilution; the work that they undertook was also shaped by contemporary conceptions of what constituted 'women's work'. The largest of the women's services, the ATS, initially opened up five different trades to women: clerk, cook, storewoman, driver and orderly, all of which, with the possible exception of driver, reflected the kinds of paid work that women had been employed in before the war. Like their colleagues in civilian employment, servicewomen were paid on a lower rate than men, a practice justified by the use of dilution and the perceived necessity of employing more than one woman to do a job previously undertaken by one man. The work that women could or could not be asked to do in the services had been the subject of lengthy debate in the War Office prior to the introduction of female conscription. In particular, concern was expressed that women should not be directed into any areas of work associated with combat, such as work on the anti-aircraft sites which ringed British cities. It was eventually decided that, whilst women could be directed into the auxiliary services, they could only work on the anti aircraft sites as volunteers, thus preserving the final barrier between male combatants and female non-combatants. While women could be directed to work on anti-aircraft sites they could not be compelled to do so and, once there, they would not be able to fire the guns.

Women's work on anti-aircraft batteries was probably the most controversial aspect of their wartime employment in Britain. Women were employed on the sites as a means of replacing men who were increasingly 'combed out' for use with the Regular Army overseas. By 1942, more women than men were working on the anti-aircraft sites and approximately 50 per cent of new recruits to the ATS were choosing to work in Air Defence.[10] However, although women working on the gun sites worked with and alongside men, undertaking every aspect of the work except firing the guns, they remained officially non-combatant, were paid approximately two-thirds of the equivalent male wages and were unable to receive service medals. This distinction, whilst it may have acted to preserve the morale and the masculinity of the men on the anti-aircraft sites, did little to safeguard women on the sites from physical danger, or from attacks upon their femininity and their morality. Private Nora Caveney, aged just 18, was the first fatality amongst members of the ATS working on the anti-aircraft sites, hit by a bomb splinter whilst on duty. In total, 335 members of the ATS were killed during the war, 83 of these serving with Air Defence on the anti-aircraft sites.[11] Despite this, women on the gun sites were subject to continual rumours regarding their alleged immorality and promiscuity. Working closely with men, at night, often in isolated positions, in the imagined excitement of battle, these women were more vulnerable than others to the whispering campaign which dubbed the ATS the 'All Tarts Unit', or the OTS the 'Officers' Ground Sheets'. The integration of women into the anti-aircraft sites proved to be an operational success; the challenge that their position there offered to existing conceptions of gender was less easy to negotiate.

In all areas of women's work during the war, the desire to maintain distinctions of gender shaped and modified the employment of women. This impacted upon the processes by which they were registered and conscripted, the types of work that they undertook, the pay they received and, in the case of women in the auxiliary forces, the designation of non-combatant which prevented them from being awarded combat medals. Despite the necessity of utilising women's labour alongside men's in order to mobilise the nation fully for the war effort, discourses of gender which positioned men and women, masculinity and femininity as binary opposites, with the masculine being closely linked with the military and the feminine closely linked with the home, remained extremely powerful throughout the war. The next section of this chapter will explore this relationship further.

Women and the Wartime Home

Alongside wartime entreaties to women to leave the home and take up necessary wartime work, to position themselves as public, rather than private, citizens, was a contradictory discourse, which emphasised the importance of women's role in maintaining the wartime home. With men being conscripted from the outbreak of war, women were increasingly responsible not only for the material management of the home, but also for its symbolic maintenance. The preservation of the familial home amongst the many disruptions of wartime was understood as having not only

---

10   Vera Douie, *Daughters of Britain: An Account of the Work of British Women During the Second World War* (Oxford: George Ronald, 1949), p. 34.

11   <http://www.atsremembered.pwp.blueyonder.co.uk/CWGCpdf> [accessed 21 June 2008].

practical, but also symbolic and propagandist importance. With men conscripted into service away from the home, women became ever more closely linked with both the home and the home front, the term used to describe the geographic nation at war and which, as Antonia Lant has suggested, can be understood as a way of attempting to represent the nation as home, and thus women's work away from the domestic setting as an extension of that carried out within the home.[12] It is exactly this discourse that is mobilised in the film *Millions Like Us*, made in 1942 to persuade more women to volunteer for factory work, in which the key character, Celia, who could avoid conscription because she was caring for her widowed father, chose not to do so, instead taking up paid work on the home front. Despite this move away from the family home, Celia is represented throughout the film as domesticated and feminine, her gender remaining unthreatened by her move into an area of employment broadly understood as masculine. Mobilised men were reassured that the homes they were fighting to defend were still present in some form or other: an article in the *Sunday Pictorial*, published during the Battle of Britain in June 1940, when the threat of invasion was at its strongest, reassured its readers that 'while the men are away (women) are keeping the home front going'. The housewife as defender of not only home but also nation was asserted in the article's claim that 'Britain's second line of defence is your house, our house, my house, and the house next door … more and more women are being left behind to hold that second line of defence.'[13] Early on in the war, women's magazines urged their readers not to be swept up in the excitement of war and to remember that domestic and family work was of equal importance with the, apparently, more glamorous and exciting public roles that were becoming available. The novelist Storm Jameson, writing in *Woman's Journal* in the autumn of 1939, urged her readers to 'guard against that peculiar excitement to which some women succumb in wartime', rejecting the appeal of war work for the equally important but less glamorous work of maintaining the family home. Jameson looked back to World War I as a means of warning her readers that: '[I]n the last war many men were bitterly disappointed when they came home … they came back to find that we had changed. … It will be a disgrace if this happens again. Even in small things we must try to keep their home "intact".'[14] Keeping the home intact in the face of conscription, evacuation, bombardment and shortages was the job of women in wartime.

However, many of the women who were attempting to manage the wartime home were also trying to hold down jobs in wartime industries. This 'dual burden' of paid and unpaid labour was compounded by the specific difficulties of wartime, as, with commodity shortages outweighing those of World War I, women found themselves spending long hours both queuing for food and undertaking the tasks of cooking and cleaning in conditions that were impaired by a lack of new household goods. The government policy of 'make do and mend' encouraged

---

12   Lant, p. 15.

13   *Sunday Pictorial* (8 June 1940), pp. 10–11.

14   S. Jameson, cited in J. Waller and M. Vaughan-Rees, *Women in Wartime: The Role of Women's Magazines* (London: Macdonald, 1987), p. 14.

these women to see undertaking household work under conditions of adversity as their patriotic duty. Newspapers and magazines were full of advice to their female readers: among the more unlikely tips listed by Angus Calder in *The People's War* are suggestions that unrationed sheeps' heads would be a good source of protein and that cormorant eggs be used for baking.[15] 'Make do and mend' leaflets, issued by the Board of Trade, advised mothers on how to let out children's clothes, as few new clothes were available, how to carry out simple household repairs, and how to prepare for the arrival of a new baby when goods were scarce.[16] Despite the rather jolly nature of much of the advice, the realities of life for the working woman with household responsibilities can be represented by the following account of daily life from a 40-year-old mother of six:

> *I get up at 5 in the morning and get the worst of my housework done, and the children all washed and dressed, and I do the washing up and get my dinner started so it'll only need a warm up in the evening. Then I go to work and I come back at 9.30 in the evening and give them all their supper and tidy up a bit. I seem to manage.*[17]

While the conditions described here could be alleviated for women of the upper and middle classes, who were more likely than others to be in a position to afford access to childcare and to some domestic support, the responsibility for maintaining the family home was understood during the war as being a specifically feminine responsibility.

The government and employers did attempt to alleviate the double burden of paid work and housework to some extent, as it was recognised that the level of unofficial absences amongst women workers had the potential to impact on productivity. This intervention was, however, limited. The amount of time that had to be spent on shopping in wartime, with consumers chasing after scarce goods and often queuing for hours once they were discovered, led industrialists to petition the government to provide a solution to the problem of the high rate of absenteeism amongst married women that this was perceived to be causing. A variety of schemes were suggested and trialled, including priority shopping cards for munitions workers, factories opening stores for their workers, and the registration of shoppers with specific shops, but these were all eventually rejected as either interfering with the market or, in the case of the priority cards scheme, causing resentment amongst other customers. Women with the dual burden of paid work and housework increasingly had to rely upon neighbours, relatives and older children to do their shopping for them. Although many factory employers decided to recognise the time-consuming nature of shopping in wartime, and to regulate

---

15   A. Calder, *The People's War* (London: Pimlico, 1969), p. 380.
16   Ministry of Trade, Make Do and Mend Leaflets, reproduced as *Make Do and Mend: Keeping Family and Home Afloat on War Rations* (London: Michael O'Mara, 2007).
17   G. Braybon and P. Summerfield, *Out of the Cage: Women's Experiences in Two World Wars* (London: Pandora, 1987), pp. 235–6.

this by providing 'shopping leave', this was unpaid, and simply regularised the patterns of absenteeism, rather than alleviating the demands of balancing domestic management with paid work.

Probably of more practical help to working women was the growth of communal feeding centres such as 'British Restaurants' and the development of time and labour-saving devices and products for the home. Manufacturers of convenience foods and household devices such as vacuum cleaners and washing machines responded to the needs of the wartime home. Wartime advertisements for domestic goods demonstrate the emphasis on time-saving that dominated discourses on household management during the war. An advert for 'Rinso' washing powder was headlined: 'Mrs Green turns out tops for ammunition boxes – 1 every 3 seconds – then does washing for family after 8 and a half hour day' and concluded that 'Rinso's no end of help to busy folk like me … not that I'd be happy if I wasn't doing my bit to get this war over and won.'[18] Similarly, an advert from 1941 headed 'Siren meals for the Smiths again' used the scenario of a busy woman, her shopping disturbed by the need to take shelter during an air raid, able to provide a hot meal for her family by cooking a ready-made 'Mrs Peeks Pudding'.[19] Hoover vacuum cleaners used an image of a woman driving a crane, headlined 'Housewife of 1944. The hand that held the Hoover drives a crane!' to promote its products, claiming that many possessors of Hoover vacuum cleaners 'now, more than ever, must bless the day they bought a Hoover to save their sorely needed time and energy'.[20] As the war dragged on, and the needs of the wartime economy grew more demanding, the pre-war emphasis on maintaining high standards of domestic maintenance shifted towards a discourse that prioritised efficiency and time management over and above pride in housework. While the domestic home had to be managed and maintained in wartime, women were encouraged to see themselves as citizens with public, as well as private, duties and responsibilities.

One of the most often cited ways in which the war impacted on the home was the provisions made by the state and by employers for childcare, most notably in the provision of workplace nurseries and the schemes to evacuate children, with their mothers if they were young, away from the cities that were expected to be the main targets for aerial bombardment. There were three main waves of evacuation away from the large cities. The first took place in the months preceding the outbreak of war in 1939, with an estimated three and a half million official and unofficial evacuees. The second wave of evacuation followed the fall of France and the Low Countries, and the beginning of the Blitz in 1940; and the third and final wave took place in the summer of 1944, as V1 and V2 rockets exploded over south-east England.[21] Evacuation was one of the key sites for the wartime intervention of the State into what had previously been understood as the private sphere of

---

18   *Picture Post* (21 February 1942).
19   *Woman's Own* (12 October 1941).
20   Waller and Vaughan-Rees, p. 109.
21   S.O. Rose, *Which People's War? National Identity and Citizenship in Wartime Britain* (Oxford: Oxford University Press, 2003), p. 57.

the home and family. The arrival of families from the urban slums in the, largely, more prosperous rural areas led to a wave of concern towards and criticism of the living standards of the urban poor. As in the nineteenth and early twentieth centuries, mothers were largely held to be responsible for the health and behaviour of their children. The class divisions of interwar Britain were made visible in a highly gendered fashion, typified by the author of a letter to the *Glasgow Herald* who claimed that 'sympathy for a woman who is too poor to procure proper food is admirable, but sympathy expressed for one who is too poor to keep a clean house and teach her children decent habits is mere sentimentality'.[22] Whilst the condition of evacuated families and children was seen to be the responsibility of individual mothers, overall responsibility for evacuation was also understood to be women's work, demonstrated by the propaganda poster which encouraged women to register to receive evacuees as 'all women love children and wish to help them'.[23] The Women's Voluntary Service (WVS) played a central role in organising evacuation and lobbied central government effectively for financial support to meet the needs of preschool-age refugee children.[24] Often in charge of billeting arrangement and called in to negotiate disagreements between evacuees and their hosts, the WVS was intimately involved in the minutiae of evacuation, and its largely middle and upper-class members in rural Britain played a key role in the management of the problems of evacuation. Whilst these problems were usually attributed to the 'dirty ... idle and unwilling to work or pull their weight' mothers of the slums, solutions to this 'problem' were also seen as a female responsibility.[25]

Evacuation was, of course, far from the only way that the family was disrupted in wartime. While individuals were asked to position themselves as public, rather than private, citizens, during the war, continuities of home and family were understood as being central to the maintenance of morale both on the home front and amongst the troops who were told one of the key things that they were fighting for was the home. As Gillian Swanson has argued, the 'common habits' of family Britain, made increasingly visible by the increased involvement of the State in domestic life were 'testimony to unity and stability'.[26] The multifarious ways in which the war threatened this stability were focused through a concern with the behaviour and activities of the women left behind to manage the home. Women's magazines were full of advice to their readers on how to manage their own and their daughters' behaviour in wartime. The newly mobile, young, single woman was a particular cause for alarm, as 'most girls have to meet their boyfriends without proper introductions nowadays', and the letters pages of magazines published numerous pleas from parents concerned about

---

22   *Glasgow Herald* (16 September 1939), cited in Rose, p. 60.
23   Imperial War Museum, Department of Art, Catalogues and Posters, ART 15707, undated.
24   J. Hinton, *Women, Social Leadership and the Second World War: Continuities of Class* (Oxford: Oxford University Press, 2002), p. 148.
25   L. Boys, 'Preliminary Report on Evacuation' (11 September 1939), cited in Hinton, p. 150.
26   G. Swanson, 'So Much Money and So Little to Spend it on: Morale, Consumption and Morality', in Gledhill and Swanson, p. 71.

the diminished lack of control they had over their daughters' lives in wartime.[27] Many of these, such as the letter that claimed the author's daughter was 'a nice girl till she started to work in a factory', were imbued with a class bias that equated decorous behaviour with the middle classes, but others, such as the letter that expressed shock at *Woman's Own* producing a booklet that told 'girls the facts of life before they get married', demonstrated a broader concern that the conditions of wartime were undermining both parental control and sexual morality more generally.[28] Married women were understood to be equally vulnerable to the increased social freedoms experienced by women in wartime. The presence in Britain of American GIs, from the winter of 1942 onwards, increased public concern about the behaviour of women on the home front, as Sonya O. Rose has argued, triggering 'the widespread perception that a wave of "moral laxity" was engulfing the country'.[29] Psychologists understood wartime to be a time of heightened sexual desire in which 'woman, granted a new-born partial freedom … has become drunk on sex' and the 'exotic'; 'unknown' GIs, with their access to consumer goods unavailable in rationed Britain, were seen to pose a particular temptation to the woman experiencing the 'freedoms' of wartime.[30] Magazines published numerous articles advising women to disregard the passing temptations of wartime and to remain faithful to absent partners, encouraging them to sublimate their desires for sex or romance in war work or organised leisure activities. Infidelity could harm not only the marriage or relationship but also, it was argued, the war effort when 'the foolish, unthinking woman' wrote to tell a man on active service of an affair causing 'an amount of damage to morale and to the war effort … probably greater than that done by the whole of Doctor Goebbels' war machine'.[31] Women who had had an affair and possibly become pregnant were sternly reminded that they had 'let down the spirit of British women, perhaps to foreign or Dominion soldiers' and to absolve themselves by 'the way of work. Work till you are too tired to mope … till you forget how much you long for "him" to kiss you and put his arms around you'.[32] It was the woman's public responsibility to maintain home and family during the war and, if needs be, rebuild it at the war's end.

Women and Reconstruction

Towards the end of the war, emphasis in Britain shifted from fighting the war and sustaining the war effort towards rebuilding the nation after the war. Whilst this

---

27 *Woman's Own* (23 March 1940).
28 *Woman's Own* (16 June 1944; 23 October 1942).
29 Rose, p. 75.
30 George Ryley Scott, *Sex Problems and Dangers in Wartime: A Book of Practical Advice for Men and Women on the Fighting and Home Fronts* (London: T. Werner Laurie, 1940), p. 70.
31 *Woman and Beauty* (November 1943), cited in Waller and Vaughan-Rees, p. 76.
32 L. Eyles, 'Rebuilding Marriages', *Woman's Own*, cited in Waller and Vaughan Rees, p. 74. No further reference given.

was strongly shaped by a desire for a more egalitarian Britain where the class and income divisions that had been so visible in the preceding years were overcome, a desire embodied in the reforms of the Beveridge Report which laid the foundations for the Welfare State, it was also formed by a desire to reconstruct gender relations as closely as possible along pre-war lines. The clearest site of gender reconstruction was in women's paid work. Whilst demobilisation was not as sudden for most women as it had been in 1918, much of women's wartime work was understood to be temporary, 'just for the duration' in a key phrase of the time, and women workers were largely expected to return to the home or to traditional areas of employment for women at the end of the war. Although the State needed to increase production as a means of boosting exports and paying off war debts, and thus maintained many of the controls over manpower, production and consumption that had been introduced during the war, attitudes towards women's employment and demobilisation were shaped by assumptions about women's domestic role. While policies shaping male demobilisation were guided by the need for manpower in the services and in industry, female demobilisation was driven by the belief that women would be returning to home, family and unpaid labour as quickly as possible, working, if they had to, part-time or in traditionally female occupations. Nursery education became the responsibility of local authorities, and hours were reorganised away from providing childcare during working hours towards the provision of more limited education and care during school hours. A survey of some of the large wartime employers of women demonstrated that many of them intended to return to pre-war practices of employment, with the four main railway companies, large city councils such as Birmingham, and industrial employers such as Unilever and Imperial Chemicals, all stating that they would cease to employ married women at the end of the war. Although some other large employers, such as the Bank of England and the BBC, decided to remove pre-war marriage bars, these decisions were qualified by comments by the Bank of England such as ' married women employed during the war were found to have disadvantages' and the BBC's statement that it would review its policy of employing married women if 'it appeared to be against public policy'.[33] Women in the services were demobilised from the summer of 1945, with married women taking priority over all others and Churchill arguing forcefully that 'all women should be free to retire as soon as possible from the services', although they were offered the opportunity to continue as volunteers for a period of two years and were eventually offered permanent support roles within the forces with the establishment of the Women's Royal Army Corps in 1948, and the Women's Royal Naval Service and the Women's Auxiliary Air Force in 1949.[34]

This gendering of employment policy went hand in hand with the gendering of the Welfare State, which assumed that the married woman was essentially dependent upon her husband. Under the system of social security benefits set out in the 1943

---

33   Appendix to *Report on Pensionability of Unestablished Civil Service, Parliamentary Papers,* 1945–46, XII, Command 6942.

34   TNA, LAB, 76/3, *Women's Auxiliary Services,* J.L. Brooke-Waddell (1956), p. 73.

Beveridge Report, the married woman working outside of the home could choose to pay a lower rate of National Insurance for which, in return, she would receive a lower rate of benefits, reflecting Beveridge's assumption that 'during marriage … most women will not be gainfully employed'.[35] Beveridge believed that these women would return to home and family, replacing the paid work of wartime with the 'vital work' of 'ensuring the adequate continuance of the British race'.[36] The post-war Welfare State thus positioned women within the domestic home, rearing children and primarily reliant on their husbands for financial support. The wartime tension between the State's need for women's labour and the ideological need for women to remain linked with the home was to be resolved by the return of the post-war woman to domesticity.

The principal address to women in reconstruction then was as wife and mother. The ensuing retreat from war work and service into the home did not mean, however, that women were no longer the subjects of social policy. Instead, schemes for the improvement of women's lives appear to have taken up much of the time of policy-makers in the mid-1940s, with plans for rest homes for tired housewives, State provision of babysitters and after-school play centres all being suggested. The new houses being built on the outskirts of towns and cities to replace the slum housing destroyed and damaged during the war were designed with hot water, gas and electricity and with enough bedrooms to accommodate the larger families women were encouraged to have following the war. Women were to be educated not only in citizenship, but also in childcare and household management through an education policy that helped to shape provision for girls in the new secondary schools; and, although women were encouraged to take an interest in public and political affairs, the key image of the post-war woman was that of a wartime worker or servicewoman returning to a normality symbolised by domesticity.

Of course, many women did desire exactly this kind of normality. After the long years of warfare, many yearned for the stability of peacetime domestic life. Mass-Observation's report on demobilisation, *The Journey Home*, found that 'the large number of opinionated women want to return to or start on domestic life', while *Woman and Beauty* reassured its readers that 'the rebirth of home life is what 99 out of every 100 of us are living for'.[37] Marriage rates increased from 14 per thousand in 1943 to 19 per thousand in 1945 and more than a quarter of brides were aged below 21.[38] Divorce rates were also on the rise, however, with 41,704 petitions for divorce being submitted in 1946, a figure not arrived at again until 1967.[39] The trend

---

35   Sir William Beveridge, *Social Insurance and Allied Services: Report by Sir William Beveridge* (London, 1942), p. 53.
36   Beveridge, p. 53.
37   Mass-Observation, *The Journey Home: A Mass-Observation Report on the Problems of Demobilisation* (London, 1944) p. 55; *Woman and Beauty* (1944), cited in Waller and Vaughan Rees, p. 125.
38   Braybon and Summerfield, p. 267.
39   C. Smart, 'Good Wives and Moral Lives: Marriage and Divorce 1937–51', in Gledhill and Swanson, p. 93.

towards the companionate marriage that had begun between the wars appears to have been strengthened by the war, with the editor of *Woman's Own* urging women who had found fulfilment in war work to 'carry forward the grand things you have learned in your courageous war service and ... take it with you when the war is over to the building of a new world in which women share equally with men'.[40] An article, published in *Woman's Magazine*, by Ella Thompson, who had served in the WAAF during the war, demonstrated the impact of the war on perceptions of married life, with Thompson equating a 'sane and sweet normality' with marriage and demobilisation whilst commenting that 'being in the WAAF has shown me the comradeship that can exist between men and women', an experience that would enable her 'to be more than a housewife. I shall be a comrade and partner to my husband ... we shall be lovers and, what is more, friends and co-workers'.[41] In common with many women at the end of the war, Thompson's experience of public war work was to be utilised to build a modern, post-war marriage. While the war may have modernised British society, it was a highly gendered process of modernisation.

Conclusions

During the war, British women moved in huge numbers from the private, domestic world of the home to the public world of work, and from part-time, traditionally feminine areas of employment to civilian and military occupations previously understood as being the preserve of men. Britain was the only participant nation to introduce female conscription during the war and, although women in other nations such as the Soviet Union may have played a more active role in military combat, British women were the only female civilian population to be subject to State-organised mobilisation on a large scale. Women were encouraged and expected to position themselves as public, rather than private, citizens for the sake of the war effort, putting the collective good above individual needs and desires. Despite this, the linkage of the home and femininity remained of enormous importance in wartime, shaping both representations of women, State policy and women's expectations of their lives. Although peacetime and demobilisation shifted the emphasis back more fully on to a more domestic femininity, there was never a complete return to the gender relations of the interwar years. For example, women made up 22 per cent of the engineering workforce in 1951, fewer than those employed in the industry in wartime, but far greater than the 10 per cent employed there in 1939.[42] Perhaps the most important transformation in women's lives wrought by the war is the hardest to quantify: women's perception of themselves.

---

40 *Woman's Own* (October 1945), cited in Waller and Vaughan-Rees, pp. 123–5.
41 E. Thompson, 'My Post-war Aims', *Woman's Magazine* (November 1944), in Waller and Vaughan-Reeves, p. 124.
42 Braybon and Summerfield, p. 264.

As Penny Summerfield's series of interviews with female veterans during the 1990s demonstrated, the impact of the war on the individual's sense of self varied greatly. Whilst the majority of the women interviewed by Summerfield did express the belief that the war had changed them, others articulated a sense of regret for lost opportunities whilst others focused on the horrors of wartime.[43] Although the uniforms of the Women at War Memorial discussed at the beginning of this chapter may have been 'taken off' at the end of the war, their impact on the wartime wearers was, at times, immense. While few historians would now want to argue that the war modernised women's lives to the extent that Arthur Marwick claimed in the 1970s, paying attention instead to the contradictory narratives of wartime, women's wartime experiences continue to shape both individual and collective identities.[44]

---

43 Penny Summerfield, *Reconstructing Women's Wartime Lives: Discourse and Subjectivity in Oral Histories of the Second World War* (Manchester: Manchester University Press, 1998), pp. 252–97.

44 Arthur Marwick, *War and Social Change in the Twentieth Century* (London: Macmillan, 1974).

PART III
MORALITY AND LAW

Ethics and the Enduring Relevance of Just War Theory in the Twenty-First Century[1]

David Whetham

Introduction

The relationship between ethics and war is at best strange, at worst, it can appear paradoxical. War is a situation in which the normal rules that govern civilised discourse in international affairs have broken down. Within a society there are many crimes that can be committed, but none is more serious than the act of deliberately taking another person's life. Yet most societies consider it perfectly consistent with this to keep a military organisation of varying size to carry out precisely this function if the circumstances so dictate. Even so, those military organisations are only allowed to carry out this function in certain ways, adhering to all sorts of legal, social and ethical constraints. Warfare, despite taking place when the normal rules of political interaction no longer apply, always has been one of the most rule-bound activities that mankind conducts and this presents something of a conundrum.

The current, broadly accepted criteria that form Just War Theory (JWT), and the long tradition from which it has developed, are the results of attempts to look at conflict within an ethical framework and, in some way, resolve this conundrum.[2] In no other walk of life are the stakes so high. JWT provides a common language for debating the rights and wrongs of conflict and an ethical framework for thinking about rights and also responsibilities and duties, even in wartime. It can help explain the difference between justifiable (and therefore legitimate) military action, and something wholly different: 'Without ethical and legal constraints on both the decision to wage it (*jus ad bellum*) and its conduct (*jus in bello*), war is nothing

---

1   This chapter is based on the article, Ethics, War and Human Rights, first published in Defence and Strategy, June 2008 <http://www.defenceandstrategy.eu/en/current-issue-1-2008/articles/ethics-war-and-human-rights.html>.

2   In the same way that the laws of war apply to armed conflicts rather than just wars, so Just War Theory applies even when a formal war has not been declared.

more than the application of brute force, logically indistinguishable from mass murder.'[3]

Such sentiments are certainly not lost on the British military:

> *The chain of command, from the government downwards, is responsible for articulating and sustaining the morality and justice of the cause in question ... [O]nly on the basis of absolute confidence in the justice and morality of the cause, can British soldiers be expected to be prepared to give their lives for others.*[4]

What this chapter will demonstrate is that JWT not only provides a common language for discussing and debating normative issues relating to the use of force, and a moral framework for explaining the difference between legitimate actions and unjustified ones; it also contains considerations that lie at the heart of sound strategic thinking.

Where Do the Just War Tradition and the Laws of War Fit In?

The type of thinking that leads to JWT fits in between two very different attitudes towards war: pacifism and realism. In many ways, JWT is a compromise between these two positions. Pacifism is a presumption against war. It argues that while evil must be opposed in the world, resorting to war and violence is always wrong. Pacifism sees a straightforward contradiction between acting morally, and the conscious, systematic and deliberate taking of life that war requires. Put simply, war is unjust and one cannot do something that is unjust whatever the reason: one cannot do evil to prevent evil. This position can come from religious, political or even pragmatic reasoning. For example, for the first three centuries AD, Christianity was broadly a pacifistic religion, taking seriously Christ's clear injunctions to non-violence found in the New Testament. Mahatma Gandhi's successful campaign to drive the British out of India in the late 1940s or the civil rights crusade of Martin Luther King Jr on behalf of African-Americans in the 1960s are both examples of politically inspired pacifism that achieved results through non-violence. One of the twentieth century's most distinguished thinkers, Bertrand Russell, articulated the very practical grounds on which war in the nuclear age (and he argued convincingly that any small war between the nuclear powers would escalate into a nuclear exchange) was no longer a viable instrument of policy:

> *Neither side can defeat the other except by defeating itself at the same time. The interests in which the two sides conflict are immeasurably less important than those in which they are at one. The first and most important of their*

---

3   Alex J. Bellamy, *Just Wars: From Cicero to Iraq* (Cambridge: Polity Press, 2006), p. 1.
4   Army Doctrine Publication, vol. 5, *Soldiering, the Military Covenant* (2002), pp. 3–13.

> common interests is survival. This has become a common interest owing to
> the nature of nuclear weapons.[5]

The logical consequence of such reasoning is that war itself must be avoided. While such arguments had a particular resonance in a period dominated by the very real threat of mutually assured destruction, clearly pacifist reasoning has found advocates throughout history. However, while providing a useful challenge to the idea of what strength really is – and the pacifist certainly provides a very profound opposition to both the realist and JWT – pacifism also has certain key limitations. Despite early persecution by the state itself, the early Christians were not faced with issues of survival from an external threat as they lived within the security provided by the Roman Empire. Once that Empire became Christianised, on the whole they, too, took up arms to defend it (see Augustine below) as they were faced with the greater evil of the destruction of Christendom. Both King and Gandhi could rely, to some extent, on the restraint of those they opposed. Would such campaigns have been possible in a totalitarian state where, as George Orwell noted, 'opponents of the regime disappear in the middle of the night and are never heard from again'?[6] The pragmatic pacifist makes a convincing argument until one is faced with a decision to intervene and save lives by using force to prevent a genocide, or to stand by and watch innocent people die when you could have prevented it.

On the other side of the argument, the realist wonders why one would need justification at all? In this context, realism is the view that moral or ethical thinking, or concepts such as 'justice', do not belong in the sphere of international relations.[7] The realist does not have to go as far as to say that such values mean absolutely nothing, just that they are alien to the world between states: the state is what makes such values possible for those who live under its protection. As there is no 'Leviathan' in the international arena, it makes no sense to talk about values, morality or ethics here either.[8] Thucydides famously captured this idea in the Melian Dialogue when the Athenians argue: 'The standard of justice depends on the equality of power to compel and that in fact the strong do what they have the power to do and the weak accept what they have to accept.'[9]

Cicero summed this view up with 'in war the law is silent'.[10] While actually arguing from the pacifist viewpoint that war required avoiding completely, not humanising (she was a Nobel Peace Laureate in 1905), Baroness Bertha von Suttner

---

5   Bertrand Russell, *Common Sense and Nuclear Warfare* (London: George Allen and Unwin, 1959), pp. 18–21.

6   Cited in Michael Walzer, *Just and Unjust Wars: A Moral Argument with Historical Illustrations*, 2nd edn (New York: Basic, 1992), p. 332.

7   For example, see Niccolò Machiavelli, *The Discourses*, ed. by Bernard Crick, trans. by Leslie J. Walker (London: Penguin, 1970), p. 515.

8   The Leviathan represents the absolute authority provided by a sovereign state.

9   Thucydides, *The History of the Peloponnesian War*, trans. by Rex Warner (London: Penguin, 1972), p. 402.

10   Cicero, *Pro Milone*, 11.

stated that 'improving the laws of war … is like regulating the temperature when boiling someone in oil'.[11] It was war itself that needed preventing, not restraining in some small way. The Baroness had a point, but the realist takes a slightly different tack, arguing that because 'war is hell', as Sherman famously stated, seeking to tame it with artificial rules is simply ridiculous and unworkable. If war is such a terrible thing, then the best that can be done is to get it over with as quickly as possible. Adhering to any kind of misguided ethical or legal limitations will simply prolong the agony and cause more suffering in the long run. As such, the realist is just as capable of arguing in ethical terms as the pacifist, even if many choose not to.

However, realism, whether descriptive or prescriptive, can itself be decidedly unrealistic when it claims that effective strategy is best served by ignoring the normative dimension of one's conduct. Military success and political success are not the same thing and successful strategy must provide a linkage between the two. To provide an historical example, the American War of Independence against the British Empire was won, effectively, at Yorktown in 1781 when the forces under George Washington accepted the surrender of the British garrison under the command of Lord Cornwallis. The surrender led to the resignation of the British prime minister and the start of the negotiations that would eventually lead to the Treaty of Paris in September 1783 and the independence of the American colonies.[12] However, sometimes a military victory can come at the expense of a political settlement and this makes any military victory hollow at best, disastrous at worse. To continue the example in a counterfactual way, if General Washington had slaughtered the British forces as they surrendered at Yorktown instead of capturing them, it would still have been a military success. However, it is probable that British public opinion would have been so outraged that rather than bringing down the government, the atrocity would have motivated the commitment of every available resource to defeat the rebel colonists. Whatever the eventual outcome of that hypothetical confrontation may have been, it is clear that the conflict could potentially have gone on for many more years precisely because of what would have been a military success. To give a more recent example, the intelligence gained by the French use of torture in Algeria in the late 1950s *may* have helped win the Battle of Algiers (although this is certainly not clear), but it certainly undermined French support, contributing to the loss of the overall war.[13] Realism can allow a conflict to escalate beyond control, and for war to become the master rather than the servant of policy. As such, it is decidedly unrealistic in many ways.

---

11   Irwin Abrams, *The Nobel Peace Prize and the Laureates: An Illustrated Biographical History 1901–2001*, centennial edn (Nantucket, MA: Science History Publications, 2001), p. 41.

12   See Don Cook, *The Long Fuse: How England Lost the American Colonies, 1760–1785* (Berkeley, CA: Avalon Travel, 2000).

13   See D. Whetham, 'Taking the Gloves Off and the Illusion of Victory', in G. Kassemeris, ed., *The Warrior's Dishonour: Barbarity, Morality and Torture in Modern Warfare* (Aldershot: Ashgate, 2006).

A Pragmatic Compromise

JWT fits in between these two positions as a pragmatic compromise. It agrees with the pacifist that war is a terrible thing that should be avoided, just not at any cost. Rather than accepting the pacifist's presumption against war, JWT states a presumption against injustice, arguing that it is sometimes morally acceptable (or even morally necessary) to fight. In this respect, JWT agrees with the realist that it is sometimes necessary to do terrible things. However, that does not mean that war should be something that is easily resorted to. Not all reasons justify going to war, and even *if* a war can be justified, it must still be fought in a way that accepts certain limits. Those limits include the recognition that individuals, both combatants and non-combatants, have certain rights, even in times of war. This is because the purpose of war is to gain a better peace. This is a principle that has been accepted in the rules that governed warfare between the city-states of Ancient Greece, through to the codification of customary international law in the nineteenth and twentieth centuries. Although often identified as a Western tradition, there is nothing incompatible with ideas, cultures and religious principles found all over the world. As such, JWT provides a common language so that the important discussions that should be had about the use of force can be conducted within a common frame of reference, even when people disagree about the specific details. Every culture, every civilisation and every religion has accepted that war must be restrained in some way.[14] But why? Precisely because military victory makes no sense unless it can be transformed into political success. Violating the basic principles of JWT makes winning harder or even impossible. Fighting wars within the ethical framework provided by JWT makes the return to peace easier and therefore allows the prospect of a genuine political victory rather than merely hollow military success.

What Does Contemporary Just War Theory Say?

The JWT has developed around two related but distinct ideas: *jus ad bellum* – what is required to justify going to war – and *jus in bello* – the limits on the use of force within war.

Jus ad Bellum

- just cause
- legitimate authority
- right intention
- the goal of the war is proportional to the offence
- reasonable chance of success
- last resort

---

14   See Paul Robinson, ed., *Just War in Comparative Perspective* (Aldershot: Ashgate, 2003).

Jus in Bello

- proportionality
- discrimination (also referred to as distinction)

Why would one want to make a distinction between the two levels? It allows us to draw a line between the decision to go to war and the actual conduct of that war. Soldiers are not responsible for the decision to go to war, but they are responsible for its conduct. Very senior military officers may straddle the line, but, as Walzer points out, this means that we know pretty well where that line should be drawn.[15] Shakespeare gets to the heart of the matter with succinct elegance:

> BATES: If [the King's] cause be wrong, our obedience to the king wipes the crime of it out of us.

> WILLIAMS: But if the cause be not good, the King himself hath a heavy reckoning to make when all those legs and arms and heads, chopp'd off in a battle …[16]

This distinction between the levels of responsibility is an important one, and can have implications for the long-term defence of the state. Vitoria, writing in the mid-sixteenth century, made it clear that:

> if subjects can not serve in war except they are first satisfied of its justice, the State would fall into grave peril and the door would be opened to wrongdoing … if subjects in a case of doubt do not follow their prince to the war, they expose themselves to the risk of betraying their State to the enemy, and this is a much more serious thing than fighting against the enemy despite a doubt.[17]

In the absence of clear evidence to the contrary, the soldiers on each side need to give their own leaders the benefit of the doubt or the state itself could be put at risk.[18] However, even while giving this warning, Vitoria still makes it clear that there are limits to how far a soldier can wash their hands of their moral responsibilities. If one were provided with clear evidence of the injustice of a war, there could be no excuse for partaking in it. Effectively, a soldier has a moral duty to disobey any

---

15   Walzer, *Just and Unjust Wars*, p. 39.

16   Shakespeare, *Henry V*, Act IV, Scene I.

17   Francisco Vitoria, *De Indis De Jure Belli*, Part III, 31.

18   Trust, of course, is a valuable commodity and it is unlikely that the benefit of the doubt will be extended to quite the same degree following the events of 2003 and the arguments employed to bolster the case for the invasion of Iraq that subsequently turned out to be questionable at best. As Descartes argued (*Meditation One*), 'it is a mark of prudence never to trust wholly in those things which have once deceived us'.

order that is clearly unjust.[19] While Vitoria was writing nearly 500 years ago, this is a theme that finds clear relevance today as every soldier has a moral and legal duty to disobey an illegal order, and cannot claim the defence of superior orders (which can, at best, only be accepted as a mitigating circumstance rather than as a defence) if he or she knowingly carries out an illegal act.

In the absence of such concerns, however, the soldiers on both sides are 'in the same boat', as it were.[20] It is impossible to know metaphysically who is really, objectively in the right.[21] No one (or rather, very few people) would knowingly fight for a cause they considered unjust. This means that there is in some sense a moral equality of combatants, no matter what side they are on. This sentiment is beautifully expressed by Ataturk on a memorial to those who fell on both sides in WWI:

> *Those heroes that shed their blood and lost their lives …. You are now lying in the soil of a friendly country …. Therefore rest in peace. There is no difference between the Johnnies and the Mehmets to us where they lie side by side now here in this country of ours.*[22]

This moral equality connects the *ad bellum* considerations to the *in bello* ones and leads to the acceptance that war should be conducted within limits. It does not matter who 'started it' – both sides will claim justice to be with them anyway – both sides are obliged to conduct their conflict justly. While one cannot make an unjust cause right by fighting it well (although those who conduct themselves in this way do not share in the blame for the war itself and can even be commended on their actions – for example Rommel in WWII),[23] one can certainly undermine a just cause by conducting it badly. The two levels, then, are clearly related, but they are also distinct.[24]

Jus ad Bellum

A just war must have a just cause. The clearest example of a just cause is self-defence owing to the invasion of one's territory. This is accepted in Article 51 of the

---

19 Francisco Vitoria, *De Indis De Jure Belli*, Part III, 26.
20 The problem of ascertaining the objective truth of an event is demonstrated by the ongoing debate over the cause of the sinking of the USS Maine in Havana Harbour in 1898, an event that precipitated the ensuing Spanish-American War, although it is still not clear whether the blast was caused by a mine or an accident on board.
21 Rather than limiting this ability to a deity alone, one can instead try to reason oneself towards a more objective position. See Thomas Nagel, *The View From Nowhere* (Oxford: Oxford University Press, 1989).
22 Kemal Atatürk Memorial, ANZAC Parade, Canberra.
23 See Walzer, *Just and Unjust Wars*, p. 38.
24 It is this separation that allows the public to support their military forces even in an otherwise unpopular war.

UN Charter, which affirms the inherent right of self-defence possessed by every state.[25] Just causes could also be the defence of a neighbour or ally (for example the liberation of Kuwait in 1991) or, increasingly, it is becoming argued in legal terms that defence of the innocent is also a just cause. This takes contemporary legal arguments back to those ethical arguments put forward by Ambrose (c. 339–397) and later Augustine (354–430) that sacrifice on behalf of the innocent and the common good are to be praised: 'Anyone who does not prevent an injury to a companion, if he can do so, is as much at fault as he who inflicts it.'[26] One can see such thinking shaping the development of the 'responsibility to protect' idea in contemporary international affairs, where if a particular state proves itself to be unwilling or unable to carry out its responsibilities to prevent human rights abuses, that responsibility must be transferred to the international community so that it can act instead, using peaceful means where possible and military force only as a last resort.[27]

Is pre-emption self-defence? Context is everything when answering this question. Morally, the problem with pre-empting a threat is that it can all too easily turn the defender into the attacker. Clearly, if one is about to be ambushed, one can fire the first shot and it still be considered self-defence. It appears common sense that this reasoning extends to states as well as individuals.[28] Sometimes a threat must be anticipated if it is to be successfully defended against, but how far can this be taken? As US National Security Advisor Condoleeza Rice argued in 2002, clearly one cannot wait until the mushroom cloud to act.[29] However, if you just decide that somebody, at some unspecified time in the future, just might become a threat to you even though they are not at this moment, attacking them cannot be considered self-defence, either legally or morally. The key to legitimacy is getting the balance right.

Unless one is acting purely in self-defence (in which case no further authority is required), the use of armed force requires a declaration by a legitimate authority. Echoing back to Roman ideas of justice, when an injury has been suffered, the offending party has to be told what it is they have done wrong, and what it is they can do to restore the situation and prevent war. This procedural requirement (to recognise the transition from one state of affairs – peace – to war and the alternative

---

25 'Nothing in the present Charter shall impair the inherent right of individual or collective self-defence if an armed attack occurs.' Thus self-defence does not require any additional authority to sanction it.

26 Ambrose, *On the Duties of the Clergy*, Book 1, Ch. 36, p. 179. In Louis J. Swift, ed. and trans., *The Early Fathers on War and Military Service* (Wilmington: Michael Glazier, 1983), pp. 101–2.

27 See the International Commission on Intervention and State Sovereignty, <http://www.iciss.ca/>.

28 Although the relationship between individual and collective self-defence has been challenged; for example, see David Rodin, *War and Self-Defence* (Oxford: Clarendon Press, 2002).

29 <http://transcripts.cnn.com/TRANSCRIPTS/0209/08/le.00.html>.

rules that now apply) can only be done by a legitimate authority.[30] It is through just such a process that the declaration of hostilities is made, setting out what the cause of the conflict is and what is required to stop the military reaction to it. This declaration is a procedural concept, but one that is nevertheless an important one. In contemporary legal terms, that legitimate authority can only come from the UN Security Council. Article 2(4) of the UN Charter declares: 'All Members shall refrain in their international relations from the threat or use of force against the territorial integrity or political independence of any state, or in any other manner inconsistent with the Purposes of the United Nations.' Everything other than actions taken in immediate self-defence requires the prior authority of the Security Council. However, in practice, if not theory, the actual power to do this still rests with individual states or regional alliances rather than exclusively with the UN.[31] States still have established procedures for legally declaring war or committing their armed forces into a conflict and these must be followed if such a deployment is to be considered just. For example, in the UK, the Royal Prerogative under which the prime minister could commit UK troops without parliamentary approval is very likely to be a thing of the past now as it is no longer seen as legitimate when parliament is supposed to be sovereign.

Most people accept that motives are relevant to the moral quality of an action. Therefore, a just war must have right intention.[32] While the just cause establishes that one is doing the right thing, right intention asks if you are doing it for the right reasons. Right intentions include creating, restoring or keeping a just peace, righting a wrong or assisting the innocent. Wrong intentions are those that seek to expand lands, enslave or convert people to your religion or ideas, hatred or revenge. If a war is motivated by these last two emotions in particular, it becomes easy for the enemy to be regarded as less than an equal which makes it far more likely that atrocities and war crimes will get committed. Of course, good intentions are often mixed up with more dubious ones. In the real world, does it really matter what the motivation for an action is? JWT recognises that states will rarely have only one reason for what they do. However, this criterion is still important as it recognises that wars fought primarily for bad motives often lead to an unjust peace, which in itself will simply sow the seeds for further conflict in the long run. This idea goes back to the time when intention was, without doubt, the most important of the just war criteria. Aquinas felt that, effectively, intent and motive were bound together so that the thing that compels us to do something also shapes what it is

---

30   To do this without legitimate authority would be piracy, or perhaps terrorism in today's popular understanding. See David Whetham, 'What Did the Romans do for U.S.?' *Journal of the Royal United Services Institute* (December 2001), vol. 146, issue 6.

31   For example, the authority for the Kosovo intervention came from the agreement by the countries of NATO and was then retrospectively legitimised by the UN.

32   Right intention was at the heart of Augustine's reluctant acceptance of war as a necessary evil, with it being justified in terms of what one was intending to achieve: a better peace. See 'City of God', Book XV, Chapter 4, in Ernest L. Fortin and Douglas Kries, eds, *Augustine: Political Writings* (Indianapolis: Hackett, 1994), p. 112.

that one is trying to do.[33] It was considered that if one had the wrong intention to begin with then no additional rules or considerations would be sufficient to prevent the 'descent into the moral abyss of war'.[34]

A just war should have a goal that is proportional to the offence that prompted that war. Of course, this can be a very subjective criterion to fulfil – after all, what price does one put on national honour? It would clearly not be proportional to invade and subjugate an entire population in response to a minor border infringement. The second part of this criterion is that the benefits of the war must outweigh the suffering it causes. How many combatant and civilian deaths are likely to result on both sides and how many can be justified by the just cause as a reason to go to war in the first place? This is a particularly difficult calculation to make in advance of military action; however, JWT asks that a credible attempt is made to answer this question before resorting to the use of force.

Going to war for a hopeless cause may be noble, but most people accept that it is unethical to sacrifice life and cause pain and suffering if it cannot change anything. Therefore, JWT asks that there be a reasonable chance of success for military action to be justified. Of course, this means that one must have a clear idea of what one's definition of success is *before* military action is pursued. This idea is closely related to the need to plan for conflict resolution rather than simply conflict termination, as this asks the protagonist to think through the *jus post bellum* – justice after the war. It is not simply about victory, but the best way to achieve the political goals that prompted the war in the first place, planning for and creating the conditions for a meaningful and lasting peace. In this way, by establishing a clear and realistic objective at the outset, mission creep can be avoided and war remains an instrument of policy rather than becoming the master of it.

The final JWT *ad bellum* criterion is that war should be a last resort. A state should only go to war when it has tried every sensible non-violent alternative first, such as diplomacy, economic sanctions, political pressure, condemnation in the UN, and so on. Of course, diplomats can always send one more letter, so how does one know when the last resort really has been reached? The last resort criterion simply means that there are no more *practical* alternatives that might achieve success that have not already been attempted.

Jus in Bello

Just as the war itself must be a proportional response to the injury suffered, the means employed in the war must be proportionate or appropriate to win and no more. The principle of proportionality requires that the damage, losses or injury resulting from any military action should not be excessive in relation to the expected military

---

33 J.D. Tooke, *The Just War in Aquinas and Grotius* (London: SPCK, 1965), p. 151.
34 Anthony Coates, 'Culture, the Enemy and the Moral Restraint of War', in Richard Sorabji and David Rodin, eds, *The Ethics of War: Shared Problems in Different Traditions* (Aldershot: Ashgate, 2007), p. 215.

advantage. Long before the JWT formula begin to emerge in a more systematised way, Plato recognised that war between the Greek city states should be restrained in certain ways that accepted the rights of the people involved in, and affected by, the hostilities. He argued that, while it was legitimate to take food to sustain oneself while passing through hostile territory, destroying the means of producing that food was not.[35] Effectively, such action was considered disproportionate in the same way that, today, destroying an entire town to neutralise one enemy sniper is likely to be disproportionate.

In this spirit, the Laws of Manu prohibited Hindus from employing poison arrows. Both Greeks and Romans, likewise, prohibited the use of poison and poisoned weapons.[36] It is the same rationale that explains the contemporary prohibition on the use of chemical and biological weapons or the poisoning of water and food supplies.[37] The parties to the 1868 St Petersburg Declaration prohibited the use of incendiary or explosive projectiles below a certain size and weight for the same reason – the same effect could be achieved with a normal solid round, so why cause additional, unnecessary suffering?[38] Certain methods of war and types of weapon are simply considered too inhumane owing to the suffering inflicted when compared to the military advantage achieved by their use.

Closely related to proportionality is the principle of discrimination. This relates to whom it is legitimate to conduct hostilities against. Plato put forward the idea that only those who are actually responsible for pursuing the dispute are to be treated as enemies.[39] Echoing Plato's point, contemporary law makes a clear separation: 'Only combatants are permitted to take a direct part in hostilities. It follows that they may be attacked. Civilians may not take a direct part in hostilities and, for so long as they refrain from doing so, are protected from attack.'[40]

There is an implicit 'deal' here. Civilians get the right not to be intentionally targeted by military forces and, in return, they have a duty not to take up arms.[41] Plato, writing in a very different environment, although one faced with many of the same issues, also argues that the defeated should not be enslaved or killed as this will otherwise stand in the way of the necessary reconciliation at the end of

---

35 Plato, *Republic*, V, ed. by E. Hamilton and H. Cairns, eds, *Plato: The Collected Dialogues* (Princeton, NJ: Princeton University Press, 1989), p. 710.

36 Adam Roberts and Richard Guelff, eds, *Documents of the Laws of War*, 2nd edn (Oxford: Oxford University Press, 1995), p. 29.

37 For example, the Geneva Gas Protocol of 1925 which prohibited 'the use in war of asphyxiating, poisonous or other gases, and of all analogous liquids, materials or devices'. See *The Manual of the Law of Armed Conflict* (Oxford: Oxford University Press, 2004), p. 11.

38 Ibid., p. 109.

39 Plato, *Republic*, V, p. 710.

40 *The Manual of the Law of Armed Conflict* (Oxford: Oxford University Press, 2004), p. 24. Referring to Additional Protocol I, Art 43 and 51.

41 Except in the case of direct self-defence, which can justify the use of arms. As explained above, self-defence requires no additional authority to be valid.

hostilities.[42] In a practical sense, there is no incentive to cease fighting if one's rights are not going to be respected afterwards – if there is to be no distinction between combatant and ex-combatant. However, deeper than this is the idea that a soldier is a legitimate object of attack precisely because he or she poses a threat as an instrument of the state or political entity against which you are engaged in hostilities. Once a soldier is wounded or surrendered and no longer capable of posing a threat, they are considered *hors de combat*. Because they are no longer capable of taking a direct part in hostilities they, too, cease to be a legitimate target.

So who is and who is not a combatant in the contemporary environment? Those who are definitely combatants include: members of the military forces; members of guerrilla forces, whether or not they are in uniform; and anyone who takes up arms in a conflict other than in direct self-defence. What about a civilian working in a munitions factory? The civilian *herself* is not a legitimate target but she is *in* a legitimate target so may well find herself under attack. The proportionality calculation would need to be made to ensure that the expected civilian deaths from such an attack were justified by the military utility of the destruction of the facility – perhaps bombing it at night when the factory floor was empty might be considered if a significant loss of life was expected. What of the 80-year-old granny knitting socks for her grandson on the front line? Is this a direct contribution to the *materiel* [equipment] required for the war effort? Are those socks a legitimate target and the little old lady vulnerable as long as she is near them? Proportionality reasoning should clearly rule out such a verdict, but it is obvious that there is a broad spectrum between the factory and the socks where difficult calculations are required.

Double Effect

Recorded history confirms the sad truth that just because civilians have the right not to be attacked, that does not mean that they do not suffer during hostilities. While non-combatants can never be legitimately targeted themselves, JWT would have become irrelevant centuries or even millennia ago if it did not recognise that, regrettably, innocent people get killed in wars. If a military operation could only be conducted with the certain knowledge that no civilians would be hurt as a result, while the world would undoubtedly be a better place, it is likely that JWT would have been abandoned long ago as unworkable. Instead, JWT accepts that sometimes the achievement of a specific aim or objective can only be satisfied by accepting a degree of 'collateral damage' – a euphemism for dead women and babies. While it would never be ethical or lawful to deliberately target a civilian population, JWT recognises that the same population may still, under certain circumstances, be affected in a negative way by military operations. Aquinas grappled with this question and articulated what later became known as the Doctrine of Double

---

42 Plato, *Republic*, V, p. 710.

Effect to explain it.[43] It is the idea that individuals are not morally responsible for a foreseeable, yet unintended side effect of an otherwise legitimate action. However, the foreseeable side effects of a military action, even while not intended, must still be proportionate to the expected military utility of the target and civilian casualties are still to be avoided as far as is possible. Therefore, the Doctrine of Double Effect cannot be used to defend the use of weapons of mass destruction against an area with a civilian population, as these weapons are so indiscriminate that the resulting civilian casualties cannot be regarded as a secondary result. This is underlined by the principle of proportionality.

Clearly the character of the conflict one is engaged with has an impact on the way the Doctrine of Double Effect is applied. For example, if one is engaged in a humanitarian operation, motivated by a desire to protect and help the civilian population and uphold their human rights, it would be inappropriate to push the burden of risk over to that same population and accept a high level of collateral damage in order to reduce the risks to one's own troops. One could argue, as such operations are more akin to police operations than military ones in many ways, that accepting *any* civilian casualties in such circumstances is to contradict the very reasoning that justifies the operation in the first place. At the very least, such operations require that military personnel accept that alternative methods of achieving one's ends may be required and that those may well require a substantial increase in risk to themselves as practices such as 'radical force protection' are abandoned.

Can the Rules Ever be Set Aside?

It seems somewhat obvious that some types of ethical considerations will feature less heavily in one's calculations when faced with a truly existential threat (or rather the way that one balances ends and means changes to reflect the circumstances). The idea of 'supreme emergency' (after a phrase used in one of Churchill's wartime speeches) was developed by the hugely influential Michael Walzer to describe an 'imminent catastrophe' to a people.[44] When faced with a genuine 'supreme emergency' of this type, the *ad bellum* side of the equation appears to weigh more heavily that the *in bello* considerations: the state takes whatever means is necessary to defend itself from such a threat, 'where one might well be required to override the rights of innocent people and shatter the war convention'.[45] Whether or not this

---

43 See Question 64: Article 7, in Thomas Aquinas, *Summa Theologica*, pp. 1,465–6.

44 See Walzer, *Just and Unjust Wars*, particularly pp. 251–68.

45 Thus, Walzer argues, given the threat Britain faced, that Bomber Command was the sole instrument available to take the war to Germany at the time, but technological limitations meant that only very large targets could be realistically attacked, the strategic bombing against German cities could be justified as necessary until other theatres of war opened up, technology improved (making it feasible to hit military targets) and,

is an ethically justifiable position has been debated at some length.[46] However, it appears obvious that, when faced with such an existential threat, most states will be prepared to go further than they otherwise would be willing to go in a 'war of choice'. Ignatieff articulates this well when he provocatively asks: 'what lesser evils may a society commit when it believes it faces the greater evil of its own destruction?'[47] However, in a discretionary conflict, where national survival is not directly at risk and perhaps even national interests themselves are not obviously at stake, the potential (and contentious) leeway offered by the 'supreme emergency' is clearly not applicable. It is the challenge of the discretionary war that we are routinely faced with today and, in this type of conflict, there is no conceivable excuse for violating the ethical norms of war.[48]

Conclusion

Success in contemporary military operations, particularly counterinsurgencies where authority and legitimacy are the prizes at stake, will likely go to the side that best 'mobilises and energises its global, regional and local support bases'.[49] Thanks to the ubiquitous nature of the contemporary media, we live in the age of the 'strategic corporal'.[50] Events in Baghdad's Abu Ghraib and Lynndie England's 'smiling poses in photos of detainee abuse' demonstrated that there were now such things as 'strategic privates', whose actions have the power to cause effects all the way up to the political level.[51] Once international, domestic and host nation support has been lost, subsequent military action almost becomes an irrelevance as it can no longer bring victory at the level that counts – the political level. There is nothing intrinsically new in this recognition of the importance of public opinion. General Keightley acknowledged it in his post-mortem of the Suez Operation in

---

most importantly, the supreme emergency itself had passed and Britain was not faced with imminent invasion and defeat. See Walzer, *Just and Unjust Wars*, Chapter 16.

46　For example, see Henry Shue, *The Impossibility of Justifying Weapons of Mass Destruction*, paper presented at the annual meeting of the American Political Science Association (Boston, MA, 28 August 2002), <http://www.allacademic.com/meta/p65596_index.html>.

47　Michael Ignatieff, *The Lesser Evil: Political Ethics in an Age of Terror* (Edinburgh: Edinburgh University Press, 2005), p. 1.

48　That is not to say that a new existential threat is inconceivable, just that this is a very high threshold and there are no current threats that come close to it.

49　David Kilcullen, 'Counter-insugency *Redux*', *Survival*, vol. 48, no. 4 (Winter 2006–07): 121.

50　See Charles Krulak, 'The Strategic Corporal: Leadership in the Three Block War', *Marines* (January 1999).

51　'Lynndie England Convicted in Abu Ghraib Trial', *USA Today* (26 September 2005).

1956, stating that 'world opinion is now an absolute principle of war and must be treated as such'.[52]

People die in wars. That is regrettable but also inescapable. Just War Theory provides a framework for distinguishing between justifiable military action within an ethical framework, and murder. As Plato recognised in the fourth century BC, a successful statesman must keep in mind that war should be a means to a better peace, rather than an end in itself.[53] This is a consideration that needs to shape and guide conduct at all levels of war.

52 Cited in T. Shaw, *Eden, Suez and the Mass Media* (London: I.B. Taurus, 1996), p. 196. See also David Whetham, 'Killing Within the Rules', *Small Wars and Insurgencies*, vol. 18, no. 4 (December 2007): 721–33.

53 Plato, *Laws*, I, p. 1,230.

Lying Down with Dogs: The Inadequacy of Machiavellianism as a Basis for US Foreign Policy

Thomas M. Kane

If you lie down with dogs, you wake up with fleas.[1]

Makers of foreign policy under the George W. Bush administration have had, at best, a complex relationship with international law and an equally complex relationship with more fundamental concepts of right and wrong. Indeed, given the enormous moral significance of their positions on the laws of war and the laws governing captives taken in armed conflict, it is difficult to discuss their attitudes toward law without discussing their attitudes toward morality. G.W. Bush's own tendency to present political issues in moral terms further blurs the distinction between his administration's legal positions and its moral principles. Thus, this chapter investigates the G.W. Bush administration's stance on legal and moral issues, and considers the implications of this stance.

G.W. Bush and his supporters have not hesitated to present their legal and moral beliefs in simple terms of good and evil. More intriguingly, they have not always aligned themselves with the former. If their characterisation of America's international rivals has been exceptionally Manichean, their willingness to advocate such widely condemned practices as torture and discretionary war has been exceptionally frank. G.W. Bush administration insider Richard Perle provided an example of this moral chiaroscuro when he co-authored a book titled *An End to Evil* even as he attracted the nickname 'Prince of Darkness'.

These discrepancies clearly contain elements of routine political hypocrisy and routine political name-calling. Nevertheless, they also highlight distinctive themes in early twenty-first-century American statecraft. Since these themes have consequences for Americans and all who interact with them, they are worth exploring in depth. The G.W. Bush administration presumably adopted its less savoury policies on the basis of pragmatism, and one of political theory's most

---

1   Traditional saying.

notorious advocates of pragmatic evil accurately predicted what many of the consequences would be.

Those who wish to make sense of early twenty-first-century American leaders' alternating relationship with evil may find that the fifteenth-century Florentine thinker Niccolo Machiavelli offers them guidance. In *The Prince*, the Florentine recommends the course that G.W. Bush and his most outspoken advisors appear to have followed. Machiavelli allows not only that it is 'well to seem merciful, faithful, humane, sincere, [and] religious' but that it is actually well 'also to be so'.[2] Having noted the genuine value of goodness, however, he adds that 'you must have the mind so disposed that when it is needful to be otherwise you may be able to change to the opposite qualities'.[3]

Machiavelli advises rulers to use evil when it is 'needful' to do so. The fact that he presents evil as a response to necessity suggests that he bases his conditional willingness to endorse evil on the principle of pragmatism. American policy-makers have advanced their morally controversial ideas on pragmatic grounds as well. The National Security Strategy of the United States of America (NSS) of September 2002 provides an instructive example, since this document outlined G.W. Bush administration thinking during the prelude to the 2003 Gulf War.

The NSS discusses the circumstances in which America might attack a regime that has not yet attacked it, as it was to do to Saddam Hussein's Baathist government of Iraq six months later. 'To forestall or prevent ... hostile acts by our adversaries, the United States will, if necessary, act preemptively.'[4] Not only does the NSS justify American action on pragmatic grounds, it also asserts the utilitarian moral principle that the case for pre-emptive action is persuasive in direct proportion to the potential consequences of inaction.[5] Stated in the abstract, the idea that extreme situations might demand correspondingly radical responses seems unlikely to trouble anyone other than the most pedantic of deontologists. The reason why the G.W. Bush administration's use of consequentialist arguments to justify such morally problematic decisions as invading Iraq is significant is that so many Americans – including ardent supporters of the administration – have been so dissatisfied with these decisions' consequences.

Perhaps unknowingly, President G.W. Bush followed Machiavelli's advice. A meaningful proportion of his constituents are unhappy with the results. Machiavelli himself, by contrast, would probably not have been either surprised or disappointed. This paper will show that the Florentine expected his policies to incur the bloodshed, financial expense, class conflict, open-ended military commitments and equally open-ended disruption of civil life that Americans have found so troubling. Moreover, Machiavelli viewed these outcomes as salutary. The

---

2   Niccolo. Machiavelli, *The Prince and The Discourses*, trans. by Luigi Ricci and Christian E. Detmold (New York: The Modern Library, 1940), p. 65.

3   Ibid., p. 65.

4   National Security Strategy of the United States of America (NSS) (Washington, DC: The White House, 2002), p. 15.

5   NSS, p. 15.

author concludes by reflecting on what those seeking to secure America and its way of life in the twenty-first century should remember about Machiavelli's nominally pragmatic advice to do ill.

Don't Mention the War

In 2003, the G.W. Bush administration demonstrated its commitment to the ruthless pragmatism of the National Security Strategy by organising a so-called 'coalition of the willing' to overthrow the Iraqi government, despite the lack of any United Nations Security Council resolution clearly authorising it to do so. There may, in fact, have been sound moral reasons for this action. Tony Blair, the British prime minister at the time, maintains that there were. G.W. Bush's critics, however, commonly portray the 2003 invasion of Iraq as an outrage. Pope John Paul II spoke for many such critics in January 2003, when he characterised all war as a 'defeat for humanity', emphasised that 'war cannot be decided upon, even when it is a matter of ensuring the common good, except as the last option and in accordance with very strict conditions', and declared 'respect for law, especially international agreements' as a key 'requirement' which state leaders would have to meet 'if entire peoples, perhaps even humanity itself, are not to sink into the abyss'.[6] The Pontiff specifically applied these principles to the unfolding conflict in Iraq.

Given that such eminent moral thinkers as the Pope explicitly linked the morality of the 2003 war to strict compliance with international law, the fact that legal scholars have been among the most vehement critics of G.W. Bush administration policies is telling. Carsten Stahn, writing in the October 2003 issue of *The American Journal of International Law*, summarised the legal community's response to the war:

> [T]he air is not filled with solemn proclamations of morality or humanitarian dedication. It is poisoned by doubt and bitterness. The damage to the international legal system is all too visible. The future of Iraq is still uncertain. Furthermore, the argument for the use of force against Iraq is open to challenge as long as there is uncertainty over the existence of Iraqi weapons of mass destruction.[7]

Not only is the 2003 Gulf War a vivid example of the G.W. Bush administration's willingness to commit morally controversial acts, it is also an equally vivid example of a policy that many Americans have come to regret. Even when the 2003 coalition appeared successful and the G.W. Bush administration enjoyed relatively high levels of public support, US officials appear to have anticipated that Americans

---

6   'Pope Warns Against War', *Catholic News Services* (13 January 2003), <http://www.americancatholic.org/News/JustWar/Iraq/papalstatement.asp> [accessed 02 July 2008].

7   Carsten Stahn, 'Enforcement of the Collective Will after Iraq', *The American Journal of International Law*, 97/4 (2003): 804.

would find the costs of war hard to bear. When the coalition attacked Iraq, the US government revived a H.W. Bush-era order which prohibited American media outlets from disseminating images of military funerals or coffins.[8] The US military justified this policy on the grounds that it protected family members of dead military personnel from journalistic intrusion. One may reasonably infer that the administration also hoped that this policy would minimise the publicity of the casualties its policies incurred.

The ban on images, however, could not conceal the fact that US forces have continued to suffer casualties, often at greater rates than they experienced during so-called 'high intensity combat' against Saddam Hussein's regular army. During America's bloodiest month in conventional campaign, April 2003, 74 US personnel died in combat.[9] America's death toll for the month of April 2004, precisely one year later, was 135.[10] Political opponents of the war, notably the bereaved mother Cindy Sheehan, have worked to draw public attention to such facts.

The financial cost of G.W. Bush's aggressive foreign policy has also risen dramatically beyond initial predictions. Lee Hudson Teslik of the US Council on Foreign Relations summarises:

> *In September 2002, White House economic adviser Lawrence B. Lindsey estimated the cost of invading Iraq could amount to between $100 billion and $200 billion. Mitch Daniels, who at the time headed the White House budget office, called Lindsey's estimates "very, very high" … and said the war would cost $50 billion to $60 billion; shortly thereafter, Lindsey left the White House. In January 2004, a report from the Congressional Budget Office (CBO) estimated the total costs of Iraq's reconstruction would land between $50 billion and $100 billion. But in October 2007, the CBO said in a new report that the United States had already spent $368 billion on its military operations in Iraq, $45 billion more in related services (veterans care, diplomatic services, training), and nearly $200 billion on top of that in Afghanistan. The CBO now estimates the costs of the Iraq war, projected out through 2017, might top $1 trillion, plus an extra $705 billion in interest payments, and says the total cost of Iraq and Afghanistan combined could reach $2.4 trillion.*[11]

The American public has, indeed, recoiled from its various losses. In January 2008, NBC News and the *Wall Street Journal* (NBC/WSJ) released results of a poll

---

8   Nicholas Wapshott, 'Diana crash photo has half the shock value of Iraq coffins', *The Times* (26 April 2004), <http://www.timesonline.co.uk/article/0,,3-1088211,00.html> [accessed 02 February 2008].

9   'Military Fatalities: By Month', <http://icasualties.org/oif/> [accessed 11 February 2008].

10 Ibid.

11 Lee Hudson Teslik, 'Iraq, Afghanistan and the US Economy', *Council on Foreign Relations Backgrounder* (4 February 2008), <http://www.cfr.org/publication/15404/> [accessed 11 February 2008].

asking whether 'removing Saddam Hussein from power was or was not worth the number of U.S. military casualties and the financial cost of the war'.[12] Fifty-nine per cent of the poll's respondents said that the price had been too high. The NBC/WSJ researchers had begun surveying Americans on that issue in 2006, and the number of respondents who found the cost of war excessive had risen continually since then.[13]

People's grief for their dead justifies itself. G.W. Bush is entitled to argue that his critics have exaggerated the financial significance of his policies. Economists disagree over the effects of wartime spending. Moreover, although the dollar cost of G.W. Bush's expenditures is spectacular, the cost in comparison to America's means is moderate by historical standards. American defence spending in 2008 amounts to approximately 6.2 per cent of America's gross domestic product (GDP).[14] This is no more than the US spent during the mid-1980s, and considerably less than it spent at the height of Cold War tension in 1962.[15]

Nevertheless, whether or not G.W. Bush's military spending is fully responsible, the American economy as of early 2008 is faltering. Inflation – commonly associated with wartime profligacy – has become an increasing threat. Meanwhile, even as money drops in purchasing power, high levels of personal debt and a shaky jobs market have left US citizens with less of it to spend. A February 2008 poll by the Associated Press confirmed that the majority of Americans surveyed felt grim about their current economic situation and pessimistic about their future.[16] Sixty-eight per cent of the Americans who responded to the poll believed that withdrawing US forces from Iraq would help the economy, and 48 per cent believed that it would help 'a great deal'.[17]

Not only are Americans circa 2008 disturbed by the costs of their country's military commitment to Iraq, they are disturbed by the lack of any visible end point. When Pew Center researchers asked Americans whether they agreed that their country should bring its troops home 'as soon as possible' the majority said yes.[18] Further questions indicated that Americans have become more concerned with the 'soon' than with the 'possible'. Over half the respondents were concerned

---

12   <http://www.pollingreport.com/iraq.htm> [accessed 11 February 2008].

13   Ibid.

14   Teslik, 'Iraq, Afghanistan and the US Economy'; <http://www.ctj.org/html/def0301. btm> [accessed 18 December 2002].

15   Teslik, 'Iraq, Afghanistan and the US Economy'; <http://www.ctj.org/html/def0301. btm> [accessed 18 December 2002].

16   Associated Press, 'AP Poll: To Fix Economy, Get Out of Iraq: Most Believe U.S. is in Recession and Quitting Iraq Would Be More Helpful Than Rebate Checks' (10 February 2008), <http://www.cbsnews.com/stories/2008/02/10/national/main3813757.shtml> [accessed 11 February 2008].

17   Associated Press, 'AP Poll: To Fix Economy, Get Out of Iraq'.

18   Jodie T. Allen, Richard Auxier and Alec Tyson, 'Deconstructing the Debate 5/15/07: How Well Did the GOP Candidates' Views Match those of their Party's Members and of the General Public', *Pew Research Center Publications* (16 May 2007), <http://pewresearch. org/pubs/479/republican-debate> [accessed 11 February 2008].

hat their country would stay in Iraq too long.[19] Only 35 per cent worried that their country would withdraw prematurely.[20]

Other Pew data confirms that overall public support for the G.W. Bush administration's campaign in Iraq has declined steadily over time.[21] When America attacked Iraq in March 2003, Pew findings suggest that 70 per cent of all Americans supported the war. By February 2007, only 40 per cent still took that position. Pew researchers also asked Americans whether they thought the war was going well. Ninety per cent of the respondents were optimistic in 2003, compared with 30 per cent four years later.[22]

One reason why the American public has shown so little commitment to what was – at first – a popular policy may be that they no longer perceive that it serves any desirable purpose. The legal justification for the war remains as valid as it ever was. Whether or not Saddam Hussein's regime was actually building weapons of mass destruction, it had still failed to comply with United Nations resolutions enjoining it to prove that it was not building such weapons. Nevertheless, the lack of evidence for a weapons programme entitled critics of the war to dismiss this point as a technicality. As Stahn predicted, this has discredited the fundamental argument in favour of overthrowing the Baathist regime.

War supporters have further reasons to feel disillusioned. In 2003, many hoped that overthrowing Saddam Hussein would be an act of compassion toward the people of Iraq. Even soldiers fresh from battle cited this among their reasons for risking their lives in combat.[23] To grasp the significance of this point, one should recall that combat troops are famed for their indifference to high-minded abstractions. From World War II onward, sociological research has confirmed the experienced soldier's axiom that troops fight for their comrades, not for any patriotic or moral ideals.[24] Events since 2003 have made the humanitarian argument for invading Iraq seem as misguided as the argument that Saddam Hussein was about to acquire nuclear weapons.

Advocates of the war have also implied that G.W. Bush's policies play a role in protecting American citizens from terrorism. As recently as 2007, Republican presidential candidates advanced this claim.[25] Since no one can know what would have happened if Saddam Hussein had remained in power, no one can know

---

19   Allen, Auxier and Tyson, 'Deconstructing the Debate'.
20   Ibid.
21   Scott Keeter, 'Trends in Public Opinion about the War in Iraq, 2003–2007', *Pew Research Center Publications* (15 March 2007), <http://pewresearch.org/pubs/431/trends-in-public-opinion-about-the-war-in-iraq-2003-2007> [accessed 11 February 2008].
22   Keeter, 'Trends in Public Opinion about the War in Iraq, 2003–2007'.
23   Leonard Wong, Thomas A. Kolditz, Raymond A. Millen and Terrence M. Potter, *Why They Fight: Combat Motivation in the Iraq War* (Carlisle, PA: Strategic Studies Institute, 2003), p. 17.
24   Ibid., p. 6.
25   Allen, Auxier and Tyson, 'Deconstructing the Debate'.

whether this argument has merit. Nevertheless, Pew data suggests that 62 per cent of the American public has rejected it.[26]

Data collected by the RAND Corporation and the Memorial Institute for the Prevention of Terrorism (MIPT) seems to justify the widespread scepticism. In 2003, the number of terrorist attacks worldwide had been steadily declining for over two years.[27] After the Western coalition invaded Iraq, the number of attacks rose steadily from 1,904 in 2003–04 to 6,672 in 2007–08.[28] The number of incidents declined to 3,479 in 2007–08 – still well over the pre-war total. Meanwhile, the US government has pressed forward with such potentially disturbing measures as detaining alleged illegal combatants without recognised due process and expanding the domestic powers of law enforcement agencies under the Patriot Act.

Even Americans who pay little attention to civil liberties or terrorism statistics are likely to have noticed the increasingly disruptive security procedures at airports. Such Americans may also recall that the air transit authorities introduced these measures in response to a 2006 plot in which over 24 terrorists intended to blow up 10 passenger aircraft travelling between Britain and the US. Despite the fact that airports had been exercising more stringent security measures ever since the attacks of 11 September 2001, the 2006 conspirators had worked out an innovative method for defeating existing baggage screening procedures by smuggling explosives on to aircraft in liquid form.[29] Those who fear such attacks or experience the resulting inconveniences are unlikely to feel that G.W. Bush's Iraq policy has made them safer.

American citizens have not only turned against their president's Iraq policies, they have turned against each other. 'In the parlance of punditry and campaign rhetoric circa 2004', scholars Nolan McCarthy, Keith T. Poole and Howard Rosenthal summarise:

> *American politics have "polarized." Scarcely a day went by without headlines such as the San Francisco Chronicle's "Where did the Middle Go? How polarized politics and a radical GOP [Grand Old Party] have put a chill on measured debate." Story after story attempted to explain the seemingly unbridgeable divide between red and blue states. Was the country divided on moral issues, national security or NASCAR?*[30]

26   Ibid.

27   <http://www.tkb.org/AboutMIPT.jsp> [accessed 11 August 2005].

28   Derived using the calculator found at Terrorist Incident Reports, Incidents To Date, <http://www.tkb.org/IncidentDateModule.jsp?startDate=01%2F01%2F2006&endDate= 01%2F01%2F2007&domInt=0&suiInt=0&filter=0&detail=0&info=&info1=&pagemode= month&imageField.x=0&imageField.y=0> [accessed 15 February 2008].

29   'Timeline: UK "terror plot" investigation', *BBC News* (7 September 2006), <http://news. bbc.co.uk/1/hi/uk/4801183.stm> [accessed 15 February 2008].

30   Nolan McCarthy, Keith T. Poole and Howard Rosenthal, *Polarized America: The Dance of Ideology and Unequal Riches* (Cambridge MA: MIT Press, 2006), p. 1.

McCarthy, Poole and Rosenthal go on to argue: 'What public commentators missed, however, was that polarization was not a solo performer but part of a tight ensemble. Polarization's partners were other fundamental changes in the American society and economy. Most important, just as American politics became increasingly divisive, economic fortunes diverged.'[31]

McCarthy, Poole and Rosenthal draw on sources ranging from US census data, US Federal Election Commission reports about various political parties' finances and an original technique for analysing ideological patterns in American legislators' voting records to demonstrate this correlation. Those authors also note a correlation between polarisation and high levels of immigration.[32] Although McCarthy, Poole and Rosenthal themselves pay comparatively little attention to foreign policy, Pew data confirm that American public opinion regarding the war has a place in the 'tight ensemble' as well.

Although increasing numbers of American citizens have come to oppose G.W. Bush's Iraq policies, those opponents come disproportionately from one political party. In April 2004, for instance, Pew researchers asked Americans whether they believed that the G.W. Bush administration's strategy of temporarily deploying additional troops to Iraq would improve the situation there. Overall, only 34 per cent of Americans were optimistic.[33] Among those who identified themselves as Republicans, however, 65 per cent predicted success.[34] By contrast, only 15 per cent of the Democrats polled were willing to concede that the deployment might achieve useful results.[35]

The mere fact that data concerning American political extremism, American economic inequality and American responses to a protracted military expedition happen to coincide does not prove that the three phenomena are connected; nor does it tell us what the connections might be. Nevertheless, those who consider the issues in more qualitative detail may infer a wide range of possible relationships among these factors. The fact that people of modest economic status are more likely to serve in the enlisted ranks of the armed forces is almost certainly important, although the tradition of martial patriotism in America's working classes complicates any simple attempt to equate socio-economic status with opinions on military action. Similar points apply to the fact that poorer people are more vulnerable to economic downturns. Thankfully, one need not work out the precise relationships among war, socio-economic status and political division to draw the more general conclusion that the three almost certainly are related, and that the combined effects of controversy over G.W. Bush's Iraq policy and socio-economic class conflict have helped to embitter American political life.

---

31 Ibid., p. 1.
32 McCarthy, Poole and Rosenthal, *Polarized America*, p. 9.
33 Allen, Auxier and Tyson, 'Deconstructing the Debate'.
34 Ibid.
35 Ibid.

Machiavelli's Shrug

Machiavelli's work accounts for both G.W. Bush's policies and their aftermath in detail. The Florentine explicitly advised the leaders of republics to wage pre-emptive war. In his *Discourses on Livy*, he presents Rome as a model for all republics to emulate. Some writers, notably Plutarch, claimed that the Romans owed much of their success to mere luck. The Florentine rejects this proposition. '[T]he good fortune which followed the Romans … would have equally attended other princes who had acted as the Romans did, and had displayed the same courage and sagacity.'[36]

Machiavelli explains:

> [I]f we examine into the cause of [Rome's] good fortune, … we shall readily find it.[37]

> [I]t is most certain that when a prince or a people attain that degree of reputation that all the neighboring princes and peoples fear to attack him, none of them will ever venture to do it except under the force of necessity.[38]

To Machiavelli, deterrence is not an end in itself. The reason why a fearsome reputation is valuable is that it allows a state to dispatch its own potential rivals without interference from others. '[I]t will be, as it were, the option of that potent prince or people to make war on such neighboring powers as may seem advantageous, whilst adroitly keeping the others quiet.'[39] If G.W. Bush did not succeed in keeping international opponents of his Iraq policy quiet, he certainly enjoyed the power to prevent any nation capable of defeating his armed forces in a direct confrontation from joining with Saddam Hussein to repel his invasion. Machiavelli goes on to cite numerous examples of instances in which the Romans destroyed other states before those states grew strong enough to threaten it.[40] From the Florentine's perspective, the fact that Saddam Hussein turned out to have only the most rudimentary arsenal of weapons of mass destruction might have appeared as a tribute to G.W. Bush's good timing.

The Florentine also anticipated the types of difficulties America has encountered since 2003. Machiavelli was acutely aware of the problems which arise in the aftermath of 'advantageous' war. Chapters 4 to 7 of *The Prince* focus on the problem of governing defeated rivals after one has conquered them. Machiavelli notes the special difficulties of maintaining control over territories which contain 'a large number of ancient nobles, recognized as such by their subjects' – a situation analogous to the numerous local potentates who have done so much to complicate

---

36 Machiavelli, *The Prince and The Discourses*, p. 280.
37 Ibid., p. 279.
38 Ibid., p. 279.
39 Ibid., p. 279.
40 Ibid., pp. 279–81.

America's occupation of Iraq.[41] Such territories, the Florentine noted, are relatively easy to invade 'but afterwards, if you wish to keep possession, infinite difficulties arise'.[42]

The Romans, Machiavelli noted, eventually overcame these difficulties by exterminating their empire's former notables and extinguishing even the memory of these potential insurrectionists.[43] This process took centuries. Accordingly, Rome – the state Machiavelli urges readers to emulate – was perpetually at war.[44] Although this prospect disturbs most Americans, it did not disturb the Florentine.

Machiavelli had little to say about the fact that perpetual war involves continual casualties, but his sanguinary advice on other issues suggests that he would not have found the losses Rome sustained in routine occupation operations upsetting. Nor did he view the financial cost of protracted military operations as an obstacle. 'Money is not the sinews of war', he declares in the title to a chapter in the *Discourses*, 'although it is commonly so considered.'[45] Since Machiavelli advised rulers to keep individuals malleable by afflicting them with 'privations', one may assume that he viewed the economic strains war places on private citizens as positively desirable.[46]

The Florentine is likely to have taken a similar attitude toward America's persisting exposure to international terrorism. 'The founders of cities are independent', Machiavelli notes in the first chapter of his *Discourses on Livy*, 'when they are people who, under the leadership of some prince or by themselves, have been obliged to fly from pestilence, war or famine, that was desolating their native country, and are seeking a new home.'[47] As states become secure and prosperous, however, citizens gain the means to indulge in 'that kind of license which inflicts injury on public as well as private interests'.[48] In such a state, 'each individual' consults only 'his own passions'.[49] This inevitably destroys the state and ensures its eventual subjugation.

In a later chapter, Machiavelli returns to this theme and suggests a remedy. 'To ensure a long existence to religious sects or republics,' the Florentine notes, 'it is necessary frequently to bring them back to their original principles.'[50] One does this, Machiavelli elaborates, by emulating the wise magistrates who governed Florence from 1434 to 1494. Those magistrates understood: '[T]hat it was necessary every five years to resume the government, and that otherwise it would be difficult

---

41   Machiavelli, *The Prince and The Discourses*, p. 16.
42   Ibid., p. 17.
43   Ibid., p. 17.
44   Ibid., p. 278.
45   Ibid., pp. 308–11.
46   Ibid., p. 109.
47   Ibid., p. 107.
48   Ibid., p. 114.
49   Ibid., p. 114.
50   Ibid., p. 397.

to maintain it. By "resuming the government" they meant to strike people with the same fear and terror as they did when they first assumed the government.'[51]

Machiavelli notes that states can receive such renewal 'either by external or internal occurrences'.[52] The Florentine describes an incident in which the Gauls helpfully restored the Romans to their original unity by sacking the city of Rome.[53] Florence's magistrates 'resumed' their city themselves, by periodically sweeping the city for 'those who, according to their principles, had conducted themselves badly' and subjecting these alleged wrongdoers to 'the extremest punishment'.[54] From a Machiavellian perspective, the terrorists who trouble America in the twenty-first century surely play a similar role to the Gauls, while also creating a pretext for the US government to behave like Florence's magistrates.

The Florentine also anticipated that war would exacerbate class conflict within a state. War forces states to seek both human and material resources from their plebeian subjects.[55] This causes the plebeians to grow both more important and more resentful. Thus, they demand more from elites. Elites, in turn come under increasing pressure to grant the plebeians' wishes. Machiavelli acknowledges that such situations are dangerous, but sees no preferable alternative.[56] Moreover, he expresses the hope that increasing the power of the plebeians will increase their commitment to the state.[57]

Conclusion

The reason why Machiavelli is able to recommend Roman imperial aggression with unqualified enthusiasm is that he never equated the freedom of republics with the freedom of citizens. He is more committed to government of the people than to government by the people or government for the people. Although Machiavelli lived too early to respond to the American founders' claim that 'governments are instituted among men' solely in order to safeguard their inhabitants' personal and inalienable rights to 'life, liberty and the pursuit of happiness', he would clearly reject it.[58] The fact that Americans have reacted against the Machiavellian consequences of their Machiavellian policy may, in fact, show that they remain more committed to the principles of their Declaration of Independence than their critics occasionally suggest. This also suggests, at a minimum, that American leaders are unwise to

---

51   Ibid., p. 400.
52   Ibid., p. 399.
53   Ibid., pp. 398–9.
54   Ibid., p. 400.
55   Ibid., pp. 125–7.
56   Ibid., pp. 125–7.
57   Ibid., pp. 125–7.
58   The text of the American Declaration of Independence comes from Pauline Maier, *American Scripture: Making the Declaration of Independence* (New York: Alfred A. Knopf, 1997), p. 236.

adopt Machiavellianism as their preferred approach, and even more so to do it explicitly.

This does, however, leave American leaders with a dilemma. Machiavelli and the G.W. Bush administration were right to note that pre-emptive war and other acts of military initiative can be advantageous. On occasions, they can be downright necessary. This leaves American leaders with the task of maximising their strategic freedom of action while minimising their exposure to moral and civic harm. If there is a simple principle for achieving this outcome, it remains to be found. Until someone discovers such a principle, America's leaders must assess the details of each issue they face for ways to achieve the best results possible given the particular situation they happen to be in. This process is neither reassuring nor intellectually satisfying, but as Machiavelli maintained in defence of his own approach, it is the alternative that 'involves fewer inconveniences'.[59]

References

Allen, Jodie T., Richard Auxier and Alec Tyson, 'Deconstructing the Debate 5/15/07: How Well Did the GOP Candidates' Views Match those of their Party's Members and of the General Public', *Pew Research Center Publications* (16 May 2007), <http://pewresearch.org/pubs/479/republican-debate> [accessed 11 February 2008]

Associated Press, 'AP Poll: To Fix Economy, Get Out of Iraq: Most Believe U.S. is in Recession and Quitting Iraq Would Be More Helpful Than Rebate Checks' (10 February 2008), http://www.cbsnews.com/stories/2008/02/10/national/main3813757.shtml [accessed 11 February 2008]

Keeter, Scott, 'Trends in Public Opinion about the War in Iraq, 2003–2007', *Pew Research Center Publications* (15 March 2007), <http://pewresearch.org/pubs/431/trends-in-public-opinion-about-the-war-in-iraq-2003-2007> [accessed 11 February 2008]

Machiavelli, Niccolo, *The Prince and The Discourses*, trans. by Luigi Ricci and Christian E. Detmold (New York: The Modern Library, 1940)

Maier, Pauline, *American Scripture: Making the Declaration of Independence* (New York: Alfred A. Knopf, 1997)

McCarthy, Nolan, Keith T. Poole and Howard Rosenthal, *Polarized America: The Dance of Ideology and Unequal Riches* (Cambridge, MA: MIT Press, 2006)

'Military Fatalities: By Month', <http://icasualties.org/oif/> [accessed 11 February 2008]

'Pope Warns Against War', *Catholic News Services*, (13 January 2003), <http://www.americancatholic.org/News/JustWar/Iraq/papalstatement.asp> [accessed 2 July 2008]

National Security Strategy of the United States of America (NSS) (Washington, DC: The White House, 2002)

---

59   Machiavelli, *The Prince and The Discourses*, pp. 127–8.

Stahn, Carsten, 'Enforcement of the Collective Will after Iraq', *The American Journal of International Law*, 97/4 (October 2003): 804–23

Teslik, Lee Hudson, 'Iraq, Afghanistan and the US Economy', *Council on Foreign Relations Backgrounder* (4 February 2008), <http://www.cfr.org/publication/15404/> [accessed 11 February 2008]

'Timeline: UK "terror plot" investigation', *BBC News* (7 September 2006), <http://news.bbc.co.uk/1/hi/uk/4801183.stm> [accessed 15 February 2008]

Unattributed online source: <http://www.tkb.org/AboutMIPT.jsp> [accessed 11 May 2005]

Unattributed online source: <http://www.ctj.org/html/def0301.btm> [accessed 11 February 2008]

Unattributed online source: <http://www.pollingreport.com/iraq.htm> [accessed 11 February 2008]

Unattributed online source: <http://www.tkb.org/IncidentDateModule.jsp?startDate=01%2F01%2F2006&endDate=01%2F01%2F2007&domInt=0&suiInt=0&filter=0&detail=0&info=&info1=&pagemode=month&imageField.x=0&imageField.y=0> [accessed 15 February 2008]

Wapshott, Nicholas, 'Diana crash photo has half the shock value of Iraq coffins', *The Times* (26 April 2004), <http://www.timesonline.co.uk/article/0,3-1088211,00.html> [accessed 2 February 2008]

Wong, Leonard, Thomas A. Kolditz, Raymond A. Millen and Terrence M. Potter, *Why They Fight: Combat Motivation in the Iraq War* (Carlisle, PA: Strategic Studies Institute, 2003)

Civilization and Savagery

Brett Bowden

O, it is excellent to have a giant's strength; but it is tyrannous to use it like a giant.[1]

How the strong treat the weak goes a long way toward determining if the strong are civilized. Restraint in the use of force is not a vice, but a virtue.[2]

Introduction: Civilization, Savagery and War

It has been suggested that civilization and war share a common heritage, that 'the cradle of civilization is also war's cradle'.[3] It has also been suggested that there 'is no document of civilization which is not at the same time a document of barbarism' or savagery.[4] This contention is thought to be particularly pertinent when applied to situations of armed conflict or the theatre of war. These suppositions are two key strands in the web of ideas linking civilization, savagery and war. Adding to the complexity of this relationship is the fact that the constituent components – civilization, savagery and war – are complex matters in and of themselves. With that in mind, this chapter seeks to situate and explain the concepts of civilization and savagery, particularly in the context of times of war.

Throughout much of organized human history, peoples, societies and states have been hierarchically divided on the basis of their proximity to the ideal of civilization. The most advanced collectives of peoples, civilized states, sit at the apex of civilizational hierarchy, while those at the other end of the scale are said to be not far removed from the state of nature. Somewhere in between these polar

---

1   Lines by Isabella in William Shakespeare, *Measure for Measure*, Act II, Scene II.
2   David Tucker, 'Fighting Barbarians', *Parameters*, 28/2 (1998): 77.
3   Ira Meistrich, 'War's Cradle: The Birthplace of Civilization is Also the Home of Culture's Nemesis', *MHQ: The Quarterly Journal of Military History*, 17/3 (2005): 85.
4   Walter Benjamin, *Illuminations*, ed. by Hannah Arendt (New York: Schocken Books, 1969), p. 256.

opposites at various stages of human and social development are barbarians and even less-developed savage peoples. Along with a capacity for sociopolitical organization and self-government,[5] means of warfare and conduct in war more generally have long been regarded as key markers of civilization, or the absence thereof. As Hannah Arendt explains, 'international law ... constitute[s] the civilized world insofar as it remains the foundation-stone of international relations even under the conditions of war'.[6] Similarly, Gerrit Gong notes that 'a "civilized" state adheres to generally accepted international law, including the laws of war'.[7] By their very nature, barbarian and savage peoples are deemed incapable of abiding by such laws. This line of thought has been extended to take in the rise of the terrorist threat, given that terrorists are thought to be capable of abiding by the rules, but are unwilling to do so.

War-making is thought to require a significant degree of organization and social cohesion. Harry Holbert Turney-High notes in *Primitive War* that the 'war complex fits with the rest of the pattern of social organization'.[8] An exemplar of the importance of society to war-making, and the qualification of civilization more generally, is J.S. Mill's observation that in 'savage communities each person shifts for himself; except in war (and even then very imperfectly) we seldom see any joint operations carried on by the union of many'.[9] According to Mill, savages and barbarians are 'incapable of acting in concert', and nowhere is the capacity for co-operation more important than in times of war: 'Look even at war, the most serious business of a barbarous people; see what a figure rude nations, or semi-civilized and enslaved nations, have made against civilized ones, from Marathon downwards. Why? Because discipline is more powerful than numbers, and discipline, that is, perfect co-operation, is an attribute of civilization.'[10]

Just as important as social cohesion and accompanying institutions is the presence of a set of values that have long been regarded as essential hallmarks of civilization. As such, it is widely thought that 'We can learn a great deal about a people's culture and the manner in which it develops by observing how they fight.'[11] Important here are the ethical and normative demands of civilization. As Jean Starobinski notes, 'as a value, civilization constitutes a political and moral norm. It is the criterion

---

5   See Brett Bowden, 'The Ideal of Civilisation: Its Origins and Socio-Political Character', *Critical Review of International Social and Political Philosophy*, 7/1 (2004): 25–50.

6   Hannah Arendt, *The Origins of Totalitarianism* (London: George Allen & Unwin, 1958), p. 462.

7   Gerrit W. Gong, *The Standard of 'Civilization' in International Society* (Oxford: Clarendon Press, 1984), pp. 14–15.

8   Harry Holbert Turney-High, *Primitive War: Its Practice and Concepts*, 2nd edn (Columbia: University of South Carolina Press, 1971), p. 23.

9   John Stuart Mill, 'Civilization', in *Essays on Politics and Culture*, ed. by Gertrude Himmelfarb (Garden City, NY: Doubleday, 1962), p. 52.

10   Mill, 'Civilization', p. 55.

11   Michael Howard, 'Constraints on Warfare', in Michael Howard, George J. Andreopolous, and Mark R. Shulman, eds, *The Laws of War: Constraints on Warfare in the Western World* (New Haven, CT: Yale University Press, 1994), p. 1.

against which barbarity, or non-civilization, is judged and condemned'.[12] A similar point is made by Anthony Pagden, who suggests that civilization 'describes a state, social, political, cultural, aesthetic – even moral and physical – which is held to be the optimum condition for all mankind, and this involves the implicit claim that only the civilized can know what it is to be civilized'.[13] This claim is important, for as Starobinski suggests, the 'historical moment in which the word *civilization* appears marks the advent of self-reflection, the emergence of consciousness that thinks it understands the nature of its own activity'. More specifically, it marks 'the moment that Western civilization becomes aware of itself reflectively, it sees itself as one civilization among others. Having achieved self-consciousness, civilization immediately discovers civilizations'.[14] But as Norbert Elias notes, it is not a case of Western civilization as one among equals, for the very concept of civilization 'expresses the self-consciousness of the West ... It sums up everything in which Western society of the last two or three centuries believes itself superior to earlier societies or "more primitive" contemporary ones'.[15]

Included in this sense of superiority is a differentiation in the moral worth attributed to civilized peoples and lesser barbarians and savages, both individually and as collectives. Examples of this abound, including early English depictions of the Irish, and subsequent European characterizations of the indigenous peoples of the Americas and elsewhere as comparable (sometimes unfavourably) to animals, insects or infants – anything but civilized human beings.[16] Such unfavourable characterizations and associated differentiations in moral worth have and continue to influence the perception and treatment of adversaries, especially in times of war; from the Crusades to the Indian Wars to the global war on terror. Inherent in the general sense of superiority are the art and ethics of war. Arising out of centuries of encounters with 'uncivilized' Others,[17] first Europe and then the West more generally proclaimed a strategic and technological capability unrivalled on the battlefield. Similarly, Europeans-cum-Westerners have laid claim to a monopoly on the moral high ground in respect to questions of *jus ad bellum* (just causes of war) and *jus in bello* (laws governing conduct of war). This does not preclude the possibility that other peoples have held similar views of their own.[18]

---

12   Jean Starobinski, *Blessings in Disguise; or The Morality of Evil* (Cambridge, MA: Harvard University Press, 1993), p. 31.

13   Anthony Pagden, 'The "Defence of Civilization" in Eighteenth-century Social Theory', *History of the Human Sciences*, 1/1 (1988): 33.

14   Starobinski, *Blessings in Disguise*, p. 32. Emphasis in original.

15   Norbert Elias, *The Civilizing Process* (Oxford: Blackwell, 2000), p. 5.

16   See Brett Bowden, *The Empire of Civilization* (Chicago: University of Chicago Press, 2009); and Edmund P. Russell III, '"Speaking of Annihilation": Mobilizing for War against Human and Insect Enemies, 1914–1945', *Journal of American History*, 82/4 (1996): 1,505–29.

17   Edward W. Said, *Orientalism* (London: Routledge & Kegan Paul, 1978).

18   See generally Michael Walzer, *Just and Unjust Wars*, 3rd edn (New York: Basic, 2000). See also John Kelsay and James Turner Johnson, eds, *Just War and Jihad: Historical and Theoretical Perspectives on War and Peace in Western and Islamic Traditions* (New York:

The Military Horizon and Savage War

The 'military horizon' was a figurative line in the sand to distinguish 'civilized' European warfare, which was supposedly organized, constrained and chivalrous, from the chaotic nature of the undisciplined and opportunistic 'primitive' warfare practiced by savages and barbarians. As Turney-High put it, the 'military horizon depends ... not upon the adequacy of weapons but the adequacy of team work, organization, and command'. Because of a perceived lack of organization and co-operation, and 'despite their face-painting and sporadic butchery', uncivilized peoples are thought to fall short of the military horizon. Thus they are deemed 'not soldiers' and nor do they 'contain the rudiments of the arts of war'.[19]

Characterizations and divisions such as these have a long history, descending from hierarchical divisions within Europe, and exacerbated from the moment European nations began to encounter peoples beyond their borders. They can be found in 1095, the year Pope Urban II (1088–1099) proclaimed the first Crusade. They are evident in Pope Innocent IV's (1243–1254) commentary on Pope Innocent III's (1198–1216) decretal *Quod super his*, in which he begins to articulate the nature of papal–infidel relations.[20] And they are implied in declarations by Sir John Davies, King James's Attorney General of Ireland, that such 'a barbarous Country must first be broken by a war, before it will be capable of good Government'.[21] The general sentiment is captured in a claim by the jurist Robert Ward, who later served in the British House of Commons and in executive posts, that if 'we look to the *Mahometan* and *Turkish* nations ... their ignorance and barbarity repels all examination .... The same inferiority in this sort of conduct, is to be found even among the Chinese .... Their wars have always been carried on with *Eastern* barbarity, and their known laws against strangers would alone demonstrate the point'.[22]

With the 'discovery' of the New World and other previously unknown lands, Amerindians and other indigenous peoples were deemed to be far less civilized than any peoples previously encountered. Relying on the various and varied accounts emanating from the frontiers of the Americas, from the tales of trappers to the more detailed accounts by early anthropological expeditions, celebrated texts such as William Robertson's *History of America* gave the following general impression:

Greenwood Press, 1991); and James Turner Johnson, *The Holy War Idea in Western and Islamic Traditions* (University Park, PA: Pennsylvania State University Press, 1997).

19 Turney-High, *Primitive War*, p. 23.

20 See Brett Bowden, 'The Colonial Origins of International Law: European Expansion and the Classical Standard of Civilisation', *Journal of the History of International Law/Revue d'histoire du droit international*, 7/1 (2005): 1–23.

21 Sir John Davies, *Historical Relations: or, A Discovery of the True Causes why Ireland was Never Entirely Subdued nor Brought under Obedience of the Crown of England until the Beginning of the Reign of King James of Happy Memory* (Dublin: Samuel Dancer, 1664), pp. 4–5.

22 Robert Ward, *An Enquiry into the Foundation and History of the Law of Nations in Europe from the Time of the Greeks and Romans to the Age of Grotius*, II vols (New York & London: Garland Publishing, 1963; reprint of 1795 edn), vol. II, pp. 3–4.

> *When polished nations have obtained the glory of victory, or have acquired an addition of territory, they may terminate a war with honor. But savages are not satisfied until they extirpate the community which is the object of their hatred. They fight not to conquer, but to destroy ... If they engage in hostilities, it is with a resolution never to see the face of the enemy in peace, but to prosecute the quarrel with immortal enmity ... With respect to their enemies, the rage of vengeance knows no bounds. When under the dominion of this passion, man becomes the most cruel of all animals. He neither pities, nor forgives, nor spares ... They place not their glory in attacking their enemies with open force. To surprise and destroy is the greatest merit of a commander, and the highest pride of his followers.*[23]

A similar, qualitative judgement was made by the influential philosopher Immanuel Kant, who claims in *Perpetual Peace* that the primary distinction between the uncivilized remnants of Europe and the savage peoples of the New World 'lies in the fact that many tribes of the latter have been eaten by their enemies, while the former know how to make better use of their conquered enemies than to dine off them'.[24] The casting of the warfare of Amerindians as savage when compared to that of Europeans or settlers made its way into such monumental documents as the United States of America's Declaration of Independence (4 July 1776), in which Thomas Jefferson charges that the British King 'has excited domestic insurrections among us, and has endeavored to bring on the inhabitants of our frontiers, the merciless Indian savages, whose known rule of warfare is an undistinguished destruction of all ages, sexes, and conditions'. As noted, such characterizations have a significant impact on the way supposedly less civilized peoples have been and continue to be treated in times of war.

The idea that organized, well-governed civilized peoples generally have an advantage over less organized, ungovernable uncivilized peoples has a long history when it comes to waging war. Georg W.F. Hegel suggests that 'it arises above all in the *Iliad* where the Greeks take the field against the Asiatics and thereby fight the first epic battles in the tremendous opposition that led to the wars which constitute in Greek history a turning-point in world-history'. He continues that in a 'similar way the Cid fights against the Moors; in Tasso and Ariosto the Christians fight against the Saracens, in Camoens the Portuguese against the Indians'. He suggests in virtually 'all the great epics we see peoples different in morals, religion, speech, in short in mind and surroundings, arrayed against one another; and we are made completely at peace by the world-historically justified victory of the higher principle over the lower which succumbs to a bravery that leaves nothing over the defeated'. The conclusion Hegel draws from this is that 'In this sense, the epics of the past describe the triumph of the West over the East, [the triumph] of European

---

23   William Robertson, *The History of America*, 12th edn, IV vols (London: Cadell and Davies, 1812), vol. II, pp. 149–54.

24   Immanuel Kant, 'Perpetual Peace', in Lewis White Beck, ed., *Kant On History* (Indianapolis: Bobbs-Merril, 1963), p. 99.

moderation, and the individual beauty of a reason that sets limits to itself.'[25] In essence, it is widely thought that the 'sedentary, civilized, and conventional typically prevail over the nomadic, barbaric, and unconventional'.[26]

It was not always the case that the supposedly more civilized triumphed over the less civilized. Adam Smith argues that in 'ancient times the opulent and civilized found it difficult to defend themselves against the poor and barbarous nations' (the victory of the barbarian hordes of Germany over the armies of Imperial Rome being an example). But as he further notes, with the coming of industrialization and commercial society the tables were quickly turned, for in 'modern times the poor and barbarous nations find it difficult to defend themselves against the opulent and civilized'. The reason Smith gives for this reverse in fortunes is that in 'modern war the great expense of firearms gives an evident advantage to the nation which can best afford the expense, and consequently to an opulent and civilized over a poor and barbarous nation'. Smith's observations on the asymmetrical nature of warfare highlight and reiterate the lopsided and almost inevitably violent nature of war between civilized and savage peoples. He concludes that the 'invention of firearms, an invention which at first sight appears to be so pernicious, is certainly favorable both to the permanency and to the extension of civilization'.[27]

More recently, David Tucker suggests that once again the greatest threat to civilized societies comes not from 'high-tech armies', but from 'savage warriors who respect none of the civilized constraints' of warfare, and 'who will do anything, absolutely anything, to gain victory'. These new savages are said to emerge from the 'deprivation of anarchic, overpopulated, and environmentally ravaged wastelands or brooding on their cultural defeat'. Supposedly they will not only 'commit these atrocities, they will enjoy doing so. Torture and rape they will consider sport; slaughtering children and the old, a pleasant afternoon's work; breaking treaties, no more trouble than taking a breath'.[28] Tucker is among a number of commentators who lament what they variously term the 'retreat of civilization', a 'return to barbarism' or the rise of 'new savagery'. For some it is sporadic, geographically or culturally isolated, but has wider ramifications in that it threatens to spill over into neighbouring regions and among diasporas. This new savagery is thought to justify the perpetuation of states or geographical zones being classified as more or less civilized, more or less savage.

Observers largely attribute this ongoing division of the world to the nationalist, ethnic and religious dimensions of the many conflicts that erupted in various regions of the world following the end of the Cold War.[29] Eric Hobsbawm, for

---

25   G.W.F. Hegel, *Aesthetics: Lectures on Fine Art*, 2 vols, trans. by T.M. Knox (Oxford: Clarendon Press, 1975), vol. 2, pp. 1,061–2.
26   Tucker, 'Fighting Barbarians', 78.
27   Adam Smith, *The Wealth of Nations* (London: T Nelson and Sons, 1869), pp. 296–7.
28   Tucker, 'Fighting Barbarians', 70.
29   For example, in the former Yugoslavia, parts of the former Soviet Union, Western Africa, the Horn of Africa, and the Great Lakes region of Central Africa, but not all of which necessarily have direct causal links with the ending of the Cold War.

instance, claims that 'barbarism has been on the increase ... and there is no sign that this increase is at an end'. It is a barbarism marked by 'the disruption and breakdown of the systems of rules and moral behaviour by which *all* societies regulate the relations among their members and, to a lesser extent, between their members and those of other societies'.[30] In a similar fashion, Clifford Poirot harks back to an earlier era, suggesting that in the Balkans in particular the collapse of communism 'produced a return to the sort of barbarism that ... was latent in late nineteenth century Germany'.[31]

Some of the most graphic and influential arguments along these lines come from journalists describing what is thought to be the largely irrational 'tribal' violence that stems from some kind of essential savagery; a remnant of incomplete 'civilizing missions' of the colonial era. The most prominent of these is Robert Kaplan's widely-read article, 'The Coming Anarchy', an apocalyptic neo-Malthusian premonition of the future of our planet and its population, as modelled on the state of affairs in Western Africa. He contends that the region is indicative of 'much of the underdeveloped world: the withering away of central governments, the rise of tribal and regional domains, the unchecked spread of disease, and the growing pervasiveness of war'.[32] Kaplan asks us to 'Think of a stretch limo in the potholed streets of New York City, where homeless beggars live. Inside the limo are the air-conditioned post-industrial regions of North America, Europe, the emerging Pacific Rim, and a few other isolated places, with their trade summitry and computer-information highways.' While on the outside 'would be a rundown, crowded planet of skinhead Cossacks and *juju* warriors, influenced by the worst refuse of Western pop culture and ancient tribal hatreds'.[33]

Demonizing the Enemy and Waging War on Savages

As noted, such characterizations and divisions of humanity have long had an impact on how different peoples or nations treat each other when they come into contact, especially in armed conflict. One of the critical questions arising out of

---

30 Eric Hobsbawm, 'Barbarism: A User's Guide', *New Left Review*, 206 (1994): 45. Emphasis in original.

31 Clifford S. Poirot Jr, 'The Return to Barbarism', *Journal of Economic Issues*, 31/1 (1997): 233. See also Clause Offe, 'Modern "Barbarity": A Micro State of Nature', *Constellations*, 2/3 (1996): 354–77.

32 Robert D. Kaplan, 'The Coming Anarchy', *The Atlantic Monthly* (February 1994): 48. See also Robert D. Kaplan, *Balkan Ghosts: A Journey through History* (London: Macmillan, 1993).

33 Kaplan, 'The Coming Anarchy', 60–62. See also Thomas F. Homer-Dixon, 'On the Threshold: Environmental Changes as Causes of Acute Conflict', *International Security*, 16/2 (1991): 76–116; 'Environmental Scarcities and Violent Conflict: Evidence from Cases', *International Security*, 19/1 (1994): 5–40; and *Environment, Scarcity, and Violence* (Princeton, NJ: Princeton University Press, 2001).

distinctions between civilized and savage peoples in times of war was posed by the jurist, Quincy Wright, in the wake of the French bombardment of Damascus in October 1925 (Syria being a French mandate at the time). Wright asked: 'Does international law require the application of laws of war to people of a different civilization?' His own thoughts were:

> The ancient Israelites are said to have denied the usual war restrictions to certain tribes against which they were sworn enemies, the ancient Greeks considered the rules of war recognized among Hellenes inapplicable to barbarians, and medieval Christian civilization took a similar attitude toward war with the infidel. An English writer [F.W. Hirst, The Arbiter in Council, p. 230] in 1906 draws attention to 'the peculiarly barbarous type of warfare which civilized Powers wage against tribes of inferior civilization. When I contemplate,' he adds, 'such modern heroes as Gordon, and Kitchener, and Roberts, I find them in affiance with slave dealers or Mandarins, or cutting down fruit trees, burning farms, concentrating women and children, protecting military trains with prisoners, bribing other prisoners to fight against their fellow countrymen. These are performances which seem to take us back to the bad old times. What a terrible tale will the recording angel have to note against England and Germany in South Africa, against France in Madagascar and Tonquin, against the United States in the Philippines, against Spain in Cuba, against the Dutch in the East Indies, against the Belgians in the Congo State.' Possibly the emphasis, in most accounts of the recent bombardment of Damascus, upon the fact that relatively slight damage was done to Europeans and Americans indicates the existence of this distinction in the moral sense of Western communities.[34]

Wright's lament of French heavy-handedness in Syria, which he equates to 'a policy of terrorism',[35] is something of an exception to the rule when it comes to self-assessments of the civilized world's conduct in its confrontations with supposedly less-civilized peoples. Responding to Wright's assessment of the legality of the French bombing of Damascus, Eldridge Colby, a captain in the United States Army, argued:

> [H]owever Professor Wright may deplore the fact … [there is] one matter which must be faced. The distinction is existent. It is based on a difference in methods of waging war and on different doctrines of decency in war. When combatants and non-combatants are practically identical among a people, and savage or semi-savage peoples take advantage of this identity to effect ruses, surprises, and massacres on the 'regular' enemies, commanders must attack their problems in entirely different ways from those in which they proceed

---

34   Quincy Wright, 'The Bombardment of Damascus', American Journal of International Law, 20/2 (1926): 266.

35   Ibid., 273.

against Western peoples. When a war is between 'regular' troops and what are termed 'irregular' troops the mind must approach differently all matters of strategy and tactics, and, necessarily also, matters of rules of war.[36]

Colby supports his argument by drawing on a range of judicial and military authorities to demonstrate that things could not be any other way. In *The Reformation of War*, Colonel J.F.C. Fuller of the British Army writes: 'In small wars against uncivilized nations, the form of warfare to be adopted must tone with the shade of culture existing in the land, by which I mean that, against peoples possessing a low civilization, war must be more brutal in type.'[37] The British *Manual of Military Law* states that 'the rules of International Law apply only to warfare between civilized nations, where both parties understand them and are prepared to carry them out. They do not apply in wars with uncivilized States and tribes'.[38] Colby further argues that the 'long list of Indian wars in which the troopers of the United States have defended and pushed westwards the frontiers of America bear eloquent testimony to the unified tribal action in war [men, women and child combatants], and to the almost universal brutality of the red-skinned fighter'.[39]

While Colby acknowledges that it is 'good to be decent', it is 'good to use proper discretion', and it is 'good to observe the decencies of international law', he insists 'it is a fact that against uncivilized people who do not know international law and do not observe it, and would take advantage of one who did, there must be something else'.[40] This gives rise to the question: how can adversaries knowingly take advantage of something they do not know exists? And does this give the other party to the conflict the right to turn their back on a set of laws they claim to abide by and which are held up as a marker of their civilization, and Civilization more generally? Colby concludes that the 'real essence of the matter is that devastation and annihilation is the principal method of warfare that savage tribes know'.[41] As such, their 'civilized' adversaries are thought to be justified in similarly adopting 'more brutal' methods in warfare between the two parties.

In speaking of this civilized–savage divide, Everett Wheeler argues that the Western tradition of warfare displays some 'tension between rival norms', or what he terms the 'Achilles ethos, advocating chivalry, pitched battle and open, direct means, and the Odysseus ethos, favoring trickery, deceit, indirect means and avoidance of pitched battle'; with terrorism cast as 'Odysseus gone mad'.[42]

---

36   Eldridge Colby, 'How to Fight Savage Tribes', *American Journal of International Law*, 21/2 (1927): 279.

37   Colby, 'Savage Tribes', 280; and J.F.C. Fuller, *The Reformation of War* (London: Hutchinson, 1923), p. 191.

38   Colby, 'Savage Tribes', 280; and Great Britain War Office, *Manual of Military Law* (London: HMSO, 1914), p. 235.

39   Colby, 'Savage Tribes', 284.

40   Ibid., 287.

41   Ibid., 285.

42   Everett L. Wheeler, 'Terrorism and Military Theory: An Historical Perspective', *Terrorism and Political Violence*, 3/1 (1991): 24, 27.

This tension or contradiction, as outlined above, is explained by Michael Howard who notes that civilized 'warfare, *bellum hostile*, was the norm within Western Christendom'. But when it came to conflict with Others, that is, 'wars against outsiders, infidels, or barbarians, the West had inherited a brutal legacy from the Romans which they termed *bellum romanum*, or *guerre mortelle*, a conflict in which no holds were barred and all those designated as enemy, whether bearing arms or not, could be indiscriminately slaughtered'.[43]

Over time there is said to be a general trend toward civilizing or constraining warfare on the basis that adversaries are recognized as fellow human beings in possession of certain rights.[44] So long as they bore arms they were a legitimate target, but once disarmed, they 'regained all the rights due to [them] as a child of God or a member of civil society'. However, if the enemy 'was not seen as a human being ... but as a member of an inferior but still menacing race, it made no difference whether he was wearing a uniform and bearing arms or not – whether indeed he was man, woman, or child. He had no more rights than a wild animal or an insect'.[45] The dehumanization or demonization of enemy Others and the brutality this gives rise to is evident throughout history. It is evident in the 'ruthlessness with which the English "pacified" Ireland', a brutality that 'was to be carried over' into the treatment of indigenous peoples by conquistadors and European settlers in the Americas. As Howard notes, the 'contrast between the manner in which the French and English soldiers treated each other, even though they were enemies, and the way they treated the Indians, provides textbook examples of the two kinds of war'.[46]

The atrocities arising from the demonization and dehumanization of adversaries and perceived enemies are also gruesomely evident in two world wars. The atrocities of the Second World War are especially well-known, both in Europe at the hands of the Nazis in particular, but also in the Pacific theatre where the fighting was described as 'brutal by the standards of the Second World War'. It was a theatre in which 'Refusal to accept surrender was the norm for both sides. Enemy wounded were generally killed out of hand. Atrocities were common and included the abuse, torture, and killing of those who did manage to surrender.' It has been suggested

---

43   Howard, 'Constraints on Warfare', p. 3.
44   For instance, the Declaration Renouncing the Use, in Time of War, of Explosive Projectiles under 400 Grammes Weight (St Petersburg, 29 November/11 December 1868), considered that 'the progress of civilization should have the effect of alleviating as much as possible the calamities of war'. In essence, the agreement's purpose was 'to examine the expediency of forbidding the use of certain projectiles in time of war between civilized nations'. In wars against uncivilized peoples, however, there were no such restraints.
45   Howard, 'Constraints on Warfare', p. 8. See also Russell, '"Speaking of Annihilation": Mobilizing for War against Human and Insect Enemies, 1914–1945'.
46   Howard, 'Constraints on Warfare', p. 5. See also James Muldoon, 'The Indian as Irishman', *Essex Institute Historical Collections*, 111 (1975): 267–89.

that 'What the fighting lacked in scale (as compared to that in Europe), it made up for in intensity and savagery.'[47]

Terrorism and the War on Terror

Even prior to 11 September 2001, terrorism was regarded as some form of contemporary 'savage war'. Wheeler contends that the 'shock of modern terrorism resembles the outrage of seventeenth- or eighteenth-century European regulars in North America when ambushed by Indians who ignored the European rules of the game'.[48] Terrorism is denounced for 'the shock value of unexpected savagery toward innocent victims [which] creates the impression of civilization teetering on the brink of anarchy'.[49] Terrorists are said to 'shuck off in particularly violent and blatant fashion the restraints that divide civil society from the state of nature',[50] with the aim of announcing that the 'whole world is a Hobbesian state of nature' devoid of civil order.[51]

In line with the military horizon and the savage war thesis, Wheeler contends that 'conventional warfare requires, above all, open battle and observance of rules', while 'terrorism like primitive warfare is unconventional in its most literal sense: the parties in conflict lack a shared set of values'. Like the warfare attributed to the savages of an earlier era, 'above all, terrorists avoid pitched battle and confrontation with regular armed forces, relying on the tactics of primitive warfare – surprise, ambush, deception, and hit-and-run maneuvers'.[52] This slide away from conventional modes of warfare, which are supposedly noble and chivalrous, is described as part of a 'murderous *reductio ad absurdum*' in which terrorists and guerrillas 'vandalize the threefold division of government, army and civilians once enforced by conventional warfare and the Westphalian and Philadelphian models'.[53]

In the immediate aftermath of the 11 September 2001 terrorist attacks, Sir John Keegan harked back to an earlier era in proclaiming that 'Westerners fight face to face, in stand-up battle, and go on until one side or the other gives in', all the while

---

47 Tarak Barkawi, 'Peoples, Homelands, and Wars? Ethnicity, the Military, and Battle among British Imperial Forces in the War against Japan', *Comparative Study in Society and History*, 46/1 (2004): 149–50. See also John W. Dower, *War Without Mercy: Race & Power in the Pacific War* (New York: Pantheon, 1986).

48 Wheeler, 'Terrorism and Military Theory', 15.

49 Ibid., 6.

50 Loren E. Lomasky, 'The Political Significance of Terrorism', in R.G. Frey and C.W. Morris, eds, *Violence, Terrorism, and Justice* (Cambridge: Cambridge University Press, 1991), p. 99.

51 Robert Phillips, 'Terrorism: Historical Roots and Moral Justifications', in M. Warner and R. Crisp, eds, *Terrorism, Protest and Power* (Aldershot: Edward Elgar, 1990), p. 77.

52 Wheeler, 'Terrorism and Military Theory', 14–15.

53 John Keane, *Reflections on Violence* (London: Verso, 1996), p. 141.

observing 'what to non-Westerners may well seem curious rules of honour'. On the other hand, 'Orientals' are said to 'shrink from pitched battle, which they often deride as a sort of game, preferring ambush, surprise, treachery and deceit as the best way to overcome an enemy'. He went on to claim that 'Relentless as opposed to surprise and sensation is the Western way of warfare.' It is said to be a style of war-making that is 'deeply injurious to the Oriental style and rhetoric of war making'. Keegan articulates what he believes to be the obvious link between the savages of the past and the savages of the present; declaring that 'Oriental war-makers, today terrorists, expect ambushes and raids to destabilize their opponents, allowing them to win further victories by horrifying outrages at a later stage.'[54]

In waging the war on terror, leaders of the Western world allied against al-Qaida and its hosts have been at pains to emphasize that the war is not a war against the Islamic or Arab worlds; it is not, they stress, a 'clash of civilizations', as made famous by Samuel Huntington.[55] Likewise, most have gone to lengths to ensure that they do not portray Islamic or Arabic civilization as inferior to Western civilization. Not all commentators, however, have felt obliged to follow suit. Keegan, for instance, concludes his observations on the war on terrorism by declaring it a 'war [that] belongs within the much larger spectrum of a far older conflict between settled, creative, productive Westerners and predatory, destructive Orientals'.[56]

In an 'Address to the Nation' from Fort Bragg on 28 June 2005, George W. Bush further underlined the notion that tactics employed by parties to a conflict reflect their degree of civility. He declared:

> We see the nature of the enemy in terrorists who exploded car bombs along a busy shopping street in Baghdad, including one outside a mosque. We see the nature of the enemy in terrorists who sent a suicide bomber to a teaching hospital in Mosul. We see the nature of the enemy in terrorists who behead civilian hostages and broadcast their atrocities for the world to see. These are savage acts of violence.

Bush went on to state that 'We're fighting against men with blind hatred – and armed with lethal weapons – who are capable of any atrocity.' These modern savages, like the Amerindians and the Vietcong before them, 'wear no uniform; they respect no laws of warfare or morality'.[57] When combined with the mantra that the war on terror is a 'war like no other' against an enemy that is 'pure evil'

---

54 John Keegan, 'Why the West will Win', *The Age* (Melbourne, 9 October 2001), p. 19. For a more favourable and balanced comparative study, see Roxanne L. Euben, *Enemy in the Mirror: Islamic Fundamentalism and the Limits of Modern Rationalism: A Work of Comparative Political Theory* (Princeton, NJ: Princeton University Press, 1999).

55 See Samuel P. Huntington, 'The Clash of Civilizations?' *Foreign Affairs*, 72/3 (1993): 22–49; and *The Clash of Civilizations and the Remaking of World Order* (London: Touchstone, 1998).

56 Keegan, 'Why the West will Win'.

57 George W. Bush, 'President Addresses Nation, Discusses Iraq, War on Terror' (28 June 2005), <http://www.whitehouse.gov/news/releases/2005/06/20050628-7.html>.

and refuses to 'fight by the rules', the inference is that this war demands tactics and means of warfare that are necessarily more brutal than might otherwise be employed.[58] In this respect it is not such a unique war.[59]

Terrorists have indeed committed atrocities, as have those fighting the war on terrorism. For the former, atrocities and acts of callousness are prescribed policy; but al-Qaida has also gone to lengths to rationalize and justify the targeting of civilians, the use of suicide bombers, and the killing of fellow Muslims.[60] Those fighting the war on terror also try to justify or explain away atrocities as isolated incidents committed by a handful of rogue troops – such as the shameful events at Abu Ghraib prison in Iraq – but they still happened and continue to happen. There have also been many other unsavoury incidents and instances, such as widespread 'collateral damage'; enough to suggest that there is something more going on than isolated incidences of brutality. The point to be made here is that just because one side, the terrorists, chooses to abandon the accepted rules of fair play it does not mean that the other party to the conflict has to follow suit and adopt 'more brutal' and indiscriminate means of warfare.

Conclusion: The Vicious Cycle of Savage War

The war on terror is just the latest circumstance in which those prosecuting the war, in response to atrocities or acts of savagery by an uncivilized foe, seek to justify a turn to any means necessary, including 'more brutal' means of warfare. As has been argued on many occasions in wars against uncivilized Others, such an evil and unscrupulously savage enemy cannot be fought using conventional means. Ironically but tragically, this all takes place in the name of Civilization and the battle of good over evil. But perhaps it is more the case that those more base instincts and uncivilized means are universal in appeal and have been at the disposal of the civilized all along. History seems to suggest as much. All too regularly adversaries dehumanize their enemy – the uncivilized savage who lacks virtue, chivalry, is beyond the pale materially and morally – in order to justify a recourse to the 'more brutal' means they claim to abhor and claim to be antithetical to the very ideal of Civilization. The dichotomy between the civilized, uniformed chivalrous combatant and the opportunistic, treacherous savage is a false one. As Aleksandr

---

58 For a good account of the persistent feature in American politics of the 'inflation, stigmatization, and dehumanization of political foes', from 'the Indian cannibal ... [to] the agents of international terrorism', see Michael Paul Rogin, *Ronald Reagan, the Movie: and Other Episodes in Political Demonology* (Berkeley: University of California Press, 1987).

59 See Brett Bowden, 'Civilization and Savagery in the Crucible of War', *Global Change, Peace & Security*, 19/1 (2007): 3–16.

60 See Quintan Wiktorowicz, 'A Genealogy of Radical Islam', *Studies in Conflict & Terrorism*, 28/2 (2005): 75–97.

Solzhenitsyn recounts in *The Gulag Archipelago*, if only it were that simple. If only there were readily identifiably evil people who could be simply weeded out. But the civilization–savagery dichotomy is not that simple, and in times of war things are even more complicated.

Particularly important in times of uncertainty and in the face of threats, especially in conflicts between peoples and combatants who are considered significantly 'different', is leadership. The demonization and dehumanization of adversaries will impact on how those adversaries are treated, or mistreated. Often, when faced with unknown threats by largely unknown or misunderstood peoples or cultures, 'identifying an enemy offers the cognitive satisfaction of certainty in uncertain times'.[61] As Sam Keen outlines in *Faces of the Enemy*, first 'we create the enemy. Before the weapon comes the image. We *think* others to death and then invent the battle-axe or the ballistic missiles with which to actually kill them. Propaganda precedes technology'.[62]

Moreover, as Colonel Anthony Hartle of the US Military Academy notes, the 'fear and violence of warfare incite brutal and inhumane actions'. And atrocities '*will* occur without strong leadership and focused training'.[63] Irrespective of time and place, whether it is Amerindians in the New World, the world wars, the Rwandan genocide, or the war on terror, 'large-scale atrocities occur when governments or military institutions foster fears and sanction brutality … When official doctrine and guidance demonize the enemy and play on soldiers' fears, atrocities become inevitable'. Whether it is ambiguous statements from the head of state, leaked memos from military lawyers or intelligence gatherers, or mixed messages from commanders on the ground, 'When the chain of command tolerates excessive brutality and encourages violence targeted at prisoners or noncombatants, the only question becomes the scale of atrocities that will take place.'[64]

As Carl von Clausewitz noted in *On War*, when either side in a conflict adopts such a strategy, demonization inevitably followed by atrocities, it 'compels its opponent to follow suit; a reciprocal action is started which must lead, in theory, to extremes'.[65] And thus the vicious cycle of savage war endlessly repeats itself until one side ultimately prevails. But as Arnold Toynbee notes, 'We have to remember that the annals of this warfare between "civilization" and "barbarism" have been written almost exclusively by the scribes of the "civilized" camp.'[66] So while it is the victors that are left to proclaim their motives and methods as civilized, victory in itself being proof enough, the vanquished are invariably cast as the morally

61   David Keen, 'War without End? Magic, Propaganda and the Hidden Functions of Counter-terror', *Journal of International Development*, 18/1 (2006): 95.
62   Sam Keen, *Faces of the Enemy: Reflections of the Hostile Imagination* (San Francisco: Harper & Row, 1991), p. 10. Emphasis in original.
63   Anthony E. Hartle, 'Atrocities in War: Dirty Hands and Noncombatants', *Social Research*, 69/4 (2002): 965. Emphasis in original.
64   Ibid., 966.
65   Carl von Clausewitz, *On War* (Princeton, NJ: Princeton University Press, 1976), p. 77.
66   Arnold J. Toynbee, *A Study of History*, 2 vols, abridged by D.C. Somervell (Oxford: Oxford University Press, 1947), vol. 1, p. 420.

and materially inferior savage aggressor who got nothing less than they deserved – right or wrong. In concluding, it is appropriate to return to Walter Benjamin's poignantly made point with which this chapter began: there 'is no document of civilization which is not at the same time a document of barbarism' or savagery.[67] Nowhere is this more the case than in the crucible of war: savagery begets savagery. And as with every other war that has been or will ever be fought, no belligerent has a monopoly on the savagery of war.

References

Arendt, Hannah, *The Origins of Totalitarianism* (London: George Allen & Unwin, 1958)

Barkawi, Tarak, 'Peoples, Homelands, and Wars? Ethnicity, the Military, and Battle among British Imperial Forces in the War against Japan', *Comparative Study in Society and History*, 46/1 (2004): 134–63

Beck, Lewis White, ed., *Kant On History* (Indianapolis: Bobbs-Merril, 1963)

Benjamin, Walter, *Illuminations*, ed. by Hannah Arendt (New York: Schocken Books, 1969)

Bowden, Brett, 'The Ideal of Civilisation: Its Origins and Socio-Political Character', *Critical Review of International Social and Political Philosophy*, 7/1 (2004) 25–50

– – –, 'The Colonial Origins of International Law: European Expansion and the Classical Standard of Civilisation', *Journal of the History of International Law/Revue d'histoire du droit international*, 7/1 (2005): 1–23

– – –, 'Civilization and Savagery in the Crucible of War', *Global Change, Peace & Security*, 19/1 (2007): 3–16

– – –, *The Empire of Civilization* (Chicago: University of Chicago Press, 2009)

Bush, George W., 'President Addresses Nation, Discusses Iraq, War on Terror' (28 June 2005), <http://www.whitehouse.gov/news/releases/2005/06/20050628-7.html>

Clausewitz, Carl von, *On War* (Princeton, NJ: Princeton University Press, 1976)

Colby, Eldridge, 'How to Fight Savage Tribes', *American Journal of International Law*, 21/2 (1927): 279–88

Davies, Sir John, *Historical Relations: or, A Discovery of the True Causes why Ireland was Never Entirely Subdued nor Brought under Obedience of the Crown of England until the Beginning of the Reign of King James of Happy Memory* (Dublin: Samuel Dancer, 1664)

Dower, John W., *War Without Mercy: Race and Power in the Pacific War* (New York: Pantheon, 1986)

Elias, Norbert, *The Civilizing Process* (Oxford: Blackwell, 2000)

---

67 Benjamin, *Illuminations*, p. 256.

Euben, Roxanne L., *Enemy in the Mirror: Islamic Fundamentalism and the Limits of Modern Rationalism: A Work of Comparative Political Theory* (Princeton, NJ: Princeton University press, 1999)

Frey, R.G. and C.W. Morris, eds, *Violence, Terrorism, and Justice* (Cambridge: Cambridge University Press, 1991)

Fuller, J.F.C., *The Reformation of War* (London: Hutchinson, 1923)

Gong, Gerrit W., *The Standard of 'Civilization' in International Society* (Oxford: Clarendon Press, 1984)

Great Britain War Office, *Manual of Military Law* (London: HMSO, 1914)

Hartle, Anthony E., 'Atrocities in War: Dirty Hands and Noncombatants', *Social Research*, 69/4 (2002): 963–79

Hegel, G.W.F., *Aesthetics: Lectures on Fine Art*, 2 vols, trans. by T.M. Knox (Oxford: Clarendon Press, 1975)

Hobsbawm, Eric, 'Barbarism: A User's Guide,' *New Left Review*, 206 (1994): 44–54

Homer-Dixon, 'On the Threshold: Environmental Changes as Causes of Acute Conflict,' *International Security*, 16/2 (1991): 76–116

– – –, *Environment, Scarcity, and Violence* (Princeton, NJ: Princeton University Press, 2001)

Homer-Dixon, Thomas F., 'Environmental Scarcities and Violent Conflict: Evidence from Cases,' *International Security*, 19/1 (1994): 5–40

Howard, Michael, George J. Andreopolous, and Mark R. Shulman, eds, *The Laws of War: Constraints on Warfare in the Western World* (New Haven, CT: Yale University Press, 1994)

Huntington, Samuel P., 'The Clash of Civilizations?' *Foreign Affairs*, 72/3 (1993): 22–49

– – –, *The Clash of Civilizations and the Remaking of World Order* (London: Touchstone, 1998)

Johnson, James Turner, *The Holy War Idea in Western and Islamic Traditions* (University Park, PA: Pennsylvania State University Press, 1997)

Kaplan, Robert D., *Balkan Ghosts: A Journey through History* (London: Macmillan, 1993)

– – –, 'The Coming Anarchy,' *The Atlantic Monthly* (February 1994): 44–76

Keane, John, *Reflections on Violence* (London: Verso, 1996)

Keegan, John, 'Why the West will Win', *The Age* (Melbourne, 9 October 2001), p. 19.

Keen, David, 'War without End? Magic, Propaganda and the Hidden Functions of Counter-terror', *Journal of International Development*, 18/1 (2006): 87–104

Keen, Sam, *Faces of the Enemy: Reflections of the Hostile Imagination* (San Francisco: Harper & Row, 1991)

Kelsay, John and James Turner Johnson, eds, *Just War and Jihad: Historical and Theoretical Perspectives on War and Peace in Western and Islamic Traditions* (New York: Greenwood Press, 1991)

Meistrich, Ira, 'War's Cradle: The Birthplace of Civilization is Also the Home of Culture's Nemesis', *MHQ: The Quarterly Journal of Military History*, 17/3 (2005): 84–93

Mill, John Stuart, 'Civilization', in *Essays on Politics and Culture*, ed. by Gertrude Himmelfarb (Garden City, NY: Doubleday, 1962)

Muldoon, James, 'The Indian as Irishman', *Essex Institute Historical Collections*, 111 (1975): 267–89

Offe, Clause, 'Modern "Barbarity": A Micro State of Nature', *Constellations*, 2/3 (1996): 354–77

Pagden, Anthony, 'The "Defence of Civilization" in Eighteenth-century Social Theory', *History of the Human Sciences*, 1/1 (1988): 33–45

Poirot, Clifford S. Jr, 'The Return to Barbarism', *Journal of Economic Issues*, 31/1 (1997): 233

Robertson, William, *The History of America*, 12th edn, IV vols (London: Cadell and Davies, 1812)

Rogin, Michael Paul, *Ronald Reagan, the Movie: and Other Episodes in Political Demonology* (Berkeley: University of California Press, 1987)

Russell, Edmund P. III, '"Speaking of Annihilation": Mobilizing for War against Human and Insect Enemies, 1914–1945', *Journal of American History*, 82/4 (1996): 1,505–29

Said, Edward W., *Orientalism* (London: Routledge & Kegan Paul, 1978)

Shakespeare, William, *Measure for Measure*

Smith, Adam, *The Wealth of Nations* (London: T. Nelson and Sons, 1869)

Solzhenitsyn, Aleksandr, *The Gulag Archipelago, 1918–1956: An Experiment in Literary Investigation*, 2 vols (Sydney: Collins & Harvill, 1974–75)

Starobinski, Jean, *Blessings in Disguise; or The Morality of Evil* (Cambridge, MA: Harvard University Press, 1993)

Toynbee, Arnold J., *A Study of History*, 2 vols, abridged by D.C. Somervell (Oxford: Oxford University Press, 1947)

Tucker, David, 'Fighting Barbarians', *Parameters*, 28/2 (1998): 69–79

Turney-High, Harry Holbert, *Primitive War: Its Practice and Concepts*, 2nd edn (Columbia: University of South Carolina Press, 1971)

Walzer, Michael, *Just and Unjust Wars*, 3rd edn (New York: Basic, 2000)

Ward, Robert, *An Enquiry into the Foundation and History of the Law of Nations in Europe from the Time of the Greeks and Romans to the Age of Grotius*, II vols (New York & London: Garland Publishing, 1963; reprint of 1795 edn)

Warner, M. and R. Crisp, eds, *Terrorism, Protest and Power* (Aldershot: Edward Elgar, 1990)

Wheeler, Everett L., 'Terrorism and Military Theory: An Historical Perspective', *Terrorism and Political Violence*, 3/1 (1991): 6–33

Wiktorowicz, Quintan, 'A Genealogy of Radical Islam', *Studies in Conflict & Terrorism*, 28/2 (2005): 75–97

Wright, Quincy, 'The Bombardment of Damascus', *American Journal of International Law*, 20/2 (1926): 263–80

International Law: Military Force and Armed Conflict

Christopher P.M. Waters and James A. Green[1]

The Increased Relevance of International Law to Warfare

This chapter is designed to provide an overview of the legal framework applicable to the use of military force and situations of ongoing armed conflict. Since it is a chapter on law, the bulk of it will set out what the law in the context of warfare actually is. However, it will also touch upon how the law is evolving and where controversies arise in the law (although it is worth noting that controversies arise much more in the application of law to facts than with respect to the content of the law itself). In subsequent chapters, certain key legal 'flashpoints' in the area will be examined in greater detail,[2] and, as such, these topics will only be briefly noted here. This chapter aims to underpin the more particular examinations that follow with a general outline of the topic.

Before turning to the substance of the international legal provisions in the context of war, force and armed conflict, it is important to note the relevance of that law to the reality of the use of military force (something that, we lawyers tend to forget, generally involves the systematic killing of human beings, often on a vast scale).

The concept of 'war' has traditionally been viewed as being something of such fundamental importance that it cannot realistically be subject to regulation through the application of law. As former United States Secretary of State Dean Acheson famously put it during the Cuban Missile Crisis: '[L]aw simply does not deal with such questions of ultimate power. … The survival of States is not a matter of law.'[3]

---

1   Christopher Waters is Assistant Professor, Faculty of Law, University of Windsor, and James Green is Lecturer in Law, University of Reading.
2   See the chapters in this volume by Steven Haines and Tom Kane respectively.
3   Dean Acheson, speaking as part of 'Law and Conflict: Changing Patterns and Contemporary Challenges, Panel on the Cuban Quarantine: Implications for the Future: Remarks', *American Society of International Law Proceedings*, 57 (1963): 10–15, at 14.

In some quarters, this classical realist perception of the relevance of law (or lack of) in this crucial area persists. However, rather than being a bit-player, law now must be viewed as being central to the conduct of military operations. One only need think of the rise of the legal advisor in Western militaries – vetting bombing targets in Kosovo and subsequent operations – to note this phenomenon.

Some have resisted this legal creep, and suggestions have been made that operational effectiveness is reduced as a result of such 'legal encirclement'.[4] Yet others have suggested that law-making with respect to the military is an interactive process; the military is a player in determining, for example, the nature of the Armed Services Act or the relationship with humanitarian organisations in the delivery of emergency food aid.[5] Whether one welcomes or loathes the increased role of law in the conduct of military operations – and indeed with respect to various aspects of military life, including recruitment and discipline during peacetime – it appears that the law as one key framework for military decision-making is here to stay. Not surprisingly, given the pervasiveness of legal questions in Western military practice, British military officers have expressed the view that they have insufficient legal training and would like to receive greater familiarity with international law and its domestic implementation.[6]

The growing perception of law's relevance has various causes. The first of these is the strategic need to justify or defend operational decisions; States will use law strategically, as a tool to justify actions through an enabling legal framework.[7] Another is the requirement to explain to oneself and subordinates, as well as, outside of the military, civilians (both at home and in theatres of operation) and the press, the legal basis for a mission. The threat of personal liability for one's actions (or those of subordinates under the rubric of command responsibility) is also a natural motivator in wanting to know the law. To these reasons might be added the fact that law and order and rule of law reform are often central aspects of a mission. Officers may need to be familiar with the legal framework to successfully pursue mission goals. Unfortunately, at present, lack of training – and, arguably, failures in leadership in terms of setting out in unambiguous terms the need for strict compliance with law – have led to numerous misperceptions about what the

---

4   Jenny Booth, 'Military Top Brass Attack Soldier Prosecutions', 14 July 2005, at: <http://www.timesonline.co.uk/tol/news/uk/article544087.ece>.

5   Christopher P.M. Waters, 'Is the Military Legally Encircled?' *Defence Studies*, 8 (2008): 26.

6   W.G.L. Mackinlay, 'Perceptions and Misperceptions: How are International and UK Law Perceived to Affect Military Commanders and Their Subordinates on Operations', *Defence Studies*, 7 (2007): 111.

7   As David Kennedy puts it in his masterful examination of the subject: 'Law now offers an institutional and doctrinal space for transforming the boundaries of war into strategic assets as well as a vernacular for legitimating and denouncing what happens in war.' David Kennedy, *Of War and Law* (Princeton, NJ: Princeton University Press, 2006), p. 116. See also Dino Kritsiotis, 'When States Use Armed Force', in Christian Reus-Smit, ed., *The Politics of International Law* (Cambridge: Cambridge University Press, 2004), p. 45, at pp. 47–48.

law actually is. The unwarranted fear and confusion in some quarters over the International Criminal Court's mandate well illustrates this.[8]

Understanding International Law

The focus of this chapter is on international law rather than on domestic civilian or military law. There are numerous introductory writings on international law and no more than a superficial sketch can be given here of the nature of this body of law.[9] Suffice it to say, for present purposes, that, although linked with domestic legal systems, international law represents a separate and distinct legal system. It has different sources, actors, substantive rules, methods of interpretation and enforcement. International law is primarily created between States, which are sovereign and legally equal, and it may be made in one of two ways. The first is by way of treaties (or, as they are often called, conventions), which are binding agreements akin to contracts. In the modern world, multilateral treaties relate to innumerable spheres of international life, from postal exchange to war crimes and from air travel to trade.

The second method of international law creation, customary international law, is more difficult to grasp but remains an enduring and evolving source of law, even in an era where it is sometimes overshadowed by the rise of treaty law. It is created through State practice that is largely constant and uniform, combined with an acceptance that the practice is conducted as part of a legal right or obligation. Both the objective actions that constitute State practice and the subjective element (often referred to as *opinio juris*) – the understanding that the State practice is governed by law and is not merely habit – are needed for a practice to be considered customary *law*. For instance, while naval vessels may salute each other at sea with some consistency, there is no sense that there is a 'legal' obligation to do so and therefore no customary international law is created. By contrast, allowing free passage of ships on the high seas is both State practice and perceived as a binding legal norm by States themselves. The free passage rule thus represents customary international law. In addition to treaties and customs, it should be noted that general principles of law from around the world and the resolutions and practices of international organisations also contribute to our understanding of what international rules exist.

---

8   On widespread misunderstanding of the Court, see Mackinlay, 'Perceptions and Misperceptions: How are International and UK Law Perceived to Affect Military Commanders and Their Subordinates on Operations'.

9   For a clear and recent introductory account of international law, see Vaughan Lowe, *International Law* (Oxford: Oxford University Press, 2007). For further readings on the law governing the use of force and international humanitarian law, see respectively Christine Gray, *International Law and the Use of Force*, 3rd edn (Oxford: Oxford University Press, 2008) and Yoram Dinstein, *The Conduct of Hostilities Under the Law of International Armed Conflict* (Cambridge: Cambridge University Press, 2004).

It will be evident that unlike the prototypical domestic legal system, which can be categorised as vertical (a legislature centrally passing binding laws on all citizen-subjects), international law is created 'horizontally' between States. There is, for example, no international legislative body capable of passing laws that will be automatically enforced by an international police force. Although the UN apparatus may play some of the roles played by domestic governance institutions, international law is primarily set, interpreted and enforced by States themselves. In other words, unlike in other legal systems, those that are bound by the law must *consent* to be bound by it. This is, in one sense, international law's weakness. Having said this, international law has huge impact on the relations between States, as well as on the individual lives of the citizens living within those States. International law may be rather different from traditional perceptions of what a 'legal system' is like, and it is undoubtedly far from perfect, but it is nonetheless a functioning and distinct normative system and, moreover, one that is crucial for human development, particularly in the context of situations like the use of military force and the conduct of armed conflicts.[10]

The Two Branches of the Law: The When and the How

There are two generally recognised branches of international law that relate to military force and armed conflict. The first branch is the *jus ad bellum*, which may also be referred to as the law on the use of force. It is concerned with whether resort to force is lawful or unlawful. This is the 'when' of war: when – under what circumstances – is the use of military force lawful? The second branch is the *jus in bello*, which is sometimes also known as either international humanitarian law (IHL) or as the law of armed conflict. This branch deals with the manner in which hostilities can be conducted once force is being employed (regardless of whether or not the use of force was lawful or unlawful under the *jus ad bellum*). This, then, is the 'how' of war.

These two branches of international law are conceptually distinct, but inevitably interrelate to some extent: the two categories are far from watertight. For example, concepts of 'necessity' and 'proportionality' (as mechanisms for assessing lawfulness) are present in both the *jus ad bellum* and the *jus in bello*.[11] Nonetheless, these two branches of the law will be treated as separate sections of this chapter. Before moving on, it is worth noting that it has also become fashionable to speak of the *jus post-bellum*, a third branch of law that deals with peace agreements and transitional justice. This post-conflict branch will not, however, be further discussed here.[12]

---

10   James A. Green, 'An Unusual Silence', *New Law Journal*, 157 (2007): 1,478–9.

11   See, generally, Judith Gardam, *Necessity, Proportionality and the Use of Force by States* (Cambridge: Cambridge University Press, 2004).

12   For more, see Carsten Stahn, '*Jus ad Bellum, Jus in Bello … Jus Post-Bellum?* – Rethinking the Conception of the Law of Armed Force', *European Journal of International Law*, 17 (2006): 243.

Jus ad Bellum

Legal limitation of a State's right to resort to war is a relatively new phenomenon. Traditionally, it has been the legal right of States to opt for warfare with total discretion. Admittedly, the modern legal rules have their roots in a long-standing tradition that war was only legitimate if it was 'just'.[13] However, this doctrine – which can be traced back at least as far as Cicero, but which was significantly developed by later theologians – was essentially an issue of morality or righteousness: it was not until the twentieth century that the 'just war' doctrine resulted in any specific legal obligations. Moreover, it is questionable how ethical the avowedly 'moral' just war doctrine in fact was: one man's 'just war' is inevitably another's aggressive conquest.

In the early part of the twentieth century, the first attempts were made to limit the discretion of States in opting for war as a policy instrument. For example, the Covenant of the League of Nations allowed for a 'cooling off' period before resort to arms was permissible.[14] In reality, though, the Covenant did little more than place the legal restriction of the resort to warfare on the international agenda. More notably, the 1928 Kellogg-Briand Pact explicitly sought – for the first time in human history – to outlaw war. This treaty stated: 'The High Contracting Parties solemnly declare in the names of their respective peoples that they condemn recourse to war for the solution of international controversies, and renounce it, as an instrument of national policy in their relations with one another.'[15] The ultimate failure of the League and the Pact are obvious, however, and, while of historical interest, these instruments only provide a backdrop to the post-1945 regime of the UN Charter.

The Charter was adopted explicitly to prevent further world war and it not only seeks to prohibit the threat and use of 'force' (a broader notion than the formal term of 'war' used in the Kellogg-Briand Pact) but provides for a centralised response to breaches of the prohibition. The basic rule on the use of force is contained in Article 2(4):

> *All States shall refrain from the threat or use of force against the territorial integrity or political independence of any State, or in any other manner inconsistent with the Purposes of the United Nations.*

Despite the fact that there appears to be some ambiguity in the language of Article 2(4), which a small minority of States have sought to explore (Argentina in the Falklands dispute claiming it was not in breach of Article 2(4) because it was reclaiming its own 'territorial integrity'), the Article has been interpreted by most

---

13 See Jean B. Elshtain, 'The Just War Tradition and Natural Law', *Fordham International Law Journal*, 28 (2004–2005): 751.

14 Covenant of the League of Nations (1919), Article 12.

15 General Treaty for the Renunciation of War (1928), Article 1. The treaty is colloquially known as the 'Kellogg-Briand Pact' after the American Secretary of State and his French counterpart at the time; it is also sometimes referred to as the 'Pact of Paris'.

States and scholars as a broad prohibition on the use of force – all uses of military force fall under the scope of the prohibition,[16] at least *prima facie*.[17] For example, what may be called 'indirect force' is considered to be a breach of the prohibition: the use of armed militia groups to make incursions into another State would contravene Article 2(4).[18] The Charter, which is ultimately a treaty (albeit one that has a quasi-constitutional character) has been ratified by all members of the UN. It is also widely recognised that Article 2(4) represents customary international law on the subject of the use of force. Thus, if a State that is not a member of the UN were to embark on an aggressive war, such action would still be unlawful. As a legal norm, then, Article 2(4) may be said to be 'universal' both in terms of content and application. Indeed, it should be noted that not only is force prohibited under the Charter, but States are under a positive duty to seek to resolve their disputes peacefully.[19] It should always be borne in mind that the peaceful settlement of disputes – through negotiation, mediation, arbitration, adjudication and 'good offices' – is the usual course of action in the vast majority of international disputes that arise.

Although Article 2(4) essentially represents a blanket prohibition on the use of military force, there are two universally accepted exceptions to the prohibition that may be found elsewhere in the Charter. The first of these is the use of force pursuant to the collective security measures as part of the UN framework. When the 15-member Security Council decides that there has been a threat to the peace, a beach of the peace, or an act of aggression, it may order States to act (or desist from acting) in a certain manner. To implement its will in such matters, the Security Council may, if it feels it necessary, impose measures 'not involving the use of armed force'.[20] These measures can include economic or political sanctions (increasingly becoming 'smarter' and more targeted against individuals or elites within a State) or other measures such as a weapons inspection regime or the establishment of an international criminal tribunal (tribunals of this kind were established for both the former Yugoslavia and Rwanda). However, if such non-forcible measures are deemed inadequate, the Security Council may 'take such action by air, sea, or land forces as may be necessary to maintain or restore international peace and security'.[21] In other words, the Council may lawfully sanction the use of military force.

As the UN as currently constituted has no standing forces, the Security Council may delegate enforcement action to a regional security organisation (such as NATO) or to a coalition of States. During the Cold War, with deadlock amongst the

---

16   Although not 'economic' or 'political' force.

17   Though this perhaps has more to do with political acceptance of the prohibition following the Second World War than with the clarity of the legal language used in Article 2(4). See Kritsiotis, 'When States Use Armed Force', pp. 57–58.

18   See, generally, the principles adopted by the UN General Assembly, by consensus, in the Declaration on Principles of International Law Friendly Relations And Co-Operation Among States in Accordance with the Charter of the United Nations, GA Res. 2,625 (XXV), 1970.

19   UN Charter, Article 2(3).

20   UN Charter, Article 41.

21   UN Charter, Article 42.

five veto-wielding permanent members on the Security Council, the enforcement provisions were largely 'dead letter'. However, with the end of the Cold War, more robust Security Council action was possible. Beginning with the grant of authority to the United States-led 'coalition of the willing' following the 1990 invasion of Kuwait by Iraq, an era of Charter sanctioned forceful intervention was ushered in (although this is not to imply that the Security Council is, in the post-Cold War world, immune to political deadlock and sporadic periods of ineffectuality, as inaction over the recent Russia-Georgia conflict shows).

The most controversial use of Security Council Resolutions to justify the use of force came with the 2003 intervention in Iraq by United States/United Kingdom led forces. Both the United States and the United Kingdom purported to find legal basis for their operations under Security Council grants of authority from the first Gulf War coalition, which, they argued, were automatically reinstated by Iraq's failure to comply with the weapons inspection regime put in place after the 1990 intervention in Iraq.[22] This legal argument has been condemned by most international lawyers in the United Kingdom who have argued that, among other things, such reasoning is contrary to the purposes and principles of the United Nations and represents a turning of backs of the historic 'transatlantic commitment to international law'.[23] What is clear is that whilst the dispute over the interpretation of the Security Council Resolutions was a body blow to the collective security system, it was not a lethal blow as was feared in many camps in 2003. The taste for open-ended 'peace enforcement' missions may have subsided somewhat, but the Security Council maintains a busy agenda and has taken action on such matters as terrorist financing and peacekeeping. Indeed, the Western European public reaction to the intervention in Iraq may be seen as actually strengthening the position of international law – a breach of the law in Iraq has had significant political ramifications for the Labour government, for example.

The second exception to the prohibition on the use of force is the right to self-defence, which the Charter itself refers to as an 'inherent' right. Article 51 provides that:

> *Nothing in the present Charter shall impair the inherent right of individual or collective self-defence if an armed attack occurs against a Member of the*

---

22   In brief, the argument goes that Resolution 678 (1990) authorised force against Iraq in part to 'restore peace and security to the area'. Resolution 687 (1991) set out ceasefire conditions which included Iraq's compliance with a weapons inspection regime. When those ceasefire conditions were breached by Iraq's non-compliance, as recognised by Security Council Resolution 1,441 (2002), Resolution 678 was revived. For more detail see 'The Advice of the United Kingdom Attorney-General, Lord Goldsmith, on The Legal Basis For the Use of Force Against Iraq', 17 March 2003, at: <http://www.number-10.gov.uk/output/Page3287.asp>. It should be noted that, unlike the United Kingdom, the United States also set out a secondary legal argument that was even more shaky, based upon a notion of pre-emptive self-defence (something that will be discussed below), see UN Doc. S/2003/351.

23   Philippe Sands, *Lawless World* (London: Allen Lane, 2005), p. 225.

> *United Nations, until the Security Council has taken measures necessary to maintain international peace and security. Measures taken by Members in the exercise of this right of self-defence shall be immediately reported to the Security Council and shall not in any way affect the authority and responsibility of the Security Council under the present Charter to take at any time such action as it deems necessary in order to maintain or restore international peace and security.*

The most crucial aspect of this passage is that it holds that the use of force in self-defence is only lawful if taken in response to an 'armed attack'. This means that political or economic pressure does not give rise to the right to use military force; a State claiming self-defence must have suffered military force against it. Moreover, an armed attack constitutes a *qualitatively grave* use of force.[24] In other words, it is not merely the case that a State may meet force with force. Only the gravest uses of force ('armed attacks') allow the victim State to use military force in response. Of course, this begs the question: how grave is grave? In general, though, this simply means that comparatively minor instances of force (such as an isolated border skirmish, for example), will not trigger the right of self-defence in and of themselves.[25]

It is clear that an armed attack may be 'indirect', in that it may come from 'non-regular' forces. A good example of this would be an attack by mercenary forces directed by a State, as occurred in the Seychelles in 1981. It is argued by some that this concept extends to wholly non-State actors, such as terrorist forces operating from within the territory of a 'host' State. Thus, it was claimed by the United States following 9/11 that an attack by al-Qaeda constituted an armed attack allowing for a lawful military response against Afghanistan. Operation Enduring Freedom was generally accepted as a lawful action of self-defence; however, most international lawyers would argue that there must be at least some level of involvement by a State in the conduct of the non-State actor before this action can constitute an armed attack. How much State involvement is necessary, however, remains open to debate.[26]

Article 51 also holds that self-defence can be collective; that is to say that a State may use force to aid another State that has suffered an armed attack against it. This permits, for example, NATO-style agreements that provide that an attack on one State is an attack on all. Similarly, it allows for an individual State of superior

---

24 As the International Court of Justice (ICJ) has put it, an armed attack constitutes 'the most grave form of the use of force', *Military and Paramilitary Activities in and Against Nicaragua (Nicaragua v. United States of America)* merits, (1986) ICJ Rep. 14 (hereinafter '*Nicaragua*'), para. 191.

25 However, it is possible that numerous 'minor' attacks may be taken cumulatively to constitute a 'grave' armed attack, see Derek W. Bowett, 'Reprisals Involving Recourse to Armed Force', *American Journal of International Law*, 66 (1972): 1, p. 5.

26 For example, contrast the views expressed by Kimberley N. Trapp, 'Back to Basics: Necessity, Proportionality and the Right of Self-Defence Against Non-State Terrorist Actors', *International and Comparative Law Quarterly*, 56 (2007): 141 with the position taken by Ian Scobbie, 'Words My Mother Never Taught Me: In Defence of the International Court', *American Journal of International Law*, 99 (2005): 76, pp. 80–81.

military might to come to the aid of a weaker State under attack. However, a 'white knight' State cannot make the decision to intervene on behalf of another unilaterally. The State that has suffered the grave use of force against it must declare itself to be the victim of an armed attack and, moreover, it must specifically request military aid from the responding State in repelling that attack.[27]

Additionally, there are what might be called procedural aspects to Article 51 in relation to Security Council action. First, States have an obligation to report any self-defence actions to the Security Council (something that initially was poorly maintained, but in the last 20 years has become common practice). Second, and perhaps more importantly, the right of self-defence is terminated once the Security Council has taken measures to deal with the situation.[28]

Article 51 alone does not tell the whole story with regard to the law concerning self-defence actions, however. Crucially, this area is also governed by customary international law. Indeed, there are fundamental legal criteria for self-defence that are not present in Article 51, but instead can only be found in custom. The traditional starting point for understanding these customary legal rules on self-defence is the *Caroline* incident of 1987, which occurred in the context of the Canadian rebellion against British rule. The *Caroline* was a privately-owned American steamer that had been used to supply munitions and American nationals to support attacks against British assets in Canada. Whilst it was docked at Schlosser, in United States territory, it was attacked by British-Canadian forces, who set fire to the vessel and towed it over Niagara Falls.

A protracted diplomatic exchange ensued, which culminated in a number of correspondences between the new United States Secretary of State Daniel Webster and the British Special Representative to the United States, Lord Ashburton. The formulation that came out of that exchange of letters was that – for a military action to constitute lawful self-defence – there had to be 'a necessity of self defence, instant, overwhelming, leaving no choice of means, and no moment for deliberation' and that the response could not be 'unreasonable or excessive'.[29] These phrases have since been distilled into two universally accepted key criteria: self-defence must be both *necessary* and *proportionate*.[30] It is here that debates most often arise as to whether a response – say the United States-led intervention in Afghanistan of 2001 – was necessary and proportionate; and, often, there can be no mechanical or formulaic response to that question.

---

27 *Nicaragua*, merits, paras 195 and 199.
28 Although whether these 'measures' need to be effective or simply in existence is debateable; see D.W. Greig, 'Self-Defence and the Security Council: What Does Article 51 Require?' *International and Comparative Law Quarterly*, 40 (1991): 366, pp. 389–99.
29 Letter dated 27 July 1842, from Daniel Webster to Lord Ashburton, *British and Foreign State Papers*, Vol. XXX (1841–1842), pp. 193–4, extract taken from Webster's earlier letter to Henry S. Fox dated 24 April 1841, *British and Foreign State Papers*, Vol. XXIX (1840–1841), pp. 1,137–8.
30 James A. Green, 'Docking the *Caroline*: Understanding the Relevance of the Formula in Contemporary Customary International Law Concerning Self-Defence', *Cardozo Journal of International and Comparative Law*, 14 (2006): 429.

One further area of controversy in the area of self-defence is with respect to responses against apparent threats of force that have not yet materialised. Must the attack have actually occurred, as suggested by a strict reading of Article 51, or can a response be taken against an attack that is merely 'imminent'? What about pre-emptory attacks against non-imminent threats, as suggested by the so called 'Bush Doctrine', which was first set out by the United States in 2002?[31] There is a volume of scholarly literature on this topic, but State practice suggests that anticipatory self-defence in the face of imminent attack will in certain circumstances be lawful, while a broader pre-emptory right taken in response to a non-imminent threat – such as a 'preventative' attack on an installation in State A that might be making weapons to be used at some point in the future against State B – would be unlawful. Thus, the Israeli strike on the Iraqi nuclear reactor at Osiraq in 1981 was broadly condemned as unlawful, on the basis that the perceived threat could not be considered to be imminent. Quite clearly, claims of a broad pre-emptory right of self-defence are open to unilateral abuse and threaten the basic Charter regime on the use of force. It is primarily for this reason that States have rejected the doctrine as being contrary to international law.[32]

In addition to the two universally accepted exceptions to the prohibition contained in Article 2(4), there are a number of other proposed exceptions to the restriction on the use of force. Some of these are of highly dubious merit, such as the use of force to promote democracy, or the support of 'national liberation movements' in internal conflicts. A more credible, albeit controversial, contender is so-called 'humanitarian intervention'. That the Security Council can intervene on humanitarian grounds is now uncontroversial, but whether States may unilaterally use force to protect the human rights of non-nationals in another State in instances where the Security Council is unwilling or unable to take action – such as was the situation in Kosovo in 1999 – has been a long-standing academic 'hot potato'. Humanitarian intervention will be discussed further in the following chapter by Professor Haines, so we will not dwell on it any more here.

Before concluding this section, it is necessary to turn to an organisation that has been previously unconcerned with the *jus ad bellum*: the military. While traditionally an active participant in the creation and development of the *jus in bello*, Western militaries under the doctrine of civilian supremacy have essentially not concerned themselves with the question of whether or not a conflict is lawful. For the most part, it is fair to say, military forces will simply adopt the view on the *jus ad bellum* held by civilian overseers, and the extent to which commanders must grapple with

---

31   National Security Strategy of the United States of America, September 2002, at: <http://www.whitehouse.gov/nsc/nss.html>.

32   A rather stark example of the general rejection by States of the doctrine of 'non-imminent' pre-emptive self-defence is the categorical rejection of the concept by the 114-member Non-Aligned Movement in the declaration that emerged from that organisation's 14th summit in Havana in September 2006, 14th Summit of Heads of State or Government of the Non-Aligned Movement, Final Document, Havana, 11–16 September 2006, NAM 2006/Doc.1/Rev.3, at: <http://www.cubanoal.cu/ingles/index.html>.

the *jus ad bellum* will be limited to an interpretive rather than decision-making role. This limited, though important, engagement may involve interpreting the mandate of a military presence as set out in a Security Council Resolution, advising on the proportionality of using particular tactics after a decision to engage in self-defence has been made, or, in cases where soldiers are in a foreign State with the latter's consent – such as in classical peacekeeping missions – interpreting the agreement that makes the visiting forces' presence lawful. The latter agreements are typically called status of forces agreements (SOFAs) and govern a variety of matters ranging from the geographical and territorial scope for military activities to criminal jurisdiction over soldiers and compensation to civilians for damage caused by the visiting forces.[33]

Moreover, the traditional 'hands off' approach of the Western military to wider legal issues concerning the *jus ad bellum* is slowly being replaced by a somewhat more critical stance, as evidenced by reports that the British Chief of Defence Staff at the time of the invasion insisted on a government legal opinion that the war was legal before committing his armed forces to action.[34] At a 'grass roots' level, lawfulness matters as well, as suggested by calls for the Military Covenant to be rethought. For example, in an open letter to the prime minister published in the *Independent on Sunday*, the signatories – who include family members of active and deceased service people – demanded 'the right [of British service people] to expect any war to be lawful'.[35]

It is important to be realistic about the weakness of the international legal regime governing the use of military force. Some scholars, from the classical realist perspective, understandably view this area of the law with cynicism. It is largely agreed – at least outside of the United States – that the use of force in Iraq was unlawful. This unlawfulness did not stop the intervention from occurring, however; nor did it lead to much in the way of tangible recriminations for the United States or the United Kingdom. Yet it is also important to keep in mind that breaches of the prohibition on the use of force have become the exception, not the rule. We now have a legal prohibition on the use of military force for the first time in human history – this in itself sets the UN system apart as a monumental step in the right direction, irrespective of its imperfections. No State has ever claimed to be exempt from the Charter regime on the use of force. When States do use force, justification is always sought under an exception to the basic prohibition. The Charter regime has shaped the way in which States perceive their options. For example, aggressive war for territorial conquest is now a non-starter. The influence on State behaviour

---

33 The leading book on this subject is Dieter Fleck, ed., *The Handbook of the Law of Visiting Forces* (Oxford: Oxford University Press, 2001).

34 Antony Barnett and Martin Bright, 'British Military Chief Reveals New Legal Fears over Iraq War', *The Observer*, 1 May 2005, at: <www.guardian.co.uk/politics/2005/may/01/uk.iraq>.

35 Terri Judd, Sophie Goodchild, Andrew Johnson, Lauren Veevers and Kim Sengupta, 'The Betrayal of British Fighting Men and Women', *The Independent*, at: <http://news.independent.co.uk/uk/politics/article2347537.ece>.

may or may not be affected by perceptions of legitimacy, or the law's 'compliance pull'. It may be mostly that States take the view that their long-term self-interest is tied up with a predictable and stable world order. However, it is no longer the case that States may ignore the *jus ad bellum* entirely.[36]

Jus in Bello

In a broad sense, IHL is the body of law that seeks to protect the 'victims' of warfare (or, more accurately, of *armed conflict*). Be it civilians caught up in a conflict, or combatants that have been wounded or captured, IHL sets down legal requirements that such persons be treated with reference to basic, humane standards. As such, for all its complexity, the key principle of IHL is that people who – for whatever reason – are not engaged in active fighting must be treated humanely and that conflict must be conducted in a manner that reflects this.

The ideas underlying IHL find resonance in ancient notions such as chivalry and a warrior's honour. Most cultural and religious traditions can be plumbed for examples of 'proto-IHL' protection afforded to civilians (such as women and children) or special classes of fighters (such as those carrying a white flag). The origins of its modern and multilateral incarnation, however, can be traced to the latter half of the nineteenth century in Europe.[37] In fact, the story of IHL is most often – somewhat simplistically – grounded in a particular European battlefield. In 1859, during the Battle of Solferino in the war for Italian unification, a travelling Swiss businessman, Henri Dunant, witnessed battlefield carnage on a massive scale. Together with local citizens, he collected and cared for the wounded who had been left on the battlefield. Touched by what he had seen and convinced of the need for action, Dunant wrote a tract entitled *A Memory of Solferino*, in which he suggested the need to create a relief group to address the inadequacy of army medical services. He also asked the militaries of various countries whether they could formulate 'some international principle, sanctioned by a convention and inviolate in character, which, once agreed upon and ratified, might constitute the basis for societies for the relief of the wounded in the different European countries'.[38] The group formed in 1863 to continue the agenda suggested by Dunant was the International Committee of the Red Cross (ICRC), an organisation that remains the guardian of much of IHL. At the urging of the ICRC, the Swiss government agreed to convene a diplomatic conference which resulted in the 1864 Geneva Convention for the Amelioration of the Condition of the Wounded in Armies in the Field and set the stage for a multilateral treaty regime that continues to evolve to this day.

---

36 Take, for example, the situation following the Israeli raid on Tall al-Abyad in Syria in September 2007. See James A. Green, 'An Unusual Silence'.
37 Though the first modern codification of humanitarian law is often credited to the Leiber Code issued to Union troops during the United States civil war.
38 ICRC, 'From the Battle of Solferino to the Eve of the First World War' (2004), at: <http://icrc.org/web/eng/siteeng0.nsf/html/57JNVP>.

The most important IHL treaties today are the four Geneva Conventions (GCs) of 1949 and the additional protocols to the GCs.[39] The GCs are almost universally ratified (ratification is a process whereby a State formally agrees to be bound) with 194 States party. They cover victims of land (GC I) and sea (GC II) warfare, prisoners of war (GC III) and the treatment of civilians (GC IV). In 1977 two additional protocols (APs) were created to fill gaps left by the 1949 set of treaties and to recognise the evolving nature of warfare. AP I more clearly addresses the conduct of hostilities (for example, prohibiting weapons that cause superfluous injury) and additional types of combat (notably aerial warfare). AP II addresses civil wars (or, to use the language of IHL, 'non-international armed conflicts') and supplements the minimal protections provided for victims of civil wars in the GCs themselves.[40] Given that a clear majority of the victims of warfare are victims of civil wars, AP II is perhaps particularly important, though it has been ratified by fewer States than AP I and certainly than the GCs themselves. AP III of 2005 was made to deal with the discrete issue of the emblem of protection. The red crystal – a symbol without possible religious connotations – was adopted to stand beside the red cross and red crescent as internationally recognised symbols to be used on, among other things, medical transport vehicles.

In addition to the GCs, there are roughly 20 additional, important IHL treaties – on issues ranging from child soldiers to cultural property to laser-blinding weapons – including, most recently, the Convention on Cluster Munitions of 2008. They have been subscribed to with varying degrees of support. In addition to the IHL treaty regime, customary international law also provides IHL content. The ICRC in 2005 completed an exhaustive review of customary international law – by among other

---

39   Convention (I) for the Amelioration of the Condition of the Wounded and Sick in Armed Forces in the Field. Geneva, 12 August 1949; Convention (II) for the Amelioration of the Condition of Wounded, Sick and Shipwrecked Members of Armed Forces at Sea. Geneva, 12 August 1949; Convention (III) relative to the Treatment of Prisoners of War. Geneva, 12 August 1949; Convention (IV) relative to the Protection of Civilian Persons in Time of War. Geneva, 12 August 1949; Protocol Additional to the Geneva Conventions of 12 August 1949, and relating to the Protection of Victims of International Armed Conflicts (Protocol I); 8 June 1977, Protocol Additional to the Geneva Conventions of 12 August 1949, and relating to the Protection of Victims of Non-International Armed Conflicts (Protocol II), 8 June 1977; Protocol Additional to the Geneva Conventions of 12 August 1949, and relating to the Adoption of an Additional Distinctive Emblem (Protocol III), 8 December 2005. The text of these and all other IHL treaties can be found on the ICRC website, at: <www.icrc.org>.

40   Common Article 3 of the GCs has been described by the ICJ as setting out 'elementary considerations of humanity', *Corfu Channel (United Kingdom v. Albania)*, merits (1949) ICJ Rep. 4, p. 22. It requires that those not taking part in hostilities – including non-combatants and detainees – should be treated humanely. Acts such as torture, murder and the passing of sentences without guarantees of judicial fairness are specifically prohibited. The United States Supreme Court recently held that Common Article 3 is the appropriate IHL framework to be applied by American forces in the 'War Against Terrorism': *Hamdan v. Rumsfeld* 126 S.Ct. 2749 (2006).

things, surveying military manuals – to determine the customary rules.[41] The ICRC study had more than 200 contributors, and comprised two volumes that together ran to over 5,000 pages of text. This should go some way to illustrating the vast scope of the customary IHL rules.

Finally, it is worth briefly noting that international human rights – rights guaranteed to individuals vis-à-vis governments through a separate though overlapping treaty regime from IHL – may also apply. Rights do not automatically cease to exist in times of armed conflict. For example, while in national emergencies States may derogate from some rights; others, such as freedom from torture, are non-derogable.[42]

The modern IHL regime – rooted in the GCs, but expanded across numerous other treaties and in customary international law – is large and complex. There is certainly not space here to even begin to delve into the specific protections provided for under the GCs or elsewhere. Given this complexity, mastering the body of IHL and related areas is, in practical terms, a challenge for any military or civilian lawyer and, clearly, non-legally trained officers and enlisted personnel are not expected to have a detailed knowledge of the law. In modern militaries, rules of engagement (ROE) will have been vetted by lawyers to ensure compliance with IHL principles and, for the most part, will provide an adequate guide to some basic questions, notably, 'when to shoot and when not to shoot'. However, rules of engagement – no matter how comprehensive – cannot cover the many detailed aspects of IHL or anticipate all the eventualities that may arise on the battlefield. Officers must therefore be alert to legal issues that may arise. What if, for example, in a multi-national force, rules of engagement on the treatment of detainees differ? Military manuals (such as the United Kingdom's *Manual of the Law of Armed Conflict*),[43] specialised personnel (for example military police specifically trained to handle prisoner of war matters) and legal advisors (who are being increasingly deployed operationally) are among the resources to which a commander might turn where there is uncertainty. There is no substitute, however, for a commander's mastery of key IHL concepts as, ultimately, it will be commanders and not advisors who take decisions for which they are answerable.

---

41   J.-M. Henckaerts and L. Doswald Beck, eds, *Customary International Humanitarian Law: Vol. I, Vol. II (Parts 1 and 2)*, ICRC Study (Cambridge: Cambridge University Press, 2005).

42   A good primer on the overlap of the two regimes is ICRC, 'International Humanitarian Law and International Human Rights Law: Similarities and Differences', 2003, at: <http://www.icrc.org/web/eng/siteeng0.nsf/html/57JR8L>. Another debate has been over the exact territorial reach of human rights. Does, for example, the European Convention of Human Rights apply to the actions of British soldiers in Iraq? The House of Lords recently held that European Convention Rights did apply in a case where an Iraqi civilian was killed while in British custody, though not where civilians were killed by British soldiers on patrol: *R (on the application of Al-Skeini and others)* v. *Secretary of State for Defence*, 13 June 2007 (HL).

43   Ministry of Defence, *The Manual of the Law of Armed Conflict* (Oxford: Oxford University Press, 2004).

While quite properly insisting that a distillation of the rules cannot act as a substitute for the text of the treaties themselves, the ICRC has put forward seven basic rules that go a long distance towards sketching the crux of IHL. They are as follows:[44]

1. Persons hors de combat [in other words those taken prisoner or wounded/ injured] and those who do not take a direct part in hostilities are entitled to respect for their lives and their moral and physical integrity. They shall in all circumstances be protected and treated humanely without any adverse distinction.
2. It is forbidden to kill or injure an enemy who surrenders or who is hors de combat.
3. The wounded and sick shall be collected and cared for by the party to the conflict which has them in its power. Protection also covers medical personnel, establishments, transports and equipment. The emblem of the red cross or the red crescent [and now the red crystal] is the sign of such protection and must be respected.
4. Captured combatants and civilians under the authority of an adverse party are entitled to respect for their lives, dignity, personal rights and convictions. They shall be protected against all acts of violence and reprisals. They shall have the right to correspond with their families and to receive relief.
5. Everyone shall be entitled to benefit from fundamental judicial guarantees. No one shall be held responsible for an act he has not committed. No one shall be subjected to physical or mental torture, corporal punishment or cruel or degrading treatment.
6. Parties to a conflict and members of their armed forces do not have an unlimited choice of methods and means of warfare. It is prohibited to employ weapons or methods of warfare of a nature to cause unnecessary losses or excessive suffering.
7. Parties to a conflict shall at all times distinguish between the civilian population and combatants in order to spare civilian population and property. Neither the civilian population as such nor civilian persons shall be the object of attack. Attacks shall be directed solely against military objectives.

Many points of clarification could be made here, but let us content ourselves with just one, albeit a clarification that goes to the heart of the internal tensions within IHL. Underlying several of the seven rules is the principle of distinction: the notion that fighters should distinguish between civilians and combatants and between civilian and military objects. To the extent that this means that civilians should never be specifically targeted, the rule is unambiguous. What if, however, in pursuing a legitimate military target, civilians will be harmed? The rule is that the harm to

---

44   ICRC, Basic rules of the Geneva Conventions and their Additional Protocols, 1988, at: <http://icrc.org/Web/Eng/siteeng0.nsf/htmlall/p0365/$File/ICRC_002_0365_BASIC_ RULES_GENEVA_CONVENTIONS.PDF!Open>.

civilians cannot be unnecessary or excessive – in other words, *disproportionate* – to the military importance of the military objective. To put it another way, military logic or military necessity is to be balanced against the principle of distinction, with 'proportionality' acting as the fulcrum. When one civilian nightwatchman will be killed in an attack on a major munitions dump, the harm to civilians will obviously not be disproportionate. Similarly, an air strike that will kill dozens of civilians as the price for killing one mid-ranking enemy officer will be disproportionate.

The problem comes in the grey areas, with different militaries taking different approaches. What is clear for most observers is the essential permissiveness of IHL itself as it now stands. As the British MOD *Manual on the Law of Armed Conflict* puts it: 'The Law of Armed Conflict is consistent with the economic and efficient use of force. It is intended to minimise the suffering caused by armed conflict rather than impede military efficiency.'[45] While some specific acts or weapons are prohibited, in general the 'balancing' is often tipped towards military necessity, at least in current practice. Whether the generally permissive nature of IHL is *desirable* is essentially a non-legal question. As such, it is one major reason why ethics remains an important part of the military decision-making calculus: what is legally permitted may be unethical or simply, especially in the context of counterinsurgency, imprudent.

Having sketched out the nature of IHL, a fair question remains: is there any way of enforcing it? The answer is that, for the most part, IHL is difficult to enforce. Therefore, the most important means of ensuring the successful implementation and application of the law is the training and dissemination of IHL, particularly amongst the military personnel that deal with decision-making on the ground.

Similarly, of the – far from comprehensive – methods of enforcement that do exist, perhaps the most important is what may be termed 'political enforcement'. It is in States' interests to be seen to be acting in conformity with the law, especially when the law requires the State to act in a humane manner. This may not sound as desirable as humanitarian protection for its own sake, but to some extent it is the reality. Political pressure on States to conform with the law comes from all manner of sources, including 'naming and shaming' type activities on the part of non-governmental organisations, judicial complaints against States by individuals or other States and, not by any means least, the individual citizens of the State concerned.

A more concrete method of enforcement is the concept of a 'protecting power' – a neutral State that essentially undertakes to ensure, so far as possible, that the rules of IHL are being upheld by the parties in conflict or by an occupying power. Both Switzerland and Sweden performed this role in Europe during the Second World War. The obvious drawback with this method is that it requires a neutral State to come forward to perform the protecting power role and also requires that the States in conflict allow it to effectively do so. As such, this method of enforcement has, to a large extent, fallen into disuse. Today, the ICRC essentially takes on an equivalent role where possible, through processes of monitoring and reporting.

---

45   See *The Manual of the Law of Armed Conflict*, p. 21.

Another way to enforce IHL is through individual criminal accountability. Thus, war crimes trials of individuals can be conducted by national authorities or by an international ad hoc criminal tribunal (such as the International Criminal Tribunal for the Former Yugoslavia and the International Criminal Tribunal for Rwanda). Those committing war crimes, genocide or crimes against humanity may also be tried by the International Criminal Court (ICC), a permanent, independent court created by a 1998 treaty with 106 States participating. If there is a national or territorial connection of a suspected individual criminal to a State party, and that State has proven unwilling or unable to investigate or prosecute, the ICC may take that case over. As important as the ICC is in the fight against impunity, however, it only has a mandate to go after 'big fish'; in the words of the treaty establishing the Court, '[t]he jurisdiction of the Court shall be limited to the most serious crimes of concern to the international community as a whole'.

Thus, whilst problems with the enforcement of IHL remain, there are methods in place to ensure compliance. However, the success of IHL currently rests more on its wider implementation through education and dissemination, and through the political capital that is generated through adherence, rather than any specific enforcement mechanism.

Conclusion

For the most part, international law is followed by States. On the rare occasions where it is breached, the consequences are usually comparatively minor, and legal disputes are, in the vast majority of instances, resolved through peaceful means. Adherence to the norms of the twin systems of the *jus ad bellum* and the *jus in bello* is – as with international law more generally – the rule and not the exception; breaches of the law are much rarer than is commonly perceived. Unfortunately, in the case of the particular areas of international law we are here discussing, the failures of the law that do occur have dramatic (and deadly) consequences. When considering international law, we think of Gaza, or the abuses of Abu Ghraib, or – perhaps most appallingly – recent failures in Africa: take Rwanda or Darfur as two examples amongst many. We do not think of how international law allows us to fly to Moscow, or how we receive post from a friend in Vancouver. This perception is quite correct, because it is at the fundamental margins – in the areas such as the use of force and conduct of armed conflict – that the most work needs to be done. It is here that breaches do the most harm.

This chapter has sketched out how international law seeks to minimise such harm. We have examined international law's prohibition on the use of force and the scope of the exceptions to that prohibition. We then turned to the tools provided by international law that can be used to protect victims of armed conflict, should the prohibition be breached or should an exception to it apply. In both the *jus ad bellum* and the *jus in bello* the core rules themselves are generally clear, albeit that they can at times be rather dense. Moreover, law is playing an ever-increasing role in the reality of military force and armed conflict. There remain significant concerns with regard to the application of the law and, importantly, its enforcement. Nonetheless, international law is here to stay as a major factor in the conduct of warfare.

Humanitarian Intervention: Genocide, Crimes against Humanity and the Use of Force

Steven Haines[1]

The fact of genocide long preceded the word coined to describe it.[2] It also continues long after the coming into force of the international convention intended to eliminate it.[3] Given the millions that have died or suffered through genocide, it is a sad fact that only a fraction of the perpetrators of the crime have ever been brought to justice. Just under a million were massacred in Rwanda. Over 100,000 suspects have been identified. Fewer than 10,000 have been prosecuted in Rwandan courts, and the International Criminal Tribunal for Rwanda has had just 74 brought before it to date. We have a long way to go before we can say with confidence that the

---

1 Steven Haines is Head of the Security and Rule of Law Programme at the Geneva Centre for Security Policy and formerly Professor of Strategy and the Law of Military Operations within the University of London. From 1971 to 2003 he was an officer in the Royal Navy, his most recent operational deployments being to Kosovo and Sierra Leone in 2001. His research spans the twin fields of international relations and international law in general and strategic studies and the law of military operations in particular. While a staff officer in the Ministry of Defence he wrote the UK's strategic doctrine (*British Defence Doctrine*, 2001) and chaired the Editorial Board of the official *Manual of the Law of Armed Conflict* published in 2004. While a Visiting Fellow at St Antony's College, Oxford, he was invited to participate in the work of the International Commission on Intervention and State Sovereignty and was a named contributor to its report (*Responsibility to Protect*) presented to UN Secretary General Kofi Annan in December 2001.
2 The term 'genocide' was coined by Raphael Lemkin in a book he wrote in 1944 (R. Lemkin, *Axis Rule in Occupied Europe: Laws of Occupation, Analysis of Government, Proposals for Redress* (Washington: Carnegie Endowment for World Peace, 1944)). Within two years the term had been accepted to the point at which it was used in indictments at Nuremberg.
3 1948 Convention of the Prevention and Punishment of the Crime of Genocide.

perpetrators of all acts of genocide will be punished. Prevention is likely to be better and more effective than the cure.

This was certainly what the leaders of NATO thought in 1999. In the spring of that year, the Alliance waged a 78-day air campaign against Serbia, the rationale for which was the need to prevent atrocities of a genocidal nature and intensity being committed by Serbs against ethnic Albanians in the province of Kosovo. After the experience of Rwanda and Srebrenica, opting to do nothing was not a serious option for the Alliance. Something had to be done to prevent a further genocide. Humanitarian intervention was NATO's response.

The law seemed not to allow for this. Only the Security Council can authorise intervention and was unlikely to do so because one of its permanent members – Russia – would not allow it. NATO intervened anyway, with member states asserting the legitimacy of their action. Were they indeed right to do so? This question remains important 10 years after Kosovo because extreme crimes against humanity continue to be committed. Be it ethnic cleansing in the Darfur region of Sudan, the reckless and wanton destruction of the Zimbabwean economy, or the deliberate prevention, by the military government, of foreign aid reaching disaster victims in Burma, man-made or exacerbated humanitarian catastrophe remains a feature of the international system.

To answer the question – is humanitarian intervention lawful or legitimate? – we need to understand something of the nature of international law and how it has developed to date, especially that part of it relating to the use of force.

The Changing Bases of International Law

The history of international law, since the birth of the modern Westphalian state system in the seventeenth century, has been characterised in particular by a struggle for supremacy between the Natural Law and Positive Law traditions. The former regards the international legal system as the product of a 'top down' process while the latter sees it as fundamentally 'bottom up'.

In the Natural Law tradition there is an acceptance that even ruling sovereigns must acknowledge their obligation to be bound by certain principles established by some form of higher authority. In the pre-Westphalian era, Natural Law had a religious basis (and flowed from God) but, from the seventeenth century onwards, it was increasingly determined by resort to human reason.[4] The legitimacy of resort to force (the *jus ad bellum*) was determined by reference to the Christian doctrine of Just War.[5]

---

4   A shift most notably associated with the work of the seventeenth-century Dutch lawyer Hugo de Groot (or Grotius), who came to be described as the father of modern international law.

5   The development of Just War doctrine has recently been subjected to an extremely thorough and powerful analysis (A. Bellamy, *Just Wars: From Cicero to Iraq* (Cambridge:

In the Positive Law tradition, the principal assumption is that the source of international law, which governs relations between states, is the will of those sovereign states themselves.[6] States acknowledge no higher law than that by which they have themselves agreed to be bound. Agreement is demonstrated either by practice (customary law) or by formal agreements (treaty law). The practice of states, driven by the need for security, influenced the development of the law, with the legitimacy of the use of force determined by the needs of interest rather than justice.[7]

The influence of both the Natural and the Positive Law traditions has always been in evidence, with neither prevailing to the total exclusion of the other. Nevertheless, from the seventeenth century onwards, Natural Law declined as Positive Law gained the ascendant. Positive Law's rise to undeniable pre-eminence was simply a consequence of political developments and realities within a Europe increasingly governed by balance of power and *raison d'état*. Neither the waning influence of religion nor the waxing influence of reason within the Natural Law tradition could either prevent its decline or stem the eventual rise of Positivism.

The demands of balance of power politics gave rise to the perception that warfare was merely an instrument of state policy in pursuit of national interest. By the time of the Napoleonic Wars, sovereigns believed that they had an unrestrained right to go to war, when, where and for whatever reason associated with the needs of the balance of power – and that the demands of military necessity overcame any moral or legal limits on the conduct of hostilities.[8] This attitude is reflected in the

---

Polity Press, 2006)) in which it is argued that there are Natural Law, Positive Law and Realist influences within modern Just War. This leads to the assertion that the *jus ad bellum* in particular has always been subject to Just War thinking. In other words, Just War has not suffered decline or ascent; it has merely changed in character over time, with different influences brought to bear upon it. While acknowledging Bellamy's excellent analysis, this author prefers, on balance, the narrower view that Just War is a Natural Law (and largely a religious based) doctrine whose influence was greatly undermined as Natural Law itself changed in character and suffered decline.

6   Jean Bodin, the sixteenth-century philosopher most closely associated with the emergence of sovereignty as a defining feature of states, regarded it as indivisible; sovereigns were answerable to no higher authority in relation to the conduct of political affairs (see J.H. Franklin, 'Introduction', in J. Bodin, *On Sovereignty: Four Chapters from the Six Books of the Commonwealth* (Cambridge: Cambridge Texts on the History of Political Thought, Cambridge University Press, 1992), pp. ix–xxvi, xiii). Grotius concurred, and noted the power of the sovereign 'that is called Supreme, whose acts are not subject to another's Power so that they cannot be made void by another human Will', quoted in Hugo Grotius, *The Rights of War and Peace, Book I*, ed. by R. Tuck (Indianapolis: Liberty Fund, 2005), p. 259. Grotius is here, of course, stressing the lack of any temporal power above that of the sovereign.

7   See S.C. Neff, *War and the Law of Nations* (Cambridge: Cambridge University Press, 2005). To quote Neff, at p. 170: 'Positivism was … a thoroughly unspeculative philosophy, rooted in the brute facts of real life as they actually stood, rather than in the wispy ideals of theologians or in the "metaphysical" subtleties of natural lawyers.'

8   Bellamy, *Just War*, p. 89.

claim made famous by Clausewitz that war is simply 'a continuation of political intercourse carried on with other means'.[9]

Clausewitz also famously rejected the view that international law could provide a significant restraint on the use of force.[10] In the first substantive paragraph of his great work *On War* he stated that: 'Attached to force are certain self-imposed, imperceptible limitations hardly worth mentioning, known as international law and custom, but they scarcely weaken it.'[11]

The nineteenth and early twentieth century was the high period of Positivism in international law. It complemented Realism, frequently regarded as the default approach to international politics, which seems to come fully into its own in historic periods of multi-polar interstate rivalry that are conducive to balance of power politics.[12] International law evolved in Europe in a manner consistent with the ebb and flow of great power politics. The political climate was not conducive to the development of Natural Law. Positive Law was pre-eminent and gave rise to a legalist approach – and to the acceptance of a legalist paradigm relating to the use of force which privileged sovereignty and the twin principles of political independence and territorial integrity above all else.[13] It did so by eventually outlawing aggression and stressing the norm of non-intervention.

---

9   C. von Clausewitz, *On War*, ed. and trans. by M. Howard and P. Paret (Princeton, NJ: Princeton University Press, 1984), p. 87.

10   He did at one point highlight the need for proportionality in the conduct of war, stressing in particular the imperative for military forces to concentrate their efforts on attacking military targets. However, while this might be interpreted as supportive of the *jus in bello* legal principle of proportionality, it was essentially a pragmatic and practical appeal reflecting the principle of war relating to the economy of effort, rather than a morally based call for humanitarianism. He argued that the killing of prisoners or the destruction of cities should be avoided because good generals recognised that to do such would not be an intelligent or an effective use of force, but merely a 'crude expression of instinct'. Clausewitz, *On War*, p. 76.

11   Clausewitz, *On War*, p. 75. It is not known to what extent Clausewitz was aware of the writings of legal philosophers, but his view certainly chimes well with that of Bynkershoek, for whom all forms of force were lawful. If restraints were applied to the application of force they were applied out of charity and not as a result of any legal obligation.

12   Whether one examines the relations between the city states of Ancient Greece or of Renaissance Italy, or the great powers of seventeenth, eighteenth and nineteenth-century Europe, one sees circumstances that lend themselves well to Realist interpretations of politics and strategy. See M. Sheehan, *The Balance of Power: History and Theory* (London: Routledge, 1996), in particular Chapter 2 at pp. 24–52.

13   Leo Kuper provides an excellent quote that neatly conveys the positivist and legalist approach based on strict assumptions about state sovereignty, political independence and territorial integrity. Henry Morgenthau was US Ambassador in Turkey between 1913 and 1916. Deeply concerned about the massacre of Armenians, he favoured intervention. Nevertheless, he was profoundly frustrated by legalism. As he stated in his memoirs: 'Technically, of course, I had no right to interfere. According to the cold-blooded legalities of the situation, the treatment of Turkish subjects by the Turkish government was purely a domestic affair.' *Ambassador Morgenthau's Story*

The Use of Force and the Legalist Paradigm

The catastrophic outbreak of war in the summer of 1914 ended what many in Europe had assumed was a century of peace and stability.[14] The end of the war that followed was only achieved by the involvement of the United States – essentially, the European great power system had proved itself incapable of further effective self-regulation. When war ended, US President Woodrow Wilson proposed a radically new approach to international politics that would see even the great powers reduced in military capacity to the point where unilateral aggressive war would be untenable. Force would still be a feature of the system, but only in the sense that collective enforcement would be possible through the decision-making process of a global organisation responsible for managing the system.[15] The League of Nations failed to live up to Wilson's ideal but it certainly did change things to a degree. The Covenant of the League of Nations, from which the League drew its authority, was the first multilateral attempt formally to challenge the legitimacy of resort to war. Liberal notions that war could be reduced in importance within the international system gained ground. Today, it is generally believed that war should no longer be relied upon routinely to maintain equilibrium between the great powers. This is the essence of the legalist paradigm.

Michael Walzer, in his classic treatment of Just War, outlines the following six propositions as forming the essential elements of this paradigm:

1. There exists an international society of independent states;
2. This international society has a law that establishes the rights of its members – above all, the rights of territorial integrity and political independence;
3. Any use of force or imminent threat of force by one state against the political sovereignty or territorial integrity of another constitutes aggression and is a criminal act;
4. Aggression justifies two kinds of violent response: a war of self-defence by the victim and a war of law enforcement by the victim and any other member of international society;
5. Nothing but aggression can justify war;
6. Once the aggressor state has been repulsed it can also be punished.[16]

(1918), pp. 328–9, quoted in L. Kuper, *Genocide: Its Political Use in the Twentieth Century* (Harmondsworth: Pelican, 1981), p. 161.

14   Appearances can be deceptive, however. There were 14 wars between great powers in Europe between 1815 and 1914, most notable of which were the Crimean War of 1853–56 and the Franco-Prussian War of 1870–71. What was absent was general, multilateral, great power war on the scale of the Revolutionary and Napoleonic Wars. See S. Halperin, *War and Social Change in Modern Europe: The Great Transformation Revisited* (Cambridge: Cambridge University Press, 2004), p. 6.

15   See M. Wight, *Power Politics* (ed. by H. Bull and C. Holbraad) (Harmondsworth: Penguin, 1979), in particular Chapter 19 on the League of Nations, pp. 200–15.

16   M. Walzer, *Just and Unjust Wars: A Moral Argument with Historical Illustrations*, 3rd edn (New York: Basic, 2000), pp. 58–63.

The paradigm reflects the objective of liberals in the Wilsonian mould to rid the international system of the worst excesses of war. It is encapsulated in the Covenant, the Kellogg-Briand Pact and the UN Charter. It is principally about the maintenance of order within the international state system. Order is an essential prerequisite for the pursuit of justice but the order one creates tends to determine the level of justice that is achievable. The legalist paradigm privileges interstate justice; it does little or nothing for the advancement of either individual or cosmopolitan notions of justice.[17] This seems odd when one appreciates that the UN Charter, the principal documentary source of the legalist paradigm, certainly advances more than merely interstate justice. Importantly, it introduces human rights, thereby giving scope for the provision of justice to the individual.

The Emergence of Human Rights and the Re-Emergence of Natural Law

Before the Second World War, there was no international human rights law. Indeed, the prevailing legal view at that time was that sovereign states could act almost with impunity within their own territories.[18] The Holocaust changed this. It raised human rights to an unprecedented level of concern and resulted in a significant human rights input to the UN Charter. The statesmen who signed the document articulated their concern in the preamble to the *Charter* in which 'fundamental human rights', 'justice and respect for the obligations arising from treaties and other sources of international law' were prominent.[19]

Once the UN was functioning as an organisation, genocide, crimes against humanity and human rights in general were quickly placed on its agenda. An early UN General Assembly resolution gave birth to the Genocide Convention, which was followed by the Universal Declaration of Human Rights.[20] The combined

---

17 To use Hedley Bull's categorisation of justice in world politics. See H. Bull, *The Anarchical Society: A Study of Order in World Politics*, 3rd edn (Basingstoke: Palgrave, 2002), pp. 75–82.

18 Although one should stress that this was merely the prevailing view and not one universally supported. For an account of the historical antecedents of international human rights law see H.J. Steiner and P. Alston, *International Human Rights in Context: Law, Politics, Morals* (Oxford: Clarendon Press, 1996), pp. 59–116. See in particular in Steiner and Alston at pp. 113–15 the extract from L. Henkin, International Law: Politics, Values and Functions, 216 *Collected Courses of Hague Academy of International Law* 13 (1989), vol. I: 208.

19 It actually took the efforts of a small group of consultants employed by the US government to advise on the drafting of the Charter to achieve mention of human rights within it. See S.C. Schlesinger, *Act of Creation: The Founding of the United Nations* (Boulder, CO: Westview, 2003), p. 124.

20 See the account of the UN's role in the advancement of human rights in P. Kennedy, *The Parliament of Man: The United Nations and the Quest for World Government* (London:

effects of war and genocide had prompted a substantial review of the nature of the human condition and focused jurisprudential attention on individual rights at the expense of absolutist notions of sovereignty. This massively significant development has served fundamentally to shift international law back along the Natural Law/Positive Law axis, towards the former and away from the latter.[21]

After 1945 the new universal human rights system developed apace. The equally new notion of *jus cogens*, or peremptory norms of international law, which cannot be breached under any circumstances, included crimes against humanity and genocide. Significantly, this was acknowledged in 1970 by the International Court of Justice, when it recognised that states could no longer expect to act with impunity within their borders if their domestic actions breached *jus cogens*.[22]

If states grossly abuse their own citizens' human rights, is there a lawful means by which others can intervene to prevent and punish? While it is encouraging that today there is something called international human rights law, for it to be truly influential there has to be some means of enforcing it. If something profoundly dreadful is happening within a state, it would seem reasonable for others to intervene to stop it. It is the United Nations that has the leading role within the legalist paradigm to resort to the use of force in such circumstances. With the emergence of human rights considerations and the shift back towards a Natural Law approach, the law relating to the use of force and the role of the UN in legitimising it has revived interest in Just War.

Penguin and Allen Lane, 2006), Chapter 6, pp. 177–205. See also Genocide Resolution (General Assembly Resolution 95(I)) and the Universal Declaration of Human Rights 1948 (General Assembly Resolution 217A(III)).

21 Although the idea of human rights certainly sits more comfortably within the Natural Law tradition, it should be stressed that Positivism emphatically does not exclude them. Responsible liberal-minded states will help to develop human rights law at the international level through both their practice and their willingness to be bound by formal agreement (treaty law), in the Positivist tradition. It is, nevertheless, the case that the actual practice of many states is inconsistent with treaty law, even that to which they have become party. They may argue a difference of interpretation of the words of treaty commitments. However, others may regard the actions of such states as an affront to human reason – hence the renewed relevance of the Natural Law approach.

22 *Jus cogens* is a body of overriding principles (peremptory norms) of international law, established in customary law and not amenable to being set aside in treaty law (see Vienna Convention on the Law of Treaties Article 53). There is some controversy as to which principles are included within *jus cogens* but the least controversial are the rules prohibiting the aggressive use of force, those prohibiting genocide and crimes against humanity, the principle of racial non-discrimination, and the rules prohibiting piracy and the slave trade. It was *jus cogens* to which the ICJ referred in Barcelona Traction (Barcelona Traction Case, *ICJ Reports*, 1964, p. 6). For the views of a distinguished contemporary publicist see, for example, the discussion in I. Brownlie, *Principles of Public International Law*, 6th edn (Oxford: Oxford University Press, 2003), pp. 488–90.

The UN Charter and the Just War Doctrine

The Just War doctrine was the core of the traditional *jus ad bellum* governing resort to force. The doctrine stated that war could be waged legitimately by states, but only if it met certain essential criteria. The first was that the decision to use force could only be made by a legitimate authority: a ruling king or prince. Today this is generally assumed to mean a sovereign state, or a collection of sovereign states. Second, war must be waged for a just cause, such as for reasons of self-defence in response to aggression or for the purpose of righting a wrong or rectifying an injustice. Closely linked to this is the requirement for war to be waged for a morally defensible purpose or right intention. Fourth, war must be the ultimate resort, with all other remedies either most unlikely to succeed or having been tried and found wanting.[23] Fifth, there must be a reasonable chance of success. Without that, war might be futile and lead to unnecessary suffering. Six, the principle of proportionality must be applied in order that the likely good to be achieved is estimated to exceed the harm that will undoubtedly be done in waging war. Seven, war must be declared. Finally, war must be waged in accordance with the rules of combat (or *jus in bello*) in order that it is not deemed immoral or inhumane.[24]

The UN Charter, following the Covenant of the League of Nations and the 1928 Kellogg-Briand Pact, is assumed to have outlawed war and then rendered Just War doctrine redundant. However, what is most remarkable about the UN Charter is the extent to which it reflects Just War doctrine. The arrangements incorporated in it effectively codify what had previously been a set of rules forming either a part of customary law or a set of general principles governing states' resort to force.

To emphasise this let us examine the evidence. First, granting the UN the authority to apply military sanctions against transgressor states institutionalised the collective sovereign authority to wage war. In terms of just cause, the inherent right of self-defence was enshrined in Article 51 and the ability to rectify an injustice was contained in the general provisions on sanctions in Chapter VII. War as the ultimate resort is reflected in the essential trinity of sanctions: diplomatic, economic and military, with the latter applied if the former two either 'would be inadequate or … proved to be inadequate' (Article 42 of the Charter). The prospect of success and the need for proportionality are conditions to be weighed and decided upon by the Security Council. The need for a declaration of war is covered by UN Security

---

23   It is a common misperception that war must be a last resort, implying that all other means of persuasion must be tried first. This has never been the case. If other means would be manifestly ineffective, war may well be the legitimate first resort – but still the ultimate. This is reflected in Article 42 of the UN Charter.

24   These eight criteria by which a decision to go to war may be judged just are not universally accepted. The seventh – the need for a declaration – is frequently not included. As an example see M.R. Amstutz, *International Ethics: Concepts, Theories and Cases in Global Politics* (Lanham, MD: Rowman and Littlefield, 1999), p. 101 for a checklist of criteria in which this criterion is not included. There is a common myth that wars before 1945 were declared but after that date were not. This is not the place to debate this issue and, for the sake of argument, we include the need for war to be declared.

Council resolutions announcing the intention to embark on enforcement. Finally, the modern law of war (or international humanitarian law) owes its origins to the traditional *jus in bello*. War, while regrettable, is to be conducted in accordance with international law. This in itself is recognition of war's continuing relevance within the international system. It is often forgotten that the UN, by virtue of its powers under Chapter VII of its Charter, is a coercive organisation. Far from rendering Just War obsolete, the UN Charter declares its relevance and potential legitimacy within the international system. The modern version of the doctrine will determine the legitimacy of intervention.

Intervention or Non-Intervention?

Intervention is defined in international law as 'the forcible or dictatorial interference of a state in the affairs of another state, calculated to impose certain conduct or consequences on that other state'.[25] It is *prima facie* unlawful. In the UN Charter, Article 2(7) states that not even the UN itself is to 'intervene in matters which are essentially within the domestic jurisdiction of any state ...'. This seems to preclude intervention, even at the behest of the Security Council. Is this indeed the case? As Vincent stresses in his classic study of non-intervention, there can be both Naturalist and Positivist arguments both ways – in favour of and against intervention.[26] The orthodoxy in both, however, is that non-intervention is the norm, with intervention only justified exceptionally. This is related to political independence and territorial integrity, themselves linked to sovereignty. All are recognised within the UN Charter and reflected in the legalist paradigm.

In *Perpetual Peace*, Immanuel Kant argued that non-intervention allowed people in a democratic society to work out for themselves the domestic political arrangements that would best suit them and allow them to determine the norms by which they wished to be governed.[27] People have the right to choose. J.S. Mill argued that it would be a grave mistake to export a way of life to a people who were not yet adequately prepared to live in that manner. Liberal democratic society (for it is that which both Kant and Mill were envisaging) cannot be imposed but must develop from within. Even intervention to introduce a democratic form of government could lead, ironically, to a form of tyranny if it were opposed and

---

25 From Sir R. Jennings and Sir A. Watts, *Oppenheim's International Law Volume I: Peace (Introduction and Part I)*, 9th edn (London: Longman, 1996), p. 104.

26 R.J. Vincent, *Nonintervention and International Order* (Princeton, NJ: Princeton University Press, 1974). See in particular Chapter 2, pp. 20–44.

27 See Preliminary Article No. 5 (No nation shall forcibly interfere with the constitution and government of another) in I. Kant, *Perpetual Peace and Other Essays*, trans. by T. Humphrey (Indianapolis: Hackett, 1983), p. 109.

consequently had to be imposed by force.[28] These arguments for non-intervention lead to the conclusion reached in the legalist paradigm – that intervention is *prima facie* aggression and a breach of *jus cogens*.

How does one counter non-interventionist arguments with liberal justifications for intervention? Michael Walzer, while recognising the pre-eminence of the non-interventionist approach, acknowledges three possible situations in which intervention might be justified: secession; civil war; and humanitarian intervention.[29] We will pass by the first two of these and concentrate on that which is the focus of this chapter: humanitarian intervention.

The Past Practice of Humanitarian Intervention

The orthodox claim underpinning humanitarian intervention is that if there is evidence of an impending or actual humanitarian catastrophe – particularly one that is man-made – states have a right (but, importantly, not an obligation) to intervene in another state to protect those under threat. While non-interventionism prevailed during the high period of legal Positivism, and was adopted as the legalist norm thereafter, there were instances in the nineteenth century of humanitarian intervention that defied this trend. In particular, there was a series of interventions to protect Christian groups within areas of Turkish rule. Britain, France and Russia intervened in Greece between 1827 and 1830 following massacres of Greek Christians by Turks, the eventual outcome of which was Greek independence. In 1860, six thousand French troops intervened in what is now Lebanon to protect Maronite Christians from persecution by the majority Muslim population in the area. In 1877, Russia intervened in Bosnia, Herzegovina and Bulgaria, again to protect the interests of Christian minorities. Away from Europe, the US intervened in Cuba in 1898, 'in the cause of humanity and to put an end to the barbarities, bloodshed, starvation and horrible miseries now existing there', to quote President McKinley's message to Congress. He went on to say: 'It is no answer to say this is all in another country, belonging to another nation [Spain], and therefore none of our business …'[30]

In the interwar years, the record of the League in crisis response in Europe and elsewhere, including the early stages of what came to be known as the Holocaust, was unimpressive to say the least. In 1938, a leading British international lawyer was prompted to reach the following reluctant conclusion:

---

28 See the discussion in M.W. Doyle, *Ways of War and Peace* (New York and London: W.W. Norton, 1997), pp. 394–6.

29 Walzer, *Just and Unjust Wars*, as n. 15, Chapter 6 on 'Intervention', at pp. 86–108.

30 Examples and the McKinley quote taken from F.K. Abiew, *The Evolution of the Doctrine and Practice of Humanitarian Intervention* (The Hague: Kluwer Law International, 1999), pp. 44–54.

... in practice we no longer insist that States shall conform to any common standards of justice, religious toleration and internal government. Whatever atrocities may be committed in foreign countries, we now say they are no concern of ours. Conduct which in the nineteenth century would have placed a government outside the pale of civilised society is now deemed to be no obstacle to diplomatic friendship. This means in fact that we have abandoned the old distinction between civilised and uncivilised states.[31]

After the Second World War several interventions had significant humanitarian dimensions: the Congo (1964); the Dominican Republic (1965); East Pakistan (1971); Cambodia/Kampuchea (1978); and Uganda (1979). Both the Congo and Dominican Republic interventions were what are these days described as non-combatant evacuation operations, in which states intervene to rescue their own citizens under threat. The East Pakistan, Cambodian and Ugandan interventions were, however, markedly different. All involved large-scale invasions following massive humanitarian crises involving crimes against humanity, and all resulted in changes of regime in the countries concerned. None was mandated by the UN. Significantly, none was justified by reference to a perceived right of humanitarian intervention either – although the UN Charter rules were acknowledged, with arguments based on self-defence deployed in all cases.[32]

Humanitarian Intervention in the 1990s

The 1990s saw a substantial increase in military operations, many fully mandated by the UN but some not. Immediate post-Cold War examples of humanitarian intervention include: Liberia (1990–95); Northern Iraq (1991); Somalia (1992–95); Bosnia (1992–95); Rwanda (1994); and Haiti (1994). All set the scene for the NATO intervention in Kosovo (1999).

Liberia was authorised by the Economic Community of West African States (ECOWAS) and not by the UN. The ECOWAS Monitoring Group (ECOMOG) deployed for over two years before the UN Security Council adopted a resolution retrospectively endorsing ECOWAS's efforts.[33] This was an example of collective humanitarian intervention without prior UN approval; it set an important precedent.

In the wake of Iraq's defeat in the 1991 Gulf War, Britain, the US and France imposed no-fly zones in both Northern and Southern Iraq to protect minority groups within Iraq from persecution by the Ba'athist regime. These were not approved by

---

31   Professor H.A. Smith in *The Listener* (26 January 1938), quoted in Abiew, as n. 29, p. 57.

32   T.M. Franck, 'Interpretation and Change in the Law of Humanitarian Intervention', in J.L. Holzgrefe and R.O. Keohane, *Humanitarian Intervention: Ethical, Legal and Political Dilemmas* (Cambridge: Cambridge University Press, 2003), pp. 204–31, at pp. 216–19.

33   UNSCR 788 (1992).

the Security Council. UN Security Council Resolution 688 (1991) condemned the Iraqi repression of minorities but notably did not provide a specific mandate for further military action.

After 1991, the UN became more involved. In December 1992, a Chapter VII mandate provided for the use, in Somalia, of 'all necessary means', a phrase that became synonymous with approval to use whatever military force was necessary to achieve the objectives of an intervention. The US-led force UNITAF intervened and successfully conducted Operation Restore Hope. Subsequently, however, the situation deteriorated markedly following the deployment of UNOSOM II. In Mogadishu in October 1993, US forces suffered heavy casualties, with 12 killed, 75 wounded and six missing in action. UNOSOM II's mandate expired in March 1995; it was not renewed and UN forces withdrew. Overall, the UN operations in Somalia were a failure.

Bosnia also proved problematic. The complex mixture of Muslim and Serb communities provided a recipe for extremely bloody ethnic violence. Bosnian Serbs, supported by Serbia itself, pursued a policy of ethnic cleansing. The UN authorised a protection force (UNPROFOR) in February 1992 but provided an inadequate mandate for the circumstances. By August of 1992 it was obvious that something more was required and a Chapter VII mandate was provided. The operation in Bosnia became more robust until finally the imposition of a no-fly zone and NATO's bombing of Serb positions achieved a breakthrough. Negotiations for a ceasefire and eventual peace agreement produced the Dayton Accords in December 1995.

The Rwandan genocide of 1994 provides graphic evidence of the potential consequences of a lack of intervention. There was a UN-authorised force (UNAMIR) in Rwanda throughout the period in which genocide was committed. Initially 2,700 strong, it was reduced to a skeleton force of 270, while the genocide was in progress, in order to reduce the risk to UN personnel. A French intervention, code-named Operation Turquoise and authorised by the Security Council, was mounted in June 1994; it had some positive impact but overall did little to prevent the continuation of an appalling massacre. Rwanda was not an example of non-intervention (that would have been predicated on the principle that what Rwandans got up to was their own business and not that of the international community). The principles underpinning humanitarian intervention were clearly acknowledged – and then, disgracefully, absolutely nothing was done to give effect to them.

In July 1994, the Security Council authorised a US-led multinational force (MNF) to intervene in Haiti to restore the democratically elected government of President Jean Bertrand Aristide. This was successful and was replaced by a UN force (UNMIH) in March 1995. This was a fully authorised humanitarian intervention with a specific Chapter VII mandate from the Security Council.

By the mid-1990s, therefore, there had been a number of military operations that had indicated a significant degree of practice in relation to humanitarian intervention. Until the 1990s, even advocates of humanitarian intervention had fallen short of claiming that the right of humanitarian intervention was well established and recognised in international law.[34] In 1986, the British Foreign and Commonwealth Office (FCO), in a review of the law relating to intervention, had concluded that 'the best case that can be made in support of humanitarian intervention is that it cannot be said to be unambiguously illegal'.[35] This comment might be dismissed as a fine example of diplomatic double-speak – but it reflected the legal reality at the time and the FCO's reticence was entirely understandable. Once we examine the situation in the 1990s, however, we detect a shift in opinion. By 1993, following the experience of Liberia and Northern Iraq and while the crises in Somalia and Bosnia were being played out, one of Britain's leading international lawyers specialising in the law relating to the use of force felt able to comment: 'It seems that the law on humanitarian intervention has changed, both for the United Nations *and for individual states*. It is no longer tenable to assert that whenever a government massacres its own people or a state collapses into anarchy, international law forbids military intervention altogether.'[36]

Kosovo

The decision by NATO leaders to use force against Serbia in the spring of 1999 has to be seen against the backdrop of previous experience, especially that during the immediate past. NATO took action without a UN Security Council mandate because, while humanitarian intervention was viewed as an imperative, a UN mandate was impossible against a certain Russian veto. The interventions in Liberia and Northern Iraq set important precedents for further actions without specific UN Security Council approval. The Liberian intervention by a significant regional organisation was especially significant in this respect. The Northern Iraq precedent was important as it had involved three NATO members breaching strict UN law; having done so once before, it was easier for them to do so again. Nevertheless, while Liberia and Northern Iraq were important, their significance

---

34 Claims that a pre-existing customary right of humanitarian intervention had survived the coming into force of the UN Charter in 1945 were unconvincing, given both the absence of any obvious practice during the League of Nations era and the reluctance of states to rely on humanitarian arguments to justify interventions in the later stages of the Cold War.

35 See UK Foreign Office Policy Document No. 148 in D.J. Harris, *Cases and Materials on International Law*, 5th edn (London: Sweet and Maxwell, 1998), pp. 917–18 (previously published in *British Yearbook of International Law*, vol. 57 (1986) and quoted in I. Brownlie and C. Apperley, 'Kosovo Crisis Inquiry: Memorandum on the International Law Aspects', in *International and Comparative Law Quarterly*, vol. 49, pt 4 (October 2000), pp. 878–905, p. 888). In fact, the FCO document is deeply sceptical about the existence of any customary right of humanitarian intervention.

36 C.J. Greenwood, 'Is there a right of humanitarian intervention?', *World Today* (February 1993), pp. 34–40 (emphasis added).

pales in comparison with the profound impact of events in Rwanda – and closer to home, in Bosnia, especially the massacre in Srebrenica.[37]

By the end of January 1999, over 200,000 Kosovar Albanians had been either deliberately driven from their homes or rendered homeless by Serb military action. On 15 January, 45 Albanian civilians were massacred in the town of Racak. This massacre in particular focused minds in NATO capitals. It was seen, very simply, as a sign of what might well transpire unless the Milosevic government in Belgrade could be persuaded to withdraw Serbian forces from the province and restore the autonomy it had enjoyed until it had been withdrawn exactly 10 years earlier. The NATO response was to invite both Serbia and the Kosovar Albanians to send delegations to talks at Rambouillet. Belgrade demonstrated its disinterest in these talks by continuing to bombard villages in Kosovo with the result that by mid-March a further 60,000 Kosovo Albanians had been rendered homeless. At the talks, NATO attempted a compromise that assured Belgrade continuing sovereignty over Kosovo in return for provincial autonomy and the insertion of a NATO military force to ensure compliance. Belgrade rejected this solution and, in so doing, prompted NATO to resort to force.[38]

Given the extent of ethnic cleansing and killings from January to March 1999, it was not unreasonable to assume that a major crime against humanity, probably genocide, was about to be committed by Serbia against Kosovar Albanians. Indeed, there had already been a major crime against humanity committed by March 1999. The question was just how much more serious that crime would become if the Serbs were left to their own devices. The fear was that they intended forcing all Kosovar Albanians out of Kosovo, leaving it as a purely Serbian province and a fully integrated part of Serbia proper.

NATO's intervention divided legal opinion, no better demonstrated than in the contrasting views of the distinguished group of British international lawyers invited to give evidence to a Parliamentary enquiry into Kosovo, the report of which was published in 2000.[39] A brief justification had been provided by the Secretary of State

---

37 Some have argued that the NATO claim that ethnic cleansing or genocide was a significant risk was simply a smokescreen to allow the Alliance to act for other, un-stated, reasons. This argument is rejected here. The author was serving on the Central (Policy Area) Staff in the UK Ministry of Defence at the time and is in no doubt whatsoever that the motive for intervention was directly related to the humanitarian and other consequences of what was regarded as a high risk of ethnic cleansing, particularly following the massacre at Racak in January 1999.

38 For an authoritative account of events in Kosovo in the period from January 1999 to the commencement of the NATO air campaign against Serbia on 24 March 1999, see Independent International Commission on Kosovo, *Kosovo Report* (Oxford: Oxford University Press, 2000), pp. 78–83. See also the account in A. Weymouth and S. Henig, *The Kosovo Crisis: The Last American War in Europe?* (London: Reuters, 2001), pp. 86–88).

39 *4th Report of the House of Commons Foreign Affairs Committee* (HC28-I) and Appendices (HC28-II) dated 7 June 2000. The written evidence of leading British based international lawyers, Ian Brownlie, Christine Chinkin, Christopher Greenwood and Vaughan Lowe were conveniently published in: A. Boyle, 'Kosovo: House of Commons Foreign Affairs

for Defence in a statement to the House of Commons the day after the air campaign commenced, which stated:

> ... that the Government was in no doubt that NATO is acting within international law and that the use of force ... can be justified as an exceptional measure in support of purposes laid down by the UN Secretary General, but without the Council's express authorisation, where that is the only means to avert an immediate and overwhelming humanitarian catastrophe.[40]

The orthodox view in tune with the pre-existing legalist paradigm was expressed forcefully to the Committee by Brownlie, who regarded NATO's actions as unlawful and who argued that humanitarian intervention has no place in either customary law or in the UN Charter (except, of course, when authorised by the Security Council under Chapter VII).[41] In stark contrast, Greenwood concluded that:

> The NATO operation raised fundamental questions about the nature of modern international law and the values which it is designed to protect ... I believe that the resort to force in this case was a legitimate exercise of the right of humanitarian intervention recognised by international law and was consistent with the relevant Security Council Resolutions.[42]

Between these two extremes, Lowe and Chinkin provided justification in law for the conclusion that NATO's action was at the same time both unlawful and legitimate. Lowe argued that 'there is no clear legal justification for the NATO action but it is desirable that such ... be allowed to emerge in customary international law'.[43] Chinkin did 'not consider that the accumulative effect is to bestow legality'. Nevertheless, she also concluded:

> [While NATO's operation] does not fall under any of the doctrines of international law permitting the use of force, the cumulative effects of the arguments may be thought to be persuasive. The Security Council ... did not condemn it; humanitarian considerations were important and the subsequent Peace Plan has been made operational with Security Council authorisation

---

Committee 4th Report, June 2000', in *International and Comparative Law Quarterly*, vol. 49, pt 4 (October 2000), pp. 876–943.

40   *Report*, as n. 37, vol. II, p. 1.

41   See I. Brownlie and C. Apperly, 'Kosovo Crisis Inquiry: Memorandum on the International Law Aspects', in *International and Comparative Law Quarterly*, vol. 49, pt 4 (October 2000), pp. 878–905, at p. 904.

42   C. Greenwood, 'International Law and the NATO Intervention in Kosovo', in *International and Comparative Law Quarterly*, vol. 49, pt 4 (October 2000), pp. 926–34, at pp. 933–4.

43   V. Lowe, 'International Legal Issues Arising in the Kosovo Crisis', in *International and Comparative Law Quarterly*, vol. 49, pt 4 (October 2000), pp. 934–43, at p. 941.

> ... *What is clear is that the NATO intervention is leading international law into new areas.*[44]

Given the extent to which the Security Council has been prepared to rule that humanitarian abuse poses a threat to international peace and security, the legalist paradigm has arguably been modified slightly in relation to intervention. Humanitarian intervention is certainly now permitted if the Security Council authorises it. When no mandate is likely, however, the legitimacy of intervention remains, on balance, ambiguous. Looked at from a Positivist perspective, neither treaty law nor customary law provides any evidence of a shift of sufficient magnitude to render unauthorised humanitarian intervention lawful. Nevertheless, if we accept that the Natural Law tradition has become more influential in recent years, especially in the light of the development of a universal human rights regime, might it be the case that the plight of large numbers of innocent victims ought to result in the privileging of individual rights over states' rights?

Rights or Responsibilities to Protect?

The idea that humanitarian intervention has as its basis the right of states to intervene when another state breaches its obligations to the wider international community by abusing its own citizens, is a Positivist approach that privileges the state over the individual. It is predicated on the assumption that individuals are merely objects of the law and not subjects endowed with their own rights and obligations. Arguably, since the emergence of international human rights law, this approach is becoming increasingly inappropriate, but it remains the principal way in which international law deals with the problem, nevertheless.

Following NATO's intervention over Kosovo and the legal controversy that was generated by it, a significant attempt was made to redraw the relationship between states and individuals. The Canadian government initiated an international commission to address the dilemma created by humanitarian crises. It was directly prompted by the controversy generated by Kosovo but its principal focus was to be on how the need for intervention in extreme circumstances of human rights abuse could be squared with the powerful norm of non-intervention, which itself reflected the most fundamental of all principles within the international state system: sovereignty.

The International Commission on Intervention and State Sovereignty (ICISS) was convened initially in 2000 and reported eventually to the UN Secretary General

---

44 C. Chinkin, 'The Legality of NATO's Action in the Former Republic of Yugoslavia (FRY) Under International Law', in *International and Comparative Law Quarterly*, vol. 49, pt 4 (October 2000), pp. 910–25, at p. 925.

in December 2001.[45] Much of its report was to become especially significant in the context of Kofi Annan's UN reform agenda.[46]

By far the most significant idea to come from the process was the concept of a 'responsibility to protect'. This first emerged at the ICISS's third round table meeting, in London in February 2001, when it was suggested that the notion of a right to intervene, while logical in a strictly legal sense, was singularly inappropriate when applied to the protection of human rights.[47] In some way there needed to be an acceptance that the international community had some degree of obligation relative to the human rights of individuals and communities being abused. While a right of intervention was inappropriate, it was also equally inappropriate to establish an obligation or duty to intervene, not least because that implied that the international community would have no choice but to resort to force as soon as a threshold of abuse had been breached. This degree of obligatory commitment is not something to which any responsible statesman would be prepared to subscribe. Nevertheless, there was general agreement within the round table that the right to intervene should be replaced by some degree of obligation or duty. The commissioners present (Gareth Evans, Mohamed Sahnoun and Michael Ignatieff) suggested that it might be helpful to think in terms of a 'responsibility to protect'.[48] This phrase caught on and was eventually used as the title of the commission's report, since when it has become something of a mantra within the human rights discourse.

---

45   ICISS, *The Responsibility to Protect: Report of the International Commission on Intervention and State Sovereignty* (and Supplementary Volume) (Ottawa: International Development Research Centre, 2001).

46   The ICISS Report was studied by Annan and the Secretariat in New York and eventually passed to a High Level Panel convened by Annan to propose a way forward for UN reform. The Panel took the ideas from the ICISS and incorporated them in its own report (United Nations, *A More Secure World: Our Shared Responsibility – Report of the Secretary General's High Level Panel on Threats, Challenges and Change* (New York, 2004)). Annan then followed the High Level Panel's report with his own reaction prepared in advance of the UN summit in 2005 (United Nations, *In Larger Freedom: Towards Development, Security and Human Rights for All* (New York, 2005)).

47   The author provided a paper to the ICISS which urged a shift from rights to obligations. Although he is a named contributor to the ICISS report, the paper did not form a part of the published report itself and was only published, in modified form, three years later as S. Haines, 'Genocide, Humanitarian Intervention and International Law', in M. Mason, ed., *Hudson Papers Volume II* (Ministry of Defence (Naval Staff) and Oxford University Hudson Trust, 2004).

48   See ICISS Report, Supplementary Volume, as n. 43, for a brief account of the London Round Table at pp. 358–361. Gareth Evans, one of the two co-chairmen of the ICISS, has recently given his own account of the process that led to the emergence of the notion of a 'responsibility to protect'. The commission had discussed the idea before the London Round Table. Support for it there and at subsequent round table meetings worldwide convinced the ICISS to champion the idea. See G. Evans, *The Responsibility to Protect: Ending Mass Atrocity Crimes Once and For All* (Washington, DC: Brookings Institution Press, 2008), in particular Chapter 2, pp. 31–54.

Has 'responsibility to protect' had any effect on the law relating to the use of force? On one level (the theoretical) it arguably has but on another (the practical) it would not appear to have had any impact at all. The reason is that, while the ideas behind such a responsibility are certainly both attractive and persuasive, especially in liberal circles, it has not so far produced any significant shift in state practice in relation to humanitarian intervention. Indeed, while the 1990s were arguably the decade of humanitarian intervention, the decade since has been dominated by the terrorist attacks on New York and Washington in September 2001, the subsequent invasions of Afghanistan and Iraq and the so-called 'global war on terrorism'. Humanitarian intervention has taken a back seat. It is not that there have been no instances in which it might have been justified; humanitarian crises have certainly not reduced in number or intensity. But those states that have the capacity for such interventions, either alone or in coalition with others, have not been inclined to embark on them. The US and Britain, for example, have had serious preoccupations elsewhere that have effectively closed off the possibilities of intervention, particularly in the most obvious case – to prevent genocide in the Darfur region of Sudan. Unfortunately, state practice combined with *opinio juris* remains an important source of international law and a clear and persistent shift in practice is needed for the law to change by the influence of shifting practice.

The ICISS report's contents certainly progressed through Annan's UN reform process, which many hoped would result in significant changes in the way that the UN conducted its business. The ICISS's report, *Responsibility to Protect*, was an important influence on the Secretary General's High Level Panel on Threats, Challenges and Change (on which Gareth Evans, co-chairman of the ICISS, also served). The High Level Panel's own report (A More Secure World: Our Shared Responsibility) was used by Kofi Annan as an important source document for his own report prepared to inform the UN Summit in 2005 (In Larger Freedom: Towards Development, Security and Human Rights for All).

While all of this augured well for the prospect of reform, ultimately the reform process was stalled. The sorts of changes that would have been required fully to bring to fruition the sorts of developments many were advocating would ideally have required a change to the law of the UN Charter – effectively, formal substantive changes to the *Charter* and to the Security Council's constitution and procedures. Unfortunately, suggestions for reform were largely unsuccessful when it came to the world summit in 2005. The reform agenda was halted by the combined effects of Annan's rapidly declining authority (caused by his impending retirement and the so-called 'oil for food scandal') and US opposition most vocally obvious in the statements of US Permanent Representative to the UN John Bolton. The failure of Annan's UN reform agenda meant no change in treaty law (the UN Charter itself).

With no change to the relevant treaty law and no significant evidence of state practice to support a normative shift, the law on humanitarian intervention arguably remains precisely where it was in 1999. It is even possible to argue that the lack of practice since then actually challenges the conclusions of many international lawyers at the time that Kosovo was unlawful yet legitimate – and that the law should and would develop in favour of humanitarian intervention; perhaps it should but it certainly has not done so as yet. Having said this, it would be wrong not to acknowledge at least one development that could ultimately come to be seen as significant in the development of a norm under the heading of 'responsibility to protect'. The UN General Assembly endorsed the idea in the 2005 World Summit Outcome document and the UN Security Council went on to quote 'responsibility to protect' in a 2006 UNSC resolution dealing with the protection of civilians in armed conflict.[49] These two documents may well have consigned the notion of a 'right of humanitarian intervention' to history, replacing it with a 'responsibility to protect' that can provide the justification behind a decision to intervene. If so the sovereign rights of states have given way to the rights of individuals under threat, generating a correlative obligation on the part of states. Hence the assertion that the theoretical underpinning for intervention has changed despite there having been no obvious practical consequence in terms of actual practice.

What now for the future of humanitarian intervention? It is by no means clear. For the moment there is no practical enthusiasm for human intervention amongst states despite there being no lack of humanitarian crises to provide opportunities for the international community to give meaning to a responsibility to protect. As this chapter is written, Sudan and Zimbabwe offer striking examples of just the sorts of crises to which such a responsibility might apply. The acceptance that other priorities have probably prevented action in these instances does not necessarily mean an end to the development of either the idea of responsibility to protect or the ultimate means of meeting that responsibility – humanitarian intervention. Assuming that there is scope for it to develop further in the future, there is one issue in particular that requires some attention – what ought to be the trigger for military intervention?

Genocide or Crimes against Humanity?

What degree of abuse of human rights would 'shock the conscience of mankind'? A particularly onerous and systematic breach of human rights will certainly constitute a 'crime against humanity'. This phrase clearly suggests something altogether more serious than the bulk of general breaches of the wide range of so-called 'human rights standards' existing today. Genocide is a particular form of crime against humanity, separately and deliberately defined in a convention devoted to it – the 1948 Convention on the Prevention and Punishment of the Crime of Genocide – and assumed invariably to shock the conscience of mankind.

Unfortunately, 'genocide' is a problematic term. We instinctively understand what is meant by it but as soon as we try to define it we encounter difficulties.

---

49   See *2005 World Summit Outcome*, UN Doc. A/RES/60/1 (New York: United Nations, 24 Oct 2005), paras 138–140; and UN Security Council Resolution 1674 (2006) of 28 April 2006.

Attempts at interpreting what is and what is not genocide can produce apparently absurd conclusions. The actions of the Pol Pot regime in the 'killing fields' of Cambodia between 1975 and 1979, resulting in an estimated two million deaths, are not unambiguously genocide as defined in the Genocide Convention. Using that same definition, if an individual caused serious bodily or mental harm to just three or four people he may be personally guilty of genocide. The key determinant is intent and not the scale of humanitarian abuse. The intention must be to 'destroy, in whole or in part, a national, ethnical, racial or religious group, as such'.[50] It is precise motive that distinguishes genocide in international law.[51] As Schabas has noted: 'Where the specified intent is not established, the act remains punishable, but not as genocide. It may be classified as a crime against humanity or it may be simply a crime under ordinary criminal law.'[52]

In 2005, the International Commission of Inquiry on Darfur submitted its report to the UN Secretary General. It had been expected to conclude that genocide was being committed. It concluded that there were indeed serious crimes against humanity and breaches of international humanitarian law being committed – but not genocide. Motive was the crucial issue. Nevertheless, the Commission went on to say that 'offences such as the crimes against humanity and war crimes that have been committed in Darfur may be no less serious and heinous than genocide'.[53]

This conclusion is of some significance in the context of humanitarian intervention. It has been argued that a breach of the non-intervention principle can only be justified as a response to genocide, it being by far the most dreadful

---

50   1948 Convention on the Prevention and Punishment of the Crime of Genocide, Article 2. In the case of Cambodia there has been some hesitation about labelling the killing of almost two million Cambodians (over 20 per cent of the total population) as genocide. The killings were politically motivated and, although ethnic Vietnamese and Chinese as well as Muslims and Buddhists were included in the list of victims, in the main the killings were arguably not intended systematically to destroy a particular national, ethnic, racial or religious group – the strict requirement to meet the definition in the Genocide Convention.

51   Actual examples of convictions on charges of genocide and a subsequent successful appeal serve to illustrate this point. The International Criminal Tribunal for the Former Yugoslavia sentenced General Radislav Krstic to 46 years' imprisonment in its first genocide conviction in August 2001. This was for the killing of over 7,500 Bosniak men in Srebrenica in July 1995. One of Krstic's subordinate commanders, Vidoje Blagojevic, having been convicted in 2005 of complicity in genocide and sentenced to 18 years' imprisonment, had his sentence reduced to 15 years, in May 2007, after the Appeals Chamber ruled that the Trial Chamber had erred in convicting him of genocide as it was not clear beyond a reasonable doubt that he knew of the main perpetrator's genocidal intent; his convictions for crimes against humanity and violations of the laws and customs of war were upheld.

52   W.A. Schabas, *Genocide in International Law* (Cambridge: Cambridge University Press, 2000), p. 214.

53   Report of the International Commission of Enquiry on Darfur to the United Nations Secretary General (Geneva: United Nations, 25 January 2005), p. 4.

of crimes,[54] with a treaty law obligation to prevent and punish it.[55] Nevertheless, as the discussion of definition illustrates, 'genocide' may be an inappropriate label. If so, surely it would be wrong to rule out intervention simply because it cannot be labelled as 'genocide' despite it being manifestly obvious that something profoundly dreadful has occurred.

Definitional difficulties may prove politically useful, with an apparent lack of a clear-cut case of genocide providing an excuse for taking no action, despite profoundly serious crimes against humanity being committed. This was arguably the case in relation to Rwanda and, more recently, Sudan. The US government is reputed to have avoided official use of the term 'genocide' in relation to Rwanda, deliberately to avoid its obligations as a party to the Genocide Convention. In the case of Sudan, the International Commission's decision not to describe the humanitarian catastrophe in Darfur as genocide may have given both Britain and the US a convenient excuse for not providing forces for a military intervention (particularly convenient, given their preoccupation with demanding military operations in both Iraq and Afghanistan).

The term 'genocide' has arguably been rather unhelpful. Perhaps the International Commission's conclusion that there was little evidence of genocidal intent in Sudan may eventually prove more significant than it currently appears. It might come to serve to convince all concerned that it ought to be crimes against humanity, in all their forms, that are accorded the pre-eminent significance that, since 1948, has been granted to genocide alone.

Concluding Comments

International law is in a state of flux, as it always is. What we are witnessing at present, however, is a potential paradigm shift. Positive Law, having dominated the international legal system for most of the Westphalian era, is under mounting threat from a Natural Law revival. There is a causal connection between the emergence of international human rights law since 1945 and this potential shift. As with many causal connections, however, it is not always easy to determine which of the two sides of the equation is most responsible for the change.

While the universal human rights regime developed after 1945, it was during the 1990s that profound international concern about gross violations of human rights was able to influence decisions about intervention in sovereign states. Again, the precise nature of a causal relationship – between the incidence of UN authorised

---

54 The author himself tended to use genocide as the threshold test to justify humanitarian intervention, for precisely this reason. For such an argument, put to the ICISS in 2001, see S. Haines, 'Genocide, Humanitarian Intervention and International Law', in M. Mason, ed., Hudson Papers Volume II (Ministry of Defence (Naval Staff) and Oxford University Hudson Trust, 2004).

55 Genocide Convention, Article 1.

military operations and the end of the Cold War – is by no means entirely certain. The facts, however, do tend to speak for themselves. The pre-existing legalist paradigm on the use of force was under challenge. The key question was to do with the extent to which states could continue to argue that actions taken within their domestic jurisdiction remained their business and not that of the international community. When Article 2(7) of the UN Charter was drawn up in 1945, the prevailing view was strongly non-interventionist. It remains non-interventionist today, but there is a new interpretation being placed on the words 'essentially within the domestic jurisdiction of any state'. Something may well be within domestic jurisdiction, but arguably it may not be 'essentially' an exclusively domestic matter, as the ICJ stated in *Barcelona Traction*. That much is clear from UN practice and the Security Council's willingness to authorise humanitarian interventions during the 1990s.

Although the UN has legal personality itself, essentially it is the member states, individually or collectively, which have to meet their obligations resulting from international law. This is especially the case in relation to *jus cogens*. It is, arguably, simply not good enough for states to hide behind the inherent political shortcomings of an organisation that they themselves created, in order to avoid meeting their broader legal obligations. It is also regrettable that a willingness among a significant regional grouping of states to meet a substantial humanitarian obligation, must necessarily be thwarted by a single veto in the Security Council emanating from outwith that region. Some may argue that Article 103 of the Charter reflects such a suggestion. Certainly it obliges states to comply with their obligations under the Charter rather than with any other international obligations if there is a conflict between the two. This sanctions the precedence of the Charter over obligations arising from other agreements.[56] It certainly does not oblige states completely to ignore their other obligations, however.

Although we are far from the point at which we can claim that 'responsibility to protect' is a principle enshrined in international law, there is no doubt that this is one of the influences that is now being brought to bear on the existing paradigm for the use of force. A great many statesmen have talked about it in positive terms, although their words have not so far been turned into actions. It was even recently invoked by Pope Benedict XVI on his visit to the United Nations in New York on 18 April 2008.[57] Could it be that it becomes accepted as a principle of Natural Law and, if so, how will this influence both the legalist paradigm and future state practice?

If responsibility to protect does affect the paradigm and cause a shift, then the issue of threshold comes to the fore. 'Genocide versus crimes against humanity' implies a dispute about terminology. To the victims of either, each looks pretty much like the other at the point at which it is being committed.

---

56 See B. Conforti, *The Law and Practice of the United Nations* (The Hague: Kluwer Law International, 1996), p. 276.

57 See Vatican website: <http://www.vatican.va/holy_father/benedict_xvi/speeches/2008/april/documents/hf_ben-xvi_spe_20080418_un-visit_en.html>.

"Forgetful Warriors": Neglected Lessons on Leadership from Plato's Republic

George R. Lucas

Toward the middle of Plato's *Republic*,[1] Socrates is portrayed as offering a somewhat unusual piece of advice concerning warriors and leadership. The advice is buried in the midst of a lengthy and somewhat rambling discussion, extending from Book III through VII, concerning the selection and education of a nation's warriors and, ultimately, its political leaders. The commentary I wish to highlight occurs early in Book VI, immediately after the better-known discussions in Book V that culminate in Socrates' famous suggestion that philosophers alone are qualified to rule the State [473 d].

The wide-ranging discussion to this point has led to consensus among the dinner-party participants that the proper education and training of the warrior and leader is a curriculum in what Socrates explicitly terms "military science" [πολεμική].[2] Such a curriculum properly consists (Socrates maintains) in a careful study of the core subjects that we now identify as "the liberal arts." Having early on [Book III] discussed gymnastics, and "music" (which, with due caution about their heady effects on the young, encompasses literature and poetry), Socrates subsequently adds to these studies of "imitative" and transient subjects the study of what is timeless and enduring,[3] as the course of study that will prove "most useful for

---

1   I have used the translation by Raymond Larson, with introduction by Eva T.H. Brann (Chicago: AHM Publishing/Crofts Classics, 1979). All references, citations in square brackets in the text, and discussion of terminology and translations refer to the Loeb Classic edition of the original Greek, edited by Paul Shorey (Cambridge: Harvard University Press, 1994), and to Liddell and Scott, *Greek–English Lexicon*, 7th edn (Oxford: Clarendon Press, 1975).

2   [522 c]—also translated as "the art of war," or "warlike exercises" in Plato and Thucydides.

3   It is core Platonic doctrine, of course, that the study of the transient is of less importance than the study of what abides, and also (according to the simile of "the divided line") that the study of imitations of genuine things (for example, art and poetry) is

warriors." [Book VI, 521 d] These "higher" subjects include arithemetic (so that we might reliably inventory our ships and hoplites), geometry (so that we may size up the battlefield terrain, organize the proper number of hoplites into each phalynx, and deploy ships and troops to military advantage), astronomy (so that we might navigate the ships and position soldiers properly), and finally, dialectic, so that we might gain the wisdom and judgment to lead—that is, the capacity to recognize, as Sun Tzu also counsels, exactly when and where to engage the enemy, and when to refrain from battle.

Concerning the former subjects: in contrast to our modern tendency to emphasize the physical training of warriors, Socrates advises that too much poetry makes a person soft and dreamy, but too little renders them ignorant and incapable of sound judgment. [Book III, 411–12] Concerning the latter subjects, and especially dialectic: the often caricatured and somewhat misconstrued argument about philosophers in this regard is, in fact, a claim that the individuals who can best be expected to profit from such a curriculum are those rare individuals who innately posses what Socrates terms a "philosophic soul"—that is, these rare individuals are consumed by a love of learning for its own sake, together with a desire to understand what is unchangingly good and true amidst the bewildering backdrop of fleeting and transient opinion. Socrates and his companions concur that only such individuals, possessed of such learning, can be vouchsafed to place the welfare of the State and its citizens ahead of their own.

To the skeptics and nay-sayers, moreover, who doubt the efficacy of such knowledge for the practice of military leadership, Socrates offers the amusing but telling allegory of a "topsy-turvy" ship:

> Imagine a situation like this, on one ship or many: a captain who outstrips everyone on board in size and strength, but [is also] nearsighted, partially deaf, and with [a] knowledge of sailing to match; sailors in mutiny over navigation, each thinking that he ought to steer, though none has learned the skill or can point to his teacher or to the time when he learned it, who deny in fact that navigation can even be taught, and are ready to cut down anyone who says that it can, always swarming around the captain and begging for the wheel ... and on top of it all, they praise as a navigator and sailor with a [true] knowledge of shipcraft the man who [in fact] is sharpest [simply] at persuading or coercing the captain into letting him [steer] ... refusing even to hear that a navigator must necessarily study the seasons and climates, the

---

correspondingly of lesser value than a direct encounter with the things themselves. That does not mean that imitation and right example are without value, however. Socrates counsels: "If we want to keep to our original idea that our [phulaké, warriors and leaders] must be freed from all other crafts to be painstaking craftsmen of their city's freedom, pursuing nothing that doesn't contribute to this end, then they mustn't do or imitate anything else. If they imitate anything, it must, from childhood on, be men with qualities befitting a [phulaké]: courage, temperance, liberality, reverence, and so on." [Book III, 395 c, my emphasis].

sky, the stars, the winds and everything else that pertains to his craft if he's to become a true shipmaster ... and [persisting in] disbelieving that there is a skill or practice of steering that can be acquired along with navigation. In such a state of affairs, is it any wonder that the true navigator is called a useless, babbling stargazer by the crews of such topsy-turvy ships? [Book VI, 488 b–e, my emphasis][4]

All these provisional findings converge toward a discussion of the characteristics of individuals that might distinguish them as suitable or unsuitable candidates for selection and education as warriors and leaders. If we seek to identify and enlist the right kind of individuals to study in our leadership development curriculum,[5] and groom them as future guardians of the State (bearing in mind that any such individual will naturally be reluctant to assume the mantle of leadership), then, Socrates observes: "... we must first understand their nature. If we can agree on that [that is, on what that essential nature consists of], then I think we'll also agree ... that no one else should lead in the cities" [485 a].

He then begins to outline, with the help of his dinner companions, a provisional checklist of the ἀρετή[6] — the excellences, the necessary and sufficient characteristics — that such individuals would possess as constituting their *physis*, their nature. They would, for example, love the truth for its own sake, and seek ever the knowledge of that which abides, rather than trafficking in the constantly-changing and usually uninformed opinions of society. [485 b–c] They will be concerned only with pleasures of the soul, rather than desires of the body, and so will be temperate rather than greedy or extravagant. They will not be slavish or petty; they will be orderly, but not cowardly or boastful [486 b]; and, in order to determine whether an

---

4   The transparent comparison of such shipboard nonsense to analogous beliefs in the "ship of State," about the relative importance of the study of ethics for the practice of leadership, helps midshipmen and cadets understand that their elders' widespread opinions that such subjects cannot be taught, or that their study serves no useful purpose, is hardly a modern (let alone a very sophisticated) conceit.

5   It is more customary to render Φύλάκή as "guardians," and the excellence or fittingness to serve in this capacity as Φύλάκική ("guardianship"), whereas a "leader" is customarily translated as ἀρχον. The latter is a *de facto* designation, however, for example, for royalty, or for one of the nine magistrates of Athens, or for Agamemnon at Troy. The magistrates were corrupt and unjust, and Agamemnon was incompetent and tyrannical. Φύλάκή, in Plato's account, is a normative designation of merit, earned not conferred, and one who is a *phulaké* has already had to prove himself (or herself) incapable of being tyrannical, corrupt, or incompetent. Hence it seems clear in context that "leaders" and "leadership" would be as apt or even more apt translations into English. Thus "guardianship" or leadership is the property of "citizens [who] have a knowledge, not of something in the city but of the city as a whole, that judges and deliberates how she may have the best relations with herself and other cities." [428 d]

6   Again, though *arête* is translated as "virtue," it shares the same root as Ares, the Greek goddess of war, and connotes those excellences (like courage) most conducive to the warrior.

individual possesses a soul suitable for the life of the warrior and the leader or not, Socrates advises Glaucon, "you'll examine it from childhood up to see whether it is gentle and just, or savage and unsociable" [486 c].

Plato is renowned (and sometimes reviled) for this kind of indifferent, other-worldly asceticism, and we might well wonder, perhaps with some amusement, to what extent his own list of essential virtues constitutes an exhaustive or even fully appropriate set of criteria for those who aspire to become military cadets or midshipmen today. In the midst of this discourse, however, Socrates unexpectedly offers the brief and somewhat unusual addition to the list of essential leadership traits to which I would like to call your attention today. He warns: "If he [the candidate] is *full of forgetfulness*, won't he be empty of knowledge? ... Therefore we won't admit a *forgetful soul* to our [community of leader-candidates]; [instead], *we'll seek out the one that remembers*" [486 d, my emphases].

Scholars of Plato's writings are, of course, quite familiar with the theme of memory and forgetting in Platonic dialogues generally. But what are we to make of this reference, in this particular context, in which we are explicitly invited to consider the essential and necessary characteristics of the soul requisite for candidacy as effective warriors and, ultimately, as the State's leaders? What sort of "forgetfulness" is it that Socrates has in mind that would so decidedly disqualify a person for prospective future service as a warrior and guardian of the State?

There are, in the larger Platonic corpus, all sorts of references to forgetting and forgetfulness, of the sort that the German philosopher, Martin Heidegger, found extremely suggestive. Not all of these references have a negative connotation, as the reference above clearly does. For example, the forgetting that takes place in the "Myth of Er," in Book X at the end of the *Republic*, in which righteous souls are cleansed and reborn by crossing the "river of Lethe" in the underworld [610 c], seems to be a neutral if not a positive event (see below). Indeed, despite Heidegger's interest in this theme in Plato and the pre-Socratics, the fascinating topic of forgetting in Plato's dialogues generally has been slighted in favor of his more conventional discussions of remembering—that is, the so-called Platonic Doctrine of Recollection.[7]

The *amnesia* mentioned in this passage that I have highlighted, however, does not appear to be a constructive form of forgetfulness, but something that is negative and destructive, and to be avoided at all costs in the life of the warrior and leader. What sort of "forgetting" is this? All Socrates offers by way of illustration is the student or candidate who has difficulty learning, or cannot retain what he learns. So, not surprisingly, we recognize by analogy that the individual who cannot remember where he has put his rifle or his uniform, let alone remember how to clean, wear, or discharge them is incompetent, and not suitable as a warrior or a leader. The student who is weak-minded, and cannot remember or retain his or her trigonometric identities or derivative forms in calculus, or cannot master the

---

7   The sole exception is a remarkable dissertation by Patricia J. Cook, "Memory and Forgetting in the Dialogues of Plato" (Atlanta, GA: Emory University, 1992), which regrettably remains unpublished.

essential regulations of the military code of conduct, is likewise "forgetful" and (we might therefore suppose) not very promising as a candidate to fight for and protect, let alone lead the State.

Something about the entire, remarkable sweep of this discussion in the *Republic*, however, leads me to believe that Plato had more in mind than simple intellectual incompetence. He has, after all, taken pains (and as my mentor, Admiral Stockdale himself, might observe, quite a few rolls of parchment) to allow Socrates and his companions to explore the wider nature of leadership, and of the quest for leaders who would "not turn on us, but would love the State more than themselves." And likewise, we know many fine candidates for commissioning who may not be "the sharpest tools in the shed" when it comes to remembering mathematical formulae, or keeping track of their car keys, but still seem to us exemplary candidates for service to their country.

At this point in Plato's most famous dialogue, we are in fact primarily concerned with the themes of character and moral courage, and the kinds of properties and preparations that will, when combined, produce leaders of character, and warriors of moral courage, who can be relied upon to resist the temptations of power and corruption, and counted upon to do their duty in behalf of their fellow citizens and the State. What sort of "forgetting," then, would it be that might threaten so gravely these desirable outcomes as to be specifically denounced and decried? Let me follow good Platonic practice, and sketch a hypothesis—one that, I believe, comes close to teasing out Plato's deeper meaning.

A few years after the end of the Cold War, following the final collapse of the Berlin Wall in the fall of 1989, a retired former Soviet army officer, Colonel Vladimir Malinin, related how he and his wife, Yevgenia, first learned for themselves of how the Soviet State dealt with political prisoners:

> *Yevgenia, an archivist for the state prison system, accidentally discovered a secret report written to Soviet leader Nikita Khrushchev by the director of the camps administration in the Far East. The report recited a litany of horrors that shocked the couple out of their previous unquestioning devotion to the Soviet state. According to Mr Malinin, the report recounted that 17.5 million people had been imprisoned in a sprawling network of labor camps for political prisoners in the Kolyma River valley north of Magadan between 1933 and 1952. Of those, the report said, 16.3 million had died of exhaustion or illness and another 85,877 had been shot to death. Having stumbled upon such forbidden knowledge, Mr Malinin said, he agonized over it for months, then finally shared his secret and sought advice from a friend named Ivan Chistiakov, who held a high position in the Magadan regional administration. "He told me, 'It's better you forget all about it'," Mr. Malinin said.*[8]

---

8   *Newsday* article on Soviet prison camps, reprinted in *The Baltimore Sun*, "Photo helps ex-Soviet officer recall US prisoner" (Monday, September 20, 1993), p. 3A.

Likewise, at the relatively advanced age of 76, a former Japanese Army physician decided to break a long-standing code of silence and denial and speak out for the record concerning Japanese military atrocities during World War II. At issue were allegations, never acknowledged by the Japanese, that army doctors had conducted a variety of cruel and scientifically unwarranted experiments on Chinese and Korean prisoners of war. The physician, Dr Ken Yuasa, remarked: "I must confess, with embarrassment for myself and the country, because I strongly believe everyone should know the truth. If I don't tell my story, *what the Japanese military has done will be forgotten* [erased from history]."[9]

Forgetting, it would seem, is not always about mere dull-wittedness or simple-mindedness. Rather than being unavoidable or inescapable, it is often intentional. Forgetting, indeed, is the stock-in-trade of tyranny. What Col. Malinin uncovered was a strategy to *suppress* the deeds of an evil regime. Dr Yuasa, by comparison, finally refused to condone *repression*, a conspiracy of silence and denial concerning medical and pseudo-scientific activities that violated established, universal codes of decency and humanity. The motivations in both instances are literally to cast these black deeds into historical oblivion, to have them (and the guilt of their perpetrators) *erased from history*. "We would not want the forgetful ones to be our warriors, or our leaders," Socrates warns us.

Both strategies very nearly succeeded, save that someone, somewhere, chose instead to "remember," for remembering is an act of caring. Czech author Milan Kundera maintains, in his *Book of Laughter and Forgetting*, that "the only reason people want to be masters of the future is to change the past."[10] Tyrants often see the need for this social or cultural amnesia, this need "to change the past," either to hide what they have done or to disguise or distort what they propose to do. They threaten to succeed only when the rest of us cease to care.[11]

"Therefore," Socrates concludes, "we won't admit a *forgetful soul* to our [community of leader-candidates]; [instead], we'll seek out the one that remembers." Could Plato be intimating something like this? It is not merely that we don't want dim or dull-witted or thoughtless people to serve as our warriors and leaders. Even more we desire to exclude tyrants, for whom forgetfulness, cultural amnesia, is itself an instrument of ruthless, unprincipled political power? There are some things, terrible things, about which it is not finally "better that we forget all about it."[12]

---

9   Dr Yuasa, imprisoned for three years as a war criminal at the conclusion of WWII, as quoted in an Associated Press article on Japanese war crimes in *The Baltimore Sun* (Tuesday, September 7, 1993), p. 7A [my emphasis].

10   Milan Kundera, *The Book of Laughter and Forgetting*, trans. by Michael Henry Heim (London: Penguin, 1983), p. 22.

11   Heidegger himself famously, if somewhat obscurely observes that "Care [*Sorge*] is the Being of Dasein." See *Being and Time* (1925), trans. by John Macquarrie and Edward Robinson (New York: Harper, 1962), pp. 225–41.

12   My reading is consistent with an earlier comment by Socrates [in Book III] concerning the method of educating potential guardians who would, later in life, transition from the role of warrior-protector to leader. For these, Socrates states: "we must examine the

Lest my proposal sound like the worst kind of postmodernist anachronism, consider that several, and very likely most of the characters with whom Plato populates his splendid dialogue are, or rather were, in their real life, ghosts. Several of the voices gathered around that dinner table in this dialogue—offering hypotheses about justice, moral virtue, a functional military science curriculum, leadership, and the State (including Socrates and Polemarchus surely, and on some less certain accounts, Plato's brothers, Glaucon and Adeimantus, as well)—were, in real life, victims in the ancient "reign of terror" that followed hard upon the defeat of Athens in the Peloponnesian war. Only the author of the dialogue, who lies hidden, concealed within it, was for certain spared. The very presence of these forgotten ghosts in that dialogue is an act of remembrance, recollection, resurrection—an act of care, one that inhibits the otherwise-inevitable forgetfulness that is the cloak of tyranny and injustice.

And what is it that these forgotten ghosts discuss? Only a few pages earlier (15, to be exact), toward the end of Book V, they discuss the terrible things that were done by Athenians in that war. Here Socrates gives what is generally regarded as the earliest systematic discussion in all of world history of what we now term *jus in bello*, the laws of war, the proper conduct of war, and the proper restraints that the warrior should observe, by asking the question we still have before us at this conference today: "how shall our warriors act toward the enemy?" [469 c] The ensuing discussion, to be sure, is only about what Greeks have done (and should not have done) to other Greeks. But we recognize it as an acknowledgment of what those who enjoy a moral status or standing owe to others who have an equivalent moral standing—what, in our idiom, human beings owe to other human beings who are not animals or ruthless barbarians.

For example, should we enslave our enemies, Socrates asks, or should we abolish this practice? What about plundering the dead in a battle? "Is it good to take anything but their armor, or is that just an excuse for cowards to avoid facing the enemy by pretending to do something necessary in poking around with the dead?" What about ravaging the land and burning the houses of adversaries? What about treating every man, woman, and child in a neighboring hostile or neutral State as our enemies, and killing or enslaving them after defeating them?

Would not these acts, Socrates asks, seem unreasonable and excessive? "Shall we make it a law for our leaders and warriors not to ravage land or burn houses," he asks? Shouldn't our warriors refuse to engage in such atrocities and instead pursue the quarrel only with sufficient force to resolve the dispute, regarding enemy

---

guardians and choose the ones who all their lives appear eager to do whatever they think will be advantageous to the city and who refuse to do anything harmful. ... It seems to me they must be watched at every stage of life, to make sure they guard this conviction—always to do whatever seems best for the city—*and not forgetfully drop it through beguilement or force*" [412 e]. As a result, Socrates suggests, "[f]rom childhood up ... we must set them tasks that especially deceive and *make one forget such convictions*. We must watch them carefully and *choose the one who remembers and is hard to deceive*, and reject the rest" [413 d, my emphases].

combatants as potential future allies with whom they may one day be reconciled, and so refuse arbitrarily to burn their land, raze their houses, or to punish all of them indiscriminately with death or slavery? Wouldn't we want our warriors, Socrates asks, to behave with this kind of disciplined restraint? We would want our warriors not to "forget themselves" [469 c–471 c].

The argument here seems quite clearly to be that those individuals who are prone to this special kind of forgetfulness are precisely those who would be most likely to commit war crimes. We would not want the forgetful ones to be our warriors and leaders, because they might forget themselves, forget who they are, and so engage in all sorts of terrible deeds in war. Socrates refers in passing illustration to Homer's mythic hero, Achilles, who, in his raging, "forgets himself" and disgraces himself in the wanton and cruel desecration of the noble Hector. Sadly, however, the true historical referents for these discussions were not the mythical heroes of the long-distant past, but the Athenians themselves. In marked contrast to the advice emanating from the ghosts of their victims around the dinner table, the Athenians had certainly forgotten themselves, and had done all of the terrible things mentioned to one another, repeatedly: they had looted the dead, razed houses, burned neighboring cities, and slaughtered or enslaved their citizens—and, in the end, they had, during Plato's lifetime, turned upon one another, adding fratricide to their list of atrocities in an unjust cause. It seems quite reasonable to believe that, as Plato worked out this dialogue, he had before him the same memories as those of Thucydides, of what actual warriors had actually done, for example, at Melos.

In recounting that terrible and cruel encounter, Thucydides is often portrayed as an advocate of what we have come to call "moral realism." The so-called "Melian dialogues" are virtually required reading in every introductory course in political science, where they are solemnly offered by guileless instructors as proof of the irrelevance of ethics in politics and international relations. Moral realism, or *realpolitik*, is the modern name formally given to the doctrine that the Athenians themselves espouse at the alleged meeting of their emissaries with the elders of Melos, that "ethics" is all about appearances, when in reality, the strong do as they will, and the weak are condemned to seek as good a bargain as they can obtain.[13]

The author of *The Peloponnesian Wars*, however, had a very different lesson in mind. Thucydides was a historian who first patterned historical narrative after Greek tragedy. As the disappointed and exiled Athenian general recounts the events of that lengthy war, the dismal end is already known to all his readers, and is throughout prefigured in the proud beginnings he relates. The tragedy of Athens works itself out relentlessly and remorselessly to its inevitable conclusion. The sin, as in all Greek drama, is *hybris*, arrogant pride, perfectly and poignantly captured in the Athenians' haughty and contemptuous manner of addressing the elders of this neutral city. The lesson is hardly that "ethics does not matter." Quite

---

13   Recall that toward the conclusion of Book I Plato has the rival tutor, Thrasymachus, offer a highly similar account of the "true" relationship of justice to unprincipled power, only to have that doctrine's incoherence and self-contradiction exposed easily by Socrates.

the opposite, the clear moral of this story is what will happen to a people or a nation that loses sight of its moral compass, and forgets its way.

After Melos, who can shed a tear for the ultimate and inevitable fate of the Athenians themselves? They get what they themselves have given, and no worse than they deserve. We find ourselves wondering, as we read Thucydides' account of the relentless siege, persecution, and destruction of those who posed no threat, meant no harm, and had asked only to be left alone: is this what democracy, and the highest humanistic ideals of Greek civilization and culture, have come to?[14] The great democratic experiment forged under Pericles, the shining city on the hill, has been forgotten. The Athenians, in their arrogance and cruelty, have forgotten themselves, and engaged in all manner of terrible excesses in war. Many of Plato's dinner-table philosophers were, in real life, among the last of Athens' victims, as that defeated society crumbled amidst recrimination, suspicion, and vilification following its military defeat.

More than two millennia later, an American Army helicopter pilot, flying a reconnaissance mission low over the treetops in central Vietnam, came across a terrifying sight. He saw his own troops systematically rounding up and executing unarmed and helpless old men, women, and children in a small village below. Chief Warrant Officer Hugh W. Thompson was a shy, humble, plain-spoken and largely uneducated man. He had certainly never read Plato. When he was asked, some 30 years later, however, why he landed his helicopter, pointed his weapon at his own soldiers, and thereby stopped the My Lai massacre, he answered: "Those men down there that day had *forgotten* what we had come here to do."[15] We would not want the forgetful ones to be our warriors, or our leaders. When Major General Anthony Taguba, US Army, was asked to summarize the findings of the commission he headed, investigating the abuse and torture of prisoners at Abu Ghraib, he summarized the problem as a failure of leadership: "Those men and women forgot their mission, forgot their core values, they forgot themselves," he explained.[16]

It is thus not the forgetting of our wallet, or car keys, or even of mathematical formulae or legal cases that is to be avoided. Rather, it is the warrior's or the leader's *forgetting themselves* that is the unacceptable tragedy. We must not, Socrates warns, allow the forgetful ones to be our warriors or our leaders, lest in politics or in battle, they "forget themselves," and engage in all kinds of terrible atrocities. The Athenians "forgot themselves." Such forgetting occurs all the time, and is a

---

14   For this interpretation of Thucydides, which now enjoys wide currency, see the first chapter of Martin L. Cook, *The Moral Warrior* (Albany, NY: State University of New York Press, 2004), Chapter 1.

15   Cf. the case study on Hugh Thompson in Rick Rubel and George Lucas, eds, *Case Studies in Military Ethics* (New York: Pearson Publishers, 2005).

16   *Viva voce*, in discussions following his lecture at the US Naval Academy, during which it was clear that the "forgetting" involved was not confined to a few reserve enlisted personnel, but extended to the highest reaches of command. Cf. "Ethical Leadership, Your Challenge, Your Responsibility," 11th Annual Stutt Lecture (March 22, 2005).

constant danger, in Rwanda, at My Lai or in Abu Ghraib, in Somalia, Bosnia, or Sudan. Those who are forgetful engage in all kinds of terrible behavior, Socrates warns. We would not wish these forgetful ones to be our guardians, our leaders, our warriors.

Warriors, as guardians and protectors of the State, do not *do* these terrible things—they themselves do not massacre, torture, or enslave the innocent. Rather, they themselves exist in order to *prevent* such terrible things from occurring, or *stop* them whenever and wherever encountered. Warriors themselves must always care, and must never become complicit in these ongoing acts of loss and forgetfulness.

In my country, and in the nations represented among the contributors to this volume, military service as a profession is now clearly linked to its high moral purpose in the defense of liberty, the protection of the most basic human rights, enforcing justice, and upholding the rule of law. The high moral purpose of military service is not simply the "defense of the homeland," but in protecting homelands that are themselves morally deserving of such defense. The role of the modern warrior is the never-ending struggle against the abuse of power by tyrants and criminals, as portrayed in the foregoing examples, and the protection of the vulnerable rights and liberties of their prospective victims. Warriors, as distinct from tyrants and criminals, use force reluctantly, and only when necessary, for this sole purpose: to protect the well-being of others, and never simply to harm them.

Warriors, of course, have not always remembered these things. And neither have the nations that select, educate, and deploy them. Remembering is an ongoing act of reminding, recollecting, and caring. Some might think it hypocritical or presumptuous of an American citizen, at present, to utter such sentiments. "Has not your own nation," critics may ask, "forgotten itself, just like Athens did, as you likewise emerged somewhat unintentionally and unexpectedly from the Cold War as the world's sole remaining superpower? Did your nation not 'forget itself' by responding to terrorist attacks with torture, or with unauthorized war, or with domestic legislation (like the 'Patriot Act') abridging the rights of its own citizens at home?"

I am less certain than many critics that all of these charges are entirely true, or completely fair. What I would acknowledge is that, regardless of the arguments and interpretations attached to each of these specific charges, it is wise to confront them as cautionary tales of how easy it is for citizens and elected leaders to forget, and lose their way. As in Athens itself, such forgetting is the ever-present danger of democracy—as Socrates portrays it, "going here and there after transient opinion."

What is genuinely new, different, and to my mind, hopeful, is that we have unquestionably committed in my country to ensuring that our nation's *warriors* will not be so forgetful. Our students and future warriors are strictly counseled to stand by respectfully, and place themselves outside the realm of public political discourse. Theirs is not to participate, take sides, or become partisans in that discourse, but to protect the rights and liberties of those citizens who do. Their role is, as Socrates advocates, "to care about the State more than themselves."

To this end, we now have a system of education not unlike that which Socrates recommended. Our warriors not only reflect upon the irreducible foundations of military leadership in justice and the Good. They also study the dangers of forgetting. From Melos to My Lai, from Achilles to Abu Ghraib, from Syracuse to Somalia, and on to Rwanda, Bosnia, and Sudan: they study warrior memory, and the dangers of forgetting. They are encouraged to reflect, through these case studies, upon the noble things expected of warriors (in contrast to murderers, tyrants, and terrorists), as well as upon the terrible things that otherwise ordinary, decent people may allow themselves to do, when they forget who they are.[17]

They remember that warriors abide by a code that is invariant, timeless, and eternal, and they remember the tenets of that code, the "Warrior's Honor": to use force reluctantly, and as a last resort, and only insofar as is necessary to attain their lawful and just ends; to respect the immunity of non-combatants, even when their enemies forget this, and to remember that they themselves must never become like their enemies in this respect.[18] Most of all, they are encouraged to remember that no abstract cause or principle is more important than those citizens who are its alleged beneficiaries. Thus no cause or principle is ever sufficient to justify instrumentalizing its likely beneficiaries for the sake of its attainment. Warriors do not break the law in order to uphold it, nor violate basic rights in order to defend them.

Warriors must never forget these things. In remembrance of these things lies the warrior's honor and moral strength, the trust of their nation, and the well-being of the world's nations and peoples whom they have sworn to serve and protect. And if we, too, continue to listen (as Socrates advises):

> [Such lessons] may preserve us, and we shall cross the River of Lethe without defiling our souls. And if we believe what I say ... we shall ever hold to the upward path, and practice justice with knowledge in all that we do ... and when, like victorious athletes collecting their spoils, we have won the prize for justice, both here and in the thousand-year journey we have gone through, we shall fare well. [Book X, conclusion]

---

17 One of the cases featured early on in the development of my institution's character education program was the compelling book by Christopher Browning, *Ordinary Men: Reserve Police Battalion 101 and the "Final Solution" in Poland* (New York: HarperCollins, 1993).

18 This phrase is taken from the title of a book by Michael Ignatieff, *The Warrior's Honour: Ethnic War and the Modern Conscience* (Toronto, CA: Penguin, 1998); these specific tenets are outlined by him at a lecture at the Naval Academy on "virtual war" in the aftermath of the attack on the USS Cole (March, 2002). The broader concept of a "code of the warrior" is hauntingly summarized in a remarkable book of that title by Shannon E. French, *The Code of the Warrior: Exploring Warrior Values Past and Present* (Lanham, MD: Rowman and Littlefield, 2003).

PART IV
PERCEPTIONS AND
REPRESENTATIONS
OF WARFARE

Land of Ghosts?
Memories of War in the Balkans

Patrick Finney

In September 1990, sitting in his Sarajevo apartment quaffing plum brandy, the future leader of the Bosnian Serbs Radovan Karadžić speculated with dark foreboding about the escalating tension in Yugoslavia. Addressing a Western journalist, he depicted a people still haunted by the legacy of the murderous oppression they had experienced at the hands of the collaborationist Croatian Ustaša in the Second World War. 'Serbs here are ready for war. If someone forces them to live as a national minority, they are ready for war. This nation remembers well the genocide. The memory of those events is still a living memory, a terrible living memory. The terror has survived fifty years.'[1] There could be no more pellucid illustration of how participants in the conflicts in former Yugoslavia ubiquitously and insistently framed them with reference to historical rivalries, injustices and trauma. Numerous external commentators accepted the claims of nationalist demagogues at face value and consequently represented these wars as historically determined, almost natural phenomena in a region inhabited by exotic primitives in thrall to primordial hatreds and a cyclical history of vicious blood-letting.[2] Such caricatural views did not find much favour in scholarly work, which instead devoted considerable effort not only to unravelling the 'Balkanist' Western prejudices that underpinned them but also to elaborating more sophisticated interpretations of the origins and nature of the Yugoslav wars.[3] While rejecting determinism, and often struggling to gauge its precise significance as a variable, these alternative explanations nonetheless generally accepted that 'memory mattered and exercised

---

1   Chuck Sudetic, *Blood and Vengeance: One Family's Story of the War in Bosnia* (New York: W.W. Norton, 1998), pp. 83–4.

2   Most notoriously, Robert D. Kaplan, *Balkan Ghosts: A Journey through History* (New York: St Martin's Press, 1993).

3   For a summary, see Jasna Dragović-Soso, 'Why Did Yugoslavia Disintegrate? An Overview of Contending Explanations', in Lenard J. Cohen and Jasna Dragović-Soso, eds, *State Collapse in South-Eastern Europe: New Perspectives on Yugoslavia's Disintegration* (West Lafayette, IN: Purdue University Press, 2007), pp. 1–39.

power' in former Yugoslavia.[4] From this point of departure, the following essay offers a necessarily schematic discussion of some of the interconnections between memory, identity and war in the modern Balkans.[5]

The study of collective memory is a vibrant interdisciplinary field, and the memory of the dislocating experience of war lies at its very heart.[6] A ceaselessly proliferating scholarship illuminates how memories of the Holocaust, two world wars and numerous 'lesser' conflicts have been negotiated through subsequent decades by governments, societies, sectional interest groups and individuals, and the intersection of that process with other political and cultural discourses. The intimate interconnection between war memory and national identity has emerged as a pre-eminent theme here. Modern warfare strains loyalties and brings issues of belonging into exquisite relief, not least when nation states face the existential danger of 'the threat of extinction, a threat that resonates long past the cessation of hostilities'.[7] Post-war, political leaders and other agents with cultural authority accommodate the sacrifices made, hardships endured and even crimes committed within positive narratives of the national past, articulated through diverse media, and thus rationalise, justify and domesticate them. In victory or defeat, overtly or surreptitiously, such public collective remembering helps societies overcome wartime traumas and, simultaneously, reconstitutes the political and national community.[8] Cultural historians have documented the nuances of these developments in myriad national cases, and military and international historians have lately begun to recognise the potential pertinence of this work. Given their distinctive sub-disciplinary concerns, their specific interest is usually in how elite

---

4   Quote from Jan-Werner Müller, 'Introduction: The Power of Memory, the Memory of Power and the Power over Memory', in Jan-Werner Müller, ed., *Memory and Power in Post-War Europe: Studies in the Presence of the Past* (Cambridge: Cambridge University Press, 2002), p. 2.

5   Treating 'the Balkans' as a coherent unified subject here is perhaps a somewhat 'Balkanist' move in so far as it elides significant differences in political culture, historical experience and collective mentality amongst the various countries of the region, but constraints of space dictate a somewhat generalised treatment.

6   A whole essay could be taken up with a definition of 'collective memory'. I use the term very broadly here to denote narratives, symbols and images embodied in a wide variety of cultural forms that circulate within a collectivity and form a social frame of reference. This frame endows the collectivity with cohesion and helps its members to orientate themselves for action in the world. Official efforts to exert control over its content can be potent, but collective memory is always processual, unstable, contested and, perhaps somewhat ironically, by no means unified. It is also quintessentially performative: 'In truth … there is no such thing as memory; there is only the activity of remembering' (Jeffrey K. Olick, *In the House of the Hangman: The Agonies of German Defeat, 1943–1949* (Chicago: University of Chicago Press, 2005), p. 20).

7   Quote from Wolfgang Schivelbusch, *The Culture of Defeat: On National Trauma, Mourning, and Recovery*, trans. by Jefferson Chase (London: Granta, 2003), p. 5.

8   See, for example, Richard Ned Lebow, Wulf Kansteiner and Claudio Fogu, eds, *The Politics of Memory in Postwar Europe* (Durham, NC: Duke University Press, 2006).

and popular understandings of the past and of the self condition perceptions, delimit policy options and shape responses in subsequent crises and conflicts.[9]

The formation of nation states in the Balkans in the nineteenth and early twentieth centuries was accompanied by the development of nationalist ideologies in which warfare figured prominently.[10] Mythological memories of past conflicts – especially against the Ottoman Turks – and heroic ancestors were among the key cultural resources deployed by elites attempting to create cohesive communities in which loyalty to the nation was the prime marker of identity. The Serbian rediscovery of the epic 1389 battle of Kosovo is most notorious here, but one could equally adduce the Romanian instrumentalisation of the sixteenth-century warrior prince Mihai Viteazul ('Michael the Brave').[11] These ideologies served to mobilise populations behind irredentist claims; and subsequent military campaigns to extend and secure the putative patrimony generated fresh antagonisms, unsettled scores and national martyrs. For example, the posthumous veneration of Pavlos Melas, a Greek patriot killed in Macedonia in 1904, inspired countless other Greeks to join the armed struggle with Bulgaria and the Ottomans for control of that region.[12] It is important to recognise that such martial myths were far from untypical in the age of romantic nationalism: 'Across Europe – from Ireland to Poland – poetic visionaries dreamed of resurrection, sacrifice and blood spilled for the sake of the nation's future.' Moreover, 'the emergence of Balkan epics of bloodshed and national unity' was the product of the exigencies of nation-building in a specific set of political, social and economic circumstances rather than a genetic predisposition towards violent feuding.[13] Yet this said, it is hard to deny that contingencies in the Balkans did favour 'a particularly intensive reference to wars in the collective historical consciousness': 'the fact that almost all Balkan nation-states were the immediate product of wars' meant that 'the tradition of myth-building and the glorification of military violence' became 'a particularly attractive instrument for the strategy of nation-building'.[14]

---

9   Robert M. Citino, 'Military Histories Old and New: A Reintroduction', *American Historical Review*, 112/4 (2007): 1,070–90; Robert D. Schulzinger, 'Memory and Understanding U.S. Foreign Relations', in Michael J. Hogan and Thomas G. Paterson, eds, *Explaining the History of American Foreign Relations*, 2nd edn (Cambridge: Cambridge University Press, 2004), pp. 336–52.

10   Victor Roudometof, *Nationalism, Globalization, and Orthodoxy: The Social Origins of Ethnic Conflict in the Balkans* (Westport, CT: Greenwood Press, 2001).

11   Florian Bieber, 'Nationalist Mobilization and Stories of Serb Suffering: The Kosovo Myth from 600th Anniversary to the Present', *Rethinking History*, 6/1 (2002): 95–9; Lucian Boia, *History and Myth in Romanian Consciousness* (Budapest: Central European University Press, 2001), pp. 39–42.

12   Anastasia Karakasidou, 'Affections of a Greek Hero: Pavlos Melas and Heroic Representations in Greece', in Maria Todorova, ed., *Balkan Identities: Nation and Memory* (London: Hurst, 2004), pp. 197–232.

13   Mark Mazower, *The Balkans* (London: Weidenfeld & Nicolson, 2000), p. 133.

14   Wolfgang Hoepken, 'War, Memory, and Education in a Fragmented Society: The Case of Yugoslavia', *East European Politics and Societies*, 13/1 (1999): 191–2.

With the demise of the Ottoman and Habsburg empires, the post-First World War peace settlements established a territorial configuration of nation states in the Balkans that endured in broad terms until the last decade of the twentieth century. The intensity of nation-building efforts scarcely abated, however, as modernising reformers grappled with the challenge of integrating new territories and diverse populations into expanded states. Simultaneously, old international rivalries persisted, in some instances sharpened by the revisionist aspirations of those vanquished in the First World War. Profound economic problems, struggles to stabilise constitutional forms and the machinations of the great powers in the region also contributed to a pervasive sense of insecurity. In these circumstances, it is perfectly explicable that war memory still played an important role as 'a tool for national identity management'. State-controlled education, for example, continued to 'show the legitimacy of war to fulfil national interests and to present wars as examples from the past of how to behave and how to defend those national interests'.[15]

The memorialisation of the First World War was also closely bound up with such integrative projects. Thus, in Romania, the construction of over 3,500 statues and commemorative sites and the institution of Heroes' Day (on the Orthodox holiday of the Ascension) were important unifying and homogenising gestures.[16] In the very different context of Yugoslavia, on the other hand, memorialisation did little to overcome fissures in the body politic. Commemoration here focused overwhelmingly on ceremonies and cemeteries for Serbia's military dead: 'Croat and Slovene losses on the defeated Habsburg side were left unrecognized', fostering further resentment at Serbian domination of the new state.[17] Even if liberal reformers tended to be the most ardent centralisers in the interwar years, the emergence of various extreme nationalist movements as the 1930s wore on also ensured continued visibility for martial tropes. So when the Greek dictator Ioannis Metaxas reached back into the classical past, for symbolic antecedents for his Fourth of August Regime, he turned not to decadent and democratic Athens but to militaristic and autocratic Sparta.[18]

While acknowledging the prevalence of these violent memories, it remains important once more to contextualise them. The historical imaginaries of Balkan nations were not solely comprised of recollections of internecine conflicts; artistic and scientific achievements demonstrating civilisational superiority were also routinely lauded. Nor were national identities unitary: this was an age of intense ideological contestation and very different visions of the national essence were

---

15   Ibid., 193.
16   Maria Bucur, 'Edifices of the Past: War Memorials and Heroes in Twentieth-Century Romania', in Todorova, ed., *Balkan Identities*, pp. 163–71.
17   John R. Lampe, *Balkans into Southeastern Europe: A Century of War and Transition* (Basingstoke: Palgrave Macmillan, 2006), p. 100.
18   Philip Carabott, 'Monumental Visions: The Past in Metaxas' Weltanschauung', in Keith S. Brown and Yannis Hamilakis, eds, *The Usable Past: Greek Metahistories* (Lanham, MD: Lexington, 2003), pp. 29–31.

offered by agrarian radicals, communists, liberals and the authoritarian right. Such ideological commitments could also entail transnational affiliations which cut across the primacy of the nation, even if – as the example of Balkan communism's plans for radical territorial revision in the age of the Comintern demonstrates – these were not necessarily conducive to international harmony.[19] By the same token, elite endeavours to instrumentalise war memory in the service of identity construction were often resisted: witness the diverse critical responses of intellectuals and the wider populace to official Bulgarian attempts to promote a 'supercharged militaristic patriotism' through representation of the experience of the First World War.[20] It was also certainly not the case that Balkan states were simply helpless captives of the legacy of a violent past. Although Albanian nationalism had its own inspirational 'immortal hero' in the shape of the fifteenth-century warrior Skenderbeg, weakness and underdevelopment in the interwar years dictated concentration on survival and the eschewing of any efforts at mass patriotic agitation or the pursuit of irredentism.[21] Greece and Turkey had been involved in the bitterest of armed conflicts between 1919 and 1923, but even this very recent antagonism with centuries-old resonances proved susceptible to amelioration (if not, admittedly, outright resolution) through prudent statecraft, with the signature of the reconciliatory 1930 Ankara accords.[22] Similarly, there were significant moves towards regional anti-revisionist cooperation in the 1930s as the rising Axis menace began to impinge upon the region.[23] Moreover, it should not be forgotten that the 'Balkan states wanted war neither in 1914 nor in 1939'; in both cases, it was imposed from outside.[24]

The Second World War plunged the Balkans into a maelstrom of violence. A complex three-way struggle between Axis occupation forces, collaborationist regimes and resistance movements was overlaid and intertwined with a class-based civil war waged by communists against traditional elites and inter-ethnic blood-letting, in which old antagonisms took on unprecedentedly ferocious, even genocidal, forms. Historical rationalisations and symbolism loomed large. The collaborationist Ustaša regime, for example, exploited years of pent-up resentment

---

19 For a classic case study in these complexities, see Evangelos Kofos, *Nationalism and Communism in Macedonia* (Thessaloniki, 1964), pp. 57–94.

20 Snezhana Dimitrova, '"My War is not Your War": The Bulgarian Debate on the Great War', *Rethinking History*, 6/1 (2002): 15–34; quote at 28.

21 Quote from Kristo Frasheri, *The History of Albania (A Brief Survey)* (Tirana, 1964), p. 86; Robert C. Austin, 'Greater Albania: The Albanian State and the Question of Kosovo, 1912–2001', in John R. Lampe and Mark Mazower, eds, *Ideologies and National Identities: The Case of Twentieth-Century Southeastern Europe* (Budapest: Central European University Press, 2004), pp. 237–42.

22 Bruce Clark, *Twice a Stranger: How Mass Expulsion Forged Modern Greece and Turkey* (London: Granta, 2007), pp. 201–22.

23 Tom Gallagher, *Outcast Europe: The Balkans, 1789–1989* (London: Routledge, 2001), pp. 103–26.

24 Misha Glenny, *The Balkans, 1804–1999: Nationalism, War and the Great Powers* (London: Granta, 2000), p. 457.

at Serbian supremacy in the first Yugoslavia, symbolised by the martyr's death of nationalist leader Stjepan Radić at the hands of a Serb politician in 1928, and regarded itself as the culmination of the long Croatian struggle for independent statehood against a succession of domineering others.[25] The Serbian royalist and nationalist movement led by Draža Mihailović – which occupied a somewhat ambiguous position in the matrix of collaboration and resistance – conversely adopted the sobriquet 'Četniks', 'the traditional name of rural Serb bands resisting Ottoman forces'.[26] To be sure, power political motives mingled with historical grievances. The harshness of the Bulgarian occupation regime in Greek Macedonia and Thrace owed something to a sense of exultation at the final acquisition (or 'recovery') of territories that had lain at the core of Bulgarian national aspirations since the abortive treaty of San Stefano in 1878.[27] Determination to retain these long-coveted lands underpinned Bulgaria's brutal policy of colonisation and the extirpation of Greek culture: 'for some Balkan states ... this war was not just about military victory but about permanent demographic engineering in new territories'.[28]

If the cruel savagery of the war in the Balkans is undeniable, however, it is important not to view it as 'the spontaneous eruption of primeval hatreds'.[29] Rather it was Nazi policy deliberately to exploit latent animosities in the region – so in Yugoslavia, '[a]ll claims were accepted, all separatisms encouraged, all tensions exacerbated' – while also infusing them with a novel biological racism, in the context of the desperate straits of total war in which previous civilised norms became utterly moot.[30] Some elements of the conflict are, moreover, hardly explicable through the frame of memory. The struggle waged by Tito's communist partisans, for example, was future-oriented, in so far as its main goal was the establishment of a multi-ethnic socialist Yugoslavia (though, of course, all communists viewed the world through the historical prism of class struggle). Yet, throughout the region, whatever the fine detail of motivation, the sanguinary experience of this war generated a fresh catalogue of historical traumas, unsettled scores and poisonous legacies which had to be negotiated during post-war reconstruction and beyond, and which would remain available for exploitation with baleful consequences in the future.

As across the rest of Europe, the development of collective memories of the Second World War in the Balkans was heavily conditioned by post-war political

---

25 Sabrina P. Ramet, 'The NDH – An Introduction', *Totalitarian Movements and Political Religions*, 7/4 (2006): 399–408.

26 Lampe, *Balkans into Southeastern Europe*, p. 160.

27 On the occupation and its legacy, see Xanthippi Kotzageorgi-Zymari and Tassos Hadjianastassiou, 'Memories of the Bulgarian Occupation of Eastern Macedonia: Three Generations', in Mark Mazower, ed., *After the War Was Over: Reconstructing the Family, Nation, and State in Greece, 1943–1960* (Princeton, NJ: Princeton University Press, 2000), pp. 273–92. Bulgaria had previously seen its expansionist ambitions thwarted in the 1912–1913 Balkan Wars and the First World War.

28 Mazower, *The Balkans*, p. 111.

29 Ibid., p. 129.

30 Quote from Stevan K. Pavlowitch, *A History of the Balkans, 1804–1945* (London: Longman, 1999), p. 311.

imperatives, especially those generated by the nascent Cold War. Given the slightly problematic democratic credentials of the newly-established communist regimes, the insistent construal of the war in ideological terms as a virtuous anti-fascist struggle was for them a crucial mechanism of legitimation. That said, as Balkan states over time developed their own variants of 'national communism', collective memory increasingly hybridised familiar nationalist and novel communist tropes. Bulgaria and Romania faced a particular dilemma here: as allies of Nazi Germany, they had gone to war in large part to secure traditional national territorial aspirations which the communist successor governments did not necessarily repudiate; yet, simultaneously, the war 'had to be remembered as the political adventure of a "native fascist bourgeoisie", and each country's defeat in the war had to be praised as the birth of a new political order'.[31] In Bulgaria, official remembrance policies prior to the later 1960s focused on 'the memory of the Soviet soldiers, partisans and antifascists' and the 'socialist victory' after the Second World War to the virtual exclusion of other actors and epochs. Subsequently, however, policy shifted and the traditional heroes of the national liberation struggle from the medieval period onwards began to be rediscovered and celebrated anew, as the past was reinterpreted 'as coherent and contiguous with the socialist framework'. Aligning nineteenth-century freedom fighters with partisan resisters, the national past was ideologised just as the ideology's vision was nationalised.[32]

The specificities of this process were somewhat different in Romania. Initial memorialisation policy focused on lauding the achievements of the victorious Red Army and of those Romanian soldiers who had fought alongside them after the country's volte-face in August 1944. The fate of Romanian soldiers who had fallen previously, fighting for the Axis, was entirely marginalised. (Jewish victims of the Holocaust on Romanian soil were also largely ignored, owing to murky issues of complicity, lingering anti-Semitism and the fact that ethnic difference was elided within the communist anti-fascist narrative.[33]) Once Romanian communism began to take an increasingly independent turn after the withdrawal of the Red Army in 1958, a rapprochement with more traditional nationalist rhetoric proved useful here too, but with a pointedly anti-Russian purpose. The 'vigorous revival of national ideology' proceeded apace under Nicolae Ceauşescu, who co-opted Romania's medieval national heroes such as Michael the Brave as the direct antecedents of the Romanian communist party in an ongoing struggle for independence: 'in the past Romanians had had to fight against the Ottomans; under Ceauşescu they

---

31 Hoepken, 'War, Memory, and Education', 195.

32 Nikolai Voukov, 'Representing the Nation's Past: National History Monuments in Socialist and Post-Socialist Bulgaria', unpublished paper, <http://www.hks.harvard.edu/kokkalis/GSW7/Nikolai%20Voukov%20_paper_.pdf> [accessed 27 June 2008]; quotes at pp. 4–6. That Russia had long been a patron of Bulgarian national aspirations, just as Bulgarian communism remained solidly Russophile, assisted with the construction of this narrative. The Russo-Turkish War of 1877–1878 was also a partial exception to the general initial neglect of pre-1940s history.

33 Bucur, 'Edifices of the Past', pp. 171–7.

had to oppose the Soviets'.[34] This nationalist turn also had an anti-Hungarian twist, and the regime began to invest considerable resources in documenting and commemorating atrocities purportedly committed by occupying Hungarian forces in northern Transylvania between 1940 and 1944 which had previously been rendered taboo by the dictates of socialist fraternity.[35]

The remembering of diverse conflicts – and its inevitable concomitant of strategic forgetting – also continued to be an integral part of the fabric of national identity in Greece. Though Greece remained outside the Soviet bloc, Cold War exigencies were still important because of the problematic legacy of the civil war in which royalists vanquished communists between 1946 and 1949. The communists had dominated the resistance to the Axis in the Second World War, but their subsequent defeat and the establishment of a profoundly conservative, post-war political order meant that their cause was retrospectively discredited, stigmatised as unpatriotic: resistance fighters were imprisoned, collaborators and war criminals were rehabilitated and extensive commemoration was shunned.[36] 'Through the 1950s, the Greek state remained faithful to a Cold War vision of the war, unwilling either to praise the resistance or to condemn collaborators. Silence and repression were the main elements of its policy.' Public pressure for a revision of official attitudes escalated through the 1960s, as former resisters queried whether an establishment subservient to the United States was entitled to claim the patriotic high ground, but then, under the 'Colonels', persecution of the left only intensified. The fall of the junta in 1974, however, demonstrated the bankruptcy of this agenda and 'opened the floodgates' for a more widespread engagement with the wartime past. Official recognition of the resistance as a national liberation struggle was duly accorded in 1982. That said, this reconciliatory nationalist vision was, perhaps perforce, somewhat anodyne and depoliticising, as it 'smoothed away the memories of social division and skated over equally dark areas of ethnic complexity'.[37]

---

34 Dragoş Petrescu, 'Communist Legacies in the "New Europe": History, Ethnicity, and the Creation of a "Socialist" Nation in Romania, 1945–1989', in Konrad H. Jarausch and Thomas Lindenberger, eds, *Conflicted Memories: Europeanizing Contemporary Histories* (New York: Berghahn, 2007), pp. 37–54; quotes at pp. 39, 43.

35 Maria Bucur, 'Treznea: Trauma, Nationalism and the Memory of World War II in Romania', *Rethinking History*, 6/1 (2002): 35–55.

36 28 October – the anniversary of Metaxas' famous 'no' to Mussolini in 1940 – was declared a national holiday in 1944 and was subsequently the main occasion for public Second World War remembrance. The goal of reinforcing conservative patriotic sentiment through commemoration was facilitated by thus focusing on the beginning of the war, highlighting a moment of defiant resistance to a foreign would-be occupying power and sidelining the schisms of the subsequent occupation. See Anastasia Karakasidou, 'Protocol and Pageantry: Celebrating the Nation in Northern Greece', in Mazower, ed., *After the War Was Over*, pp. 221–46.

37 Mark Mazower, 'The Cold War and the Appropriation of Memory: Greece after Liberation', in István Deák, Jan T. Gross and Tony Judt, eds, *The Politics of Retribution in Europe: World War II and its Aftermath* (Princeton, NJ: Princeton University Press, 2000), pp. 212–32; quotes at pp. 221, 229; David Close, 'The Road to Reconciliation? The Greek

Different layers of war memory were also constantly interlaced in the Greek case. The claim that modern Hellenes were the rightful heirs of the legacy of ancient Greece was a foundational element in nationalist discourse. Consequently, during the Cold War, the right persistently mobilised classical antiquity as a resource in its efforts to re-educate dissidents and to reinstate them into the virtuous national community.[38] In at least one instance, in the late 1960s, this strategy was also deployed in connection with the commemoration of the Second World War. The junta sponsored the erection of a war memorial in the city of Komotini in Thrace, which deployed a monumental classical aesthetic and was festooned with images of Mycenaean armaments, including spears, shields and a huge bronze sword. This 'grandiose and severe structure' gestured towards 'monumental symmetry, timeless dignity and ethical austerity', and its abstract form enabled it to skirt the political contestation that still surrounded the war. It became the focus for official commemorations of all Greece's past wars, thus vocalising a nationalist discourse that 'exploited all references to past glory and accentuated Greek eminence at all points in history'. 'The Sword', as it was dubbed, was therefore intended both to buttress the regime's legitimacy, by locating it within a heroic narrative, and to inculcate a martial nationalism in the public.[39] Its failure to achieve these ends demonstrates the general point that the efficacy of symbolic politics is not guaranteed: the puissance of any given intervention, however carefully crafted, will be heavily dependent upon the wider field of political and social forces within which it is located.

The most sustained official efforts to manage collective memory of the Second World War occurred in Yugoslavia, and these have been deemed especially portentous because of the link between nationalist myths and the outbreak of further violence in the 1990s. The conflict was extraordinarily visible in socialist Yugoslav culture: 'almost all symbolic forms of historical memory, such as memorials or official holidays, were dedicated to the memory of the war'. Moreover, the propagation of an authorised version of the war was absolutely central in manufacturing legitimacy for the communist regime and attempting to instil a common sense of identity amongst disparate peoples, arguably even more important than was the comparable myth of the Great Patriotic War in the Soviet Union. 'It was hoped that remembering the common fight and suffering during the war would help to create consensus in a society that was burdened not only by extreme ethnic, cultural, and

Civil War and the Politics of Memory in the 1980s', in Philip Carabott and Thanasis D. Sfikas, eds, *The Greek Civil War: Essays on a Conflict of Exceptionalism and Silences* (Aldershot: Ashgate, 2004), pp. 257–78.

38 See, for example, Yannis Hamilakis, '"The Other Parthenon": Antiquity and National Memory at Makronisos', *Journal of Modern Greek Studies*, 20/2 (2002): 307–38.

39 Iro Katsaridou and Anastasia Konogiorgi, 'Commemorating World War II in Northern Greece: Controversy and Reconsideration', *Forum for Modern Language Studies*, 44/2 (2008): 140–6; quotes at 143–4.

religious fragmentation but also by the unfavorable experiences of living together in one state.'[40]

The master narrative of the war reduced its ambiguities and complexities to a Manichaean struggle between Tito's righteous communist partisans and all other participants, construed as the forces of fascist reaction and counter-revolution. The 'political, military, and moral superiority' of the multi-ethnic partisans, together with their overwhelming popularity across the constituent parts of Yugoslavia, was insistently affirmed, and any suggestion that they had committed excesses or even mistakes was prohibited. The 'war of national liberation' and class conflict templates deployed here meant sidelining the ethnic dimensions of the war entirely. Ethnic violence and war crimes were blamed on the bourgeoisie on all sides, but no nation was deemed especially guilty and, in any case, such events were marginal to the central emplotment. The incessant reinscription of this rendering in education, academic historiography and public memorialising obviously supported both the authority of the communist party and the official ideology of 'brotherhood and unity' between nations. That said, this myth-making was also fraught with tensions. In suppressing the complexities of the war and perpetuating certain outright falsehoods, it established a dissonance between private memory and official mantras and left significant blank spots which would make it vulnerable to assault if communism's 'monopoly on discourse and interpretation' was weakened.[41]

After Tito's death in 1980, mounting challenges to the regime's sanctioned readings did indeed accompany the fragmentation of political, economic and social order and the waning of communist legitimacy.[42] Up to a point, the logic here was simply destructive, as historians, novelists and film-makers broached taboos and questioned long-standing shibboleths, tarnishing the pristine past upon which communism had grounded itself. Vladimir Dedijer's 1981 biography of Tito was symptomatic here, as it presented him as a 'lecher and schemer, dissembler and master of craftiness, bon vivant and tyrant', and also revealed details of secret negotiations between the partisans and the Nazis in 1943 which whiffed of collaboration.[43] Dedijer's 'disclosures made it impossible to defend the infallibility both of the revolution and its leader and gave rise to a full-scale reinterpretation of the history of the Yugoslav communist movement in the interwar and wartime years'.[44]

In relation to the war, this reappraisal highlighted the repressive brutality of Tito towards his opponents and posed unwonted questions about the ethnic

---

40   Hoepken, 'War, Memory, and Education', 196–7.

41   Ibid., 197–202; quotes at 197, 202.

42   Dejan Djokić, 'The Second World War II: Discourses of Reconciliation in Serbia and Croatia in the Late 1980s and Early 1990s', *Journal of Southern Europe and the Balkans*, 4/2 (2002): 127–39. This conjuncture was hardly unique to Yugoslavia, of course: cf. Robert W. Davies, *Soviet History in the Gorbachev Revolution* (London: Macmillan, 1989).

43   Ivo Banac, 'Historiography of the Countries of Eastern Europe: Yugoslavia', *American Historical Review*, 97/4 (1992): 1,093.

44   Jasna Dragović-Soso, *'Saviours of the Nation': Serbia's Intellectual Opposition and the Revival of Nationalism* (London: Hurst, 2002), p. 78.

aspects of the conflict. Serbian historians, for example, rehabilitated the Četniks as a genuine resistance force that had been the victim of communist machinations to acquire pre-eminence in the anti-fascist struggle (though a simultaneous, somewhat contradictory, claim held that Serbs had predominated in the partisan movement).[45] This rediscovery of the suppressed ethnic 'realities' of the war illustrated how the critique of official memory gradually shaded into a project of constructing alternative visions of the past that could ground nationalist identities and polities in the present.

> *Just as a common memory of the war had played a central role in legitimizing the common Yugoslav state, the separate and diverging memories were now used to support the policy of the country's dissolution. The memory of the last war thus contributed to preparing people for the new war that was to come.*[46]

Memory did not, of course, cause the break-up of Yugoslavia: this was a complex political process in which numerous and diverse long and short-term factors were operative, the relative significance of which scholars still fiercely debate.[47] Yet Tito's problematic historical engineering in the name of integration facilitated the subsequent utilisation of memory in disintegrative nationalist mobilisation. The restriction of the parameters of discussion ensured that a diverse multi-ethnic society was never able to debate maturely how to handle the complex and divisive legacy from the past or to elaborate a truly unifying social memory. Simultaneously, the venerative character of war memory and its enshrinement as an authoritative lexicon for the articulation of political aspirations helped to naturalise violence and make further wars imaginable.[48]

In Serbia, politicians and intellectuals collaborated in scripting a national history of suffering, injustice and victimisation that proved particularly potent and destructive. At its heart lay a revivified Kosovo myth, an epic tale of past glory and traumatic defeat which also offered the consolation of divine election and promise

---

45 Ibid., pp. 100–103; Marko Attila Hoare, 'Whose is the Partisan Movement? Serbs, Croats and the Legacy of a Shared Resistance', *Journal of Slavic Military Studies*, 15/4 (2002): 32–3.

46 Hoepken, 'War, Memory, and Education', 207.

47 Dragović-Soso, 'Why Did Yugoslavia Disintegrate?' identifies five main approaches in the literature. Memory is generally rendered epiphenomenal in those focusing on the flawed nature of Yugoslavism as an ideology, the structural weakness of socialist Yugoslavia or the malign influence of external (that is, Western) powers. It figures more prominently in interpretations premised upon 'ancient hatreds' and in those that seek to trace how the decisions and actions of political and intellectual agents transformed a systemic crisis into a violent dissolution. See, further, Cohen and Dragović-Soso, eds, *State Collapse in South-Eastern Europe* and Sabrina P. Ramet, *Thinking about Yugoslavia: Scholarly Debates about the Yugoslav Breakup and the Wars in Bosnia and Kosovo* (Cambridge: Cambridge University Press, 2005).

48 Hoepken, 'War, Memory, and Education', 203–7.

of vengeful, resurrected grandeur.[49] The utility of such a myth for Slobodan Milošević's efforts first to enhance Serbian authority within Yugoslavia and then to carve out an expanded 'Greater Serbia' quickly became apparent. Complementing this core fable was a revisionist discourse on the history of Yugoslavia which argued that Serbs had been the victims of consistent discrimination: constitutional and administrative arrangements had denied the nation its historic borders and institutionalised its economic exploitation, while Serbs living in Kosovo, Croatia and Bosnia had been systematically persecuted.[50] The invocation of the trope of genocide transmuted fears of oppression into hysteria about possible physical annihilation. Here, the rewriting of the Second World War era was absolutely central. The wholesale slaughter of Serbs by the Croatian Ustaša, which had been elided in the official communist narrative, became the focus of intense publicity. Vastly inflated estimates of the numbers of Serbian victims were put into circulation and the Ustaša camp at Jasenovac, the Golgotha of the putative Serbian 'holocaust', became the supreme symbol of a continuous history of victimhood.[51]

It is important to note that the Milošević regime 'had other weapons in its ideological armoury' as well and that its deployment of nationalist rhetoric was neither unremitting nor unnuanced.[52] (Equally, despite his undoubted responsibility, it is an oversimplification to present Milošević as the sole active agent in Yugoslav disintegration, or his policy as consistently embodying a predetermined strategy to create an expanded Serbian state.[53]) Yet, towards the end of the 1980s, a palpable nationalist frenzy nonetheless engulfed Serbian political and popular culture, and a whole gamut of symbolic references to the Second World War contributed significantly to it.[54] The excavation of the mass graves of victims of Ustaša atrocities and the reburial of the exhumed corpses with elaborate theatrical ceremony was the most startlingly literal illustration of this.[55] Extensive and lurid media coverage

---

49   For a full discussion, see Branimir Anzulović, *Heavenly Serbia: From Myth to Genocide* (New York and London: New York University Press, 1999).

50   David Bruce MacDonald, *Balkan Holocausts? Serbian and Croatian Victim-Centred Propaganda and the War in Yugoslavia* (Manchester: Manchester University Press, 2002), pp. 63–97, 183–219.

51   Dragović-Soso, *'Saviours of the Nation'*, pp. 100–114. For more detail on Second World War revisionism, see MacDonald, *Balkan Holocausts?* pp. 132–82.

52   Bieber, 'Nationalist Mobilization', 103.

53   Dragović-Soso, 'Why Did Yugoslavia Disintegrate?' in Cohen and Dragović-Soso, eds, *State Collapse in South-Eastern Europe*, pp. 14–18; Eric Gordy, 'Destruction of the Yugoslav Federation: Policy or Confluence of Tactics?' in Cohen and Dragović-Soso, eds, *State Collapse in South-Eastern Europe*, pp. 281–99.

54   On the 'nationalisation' of Serbia, see Nebojša Popov, ed., *The Road to War in Serbia: Trauma and Catharsis* (Budapest: Central European University Press, 2000); cf. the revisionist arguments – stressing, inter alia, oppositional currents – of Janine Natalya Clark, *Serbia in the Shadow of Milošević: The Legacy of Conflict in the Balkans* (London: I.B. Taurus, 2008).

55   Bette Denich, 'Dismembering Yugoslavia: Nationalist Ideologies and the Symbolic Revival of Genocide', *American Ethnologist*, 21/2 (1994): 367–90.

of these reinterments revelled in 'a pornography of victimhood'.[56] Fomenting 'a sense of existential crisis that could be harnessed for a more belligerent and uncompromising policy', the unrelenting promotion of the genocide thematic was especially ominous as the Milošević regime began to ratchet up its professed concern for the fate of Serbian minorities living beyond the bounds of the republic proper.[57] It is sadly not uncommon for pernicious, exclusionary and aggressive nationalist projects thus to be founded upon sentimental rhetorics of self-pity and self-defence. They also typically entail the identification of demonised others, which in this case included not only the Western powers that came to look askance at Serbian expansionism but also, and most importantly, the Croats who constituted its immediate object at the beginning of the wars of succession.

A nationalist upsurge in Croatia paralleled that in Serbia. Even though the Croatian leader Franjo Tuđman is often characterised as a more authentic nationalist than Milošević – the former a true believer, the latter essentially an opportunist – the emergence of Croatian nationalism is nonetheless often emplotted as a reaction to developments in Serbia.[58] There is some truth in this, though a distinctive Croatian historical consciousness of sorts had persisted through the Tito era; moreover, it is generally preferable to conceive of a dynamic interaction between these competing nationalisms in an escalating spiral of distrust. The claims of Serbian nationalists about wartime genocide could not but intimidate the Croats, and their response directly challenged extravagant contentions about total Serbian casualties, and those at Jasenovac in particular, thus tending to minimise rather than maximise Croatian historical guilt. Moreover, Croats also went on the offensive, raising the issue of Četnik and partisan atrocities against Croats in a deliberate strategy of historical offsetting. The massacre of several thousand opponents of the partisans at Bleiburg at the close of the war was the emblematic crime here, symbolising that Croats had also been 'victims of wartime terror' and sustaining their own counter-narrative of historical victimhood.[59]

The broader historical imaginary of Croatian nationalism synthesised several somewhat contradictory elements. On the one hand, Tuđman claimed title to the anti-fascist partisan heritage from the 'national liberation struggle' of 1941–1945, asserting in a mirror image of Serbian pretensions that Croats had been the dominant ethnic group within the movement and continuing to revere Tito, himself, of course, a Croat. This was obviously intended to defuse the allegation that all Croats had been Nazi collaborators, which was potentially damning given broader discursive norms about the 'good war'. On the other hand, the legacy of

---

56 Michael Sells, 'Crosses of Blood: Sacred Space, Religion, and Violence in Bosnia-Hercegovina', *Sociology of Religion*, 64/3 (2003): 313. Sells underlines the religious dimension of the post-Tito nationalist movements.

57 Quote from Dragović-Soso, 'Why Did Yugoslavia Disintegrate?' in Cohen and Dragović-Soso, eds, *State Collapse in South-Eastern Europe*, p. 19.

58 For example, Laura Silber and Allan Little, *The Death of Yugoslavia* (London: Penguin, 1995), pp. 87–97.

59 Hoepken, 'War, Memory, and Education', 212–15; quote at 215.

the 'independent' Ustaša state also had an undeniable utility for the construction of a positive foundation for contemporary Croatia. So, although it was not officially rehabilitated by Tuđman, there was nonetheless a shift to a perniciously ambivalent treatment and 'the insertion of elements of the Ustasha heritage into Croatian public life'. This largely took symbolic form, with the renaming of streets after Ustaša-related figures and the adoption of national emblems that had formerly been tainted by association with that regime.[60] Tuđman declared that the Ustaša was 'not only a quisling organisation and a Fascist crime, but … also an expression of the Croatian nation's historic desire for an independent homeland'. This 'peculiar phraseology' suggested that the regime 'was the malevolent manifestation of a benign impulse'.[61]

The tension within this Croatian project is partly explained by the diverse audiences that Tuđman was attempting to satisfy, from ultranationalists in the Croatian diaspora who provided substantial funds for his movement to Western governments wary of any hint of neo-Nazi revisionism. Yet it also illustrated how, in seeking to accumulate symbolic capital, the Croats mobilised all possible resources, positioning themselves simultaneously as victims of genocide, leaders of the anti-fascist resistance and inheritors of – yet also 'conscientious objectors' from – the Ustaša regime. The finesses entailed here discernibly contributed to the cycle of mutual recrimination and, ultimately, violence. Tuđman relativised Croatian support for the Ustaša, by claiming that where it existed it was in essence self-defensive, driven by fears of Serbian oppression rather than ideological sympathy for fascism. In the febrile atmosphere of the last years of Yugoslavia, any hint of resuscitation of that regime – when combined with concurrent, allegedly discriminatory, legislation against Croatia's Serbian minority – was sufficient to exacerbate Serbian alarm about incipient renewed genocide.[62]

In these and myriad other ways, conflicting memories of war were prominent in the political controversies preceding the onset of armed struggle between Serbia and Croatia in 1991.[63] The same was true of the subsequent conflict in Bosnia between 1992 and 1995. Both Serbian and Croatian nationalists advanced historically grounded claims to Bosnian territory, and 1940s massacres – of Serbs by Croats and Bosnian Muslims, and of Croats and Bosnian Muslims by Četniks – were mobilised as frames for contemporary politics, thus further envenoming inter-communal relations.[64] Equally, the warring parties often labelled themselves

---

60   Hoare, 'Whose is the Partisan Movement?' 35–8; quote at 37.

61   Marcus Tanner, *Croatia: A Nation Forged in War* (New Haven, CT: Yale University Press, 1997), p. 223.

62   MacDonald, *Balkan Holocausts?* pp. 135–8, 177; quote at p. 177. On anti-Serb legislation, see Robert M. Hayden, 'Constitutional Nationalism in the Formerly Yugoslav Republics', *Slavic Review*, 51/4 (1992): 654–73.

63   Other interesting treatments – from an anti-Serbian viewpoint – are contained in Stjepan G. Meštrović, ed., *Genocide after Emotion: The Postemotional Balkan War* (London: Routledge, 1996).

64   For an account of the Bosnian war alive to historical parallels, see Marko Attila Hoare, *The History of Bosnia: From the Middle Ages to the Present Day* (London: Saqi, 2007), pp. 338–402.

or their antagonists with historically resonant appellations such as Četnik, Ustaša and Turk.[65] It has even been suggested that the ritualised form given to Serbian mass rapes of Bosnian Muslim women – a signal crime within an iniquitous war – requires 'a culture-specific explanation ... as a projection that has its origins inside of the powerfully invested narratives of Serb cultural memory', a storehouse that includes 'the humiliating memory of rape by the Turk'.[66]

Once such atrocities began to be committed, of course, they might perpetuate and intensify the momentum of violence regardless of how they were externally represented. Yet, in fact, they were immediately embroiled in the symbolic battle between the participants, as past injustices were rhetorically balanced against present and mastery over naming assumed paramount significance – especially as regards the applicability of the politically and ethically-charged term 'genocide'.[67] The pervasiveness of this figurative mediation indicates the importance of not overstating the raw determining power or unprompted innocence of memory. Just as propaganda and paramilitary violence were deployed to incite hatred, so elites were quite capable of cynically invoking alleged antique grievances and traumas to gain advantage: one exasperated American envoy clearly recognised this when he insisted that the Bosnian Serbs should not obfuscate negotiations with 'a lot of historical bullshit'. Thus Ger Duijzings has argued that while history undoubtedly weighed heavily in Bosnia and conditioned agency, it did not efface personal choice or responsibility.[68]

The issue of what precise work memory was doing here remains deeply contested. The initial, dominant mode of framing these conflicts amongst Western observers attributed them to an uncontrived upsurge of primal bloodlust, and this tended to ascribe very tangible agency to the memory of past conflicts whilst also encouraging a policy of non-intervention on the grounds that such deep-rooted antagonisms were intractable. From the mid-1990s, however, an alternative conceptualisation found favour with the adoption of what Lenard Cohen has dubbed 'the paradise lost/loathsome leaders perspective'. This stressed periods of peaceful coexistence rather than violence in Balkan history and the role of 'self-aggrandizing nationalist leaders who have whipped up ethnic antagonisms in order to suit their political agendas': in this view, hatreds were 'instrumentally constructed or imagined by ambitious and unscrupulous' elites, which diminished their objective significance. This paradigm rendered conflict in the Balkans potentially susceptible to resolution

---

65   Ben Lieberman, 'Nationalist Narratives, Violence between Neighbours and Ethnic Cleansing in Bosnia-Hercegovina: A Case of Cognitive Dissonance?' *Journal of Genocide Research*, 8/3 (2006): 301–7.

66   Lynda E. Boose, 'Crossing the River Drina: Bosnian Rape Camps, Turkish Impalement, and Serb Cultural Memory', *Signs*, 28/1 (2002): 71–96; quotes at 93.

67   Robert M. Hayden, 'Mass Killings and Images of Genocide in Bosnia, 1941–5 and 1992–5', in Dan Stone, ed., *The Historiography of Genocide* (London: Palgrave Macmillan, 2008), pp. 487–516.

68   Ger Duijzings, 'Appendix IV: History and Reminders in East Bosnia', in *Nederlands Instituut voor Oorlogsdocumentatie, Srebrenica: A 'Safe' Area* (Amsterdam, 2003), <http://193.173.80.81/srebrenica/> [accessed 7 July 2008]; quoting Richard Holbrooke.

provided the international community took robust action against renegade leaders, and coincided with the emergence of just such a policy, directed principally against Milošević and the Serbs in the closing stages of the Bosnian war and then in Kosovo in 1999. (The nature of the relationship between the changes in perception and in policy remains moot.)[69]

This involved the substitution of one extreme oversimplification for another; yet the issue of how to strike a balance between the undoubted facts of unplanned, grassroots national mobilisation and elite construction of new forms of national identity, premised upon the manipulation of fears and memories, is intensely problematic. The fact that elite discourses became so prevalent and potent suggests that they must have resonated on some level with certain personal, family or local memories or cumulative resentments that had not formerly enjoyed official sanction.[70] That said, proper scepticism about the alleged liberation or return of repressed traumatic memory and awareness of 'the danger of attributing a straightforward causal role to recollections of past events' are essential.[71]

The issue of Western perceptions is also germane for gauging how far Balkan actors were unique in filtering contemporary affairs through the prisms of remembered conflicts. For it is an irony that the United States, Great Britain and other external powers often appeared to be equally wholly encapsulated by violent memories and historical trauma. The initial acceptance on its own terms of demagogic rhetoric about ancient hatreds and the adoption of a policy of non-intervention were inextricably intertwined with a 'Vietnam syndrome' ('or its 1990s equivalent, Somalia syndrome'): with enmities so entrenched, amongst peoples with proud and brutal martial traditions, intervention would have led to heavy Western casualties in a bloody quagmire.[72] Critics of this stance, rejecting the relativising 'civil war' frame and identifying Serbian aggression as the prime cause of the conflicts, conversely invoked the spectre of Munich: in cravenly standing by and permitting genocidal atrocity, the West was guilty of callous and shameful appeasement.[73] The slaughter at Srebrenica, coupled with the gradual emergence of a new norm of humanitarian intervention, sealed the ascendancy of this latter perspective and equivocation gave way to the 'Nazifying' of the Serbs. This reached its apogee during the Kosovo war in 1999 when Milošević was firmly branded a

---

69 Lenard J. Cohen, *Serpent in the Bosom: The Rise and Fall of Slobodan Milošević*, rev. edn (Boulder, CO: Westview, 2002), pp. 451–64; quotes at p. 454.

70 Dragović-Soso, 'Why Did Yugoslavia Disintegrate?' pp. 20–23.

71 Stef Jansen, 'The Violence of Memories: Local Narratives of the Past after Ethnic Cleansing in Croatia', *Rethinking History*, 6/1 (2002): 77–93; quote at 77. Memory's power is perhaps overstated in Ilana R. Bet-El, 'Unimagined Communities: The Power of Memory and the Conflict in the Former Yugoslavia', in Müller, ed., *Memory and Power in Post-War Europe*, pp. 206–22.

72 James J. Sadkovich, *The U.S. Media and Yugoslavia, 1991–1995* (Westport, CT: Praeger, 1998), pp. 146–8; quote at p. 146.

73 Brendan Simms, *Unfinest Hour: Britain and the Destruction of Bosnia*, rev. edn (London: Penguin, 2002), p. 332 and passim.

new Hitler and his treatment of the Kosovo Albanians a genocidal reprise.[74] Fuelled by the general boom in consciousness of the Second World War as the cycle of 60th anniversary commemorations geared up, and with public debate and political rhetoric replete with references to Hitler, appeasement and the Holocaust, it often seemed as if that conflict was being replayed wholesale in the south-eastern corner of Europe. That said, this rendering did not entirely marginalise other martial analogies, including multiple different readings of the lessons of Vietnam and of 1914 when the Balkans had served as the powder-keg of Europe.[75]

Following the end of outright hostilities, negotiating memories of multiple wars is now integral to political transition, peace-building and reconciliation. Post-conflict stabilisation is, of course, an enormously complex transaction that encompasses many factors, including the creation of viable and legitimate political institutions, economic development, reintegration of displaced persons, security sector reform, social reconstruction, and the promotion of human and minority rights.[76] The international community has been very heavily engaged in peace-building efforts in the region – especially under the auspices of the Stability Pact for South Eastern Europe – and early recognised that managing violent memories must also constitute part of the agenda: thus, mindful of the role the media had previously played in disseminating inflammatory propaganda, in 1997 North Atlantic Treaty Organisation (NATO) peacekeepers seized Bosnian Serb television transmitters to prevent the broadcast of egregiously nationalist representations of the past war.[77] The International Criminal Tribunal for the Former Yugoslavia (ICTY) is perhaps the pre-eminent single international instrument designed to manage memory. It aims to deliver justice to victims, to punish and remove from the scene the most flagrant perpetrators of war crimes, to establish an authoritative and impartial historical record, and to deter future crimes, all in the name of promoting reconciliation and sustainable peace.[78] The ICTY's efficacy in achieving

---

74   Mick Hume, 'Nazifying the Serbs, from Bosnia to Kosovo', in Philip Hammond and Edward S. Herman, eds, *Degraded Capability: The Media and the Kosovo Crisis* (London: Pluto, 2000), pp. 70–78. Hume had his own, rather dubious agenda, here: see Marko Attila Hoare, 'Genocide in the Former Yugoslavia: A Critique of Left Revisionism's Denial', *Journal of Genocide Research*, 5/4 (2003): 543–63.

75   George C. Herring, 'Analogies at War: The United States, the Conflict in Kosovo, and the Uses of History', in Albrecht Schnabel and Ramesh Thakur, eds, *Kosovo and the Challenge of Humanitarian Intervention: Selective Indignation, Collective Action, and International Citizenship* (Tokyo: United Nations University Press, 2000), pp. 347–59; Roland Paris, 'Kosovo and the Metaphor War', *Political Science Quarterly*, 117/3 (2002): 423–50.

76   Brad K. Blitz, ed., *War and Change in the Balkans: Nationalism, Conflict and Cooperation* (Cambridge: Cambridge University Press, 2006).

77   Monroe E. Price, 'Memory, the Media and NATO: Information Intervention in Bosnia-Hercegovina', in Müller, ed., *Memory and Power in Post-War Europe*, pp. 137–54. NATO forces also objected to being branded as Nazis by the Bosnian-Serb broadcasts.

78   Janine Natalya Clark, 'The 3 "Rs": Retributive Justice, Restorative Justice, and Reconciliation', *Contemporary Justice Review*, forthcoming.

these ends, and indeed its very legitimacy, is much contested.[79] Yet, while it is no panacea, it has made a palpable contribution to societal reconciliation. Moreover, the insistence of the European Union (EU) that full cooperation with the ICTY is an essential prerequisite for accession negotiations demonstrates the international community's belief in the intimate interconnections between war memory, justice and peace.[80]

The normative mnemonic demands of the drive towards integration into Euro-Atlantic institutions are one key factor promoting a frank coming to terms with the recent past. Yet, important domestic, political and social forces are driving in the same direction, especially since the sidelining following death, ICTY indictment or electoral defeat of many key nationalist leaders. For example, when elections in Croatia in 2000, after Tuđman's death, brought to power a liberal government committed to European integration and cooperation with the ICTY it seemed to mark a sea change after the nationalist rigidities of the 1990s.[81] Subsequent governments have broadly maintained this trajectory, though progress on the war criminals issue has proved slightly rocky and recidivist nationalism and a measure of Ustaša nostalgia persist.[82]

In Serbia, the ousting of Milošević in 2000 opened up space for a more pluralist politics, but the issue of whether the country should turn its back on heavenly myths and embrace 'Europe' continues to be fiercely contested, embittered by the status of Kosovo. Some commentators stress the increasing strength of liberal reformist attitudes, whether manifested in the healthy civil society activism of peace-building non-governmental organisations or the moderate and restrained tone of the commemorations held in 2004 to mark the bicentenary of the first Serbian uprising against Ottoman rule.[83] Others discern a xenophobic nation still in denial about its historical wrongdoings and wallowing in a lingering sense of victimhood.[84] The extent to which it will be possible to secure political stability

---

79 For one positive argument, see James Gow, 'The ICTY, War Crimes Enforcement and Dayton: The Ghost in the Machine', in Marc Weller and Stefan Wolff, eds, *International State-Building after Violent Conflict: Bosnia Ten Years after Dayton* (London: Routledge, 2008), pp. 47–63; for a full-blooded critique, see John Laughland, *Travesty: The Trial of Slobodan Milošević and the Corruption of International Justice* (London: Pluto, 2007).

80 Rachel Kerr, 'Peace through Justice? The International Criminal Tribunal for the Former Yugoslavia', *Southeast European and Black Sea Studies*, 7/3 (2007): 373–85.

81 Rose Lindsey, 'Remembering Vukovar, Forgetting Vukovar: Constructing National Identity through the Memory of Catastrophe in Croatia', in Peter Gray and Kendrick Oliver, eds, The Memory of Catastrophe (Manchester: Manchester University Press, 2004), pp. 190–204.

82 Kerr, 'Peace through Justice?', 381–2; Nicholas Wood, 'Fascist Overtones from Blithely Oblivious Rock Fans', *New York Times* (2 July 2007), <http://www.nytimes.com/2007/07/02/world/europe/02croatia.html> [accessed 9 July 2007].

83 See, respectively, Clark, 'The 3 "Rs"', and Dejan Djokić, 'Coming to Terms with the Past: Yugoslavia', *History Today*, 54/6 (2004): 19.

84 Sabrina P. Ramet, 'The Denial Syndrome and its Consequences: Serbian Political Culture since 2000', *Communist and Post-Communist Studies*, 40/1 (2007): 41–58.

and prosperity on the basis of an honest accounting with intertwined pasts is therefore open to question. Disturbing nationalist views on the memory of the wars of the 1990s and of the Second World War – patriotically denying war crimes and defending fascist collaborators as true patriots – are still very apparent in popular culture and education.[85]

In the fractured polity of Bosnia, competitive victimhood over past atrocities continues to be an irritant to political progress. For Bosnian Muslims the genocide at Srebrenica remains a festering sore, but Bosnian Serbs, in riposte, invoke the memory of their own dead in numerous conflicts, for instance by erecting gory new memorials to victims of Ustaša cruelties.[86] Nevertheless, even if external pressure from the international community is at present more potent than bottom-up sentiment for reconciliation, there is some cause for optimism that, in due course, older animosities may be transcended. One hopeful milestone was passed in 2004 when the government of the Bosnian Serb Republic offered an official apology for Srebrenica.[87]

Large swathes of the Balkans were, of course, not directly touched by the Yugoslav wars, but here, too, memories of conflict were still profoundly implicated in domestic and international politics. The long-running dispute between Greece and the Former Yugoslav Republic of Macedonia over the latter's sobriquet and status encompassed an intense controversy over symbols and territorial claims ostensibly rooted in the mists of antiquity; but the Greeks were, at bottom, determined to defend a territorial settlement that was a highly contingent outcome of a series of conflicts beginning in the nineteenth century anti-Ottoman liberation struggle, and the memory of numerous heroic participants in these, such as Pavlos Melas, was explicitly mobilised in the cause.[88] The transitions to democracy in Bulgaria and Romania had an important mnemonic dimension, as existing narratives of the national past had to be revised in the process of historicising the experience of communism. Rejection of the communist heritage could sometimes take dramatic symbolic form, as with the demolition of the mausoleum of Georgi Dimitrov in Sofia, but also entailed a somewhat problematic rehabilitation of pre-communist nationalist leaders tainted by association with fascism.[89] In Romania, argument swirled around history education in the 1990s, as the EU exerted pressure for a revision of rather chauvinist textbooks that were clearly intended to inculcate a patriotic identity. Less ethnocentric versions – with a reduced emphasis on national heroes and the emergence of the nation through warfare – were introduced in

85   Nicole Münnich, 'Conference Report: Revisionism in Serbia', *H-Soz-u-Kult* (5 December 2007), <http://hsozkult.geschichte.hu-berlin.de/tagungsberichte/id=1794&count=160&r ecno=15&sort=datum&order=down&geschichte=69> [accessed 6 July 2008].
86   Paul B. Miller, 'Contested Memories: The Bosnian Genocide in Serb and Muslim Minds', *Journal of Genocide Research*, 8/3 (2006): 311–24.
87   Hoare, *History of Bosnia*, pp. 402–11.
88   For an overview, see Victor Roudometof, *Collective Memory, National Identity, and Ethnic Conflict: Greece, Bulgaria, and the Macedonian Question* (Westport, CT: Praeger, 2002).
89   Maria Todorova, 'The Mausoleum of Georgi Dimitrov as Lieu de Mémoire', *Journal of Modern History*, 78/2 (2006): 377–411.

1999, but proved controversial.[90] Romania, in common with numerous other post-communist countries, has also experienced some difficulties in coming to terms with its own complicity in the Holocaust, yet this, too, has begun to be addressed by responsible politicians and historians.[91] In both Romania and Bulgaria, the prescriptive discipline of integration with 'Europe' has had a salutary influence in tempering nationalist excesses and conducing towards more candid visions of past conflict.

This highly selective survey has sought to demonstrate that, as a consequence of the serial historical contingencies of nation-building, identity politics and international relations, memories of war have been a crucial component of political culture in the modern Balkans. Yet, acknowledging this need not entail succumbing to exoticising 'Balkanist' fallacies about a 'land of the living past'.[92] On the one hand, the very decision to focus a discussion on the problematic nature of memory perhaps risks overstating its importance, since many other variables have constantly been in play by its side, constructing identity and determining the course of foreign policy. Moreover, although successful symbolic politics must reckon with what counts as a persuasive discourse on the past within wider society, the extent to which memories of war only emerge as a feature on the landscape of politics when invoked by manipulative elites, exploiting conditions of uncertainty and insecurity, should not be understated. On the other hand, the singularity of the Balkan condition here should not be too readily assumed. The violent play of memory in the region can, in large part, be explained simply as a function of the local strength of nationalism, with its inherent 'othering' and glorification of state-making warfare; yet nationalism, of course, remains a potent political currency across the globe.[93] By the same token, thinking in time, deploying martial analogies and negotiating the problematic legacies of past conflicts are also

90   Razvan Paraianu, 'The History Textbooks Controversy in Romania', Eurozine (11 November 2005), <http://www.eurozine.com/articles/2005-11-11-paraianu-en.html> [accessed 15 June 2008].

91   Radu Ioanid, 'Revisionism in Post-Communist Romanian Political Culture: The Attempts to Rehabilitate the Perpetrators of the Holocaust', in John K. Roth and Elisabeth Maxwell, eds, Remembering for the Future: The Holocaust in an Age of Genocide. Volume 1: History (Basingstoke: Palgrave Macmillan, 2001), pp. 813–31; Cristina Petrescu and Dragoş Petrescu, 'Mastering vs. Coming to Terms with the Past: A Critical Analysis of Post-Communist Romanian Historiography', in Sorin Antohi, Balázs Trencsényi and Péter Apor, eds, Narratives Unbound: Historical Studies in Post-Communist Eastern Europe (Budapest: Central European University Press, 2007), pp. 311–408.

92   Pavlos Hatzopoulos, '"All that is, is Nationalist": Western Imaginings of the Balkans since the Yugoslav Wars', Journal of Southern Europe and the Balkans, 5/1 (2003): 37.

93   For a broad illustration, see R.J.B. Bosworth, Nationalism (Harlow: Pearson Education, 2007); for a compelling and instructive case study linking memory, national identity and war that undercuts any notion of the Balkans as unique or uniquely violent, see Walter Hixson, The Myth of American Diplomacy: National Identity and U.S. Foreign Policy (New Haven, CT: Yale University Press, 2008).

ubiquitous elements in political discourse per se. Whilst not denying the historical and cultural specificities of the Balkans, controversies over memory here thus need to be approached as political problems like any other, susceptible to rational solutions. This is the sense in which Maria Todorova has called for the trivialisation, banalisation and thus normalisation of the Balkans.[94] Such an approach might help us to grasp more clearly that the so-called 'pathologies' of the Balkans are not so very different from our own.

---

94   Maria Todorova, 'Introduction: Learning Memory, Remembering Identity', in Todorova, ed., *Balkan Identities*, p. 17.

Cinema and the Cold War:
An International Perspective

Tony Shaw

The Cold War is much in vogue on contemporary cinema screens. Just as film-makers recycled the Second World War for political and financial profit in the 1950s and 1960s, so a new generation has recently mined the rich seam of Cold War history. Some of the resulting movies have been, like many of their Second World War counterparts, unashamedly triumphalist. *In the Face of Evil: Reagan's War in Word and Deed*, for instance, an American documentary made in 2004, credits the late US actor-turned-president with having 'freed a billion slaves from their Communist masters'. Other Hollywood products, like the complex thriller *Syriana* (2005), have taken a quite different political tack by connecting US Central Intelligence Agency (CIA) machinations during the Cold War to America's present-day troubles in the Middle East. Meanwhile, films depicting the degradations faced by those who lived under communism have been in the vanguard of a 'new wave' in Central and Eastern European cinema. These include the Romanian-made *4 Months, 3 Weeks & 2 Days* (2007), the harrowing story of an illegal abortion under Nicolae Ceauşescu's dictatorship, and the German movie *The Lives of Others* (2006), a compelling, Oscar-winning critique of Stasi surveillance culture.[1]

If the Cold War is a richly contested and financially lucrative subject on film today, so it was during the conflict itself. No cinema – from the East, West, North or South – could fail to be touched in one way or another by a war that spanned four decades. Politicians of all stripes knew the value of cinematic images and realised the need to intervene in the film-making process. Their interventions took a variety of forms. The trials and tribulations faced by Hollywood leftists accused of 'un-American' activities during the McCarthy era have been well documented. So, too, have the pressures Joseph Stalin imposed on revered directors like Vsevolod Pudovkin in the late 1940s to make films that showed 'the superiority of the Soviet

---

1   <www.inthefaceofevil.com/index.html> (20 May 2008); *Variety* (21 November 2005), pp. 53, 61; *Vertigo* (April 2008), pp. 21–3; *Sight and Sound* (May 2007), pp. 16–20.

order over bourgeois democracy'.[2] Less well known but equally real, however, are the efforts the Royal Canadian Mounted Police went to during the early years of the Cold War to purge the Canadian National Film Board of suspected communists. Only recently have we learned, also, that the British Foreign Office secretly advised film-makers on how to construct plausible anti-Soviet images in the 1950s. And it was only in 2003 that the full details emerged of how, in the late 1970s, Kim Jong-il, son of the North Korean leader Kim il-Sung, kidnapped the South Korean film director Shin Sang-ok and forced him to shoot a socialist version of the 1950s Japanese monster classic *Godzilla* called *Pulgasari* (1985).[3]

That film-makers could be jailed, kidnapped, and in the case of Shin Sang-ok fed on a diet of salt, rice, grass and party indoctrination, testifies to cinema's power as a vehicle of entertainment and information throughout the Cold War. A combination of the twentieth-century communications revolution, and the Cold War's intrinsically ideological character, rendered the East–West clash a propaganda conflict par excellence. The key protagonists in this gargantuan battle for hearts and minds were the mass media. The press, radio, television and film devised and disseminated a barrage of words, sounds and images which helped not only to frame the Cold War, but which also told people what and whom to believe. Cinema's potency derived principally from its purported ability to *show* audiences the reality of the Cold War from the very outset of the conflict. Through feature films, documentaries and, before their place was taken by regular television broadcasts, newsreels, millions could *watch* 'their boys' in action in Cold War 'hot spots' like Korea, Vietnam and Angola, *see* the terrible powers unleashed by hydrogen bomb tests, and witness *with their own eyes* the dangers posed by enemy spies.

This chapter is inspired by an ongoing project comparing Soviet and American Cold War cinema, and attempts to provide the first international overview of cinema's representation of the Cold War.[4] Elsewhere I have explored the extent to which film became a tool of government propaganda during the Cold War, and what this tells us about notions of media freedom during the conflict.[5] What interests me more here is film *content* rather than agency – that is, *what* movies told people about the Cold War, *how*, and, to an extent, *why*. In particular, I want to identify and examine core themes of Cold War coverage that ran across the world of cinema between 1945 and 1990. The essay is therefore split into four sections that

---

2   Larry Ceplair and Steven Englund, *The Inquisition in Hollywood: Politics in the Film Community, 1930–1960* (Berkeley, CA: University of California Press, 1979); Sarah Davies, 'Soviet Cinema and the Early Cold War: Pudovkin's *Admiral Nakhimov* in Context', *Cold War History* (October 2003), vol. 4, no. 1: 49–70.

3   Mark Kristmanson, 'Love your Neighbour: The Royal Canadian Mounted Police and the National Film Board, 1948–53', *Film History* (1998), vol. 10, no. 3: 254–74; Tony Shaw, *British Cinema and the Cold War: The State, Propaganda and Consensus* (London: I.B. Tauris, 2000); *Guardian* (4 April 2003).

4   Tony Shaw and Denise Youngblood, *Double Vision: Soviet and American Film during the Cold War* (Lawrence, KS: University Press of Kansas, 2009).

5   Tony Shaw, *British Cinema*; and *Hollywood's Cold War* (Edinburgh: Edinburgh University Press, 2007).

look in turn at (a) how films constructed a deceptively simple but powerful picture of the enemy during the initial phase of the Cold War, explaining who was to blame for starting the conflict and why it was necessary to defeat them; (b) cinema's ambivalent attitude towards nuclear weapons; (c) how and why cinema focused so intensely on Cold War espionage; and (d) the unprecedented degree to which film provided a forum for anti-government dissent during the Cold War. Ultimately, my intention is to provide a concise but rounded picture of how mainstream cinema depicted the Cold War. I will conclude by offering some brief thoughts on film's role as a form of 'soft power' in the 45-year-long conflict.

Justifying War

The outbreak of the Cold War was slow and messy. There were no official declarations akin to those of 1914, 1939 or 1941. With one or two exceptions, like North Korea's assault on South Korea in the summer of 1950, the conflict's 'hot' wars were not prompted by sudden attacks or invasions. Instead, the most powerful belligerents slid reluctantly into the Cold War between 1945 and 1950, leaving other nations to get entangled as the conflict grew in age, depth and global complexity.

The absence of an 'evil invader' might have made it difficult for many film industries to justify going to war in the late 1940s, so soon after the devastation of the Second World War, were it not for the fact that a cultural Cold War had been simmering for three decades already across parts of Europe, Asia and North America. We now know that the US and Russian film industries, certainly, wasted little time in identifying communism and capitalism as their nations' respective 'other' in the aftermath of the 1917 Bolshevik Revolution. Images of Big Business murdering workers in silent Russian classics like *Strike* (1925) were matched by pictures of Bolshevik cruelty and economic incompetence in lesser known Hollywood dramas such as *Red Russia Revealed* (1923).[6] Images of the threat posed by fascism took precedence over these pictures for a brief period in both cinemas in the late 1930s and early 1940s. But once the Grand Alliance began to splinter in the aftermath of Adolf Hitler's death, it did not take long for the two industries to convert ideological 'other' into implacable 'enemy'.

From the late 1940s to the mid-1950s, the US and Soviet film industries dominated their respective side's Cold War cinematic offensive, telling national and international audiences that communism and capitalism were now *at war*. Not surprisingly, though rather ironically given their recent joint victory over Hitler, both industries re-crafted Second World War stereotypes to cast each other as Nazism's successor. Grigory Aleksandrov's wartime drama *Meeting on the Elbe* (1949) did this more successfully than any other Soviet movie of the era. Made

---

6   *Film Journal* (October 1972), pp. 24–33; Kevin Brownlow, *Behind the Mask of Innocence: Sex, Violence, Prejudice, Crime – Films of Social Conscience in the Silent Era* (Los Angeles, CA: University of California Press, 1990), pp. 442–62.

by one of Stalin's favourite directors, and, paradoxically perhaps, an artist best known for his entertaining American-style musical comedies, *Meeting on the Elbe* charted both US perfidy in occupied Germany, particularly the military's efforts to shelter 'useful' Nazis, and the decadence of American culture in general. For their part, Hollywood movies depicted communists as 'Red fascists'. George Seaton's docudrama-romance *The Big Lift* (1950) celebrated the US Air Force's role in defeating the 1948–49 Berlin Blockade and presented the Red Army as a tool of totalitarian aggrandisement. Made on location in collaboration with the US Defense Department's public relations directorate, *The Big Lift* was an early example of the Pentagon–Hollywood axis during the Cold War.[7]

Gestapo-style trench coats and jackboots also frequently appeared in Soviet and American features portraying the Cold War's 'enemy within' during this period. Usually they were worn by foreign ringleaders – such as US ambassador 'MacHill' in Mosfilm's Czech-based *Conspiracy of the Doomed* (1950) and the Russian trader 'Lazchenkov' in Columbia Studio's Boston-set *Walk East on Beacon* (1952) – thus making them more identifiable to audiences. Emphasising the underground threat posed by the enemy highlighted the unconventional nature of the Cold War. It also blurred the distinction between soldier and civilian, and, by demanding vigilance from everyone (mothers, sons, workmates) and everywhere (at home, in the office, in one's military unit), told audiences this was a *total* war.[8]

Soviet films took particular pleasure in playing the well-worn anti-clerical card, one of the crudest examples being *Dawn over the Neman* (1952), which portrayed a Lithuanian priest plotting with the Vatican and Washington to poison collective farm produce. Soviet cinema also enjoyed mobilising history for propaganda purposes: movies about the attempt by 'international reactionaries' and counter-revolutionaries to strangle Bolshevism at birth during the 1918–22 Russian Civil War were still being made in the 1980s.[9] American movies, on the other hand, tended to focus more on the ideological bankruptcy of communist fifth-columnists, thus countering head-on Marxism's claims to be scientifically and morally superior to capitalism. Howard Hughes's *I Married a Communist* (1949) and John Wayne's *Big Jim McLain* (1952), for example, presented the Communist Party's promises of progress and equality as at best utopian hogwash and at worst the sure-fire route to an American dictatorship.[10]

---

7   David Caute, *The Dancer Defects: The Struggle for Cultural Supremacy during the Cold War* (Oxford: Oxford University Press, 2003), pp. 134–42; Ralph Stern, 'The Big Lift (1950): Image and Identity in Blockaded Berlin', *Cinema Journal* (Winter, 2007), vol. 46, no. 2: 66–90; Lawrence Suid, *Guts and Glory: The Making of the American Military Image in Film* (Lexington, KY: University Press of Kentucky, 2002), pp. 161–2.

8   Maya Turovskya, 'Soviet Films of the Cold War', in Richard Taylor and Derek Spring, eds, *Stalinism and Soviet Cinema* (London: Routledge, 1993), pp. 131–41; James M. Skinner, 'Cliché and Convention in Hollywood's Cold War Anti-Communist Films', *North Dakota Quarterly* (Summer, 1978) pp. 35–40.

9   Caute, *Dancer*, pp. 150–53; *Soviet Film* (December 1985), pp. 8–9 for *Shores in the Fog* (USSR/Bulgaria, 1986).

10   Daniel J. Leab, 'How Red was My Valley: Hollywood, the Cold War Film, and *I Married A Communist*', *Journal of Contemporary History* (1984), vol. 19: 59–88; Ron Briley, 'John

It was not long before other film industries were putting their own spin on these demonising themes. The closest Britain came to McCarthyism on film was in 1951 with the release of *High Treason*. This thriller portrayed a communist cell exploiting Britain's weak points – its class system and strict privacy laws – in order to sabotage the nation's power supplies and thereby prepare the ground for a Soviet coup. As with most of Hollywood's subversion plots, the British authorities foil this devious plan thanks to efficient policing and public surveillance – but only just in time. The communists themselves, like those in Hollywood movies, are presented as a highly dangerous, if dysfunctional, bunch of political deviants and social misfits. Other British films made in the 1950s that depicted communist-led insurgencies in what was left of the Empire (principally Kenya and Malaya) provided further graphic proof of the Soviet Union's quest for totalitarian world domination. These were supported by government-sponsored shorts made in a number of Britain's former colonies, including Australia.[11]

By contrast, East Germany's film industry, known locally for much of the Cold War as 'Hollywood behind the Wall', stuck overwhelmingly to events at home. Throughout the 1950s, leading directors like Kurt Maetzig specialised in cataloguing the links between Nazism and Western-based political and business elites before, during and after the Second World War. Documentaries like *Holiday on Sylt* (1959) highlighted the prominent positions Nazi war criminals held in West German society, thus portraying that country as a fascist threat. At the same time, more commercially oriented features dramatised the Bonn government's efforts to destabilise its 'democratic' rival in East Berlin. Some, like the crime adventure *Circus Alarm* (1953), were designed specifically for children.[12]

A significant proportion of Cold War films produced by another new state, the People's Republic of China (PRC), during the same period also targeted young audiences, but their hatred was largely directed at the United States. *Sons of the Fisherman Island* (1959), for instance, depicted two children struggling with American-backed reactionaries 'to defend their motherland and the revolutionary cause'. America's long history of double-dealing and contempt for the Chinese people was demonstrated in *Two Generations of Swimmers* (1959), the story of a

Wayne and *Big Jim McLain* (1952): The Duke's Cold War Legacy', *Film & History* (2001), vol. 3, no. 1: 28–33.

11 Stephen Guy, '*High Treason* (1951): Britain's Cold War Fifth Column', *Historical Journal of Film, Radio and Television* (1993), vol. 13, no. 1: 35–47; Susan Carruthers, 'Two Faces of 1950s Terrorism: The Film Presentation of Mau Mau and the Malayan Emergency', *Small Wars and Insurgencies* (Spring, 1995), vol. 6, no. 1: 17–43; David McKnight, 'Australian Film and the Cultural Cold War', (27 August 2005), online at <http://beyondrightandleft. com.au/archives/2005/08/australian_film.html> (20 May 2008).

12 Mira Liehm, *The Most Important Art: East European Film after 1945* (Berkeley, CA: University of California Press, 1977), pp. 270–71; Horst Claus, 'Rebels with a Cause: The Development of the "Berlin-Filme" by Gerhard Klein and Wolfgang Kohlhaase', in Sean Alland and John Sandford, eds, *DEFA: East German Cinema, 1946–1992* (New York: Berghahn, 1999), pp. 96–8; Christiane Muckenberger, 'The Cold War in East German Feature Film', *Historical Journal of Film, Radio and Television* (1993), vol. 13, no. 1: 49–58.

Chinese champion athlete being forced to lose to his US rival in the 1930s. Other films like *The Opium War* (1959), a costume drama set a century earlier in the 1830s, reminded audiences of the unhealthy interest British imperialists had taken in China down the years. In this way, films made in both the West and the East portrayed the Cold War enemy as a clear and present danger – to individuals, to the nation, and to the wider ideological cause.[13]

Heaven and Hell

The world was segregated like never before during the Cold War. Two 'sub-universes' – the capitalist and communist spheres – coexisted, with their inhabitants mixing, for the most part, only when it suited their governments. The result was an information gap, especially about what life was really like on what came to be known as 'the other side'. This void was filled by official propaganda and intense media speculation, most of which helped characterise the Cold War as a bipolar phenomenon fought between two systems whose mores, values and politics represented mutually exclusive ways of life. Cinemas on both sides of the ideological divide reinforced this vision. Making the world appear black and white appealed to the industry's commercial instincts, especially in the West, and had the backing of government, which was essential in the East.

Film-makers in the communist world conducted extensive, often overt campaigns aimed at dazzling domestic and overseas audiences with what apparatchiks called 'the sunshine of living socialism'. Because they were technically more mature and had the scope to pool their resources, Soviet and Eastern European cinemas were at the forefront of these positive propaganda campaigns. The majority of their movies extolled communist virtues which dated back to the 1920s – comradeship, working-class solidarity, economic progress, social equality, and the joys of national, officially-sponsored high culture. As time went by, other films trumpeted new communist achievements – in space, on the sports field, in the laboratory, in industry, and so on.[14] From the 1950s onwards, PRC films echoed these communist strengths and virtues via heroic biopics and revolutionary musicals, factory-based comedies, and family-oriented melodramas drawing together China's ethnic minorities.[15] As a whole, the

---

13 *China's Screen* (October 1960 and January 1960), pp. 5–6; *Hollywood Reporter* (14 September 1978), pp. 3, 13.

14 Liehm, *The Most Important Art*; Bert Hogenkamp, 'The Sunshine of Socialism: The CPGB and Film in the 1950s', in Andy Croft, ed., *A Weapon in the Struggle: The Cultural History of the Communist Party of Great Britain* (London: Pluto, 1998), pp. 192–206; Richard Stites, 'Heaven and Hell: Soviet Propaganda Constructs the World', in Gary Rawnsley, ed., *Cold War Propaganda in the 1950s* (Basingstoke: Macmillan, 1999), pp. 85–103; Richard Taylor, Nancy Wood, Julian Graffy and Dina Iordanova, eds, *The BFI Companion to Eastern Europe and Russian Cinema* (London: British Film Institute, 2000).

15 Examples of these Chinese films are, in order of theme, *Qui Jin* (1982), *Red Guards of Lake Hong* (1961), *Big Li* (1962), *Springtime Blossom* (1960) and *A Revolutionary Family* (1960).

communist world presented itself on film as a united, peace-loving community of peoples, one protected (or 'liberated' in China's case) by a glorious military and building a happy, new society whose ultimate goal was a 'workers' paradise'.

Arguably the most vibrant and innovative of all such positive campaigns took place in Cuba where, only three months after Fidel Castro came to power in 1959, an act of law was passed declaring cinema to be a national art that was essential for the 're-education' of the Cuban people. Over the next 24 years, the Cuban Film Institute produced 112 features, approximately 900 documentary shorts, and over 1,300 weekly newsreels. Films like *Lucia* (1968), which provided a critique and ultimate celebration of Cuban society both before and after the revolution through an analysis of the changing roles of women, were highly inventive stylistically and astonished international audiences with their sophistication. Others like *Memories of Underdevelopment* (1968), the story of a bourgeois writer who decides to stay in Cuba after the revolution rather than escape with his family to Florida, even attracted plaudits in the United States, despite its economic and cultural blockade of the island. By the 1980s, Cuban cinema had provided enormous inspiration, as well as valuable production assistance, to militant film movements all over Latin America.[16]

For their part, cinema in the West did a highly effective job in promoting the benefits of capitalism. Most films did this indirectly and unwittingly, not by promulgating capitalism in a heavy-handed, strict economic sense, but instead by portraying it in lifestyle terms. In the 1950s especially, American films revelled in the material pleasures associated with the post-war economic boom, presenting America as a new, classless democracy. Many of the biggest hits of the decade – romantic comedies like *How to Marry a Millionaire* (1953), documentaries like *Cinerama Holiday* (1955) and breezy musicals like *High Society* (1956) – were lavish productions that projected America, at home and abroad, as a prosperous land of freedom, opportunity and abundance.[17] Italian, West German, Japanese and other cinemas followed suit in response to their own 'economic miracles' of the 1950s and 1960s, each subconsciously transmitting the idea that democratic capitalism laid the foundations for unprecedented levels of consumerism and what, through gritted teeth, Soviet film-makers called 'ordinary affluence'. Each, in various ways

The subject of the Cold War has yet to receive separate and sustained treatment by historians of PRC cinema. For useful background information see Paul Clark, *Chinese Cinema: Culture and Politics Since 1949* (New York: Femininst Press, 1988); Poshek Fu, *Between Shanghai and Hong Kong: The Politics of Chinese Cinemas* (Stanford, CA: Stanford University Press, 2003); Tina Mai Chen, 'Propagating the Propaganda Film: The Meaning of Film in Chinese Communist Party Writings, 1949–1965', *Modern Chinese Literature and Culture* (2003), vol. 15, no. 2: 154–93.

16   Michael Chanan, *Cuban Cinema* (Minneapolis, MN: University of Minnesota Press, 2004); David A. Cook, *A History of Narrative Film* (New York and London: W.W. Norton, 2004), pp. 814–19.

17   Cook, *Narrative*, pp. 387–40; Reinhold Wagnleitner, *Coca-Colonization and the Cold War: The Cultural Mission of the United States in Austria after the Second World War* (Chapel Hill, NC: University of North Carolina Press, 1994), pp. 230–266.

and in different sociocultural settings, celebrated the virtues of social mobility, individualism and free enterprise.[18]

Simultaneously, cinemas both in the East and in the West sought to expose what life, in their view, was really like on 'the other side'. With one eye on the Third World, Soviet films targeted America's racial strife in particular, showing that the US's claim to be a model for progress was baseless in view of the brutal discrimination black Americans experienced. Some of these were highly imaginative. Abram Room's espionage drama *Silvery Dust* (1953), for instance, showed white American fascists caging black peace partisans like monkeys in order to use them as guinea pigs for chemical warfare experiments.[19] Chinese and East European films constantly reminded audiences of the evils of the 'capitalist machine', by cataloguing social inequalities in the United States and elsewhere in the so-called 'First World'. At the same time, other movies offered Western audiences a route out of capitalist exploitation. The pioneering Dutch documentary director Joris Ivens, most of whose work from the early 1950s through to the 1980s was made in the communist world, was a leading practitioner of this sort of material. His paean to international trade unionism, *Song of the Rivers* (1954), which included a musical score by the Russian composer Dmitri Shostakovich, was reportedly seen by 250 million people.[20]

These communist-made films were far outnumbered, however, by Western depictions of the grim reality of life behind the Iron and Bamboo Curtains. Once again, Hollywood dominated this sub-genre. Beginning with *The Red Danube* in 1949 and ending with *White Nights* in 1985, both stories of defecting Russian ballet dancers who would rather die than return to their homeland, Hollywood turned out a steady stream of movies that 'opened a window' on Eastern bloc tyranny and which celebrated escapes to 'freedom'.[21] West German cinema did the same, principally by focusing on those tragically 'trapped' behind enemy lines in East Berlin.[22] In Asia, Taiwanese cinema occasionally painted lurid exposés of life on the communist-occupied mainland, perhaps the most notorious example being *The Coldest Winter in*

---

18 Réka Buckley, 'Elsa Martinelli: Italy's Audrey Hepburn', *Historical Journal of Film, Radio and Television* (August 2006), vol. 26, no. 3: 327–40; Heide Fehrenbach, *Cinema in Democratizing Germany: Reconstructing National Identity after Hitler* (Chapel Hill, NC: University of North Carolina Press, 1995); Kyoko Hirano, *Mr Smith Goes to Tokyo: Japanese Cinema under the American Occupation, 1945–1952* (Washington, DC: Smithsonian Institute, 1992); Phillip L. Gianos, *Politics and Politicians in American Film* (Westport, CT: Praeger, 1998), pp. 3–4.

19 Shaw, *Hollywood's Cold War*, pp. 171–2; Caute, *Dancer*, pp. 157–8.

20 Joris Ivens and Valdimir Pozner, *Lied der Ströme* (Berlin, 1957); Joris Ivens, *The Camera and I* (New York, 1969).

21 *Motion Picture Herald* (24 September 1949); William J. Palmer, *The Films of the Eighties: A Social History* (Carbondale, IL: Southern Illinois University Press, 1993), pp. 242–5.

22 See, for instance, *Escape from East Berlin* (1961), reviewed in *Film-Echo/Filmwoche* (31 October 1962), p. 7. See also Hans Gunther Pflaum, *Germany on Film: Theme and Content in the Cinema of the Federal Republic of Germany* (Detroit, MI: Wayne State University Press, 1990) and 'Cold-War German Cinema' [special issue], *Film History* (2006), vol. 18, no. 1: 2–103.

Peking (1981), a searing indictment of Mao Tse Tung's Cultural Revolution as told from the perspective of an English-educated scientist. Hong Kong cinema generally took a more guarded approach to its powerful neighbour, but films depicting communist China as endemically poor and a breeding ground for thieves jealously raiding its borders for rich pickings did get past the censors. Even Israeli cinema chipped in with films like *Lena* (1982), which focused on the oppression of Jews in the Soviet Union. The common theme running through these movies was the portrayal of the communist world as a vast prison wracked by state-licensed intimidation, political corruption, cultural repression, social regulation and poverty.[23]

Bombs and Monsters

The shadow of Hiroshima and Nagasaki dominated the Cold War, producing among politicians and the public alike a mixture of fear, awe, deference and protest. Myths and images of nuclear energy and weapons established before the discovery of fission – many via the cinema of the 1920s and 1930s – were expanded and refined. As Chicago sociologist Edward Shils remarked during the 1950s, a decade which marked the golden age of celluloid science fiction, 'atomic bombs made a bridge across which apocalyptic fantasies, marching from their refuge among fringe groups, invaded all society'.[24]

Like everyone else, film-makers could not but be affected by an East–West arms race that threatened to cut short their own and their families' lives so abruptly. Reactions naturally differed from one individual to another, depending partly on the country in which they worked. Some directors, such as Frenchman Alan Resnais, whose groundbreaking, poetic romantic drama *Hiroshima Mon Amour* (1959) evoked the personal horrors of nuclear bombing, consciously used film as a medium for public instruction. To many others, the whole subject offered the potential for fun, exploitative entertainment and a bulging bank balance. Hence the images of giant irradiated ants (*Them!*, USA, 1954), of aliens landing on Earth demanding an end

---

23   On *The Coldest Winter in Peking*, including the political row it caused, see *Variety* (29 April 1981), pp. 19, 22; and *Screen International* (4 April 1981), p. 24. For PRC films about life in Taiwan see Robert Chi, 'Taiwan in Mainland Chinese Cinema', in Darrell William Davis and Ru-shou Robert Chen, *Cinema Taiwan: Politics, Popularity and The Arts* (New York: Routledge, 2007), pp. 60–74. On the representation of communist China in Hong Kong film see, for instance, *Red Guards in Hong Kong* (Hong Kong, 1984), reviewed in *Variety* (4 September 1985); and Stephen Teo, *Hong Kong Cinema: The Extra Dimensions* (London: British Film Institute, 1997), pp. 207–18. On Lena see *Variety* (21 October 1981), pp. 27, 30.

24   Cited in Spencer R. Weart, *Nuclear Fear: A History of Images* (London: Harvard University Press, 1988), p. 106.

to nuclear testing (*Santo Versus the Martian Invasion*, Mexico, 1966), and of nuclear-powered superheroes battling evil princesses (*Inframan*, Hong Kong, 1975).[25]

At least 850 nuclear-related feature-length dramas were made during the Cold War. This is a remarkable figure and is matched by the number of documentaries produced, many by governments seeking to assuage public anxiety. The United States and Britain made three-quarters of these dramas, the rest coming from 34 other countries as diverse as the Philippines, Iceland, South Korea, Romania, Finland, New Zealand, Brazil, Israel, Italy and Thailand. A proportionately high number, nine per cent, emerged from Japan, *the* nuclear victim. Hardly any films – less than one per cent – were made in the Soviet Union and China, despite their membership of the nuclear club. This conspicuous reticence can be attributed to censorship, to the PRC's preference for films which glorified war (especially war fought against Japanese imperialism in the 1930s and 1940s), and to the Soviet Union's predilection for characterising their scientists and the military as communist society's 'positive heroes'.[26]

Nuclear themes appeared in virtually all film classifications, from comedy, western, musical, espionage, thriller and even hard-core pornography, to their more frequent representation in science-fiction and horror genres. Roughly speaking, cutting across national boundaries and time periods, film dealt with the nuclear issue in four ways.

First, scores of dramas and spy movies fastened on to press accounts of secret enemy agents conspiring to steal nuclear secrets or sabotage the nation's security systems. The high point for this sub-genre was the late 1940s and 1950s, followed by a mini-revival in the 1980s. Significantly, Hollywood's first fully-fledged Cold War movie, *The Iron Curtain* (1948), was based on the memoirs of a Soviet nuclear spy-cum-defector, Igor Gouzenko. The majority of these films underscored the official Cold War consensus. *The Spies* (1957), a thriller made by Henri-Georges Clouzot, nicknamed the 'French Hitchcock', was one of the few early exceptions. Set in a rundown sanatorium, *The Spies* depicted the phony inventor of a new nuclear explosive device being courted by an ultimately frenzied espionage community.[27]

Second, science-fiction and horror films exploited fears of nuclear energy and the consequences of runaway technology. Many of these adopted stereotypical imagery of the crazy scientist toying with the fabric of the universe, often using uranium-based inventions for militaristic purposes. Some, particularly in the 1950s, featured monsters brought to life by radioactive experiments – pterodactyls in *Rodan* (Japan,

25 *Image et Son* (October 1959), p. 24; *Films and Filming* (January 1960), p. 22; *Motion Picture Herald* (10 April 1954), p. 2,253; Mick Broderick, *Nuclear Movies* (London: Kegan Paul International, 1991), pp. 113, 135.

26 Broderick, *Nuclear Movies*, p. xviii; Yingjin Zhang, ed., *Encyclopedia of Chinese Film* (London: Routledge, 1998), pp. 355–6; Denise Youngblood, *Russian War Films: On the Cinema Front, 1914–2005* (Lawrence, KS: University Press of Kansas, 2007), pp. 82–186.

27 Daniel J. Leab, 'The Iron Curtain (1948): Hollywood's First Cold War Movie', *Historical Journal of Film, Radio and Television* (1988), vol. 8, no. 2: 153–88; *Image et Son* (November 1957), p. 12.

1957) or giant insects in *The Strange World of Planet X* (Britain, 1958). Others, such as *Icarus XV-I*, made in Czechoslovakia in 1963, blended gruesome radiation deaths with aliens in space. Such films are generally dismissed as Cold War kitsch these days. It is better to see them, in fact, as displaying a combination of resistance to overt discussion of the nuclear status quo and an active promotion of alternative responses to it via deeply sublimated and mythologically based 'others'.[28]

From the early 1960s onwards, a third category of films emerged reflecting and projecting increased public fears related to nuclear proliferation. One reaction to these fears was drama, another parody. The former included pictures like *The Black Box Affair* (1966), a Spanish-Italian production that showed US and Soviet agents joining forces against the Chinese to retrieve communications equipment. The latter comprised films such as *Brasil Anno 2,000* (1968), a Brazilian political satire set in the year after a Third World War, with the survivors in radically reversed class roles.[29] Both drama and parody came together in the Anglo-American James Bond series, in which the MI6 agent protected the world from nuclear annihilation at the hands of varying groups of communists, terrorists, corporate criminals or 'madmen' in search of global domination.[30] In the 1970s and 1980s, alongside these images came nihilistic post-apocalyptic survivalist fantasies. Some, like the international box-office hit *Mad Max* (Australia, 1979), were not overtly political. Others, like Poland's *O'Bi, O-Ba: The End of Civilisation* (1984), more pointedly described the trauma of survival and its ethical dilemmas.[31]

Another reaction to proliferation – and the final category of nuclear movies – was a small set of Western-made films explicitly questioning nuclear deterrence theory. The black satire *Dr Strangelove, or: How I learned to Stop Worrying and Love the Bomb* (1964), made in Britain by Hollywood exile Stanley Kubrick, blazed a trail for these cinematic critiques. Kubrick's vision of a demented Strategic Air Command chief launching an unauthorised nuclear attack on the USSR, thus triggering the Soviets' 'doomsday machine' which kills all life on earth, is, still today, regarded as one of the most powerful denunciations of nuclear deterrence theory ever produced in any medium.[32] The futuristic *Planet of the Apes* (USA, 1968), the absurdist *The Bed Sitting Room* (Britain, 1969) and, much later, *Sex Mission* (Poland, 1984), an adventure-comedy which predicted a post-apocalyptic underground society entirely populated by women and test-tube babies, all, in one way or another, owe something to *Dr Strangelove*'s dissenting images. During Mikhail Gorbachev's reign in the late 1980s, even the odd Soviet film like *Letters from a Dead Man* (1986) was

28 *Film Daily* (7 November 1957), p. 8; *Monthly Film Bulletin* (April 1958), p. 49; Broderick, *Nuclear Movies*, pp. 101–2, 118.

29 *Cahiers du Cinéma* (March 1969), p. 65: Broderick, *Nuclear Movies*, pp. 109–10.

30 James Chapman, *Licence to Thrill: A Cultural History of the James Bond Films* (London: I.B. Tauris, 1999).

31 J. Emmett Winn, '*Mad Max*, Reaganism and the Road Warrior', *Kinema* (October 1997), no. 8: 57–75; *Variety* (11 September 1985), p. 22.

32 John Baxter, *Stanley Kubrick: A Biography* (London: HarperCollins, 1997), pp. 165–98; James Naremore, *On Kubrick* (London: British Film Institute, 2007), pp. 119–37.

predicting nuclear catastrophe, though this movie's message was tempered by an optimistic ending that depicted the next generation walking towards a new life.[33]

The Spying Game

As we might expect, combat movies flourished during the Cold War. Initially the preserve of established cinemas – principally the American, British and Russian – by 1990 they had expanded across the globe, covering virtually all of the Cold War's 'hot' wars. Thus, the American film industry made gung-ho pictures about the US intervention in Korea in the 1950s. French, Algerian and Italian film-makers fought and refought the 1954–62 Franco-Algerian War, one of the dirtiest colonial conflicts of the Cold War. American, Vietnamese, Thai and Hong Kong film-makers, among others, clashed over the international conflict in Vietnam in the 1960s and early 1970s. And West German, Belgian, Lebanese, Israeli and American film-makers took different approaches to the 1975–90 Lebanese Civil War, a conflict located at the heart of one of the Cold War's strategically vital regions. It is difficult to say quite what these films, taken as a whole, added to the long history of the combat genre or what they told people about the Cold War itself. Certainly, many of them increasingly showed the brutality and complexity of late twentieth-century warfare. Conversely, a good many others – the internationally blockbusting *Rambo* series of the 1980s immediately springs to mind – extended cinema's love of wartime adventurism.[34]

Running alongside these combat movies were scores of espionage films. The Cold War provided the perfect setting for the creative exploration of this film genre, the roots of which can be traced back to the First World War era. The advent of nuclear weaponry brought with it the fear on both sides that the loss of state secrets might mean national disaster. This most obviously related to spying scientists, but it could include potential subversives in the diplomatic field and elsewhere. The threat of a nuclear Armageddon also forced the chief protagonists to fight by non-military, often clandestine means. This led to massive investment in espionage technology and the building of huge Big Brother-style national security apparatuses. Furthermore, the rich ideological nature of the Cold War highlighted the conflict's highly unusual psychological dimensions. With the notion that the Cold War was fundamentally a 'war on the mind' came fears of 'brainwashing' by 'hidden persuaders' in schools, in the media and in the workplace. In other

---

33 Jonathan Kirshner, 'Subverting the Cold War in the 1960s: *Dr Strangelove, The Manchurian Candidate*, and *The Planet of the Apes'*, *Film & History* (2000), vol. 31, no. 2: 40–44; *Films and Filming* (May 1970), p. 42; *Variety* (August 1984), p.16; *Soviet Film* (January 1987), pp. 6–8.

34 Robert J. Lentz, *Korean War Filmography: 91 English Language Features through 2000* (Jefferson, NC: McFarland, 2003); Alun Evans, *Brassey's Guide to War Films* (Washington, DC: Brassey's, 2000); Jean-Jacques Malo and Tony Williams, eds, *Vietnam War Films* (Jefferson, NC: McFarland, 1994); James Chapman, *War and Film* (London: Reaktion, 2008).

words, many people could make a direct link between national safety and almost any occupation, a connection that contained the natural ingredients for conspiracy theory and paranoia.[35]

The upshot of all of this was that espionage gave many film studios 'a licence to print money' during the Cold War. The inflation-adjusted net profit of the James Bond movies, for example – a perfect showcase for the virtues of Western spy superheroes, high-tech gadgetry and consumer capitalism – was approximately $10 billion.[36] Added to this, the cinematic espionage genre changed radically during the Cold War. As with the Cold War's combat films, spy films spread outwards from the small number of leading industries in Europe and the United States until they were eventually being made across the world. Britain, France, Italy, East Germany and Czechoslovakia became European cinema's specialists, while China, Japan and the two Koreas led the field in Asia. Even Sweden's most revered auteur, Ingmar Bergman, a noted critic of the political uses of cinema, directed an anti-Soviet spy movie during the genre's heyday of the late 1940s and early 1950s.[37] The espionage genre also expanded into a wide range of film classifications. Most spy movies of the 1940s and 1950s were thrillers or dramas, but by the later stages of the Cold War the grave threat posed by enemy agents was also being depicted in official documentaries and allegorical science-fiction fantasies. Simultaneously, spoofs, hard-boiled satires and soft-porn movies ridiculed Cold War intelligence-gathering.[38]

What might people have learned about Cold War espionage from watching these films? This depended to an extent on where they lived. With a few exceptions, from the beginning to the very end of the conflict, communist-made movies treated espionage as a deadly serious subject and accused the West of operating an insidious international spy network. Many Soviet spy films, certainly the most important ones like *Shield and Sword* (1967–68) and *Tehran-43* (1980), linked Western espionage with the threat posed to Russia during the Great Patriotic War against fascism. PRC spy films demonised nationalist underground agents or ethnic minority separatists who were plotting with foreign supporters like the CIA to explode a time bomb in a city or to disrupt social order in the region.[39]

By contrast, although they were outgunned throughout by dramas that portrayed communists as inherently devious subversives, from the early 1950s onwards Western-made films appeared parodying the Cold War spying 'game'. Once film-

35 See David Seed, *Brainwashing: The Fictions of Mind Control – A Study of Novels and Films since World War II* (Kent, OH: Kent State University Press, 2004) for movies that, like *The Manchurian Candidate* (USA, 1962), played on the brainwashing theme.

36 Stan Taylor, 'Introduction: Spying in Film and Fiction', *Intelligence and National Security* (2008), vol. 23, no. 1: 1–4; Christoph Lindner, *The James Bond Phenomenon: A Critical Reader* (Manchester: Manchester University Press, 2003).

37 Daniel J. Leab, '*This Can't Happen Here* (1950): Some Notes on Ingmar Bergman's Cold War Movie', *Historical Journal of Film, Radio and Television* (2003), vol. 23, no. 1: 73–9.

38 Wesley A. Britton, *Beyond Bond: Spies in Fiction and Film* (Westport, CT: Praeger, 2005); Toby Miller, *Spyscreen: Espionage on Film and TV from the 1930s to the 1960s* (New York: Oxford University Press, 2003).

39 Youngblood, *Russian War Films*, pp. 145–6, 188; Zhang, ed., *Encyclopedia*, p. 141.

makers felt it was safe to do so, from the mid-1960s onwards, these parodies were joined by other movies that questioned not just the fundamental ethics of espionage (which many films had done before), but also, more importantly, the very moral basis of intelligence establishments. Martin Ritt's slow, atmospheric drama *The Spy Who Came in from the Cold* (USA/Britain, 1965) provided a model for many later films, with its acutely depressing images of MI6 treachery in Cold War Berlin.[40]

As this implies, what people learned about Cold War espionage from movies also depended on the stage of the conflict in which they were made. Generally speaking, for the first two decades of the war both Eastern and Western films gave the distinct impression that the world was indeed divided between 'them' (who did the spying) and 'us' (who were spied upon). This bore no relation to reality, of course. It is a striking fact, for instance, that the Soviet Union committed no acts of sabotage on American soil during the Cold War, yet dozens of US films catalogued such 'crimes'.

From the 1960s through the 1970s, Eastern and Western espionage films then diverged, the former sticking loyally to the party line, and the latter suggesting at times that the nation's once heroic intelligence services had grown too powerful and were now the new enemy within. Hollywood's attacks on the CIA, for instance, reached a peak in the mid-1970s through such films as *Three Days of the Condor* (1975), but they continued thereafter, often treating the agency as a scapegoat for past and ongoing American misdemeanours overseas.[41] Finally, during the renewed international tensions of the early to mid-1980s, many Eastern and Western espionage films hardened their pro-government lines. *Red Dawn* (1984), for example, marked the first time since the Cold War started that Hollywood had depicted a full-blown, successful communist invasion of the United States, instigated in this case by Russian and Nicaraguan spies. On the other side, East Germany's *Lite Trap* (1982) portrayed East German agents being lured westwards by the superficial pizzazz of capitalist fashions, cars and computers.[42]

Spy novels were best-sellers in both the East and the West during the Cold War. However, it was through cinema and television that most people formed their most powerful impressions of Cold War espionage. After all, film could simplify and shed a physical light on what was a diplomatically opaque and morally complex activity. Film could make espionage look exciting and spies themselves appear sexy and brave, either in fictional scenarios or by recreating real-life Cold War incidents. Film could mesmerise audiences with purported authenticity, stylish editing or beautiful camerawork. Above all, film could put flesh on the spies' bones and thereby make espionage and the Cold War as a whole seem very real. The print media and politicians themselves consistently appropriated cinematic images of espionage, comparing the activities of the KGB, CIA, MI6 and other agencies

---

40   Alan R. Booth, 'The Development of the Espionage Film', *Intelligence and National Security* (October 1990), vol. 5, no. 4: 136–60.

41   Shaw, *Hollywood's Cold War*, pp. 249–62.

42   Harvey R. Greenberg, 'Dangerous Recuperations: *Red Dawn, Rambo,* and the New Decaturism', *Journal of Popular Film & Television* (July 1987), pp. 60–70; *Filmfaust* (December 1982), pp. 16–17; *Kino* (August 1982), pp. 43–44.

with their on-screen counterparts. Many of these images remain with us today in an updated fashion in what many cinemas across the world have identified as the new, post-Cold War enemy – the underground terrorist.[43]

Alternative Images

Many governments during the Cold War did a pretty effective job of controlling their cinemas or co-opting the nation's film-makers for their cause. In the communist world, by and large, control was exerted overtly and almost entirely from the centre. Film studios were nationalised, cultural commissars suggested propaganda themes and scrutinised the content of movies, and state organisations regulated celluloid imports and exports. In the West, most film studios supported their government's anti-communist stance chiefly because their owners and most powerful employees shared officialdom's ideological world-view; their relationship was one based, at root, on the need to protect capitalism. The democratic state could also exert influence on the film industry in two main ways: negatively, though semi-independent censorship bodies and by political pressure; and positively, by openly making Cold War movies itself or by secretly subsidising others.[44]

Notwithstanding these forms of control or influence, films were made on both sides of the political divide which deviated from the official Cold War line. This scope for dissent is what sets Cold War cinema apart from virtually all other wartime cinemas. Though its causes differ from country to country, this unorthodoxy can chiefly be attributed to the nature of the Cold War and its long duration. Governments found it relatively easy to generate and maintain film industry support during the First and Second World Wars, conflicts that lasted at most six years and in which patriotism was stirred by men dying in battle. By contrast, comparatively few people fought on conventional battlefields during the Cold War and the conflict lasted some four decades. In such circumstances, any government – democratic or dictatorial – was bound to meet some form of criticism, opposition or even resistance.

We have already seen how, from midway through the Cold War, Western, Japanese and, to a lesser extent, East European cinemas began to challenge the sanity of nuclear deterrence. We have also noted how, roughly from the same point in time, Anglo-American cinema started to question whether elements within their

---

43 On the cinematic shift from Cold War espionage to terrorism, and the depiction of terrorists in contemporary cinema generally, see, for instance, Anandam P. Kavoori and Todd Fraley, eds, *Media, Terrorism, and Theory* (Lanham, MD: Rowman and Littlefield, 2006); Carl Boggs and Tom Pollard, 'Hollywood and the Spectacle of Terrorism', *New Political Science* (2006), vol. 28, no. 3: 335–51; Lina Khatib, *Filming the Modern Middle East* (London: I.B. Tauris, 2006).

44 On how the different ways in which the Soviet and American governments influenced Cold War film-making see Shaw and Youngblood, *Double Vision*.

own intelligence services were acting as a law unto themselves. Other matters were also the subject of controversy on screen, particularly in the West. As is well known, Hollywood conducted a long and painful post-mortem on its defeat in Vietnam, with many films accusing Washington of playing politics at the troops' expense and a small minority on the left accusing the US of imperialism.[45] Reacting to events in South East Asia and at home, French Cold War cinema took a distinct turn to the left in the late 1960s and 1970s, violently satirising US foreign policy in movies like *Mister Freedom* (1970). Even South Africa, an ardently anti-communist state throughout the Cold War, made fun of superpower diplomacy in *After You, Comrade* (1967).[46] When detente gave way to renewed East–West tensions in the early 1980s, a number of young Western film-makers expressed contempt both for their governments' foreign policies and, significantly, for the malevolent role the media had played in stoking the fires of anti-communism in the 1940s and 1950s.[47] Several films, like the acerbic, Liverpool-based romantic comedy *A Letter to Brezhnev* (1985), demanded an immediate end to the Cold War.[48]

While no film-makers in the communist world went quite this far during the latter stages of the Cold War, it is important that we revise the common misconception that Eastern bloc cinema remained politically straitjacketed throughout the conflict. Most Eastern European cinemas, including that of the Soviet Union itself, reflected the cultural 'thaw' inspired by the Russian leader Nikita Khrushchev in the late 1950s in their bolder investigation of social issues. Movies during this period, and those associated with the 'new wave' of film-making in Bulgaria, Czechoslovakia, Hungary and Poland in the 1960s, were allowed to show that communism was far from perfect.[49] During the 1970s, Soviet cinema opened up to the point of collaborating on productions with Hollywood. This reached a peak with *The Bluebird* (1976), a bloated, star-studded fairy tale about a young girl's search for true happiness, which flopped at the box office.[50]

Chinese cinema, too, was subject to fewer state constraints in the late 1970s and early 1980s than at any point since the communists' accession to power in 1949. During this period, films exposed the evils of the Cultural Revolution, called for a democratisation of political life, and moved closer to the aspirations

---

45   Jeremy M. Devine, *Vietnam at 24 Frames a Second: A Critical and Thematic Analysis of Over 400 Films about the Vietnam War* (Jefferson, NC: McFarland, 1995).

46   *Films and Filming* (April 1969), pp. 42–3; *Positif* (April 1969), pp. 65–6, *Monthly Film Bulletin* (October 1967), p. 155.

47   See, for instance, *Hearts and Minds* (USA, 1974) in *Jump Cut* (July 1975), pp. 3–5; and *The Atomic Cafe* (USA, 1982) in *Cinéaste* (September 1982), pp. 39–41.

48   Tony Shaw, 'From Liverpool to Russia, With Love: *A Letter to Brezhnev* and Cold War Cinematic Dissent in 1980s Britain', *Contemporary British History* (June 2005), vol. 19, no. 2: 243–62.

49   Josephine Woll, *Real Images: Soviet Cinema and the Thaw* (London: Tauris, 2000); Taylor et al., *BFI Companion*, pp. 1–4; Joshua Feinstein, *The Triumph of the Ordinary: Depictions of Daily Life in the East German Cinema, 1949–1989* (Chapel Hill, NC: University of North Carolina Press, 2002).

50   *Soviet Film* (December 1976), pp. 13–16; *Variety* (12 May 1976), p. 34.

of their audiences and away from the dictates of the Communist Party elite.[51] Finally, encouraged by Mikhail Gorbachev's liberalisation programmes in the late 1980s, Soviet cinema entered a brief and final phase questioning many of the communist state's core values. One film, Marina Goldovskaya's remarkably candid documentary *Solovki Power* (1988), exposed the whole history of the Soviet Union's notorious northern labour camp complex. Others covered a range of hitherto taboo subjects: from drugs and prostitution to underemployment and the inequities of military service. Such films opened a window on a parallel reality long known to exist but scarcely acknowledged officially. A number mirrored the sort of images cinema in the West had been transmitting about the Soviet Union for decades. They testify to the considerable distance the Soviet film industry had travelled since the dark, repressive days when Stalin censored films personally.[52]

And the Winner is ...

Film-makers made hay with the Cold War, plundering the conflict for profit and propaganda from beginning to end. The result was the longest international, cinematic war on record and one that, given television's worldwide ubiquity since the 1970s and the recent arrival of the Internet, is unlikely to be surpassed. Films addressed the Cold War in a myriad ways: by relating the conflict to important historical events, notably the Second World War; by dramatising actual Cold War events; by creating imaginary military and diplomatic engagements; by depicting post-nuclear war scenarios; and by embedding Cold War subtexts within apparently unrelated genres. Movies communicated attitudes, values and ideologies to millions of viewers across the globe, from the fleapits of Lagos to the Art Deco dream palaces of London. The result was countless images that enabled millions of people to grasp the 'real' meaning of a conflict that for many of them was peculiarly abstract.

Some industries engaged with the Cold War more explicitly than others. Hollywood, for instance, never tired of condemning Soviet authoritarianism and impressing on the world the stark choice between freedom and totalitarianism. A number of American directors (Sam Fuller, for instance) and actors (Sylvester Stallone is a good example) gained significantly from the roles they played in delivering such messages.[53] In contrast, many other cinemas relegated the Cold

51 Clark, *Chinese Cinema*, pp. 154–81; Chris Berry, *Postsocialist Cinema in Post-Mao China: The Cultural Revolution after the Cultural Revolution* (London: British Film Institute, 2004).

52 Taylor et al., *BFI Companion*, pp. 5–9, 85–7; Cook, *Narrative*, pp. 724–9; *American Film* (February 1990), pp. 14–15.

53 Fuller's Cold War output included two Korean War films, *Steel Helmet* and *Fixed Bayonets* (both released in 1951), the atomic secrets melodrama *Pickup on South Street* (1953), the Alaskan-based anti-Chinese atomic thriller *Hell and High Water* (1954), and an early

War to the background once the conflict had become institutionalised in the 1950s, treating it as 'part of the furniture' rather than as an ongoing crisis or a duel to the death. In the communist world, in general, films dealt with the Cold War more obliquely than in parts of the West. Movies warning of the outside threat posed by militant capitalism were made, but for the most part cinema concentrated on tracking the state's progress on the road to a socialist nirvana. Communist cinema was therefore more inward-looking, more mechanistic and political (as most people understood the word), and less likely either to be exported or to impress audiences outside the Eastern sphere if it were.

All the evidence indicates that, indeed, Western, especially American, cinema was an extremely valuable tool of 'soft power' during the Cold War – far more than its communist counterpart. We need to understand that films did not just represent issues and themes during the Cold War – nuclear weapons, espionage, and so on. They also represented the *quality* of a nation's cinema and, by extension, that nation's politico-economic system or 'way of life'. In this regard, all the signs are that Hollywood wiped the floor with its competitors during the Cold War: in terms of its high production standards, technical sophistication, lighter touch, glamorous stars and global reach. When Hollywood movies were released behind the Iron Curtain during periods of East–West cultural exchange they proved to be exceedingly popular, whereas Western audiences generally found communist films boring, outmoded and overly propagandistic. Even in Western Europe, cinema-goers often complained that, by comparison with American material, their own movies were slow-moving and pretentious. Hollywood therefore seems to have sold capitalism and the American way of life very effectively. Its supremacy in the Cold War cinematic battle might even have played a part in contributing to the West's eventual defeat of Soviet communism. Certainly, there seems little doubt that popular culture played a greater role in bringing an end to the conflict than conventional historiography allows.[54]

Vietnam War film, *China Gate* (1957). Stallone starred as Vietnam War veteran John Rambo three times in the 1980s. He also wrote, directed and starred in *Rocky IV* (1985), a massive box-office hit that pitted American Man versus Soviet Machine in the boxing ring.

54 Joseph S. Nye, *Soft Power: The Means to Success in World Politics* (New York: Public Affairs, 2004); Caute, *Dancer*, pp. 117–18, 162–3; Yale Richmond, *Cultural Exchange and the Cold War: Raising the Iron Curtain* (University Park, PA: Penn State University Press, 2003), pp. 128–32; Richard Pells, *Not Like Us: How Europeans Have Loved, Hated and Transformed American Culture since World War Two* (New York: Basic, 1997), p. 209.

Music as an Inspiration for Combat among American Soldiers in Iraq

Jonathan Pieslak

Historical Overview

Throughout history, music has inspired soldiers for combat.[1] Plato believed that music could directly affect human behavior and that certain musical modes, like Phrygian, were likely to arouse emotion and incite aggressive, members of a group sing, chant, or yell words and melodies to prepare for war or during battle itself. Soldiers of almost all cultural backgrounds have sung battle cries. Spanish soldiers, for example, shouted, "*Santiago y cierra España*" ["Saint James and attack, Spain"] during the Reconquista; Finnish cavalry warriors, Hakkapeliitat, cried, "*Hakkaa päälle*" ["Cut them down"] in the Thirty Years War (1618–48); and Japanese pilots screamed, "*Bonzai*" ["Ten thousand years"] as a battle cry in WWII. Certain musical instruments, like bagpipes, have historical roots in inspiring soldiers for combat. In *The Piper in Peace and War*, historian C.A. Malcolm claims that pipers Allester Caddell and William Steel were commended by Scottish military leader, Alexander MacNoughton, for their playing that inspired archers in a 1627 battle against France.[2]

American military history also demonstrates how music has motivated soldiers. In the Revolutionary War (1775–83), drum and fife performers rallied troops for

1   The following article appears as an excerpt from Jonathan Pieslak, *Sound Targets: American Soldiers and Music in the Iraq War* (Bloomington, IN: Indiana University Press, 2009), with sections also reprinted from Jonathan Pieslak, "Sound Targets: Music and the War in Iraq," *Journal of Musicological Research* (2007), 26/2–3: 123–50, <http://www.informaworld.com>.

2   C.A. Malcolm, *The Piper in Peace and War* (London: John Murray, 1927; reprint. London: Hardwick Press, 1993), p. 24. It has been proposed that bagpipes motivated soldiers in combat preparation long before their documented use by Scottish clans: see the Westminster Kind Productions television series, *Bagpipes: Instrument of War*, Part 1 (1998).

battle and entertained soldiers after combat.[3] George Washington felt that music was so vital to the morale of his troops that he ordered drum and fife majors to improve the quality of music or suffer a deduction in wages:

> ... the music of the Army being in general very bad; it is expected, that the drum and fife Majors exert themselves to improve it, or they will be reduced, and their extraordinary pay taken from them. Stated hours to be assigned for all the drums and fifes, of each regiment, to attend them and practice— Nothing is more agreeable, and ornamental, than good music; every officer, for the credit of his corps, should take care to provide it.[4]

Musicians accompanied soldiers as they marched into the combat field and sometimes performed during the fighting. This practice continued in the American Civil War (1861–65). Although music often signaled commands in the battlefield, like when to attack, fire, or retreat, it also appears to have made a dramatic impact on soldiers. A regimental historian of the 14th Connecticut Volunteer Infantry wrote, "with shot and shell crashing around all about them, they played "The Star-Spangled Banner," "The Red, White, and Blue," and "Yankee Doodle" and then repeated them for fully twenty minutes. They never played better ... its effect upon the men was magical."[5] After reading, making and listening to music has been ranked as the second most popular pastime among Civil War soldiers.[6]

In the twentieth century, developments in audio technology significantly influenced how soldiers used music as an inspiration for combat. With the invention of radio, music became far more present in the lives of soldiers—one of the first uses of music on military radio was as entertainment for wounded WWI soldiers during their recovery in military hospitals.[7] In WWII, German military radio stations broadcast music to inspire troops in the combat field. Guy Sajer, a German soldier, claims that officials broadcast Wagner's *Ride of the Valkyries* over short-wave radio to motivate soldiers during many of the last battles of the war. Sajer's book, *The Forgotten Soldier*, describes a scene where he stands next to German tanks playing

---

3   The fife is a cross flute or transverse flute.

4   George Washington, *The Writings of George Washington from the Original Manuscript Sources, 1745–1799* (Washington, DC: US Government Printing Office, 1931), pp. 181–2.

5   Charles D. Page, *History of the Fourteenth Regiment Connecticut Volunteer Infantry* (Meriden, CT: Horton Publishing, 1906), pp. 120–21. Also, see similar descriptions in Kenneth E. Olson, *Music and Musket: Bands and Bandsmen of the American Civil War* (Westport, CT: Greenwood Press, 1980).

6   Bell Irvin Wiley, *The Life of Billy Yank* (Indianapolis: Bobbs-Merrill, 1952), p. 157; and Eric A. Campbell, "Civil War Music and the Common Soldier: The Experiences of Charles Wellington Reed," in Bruce C. Kelley and Mark A. Snell, eds, *Bugle Resounding: Music and Musicians of the Civil War Era* (Columbia, MO: University of Missouri Press, 2004), pp. 202–28.

7   Albert Marple, "Wireless Music for Wounded Soldiers," *The Wireless Age* (April 1918): 590, 593.

Wagner's *Ride* from their radios before an attack in Memel (Lithuania).[8] American WWII veteran Bruce Brown suggested that this was a common practice for German soldiers in the months before Germany's surrender in 1945.[9]

American WWII soldiers, however, did not appear to be involved with such clear-cut instances of music played to inspire them for combat. More often, music was employed by the US military to boost morale, rather than to explicitly motivate troops for war.[10] In 1942, the War Department established Armed Forces Radio, which later came to include television, to play popular music for soldiers. Its goal is to provide "a touch of home" to servicemen and women.[11] Live music was also a part of the efforts to boost morale. Glenn Miller's American Band of the Allied Expeditionary Forces (AEF) traveled to Europe to perform for troops on June 7, 1944, the day after D-Day. Extremely popular among soldiers, the AEF performed, according to Miller, 89 separate shows in August 1944.[12] Although some of this music may, as a secondary effect, have motivated soldiers for war, its main purpose was to reconnect soldiers with American life.

During the Vietnam War, radio stations, like the Armed Forces Vietnam Network (AFVN), continued to be closely tied to soldier life, and many Vietnam veterans recall that the AFVN was their primary source of music in the war.[13] As developments in audio technology, such as tape players and stereos, gradually became a regular part of American culture, some soldiers obtained these devices and were able to listen to recorded music of their personal preference. "Dagger X-Ray," an Operation Desert Storm combat veteran, said that he knew of occasions in Vietnam where "some units played music over horns (speakers) as they went into battle."[14] Before leaving the military camps to go on missions, some soldiers may have listened to rock music as a way to prepare psychologically for combat. While this could be true, evidence is difficult to find and corroborate. Rather, most Vietnam veterans said that they did not use music in this way.[15] If rock music was played before combat, it was not widespread and appears to have happened in isolated instances.

For American soldiers who served in Operation Desert Storm, the greater availability of portable audio devices, like small tape players, provided the

---

8   Guy Sajer, *The Forgotten Soldier* (Dulles, VA: Brassey, 1990), p. 418.

9   Bruce Brown, personal communication (Plainfield, NJ, September 12, 2006).

10   Ibid.

11   Home page of the Armed Forces Radio and Television Service [online] <www.afrts. dodmedia.osd.mil>.

12   BBC Propaganda Broadcasts, Glenn Miller and His AEF Orchestra (November 1994).

13   Online forum <http://groups.yahoo.com/group/afvn/> (July 2007). My thanks are to Christopher Sabis for initiating the discussion on this forum. Sabis's senior thesis, "Through the Soldiers' Ears: What Americans Fighting in Vietnam Heard and its Effects," from the University of Rochester provides an insightful examination of soldiers' interaction with music in Vietnam. See <http://www.geocities.com/afvn3/historymenu. html>.

14   Desert Storm website <http://phpbb2.desert-storm.com>.

15   Online forum <http://groups.yahoo.com/group/afvn/> (July 2007).

opportunity for music to play a more prevalent role as an inspiration for combat. On a recent <www.desert-storm.com> discussion forum, "Dagger X-Ray" wrote:

> As my track passed through the breach, I had AC/DC "Are You Ready?" and "Thunderstruck" playing over the track intercom system. Kinda made for a good atmosphere/feeling for all of us with headphones on. Officers inside the track didn't mind cuz it wasn't cluttering up the unit comms ... Much of the music I listened to at the time was to get myself wound up ... amped up so that I was ready for anything at that point. Being on an adrenalin rush felt good and having some AC/DC or some Megadeth accompanying it was even better.[16]

These devices allowed music, in this case hard rock and metal, to be heard in settings like military vehicles. Another Desert Storm veteran, "Achevyfan," recalls wearing out a Megadeth tape, and many Desert Storm soldiers identified hard rock/metal bands as favorites before combat (Metallica, Skid Row, Guns 'n' Roses, Judas Priest, Faith No More, and others).[17] While Desert Storm demonstrates a precedent for how soldiers in Iraq motivate themselves for possible combat through music, audio technology of the early 1990s did not allow personal music to be as readily accessible. CDs, portable CD players, and mp3 players were not yet the primary media for audio consumption, and, to a certain degree, this limited the development of music as a factor in soldiers' lives. "Achevyfan" comments: "Sure wish we had iPods then."[18]

Music as an Inspiration for Combat in Iraq

Music has become a significant source of combat inspiration for American soldiers in Iraq. The relationship between music and soldier life seems more intimate in this war since new technology allows music to be a part of soldiers' lives on and off the battlefield in unprecedented ways. Staff Sergeant (SSG) Erik Holtan, who primarily served in Baghdad as part of a Medical Readiness Team from 2004–05, explains:

> the sheer fact that music is globally accessible made it so much easier for it to play a role while deployed. Personally, I had my laptop filled with all different kinds of music, for whatever situation I was in. I used my iPod for when I traveled as well as to put me to sleep at night; sometimes to cover up the sounds of where I was, i.e. helicopter, mortars, IEDs (improvised explosive devices).[19]

---

16   Ibid., February 7, 2007 and July 8, 2007.
17   Ibid., June 14, 2007.
18   Ibid., June 14, 2007.
19   Erik Holtan, interview by the author, tape recording (New York, April 18, 2006). Some of the interviews with soldiers can be heard in their entirety at <www.soundtargets.com>.

Most soldiers listen to music daily on portable music devices like laptops, CD players, mp3 players or iPods. Tanks, Strykers and Humvees are equipped with audio and communication systems that allow soldiers to construct improvised sound systems to listen to music while on patrol; in this context, music is played within the vehicle, not broadcast outside to Iraqi civilians. Sergeant First Class (SFC) C.J. Grisham, a non-commissioned officer (NCO) who served during the initial invasion of Iraq in March 2003, describes how he and his fellow soldiers created a surround-sound system in their truck:

> We took those Lansing-type of computer speakers—the big bassy ones—we took those, we mounted them up. We created this little webbing on the top of our truck out of 550 cord. We tied up in the webbing these speakers, we did four of them, so kind of like a surround-sound system in our truck. Then, we had a laptop and CD player with all my mp3s on it and we just plugged the outlets into the laptop. And then we had a converter that you could plug the speakers into, so that was our power—that was our sound system in the truck. It looked like crap but it sounded good.[20]

The practice of constructing sound systems in military vehicles appears to be widespread and many soldiers say that they listened to music while on patrol. Specialist (SPC) Colby Buzzell, a fully automatic machine gunner in the Army Infantry who served a year-long tour in Iraq from November 2003–04 recalls: "Our vehicle had a CD player hooked up to the radio, so sometimes we would just listen to music from the speakers inside the vehicle"; and Sergeant (SGT) Neal Saunders explains that "Guys have music wired up in the back of their Bradleys, or through the CBCs in their tanks. In the Humvees, you have a little CD player with a speaker and try to turn it up as loud as you can."[21]

Given the technology that allows music to be heard more frequently and in a greater variety of settings, like military vehicles, music's role as an inspiration for combat seems stronger than in previous wars. Almost every soldier I interviewed said that they listened to music before leaving the military bases to go on patrols or in vehicles while on patrol during some point in their deployment. Within these listening contexts, metal and rap emerge as the predominant musical genres of choice. In the following interview excerpts, soldiers describe their experiences.

SPC Jennifer Atkinson, who served a one-year tour in Iraq (2005) as a photojournalist/public affairs specialist with the 3rd Infantry Division (speaking about her husband's platoon):

> My husband was there with 4th ID (Infantry Division), which was one rotation prior to mine. They were in the shit a whole lot more than I was. They would go out and before they would go out, he said he remembers listening to

---

20   C.J. Grisham, interview by the author, tape recording (New York, May 1, 2006).
21   Colby Buzzell, interview by the author, tape recording (New York, April 27, 2006); Neal Saunders, interview by the author, tape recording (New York, April 18, 2006).

a song (Lil' John's "I Don't Give a Fuck"). They would listen to it over and over and over again, and they called it their "getting crunked" song. "Getting crunked" is just getting right with whatever you have to do, and getting in the right mindset. They would play it, and it had a refrain in it … and they would just chant that over and over and over again until they were pretty much screaming it. I understand because it takes a lot to get amped up to go out there because you can go out and you don't know what's going happen. You have to be really kind of hyped up and ready for anything. It was just this loud, crude refrain that they could just repeat over and over and over again until they were ready to go out.[22]

Buzzell:

Sometimes we would go out on patrols and we'd be sitting in the back, bored, and a couple of us would have our headphones on listening to music. Some of us would have mp3 players, some of us would have CD players. … Right about when we're about to go out on a raid or a mission or something, I'd listen to Slayer to get all into it. It's kind of a surreal experience listening to Slayer out there, I can't think of a … it's just weird. It kind of got me in the mood for it; it just gets you pumped up for it. The feeling of the music, it's whatever puts you in whatever mood. … Sometimes when we were getting the vehicle ready, right, before going on a mission, our TC, which is the guy in charge of the vehicle, would play some music out of the speakers, and we'd listen to it. Or sometimes on an observation post, when we got the setup, we would play some music. One time we went out on a mission—it was a joint mission with us and the Iraqi police and it was just a patrol. We had these military intelligence guys with us and they had speakers on their Humvee— propaganda speakers so when we go in their town they'd have an interpreter say, "Hey, we come in peace," kind of thing. When we left the gate for that mission one of the MI guys had an mp3 player and he played the theme song from Rocky. What is that song they always play on parades? I forgot how it goes. It doesn't have lyrics, but every fourth of July you hear that song; and the theme from The Good, [the] Bad and the Ugly. And when he played the music, when we getting ready to go out beneath the wire, everyone was just charged. Even the Iraqis, who probably had never heard those songs before, were all getting totally pumped up to go out on the mission. It just gets you ready to go. Because sometimes your motivation is down and you're like, "I don't want to play soldier today, I don't want to do this." But then you hear The Good, [the] Bad, and the Ugly theme song and you're like, "Fuck yeah, hell yeah. I'll go out on a mission today."[23]

---

22   Jennifer Atkinson, interview by the author, tape recording (New York, May 3, 2006).
23   Buzzell, interview.

Grisham:

> The Eminem "Go to Sleep" song, it kind of got us pumped up because every time we left that camp, there was a firefight. The thing is, my job is to go out and try and make friends with people and try to convince them that it is in their best interest to tell me where the bad guys are. I'm not going out there looking for a fight, I'm not breaking down doors and all that kind of stuff. So, that kind of wears at you and you finally get yourself into that mentally that, you know what? I'm going to have to shoot at someone today, so might as well get pumped up for it. So that Eminem song, "Go to Sleep," when we got to Fallujah was kind of our anthem and before every mission we'd blare that and we'd all scream the lyrics out. Now crossing the border (from Kuwait into Iraq) Metallica was the big push, and generally on the patrols, Metallica was a big patrol one. ... Usually it was "Seek and Destroy"—was a good one, "The Four Horsemen," "One" which is a great song, and "Sanitarium," because we all felt a little crazy. It seemed like there was a Metallica song for just about every mood. ... At night-time it was quiet, whenever we do a night mission. But generally during the day we'd listen to it (in the truck). We just didn't want to listen to it loud when we were off base because we didn't want to offend anybody.[24]

SPC Joshua Revak, who served in an M-1 Abrams tank in 2005–06:

> In the communication system, there's a place where you can put in—it is like an input where you can plug in. I think it used to be for a phone and when the tanks would sit in a small group, in like a defensive position or something, the tanks would be spread out. I don't know how far apart, but they would run a landline to each tank with a phone that you crank the phone, then it rings, and they would hook it up in the communication system. And I think that's the way they would be able to hear if they had their helmets on. So instead of hooking the phones up to that, we'd take a pair of headphones and cut the wire and just hook each side of the wire up to there—all the communication systems you could plug a CD player into it. That actually helps a lot when you are on long missions. ... A lot of people couldn't even roll out without music, it soothed them or prepared them mentally. A lot of guys would listen to Drowning Pool and gangster rap to try and get really pumped up, like predator kind of music I guess, things like that, metal, hardcore, Linkin Park, stuff like that.[25]

William Thompson, an Army counter-intelligence soldier who served in 2004, stated that the Infantry soldiers in his battalion would listen to metal and rap,

---

24   Grisham, interview.
25   Joshua Revak, interview by the author, tape recording (New York, April 4, 2007).

or what he described, like Revak, as "predator music," before going on patrol.[26] Arkansas National Guardsman, "J.R." Schultz, who deployed to Baghdad in 2004, stated that Drowning Pool's "Bodies" was popular among the Infantry soldiers in his battalion.[27]

Many documentaries of the Iraq war, like *Occupation: Dreamland*, *Gunner Palace*, and *Soundtrack to War*, offer further evidence of metal and rap inspiring soldiers for combat.[28] In *Occupation: Dreamland*, a film about the Alpha Company of the 2nd Battalion of the 505th Parachute Infantry Regiment in Fallujah, soldiers watch and listen to a music video of Slayer's "Bloodline" while they put on Kevlar vests and goggles before going out on a security mission. *Gunner Palace*, a documentary by Michael Tucker, who lived with the 2/3 Field Artillery for two months in one of Uday Hussein's weekend palaces in Baghdad, features a sonic backdrop of metal and rap music provided by the soldiers. In *Soundtrack to War*, multiple soldiers make the analogy that "war itself is heavy metal," and, in fact, the original version of Gittoes' documentary was titled, *War is Heavy Metal*. Bing West's *No True Glory: A Frontline Account of the Battle for Fallujah* provides a report of troops listening to Drowning Pool's "Bodies"—a song popular among soldiers interviewed in *Soundtrack to War*—as preparation for combat "… before jumping off into attack, McCoy had the habit of gathering troops and playing at full blast (Drowning Pool's) "Let the bodies hit the floor …"[29]

While many soldiers inspire themselves for missions with metal and rap, SFC Ronald Botelho, who deployed to Iraq three times, took a different approach. He listened to music that was indigenous to Iraqi culture instead of music to make him aggressive before going out of the military camps.[30] This selection was based on his specific duties. Botelho collected information from Iraqis and said that he listened to indigenous music as a way to inform himself about local culture. He aimed to establish a connection of trust with the people:

> *I listened to a lot of the cultural music to try and get into the rhythm, particularly the rhythm and how people spoke and their body language. I had to use a translator all the time because I don't speak Arabic or Persian Farsi. And so if you have, at least in my mind, if you have an idea of how the language flowed, musically—I think I may have mentioned a couple of Arabic singers, and when I did, people's faces would light up. It's, "Oh, you know something about it, not some stupid American." I would get a little bit more*

---

26 William Thompson, interview by the author, tape recording (New York, June 22, 2007).

27 David "J.R." Schultz, interview by the author, tape recording (New York, June 22, 2007).

28 Michael Tucker, *Gunner Palace* (Palm Pictures, 2004); Ian Olds and Garrett Scott, *Occupation: Dreamland* (Greenhouse Pictures, 2005); George Gittoes, *Soundtrack to War* (Melee Entertainment, 2006).

29 Bing West, *No True Glory: A Frontline Account of the Battle for Fallujah* (New York: Bantam, 2005), p. 176.

30 Ronald Botelho, interview by the author, tape recording (New York, June 8, 2007).

forthrightness from them, a little bit more information. A lot of it is useless, but nonetheless, I would get something. So music in my field helped bridge the gap between knowing nothing and cultural awareness. ... If I could say anything else, it is bridging the cultural divide that is the most important for me. And if I think about it even harder, music played a key role in that. That is not the case for a lot of people, for most of the soldiers and what they do. It is in what I do because my job is getting information.[31]

Botelho admits that his experience was not typical. In a scene from *Soundtrack to War*, soldiers discuss the rap artists they listen to in their vehicles; and someone mentions the female singer-songwriter, Diana Krall. One of the soldiers then says: "We support you, Diana, but we just can't listen to you when we roll."[32]

Some soldiers explained that metal and rap music was effective as an inspiration for combat, even though they did not listen to this music before deploying to Iraq. SPC Mark Miner, who served in an Infantry platoon in Baghdad from September 2004–05, said: "We used to play rock in our room to pump us up before patrols. ... Before I went I never really liked heavy metal. When I was there, however, I listened to certain songs that just fit well with my moods at times."[33] In a conversation with a young woman who wished to remain anonymous, she said that her brother served in Iraq, and, since coming back, he listens to death metal constantly, even though he was not a dedicated fan before his deployment.[34] While most soldiers prefer metal and rap within the context of combat inspiration, I was curious as to what happened if a soldier did not enjoy these styles of music. Buzzell commented that soldiers who may not like metal and rap are, often times, unable to avoid the music as it is played inside a vehicle or within the helmets of the crew in a tank. He recalled a situation during Christmas 2003 when his fellow soldiers played music that was not to his liking:

One time at Christmas, we were in Samarra (Iraq), and one of the guys ordered a Chipmunks Christmas CD with Alvin, Simon, and Theodore singing Christmas carols. And he put that in the CD player in the vehicle and I couldn't take it, I'd be like, "Turn that shit off!" I fuckin' can't stand that shit because we'd be listening to it for hours and hours. And he got a big kick out of it, driving around Iraq listening to the Chipmunks. Yeah, you are screwed if you don't like what is playing. God, I still cringe when I think about that.[35]

In the process of inspiring themselves for combat, soldiers also participate in premission rituals involving specific music. As mentioned in the previous interview

---

31   Ibid.
32   Gittoes, *Soundtrack to War*.
33   Mark Miner, email communication (April 29, 2006).
34   Anonymous, personal communication (May 25, 2007).
35   Buzzell, interview.

excerpts, soldiers sometimes gather before leaving a base to listen to songs. In the scene from *Occupation Dreamland*, for example, the soldiers put on their military equipment while listening to Slayer; Grisham mentions that "Go to Sleep" was their "anthem" in Fallujah; Atkinson says that "I Don't Give a Fuck" was the pre-mission "getting crunked" song for her husband's platoon. All of these situations involve aspects of ritual where soldiers come together and participate, either by listening, or singing/yelling along with the lyrics, in organized, pre-combat actions. Many times these actions are repeated before each mission or patrol. In this way, metal and rap are a means of creating aspects of social ordering. The soldiers psychologically prepare themselves for the possibility of combat through the shared experience of music. Tia DeNora has observed that music has the capacity to function "… as a device for clarifying social order, for structuring subjectivity (desire and the temporal parameters of emotion and the emotive dimension of interaction) and for establishing a basis for collaborative action."[36] DeNora's description accurately reflects what happens in soldiers' pre-combat rituals. The music has a collective effect on the soldiers and operates as a "pretext" for action.

Music also enhances the feeling of "group-ness" or community within these rituals. By singing/screaming the lyrics of a song or listening to a song within the same physical space, soldiers create a sense of community through their common act in preparation for a common objective. Music is a means of establishing the identity of the group and supports the feeling of togetherness through a ritualized musical experience. Many soldiers claim that music helped form social groups within the military. Soldiers would frequently create and sustain friendships around their mutual enjoyment of particular popular music genres. Buzzell explained:

> *the kids that would listen to country music would all be a clique, and the kids that listen to gangster rap would all be a clique, and the kids that listen to punk would be a clique. It's sort of like, if you're at a party or with a group of people, and you listen to punk, or metal, or whatever, and you meet another person that is into punk or metal, at least you have something in common. You can start talking to them and kind of relating, and forming maybe a friendship, rather than somebody who listens to something entirely different or doesn't know anything about it. It was kind of interesting how the different cliques all kind of were into the same music.[37]*

The identity of different soldier groups or communities ("cliques") is often defined by musical preferences.

To a certain extent, soldiers are preconditioned for this type of ritual and community building. The musical environment of basic combat training (BCT)— with running and marching cadences—involves soldiers in collectively singing responses that are intended to develop camaraderie. Soldiers in BCT are taught the importance of teamwork and unity that is vital to military service, completing

---

36   Tia DeNora, *Music in Everyday Life* (New York: Cambridge University Press, 2000), p. 111.
37   Buzzell, interview.

a mission, and, in some cases, survival. The soldiers' pre-mission rituals may be considered extensions of these types of activity. The tendency of soldiers to come together around music, and to sing or yell the lyrics together, seems to have precedence in aspects of BCT.

Grisham's account of music as an inspiration for combat suggests another function of music while on patrol. He recalls that his group would listen to music during missions and that the music in this setting was beneficial to soldier concentration:

> It was always still there keeping us alert. For some reason, when we had the music on in the truck, there was less talking and, more, you were paying attention to your sector. You were on your guard a little bit more, because you were able to sustain your horizon, and you didn't have to keep up with the conversation. You just focused on the music, and focused on your sector, and made sure that you weren't getting shot at.[38]

DeNora observes that music has the power to operate as "a device with which to configure a space such that it affords some activities—concentration—more than others. ... Music affords concentration because it structures the sonic environment, because it dispels random or idiosyncratic stimuli, aesthetic or otherwise."[39] In Grisham's case, the music replaced the silence that was likely to stimulate conversation among the soldiers, and thus helped to direct their attention back to the duty at hand. Conversely, other soldiers believe that music heard while on duty, particularly in combat zones, could distract soldiers or limit their ability to hear. The effect of music in these circumstances—its ability to enhance or disrupt concentration—appears dependent on context and individual response.

Soldiers' accounts confirm that metal and rap music most often functions as an inspiration for combat, but not during combat itself. The music is a "pretext" for action, not a soundtrack to the fighting. Every soldier interviewed said that any music they listen to before combat does not continue in their minds as a real-time accompaniment to combat. Saunders commented:

> As soon as guns start firing and you're fighting your way out of an ambush, or those tanks starts going off, or those RPGs [rocket-propelled grenades] start going off, you don't fuckin' hear that music. It's all just instinct, man. It's all what you got inside of you that starts coming out.[40]

The soldiers' survival instinct and trained reactions block out sounds that are not immediately useful or relevant to combat. Buzzell, in fact, suggests that the sounds of combat become the music. Although he senses a relationship between

---

38   Grisham, interview.
39   DeNora, pp. 60–61.
40   Saunders, interview.

Slayer's music and the sounds of war, the music is decidedly not in his ears during combat.

> In combat? No. You know why? Because the explosions and the machine guns, and the shooting that's going on, that's the music. It's kind of like listening to Slayer, like that sort of shit. Listening to a two-forty fire off rounds, or a TOW missile hit something, that's music to your ears, kind of. And that sounds all twisted and wrong, but that's music in itself.[41]

Similarly, Grisham points out that even if music was playing in a tank or Humvee during combat, it seemed to disappear from the soldiers' perceptions for that time: "When shots started firing, we didn't hear anything. It's like it stopped for a little while."[42]

Metal and Rap Ideology, and Inspiration as Transformation

Most of the American soldiers interviewed for this project commented that they listened to metal and rap music before going out on patrols or missions to prepare for the possibility of combat. Soldiers frequently listen to metal or rap songs, either individually or in a group, as an inspiration for combat: Buzzell said that he listened to Slayer, which "got me in the mood for it, it just gets you pumped up;" Atkinson explained that her husband's unit would call this "getting crunked," and listened to Lil' John's "I Don't Give a Fuck" as a group before missions; Grisham and his tank mates listened to Metallica, Mudvayne, and during their assignment to Fallujah played "Go to Sleep" by DMX, featuring Eminem and Obie Trice, as a pre-mission anthem. What is it that links metal and rap music to the process of "getting crunked" before missions? How do these musical genres operate within the psychological context of combat preparation?

In terms of metal, the majority of sociocultural studies identify the concept of power as one of the most important aspects of this music. In her book, *Heavy Metal*, Deena Weinstein examines the sociocultural aspects of heavy metal music and its surrounding (sub)culture; she claims that a vital component of metal music is power. "The essential sonic element in heavy metal is power, expressed as sheer volume. Loudness is meant to overwhelm, to sweep the listener into the sound, and then to lend the listener the sense of power that the sound provides."[43] Other scholars, like Robert L. Gross, echo Weinstein's belief that the genre revolves around the concept of power: "the key element in the majority of heavy metal songs is the

---

41 Buzzell, interview.
42 Grisham, interview.
43 Deena Weinstein, *Heavy Metal: A Cultural Sociology* (New York: Macmillan, 1991), p. 23.

concept of power."[44] While the power element of metal is manifest in a variety of ways within the music (through performance, timbre, vocal articulation, rhythm, pitch, and others), it operates, not as a dominating force over the fan, but as an empowering agent. Robert Walser asserts: "the loudness and intensity of heavy metal music visibly empower fans."[45] The force of the heavy metal sound then ascribes power to the lyrical themes of the music, which Weinstein divides into two opposing categories, "Dionysian" and "Chaotic". "Dionysian" themes involve "sex, drugs, and rock and roll," and focus on forms of physical gratification and ecstasy. Conversely, "Chaotic" themes rebel against social norms and reveal a fascination with conflict, violence, and death. Robert Pielke claims that heavy metal songs demonstrating the themes of chaos have an "attitude of negation, with its emphasis on the images of death, Satanism, sexual aberration, dismemberment, and the grotesque."[46] Weinstein's categorization of heavy metal lyric themes certainly risks oversimplification and generalization, but it is useful to this study because it highlights a significant trend in metal music that is concerned with elements of war, mayhem, death, and destruction.

Almost all of the metal songs selected by soldiers as an inspiration for combat involve themes of chaos. A favorite album among soldiers is Slayer's *Reign in Blood* (1986), which is often credited as being the seminal album of the death metal subgenre. Another popular band is Metallica; their song "One," about a WWI soldier who survives a land mine explosion in which he loses his limbs, sight, hearing, and speech, was played frequently by Grisham during the initial invasion of Iraq. Drowning Pool's "Bodies" is another popular song with its repeated refrain, "Let the bodies hit the floor." In this case, however, the meaning of the lyrics has taken a different form from the original intent. Drowning Pool claim that the refrain refers to the audience "hitting the floor" of the "mosh pit" at a concert, not bodies falling to the ground from acts of violence. When these themes of chaos are combined with the notions of power inscribed in the metal sound, they provide a highly influential tool for soldiers as they prepare for combat.

In addition to themes of chaos, concepts of empowerment are essential components of metal ideology. Soldiers draw on the empowering sounds of metal music and the lyric content of chaotic themes, which involve graphic portrayals of death, destruction, and war, to prepare themselves psychologically for their combat experiences. While it makes sense that a musical genre whose primary elements involve empowerment and the thematic content of death/war would

---

44 Robert L. Gross, "Heavy Metal Music: A New Subculture in American Society," *Journal of Popular Culture* (1990), 24/1: 124. Also, see Robert Walser, *Running with the Devil: Power, Gender, and Madness in Heavy Metal Music* (Hanover, NH: Wesleyan University Press, 1993), p. 2 – "'Heavy metal' now denotes a variety of musical discourses, social practices, and cultural meanings, all of which revolve around concepts, images, and experiences of power."

45 Walser, p. 2.

46 Robert Pielke, *You Say You Want a Revolution: Rock Music in American Culture* (Chicago: Nelson-Hall, 1986), p. 202.

play an important role for soldiers as they prepare for combat, the role of music is more complex than what may be at first apparent. The majority of soldiers say that listening to metal or rap pumps them up for missions, but some also claim that part of this inspiration relates to music's psychological power to transform them outside of their normal selves. The music not only inspires them for possible combat, but artificially alters their states of mind such that they are able to handle the grotesque reality of their involvement in the war.

> War is so ugly and disgusting, and it's very inhuman. It's an inhuman thing. It's unnatural for people to kill people. It's something that no one should ever have to do; unfortunately, someone does. And we happen to be that someone sometimes. And so listening to music would artificially make you aggressive when you needed to be aggressive. If you knew you were going out and you were going to get shot at, you didn't want to go out there thinking everything was hunky-dory; you had to go out there with an aggressive mindset, hoping you wouldn't have to use that aggression. And so how it affected me is that it was really able to keep me alert. It made me — when I needed to get aggressive, I'd put some aggressive music on.[47]

Grisham highlights the music's power to keep soldiers in a state of heightened awareness, but also to make them capable of "inhuman" acts. In these instances, the music could be said to have a transformative power that removes the humanity element from human identity. Other soldiers said that metal and rap music had similar effects, to varying degrees, on their experiences as an inspiration for combat. Saunders believes that "war is people having to step outside of themselves. It is you having to become what I consider to be a monster."[48]

The idea of individuals stepping "outside of themselves" in relation to violent acts resonates with certain aspects of metal ideology. In *Running with the Devil*, Walser claims that "metal energizes the body, transforming space and social relations," and Weinstein quotes a fan as saying: "the whole point of heavy metal music is to get out of your mind."[49] In the scene from *Occupation: Dreamland* in which soldiers watch a video of Slayer's "Bloodline" before going out on patrol, a soldier says: "Yes, Slayer. I hear and obey." This comment is followed by a brief chorus of laughter, but the silence and intense stares into the television as soldiers watch the video imply the seriousness of their approach to combat preparation. Chaotic themes and notions of power appear to play a significant role for inspiring soldiers, or pumping them up, for combat. In some cases, there seems to be a transformative element to the music where the primary components of metal ideology, empowerment and chaotic themes, function as ways to artificially change

---

47 Grisham, interview.
48 Saunders, interview.
49 Walser, p. 2; Weinstein, p. 122.

the state of mind, thereby allowing soldiers to deal with the "inhumanity" of being involved in war.[50]

Certain aspects of rap ideology fit well within this framework. Specifically, soldiers tend to listen to "gangsta rap" prior to engaging in combat. In his assessment of subgenres within rap music, Adam Krims distinguishes gangsta rap as a subgenre within the larger category of "reality rap." While reality rap "undertakes the project of realism, in the classical sense, which in this context would amount to an epistemological/ontological project to map the realities of (usually black) inner city life," gangsta rap "describes gang life, or more generally, life in the ghetto from the perspective of a criminal (or liminal, transgressive) figure."[51] Reality rap refers to any lyrical theme that depicts the difficulties of human existence, usually from an urban, African-American perspective, but gangsta rap tends to isolate focus on lyrical themes that emphasize a "survival of the fittest" attitude in which the violence and death of the "other" (often contextualized in street life, gang life, or inner-city existence) are seen as fundamental components of one's own survival. Gangsta rap's rhetorical position is typically associated with criminal or deviant behavior, and violence in the form of murder with a firearm, which is one of the distinguishing features of gangsta rap within the larger category of reality rap.

The power element of gangsta rap ideology is the ability of survival and waging violence against anyone or anything that threatens survival. Power is often expressed through the lyrical theme of threatening to destroy an enemy without fear of repercussions. The world-view expressed in the lyrics seems to demonstrate the nihilistic attitudes that Cornel West describes as a "numbing detachment from others and a self-destructive disposition toward the world."[52] Grisham, for instance, said that the lyrics of "Go to Sleep" would pump them up for "the forthcoming hell of being ambushed" while stationed in Fallujah.[53] The refrain from "Go to Sleep" illustrates this point:

Now go to sleep, bitch!

Die, motherfucker, die! Time's up, bitch, close your eyes!

Go to sleep, bitch! (What?)

Why are you still alive? How many times I gotta tell you, close your eyes?

---

50   Certainly, not every soldier will engage with the music in the same way, so there may be degrees to which the music has the suggested transformative impact. For a more detailed analysis of the transformative effect of metal and rap music, see Jonathan Pieslak, *Sound Targets: American Soldiers and Music in the Iraq War.*

51   Adam Krims, *Rap Music and the Poetics of Identity* (New York: Cambridge University Press, 2000), p. 70.

52   Cornel West, *Race Matters* (New York: Vintage Press, 1994), p. 23.

53   Grisham, interview.

And go to sleep, bitch! (What?)

Die, motherfucker, die! Bye, bye, motherfucker, bye, bye![54]

Soldiers involved in the Iraq war who listen to gangsta rap appear to identify with the themes of "survival of the fittest" and violence, but not necessarily in the contexts of street gang life on which this subgenre is based. Additionally, some rap scholars, like Robin D.G. Kelley, have proposed that much of the violence glorified in gangsta rap should be understood as a deeper commentary on the reality of poor, urban existence.[55] She believes that those who disapprove of the genre as irresponsibly glamorizing gang life tend to overlook its cultural criticism, in which violence expresses a rebellion against larger social and racial oppression.[56] Despite this understanding of gangsta rap violence, most soldiers are not concerned with the possible social or racial commentary underlying the music they use for combat inspiration; rather, they relate directly to the lyrics. Their involvement with gangsta rap lyrics tends to unfold primarily on the immediate, surface level of listener identity, and, many times in the context of combat inspiration, they prefer the more explicitly violent and nihilistic songs over those with lyrics of social and racial criticism or texts expressing sexual exploitation of women, or misogyny.

Like metal music, the lyrical themes of gangsta rap ideology seem to have a transformative effect. In her book, *Rap Music and Street Consciousness*, Cheryl L. Keyes claims that "gangsta rap artists argue that the tales from the hoods range from truthful accounts to exaggerated fantasies."[57] Much of the fantasy element within these songs involves violence or physical gratification—thematic content similar to the "Chaotic" or "Dionysian" themes identified by Weinstein in metal music. In the case of soldiers in Iraq, however, the fantasy element is more about stepping outside of oneself to be able to handle the realities of war (destruction, heightened alertness, death), than entering a world of pleasurable fantasy. Talking about "Go to Sleep," Grisham says:

> *It's a very negative song, and I'm almost even embarrassed to say it was our theme song. But hey, that's what happens in war. You've got to become inhuman to do inhuman things. And, by that, I just mean shooting a weapon in the direction of a living person. … The worst part is that I didn't used to use profanity, but at some point I snapped. Now that I've returned to normal, I can't listen to this song.*[58]

---

54 Refrain from "Go to Sleep" by DMX, featuring Eminem and Obie Trice.
55 Robin D.G. Kelley, *Race Rebels: Culture, Politics, and the Black Working Class* (New York: The Free Press, 1994), pp. 183–227.
56 Ibid.
57 Cheryl L. Keyes, *Rap Music and Street Consciousness* (Chicago: University of Illinois Press, 2002), p. 4.
58 Grisham, interview.

Grisham identifies with the song in the process of becoming "inhuman" and psychologically "snapping". The process of transformation or fantasy is one in which soldiers place themselves in the position of the gang criminal and adopt the perspective towards violence and death articulated in the lyrical themes of the gangsta rap song. Some soldiers move into a state of mind outside of their "normal" selves as they prepare for combat, in order to come to terms with the reality of their surroundings; and certain aspects of gangsta rap ideology, like survival and violence, operate as important catalysts in this process.

The relationship between music and war has a long and distinct history, and this article examines only one of the many ways that music operates within the context of soldiers' lives at war. It is important to remember that the contemporary musical practices of American soldiers in Iraq are largely shaped by recent developments in audio technology. Music appears to play a more direct and significant role in the lives of soldiers than in previous American military conflicts, so much so that one soldier interviewed, who adopts the pseudonym "American Soldier," emphasized that:

> *Music was a huge thing for me while in the war; music was played a great deal in deployment. I listened to it as much as I could. I really don't know what I would have done without my iPod over there. The military ought to issue an mp3 player to every soldier![59]*

Soldiers' musical interactions are also highly variable; during deployment, they experience music in a wide variety of ways. While the study above represents those enlisted-rank soldiers who are engaged in military occupational specialties (MOS) that involve combat, many soldiers do not leave the bases regularly or encounter combat, which seems to result in a different set of musical practices. Soldiers' interactions with music vary considerably depending on factors like personal preference, ethnicity, geographic background, MOS, and rank, among others. Issues ranging from gender, sexuality, race, and religion to soldiers' acoustic guitar music, military bands, and the impact of USO-sponsored concerts seem fertile areas for further investigation. The influence of music seems more potent in the context of war than in daily life, and I would like to close with a quote from a soldier, "Major Pain," who served eight months in Afghanistan and one year in Ramadi, Iraq, which effectively speaks to this power:

> *Music can help you escape the terror and terrible things you may see. Make you think and see things back home or bring smells of a Christmas morning from home to you in a hellhole. Music can take you through a time warp and, even though for a second, can make you forget the hell around you.[60]*

---

59   "American Soldier," email communication (April 17, 2006).
60   "Major Pain," email communication (June 20, 2007).

Media War and Media Management

Stephen Badsey

The expression 'media war' was first heard in the aftermath of the Gulf War (1991, US official military designation: Operation Desert Storm), although as a concept it pre-dates that war by slightly more than a decade. It was coined to reflect a significantly new relationship in war between Western armed forces and the media, not only of greater importance than in previous wars, but also different in nature. Media war represents not (as some could perhaps be forgiven for thinking) a war conducted by the armed forces *against* the national and international news media, but rather the exploitation of the news media by the armed forces as a means of securing military victory on the battlefield. Systematic and pre-planned, media war is structured from the highest levels downwards, stretching around the globe to the centres of national policy and public opinion. It has developed as a consequence of recent increases in the news media's intrusion into the sphere of military operations, followed by an unprecedented (and politically much more controversial) intrusion by the military into the civilian sphere of the domestic media and public opinion. Although media war is closely related to public diplomacy, practised in both peace and war by governments and others, in itself it is best considered as a branch of the military art.

The resources and level of sophistication needed to fight media war mean that in practice its implementation is confined to the United States, together with Great Britain, a few other NATO and European Union countries, and Australia: all countries with democratic governments responsive to public opinion, armed forces that habitually engage in overseas military operations as a matter of governmental choice, and mass news media that operate on a global scale. For historical reasons relations between the armed forces and the media are most hostile and most problematic for the United States, which also has a continuing valid claim to dominate the international media market. Most of these countries have also been subject to propaganda attacks mounted against them through the media during military operations, both to influence policy and public opinion, and to affect the outcome on the battlefield.

Whereas, in the past, both armed forces and the media had poor institutional memories in their dealings with each other and had to learn the same lessons each time they re-engaged, media war has been institutionalised as a central part of military planning, and is employed in a systematic and (in the case of the United States) very aggressive manner, which gives the armed forces a considerable advantage in their dealings with the media. Consequently, media war has raised important issues about the relationship between the armed forces and the core values of their societies, as well as the changing nature of the mass news media and its wider role in democratic societies. Since 1991, a considerable output of scholarly books and articles has analysed the impact of this new military–media relationship, which is widely accepted among political theorists as integral to emerging new forms of conflict. However, writers on traditional military thought and strategy have generally been slow to adopt the same perspective, an important exception being the former British and NATO senior commander, General Sir Rupert Smith, who has argued that a separate military sphere no longer exists and that military operations now take place entirely within the civilian sphere, that 'we fight in every living room in the world as well as on the streets and fields of a conflict zone', with the media as 'the source of the contexts in which the acts in the theatre [of war] are played out'.[1]

Despite its wide use as an expression, media war is not recognised as a doctrinal term by any country's armed forces, and a coherent theory or consensus on its nature has not yet emerged. Perhaps in consequence, the term has sometimes been misused or misunderstood to mean merely wartime propaganda or deception.[2] Military doctrinal terms change frequently, and armed forces can be quite dismissive of anyone who fails to employ their terminology of the moment, while the media prefer to use more elastic terms which are easily understood by the public, such as 'censorship' rather than 'voluntary prior security review'. For many years the US armed forces have used 'public affairs' (PA) to describe the work of functionaries at all levels who deal with the media and issue official statements. The British preferred 'public information' up until 1992, when the newly-created ARRC, the British-led NATO headquarters designed to command many different nationalities and sub-units as required, introduced the term 'media operations' (Media Ops), and this has spread throughout British and NATO usage.[3] Since at least the First

---

1   Smith, *The Utility of Force*, pp. 285 and 391. For perspectives on the impact of the new military–media relationship see e.g. Ignatieff, *Virtual War*; Kaldor, *New and Old Wars*; McInnes, *Spectator-Sport War*; Shaw, *The New Western Way of War*; Toffler and Toffler, *War and Anti-War*.

2   Notably by both NATO (North Atlantic Treaty Organisation) and the Serbian government in the 1999 Kosovo War; see Stephen Badsey, 'Media Interaction in the Kosovo Conflict', in Badsey and Latawski, eds, *Britain, NATO and the Lessons of the Balkan Conflicts 1991–1999*, pp. 82–3.

3   ARRC stood originally for ACE (Allied Command Europe) Rapid Reaction Corps, and when Allied Command Europe was disbanded it became the Allied Rapid Reaction Corps. It has been used by NATO to command complex multinational formations, including IFOR (Implementation Force for the Dayton Accords) in Bosnia 1995–96,

World War (1914–18), almost all governments and armed forces have avoided the term 'propaganda', chiefly because there is confusion between its widespread popular meaning of malicious falsehood and its use by practitioners to mean influence which may be sometimes even benign in nature. The presently preferred military term that includes both propaganda and deception is 'psychological operations' (Psyop or Psyops), which is regarded as distinct from public affairs or media operations; however, through repeated use or misuse, the term Psyop now also carries connotations of duplicity.

If 'media' is taken to embrace the arts, including fiction, drama and music, then their relationship with warfare is probably as old as human history. Mass news media, in the sense of a commercially-owned press free from prior government censorship and protected by the law, emerged in the eighteenth century, and was seen in political theory as an important part of the liberal state and civil society first in Great Britain and the United States, before spreading through Europe and then across the world. In modern democratic theory, the media continue to carry out an essential political and social role in helping inform the electorate and shape public opinion. In the case of wars, most modern theories of public opinion place emphasis on the role of social and political elites in shaping this opinion, with the media's role in providing an early context and 'frame' for events as particularly important.[4] The military are usually disdainful of any notion of the media as part of democracy, preferring to cite their shortcomings in practice, while maintaining an equally idealised picture of themselves as defenders of their country and its values.

War reporting in the modern sense emerged from a combination of advances in politics, society and technology (particularly steam power and the telegraph) in the early nineteenth century. The idea of accuracy in reporting developed slowly, appearing first in British and European newspapers rather than in North America. But despite partisan behaviour which later ages would regard as outrageous, probably the Mexican War (1846–48) was the first to be reported by professionals. Certainly, the American Civil War (1861–65) was the first in which a democracy faced the problem of wartime military security versus press freedoms. The solution of President Abraham Lincoln's government was that the constitution should neither be preserved exactly as in peacetime nor suspended altogether, but that compromises should be worked out on a pragmatic basis, reinforced by temporary wartime legislation of draconian severity, intended as a deterrent rather than for use.[5] This preference for compromise has been the essential policy of democratic governments ever since, meaning that armed forces and the media have been obliged to work in co-operation although their interests have often clashed. The Crimean War (1854–56) saw the first clear demonstration of the way that

---

KFOR (Kosovo Force) 1999, and ISAF (International Security and Assistance Force) in Afghanistan 2006–07.

4   Siebert, Peterson and Schram, *Four Theories of the Press*, pp. 39–104; Nerone, *Last Rights*, pp. 31–124; Mueller, *War, Presidents and Public Opinion*.

5   Marszalek, *Sherman's Other War*, pp. 3–22.

the media could connect domestic public opinion with a war zone, affecting the conduct of the war while it was being fought. This reflected an unequal (in military terminology 'asymmetric') relationship between the generals and the war reporters on the battlefield: while British reporters in the Crimea had to negotiate carefully for access to their story, the political power of their newspapers back in London meant that the military could not exclude them or control them absolutely.[6] War reporters and, later, cameramen have always been constrained by these political and institutional pressures, and by the need for speed; but even so, from the early twentieth century onwards a tradition grew up of their priding themselves on their integrity and even impartiality.

As state power and awareness of the media increased, a period of more formal control and censorship of the media in war began with the Russo–Japanese War (1904–05) and lasted through to the Korean War (1950–53). It reached its height in democracies in the First World War and the Second World War (1939–45), in which national survival was perceived to be at stake and the media were enlisted into the war effort, including owners and editors being made part of government, and reporters put into military uniform. For front-line reporters and newsreel cameramen, the Second World War saw the systematic use of a 'pool' system, whereby the military granted access to a few chosen personnel whose material was then widely shared. In both world wars, the British largely maintained a media policy of what they called 'the propaganda of the facts', preferring to avoid outright falsehoods in favour of selection or omission to present the most favourable case in an understated manner, very much in the traditions of their diplomacy. This was based on the belief that long-term credibility is too important as a strategic advantage to be given up for short-term opportunism, and that the peacetime values of a society retain some importance even in war. The same view was adopted by the United States, which employed specialists in advertising to present its official case to foreign and domestic audiences. In the Second World War, General (later President) Dwight D. Eisenhower characterised the reporters within his headquarters as 'quasi-staff officers', and maintained the traditions of the Civil War by dealing with the national media pragmatically and through negotiation backed by deterrent legislation. The public also showed a clear understanding that in wartime the rules of the military–media relationship were different: temporary wartime necessities including censorship backed by the force of law were accepted, together with the expectation that the media would report military operations favourably and conceal many unpleasant truths. When the media criticised military actions, they usually did so in the name of strengthening the war effort. Critically, in both wars those in charge of propaganda and of military–media policy were predominately civilians, working in close co-ordination with national policy and grand strategy.

---

6   For histories of the military–media relationship in wartime, including its relationship to propaganda, see, for example, Carruthers, *The Media at War*; Connelly and Welch, eds, *War and the Media*; McLaughlin, *The War Correspondent*; Sweeney, *The Military and the Press*; Taylor, *Munitions of the Mind*; Young and Jessel, *The Media and the Military*.

Much of this attitude still persists: most people in democracies continue to understand that governments at war employ deception and propaganda, including withholding information from their own public for reasons of security. While Psyop is expected to include falsehood, military organisations which deal with the media in war still pride themselves on truthfulness as a matter of credibility, although they may withhold the entire truth or employ careful phrasing. The distinction was recently made by one veteran US Army press officer: 'Where neither access nor truth is appropriate, public affairs is not appropriate.'[7] Even so, some journalists see the official use of jargon and euphemisms as itself a form of lying. One constant critic, the distinguished Australian investigative reporter Phillip Knightley, gives his interpretation of military truthfulness as: '[L]ie directly only when certain that the lie will not be found out during the course of the war.'[8]

Another unchanging factor is that senior officers remain sensitive to such criticisms, and to media intrusion into their sphere of authority. The British commander of United Nations (UN) peacekeeping troops in Bosnia in 1994, Lieutenant General Sir Michael Rose, recounted with satisfaction in his memoirs that he physically assaulted a journalist who questioned his veracity, threatening further violence if it happened again.[9] Senior officers have also repeatedly shown anger and frustration at the media's refusal to accept what they are told, or to give credence to other sources, which they automatically characterise as 'propaganda' in contrast to their own 'truth'. When much of the international media took the side of the Bosnian government in 1994, Lieutenant General Rose objected: 'It is of course understandable that a Government struggling for survival should have a propaganda machine. It is not understandable that the international media should become part of that machine.'[10] In the often barbaric civil wars in Yugoslavia, Somalia and Rwanda in the early 1990s, military traditions of honesty in dealing officially with the media were placed under severe strain by the unrealistic political mandates given to the UN peacekeepers, and by hostile propaganda of the most virulent kind, to which some parts of the international media gave credence. In 1995 some UN officers resorted to outright lying to the media in order to conceal US covert action, a bombing campaign against Bosnian Serb targets which eventually became overt as Operation Deliberate Force.

Direct physical attacks against media facilities by US or NATO forces have been rare and controversial, even when these have been identified as hostile or as generating hate propaganda, the most prominent being the US bombing of the RTS television studios in Belgrade in 1999 during the Kosovo War (Operation Allied Force). Claims that reporters from friendly or neutral media have been deliberately fired upon by Western troops in wartime have been indignantly rejected by the military, but any zone of conflict is inherently a dangerous place, and there is

---

7   Colonel William M. Darley (US Army), 'Why Public Affairs is not Information Operations', *Army Magazine* (January 2005, no pagination).
8   Knightley, *The First Casualty*, p. 484.
9   Rose, *Fighting for Peace*, p. 64.
10 Rose, 'A Year in Bosnia: What has been Achieved?' p. 25.

evidence that Western reporters were deliberately targeted by at least one warring faction in Bosnia, and later in Afghanistan. In the initial invasion of Iraq in 2003 (Operation Iraqi Freedom) reporters were statistically more likely to be killed than members of the coalition armed forces. In wartime, the media have no more inherent right in law to protection provided by the military than any other civilians, and there is no undisputed media right of access to military operations. In political reality, Western armed forces have long had a moral obligation to protect or rescue reporters on a battlefield, although the military position is that they can only do this effectively if the media negotiate this protection beforehand in exchange for agreed terms of behaviour.[11]

After the Korean War, censorship and enforced military control of the media largely fell away as a practice, and in the US involvement in the Vietnam War (1961–73) reporters were allowed almost unfettered access and military assistance in the war zone. From the later twentieth century onwards, wars have been either limited in scope or undeclared, including numerous counterinsurgencies. This has produced another fundamental issue for military–media relations: a soldier risking his life in a firefight might feel entitled to the patriotic support of the media, but at the highest political levels how much governments and armed forces may demand media 'war rules' and self-censorship is always a matter for debate. The Vietnam War provoked immense controversy in the United States, amid military claims that unfavourable or biased news media coverage, particularly television news from the battlefield, had undermined public support and so produced defeat. Although often repeated, these claims were unsubstantiated and are now discredited, but a more sophisticated version of the argument may have some validity: in this view, the elites who do most to form US public opinion were genuinely divided in their support both for the Vietnam War and its conduct, and television and the press accurately reflected these divisions.[12]

The long-term importance of this experience for military–media relations was that the US military concluded that the media should never again be allowed to affect wartime public opinion in this way, that they had a duty to fight for and preserve domestic public support for their actions overseas, and that new forms of control of the media were needed. It took about a decade after Vietnam for these ideas to establish themselves in practice. After an improvised use of a media pool by the British in the Falklands War (1982, Operation Corporate), and disputes over media exclusion from the US invasion of Grenada (1983, Operation Urgent Fury), both countries agreed to the use of a wartime national media pool consisting of a small number of reporters working with military escorts, and voluntarily submitting their stories to military scrutiny beforehand. Although its first use in the US invasion of Panama (1989, Operation Just Cause) failed in an almost comic fashion, the pool system was fully implemented for the Gulf War

---

11   Cooper, 'Press Controls in Wartime' (no pagination); Payne, 'The Media as an Instrument of War', pp. 81–93.
12   Carlyle A. Thayer III, 'Vietnam: A Critical Analysis', in Young, ed., *Defence and the Media in Time of Limited War*, pp. 89–115; Hallin, *The 'Uncensored War'*.

(1991), in which pool reporters with US and British forces conformed to military agreements, while the media also employed unattached or unaccredited reporters, known as 'unilateralists' elsewhere in the war zone. In the ground phase of the war, while the British pool system functioned reasonably well from both military and press viewpoints, the US once more encountered serious problems with its pool system, resulting in further acrimony on both sides. Even so, in various forms the pool system remained the basis for front-line media coverage of US and NATO operations throughout the next decade.

In well over a century's dealings with the media, the military's strongest negotiating cards were that the national media needed to maintain long-term good relations with their government and people, and that in the war zone reporters were dependent on the military both for transport and for access to communications to get their stories home. But increasingly into the last decades of the twentieth century both of these were ceasing to be true. The media industry helped lead the way in globalisation, and with civilian satellite communications including direct television broadcasting becoming both technologically and financially viable this began to have a major impact on all aspects of society. Notably, when the Breton Woods financial system effectively collapsed in the early 1970s, the former gold standard for international money and commodity markets was replaced by a new 'information standard', greatly increasing the demand for instant news.[13] The world's first 24-hour cable television news channel was launched by CNN (Cable News Network) of Atlanta in 1980. Newspapers had long been unable to compete with television's speed of delivery and the impact of visual news, and by the 1980s they were already in decline as vehicles for mass communication, being driven either downmarket into entertainment, into partisan political commentary, or into specialist niches. Although the United States remained dominant both in international affairs and in the media industry, it could no longer assume the patriotic support of a global media, nor a battlefield free of live television images.

In the Gulf War, for the first time in warfare, British television networks used two 'forward transmission units', carried in two utility vehicles, to relay live television by satellite from the battlefield, by agreement with the British armed forces. The Iraqi regime repeatedly sought to exploit Western media, including allowing reporters to remain in Baghdad to broadcast (in CNN's case throughout the war). But the great media surprise of the war was how a highly co-ordinated US media policy at the highest levels had provided newsworthy images and narratives for the media, controlled the story, and successfully blocked negative or critical reports. The US military had drawn on their experiences of the previous decade and analysed future media trends to produce a new approach, while also relying on an innate hostility towards the media from many of their lower level commanders.[14]

The ideas and mechanisms that led to media war had their origins as far back as the start of the Cold War, when in 1947 the newly-created CIA (Central Intelligence

---

13   Read, *The Power of News*, pp. 397–406.
14   For the media in the 1991 Gulf War see, for example, Bennett and Paletz, eds, *Taken By Storm*; Taylor, *War and the Media*.

Agency) was placed in charge of psychological operations as part of US covert action around the world. In 1961 the Pentagon was made part-responsible with the CIA for covert operations, and 'political-psychological activities' were made part of the new Special Forces (Green Berets) remit. Meanwhile, the United States sought to prevent covert action from affecting its own democratic processes. In 1948 the Information and Educational Exchange Act (Smith-Mundt Act), while authorising the US government to disseminate propaganda ('information') abroad, made it illegal to do so at home, a position strengthened by the 1972 Foreign Relations Authorization Act. The object of this decision was to preserve the older tradition of truthfulness in public diplomacy, since it barred the State Department from conducting covert propaganda, while in Great Britain in the same period covert propaganda continued to be run by the Foreign Office. This US approach to covert action viewed propaganda (and sometimes media relations) as a branch of warfare governed by military imperatives, in contrast to the older tradition that it was a branch of diplomacy conducted during wartime.[15]

Another important factor in developing media war was the radical change in US warfighting doctrine after Vietnam, away from counterinsurgency and towards NATO and the defence of Western Europe, where US forces were located alongside those of the Federal Republic of [West] Germany. The US armed forces already took many of their ideas and traditions from the Germans, especially the doctrine of 'mission accomplishment', an almost obsessive emphasis on carrying out plans and orders regardless of changing circumstances or non-military factors, so in the late 1970s the US armed forces turned to their West German allies for methods of defeating a possible Soviet invasion. The West German Bundeswehr, in turn, still retained many of the ideas of the Imperial German Army and the Wehrmacht, including a heavy emphasis on victory through the primacy of battlefield skills. This had long been associated with an innovative and high-tempo German style of warfighting known commonly (although strictly inaccurately) as *Blitzkrieg* [lightning war].[16] From the early 1980s, the US armed forces adopted these German ideas in a form known as 'maneuver war', stressing the defeat of the enemy on the battlefield by attacking vulnerabilities in an utterly ruthless fashion. One US Army officer described maneuver war as 'a kick in the groin, a poke in the eye, a stab in the back. It is quick, violent for a moment, and unfair'; while an equally approving US Marines officer identified the soldiers needed for it as 'aggressive, independent, intuitive, curious, intellectual – and a man who knows that you go for the kill'.[17] In a spirit of NATO solidarity, maneuver war was also adopted by the British in

---

15 Lieutenant Colonel Frank L. Goldstein (PhD) USAF, Psychological Operations: A Plan for Success', in Hayden, ed., *Shadow War*, pp. 95–102; Prados, *Presidents' Secret Wars: CIA and Pentagon Covert Operations from World War II through Iranscam*, pp. 208–10 and 242; Treverton, *Covert Action*, p. 35; Lashmar and Oliver, *Britain's Secret Propaganda War 1948–1977*.

16 Trauschweizer, 'Learning with an Ally', *The Journal of Military History* (April 2008), vol. 72, no. 2: 477–508; Atkinson, *Crusade*, p. 250.

17 Leonard, *The Art of Maneuver*, p. 61; Hayden, *Warfighting*, p. 77.

the later 1980s, but with a characteristic twist as 'the manoeuvrist approach', a way of thinking and planning that the British claimed would be applicable to all forms of military operations including peacekeeping.[18] Long before the 2003 invasion of Iraq the US armed forces, and to some extent their NATO partners including the British, had absorbed deeply into their thinking the view that nothing should stand in the way of the mission they had been given, that victory on the battlefield was paramount, and that relations with the media were just another weapon to help bring this about.

These doctrines were adopted by US and NATO armed forces in the belief that nothing less could deter, or if necessary win, a non-nuclear Third World War in Europe. The success of maneuver war in 1991 in the Gulf War also gave it a tremendous boost in military popularity. But all this took place just as the strategic basis for its adoption changed with the end of the Cold War; for the foreseeable future military interventions overseas would be matters of governmental choice needing public support and approval. This presented a list of problems. The Vietnam War had provoked a revival of 'just war' theory and a lively debate among Western intellectuals on the ethics of such wars. Another lesson of Vietnam and subsequent smaller wars was that American and other Western publics were – rightly or wrongly – believed to be highly sensitive to casualties in war, especially civilian deaths, even on the other side.[19] A further problem was whether it was possible to divorce the purely technical and methodological aspects of the historic German approach to warfare from its accompanying traditions of brutality, particularly towards civilians; and whether such methods were appropriate for the armed forces of democratic countries. Recent works of scholarship have increasingly identified this extreme brutality not as an aberration of the Nazi era but as central to German warfighting from the later nineteenth century onwards, and draw a link to the 'unfair war' practised by the United States. 'Like the Wehrmacht', argued one British scholar in 2004, 'we've descended into barbarity.'[20] Whatever the merits of this particular argument, there was a dimension to this warfighting doctrine that made its presentation by the media controversial: watching the destruction wrought by coalition forces in the Gulf War, one senior British officer speculated whether 'commanders can now be ruthless enough, in a television age, to pursue the enemy to the limit, if the stakes are anything less than national survival'.[21] But, although critics complained that the image of the war had been 'sanitised' for public consumption, as long as these methods produced swift victory such complaints appear to have had little impact on domestic mass public opinion.

---

18   Army Code 71451: Design for Military Operations: the British Military Doctrine (MoD, 1996), pp. 4–21; Joint Warfare Publication 3–50 Peace Support Operations (MoD, 1998), pp. 3–10; McInnes, *Hot War, Cold War*.

19   Hugh Smith, 'The Last Casualty? Public Perceptions of Bearable Cost in a Democracy', in Evans and Ryan, eds, *The Human Face of Warfare*, pp. 54–83.

20   Professor Richard Overy, quoted in the editor's introduction to Kassimeris, ed., *The Barbarisation of Warfare*, p. 2.

21   Cordingley, *In the Eye of the Storm*, p. 254.

The experience of the Gulf War reinforced the US military consensus that dramatically swift and successful victories could be won by elite and technologically sophisticated forces. This culminated in 1996 in the announcement by the US National Defense University in Washington of the twin concepts of 'rapid dominance' and 'shock and awe', the latter term being adopted in 2003 for the invasion of Iraq by US Secretary of Defense Donald Rumsfeld and his theatre commander, General Tommy Ray Franks. As envisaged in 1996, the goal of rapid dominance was to merge a swift and violent physical attack on an enemy with attacks on his perception of events, so overwhelming him in every sense while keeping total losses and damage to a minimum.[22]

Meanwhile, the United States and other Western countries found themselves engaged in very different kinds of military operations, starting in 1991 with humanitarian assistance to the Kurds of northern Iraq (Operation Provide Comfort). Relationships between the military and the media in these operations varied depending on the level of success achieved; but some peacekeepers, particularly in Bosnia, found that some Western reporters were prepared to co-operate very closely with them, to help enforce ceasefires or condemn atrocities by making them global news, adding to the military belief that the media was a weapon to be exploited. Nevertheless, these operations, loosely characterised as peacekeeping or even as 'humanitarian war', gave rise to the conviction that the military–media relationship had once more swung in the media's favour with the 'CNN effect', a belief that live television coverage of humanitarian disasters had a very direct impact on governments and public opinion, leading to demands for the commitment of troops to the region, followed by equally swift demands for their withdrawal once casualties were taken or the situation proved problematic. As with other myths about the power of the media, evidence to support this simple view of the CNN effect is lacking or unconvincing, except perhaps in the earliest cases, including the joint UN/US intervention in Somalia (1992–94, Operation Restore Hope). A more sophisticated interpretation of the evidence may be valid: direct satellite broadcasting from the war zone had for the first time made mass public opinion an important factor in the diplomacy of using force overseas, intruding into a traditionally elite sphere of decision making.[23] But it is equally possible that on some occasions politicians may have made use of shocking media images as a cover to help implement policies on which they had already decided.

By the mid-1990s it seemed to Western armed forces that the rules of the media war had swung against them, and that it was time to redress the balance.[24] Further advances in commercial media technology were rapidly removing the last vestiges

---

22 Ullman and Wade, *Shock and Awe: Achieving Rapid Dominance*, pp. xi and xxiv; Gordon and Trainor, *Cobra II: The Inside Story of the Invasion and Occupation of Iraq*, p. 44.

23 Robinson, *The CNN Effect*, pp. 117–31; Bellamy, *Knights in White Armour*, pp. 100–123; Badsey, The and UN "Peacekeeping" since the Gulf War', pp. 13–15.

24 Edwards, 'The Military–Media Relationship: A Time To Redress the Balance?' pp. 43–9; Ripley, *Operation Deliberate Force*, especially the foreword by Nik Gowing, pp. 6–7; Smith, *The Utility of Force*, pp. 353–4.

of military control in a war zone, short of physical restraint. Mobile (cellular) telephones, digital cameras and satellite global positioning systems were becoming commonplace. The World Wide Web was launched in 1992 and, by the end of the decade, live pictures could be transmitted worldwide by a portable computer the size of a large notebook. Building on their previous experiences, the response of most Western armed forces, led by the United States, was to recognise that the media could no longer be controlled or coerced, and to adopt the techniques of public relations and lobbying used by governments and by large commercial firms in the public sphere in peacetime, in order to win over the media and 'court' them into doing their bidding.[25] In a development from the pool system, the US armed forces experimented with 'embedding' reporters, first in 1994 in their intervention in Haiti (Operation Restore Democracy), and then from 1995 onwards in IFOR in Bosnia. In this approach, large numbers of reporters known as 'embeds' are each attached to live and work with a specific small military unit for an extended period, with agreed rules for what they can report but no official check on specific stories, allowing them to send material as events unfold. This method greatly increases the likelihood of the embeds bonding with the military and adopting their perspective on events.

Among the media's strong cards in the developing media war has been that it is they who have mostly presented military behaviour to the wider public. But, building on trends that had been visible in the 1970s, by the last decade of the twentieth century a transformation of the media was underway, at least as great as that of the early nineteenth century which originally created war reporters. With this transformation, even the mass news media's historical role as part of the democratic process is being called into question, and with it by implication any obligation towards the media from the armed forces.[26] Globalisation in financial terms has concentrated the dominant ownership of communications and entertainment media into the hands of a few international companies, while at the same time diversifying and fragmenting the news media into many different outlets, diluting the idea of a national new media and weakening the dominant position of the United States in the media market. Websites have flourished, including personal commutations by soldiers from war zones, increasingly bypassing the media's role as an interpreter of events. Just as television had forced a change in newspapers, so websites have forced television news downmarket into a softer 'infotainment' style. More news product often results in less information to the public and an increase in opportunities for propaganda and censorship by the powerful.[27] The news media have always been dependent on official or reliable sources; now, starved of staff and resources by the increase in high-speed media outlets and the demand for continuous global ('24/7') news, newspapers and television have come to depend

---

25   Charles C. Moskos, 'Towards a Postmodern Military: The United States as a Paradigm', in Moskos, Williams and Segal, *The Postmodern Military*, pp. 19–21.

26   Schudson, *The Power of News*, pp. 189–223.

27   Gorman and McLean, *Media and Society in the Twentieth Century*, pp. 209–27; Alleyne, *News Revolution*, pp. 89–140.

increasingly on pre-packaged stories supplied to them, complete with visuals and quotations, by government departments and public relations firms. Once more, an old if controversial practice has being institutionalised and applied systematically, including by the armed forces in the name of generating public support for their activities and operations. In adopting this policy of packaging news for the media on such scale and in such a highly systematised manner, the military appear to have crossed an important line by intruding into domestic politics in an unprecedented fashion.

A prominent feature of the Gulf War had been an increased importance for electronic warfare, including space-based systems and computers collectively described by the new doctrinal term 'information warfare'. In August 1996 the Pentagon combined this with the basic concepts of 'shock and awe' in a new US Army manual on 'information operations' (IO) which vastly broadened the concept and its definition, expanding electronic warfare into 'command and control warfare' (C2W), including Psyop, and placing public affairs and the closely related activity of civil affairs (CA) within the same over-arching activity. For a while this caused some confusion as other nations' armed forces continued to think of information operations as solely related to electronics, radios and computers. Two years later a joint US armed forces doctrine for information operations withdrew slightly from this position, placing public affairs among activities that might contribute to 'offensive IO'.[28] Then US government perceptions were dramatically changed by the al-Qaeda terrorist attacks on New York and Washington on 11 September 2001 ('9/11'). Announcing a 'global war on terror' (renamed the 'long war' in 2006) the US government and its armed forces immediately adopted a war mentality (a phrase that is well understood if little analysed), including a belief that wartime media rules were now in force. Most of the media trouble that followed has been a reflection of the extent to which US public opinion, and that in other countries, either shared or did not share this perception. As well as the protracted fighting in Afghanistan which began that year under Operation Enduring Freedom, in late 2001 the US government launched an Office of Strategic Influence to disseminate propaganda, only to close it early the following year amid claims that it was targeting US domestic media. But, following the invasion of Iraq, in October 2003 the Pentagon continued with an 'information operations roadmap', further blurring the distinction between propaganda aimed at its enemies and military relations with the domestic media.[29]

As criticisms and problems over US policy towards the media both in Iraq and in the global war on terror increased, civilian practitioners of public diplomacy scarcely concealed their view that the military lacked the political sophistication

---

28   Joint Publication 3–13 Joint Doctrine for Information Operations (US Department of Defense, 9 October 1998), pp. II-6 and B-F-2.
29   Information Operations Roadmap (US Department of Defense, 30 October 2003), p. 26; this document was released under the Freedom of Information Act in 2006 and is available on the website of the National Security Archive at George Washington University.

to handle such a policy, including the ability to distinguish between bending the rules and throwing them away. Some even see the origins of the problem in President Kennedy's decision to remove the CIA's leading role in covert operations and counterinsurgency.[30] But experienced US and British military specialists in public affairs have also challenged the new thinking on information operations as inappropriate, as well as counterproductive in the long term.[31] The dispute reached the highest levels when, in September 2004, the professional head of the US armed forces, Chairman of the Joint Chiefs of Staff General Richard B. Myers, issued a memorandum stipulating a return to the traditional (and legal) doctrine that information operations and public affairs were separate activities, not to be intermingled.[32]

Distinguishing between treating military–media relations as a part of information operations, rather than as an activity running in parallel, might appear to be hair-splitting; but for specialists another important line had been crossed. Stripped of its doctrinal sophistry and applied to the real world, the new US information operations doctrine was encouraging the military from policy levels downwards to think of the media in terms of propaganda and deception, regardless of the wider and long-term political consequences. The practical results first became apparent in the Kosovo War, with friction evident between the US military and traditional – often civilian – practitioners of media relations within NATO.[33] As the new doctrine spread worldwide, the Australians in their UN peacekeeping operation in East Timor (2000, Operation Stabilise) took information operations to mean very much what the National Defense University had intended by shock and awe: any activity from public affairs to physical attack that could be used to manipulate the enemy's perceptions in support of victory.[34]

By the invasion of Iraq in 2003, domestic cynicism regarding US (and to some extent British) media policy in wars and the ability of the media to counteract it had grown considerably, with critics from the mainstream of the opinion-forming elites stating openly that their governments were engaged in propaganda and deception, and that the media were powerless to prevent this.[35] The role of the media in the invasion of Iraq was particularly prominent, since the US war plan identified the dictator Saddam Hussein's propaganda image with the Iraqi people as an important aspect of his power, and stipulated the destruction of 'regime

---

30   Quoted from a first-hand encounter by Davies, *Flat Earth News*, p. 244.
31   Darley, 'Why Public Affairs is not Information Operations'; Tatham, *Losing Arab Hearts and Minds*.
32   Quoted in Cox, 'Information Operations in Operations Enduring Freedom and Iraqi Freedom – What Went Wrong?' p. 83.
33   Stephen Badsey, 'Media Interaction in the Kosovo Conflict', in Badsey and Latawski, eds, *Britain, NATO and the Lessons of the Balkan Conflicts 1991–1999*, pp. 81–2.
34   Beasley, 'Information Operations during Operation Stabilise in East Timor', pp. 1–4 and 32–34.
35   Professor Carolyn Marvin, Annenberg School for Communication, University of Pennsylvania, quoted in 'Hyped hero Jessica Lynch returns home', Reuters (22 July 2003).

targets' such as wall posters and statues. This culminated in the symbolic toppling of a statue of Saddam in Baghdad, at a location allegedly selected by the Americans in advance and stage-managed for the Iraqi population and global media. As an illustration of what media war has become, this televised image was then written into President George W. Bush's speech a few days later declaring the end of 'major combat operations' in Iraq. 'In the image of falling statues,' the president claimed, 'we have witnessed the arrival of a new era.'[36]

The identification of regime targets meant that the invading coalition sought to maximise live television coverage of their destruction by their attacking forces. In consequence, although the invasion featured other familiar aspects of media war, such as unilateralists, Western reporters in Baghdad, and tight co-ordination of the US media message, US official policy placed its greatest emphasis on embeds, of which more than 760 were accredited to the US armed forces, together with over 2,200 media personnel registered with the coalition headquarters.[37] Whereas in 1991 the United States had emphasised news from its military headquarters in the region, CENTCOM (Central Command), this time CENTCOM was marginalised and the news came chiefly from Washington and from the front lines. The result was that most media attention was paid to the instant images that the military needed as the invasion progressed, but the pictures and anecdotes sent back by the embeds gave only the most impressionistic view of events. The television media were left bewildered: the military had granted them open access and unrestricted transmission, and the result was that they failed to report the war. Newspaper journalists, with the extra time to investigate and to write their stories, provided most of the best reporting, but their work made much less impact except with elites. It was hard not to conclude that the military had identified and exploited the media's demand for instant news and visuals, and had manipulated them into playing their desired role in the wider war plan.

Operation Iraqi Freedom was probably exceptional in that the media featured as such a central part of the overall military planning. But in the insurgency following the invasion, media war continued to play a large role in US military thinking and fighting. In April 2004, US Marines launched a major attack on the town of Fallujah in northern Iraq, using heavy firepower, with considerable destruction and civilian loss of life. After a few days the Marines were forced to halt, owing to opposition from the Iraqi interim government and wider national and international condemnation. The US military response was not to question their own methods, but to conclude that they had been defeated by superior enemy manipulation of the media. With echoes of the mythology of Vietnam, one influential commentator claimed that the Marines 'weren't beaten by the terrorists and insurgents'; rather,

---

36   White House Press Release, 'President Bush Announces Major Combat Operations in Iraq have Ended: Remarks by the President from the USS Abraham Lincoln at Sea off the Coast of San Diego, California' (1 May 2003); Rutherford, *Weapons of Mass Persuasion*, pp. 177–9; Rampton, Sheldon and Stauber, *Weapons of Mass Deception*.

37   Bryan Whitman, 'The Birth of Embedding as Pentagon War Policy', in Katovsky and Carlson, eds, *Embedded*, pp. 203–9.

'they were beaten by al-Jazeera', the independently-minded Arab satellite television station.[38] In consequence (and despite the previously firm ruling by General Myers), when the attack was renewed in November by the US Army, it included an elaborate propaganda offensive intended to neutralise the insurgents' access to the media, while simultaneously feeding the media pre-prepared and packaged visuals and stories, in the manner of a civilian public relations firm, in order to dictate the narrative of the battle. The senior US Army officer involved, Lieutenant General Thomas F. Metz, triumphantly characterised this approach as 'bridging the firewall' between public affairs and information operations, and as a pointer to military success in the future.[39]

References

Alleyne, Mark D., *News Revolution: Political and Economic Decisions about Global Information* (New York: St Martin's Press, 1997)

Army Code 71451: Design for Military Operations: The British Military Doctrine (MoD, 1996)

Atkinson, Rick, *Crusade: The Untold Story of the Persian Gulf War* (New York: Houghton Mifflin Harcourt, 1993)

Badsey, Stephen, 'The Media and UN "Peacekeeping" since the Gulf War', *Journal of Conflict Studies* (1997), vol. 17, no. 1: 17–27

Badsey, Stephen and Paul Latawski, eds, *Britain, NATO and the Lessons of the Balkan Conflicts 1991–1999* (London: Frank Cass, 2004)

Beasley, Major Kent, 'Information Operations during Operation Stabilise in East Timor', (Working Paper Number 120: Land Warfare Studies Centre (Australia), August 2002)

Bellamy, Christopher, *Knights in White Armour: The New Art of War and Peace* (London: Hutchinson, 1996)

Bennett, W. Lance and David L. Paletz, eds, *Taken By Storm: The Media, Public Opinion and U.S. Foreign Policy in the Gulf War* (Chicago: University of Chicago Press, 1994)

Carruthers, Susan L, *The Media at War* (London: Macmillan, 2000)

Connelly, Mark and David Welch, eds, *War and the Media: Reportage and Propaganda 1900–2003* (London: I.B. Tauris, 2005)

Cooper, Stephen D., 'Press Controls in Wartime: The Legal, Historical and Institutional Context', *American Communication Journal* (Summer, 2003), vol. 6, issue 4

Cordingley, Major General Patrick, *In the Eye of the Storm: Commanding the Desert Rats in the Gulf War* (London: Hodder and Stoughton, 1996)

---

38   Ralph Peters, quoted in Payne, 'The Media as an Instrument of War', p. 82.
39   Metz et al., 'Massing Effects in the Information Domain', pp. 2–12.

Cox, Major Joseph L. (US Army), 'Information Operations in Operations Enduring Freedom and Iraqi Freedom – What Went Wrong?' (Fort Leavenworth, KS: Monograph, School of Advanced Military Studies (SAMS), United States Army Command and General Staff College, 2006)

Darley, Colonel William M. (US Army), 'Why Public Affairs is not Information Operations', *Army Magazine* (January, 2005)

Davies, Nick, *Flat Earth News* (London: Chatto and Windus, 2008)

Edwards, Major P.W.D., 'The Military–Media Relationship: A Time to Redress the Balance?' *Journal of the Royal United Services Institute for Defence Studies* (October 1998), vol. 143, issue 5

Evans, Michael and Alan Ryan, eds, *The Human Face of Warfare: Killing, Fear & Chaos in Battle* (St Leonard's, NSW: Allen & Unwin, 2000)

Gordon, Michael and Bernard Trainor, *Cobra II: The Inside Story of the Invasion and Occupation of Iraq* (London: Atlantic Books, 2006)

Gorman, Lyn and David McLean, *Media and Society in the Twentieth Century: A Historical Introduction* (Oxford: Blackwell, 2003)

Hallin, Daniel C., *The 'Uncensored War': The Media and Vietnam* (Oxford: Oxford University Press, 1986)

Hayden, Lieutenant Colonel H.T. (USMC), ed., Shadow War: Special Operations and Low Intensity Conflict (Vista, CA: Pacific Aero Press, 1992)

– – –, *Warfighting: Maneuver Warfare in the U.S. Marine Corps* (Mechanicsburg, PA: Stackpole, 1995)

Ignatieff, Michael, *Virtual War: Kosovo and Beyond* (London: Vintage, 2001)

Information Operations Roadmap (US Department of Defense, 30 October 2003)

Joint Publication 3–13 Joint Doctrine for Information Operations (US Department of Defense, 9 October 1998)

Joint Warfare Publication 3–50 Peace Support Operations (MoD, 1998)

Kaldor, Mary, *New and Old Wars: Organized Violence in a Global Era* (Palo Alto, CA: Stanford University Press, 1999)

Kassimeris, George, ed., *The Barbarisation of Warfare* (London: Hurst, 2006)

Katovsky, Bill and Timothy Carlson, eds, *Embedded: The Media at War in Iraq – an Oral History* (Guilford, CT: Lyons Press, 2003)

Knightley, Phillip, *The First Casualty: The War Correspondent as Hero and Myth-Maker from the Crimea to Kosovo*, rev. edn (London: Prion, 2000)

Lashmar, Paul and James Oliver, *Britain's Secret Propaganda War 1948–1977* (Thrupp: Sutton, 1998)

Leonard, Lieutenant Colonel Robert R., *The Art of Maneuver: Maneuver-Warfare Theory and AirLand Battle* (Novato, CA: Presidio Press, 1991)

Marszalek, John F., *Sherman's Other War: The General and the Civil War Press* (Memphis, TN: Memphis State University Press, 1981)

McInnes, Colin, *Hot War, Cold War: The British Army's Way in Warfare 1945–95* (London: Brassey's, 1996)

– – –, Spectator-Sport War: The West and Contemporary Conflict (Boulder, CO: Lynne Rienner, 2002)

McLaughlin, Greg, *The War Correspondent* (London: Pluto, 2002)

Metz, Lieutenant General Thomas F. et al., 'Massing Effects in the Information Domain: A Case Study in Aggressive Information Operations', *Military Review* (May–June 2006)

Moskos, Charles C., John A. Williams and David R. Segal, eds, *The Postmodern Military: Armed Forces after the Cold War* (New York: Oxford University Press, 2000)

Mueller, John E., *War, Presidents and Public Opinion* (New York: Lanham, 1985)

Nerone, John C., ed., *Last Rights: Revising Four Theories of the Press* (Urbana, IL: University of Illinois Press, 1995)

Payne, Kenneth, 'The Media as an Instrument of War', *Parameters* (Spring, 2005)

Prados, John, *Presidents' Secret Wars: CIA and Pentagon Covert Operations from World War II through Iranscam*, rev. edn (New York: William Morrow, 1988)

Rampton, Sheldon and John Stauber, *Weapons of Mass Deception: The Uses of Propaganda in Bush's War on Iraq* (New York: Tarcher, 2003)

Read, Donald, *The Power of News: The History of Reuters* (Oxford: Oxford University Press, 1992)

Ripley, Tim, *Operation Deliberate Force: The UN and NATO Campaign in Bosnia 1995* (Lancaster: CDISS, 1999)

Robinson, Piers, *The CNN Effect: The Myth of News, Foreign Policy and Intervention* (London: Routledge, 2002)

Rose, General Sir Michael, 'A Year in Bosnia: What has been Achieved?' *Journal of the Royal United Services Institute for Defence Studies* (June 1995), vol. 140, issue 3

———, *Fighting for Peace: Bosnia 1994* (London: Harvill, 1998)

Rutherford, Paul, *Weapons of Mass Persuasion: Marketing the War Against Iraq* (Toronto: University of Toronto Press, 2004)

Schudson, Michael, *The Power of News* (Cambridge, MA: Harvard University Press, 1995)

Shaw, Martin, *The New Western Way of War* (London: Polity, 2005)

Siebert, Fred S., Theodore Peterson and William Schram, *Four Theories of the Press* (Urbana, IL: University of Illinois Press, 1963)

Smith, General Sir Rupert, *The Utility of Force: The Art of War in the Modern World* (London: Alan Lane, 2005)

Sweeney, Michael S., *The Military and the Press: An Uneasy Truce* (Evanston, IL: Northwestern University Press, 2006)

Tatham, Steve, *Losing Arab Hearts and Minds: The Coalition, Al Jazeera and Muslim Public Opinion* (London: Hurst, 2006)

Taylor, Philip M., War and the Media: Propaganda and Persuasion in the Gulf War (Manchester: Manchester University Press, 1992)

———, *Munitions of the Mind: A History of Propaganda from the Ancient World to the Present Day*, rev. edn (Manchester: Manchester University Press, 1995)

Toffler, Alvin and Heidi Toffler, *War and Anti-War: Survival at the Dawn of the 21st Century* (New York: Little, Brown, 1993)

Trauschweizer, Ingo Wolfgang, 'Learning with an Ally: The US Army and the Bundeswehr in the Cold War', *The Journal of Military History* (April 2008), vol. 72, no. 2

Treverton, Gregory F., *Covert Action: The Limits of Intervention in the Postwar World* (New York: Basic Books, 1987)

Ullman, Harlan K. and James P. Wade, *Shock and Awe: Achieving Rapid Dominance* (Washington, DC: National Defense University, 1996)

Young, Peter, ed., *Defence and the Media in Time of Limited War* (London: Frank Cass, 1992)

Young, Peter and Peter Jessel, *The Media and the Military: From the Crimea to Desert Strike* (Melbourne: Macmillan, 1997)

From Psychological Warfare to Information Operations and Back Again

Philip M. Taylor

The psychological dimension of warfare has been a key element of conflict throughout history. Successful military commanders in the ancient world from Alexander the Great to Hannibal to Julius Caesar instinctively factored into their decision-making certain actions or gestures that were designed to raise the morale of their own troops and undermine the will of their opponents. This front-line or combat propaganda was also extended beyond the battlefield to the 'home front' in order to sustain popular support for warfare amongst civilians, especially the families and friends of soldiers. As communications improved through the arrival of new technologies, especially from the mid-nineteenth century onwards, battlefields became much more public 'spaces', not just for those soldiers fighting on them or for those civilians caught up in them, but also for a distant reading and – later – viewing public. And what that public thought about the sacrifices or successes of its soldiers became more and more important in the wake of the spread of mass participatory democracy and the ability of voters to influence political decision-making. In short, in the age of mass communications, perceptions of war have moved from the periphery to the centre stage of conflict for soldiers and civilians alike, while the speed with which information passes from the battlefield to the home front, and vice versa, has been transformed from weeks and days to minutes and seconds. Now, war reports are often live (that is, in 'real-time'). In other words, the 'theatre of war' has assumed a whole new meaning in which audience perceptions of, and reactions to, military performance have become a critical part of the outcome.

This is not to suggest that those perceptions of warfare were or, even today in the age of real-time reporting, are the same. The gap between image and reality remains quite wide. In World War I, soldiers returning home on leave often found themselves surrounded by a public infinitely more bellicose or hateful towards the enemy than they were themselves, despite, or maybe because of, their own real experiences. In Britain, for example, atrocity propaganda about the 'Beastly

Hun' raping and pillaging his way through 'Poor Little Belgium' even gained authoritative credence from the 1915 Bryce Report when, in fact, the reality of German 'barbarism' was quite different. On the Western front, as the war dragged on through its first, second and third Christmasses, there was a growing realisation that new kinds of weapons would be needed to break the stalemate. Gas was tried, then tanks and planes, but the casualties continued to mount, requiring the British to introduce conscription for the first time in 1916. Then came the Somme and Paschendaele. Something other than physical force was clearly required to make a breakthrough and a solution was sought in psychological warfare.

Although the Department of Enemy Propaganda at Crewe House was finally created early in 1918, the use of these 'munitions of the mind' had admittedly been going on for some time. As a young German soldier called Adolf Hitler later wrote:

> With the year 1915, enemy propaganda began in our country, after 1916 it became more and more intensive, till finally, at the beginning of the year 1918, it swelled to a positive flood. Now the results of this seduction could be seen at every step. The army gradually learned to think as the enemy wanted it to.[1]

Although clearly exaggerated – a rationalisation for defeat rather than an explanation of it – the very fact that Hitler devoted two chapters in *Mein Kampf* to the subject of propaganda and, of course, subsequently exploited in Nazi Germany from 1933–45, the lesson he had learned from the Great War was that modern propaganda and psychological warfare had come of age. While the victorious Allies largely dismantled their wartime propaganda machinery in 1918, the emerging totalitarian regimes in Fascist Italy, Stalin's Russia and Nazi Germany placed propaganda at the very centre of peacetime politics. When Hitler came to power in 1933, he delegated the new Ministry of Public Enlightenment and Propaganda to Dr Josef Goebbels, who immediately began creating the first efficient modern propaganda state geared up to wage war.

Meanwhile, military thinkers like Liddell Hart realised that future warfare would require an 'indirect approach', fighting enemies psychologically by striking at their will to fight rather than attempting to overcome them physically in conflicts that would inevitably turn into bloodbaths for victor and vanquished alike. War, he believed, had become a struggle of the mind over the physical body; what he termed 'the perfection of strategy', if it could ever be achieved, would consist of the 'destruction of the enemy's armed forces through their unarming by surrender' without the need for any fighting at all.[2]

---

1   Adolf Hitler, *Mein Kampf* (1925–26), with an introduction by D.C. Watt (London: Hutchinson, 1960), p. 170.
2   B.H. Liddell Hart, *The Decisive Wars of History: A Study in Strategy* (Boston: Little, Brown, 1929), pp. 153–4.

Although the experience of 'industrialised warfare' between 1914 and 1918 clearly shaped such thoughts within the context of the 'war to end all wars', Liddell Hart was echoing the ideas of the ancient Chinese writer Sun Tzu, whose *The Art of War* he would later co-write an introduction for.[3] Particularly relevant is Sun Tzu's maxim: 'To win one hundred victories in one hundred battles is not the acme of skill. To subdue the enemy without fighting is the acme of skill.'[4] The history of warfare is replete with examples of failing to apply this maxim, although it underlies claims that the West did 'win' the Cold War against the Soviet Union without recourse to global thermonuclear conflagration. Alternatively, it could be argued that the Cold War was never a 'hot' conflict that could be waged with nuclear weapons because of the likelihood of mutual assured destruction. Rather, it was a contest of ideas, of competing ideologies – what Joseph Nye would later call 'soft power' – in which the deployment of attractive arguments and ideas were the principal weapons. It was, in effect, a war of words – indeed a psychological war.

It is in this wider context that we need to consider planned military information activities in support of military operations, both on the battlefield and beyond. In World War I, organised psychological warfare was developed relatively late in the conflict and involved primarily the use of leaflets and loudspeakers to transmit messages to enemy soldiers. The British mainly used balloons to distribute leaflets on the Western front because the Germans had threatened to treat any captured pilots who air-dropped such literature over their lines as war criminals rather than as conventional prisoners of war. Although contemporary soldiers like Hitler and his commander-in-chief, General Ludendorff, claimed that such leaflets hypnotised German soldiers 'like a rabbit is by a snake', modern historians have questioned their effectiveness.[5] While it is certainly true that such claims shifted the blame for defeat away from the German Army, which suited post-war theories about Germany being 'stabbed in the back', Allied psychological warfare campaigns on the southern front against the Austro-Hungarian Army do seem to have been particularly effective in prompting an internal collapse within the dual monarchy.[6]

When Britain again declared war on Germany on 3 September 1939, the very first mission of the RAF, on the opening night of the conflict, was to drop 13 tons of leaflets over Hamburg, Bremen and the Ruhr urging the German people not to support 'Hitler's War'. Later that month, balloons were deployed from France but, after the fall of that country in June 1940, it was left primarily to the RAF to disseminate leaflets in what were termed 'nickel raids'. While this early deployment of propaganda – or what the British would label 'political warfare' – reveals just how far thinking about psychological weapons had progressed since 1918, many

---

3   Sun Tzu, *The Art of War* (6th century BC), trans. with an introduction by Samuel B. Griffith and B.H. Liddell Hart (Oxford: Oxford University Press, 1988).

4   *The Art of War*, Chapter 3, p. 68.

5   Michael Balfour, *Propaganda in War, 1939–1945* (London: Routledge & Kegan Paul, 1979).

6   Mark Cornwall, *The Undermining of Austria-Hungary: The Battle for Hearts and Minds* (Basingstoke: Macmillan; New York: St Martin's Press, 2000).

pilots resented having to risk their lives dropping 'paper bullets' over enemy territory.[7] They felt their role was to fight, not to persuade. However, dropping leaflets remains an important element in the deployment of armed forces today.

Soldiers who are trained to fight battles do not always appreciate the importance of the psychological dimension of conflict in assisting their mission. In World War II, it proved extremely difficult to persuade German soldiers to surrender, while Japanese soldiers were renowned for dying rather than be captured. Following the entrance of the USA into the war after Pearl Harbour in December 1941, the Americans introduced the phrase 'psychological warfare' to support their military effort. By that time, the British had created the Political Warfare Executive (PWE) and had begun experimenting with a new method of dissemination, namely radio. It was illegal – under penalty of death – in Germany and occupied Europe to listen to foreign radio broadcasts, including those of the BBC. How to get the Allied message across to audiences who dared listen only in fear was therefore a challenging problem. In the PWE, Sefton Delmer came up with the idea of 'black' or covert radio stations (code-named 'research units') which appeared to emanate from inside occupied Europe but in fact originated from within Britain.[8] They gave the impression of disaffected German soldiers or resistance fighters communicating with each other, when really they came from transmitters at Woburn Abbey. Although Goebbels feared these broadcasts, their impact in a Gestapo monitored environment was probably slight.

In a 'total war', however, any and every weapon is worth trying. The Americans even created a dedicated airborne leaflet dropping capability, the 406th Night Leaflet Squadron, and when the Supreme Headquarters of the Allied Expeditionary Force (SHAEF[9]) was created under General Eisenhower, it contained a Psychological Warfare Division (PWD). By the end of the war, billions of leaflets had been dropped over Axis lines while the ability to penetrate radio messages deep into Germany had been greatly helped by the Allied capture of Radio Luxembourg in 1944. While the German Army fought on until it became futile and it took two atomic bombs to force Japan's surrender, no claims similar to those in 1918 could be made about the impact of psychological warfare. Intelligence historians can make a good case for 'Ultra' and 'Station X' having shortened World War II by a couple of years. No such claims can really be made for the PWE or PWD. This may, in part, be due to the militaristic indoctrination of German and Japanese soldiers and their psychological resistance to Allied appeals. But it was also a fact that the Allied policy of unconditional surrender, announced following the Casablanca Conference of 1942, did something that no amount of Goebbels-inspired Nazi propaganda over the previous decade had been able to achieve: it connected the German people to the fate of the Nazi Party. The message was simple: surrender unconditionally this

---

7   American pilots, following their entry into the war in December 1941, called them 'bullshit bombs'.

8   Sefton Delmer, *Black Boomerang: An Autobiography* (London: Secker & Warburg, 1962).

9   SHAEF was the forerunner of SHAPE, NATO's Supreme Headquarters of the Allied Powers in Europe.

time and face extremely unpleasant consequences, or fight to the bitter end. When policy and presentation become desynchronised, no amount of skilful propaganda can compensate if the policy is unpopular.

Partly as a consequence of the inability to claim that psychological warfare helped to shorten the war – indeed, it may even have lengthened it – its practice went into decline after 1945. Instead, Allied representatives went about changing hearts and minds in occupied Germany and Japan through what they called 'political re-education'. Everything from school textbooks to media law was transformed in order to convert what was believed to be a militaristic mindset cultivated by a generation of anti-democratic propaganda; and it was recognised that it would take several generations of occupation and the democratic reform of civil society to achieve this conversion. Today, it would be called 'nation-building', although the success of what was achieved in post-war Germany and Japan appears to have been forgotten in the planning for the Iraqi invasion of 2003.

Internationally, another war was brewing in the late 1940s. The Cold War was a new type of war, which evolved into a struggle between two completely different political ideologies and, as such, was every inch a Manichean psychological struggle between western democracies and the Communist bloc. Such a confrontation had been brewing since the 1917 Russian Revolution and the Soviets had been quick to build the world's most powerful radio transmitter in the 1920s to promote its anti-capitalist ideology amongst the 'workers of the world'. A common enemy in the form of Hitler had put the contest on hold from 1941 to 1945 but by the end of the 1940s the United States and the Soviet Union were squaring up to each other over the Berlin Blockade. With the outbreak of the Korean War in 1950, the struggle went global. And although psychological warfare leaflets and radio broadcasts featured once again, it was at the wider strategic level that the conflict was being waged, especially as the European empires dismantled their colonial links in the 'Third World'. The Voice of America, created in 1942, was joined by Radio Free Europe (RFE) and Radio Liberty (RL, respectively for Eastern European and Russian audiences) to compete with Radio Moscow, while what has been termed a 'cultural cold war' extended to medical research, Olympic Games, films and the new medium of television. The space race in the 1960s facilitated the launch of satellites which internationalised television and made it a key weapon, with each side competing to gain the allegiance of global audiences.

The advent of nuclear weapons caused them to become a central theme of this propaganda war, both at home and abroad. Although their first strike launch might trigger the aggressor's own annihilation, each side had to justify massive military expenditure to their own public by painting the other side as a face of the enemy or aggressor. This bipolarisation of the world into two armed camps was accompanied by the creation of propaganda machineries with global reach. In America, the United States Information Agency (USIA) was created in 1953 while, around the same time, the Psychological Operations School was founded at Fort Bragg. In Britain, the Information Research Department was set up secretly, inter alia, to plant anti-communist articles in newspapers while the Soviets went about infiltrating, or even creating their own, front organisations to spread their ideology and discredit that of their opponents.

Much of this activity was covert and conducted by the intelligence services. RFE and RL were initially financed by the CIA. Soviet 'active measures' – as they preferred to call them – included the disseminating of *disinformatzia* [disinformation], for example, spreading the story, towards the end of the Cold War, that AIDS had been created as an offshoot of an American biological warfare experiment. During the 1950s and early 1960s, the fog of propaganda had become so thick that the two superpowers almost came to nuclear blows during the Cuban Missile Crisis and the leaders of both sides realised that they would have to talk directly to each other rather than through 'radio diplomacy' if further misunderstandings were not to occur. A direct hotline between the Kremlin and the White House was set up as a result.

The psychological war did not stop, however; it merely shifted into new battle spaces such as Vietnam. In the 1950s, Britain had demonstrated the value of what were now being called 'psychological operations' (PSYOPS) in the Malayan emergency, when General Templar used them as a means of isolating communist insurgents from the general population. The Americans would need to turn this psychological tool into a weapon in Vietnam, especially after 500,000 of their troops were in theatre after 1965. Many senior American commanders would later claim that they lost the war not on the battlefields of South East Asia but in the living rooms of Middle America, where the television set had become a feature of nearly every household. Surveys revealed that people were beginning to trust television news more than any other source of information and from the mid to late 1960s onwards televisual images were transformed from the traditional black and white of the cinema newsreels into full-blown colour, bringing the horrific, ugly 'reality' of war even closer to home. Images of naked, napalm-covered children or executed Vietcong suspects are thought to have undermined US popular support for the Vietnam War, especially after the 1968 Tet Offensive.

The war lasted for seven more years, however, during which time President Nixon, elected in 1968, was re-elected in 1972 – hardly an indication of unpopularity. Although US troops were withdrawn from Vietnam the following year, it was the Watergate scandal which brought Nixon down rather than the Vietnam War and its graphic television images. This knowledge should temper arguments about whether the US military was 'stabbed in the back' by the media over Vietnam, although the belief that it had been was to usher in a whole new era of factoring into the waging of war the psychological dimension of conflict as being equally important as, if not more so than, the kinetic element.

Following defeat in Vietnam, US military PSYOP went into decline until President Reagan was elected in 1980, just as the Soviets were becoming embroiled in Afghanistan, their own 'Vietnam'.[10] Reagan's nickname was 'the Great Communicator' and, from his past career as a Hollywood movie actor, he understood the power of communications to change minds only too well.

---

10   Note that the American version is PSYOP, without the final 'S' used by other nations.

He escalated US broadcasts to behind the Iron Curtain, increased the strategic activities, now being described as 'public diplomacy', of the USIA, and he set the timeframe for the struggle against what he called the 'Evil Empire'. What perhaps frightened the Soviets more than anything was Reagan's promise to deliver a 'Star Wars' programme which would extend the psychological battle into outer space.

The Soviets got bogged down in Afghanistan and underwent a series of leadership changes brought about by the deaths of old-guard premiers. So Reagan watched with dismay when, in 1982, the British decided to reclaim the Falkland Islands, which had been seized by Argentina, Reagan's chosen South American proxy for spearheading the fight against communism in Latin America. Reagan's decision to back Britain was not just down to the 'special relationship' between the nations: British prime minister Margaret Thatcher was a fellow anti-communist traveller who had made the controversial decision to allow US missiles to be based on UK soil.

Although the British forces had no psychological operations capability to speak of when fighting to liberate the Falklands, they did allow 29 journalists to accompany them and it was through these journalists that the propaganda war ended up being waged. From World War I through World War II and beyond – with the single exception of the Suez Campaign of 1956 – the British media could largely be relied upon to support a national war effort. This was because most of Britain's wars had been perceived as both just and justified. The Falklands conflict was no different, although the excessively jingoistic headlines of *The Sun* newspaper ('UP YOURS GALTIERI!', 'ARGIE BARGEY' and 'GOTCHA') resulted in a downturn in readership. Problems occurred not with the reporters at sea, where they came to identify with the troops whose hopes and fears they shared, but back in London, where the Ministry of Defence often delayed information or said very little at all. Indeed, some television news reports from the South Atlantic took longer to reach home than the despatches via telegraph of the first war correspondents covering the Crimean War a century and a quarter earlier.[11] In the years following the Falklands conflict, information vacuums would not be an option.

The 1980s witnessed advances in communications technologies that were to revolutionise the psychological dimension of conflict. The arrival of the domestic computer, the fax machine, the brick-sized satellite telephone and the release into the public sphere of the Internet transformed global communications flows. CNN was founded in 1980 as the first 24-hour-a-day TV news station – although it did not earn global prominence until the 1991 Persian Gulf War. By then, the Soviet Union had collapsed; while television images of young Eastern Europeans throwing off their communist shackles in Poland, East Germany, Czechoslovakia and Romania had followed in domino effect from the moment that iconic images of the Berlin Wall being torn down had been broadcast live around the world. The KGB nicknamed the western international radio broadcasts of the BBC, Voice of America, the RL and RFE 'the voices'. Reagan and Thatcher, in their dealings

---

11   See Paul L. Moorcraft and Philip M. Taylor, *Shooting the Messenger: The Political Impact of War Reporting* (Dulles, VA: Potomac Books, 2008).

with a new-generation Soviet leader in the form of Mikhail Gorbachev, persuaded him to cease jamming 'the voices', whereupon the whisper of freedom became a welcome roar. Although we will never know with certainty what precise role international communications played in ending the Cold War, it is impossible to see its termination without them.

Reagan not only reinvigorated US public diplomacy efforts but also ordered a review of military psychological operations capabilities. This resulted in two Department of Defense PSYOP 'master plans', one in 1985 and another in 1990 in light of the experience of the 1989 Panama invasion. General Noriega, under siege, had been driven to surrender by the noise emanating from loudspeakers deployed by Fort Bragg's teams in Panama City, and this success helped to ensure that any plans to liberate Kuwait following the Iraqi invasion of August 1990 would incorporate PSYOP right from the beginning. Policy and military psychology work most effectively when they work in synchronisation. This is one of the reasons why the PSYOP campaign supporting Operation Desert Storm was so important in reviving the practice in the post-Cold War years.

During Desert Storm, the American armed forces – who were the only members of the 30-strong 'coalition of the willing' with a PSYOP capability at that time – dropped almost 30 million leaflets on receptive Iraqi soldiers in occupied Kuwait and southern Iraq. These were reinforced by broadcasts from their airborne PSYOP platform known as Volant (later Commando) Solo. This was a converted EC130 Hercules aircraft carrying dedicated radio and television transmission equipment in all frequencies and formats. The Iraqis tried to respond with their updated version of Tokyo Rose, known as Baghdad Betty, promising the 'mother of all battles'. But, following the success of a deception campaign designed to convince the Iraqis that the coalition would liberate Kuwait from the sea rather than by the planned 'left hook' by land,[12] Iraqi forces surrendered in their tens of thousands and withdrew from Kuwait, taking heavy casualties.[13] It was the 'mother of all defeats' and one of the most one-sided military conflicts in history. The vast majority of Iraqi prisoners of war claimed that they had heard American PSYOP messages and had conformed to behaviour desired by those messages – which were essentially of the 'surrender or die' variety.

The era of PSYOP as a 'combat force multiplier' had arrived. The lesson taken was that PSYOP could actually save the lives of enemy forces – 'Our motto is electrons, not bullets' – and, as a non-lethal weapon, persuasion seemed morally more acceptable than military force designed to kill an enemy. It resonated well

---

12   This was what coalition supreme commander General Norman Schwarzkopf described as his 'Hail Mary play', drawing his analogy from American football, when a quarterback tries one last-ditch throw to a receiver to win a game. Although the deception campaign was primarily directed at the Iraqi armed forces, the western media got caught up in it, causing considerable controversy after the war. See Philip M. Taylor, *War and the Media: Propaganda and Persuasion during the Gulf War*, 2nd edn (Manchester: Manchester University Press, 1997), pp. 134–5.

13   A total of 59,000 Iraqi troops surrendered before the end of the war.

with President Bush's calls for a new world order to succeed the era of the Cold War, although what precisely he meant by that remained vague and undeveloped. The first signs that international affairs had really changed came in the aftermath of Desert Storm with a 'humanitarian intervention' to help the Kurds of northern Iraq (Operation Provide Comfort) following their uprising against Saddam Hussein. Again, PSYOP products accompanied the airdrops, thereby extending their target audience from traditional enemy soldiers to friendly civilians. Little noticed at the time, however, was the plight of the Shi'ites in southern Iraq, who had also risen up against Saddam but who received no outside help and were brutally crushed. The Kurdish plight was broadcast on CNN but not that of the Shi'ites. This, as we shall see, was to have dangerous long-term consequences.

Debates then arose about a 'CNN effect', asking whether 'real-time' television had the power to drive, rather than follow, the foreign-policy-making process. It was, at the time, an interesting new development in the role of the media and communications in covering international conflicts which was to influence the military–media dynamic, although it has since been discredited by serious academic research.[14]. In the Balkan conflict which rapidly followed the Middle East Crisis, another, related idea was promulgated by BBC journalist Martin Bell, namely 'journalism of attachment', by which he meant that war reporters should do more to prompt the international community to intervene in civil wars where innocents were caught up in conflict and genocide.[15] It was the Balkan wars which eventually forced other NATO nations to take public affairs more seriously than they had done in the past.

Meanwhile, within military circles there was much talk of a revolution in military affairs, prompted by the experience of the 1991 Gulf War as the 'first information war'.[16] As we have seen, information and communications have always been important in warfare but what Desert Storm seemed to have demonstrated was that wars in the future would have their outcomes determined by the integration of new communications technologies into both kinetic and non-kinetic fighting. There emerged the idea of 'command and control warfare' (C2W), which evolved over the next decade into C4I (command, control, communications and computing, plus intelligence). After all, cameras had been mounted on precision-guided weapons such as cruise missiles and guided by GPS systems and satellites which were able to hit their targets with unprecedented accuracy, thanks to computer-based technology. Only after Desert Storm did it emerge that barely 10 per cent of the ordinance dropped on Iraq was 'smart'.

---

14   See, in particular, the work of Steven Livingstone and Piers Robinson.

15   Martin Bell, *In Harm's Way: Confessions of a War Zone Thug* (London: Hamish Hamilton, 1995).

16   Alan D. Campen, ed., *The First Information War: The Story of Communications, Computers, and Intelligence Systems in the Persian Gulf War* (Fairfax, VA: AFCEA International Press, 1992).

Once the World Wide Web became available after 1989 as the accessible front page of the Internet, another information space started to open up at phenomenal, prompting fears of an 'electronic Pearl Harbour'. There was much talk of 'cyberwar', 'hacker warfare' and a whole host of other terms that became subsumed in the phrase 'information warfare' (IW). There are essentially four components to this: 1) influence activities; 2) information assurance, computer network defence and operational security; 3) deception; and 4) electronic warfare and computer network attack. Early debates were dominated by discussion of components 2–4, which are essentially Internet-age equivalents of Cold War signals intelligence (SIGINT). Less attention has been given to the influence component, which is a variation on human intelligence (HUMINT) including counter-propaganda, PSYOP, public affairs and public diplomacy. Indeed, in 1999, during the last months of the Clinton administration, it was decided both to close down the United States Information Agency and to dramatically reduce international broadcasting. Despite all the talk about IW, which was then evolving into 'information operations' (IO) in much the same way as PSYWAR was relabelled PSYOPS in the 1950s, the theory was stronger than the reality.

The Serbs were to expose this in 1999 during their conflict with NATO over Kosovo. For several years, other NATO partners including Britain and Germany had been developing their own PSYOPS capabilities. These were now placed under the umbrella of 'information operations', for which there was a small cell at SHAPE. The Americans still had the largest capability and managed to drop over 100 million leaflets over Serbia and Kosovo. But the Serb armed forces were no Iraqis; they were professional volunteer forces defending a province of their homeland from those they labelled 'Kosovan terrorists'.[17] As the 1940 London Blitz showed, bombing tends to increase rather than shatter the morale of recipients. The situation in 1999 proved to be no different as NATO launched its air war to drive the Serbs from Kosovo. Ground forces were only deployed after this had been achieved but, in the meantime, the Milosevic regime had rallied the Serbs, branded NATO as Nazi aggressors (since there was no UN resolution authorising the NATO attack) and skilfully exploited NATO bombing mistakes at press conferences and on television. Belgrade also proved adept at using the Internet, bringing down NATO servers and bombarding chat rooms with anti-NATO sentiments and videos: <www.1>.

Despite NATO countries having taken great strides in professionalising public affairs in the few years prior to Kosovo, the multinational nature of the alliance made it particularly difficult for all nations to agree on a unified policy. The Greek government, for example, found itself in a difficult position with its public openly hostile to the conflict. There was no UN mandate for Operation Allied Force. The Serbs proved the new importance of the media and communications in asymmetric warfare; they knew that they could not defy NATO militarily but that they could fight them in the information space which was now global, digital and instantaneous.

---

17   Indeed, the Kosovo Liberation Army was also labelled a terrorist organisation by the CIA at that time.

The weak could now fight the strong using the media and communications as a 'battlespace', while the Internet made information warfare possible even when NATO forces temporarily took out Radio Television Serbia in an air strike. Whether this new information 'front' made any difference to the outcome is dubious, but it did offer valuable lessons for a new kind of enemy in the form of international terrorism.

The terrorist attacks on New York and Washington on 11 September 2001 indicate the importance of the new global information battlespace. The destruction of the second tower of the World Trade Centre was captured live on television by New York TV traffic helicopters on their routine rush-hour duties.[18] The reaction of many people was that 'it was like watching a movie' – which was precisely the point of this propaganda of the deed. The terrorists were waging an asymmetric strike against a world superpower and they understood only too well the importance of the media and communications in their extremist campaign. This is because terrorism is 10 per cent violence and 90 per cent propaganda. Terrorism is the ultimate form of asymmetric psychological warfare in the information age.

The United States responded to 9/11 with 90 per cent violence (that is, war) and 10 per cent propaganda, then labelled 'perception management', changed to 'strategic communications' in 2005. President Bush junior declared war on terror, although he initially, and disastrously, called it a 'crusade' – in psychological warfare, words are crucial. The first battle of the 'global war on terror' was to be in Afghanistan where the Taliban seized power a few years after the Russians ignominiously withdrew. The Taliban had permitted the terrorist organisation Al-Qaida to create training camps in their country and Al-Qaida had been identified as the principal conspirator behind the 9/11 attacks. Kabul fell to Anglo-American special forces and their proxy Northern Alliance by December 2001 and, once again, millions of leaflets were dropped explaining that they were not foreign invaders but, rather, liberators expelling foreign terrorists from Afghanistan. The Taliban had banned television, so cinematic images of 9/11 had not reached Afghanistan's population. Commando Solo was confined to broadcasting radio messages received via air-dropped wind-up radios supplied by American PSYOP teams.

Although there was disquiet in some Muslim countries, most countries understood the reasons for the Afghan expedition. *Le Monde's* famous headline on the day after 9/11, 'We are all Americans', encapsulated the mood of worldwide sympathy for what had happened. But what was to follow was a strategic communications disaster. By regarding the information front as a supporting element of the military campaign, the US handed the psychological initiative to Al-Qaida, which viewed the information front as the main battlefield of its extreme jihadist struggle. In the years that followed, anti-Americanism grew to unprecedented levels worldwide and the US found itself caught on the defensive in justifying its alleged 'crusade' against Islam. Even the Taliban prior to its fall

---

18   The strike on the first tower, 16 minutes earlier, was also captured on film by a French documentary film team working with the New York Fire Brigade, but it was not broadcast until many hours later.

had proved more nimble at manipulating the media – at least until a coalition information centre was established in Islamabad to match Taliban claims about 'collateral damage'. And because Washington had chosen to respond militarily, it was the soldiers who were tasked with fighting the information war. It was military doctrine relating to information operations which prevailed when a global struggle for 'hearts and minds' really required a softer touch – or 'soft power'.

Not that US public diplomacy – now undergoing an unprecedented public debate in response to the much vaunted question, 'Why do they hate us?' – had all the solutions to mounting anti-Americanism. New initiatives were tried by the post-USIA State Department, such as the establishment of Radio Sawa and Al-Hurra TV targeting the Middle East. But when, in March 2003, the US attacked Iraq to facilitate 'regime change' force was once again shown to prevail over persuasion. The new 'coalition of the willing' in fact consists of only four nations (USA, Britain, Poland and Australia) and, unlike in 1991, there was no UN mandate and there were no Arab partners. Although Baghdad fell relatively quickly, Saddam Hussein took several more months to find and a couple more years to execute. But the USA's problems were only just beginning as Al-Qaida and its associates switched focus from Afghanistan to Iraq in order to intensify the insurgency against another western 'invasion' of a Muslim country.

In the US itself, public opinion was initially behind both wars. Seventy per cent of Americans in one poll were found to believe that Saddam had been behind the 9/11 attacks, while both Washington and London argued that the war in Iraq was to capture and destroy Iraq's weapons of mass destruction. When none were found, and as the insurgency intensified, the controversy about this already-controversial war also intensified. Evidence that deception had crept into the Pentagon's 'strategic communications' efforts was found in the form of the Office of Strategic Influence (OSI), established after 9/11 to wage information operations beyond the battlefields of Afghanistan and Iraq in the wider strategic information space of world public opinion. A declassified 'information operations roadmap' revealed that the Pentagon was attempting to harmonise the three main pillars of influence activities, namely IO, public diplomacy and public affairs. The problem was that, under the 1948 Smith-Mundt Act, the US government was expressly prohibited from conducting propaganda against its own citizens. While Washington denied that it was doing so, American journalists knew that much of their information was gathered from sources overseas – and that those sources were fair game for US deception and black propaganda operations. Following a media outcry, the OSI was closed down – although other shadowy organisations like the Office of Special Plans and the White House Iraq Group came and went in its aftermath.

Abroad, all this served to undermine the credibility of America's message as a force for good in the world. Although the global war on terror was rebranded as 'the Long War', events in Iraq's Abu Ghraib prison and images of captured Muslim 'terrorists' in America's Guantanamo Bay prison incensed Muslim observers, prompting further Al-Qaida-related attacks in Bali, Istanbul, Madrid and London, amongst other places. It was becoming clear that US strategic communications was failing to persuade many in the Muslim world that the Long War was not a 'clash of civilisations', prompting US envoy Richard Holbrooke famously to question why a man in a cave was able to out-communicate the most advanced communication nation in the world.

The answer lies partly within Al-Qaida and its leader Osama bin Laden's skilled use of propaganda, especially on the Internet. Jihadist websites grew in number from about five in 2001 to 5,000 in 2007, and were peppered with multi-media presentations distributed by their dedicated media production centre know as As-Sahab. Because of Smith-Mundt, the US was slow to use the Internet, finding it difficult to draw a line between foreign and domestic audiences. Another serious issue was the decades-long turf war between the State Department, responsible for public diplomacy, and the Department of Defense, responsible for information operations. Simply put, the soft power strategic messages of the former were being undermined by the hard power operational activities of the latter. But both were failing at the strategic level and mainly because of Islamic resentment, not at American communications but at American foreign policy under Bush. His doctrine consisted of hunting down terrorists wherever they reside, branding certain countries as part of an 'Axis of Evil', carrying out pre-emptive strikes against those targets and aggressively promoting American style democracy. In a climate generated by such of Bush's phrases as 'You are either with us or against us' or 'There is no neutral ground', international terrorism flourished under the cloak of a distorted religious ideology perpetuated by Al-Qaida propagandists and their sympathisers.

Perhaps terrorists were able to do this because they understood the importance of psychological warfare more than democracies understood strategic communications. Places like Washington are highly bureaucratic and slow to make decisions, and they are riddled with rivalries and personality clashes. A terrorist network is more nimble, more united in its goals, and it plays by different rules – characteristics which give it a vital edge in an information war waged on websites such as YouTube or My Space. Seven years after 9/11 – a period longer than the duration of World War II – there are some signs that the Long War is finally being accepted as a long conflict of ideas. Its principal weapons need to be not tanks, planes or armies, but rather words, values and, above all, actions, especially in places like the Middle East. But there is still no clear idea of what victory in this information war should look like or whether soft power will prevail over hard.

When Desert Storm was heralded as the first information-age war, a little noticed breach of the information rules of engagement was sowing the seeds of future conflict. Black broadcasts, emanating from unknown coalition sources,[19] were encouraging the Kurds of northern Iraq and the Shi'ites of the south to rise up and overthrow Saddam Hussein. This was not part of expressed coalition strategy a decade before 'regime change' became an essential part of the Bush doctrine. UN mandates at the time permitted 'all necessary means' only to expel Iraqi forces from Kuwait rather than to go after Saddam in Baghdad, as many hawks wanted.

---

19   These were very likely members of the CIA, as testified by disgruntled Iraqi broadcasters later on CNN.

The uprisings were then brutally crushed by Saddam's forces. This black blowback was seriously to hinder the later coalition's effort to impose regime change in 2003. When British forces reached Basra, they realised that enormous resentment still festered amongst the Shias and produced a reassuring PSYOPS leaflet which stated: 'This time we won't abandon you.' The 1991 blowback also goes a long way to explaining why coalition forces were greeted as invaders in 2003 rather than as liberators to be showered with flower petals. Moreover, a good deal of the 2003 PSYOPS messages were designed to persuade Iraqi forces to 'go home' rather than surrender – which thousands did, but taking their weapons with them. The Iraqi insurgency, which took the lives of more American soldiers than the actual combat phase, owed its roots to the lack of adequate planning for the post-combat phase of Operation Iraqi Freedom.

There was another, more significant, legacy from 1991. A certain Saudi Arabian who had been funding mujahedeen fighters in Afghanistan against the godless Soviet forces throughout the 1980s watched in disbelief and mounting fury as his native government allowed half a million 'infidel' troops (men and women) to station themselves in the Holy Land of Mecca, not only during Desert Shield and Desert Storm but also remaining there in the years that followed. His name was Osama bin Laden.

Small Wars and Telecommunication

Thomas Rid

Information technology has fundamentally affected the way modern armies operate. Technology has made journalism more intrusive, faster, and independent from military logistics even in remote areas. Deepening Internet penetration everywhere has turned the civilian populations at home and in theater into keen observers and commentators of military action. And—most significantly—improved "network-enabled" command-and-control technology has made regular armies far more lethal and efficient.[1] But changes in telecommunication have had an even more revolutionary impact on irregular forces.[2]

---

1   One of the best histories of war reporting is Phillip Knightley, *The First Casualty: From the Crimea to Vietnam: The War Correspondent as Hero, Propagandist and Myth Maker* (New York: Harcourt Brace Jovanovich, 1975). See also Susan L. Carruthers, *The Media at War* (New York: St Martin's Press, 2000); Frank Aukofer, and William P. Lawrence, *America's Team: The Odd Couple: A Report on the Relationship between the Military and the Media* (Nashville: The Freedom Forum First Amendment Center, 1995); Daniel C. Hallin, *The "Uncensored War": The Media and Vietnam* (Oxford: Oxford University Press, 1986); John J. Fialka, *Hotel Warriors: Covering the Gulf War* (Baltimore: Hopkins University Press, 1991); William M. Hammond, *Public Affairs: The Military and the Media, 1962–1968* (Washington: Center of Military History, 1988); William M. Hammond, *Public Affairs: The Military and the Media, 1968–1973* (Seattle: University Press of the Pacific, 2002); Thomas Rid, *War and Media Operations: The US Military and the Press from Vietnam to Iraq* (London: Routledge, 2007). For armies in the information age see Alvin Toffler, and Heidi Toffler, *War and Anti-War: Making Sense of Today's Global Chaos* (New York: Grand Central, 1993); John Arquilla, and David Ronfeldt, *In Athena's Camp: Preparing for Conflict in the Information Age* (Santa Monica: Rand, 1997); Thomas X. Hammes, *The Sling and the Stone: On War in the 21st Century* (St Paul, MN: Zenith Press, 2006). Specifically on the debate on military "transformation", a good critique is Williamson Murray, "Clausewitz Out, Computer In: Military Culture and Technological Hubris," *The National Interest* (Summer, 1997), vol. 48: , Summer, 57–64. For a good introduction to war blogs see John Hockenberry, "The Blogs of War," *Wired Magazine* (August 13, 2005).
2   On the history of telecommunications see George P. Oslin, *The Story of Telecommunications* (Macon, GA: Mercer University Press, 1992); Anton A. Huurdeman, *The Worldwide*

The differences between big war and small war, between regular armies and irregular armed groups, between the counterinsurgent and the insurgent, are manifold.[3] Yet one disparity is most fundamental: the counterinsurgent is almost always older than the insurgent. Put inversely, a resistance movement, formed to oppose established authority, is in nearly all cases younger than its adversary. A successful rebellion therefore grows from weak to strong while the government authority loses strength and weakens. Counterinsurgent forces, usually, are well-established regular military organizations, with a large bureaucracy, a professional officer corps, a complex logistics organization, and sophisticated weapons platforms. Insurgent forces are not. This simple observation has far reaching consequences for the use of information technology and the media.

All insurgencies are improvised, at least initially. Irregular fighters, therefore, have fewer resources, no sophisticated bureaucratic apparatus, no system of equipped and specialized units, no established routines and procedures, and only fresh and untested experience and expertise. Ingenuity and learning, therefore, are existential. This applies to the use of information technology and the media: for irregular forces telecommunication is operational and existential; for regular armies it has long been a side activity and a luxury.

The history of irregular media operations is complex and fractured; generalizations are difficult. Yet it is possible to isolate three large and overlapping historical phases. First, throughout the nineteenth century, irregular forces saw the state's telecommunication facilities as a target that could be physically attacked to weaken the armies and the authority of states and empires. Second, for most of the twentieth century, irregulars slowly but successfully began using the mass media as a weapon. Telecommunications, or more specifically the press, were used to attack the moral support and integrity of opposing political entities. Eventually, in the early twenty-first century, a third phase began: irregular movements started using commoditized information technologies as an operating platform. Before plunging into examples to illustrate this three-tiered development, it is first in order to understand the philosophical underpinnings of telecommunication's violent history, Clausewitz's three escalations of war. Only then will it become evident how significant the year 2000 truly is in the history of armed conflict.

The Utility of Communication

Almost any use of military force is, first and foremost, an act of communication. "War is an act of force to compel the enemy to do our will," wrote Carl von Clausewitz. The philosopher of war was writing about the collective use of force, of clashing political entities. War, Clausewitz argued, is always permeated by politics. "How

---

History of Telecommunications (New York: J. Wiley, 2003).

3   For a good introduction to the theory of small war see Walter Laqueur, *Guerrilla: A Historical and Critical Study*, vol. 4 (Boston: Little, Brown, 1976).

could it be otherwise?" he asked. When the diplomatic communiqués fall silent and the weapons begin speaking, the political motivations of the warring parties remain unaffected, Clausewitz argued. War remains an instrument for a political purpose, a continuation of political intercourse by other means. Yet it is the form of the interaction that fundamentally changes as missiles take the place of missives. "Isn't war just another way of writing and speaking their [the people's and the government's] thoughts?" Clausewitz rhetorically asked. He then continued with a widely quoted aphorism: "War has its own grammar, but not its own logic."[4] Armed conflict is not a realm of its own; it remains a form of politics, and therefore political communication.

Perhaps no author grasped war better than Clausewitz. Given the spirit of *On War* and the author's treatment of politics and occasionally communication, it is a reasonable assumption that Clausewitz would have dedicated a significant section of his work to the mass media, had he not written in the Germany of the 1820s, even before the invention of the telegraph, let alone television or the Internet. Yet *On War* is an excellent starting point for understanding the role of communication in war, and by extension that of the media and the Web.

Clausewitz starts his discussion of war with the image of a competition, a struggle between two opponents—he actually uses the analogy of two wrestlers. Each side's overarching *purpose* is to impose its will on the other one. Both therefore have the same *objective*: to render the other one "defenseless." Both use the same *means*, physical force. He proceeded from these three basic but abstract elements of war, purpose, objective, and means: if both adversaries would relentlessly focus on their objective and increase the use of force, they would "give the other side the law [of action]." Each side would, as a necessary consequence, be forced to react to the other's reaction, back and forth, without bounds and without limitations. Clausewitz then identified three escalations (*Wechselwirkungen*): first, the mutual increase of the physical means—an escalation of force; second, the mutual increase of the psychological impetus, or objective, to succeed before the other side does— an escalation of will; and third, the combination of both force and will, a couple that cannot be divided—an escalation of effort (*Anstrengung der Kräfte*). Clausewitz makes it very clear that such a concept of war is possible only in "the abstract realm of pure notions," pushed to the extremes by man's "restless reason," artificially isolated from actual political influences and logistical difficulties. Such an abstract theory, he wrote, would be "a mere book law, and nothing for the real world."[5]

---

4   The entire passage, which has been somewhat liberally translated by Paret and Howard, reads as follows: "Hören denn mit den diplomatischen Noten je die politischen Verhältnisse verschiedener Völker und Regierungen auf? Ist nicht der Krieg bloß eine andere Art von Schrift und Sprache ihres Denkens? Er hat freilich seine eigene Grammatik, aber nicht seine eigene Logik." Carl von Clausewitz, *Vom Kriege* [On War, 1832], trans. by M. Howard and P. Paret (Berlin: Ullstein, 1980), Book VIII, Chapter 6, p. 683.

5   Ibid., p. 31.

Absolute war, he unequivocally makes clear, does not exist in reality.[6] The war that we observe in reality is tamed and "moderated" by time, by friction, by decisions, by human error, by logistics, by chance, even by the weather. And most importantly it is never isolated from political motivations and influences. Clausewitz calls this real war, in a purely descriptive sense. Real war can nevertheless approximate absolute war, although it can never be reached entirely. That would be physically and politically impossible—war cannot be isolated from politics. The Prussian philosopher of war was only writing about conventional state-on-state war. He was not writing about irregular war, or small war, where the military capabilities of one side—and therefore the potential for the first mutual escalation, the escalation of force—are very limited. The insurgent does not have the military capabilities and means to push his adversary to extremes.

Communication, now, is tightly connected to this distinction in absolute war and real war. Absolute war would not only be isolated from politics, but also from communication. The first escalation, the escalation of force, presupposes that a collective military actor—composed of an army, navy, air force, many layers of hierarchy scattered across large areas of operation, all in sync with the political leadership in the capital—works and communicates smoothly and efficiently. It presupposes a sturdy command-and-control setup. In any modern force, for the past two hundred years, this setup is heavily reliant on telecommunications. The second escalation, the escalation of will, presupposes that a political body, a nation or state, backs up the use of military force morally, economically, and politically— a rule that applies in any political system, but with particular urgency in any democratic system. The second escalation, in other words, presupposes a robust public opinion, continually informed about the war by the government and the mass media.

The more escalated and powerful the use of force, for instance the aerial bombardment of an entire country, the less need there is for a separate channel to amplify the use of force through its reportage and dissemination in the news. Perhaps the most extreme example is the maximum use of force through nuclear weapons: if a country's industrial center and the majority of its cities would be wiped out, it would be nearly irrelevant how the few remaining survivors of that country receive the news. On the other end of the spectrum is a minimal use of force by insurgents, such as kidnappings or the killing of a single person, often selected for no other reason than ethnic affiliation or by pure chance, for instance Nicholas Berg's beheading. Such acts of force have a negligible or no physical impact on the opponent the perpetrators are intending to attack. These operations gain their moral and psychological force only through their representation and their widespread coverage in the news media. A general rule can be derived from this observation: the smaller the physical power of force, the larger the need for

---

6   Absolute war is frequently confused with total war. The two ideas are entirely unrelated. Confusion may result from a superficial reading (or in fact no reading at all) of *On War*, or an intentionally misconstrued argument.

psychological amplification. It follows that insurgents have to compensate in the psychological dimension for a lack of force in the physical domain.

Three imperatives for insurgent movements can be derived from this: first is to attack the regular army's capability to escalate force, its command-and-control network; second is to attack the state's capability to escalate its political will, its public opinion; and third is to build up, maintain, and protect your own capabilities to escalate both force and will. This is what irregular movements have done and what they continue to do: in the nineteenth century they attacked their adversary's command-and-control network; in the twentieth century they attacked public opinion; and in the twenty-first century they are using commoditized telecommunications to build up and protect their own capabilities with more sophistication than ever before.

Target

On August 23, 1793, the *levée en masse*, or conscription, was decreed in revolutionary France by the National Convention. The law was a milestone in the creation of modern armies.[7] Exactly one year later, another, perhaps more important milestone in human history was reached: transport and communication were divorced, marking the birth of modern telecommunication. Since ancient times the most common form of long-distance communication was to send messages or letters by carriers and dispatch riders. The optical telegraph, or semaphore, first broke the physical link between messenger and message. The idea of semaphore was to convey information through visual signals, such as smoke, fires, lights, and flashes created by pivoting shutters and blades. The first modern system was built in 1794 by Claude Chappe and his three brothers, initially for military purposes. The first line, with 19 stations across a distance of 190 kilometers, was completed on July 16, 1794. Then, on August 15, 1794, the era of telecommunications began: the new telegraph was used for the first time to report that the French general Armand Samuel de Marescot had liberated of the city of Le Quesnoy from Austrians troops after nearly one year of occupation, about 200 kilometers north of Paris. The Convention received the news only one hour after the battle's end.[8]

---

7   Incidentally, it helped trigger one of Europe's most violent insurrections in the Vendée. See Peter Paret, *Internal War and Pacification: The Vendée, 1789–1796* (Princeton, NJ: Princeton University Press, 1961).

8   Jeremy M. Norman, *From Gutenberg to the Internet: A Sourcebook on the History of Information Technology* (Novato, CA: HistoryofScience.com, 2005), p. 173; Gerard J. Holzmann and Björn Pehrson, *The Early History of Data Networks* (Los Alamitos, CA: IEEE Computer Society Press, 1995), p. 64. Again, an excellent history is Huurdeman, *The Worldwide History of Telecommunications*, p. 24.

Napoleon developed the system and used the telegraph to stay in touch with Paris from places as far away as Russia, Chappe wrote.[9] Already in 1810, fixed installations ran west from Paris to Brest, north to Amsterdam, east to Mainz in Germany, and south-east to Lyons and then across northern Italy to Milan and Venice.[10] Operators in the towers waited for semaphore signals from their neighboring tower, took notes, checked for errors, and quickly passed the encrypted signals on to the next tower. The French government used the system until it was superseded by the electric telegraph in 1852. Optical telegraphy had several downsides. It was clumsy; it was slow to operate, with one character consuming about 30 seconds, the speed and viability heavily affected by snow and rain; it was limited by geography; it was an easy military target, as the signals could simply be intercepted—and, most importantly, it was exceedingly expensive to build, operate and maintain. Optical telegraphy could only be afforded by the state and only for the most urgent and important military or political purposes—a trend that would persist for the next 200 years.

The electrical telegraph ended the use of semaphore (except in naval affairs). The telegraph's history is tied equally closely to revolution and war. It was developed and patented in the United States by Samuel Morse in 1837 and first operated, between Baltimore and Washington, DC, on May 24, 1844. "What hath God wrought?" was the world's first electric memo. This groundbreaking invention was, of course, of high political and military value. America and Europe began to wire the world. In the same year that Moltke and Bismarck conquered Paris, in 1871, Antonio Meucci filed a patent for the "sound telegraph" in the US Patent Office. The first transmission in clear and comprehensible speech is recorded to have taken place five years later, on March 10, 1876, when Alexander Graham Bell shouted into his experimental device: "Mr Watson, come here, I want to see you."[11] Several inventors claimed to have invented the telephone, but Bell was the first to patent "[t]he method of and apparatus for transmitting vocal or other sounds telegraphically."[12] He filed the specification on February 14, 1876.

In irregular conflicts, it should be stressed, these technologies, almost without exception, were used only by one side—by the state and by big armies. Bands of rebels could not even dream of maintaining a telegraph or telephone network for their own advantage. Instead, they turned the technology into a disadvantage for their enemies and attacked telegraph posts and wires. Examples abound. In the district of the 10th German Division, just outside Paris in 1870, a Dragoner-patrol

---

9   Ignace Urbain Jean Chappe, *Histoire de la télégraphie* (Paris, 1824), p. 130. On optical telegraphs see Alexander J. Field, "French Optical Telegraphy, 1793–1855: Hardware, Software, Administration," *Technology and Culture* (April 1994), vol. 35: 315–47; Duane Koenig, "Telegraphs and Telegrams in Revolutionary France," *The Scientific Monthly* (1944), vol. 59, issue 6: 431–7.

10   Chappe, *Histoire de la télégraphie*, pp. 129–31.

11   Robert V. Bruce, *Bell* (Ithaca, NY: Cornell University Press, 1990), p. 181.

12   Bell's specification is reproduced in George Bartlett, and Prescott, *The Speaking Telephone, Talking Phonograph, and Other Novelties* (New York: D. Appleton, 1878), p. 205 onwards.

caught a civilian trying to sabotage telegraph wires. The man, who was from the wealthy class of landowners, was instantly court-martialed. When he was asked for his motivation, he said, "in the most dignified posture," in the words of a German officer who was present, "because I am a Frenchman!" When the judge wanted to know what he had hoped to achieve, the man said he wanted to give an example to his compatriots so that they all would rise. He kept the noblest countenance when he faced the firing squad.[13]

At that time the telegraph network in North America was expanded as well. The first transcontinental line had been completed on October 24, 1861 between Omaha, Nebraska, and Sacramento, California. Soon Native Americans found out that the "talking wire" was used to pass on military information, and attacked it. While the Cheyenne were on warpaths in 1864 and 1865 in Nebraska and Wyoming, the government could not protect the lines: poles and stations were burned, and wires were ripped down. Station operators, often alone in remote areas with their horse and dog, were easy targets. Some could do nothing but helplessly cable about the impending deadly attacks on their shacks.[14]

The telegraph also played an important role in one of the classic counterinsurgencies of the period, the Philippine War from 1899 to 1902. At the end of July 1900, the US government had laid 2,931 miles of land telegraph and telephone lines, and more than 200 miles of cable. Built primarily for use by the US Army, the system was operated and maintained by the Signal Corps. Four hundred and fifty telegraph offices had been opened, sparsely staffed with just 25 officers and 350 men. Insurgents constantly attacked the lines. In the northern Luzon province, rebels cut wires, removed large sections, and felled the poles. In July alone, the lines were cut 13 times and nearly 6,000 yards of wire were removed by the insurgents, reported Lieutenant Colonel James Allen, the Chief Signal Officer of the Division of the Philippines.[15] Attacking and removing telegraph wires was a common tactic among insurgents, from the Cuban War of Independence against the Spanish after 1895 to the Macedonian Insurrection against the Turks in 1903.

Even in the war that ended the Belle Epoche in Europe, the First World War, the telegraph remained a target of irregular forces. T.E. Lawrence—as Lawrence of Arabia one of the world's best-known insurgents—masterfully used the Ottomans' technological superiority against them. By 1914 the Turks made heavy use of telegraph links for the strategic command of their forces. Yet the system, not unlike some of today's most sophisticated command-and-control systems, had negative side effects:

---

13   The anecdote comes from Albrecht von Boguslawski, *Der kleine Krieg und seine Bedeutung für die Gegenwart* (Berlin: Friedrich Luckhardt, 1881), pp. 21–2n.

14   Huurdeman, *The Worldwide History of Telecommunications*, p. 100; Oslin, *The Story of Telecommunications*, p. 112.

15   Annual Reports of the US War Department for the Fiscal Year Ended June 30, 1901 (Washington: Government Printing Office, 1901), p. 1,009.

> *Young and I cut the telegraph, here an important network of trunk and local lines, indeed the Palestine army's main link with their homeland. It was pleasant to imagine Linan von Sandars' fresh curse, in Nazareth, as each severed wire tangled back from the clippers. We did them slowly, with ceremony, to draw out the indignation. The Turks' hopeless lack of initiative made their army a "directed" one, so that by destroying the telegraphs we went far towards turning them into a leaderless mob.*[16]

Garland, a British officer and specialist for explosives, taught Feisal's army to cut the Ottomans' lines, with his "own devices for mining trains and felling telegraphs and cutting metals." Lawrence himself occasionally climbed poles and cut cables—one time nearly falling down—then took the loose wire endings, tied them to camels, and rode on, ripping down the wire and dragging the poles behind him, until the weight got too heavy for the animals to pull.[17]

Weapon

In the twentieth century, insurgents and irregular fighters still saw their adversaries' telecommunication facilities as an Achilles heel, although attacking them would become progressively more difficult. Wooden telegraph posts were easy targets even for primitive fighters. That did not apply to the technology that succeeded the telegraph—electromagnetic energy emitted on the electromagnetic spectrum's radio-frequency range, the vehicle for the early wireless communication, could not be burned, felled, or torn down. The way insurgents took advantage of telecommunications forcibly began to change.

Europe and America were mostly focused on big state-on-state war from 1914 to 1945. When colonial empires began to crumble after the Second World War, irregular movements had to experiment with the new conditions of mass communication. The outbreak of the Great War and high-flying nationalism—along with rising literacy rates—produced a huge news–media market. Newspaper circulation across Europe skyrocketed and radio receivers became more widespread. The spread of newspapers and the invention of radio in particular, helped extend the government's persuasive powers to the masses. This effect, naturally, was attractive for insurgents too, but it initially remained intensive and costly to resource for most insurgencies. Irgun and Lehi, two militant Zionist groups during the 1930s and 1940s, operated radio stations to bolster their cause against the British authorities in Palestine. Nasser's *Sawt al-Arab* [Voice of the Arabs] became a popular outlet in the mid-1950s, when inexpensive transistor radios spread to the illiterate poor, even in more remote cities and villages across the Arabic world. By 1957, Cairo, with a stronger transmitter, started to tailor its messages to regional audiences

---

16   T.E. Lawrence, *Seven Pillars of Wisdom* (London: Bernard Shaw, 1926), p. 620.
17   Ibid., p. 208.

and blared a constant stream of inflammatory anti-colonialist propaganda into the Maghreb, fuelling the insurgency in Algeria against the French.[18] In stark contrast to regular forces, irregulars—by and large—did not use radio tactically with great skill.[19] If radio was used, it was mostly as a tool to communicate with friendly constituencies. Although even less efficiently, radio was sometimes used by well-organized insurgent forces as a military command-and-control device, examples of which are the Viet Minh and General Vo Nguyen Giap's use of radio to coordinate an impressively large force in the Battle of Dien Bien Phu.

After the Second World War, a broader trend gained contours: already in the Malayan Emergency after 1948, public opinion gained importance in theater, although telecommunication was mostly used by the British authorities while the communists relied on posters and leaflets.[20] A similar dynamic can be observed in the French war in Algeria after 1954.[21] The first dramatic example of this new trend is the Tet Offensive in Vietnam in January and February 1968.[22] William Westmoreland declared in a speech in November 1967 in the National Press Club that the enemy could no longer conduct major operations near South Vietnam's cities. "[Success] lies within our grasp," he declared somewhat optimistically.[23] Less than three months later the Vietcong, supported by the North Vietnamese Army, attacked with an estimated strength of 67,000 troops. For a brief but chaotic moment the onslaught turned Saigon into a war zone, and a small group of enemy troops even penetrated the US embassy in Saigon. Although approximately 14,000 South Vietnamese and 4,000 American soldiers were killed, the attack was a massive defeat for the North. After a few weeks the North's units were driven out of every city they attacked, and their military infrastructure and equipment was destroyed. The attackers suffered horrendous human losses, probably between 45,000 and 84,000 men.

On the morning of February 1, 1968, in Fort Leavenworth, a young officer named Powell, who later would become the chairman of the Joint Chiefs of Staff,

18　Alistair Horne, *A Savage War of Peace: Algeria 1954–1962* (New York: NYRB Classics, 1977; 2nd edn 2006), p. 85. For a general history of propaganda see Philip M. Taylor, *Munitions of the Mind* (Manchester: Manchester University Press, 2003). For a specific analysis of the media role in small wars (from the government's point of view) see Susan L. Carruthers, *Winning Hearts and Minds: British Governments, the Media and Colonial Counter-Insurgency 1944–1960* (Leicester: Leicester University Press, 1995).

19　Dean Juniper, "The First World War and Radio Development," *History Today* (2004), vol. 54, no. 5: 32–8; William R. Blair, "Army Radio in Peace and War," *Annals of the American Academy of Political and Social Science* (March 1929), vol. 142: 86–9.

20　In fact, the expression "battle for the hearts and minds" originated in that war. See Anthony Short, *The Communist Insurrection in Malaya, 1948–1960* (New York: Crane, Russak, 1975), p. 416.

21　Yves Courrière, *La guerre d'Algérie* (Paris: Fayard, 2001).

22　For a more detailed treatment see Peter Braestrup, *Big Story: How the American Press and Television Reported and Interpreted the Crisis of Tet 1968 in Vietnam and Washington* (Novato, CA: Presidio, 1994).

23　Don Oberdorfer, *Tet!* (New York: Garden City, 1971), p. 105.

came out of his bedroom, put on the coffee-pot, turned on the TV news, and was shocked—as were many of his compatriots. The screen showed US marines as they were fighting in the American embassy in Saigon, and Vietnamese forces battling in front of the presidential palace in the heart of the ally's capital. The attack on the embassy received intense TV coverage and it was probably the first battle in Vietnam that made sense to many Americans. Finally they could see the adversary. "The images beamed into American living rooms of a once faceless enemy suddenly popping up in the middle of South Vietnam's capital had a profound effect on public opinion," Powell remarked later. He added, with respect to the consequences of the newscasts: "Tet marked a turning point, raising doubts in the minds of moderate Americans, not just hippies and campus radicals, about the worth of this conflict, and the antiwar movement intensified."[24] Probably more than anyone else Walter Cronkite spoke for moderate, ordinary Americans. He was host of *CBS Evening News*, the first consistently popular half-hour news show; President John F. Kennedy himself had inaugurated the first edition. Cronkite was equally shocked by the events in Vietnam of that early February. The anchorman remembers reading the news agency tapes in the newsroom in New York after the reports were coming in: "What the hell is going on? I thought we were winning the war?"[25] Cronkite, a veteran correspondent of the Second World War, decided to travel to Vietnam to inspect the situation. He toured the country and met with senior officers, even with Creighton Abrams, Westmoreland's successor, whom he knew as a colonel from the Battle of the Bulge. He was still shocked by what he saw in Vietnam and became convinced that the war was lost. When Cronkite returned from the trip, he commented in heavy and memorable words on Tet in a CBS News Special, *Report from Vietnam by Walter Cronkite*: "The only national way out then will be to negotiate, not as victors, but as an honorable people who lived up to their pledge to defend democracy, and did the best they could."[26] This was Walter Cronkite calling to accept defeat in Vietnam. After his remarks—the impact of which cannot be underestimated—President Lyndon B. Johnson reportedly concluded: "If I've lost Cronkite, I've lost Middle America."[27] A few weeks later the incumbent announced that he would not run for the presidency a second time.

The Tet Offensive was the idea of General Nguyen Chi Thanh. He realized that the US was fighting in an alien environment, and that Westmoreland was overconfident and "arrogant."[28] The North Vietnamese were also overconfident when they launched the Tet Offensive; they failed to achieve many military objectives and suffered heavy losses. But they succeeded in one critical point: "[I]n

---

24 Colin L. Powell, and Joseph E. Persico, *My American Journey* (New York: Random House, 1995), p. 120.

25 Walter Cronkite; quoted in Oberdorfer, *Tet!*, p. 158.

26 Walter Cronkite on CBS News Special, February 27, 1968; Ibid., pp. 250–51.

27 Lyndon B. Johnson; quoted in Johanna Neuman, *Lights, Camera, War* (New York: St Martin's Press, 1996), p. 179.

28 Tin Bui, *Following Ho Chi Minh: Memoirs of a North Vietnamese Colonel*, trans. by J. Strowe, and D. Van (Honolulu: University of Hawaii Press, 1995), p. 62.

Saigon we planned to create a 'big bang' by occupying the U.S. Embassy," Bui Tin, a North Vietnamese colonel, wrote in his memoirs. "Tet was designed to influence American public opinion."[29]

A second example, equally spectacular, is the escalation of the so-called "Troubles" in Northern Ireland a short while later. Operation Banner, as it is officially known, was the longest campaign ever fought by the British Army, and the largest since World War II. In 1972 approximately 28,000 troops were sent into Northern Ireland, more than twice the British peak strength of Afghanistan and Iraq in 2007 combined.[30] In total, more than 250,000 members of the Regular Army served in Ulster during the campaign; over 600 were killed, 102 alone in 1972. During the course of the campaign—the word "war" was rarely used—more than 10,000 terrorist suspects were arrested, and more than 3,100 people lost their lives.

Early on, the mass media played an important role in that conflict. Six counties of the province of Ulster remained part of the United Kingdom when Ireland was given independence in 1922. The Nationalists, or Republicans, who are predominantly Catholic, see themselves as part of the Republic of Ireland; the Unionists, or Loyalists, are almost entirely Protestant and wish to remain part of the UK. The level of violence began to rise at the end of the 1960s. An Orange Order march on October 5, 1968 escalated into large-scale riots in Londonderry—it became the first fully televised event of this kind in the United Kingdom. The cameras caught the Royal Ulster Constabulary using excessive force, thereby paving the way for an escalation of the conflict. "The Troubles," as the violent conflict between the two groups became known, erupted in the summer of 1969 during a march in Londonderry when the first deaths were caused, at a time when the province had 1.8 million inhabitants.

The British Army soon introduced harsh interrogation techniques that were developed in colonial theaters during the 1950s and 1960s. Operation Demetrius was a large-scale internment policy that produced some tactical benefits. But "the information operations opportunity handed to the Republican movement was enormous," a study for the Chief of the General Staff noted in 2006. And the lesson of Demetrius was clear: the internment of large numbers of suspects, and their harsh treatment, had "a major impact on popular opinion across Ireland, in Europe and the US ... it was a major mistake."[31] The insurgents, the British slowly understood, were rooted in the local culture, spoke its patois, and were better connected than the counterinsurgents. The IRA just as easily took advantage of the violent incidents, most prominently that fateful Sunday in January 1972 in Londonderry, when 13 civil rights protestors were fatally shot by British security

---

29   Tin Bui, "How North Vietnam Won the War," *Wall Street Journal* (August 3, 1995), A8.
30   In early 2008, the British military had 7,800 forces in Afghanistan and 4,100 troops in Iraq.
31   Mike Jackson, *Operation Banner*, Vol. Army Code 71842 (London: British Army, 2006), pp. 2–7.

forces: "The events of Bloody Sunday were immediately exploited by a Republican information operation."[32]

A third example shows that the media can also be used to break the will of the superior opponent. On October 3, 1993, in the afternoon, a force of 160 troops, 19 aircraft and 12 vehicles set out from their base close to Mogadishu airport to "snatch and grab" leading figures of Mohamed Aideed's Habr Gidr clan and possibly the strongman himself. Their target was the Olympic Hotel in downtown Mogadishu. Once the Americans had stormed the hotel and captured several of the enemy fighters, the situation quickly got out of hand. The task force encountered small arms fire, and two Black Hawk helicopters were downed. The operation escalated into a pitched battle in a typical developing world urban environment: narrow streets, and civilians intermingling with enemy combatants armed with AK47s and RPGs. Delta Force, Air Force combat search and rescue assets, Navy Seals, and Army Rangers experienced more than 50 percent casualties in 18 hours, fighting against Somali paramilitaries without formal training. When the battle was over, 18 American soldiers had been killed, 84 had been wounded and one, Chief Warrant Officer Michael Durant, the pilot of one of the downed Black Hawk helicopters, had been captured. Aideed's troops celebrated their victory by desecrating the naked body of a dead US Ranger and dragging it through the dirty streets of Mogadishu. Initial hearsay reports had it that an angry mob was showing body parts as "trophies," but these were dismissed by the Pentagon. After images of the events in Mogadishu's narrow streets emerged in the news, the story spun equally out of control in Washington's Pennsylvania Avenue. Paul Watson, a print reporter from the *Toronto Star*, photographed the Ranger's abuse as he happened to be on the scene with his 35 mm pocket camera. The reporter later won a Pulitzer Prize for his picture.

What followed was intentioned. While the still photos of the battle were taken by an independent Western journalist, the moving images shown on CNN came from a questionable source. The Somali driver and stringer Mohamoud Hassan—allegedly associated with Aideed and a former freelancer for Reuters—recorded the video of the soldier's corpse being dragged and kicked through the dirt as well as the footage of Durant's interrogation.[33] Hassan had recorded the video early on 4 October and transmitted the Hi-8 cartridge through Nairobi to London from where CNN relayed the footage electronically to Atlanta.[34] Soon the grisly pictures of the dead Ranger's humiliation and the frightened face of the interrogated Durant were broadcast across the United States and the rest of the world. Given that Hassan was able to obtain the video of Durant's interrogation, where presumably no independent

---

32 Ibid., pp. 2–8.

33 David B. Stockwell, *Press Coverage in Somalia: A Case for Media Relations to be a Principle of Military Operations Other Than War* (Masters Thesis: DINFOS, 1995), p. 21; Nik Gowing, *Real Time Television Coverage of Armed Conflicts and Diplomatic Crises: Does it Pressure or Distort Foreign Policy Decisions?* (Working Paper: The Shorenstein Center, 1994), p. 48.

34 Information as given by Stockwell, who interviewed Hassan in October 2003; Stockwell, *Press Coverage in Somalia*, p. 21.

local journalist was present, the assumption seems valid that the warlord had an interest in getting the images out. It is thus a plausible and probable assumption that Aideed and his colonels had an information operations calculus in mind: they intended to penetrate their adversary's decision loop and break America's will. The images were highly successful.

Images of the naked corpse of a US soldier and the battered face and frightened voice of another captured soldier sent shockwaves through the American body politic: "The people who are dragging American bodies don't look very hungry to the people of Texas," commented Republican senator Phil Gramm, reacting to thousands of telephone calls to Capitol Hill demanding the withdrawal of US forces.[35] John McCain, an Arizona Republican on the Armed Services Committee, demanded that "Clinton's got to bring them home."[36] Not only did Congress put pressure on the president to consider pulling out of Somalia; the images had their own direct effect in the White House. National Security Advisor Anthony Lake commented later on the TV footage of the Battle of Mogadishu: the "pictures helped make us recognize that the military situation in Mogadishu had deteriorated in a way that we had not frankly recognized."[37] Bill Clinton eventually decided to withdraw.[38] The incident undermined the credibility of American military might in the eyes of its opponents for the years to come: if confronted with casualties, they concluded, the Americans would cut and run "with their tail between their legs."[39] Irregular fighters facing the world's most powerful military had come a long way indeed since their predecessors had burned telegraph poles a century or so earlier. Yet the most fundamental and truly revolutionary change still was ahead of them.

Platform

The year 2000, when the new technology investment boom reached its climax, was also a milestone for the history of armed conflict. The dot-com bubble commoditized telecommunication. Previously, only states and large companies were able to build optical telegraph chains, to shoulder the investments of laying copper wires, to create and maintain telephone networks, or to operate radio transmitters. Recipients could barely take part in the mass communication. Before 2000, the public elements of the Web had continued this *public monologue*. Particularly under the adverse conditions of warfare, the benefits of modern communication were confined to highly specialized and resourced regular armies. On the irregulars' side, only rarely did the most sophisticated and ripe insurrections acquire the

---

35   Phil Gramm; quoted in Neuman, *Lights, Camera, War*, p. 14.
36   John McCain; quoted in Bill Clinton, *My Life* (London: Random House, 2004), p. 551.
37   Anthony Lake; quoted in Gowing, *Real Time Television Coverage*, p. 48.
38   Clinton, *My Life*, pp. 551–4.
39   Michael Gordon, and Bernhard Trainor, *Cobra II: The Inside Story of the Invasion and Occupation of Iraq* (London: Atlantic Books, 2006), p. 66.

means to publish newspapers and magazines or even to run radio stations. The state-control of communication in times of war began to erode with the advent of a modern journalism that made use of the telegraph, photographs, radio, and the TV. Yet it collapsed nearly completely when several trends coincided: a fall in prices for computing, improved digital technology, overcapacity in bandwidth, and the expansion of Internet penetration and mobile phones in rich countries, emerging markets, and even in poor regions. When the demand for participation in mass communication began to soar, the companies who had survived the stock markets' wrath began to churn out the software that made this possible: the new media rose. By enabling *public dialogue*, the Web became a buzzing social platform.[40]

The developments that mesmerized entrepreneurs in the private sector showed their seductive effect on officers, soldiers, sailors, airmen, and marines in the public sector. The dot-com bubble epitomized the investors' inability accurately to understand and interpret the long-term economic significance of the Web's socio-technological changes; many heralded the advent of a "new economy" that would redefine basic economic laws. The US defense establishment, correspondingly, invested heavily in "network-centric warfare" and heralded a "new way of war" that equally redefined the laws of armed conflict. The eternal uncertainty and friction that had made warfare so unpredictable for centuries, Clausewitz's "fog of war," could finally be "lifted."[41] This near-revolution in military thinking started enthusiastically in the skies above Iraq in 1991 and received a sobering reality check in Baghdad's urban sprawl, beginning in late 2003.

Al-Qaeda's "transformation" took an entirely different form. The world's best-known and most powerful terrorist organization was forced into a virtual metamorphosis by its enemies. After the 9/11 attacks, America's best minds in the intelligence services and the military trained their sights on the group and its local insurgent offshoots. Large physical training camps in Afghanistan and elsewhere were easy targets and impossible to maintain. For the organization's leadership it became exceedingly dangerous to communicate, be it face-to-face, by messenger, by mail, by telephone, or by electronic means. Command-and-control became nearly impossible to exert.

Al-Qaeda's reaction, in essence, was to embrace the information age. One person in particular stands for this change: Mustafa bin Abd al-Qadir Setmariam Nasar, better known as Abu Mus'ab al-Suri or Umar Abd al-Hakim, jihad's most important and impressive strategic mind so far. One key to al-Suri's strategic thinking is US airpower. When some of the Afghan training camps were attacked by cruise

---

40 One of the most popular and most insightful analyses remains that of Thomas L. Friedman, *The World is Flat: A Brief History of the Twenty-First Century* (New York: Farrar, Straus and Giroux, 2004). For effects on regular armies see, for instance, Dan Baum, "What the Generals don't Know," *The New Yorker* (January 17, 2005), vol. 80, no. 43: 42; and John Robb, *Brave New War: The Next Stage of Terrorism and the End of Globalization* (Hoboken, NJ: Wiley, 2007).

41 William A. Owens, *Lifting the Fog of War* (Baltimore: Johns Hopkins University Press, 2001).

missiles in 1998, it dawned on al-Suri that not even Afghanistan's inaccessible massive mountains could provide protection from modern precision-guided munitions. After the swift US disposal of the Taliban regime and the American performance in open confrontation, this skepticism was corroborated. Fixed bases were impossible, al-Suri concluded, and American determination ruled out the establishment sanctuaries in friendly states. The tanzimat, as a consequence, became much more difficult to run. The organizations' hierarchical structure, in addition, made them easy targets for intelligence organizations that were not only able to gather intelligence from one or a few captured members, or through infiltration, but could also then paralyze or take out an entire organization in one piece.

Al-Suri distinguishes three different types of holy warfare. First come the *tanzimat* [plural; *tanzim* is Arabic for organization], which are hierarchical organizations set up locally or regionally. Examples are the Egyptian group al-Jihad, the Shabiba movement in Morocco, or the Asbat al-Ansar group in Lebanon. Al-Suri himself was a member of a typical tanzim, the Combatant Vanguard Organization in Syria. Second there are "open fronts," or large-scale insurgencies against an occupying power. Examples are the jihad in Chechnya, Bosnia, or Afghanistan against the Soviets. Al-Suri's third type of subversive war is the "jihad of individualized terrorism," single acts of terrorism organized and executed by small cells that act autonomously, without central leadership or the hierarchical setup of larger organizations. Early examples are Ramzi Yousuf's World Trade Center bombing in 1993 or Sayyid Nusayr's assassination of Rabbi Meir Kahane in 1990.[42] A skilled communicator, al-Suri summed up his alternative idea as "*nizam, la tanzim*" ["system, not organization"]. His vision for jihad was to have an "operative system" instead of an "organization for operations." He advocated templates, available for self-recruited activists and entrepreneurs with a desire to take part in the global jihad, either on their own or with a group of trusted accomplices. Connections and organizational links between the leadership and the units were thus avoided. General guidance replaced specific orders. The glue was not more than "a common aim, a common doctrinal program and a comprehensive (self-)educational program."[43]

Such a system enabled Clausewitz's escalations. First, it enabled the escalation of will: "All military schools agree that a will to fight and moral strength of the fighter is the basis for victory and good performance," al-Suri wrote.[44] For conventional armed forces with the powerful group dynamic of battle morale is already essential; but the will to fight is "the fundament for the guerrilla fighter in general and the jihadi resistance fighter in particular."[45] Entire libraries full of books and journals

---

42   Al-Suri's strategy is highly reminiscent of the "leaderless resistance" of Louis Beam, a US, right-wing, radical white supremacist writing of the early 1990s. See Louis Beam, "Leaderless Resistance," *The Seditionist* (1992), vol. 12.

43   Brynjar Lia, "Al-Suri's Doctrines for Decentralized Jihadi Training," *Terrorism Monitor* (2007), vol. 5, issue 1: 1–4, 17.

44   Ibid., p. 3; Abu Mus'ab al-Suri, *The Call to Global Islamic Resistance* (2005), p. 1,420.

45   Al-Suri, *The Call to Global Islamic Resistance*, p. 1,421.

argue the jihadists' cause. Topics range wide, from the humiliation and disgrace of Muslims, the relationship between jihad and the acquisition of knowledge, to the role of women and children and religion from a Salafi point of view. The formats include glossy books authored by recognized authorities, shorter articles often published in established periodicals, stand-alone working papers, debates, video-documentaries, audio-recorded lectures, and many more. The frequency of publications, taken in total, is impressive: in July 2007 alone, al-Qaeda affiliated entities published approximately 450 items, 90 percent of them text, nine percent videos, the remaining one percent were audio and image files. Operational or topical messages made up the vast majority of media products. Only about four percent were in-depth materials focusing on more social, political, or religious issues: 10 books, four essays, and five periodicals, estimated Daniel Kimmage.[46] The spiritual and political guidance, discussed in these books, is of the highest importance for the movement.

Second, the new platform enabled the escalation of force: training, al-Suri wrote, should be moved to "every house, every quarter and every village of the Muslim countries."[47] One of the movement's most popular and widely disseminated publications is the book *39 Ways to Serve and Participate in Jihad*. Its original author is Mohammad bin Ahmad al-Salem. The text first appeared in online forums in 2003, and the download links are updated from time to time. The book outlines how anybody can participate in the global jihad without leaving home: by praying honestly, giving money, helping to outfit a fighter or support his family, praising and encouraging the mujahideen, exposing hypocrites and defeatists, abandoning luxury, raising children to love jihad, boycotting American and British goods, but also through physical training, weapons training, marksmanship, and other preparation. One chapter deals with "electronic jihad." The Internet would be "a blessed medium," al-Salem wrote, "that benefits us greatly by making it possible for people to distribute and follow the news" and "publicize ideas and goals."[48] The *39 Ways*—the document's popularity itself is a case in point—hints at the wide span of utility of information. Such activists, (self-)radicalized and (self-)recruited online, may be entrepreneurial and decide to take action on their own. The model of individualized terrorism is facilitated by simultaneous open-front jihad, such as the wars in Afghanistan and Iraq. The West's "occupation and usurpation of Muslim land," for al-Suri, had a positive operational effect: it made the tanzimat less relevant and less necessary. Not only would the invaders and occupiers of Muslim

---

46 Kimmage, an expert on extremist media, collected the material primarily from the al-Ikhlas and al-Fallujah forums, based on "official" affiliation with known armed groups or media production companies as identified by a logo. His objective was to studied one representative month of jihadist media production. See Daniel Kimmage, "The al-Qaeda Media Nexus," *RFE/RL Special Report* (2008), p. 18.

47 Al-Suri's "training theory" is discussed in Chapter 8.6 of his manifesto, *The Call to Global Islamic Resistance*. See also Brynjar Lia, *Architect of Global Jihad: The Life of al-Qaida Strategist Abu Mus'ab al-Suri* (New York: Columbia University Press, 2008).

48 Mohammad bin Ahmad al-Salem, *39 Ways to Serve and Participate in Jihad* (Online, 2003), Chapter 34: "Electronic jihad."

lands be a potent recruiting driver, but the wars would also provide a valuable training ground for operatives of independent cells in the future. Strategically the West's post-Cold War aggression in the Muslim world, according to this line of thinking, made a reorientation necessary: the old goal of Islamic revolution in Muslim countries that were ruled by local apostates should be postponed. Instead Western interests should be attacked, both in Muslim lands and elsewhere.

America's and Europe's governments and intelligence services are beginning to recognize this new phenomenon. Thomas Fingar, the US Deputy Director of National Intelligence for Analysis, outlined the new dynamics in a congressional hearing in February 2008:

> [T]he growing use of the Internet to identify and comment with networks throughout the world offers opportunities to build relationships and gain expertise that previously were available only in overseas training camps. It is likely that such independent groups will use information on destructive tactics available on the Internet to boost their own capabilities.[49]

Conclusion

In the nineteenth century, irregular groups saw the telecommunication facilities of their state-adversaries as a target. They attacked them in an attempt to limit their opponents' ability for Clausewitz's first escalation, the escalation of force. Their success was limited. In the twentieth century, irregular fighters and rebels focused on using telecommunication as a weapon and as a force multiplier to attack their adversaries' public opinion, and moral and political support bases. Irregulars, in other words, attempted to limit their opponents' second escalation, the escalation of will. Their success was remarkable. And, also in the twentieth century, insurgents began to use mass telecommunication to bolster their own political bases. But only few insurgencies had the resources to run and maintain a mass-communication infrastructure. In the twenty-first century, terrorist and insurgent movements continue to use the media as a weapon. But commoditized global information technologies more and more serve as an operating platform, enabling irregular movements to combine both of Clausewitz's force and will escalations on their own terms—the use of militant tactics as well as the spread of ideology, in the language of modern counter-terrorism. It remains to be seen how successful this third phase will be.

At closer view, the most startling feature is a convergence between the new media and insurgent movements. Irregular movements emulate the organizing principles of "Web 2.0," which rests: on individuals and communities, not large-

---

49   Written Statement of Thomas Fingar, Deputy Director of National Intelligence for Analysis, before the US House of Representatives, Committee on Armed Services (February 13, 2008), pp. 9–10.

state bureaucracies; on anonymity, not officialdom; on unity of purpose, not unity of organization; on open-source information, not secrecy; on trust, not mistrust; and on commons-based peer-production, not command-based hierarchical operations.

The ongoing appropriation of the new media and telecommunication by violent irregular movements has an unintended and troubling effect: it has taken control out of the insurgencies' and terrorist leaders' hands. The Web has commoditized causes and tactical knowledge. The resulting decentralization of authority is raising difficult questions. Is it still possible that a would-be leader controls both the ideological debate on causes as well as "user-generated" operational activities? How is it possible to steer or even stop such a movement?

Acknowledgement

This chapter has been adapted from the original work, *War 2.0: Irregular Warfare in the Information Age*, Thomas Rid and Marc Hecker. Copyright © 2009 by Thomas Rid and Marc Hecker. Reproduced with permission of ABC-CLIO, LLC.

References

Al-Salem, Mohammad bin Ahmad, *39 Ways to Serve and Participate in Jihad* (Online, 2003)

Al-Suri, Abu Mus'ab, *The Call to Global Islamic Resistance* (2005)

Annual Reports of the US War Department for the Fiscal Year Ended June 30, 1901 (Washington: Government Printing Office, 1901)

Arquilla, John, and David Ronfeldt, *In Athena's Camp: Preparing for Conflict in the Information Age* (Santa Monica: Rand, 1997)

Aukofer, Frank, and William P. Lawrence, *America's Team: The Odd Couple: A Report on the Relationship between the Military and the Media* (Nashville: The Freedom Forum First Amendment Center, 1995)

Bartlett, George and Prescott, *The Speaking Telephone, Talking Phonograph, and Other Novelties* (New York: D. Appleton, 1878)

Baum, Dan, "What the Generals don't Know," *The New Yorker* (January 17, 2005), vol. 80, no. 43: 42

Beam, Louis, "Leaderless Resistance," *The Seditionist* (1992), vol. 12

Blair, William R., "Army Radio in Peace and War," *Annals of the American Academy of Political and Social Science* (March 1929), vol. 142: 86–9

Boguslawski, Albrecht von, *Der kleine Krieg und seine Bedeutung für die Gegenwart* (Berlin: Friedrich Luckhardt, 1881)

Braestrup, Peter, *Big Story: How the American Press and Television Reported and Interpreted the Crisis of Tet 1968 in Vietnam and Washington* (Novato, CA: Presidio, 1994)

Bruce, Robert V., *Bell* (Ithaca, NY: Cornell University Press, 1990)

Bui, Tin, *Following Ho Chi Minh: Memoirs of a North Vietnamese Colonel*, trans. by J. Strowe, and D. Van (Honolulu: University of Hawaii Press, 1995)

— — —, "How North Vietnam Won the War," *Wall Street Journal* (August 3, 1995), A8

Carruthers, Susan L., *Winning Hearts and Minds: British Governments, the Media and Colonial Counter-Insurgency 1944–1960* (Leicester: Leicester University Press, 1995)

— — —, *The Media at War* (New York: St Martin's Press, 2000)

Chappe, Ignace Urbain Jean, *Histoire de la télégraphie* (Paris, 1824)

Clausewitz, Carl von, *Vom Kriege* [On War, 1832], trans. by M. Howard and P. Paret (Berlin: Ullstein, 1980)

Clinton, Bill, *My Life* (London: Random House, 2004)

Courrière, Yves, *La guerre d'Algérie* (Paris: Fayard, 2001)

Fialka, John J., *Hotel Warriors: Covering the Gulf War* (Baltimore: Hopkins University Press, 1991)

Field, Alexander J., "French Optical Telegraphy, 1793–1855: Hardware, Software, Administration," *Technology and Culture* (April 1994), vol. 35: 315–47

Fingar, Thomas, Written Statement of Thomas Fingar, Deputy Director of National Intelligence for Analysis, before the US House of Representatives, Committee on Armed Services (February 13, 2008)

Friedman, Thomas L., *The World is Flat: A Brief History of the Twenty-First Century* (New York: Farrar, Straus and Giroux, 2004)

Gordon, Michael and Bernhard Trainor, *Cobra II: The Inside Story of the Invasion and Occupation of Iraq* (London: Atlantic Books, 2006)

Gowing, Nik, *Real Time Television Coverage of Armed Conflicts and Diplomatic Crises: Does it Pressure or Distort Foreign Policy Decisions?* (Working Paper: The Shorenstein Center, 1994)

Hallin, Daniel C., *The "Uncensored War": The Media and Vietnam* (Oxford: Oxford University Press, 1986)

Hammes, Thomas X., *The Sling and the Stone: On War in the 21st Century* (St Paul, MN: Zenith Press, 2006)

Hammond, William M., *Public Affairs: The Military and the Media, 1962–1968* (Washington: Center of Military History, 1988)

— — —, *Public Affairs: The Military and the Media, 1968–1973* (Seattle: University Press of the Pacific, 2002)

Hockenberry, John, "The Blogs of War," *Wired Magazine* (August 13, 2005)

Holzmann, Gerard J. and Björn Pehrson, *The Early History of Data Networks* (Los Alamitos, CA: IEEE Computer Society Press, 1995)

Horne, Alistair, *A Savage War of Peace: Algeria 1954–1962* (New York: NYRB Classics, 1977; 2nd edn 2006)

Huurdeman, Anton A., *The Worldwide History of Telecommunications* (New York: J. Wiley, 2003)

Jackson, Mike, *Operation Banner*, Vol. Army Code 71842 (London: British Army, 2006)

Juniper, Dean, "The First World War and Radio Development," *History Today* (2004), vol. 54, no. 5: 32–8

Knightley, Phillip, *The First Casualty: From the Crimea to Vietnam: The War Correspondent as Hero, Propagandist and Myth Maker* (New York: Harcourt Brace Jovanovich, 1975)

Kimmage, Daniel, "The al-Qaeda Media Nexus," *RFE/RL Special Report* (2008)

Koenig, Duane, "Telegraphs and Telegrams in Revolutionary France," *The Scientific Monthly* (1944), vol. 59, issue 6: 431–7

Laqueur, Walter, *Guerrilla: A Historical and Critical Study*, vol. 4 (Boston: Little, Brown, 1976)

Lawrence, T.E., *Seven Pillars of Wisdom* (London: Bernard Shaw, 1926)

Lia, Brynjar, "Al-Suri's Doctrines for Decentralized Jihadi Training," *Terrorism Monitor* (2007), vol. 5, issue 1: 1–4, 17.

— — —, *Architect of Global Jihad: The Life of al-Qaida Strategist Abu Mus'ab al-Suri* (New York: Columbia University Press, 2008)

Murray, Williamson, "Clausewitz Out, Computer In: Military Culture and Technological Hubris," *The National Interest* (Summer, 1997), vol. 48: 57–64

Neuman, Johanna, *Lights, Camera, War* (New York: St Martin's Press, 1996)

Norman, Jeremy M., *From Gutenberg to the Internet: A Sourcebook on the History of Information Technology* (Novato, CA: HistoryofScience.com, 2005)

Oberdorfer, Don, *Tet!* (New York: Garden City, 1971)

Oslin, George P., *The Story of Telecommunications* (Macon, GA: Mercer University Press, 1992)

Owens, William A., *Lifting the Fog of War* (Baltimore: Johns Hopkins University Press, 2001)

Paret, Peter, *Internal War and Pacification : The Vendée, 1789–1796* (Princeton, NJ: Princeton University Press, 1961)

Powell, Colin L. and Joseph E. Persico, *My American Journey* (New York: Random House, 1995)

Rid, Thomas, *War and Media Operations: The US Military and the Press from Vietnam to Iraq* (London: Routledge, 2007)

Robb, John, *Brave New War: The Next Stage of Terrorism and the End of Globalization* (Hoboken, NJ: Wiley, 2007)

Short, Anthony, *The Communist Insurrection in Malaya, 1948–1960* (New York: Crane, Russak, 1975)

Stockwell, David B., *Press Coverage in Somalia: A Case for Media Relations to be a Principle of Military Operations Other Than War* (Masters Thesis: DINFOS, 1995)

Taylor, Philip M., *Munitions of the Mind* (Manchester: Manchester University Press, 2003)

Toffler, Alvin and Heidi Toffler, *War and Anti-War: Making Sense of Today's Global Chaos* (New York: Grand Central, 1993)

Index

Page numbers in italics refer to tables.